Avizandum Statutes on

Scots Property, Trusts and Succession Law
2005–2006

2nd edition

Avizandum Statutes on

Scots Property, Trusts and Succession Law
2005–2006

Second edition

Editors

Andrew J M Steven LLB, PhD, Solicitor
Lecturer in Law, University of Edinburgh

Scott Wortley LLB, Solicitor
Lecturer in Law, University of Edinburgh

Avizandum Publishing Ltd
Edinburgh
2005

Published by
Avizandum Publishing Ltd
58 Candlemaker Row
Edinburgh EH1 2QE

First published 2004
2nd edition 2005

ISBN 1-904968-03-1

British Library Cataloguing in Publication Data
A catalogue record for this book is available from the British Library

Typeset by AFS Image Setters Ltd, Glasgow
Printed and bound by Bell & Bain Ltd, Glasgow

EDITORS' PREFACE

This collection, first published in 2004, aims to bring together the key statutory provisions necessary for a study of property, trusts and succession law at LLB level in Scotland. Traditionally, these subjects were treated separately and, moreover, there tended to be an emphasis on conveyancing as opposed to property law. In recent years, curricula in the universities have been revised and the subject-matter of this volume has, in a number of instances, become treated within one course.

Part I covers property law. While this can be regarded as a unitary subject, there is of course a classic division between heritable and moveable property. The law of heritable property has undergone revolutionary change in recent years, culminating in the abolition of the feudal system on 28 November 2004. This volume seeks to include all the statutory material governing the post-feudal era. In relation to moveable property, we have included a number of important provisions, notably from the Sale of Goods Act 1979.

In Part II, we have collected the main trusts and succession statutes. But it is worth noting that some of the statutes included in Part I have effect in this area too, in particular the Requirements of Writing (Scotland) Act 1995.

We have taken account of the main legislative developments since publication of the first edition, in particular the Tenements (Scotland) Act 2004, the Civil Partnership Act 2004 and the Charities and Trustee Investment (Scotland) Act 2005. In order, however, to keep the size of the volume manageable and therefore its price reasonable for students, we have required to be selective. Accordingly, even in the major legislation, such as the Title Conditions (Scotland) Act 2003, not every provision is included and those using this volume in legal practice must be aware of this. In response to helpful feedback on the first edition, we have now included some secondary legislation, notably the Land Registration (Scotland) Rules 1980. We would continue to welcome feedback as to any material omissions, which we can then address in future editions.

We greatly appreciate the help of Malcolm Combe, Chris Cooper and Diana Tansley for their assistance in bringing together the materials and checking for amendments and repeals. Our thanks also go to Margaret Cherry for her characteristic efficiency in helping to achieve publication.

The materials are intended to be up to date to June 2005. All amendments to the legislation appear in square brackets. Where part of a statutory provision has been repealed this is indicated by [. . .].

Andrew J M Steven
Scott Wortley
University of Edinburgh

July 2005

CONTENTS

PART I
PROPERTY

STATUTES

ROYAL MINES ACT 1424
(1424, c 12)

OF mynis of golde and silver

ITEM   Gif ony myne of golde or siluer be fundyn in ony lordis landis of the realme and it may be prowyt that thre halfpennys of siluer may be fynit owt of the punde of leide The lordis of parliament consentis that sik myne be the kingis as is vsuale in vthir realmys.

LEASES ACT 1449
(1449, c 18)

OF takis of landis for termes

ITEM   It is ordanit for the sauftie and fauour of the pure pepil that labouris the grunde that thai and al vthiris that has takyn or sal tak landis in tym to cum fra lordis and has termes and yeris thereof that suppose the lordis sel or analy thai landis that the takaris sall remayn with thare takis on to the ische of thare termes quhais handis at euir thai landis cum to for sic lik male as thai tuk thaim of befoir [. . .].

MINES AND METALS ACT 1592
(1592, c 31)

FOR furthering of the kingis commoditie be the Mynes and metallis

OURE Souerane Lord vnderstanding that this lang tyme bygane Nather his Maiestie nor the cuntrie hes Importit ony commoditie of the mynis and metallis quhilk in great abundance micht be easelie found in this realme to the interteynement and sustentatioun of ane greit nowmer of the liegis thairof And that the said inconvenient hes ensewit be resone Oure said souerane lord and his maist noble progenitouris wes in vse commonlie to sett the saidis haill mynis within thair dominionis to ane or tua strangearis for ane small dewtie quha nather haid substance to caus labour and wirk the hundreth pairt of ony ane of the saidis mynis nor yit instructed vtheris leigis of this realme in the knawlege thairof quhilk is mair nor notour be the doingis of the present takisman of the mynes quha nether wirkis presentlie nor hes wrocht thir mony yeiris bypast nor euir hes serchit socht nor discoverit ony new mettall sen his entrie nor hes instructit ony of the leigis of the cuntrie in that knawlege And quhilk is maist inconvenient of all hes maid na sufficient payment of the dewtie of his tak to oure souerane lordis thesaurair sua that na pairt of the said yeirlie dewtie is euir cum in the said thesauraris compt to his hienes vse and commoditie Quhairby Oure souerane lord and the haill cuntrie will sustene greit loss gif ane strangear sall bruik in this maner the haill mettallis within his maiesties dominionis but payment of ony dewtie ffor the space of xxj yeris altogidder Lyk as also in respect the richt of all mynis pertenit to his maiestie and his hienes predicessouris Thairfoir quhensoeuir ony myne or seme of mettaill wes found be ony of the leigis of this realme the same wes ather neglectit or be all moyanis possible obscurit be ressone that na pairt of the commoditie thairof micht redound to thame selffis quhairby ane greit proffite quhilk micht haue bene gottin baith to oure souerane lord and als to the cuntrie wes allutirlie owir sene And now our said souerane lord vnderstanding the inconvenientis foirsaidis To haue procedit cheiflie becaus ther wes nocht ane speciall man of witt and knawlege appointit to quhais office propirlie the owirsicht of the haill mater of the mettallis suld pertene And of quhome his Maiestie and estaitis micht seik ane compt and ressone of the adminis-tratioun of his said office that his mynis be nocht neglectit (as thay ar) dyuerse vtheris princes makand sa greit commoditie of the lyk . . . . And als oure souerane willing that all his Maiesties liegis quha will tak on hand to discouer and work the saidis mynis may haue reasonable proffite and recompence of thair panis [and] a sufficient securitie maid to thame of thair awin mynis within thair awin landis And als vnderstanding that the dewtie of the said mynis quhilk baith of the commoun law and consuetude obseruit be vther foreign princes properlie pertenis to the prince Extendis onlie to the tent part fre Thairfore our said souerane lord with auise of his estaittis in parliament hes dissoluit the saidis mynis and mettallis in safer as thay war part of his propirtie annext or ony wyis to the effect the same may be sett in few for augmentatioun of oure said souerane lordis rentall And statutis and ordanis that it salbe lesum to his hienes and his successouris . . . for reasonable compositioun to [dispone] to every erle lord barroun and vther [owner] within this realme all and quhatsumeuir mynis of gould siluer copper leid tin and vther quhatsumeuir mettallis or minerallis quhilk is or may be found within thair awin landis and heretageis with pouer to thame to seik and discouer lauboure and work the saidis mettallis and minerallis and to sell dispone or sett the mynis thairof in takkis . . . to vtheris thair subtenentis at thair pleasure as thair proper gudis and heretage And with sic vther ample priuilegeis as oure said souerane lord . . . sall think expedient for the wining and working of the saidis mettallis be cuntrie men or strangearis Payand thairfore yeirlie the saidis Erlis Lordis barounis and vtheris quha sall accept the [disposition of the saidis mynis] as said is to oure said souerane Lord and his thesaurare thair factouris and seruitouris in thair Name the Just tent part of all and haill the said gould siluer copper leid tin and vtheris minerallis quhilk salbe found and gottin yeirlie within thair saidis landis and heretageis vpoun the ground quhair the same salbe found in sic vre and qualitie as the same salbe gottin out of the erth frelie but ony deductioun . . . . Provyding that in cace ony mynis being sufficientlie discouerit to be within ony of the landis pertening to ony subiect of this realme and the lord of the ground sufficientlie aduertesit thairof and lauchfullie requirit to work the same himself befoir ane Notar [ane witness] as efferis gif he refuisses or delayis the space of thre monethis thairefter Than and in that cace It salbe lesum to our said souerane lord to [dispone the same or set the same] or tak or vtherwyis to caus work the same or to mak rycht thairof to ony vther persone at his grace pleasure That be the wilfull refuise or delay of the awnar of the ground his grace and his cuntrie be not defraudit of the commoditie of the said myne And oure said souerane lord with auise foirsaid of the parliament Declaris that this act of dissolutioun salbe per-petuall to last for all tyme cuming . [. . .]

REGISTRATION ACT 1617
(1617, c 16)

ANENT the Registratione of reuersiones Seasingis and vtheris writis

OURE Souerane Lord Considdering the gryit hurt sustened by his Maiesties Liegis by the fraudulent dealing of pairties who haveing annaliet thair Landis and ressauit gryit soumes of money thairfore Yit be thair vniust concealing of sum privat Right formarlie made by thame rendereth subsequent alienatioun done for gryit soumes of money altogidder vnproffitable whiche can not be avoyded vnles the saidis privat rightis be maid publict and patent to his hienes liegis FOR remedie whereoff and of the manye Inconvenientis whiche may ensew thairupoun HIS Maiestie with aduyis and consent of the estaittis of Parliament statutes and ordanis That thair salbe ane publick Register In the whiche all Reuersiounes regresses bandis and writtis for making of reuersiounes or regresses assignatiounes thairto dischargis of the same renunciatiounes of wodsettis and grantis off redemptioun and siclyik all instrumentis of seasing salbe registrat. [. . .] It is alwayis declared that it sall not be necessar to registrat anye bandis and wreatis for making of reuersiounes or regresses vnles seasing pas in fauoures off the pairties makeris of the saidis bandis or writtis In the whiche cace It is ordaned that the samen salbe registrat. [. . .] The extract off the whiche Register sall mak faith in all caces except where the writtis so registrated ar offered to be improvin And gif it salhappin any of the saidis writtis whiche ar appoynted to be registrat as said is not to be dewlie registrat. [. . .] Then and in that cace his maiestie with aduyse and consent foirsaid Decernis the same to mak no faithe in Judgment by way off actioun or exceptioun in preiudice of a third pairtie who hathe acquyred ane perfyit and lauchfull right to the saidis landis and heretages but preiudice alwayis to thame to vse the saidis writtis aganis the pairtye maker thairof his heiris and successoures It is alwayes declared that this present Act sall nowayis be extendit to [. . .] reuersiounes incorporate in the bodye of the Infeftmentis maid to the persounes aganis quhome the saidis reuersiounes ar vseit It is also declaired that gif anye renunciaciones or grantis of redemptioun whiche salhappin to be consignit in proces betuix pairties salbe registrat within thriescore dayes efter the daittis of the decreitis whereby the same salbe Ordaned to be gevin up to the pairties haveand right thairto The same salbe sufficient And to the effect the said register may presentlie and in all tyme cuming be the moir faithfullie keipit THAIRFORE Oure said souerane Lord with aduyis and consent foirsaid Statutes and ordanis the same registeris and registratiounes foirsaidis to be insert thairin to appertene and belang to the present Clerk of Register and his deputtis to be appoynted be him to that effect and decernis and ordanis the same Registeris to be annexed and incorporated with the said office And that the Clerk of Register present and to cum haue the said office as ane proper pairt and pertinent of the Clerk of Register his office [. . .] AND OURE SAID SOUERANE LORD with aduyse and Consent of the estaittis Decernis and Declairis this present act to haue the force strenth and effect of ane decreit and statute of parliament whiche sall have force strenth and executioun according to the tennoure thairoff in all tyme to cum. [. . .]

REAL RIGHTS ACT 1693
(1693, c 22)

Act concerning the preference of Real Rights

OUR Soveraigne Lord and Lady The King and Queens Majesties for the better clearing and determining of Competitions and Preferences of Reall Rights and Infeftments Do hereby with advice and consent of the Estates of Parliament Enact Statute and Declare That [Reall Rights in land shall in all competitions be preferable and preferred according to the date and priority of registration in the General Register of Sasines].

REGISTRATION OF LEASES (SCOTLAND) ACT 1857
(20 & 21 Vict, c 26)

AN ACT to provide for the Registration of Long Leases in Scotland, and Assignations thereof

1 Long leases, and assignations thereof registerable in Registers of Sasines

It shall be lawful to record in the general register of sasines in Scotland [. . .] probative leases, whether executed before or after the passing of this Act, for a period [exceeding twenty years] of lands heritages in Scotland [. . .], and to record respectively in the register in which any such lease as aforesaid shall have been registered, the assignations, and assignations in security of such lease, and translations thereof, all herein-after mentioned.

2 Recorded leases effectual against singular successors in the lands let

Leases registerable under this Act, and valid and binding as in a question with the granters thereof, which shall have been duly recorded, as herein provided [. . .] shall, by virtue of such registration, be effectual against any singular successor in the lands and heritages thereby let, whose [title is completed after] the date of such registration: Provided always, that, except for the purposes of this Act, it shall not be necessary to record any such lease as aforesaid, but that all such leases which would, under the existing law prior to the passing of this Act, have been valid and effectual against any such singular successor as aforesaid, shall, though not recorded, be valid and effectual against such singular successor, as well as against the granters of the said leases.

3 Assignations of recorded leases

[(1)] When any such lease as aforesaid shall have been recorded as herein provided, it shall be lawful for the party in right of such lease, and whose right is recorded in terms of this Act, but in accordance always with the conditions and stipulations of such lease, and not otherwise, to assign the same, in whole or in part, by assignation in the form as nearly as may be of the schedule (A) to this Act annexed; and the recording of such assignation shall fully and effectually vest the assignee with the right of the granter thereof in and to such lease to the extent assigned: Provided always, that such assignation shall be without prejudice to the right of hypothec, or other rights of the landlord.

[(2) Notwithstanding—

(a) any restriction imposed by subsection (1) above on the power under that subsection to assign such a lease; or

(b) any rule of law to the contrary,

it shall be, and shall be deemed always to have been, competent in an assignation under this section

[(i)] to impose conditions and make stipulations, or

[(ii) to import such conditions and stipulations,]

which, upon the recording of such assignation or the registration under the Land Registration (Scotland) Act 1979 of the assignee's interest, shall be as effectual against any singular successor of the assignee in the subjects assigned as if such assignee had been a grantee of the lease and it had been duly recorded or, as the case may be, the grantee's interest had been so registered.]

[(2A) Any person entitled to grant an assignation under this section may—

(a) execute a deed containing such conditions, or stipulations, as may be specified in an assignation under subsection (2) above; and

(b) register such conditions and stipulations in the Land Register of Scotland or, as the case may be, record the deed in the Register of Sasines,

and, subject to subsection (2C) below, on such registration or, as the case may be, recording such conditions and stipulations shall be effectual.

(2B) 'Import' in subsection (2)(ii) above means to import into itself from a deed of conditions ('deed of conditions' having the meaning given by section 122(1) of the Title Conditions (Scotland) Act 2003 (asp 9)) the terms of the conditions or stipulations; and importation in or as nearly as may be in the form set out in schedule 1 to that Act (but with the modification that for the references in that form to the terms of the title conditions there are substituted references to the terms of the conditions or stipulations) shall suffice in that regard.

(2C) Where, notwithstanding section 3(4) of the Land Registration (Scotland) Act 1979 (c 33) (creation of real right or obligation on date of registration etc), a deed provides for the postponement of effectiveness of any conditions or, as the case may be, stipulations to—

(a) a date specified in that deed (the specification being of a fixed date and not, for example, of a date determinable by reference to the occurrence of an event); or

(b) the date of—

(i) registration of an interest in land under; or

(ii) recording of,

some other deed so specified,

the conditions, or stipulations, shall take effect in accordance with such provision.]

[(3) Nothing in subsection (2) [or (2A)] above makes effectual against any successor of the assignee any obligation of periodical payment other than a payment—

(a) of rent or of an apportionment of rent;

(b) in defrayal of a contribution towards some continuing cost related to the lands and heritages subject to the lease assigned; or

(c) under a heritable security.

(4) A provision in an assignation [, or as the case may be in a deed such as is mentioned in subsection (2A) above] which purports to make effectual against any successor of the assignee any obligation of periodic payment other than one specified in paragraphs (a) to (c) of subsection (3) above shall not render the deed void or unenforceable, but the assignation [, or as the case may be the deed,] shall have, and shall be deemed always to have had, effect only to the extent (if any) that it would have had effect if it had not imposed such obligation.]

6 Translation of assignations in security. Creditor's entry to possession in default of payment

All such assignations in security as aforesaid shall, when recorded, be transferable, in whole or in part, by translation in the form as nearly as may be of the schedule (D) to this Act annexed; and the recording of such translation shall fully and effectually vest the party in whose favour it was granted with the right of the granter thereof in such assignation in security to the extent assigned; and the creditor or party in right of such assignation in security, without prejudice to the exercise of any power of sale therein contained, shall be entitled, in default of payment of the capital sum for which such assignation in security has been granted, or of a term's interest thereof, or of a term's annuity, for six months after such capital sum or term's interest or annuity shall have fallen due, to apply to the sheriff for a warrant to enter on possession of the lands and heritages leased; and the sheriff, after intimation to the lessee for the time being, and to the landlord, shall, if he see cause, grant such warrant, which shall be a sufficient title for such creditor or party to enter into possession of such lands and heritages, and to uplift the rents from any sub-tenant therein, and to sub-let the same, as freely and to the like effect as the lessee might have done: Provided always, that no such creditor or party, unless and until he enter into possession as aforesaid, shall be personally liable to the landlord in any of the obligations and prestations of the lease.

10 Adjudgers to complete right by recording abbreviate

When an adjudication of any such lease or assignation in security recorded as aforesaid shall have been obtained against the party vested in the right thereof respectively, or against the heir of such party, the recording of the abbreviate of adjudication in the register in which the lease is recorded shall complete the right of the adjudger to such lease or assignation in security.

12 Preferences regulated by date of recording transfer
All such leases executed after the passing of this Act, and all assignations, assignations in security of any such lease recorded as aforesaid, and translations thereof, and all adjudications of such leases recorded as aforesaid, or assignations in security, shall in competition be preferable according to their dates of recording.

13 Renunciations and discharges to be recorded
On the production to the keeper of the register of a renunciation of any such lease as aforesaid recorded therein, or of a discharge of any such assignation in security as aforesaid therein recorded, by or on behalf of the party appearing on the register as in right of such lease or assignation in security, which renunciation or discharge may be in the form of the schedules (G) and (H) respectively to this Act annexed, and may be endorsed on such lease or assignation in security, he shall forthwith duly record the same.

14 Entry of decree of reduction
On the production to any such keeper of an extract of a decree of reduction of any such lease, assignation, assignation in security, translation, adjudication, instrument, discharge, or renunciation recorded in the register of which he is the keeper, he shall forthwith duly record the same.

15 Mode of registering—extracts to make faith as writs registered
Leases, assignations, assignations in security, translations, adjudications, instruments, discharges, renunciations, and other writs, duly presented for registration in pursuance of this Act, shall be forthwith shortly entered in the minute book of the register in common form, and shall, with all due despatch, be fully registered in the register book, and thereafter re-delivered to the parties, with certificates of due registration thereon, which shall be probative of such registration, such certificates specifying the date of presentation, and the book and folio in which the engrossment has been made [. . .]; and the date of entry in the minute book shall be held to be the date of registration [. . .].

16 Registration equivalent to possession
   [(1)] The registration of all such leases, assignations, assignations in security, translations, adjudications [and writs of acknowledgement] as aforesaid, in manner herein provided, shall complete the right under the same respectively, to the effect of establishing a preference in virtue thereof, as effectually as if the grantee, or party in his right, had entered into the actual possession of the subjects leased under such writs respectively at the date of registration thereof.
   [(2) The registration of any such lease or other writ as aforesaid, in manner herein provided, on or after 1st September 1974, shall, without prejudice to the foregoing provisions of this section and to the provisions of section 2 of the Prescription and Limitation (Scotland) Act 1973, complete the right under the same to the effect of establishing in virtue thereof such a preference as aforesaid over the right of any party to any such lease or writ, or of any party in his right, granted after that date and not registered in manner herein provided at the time of the registration of the lease or writ first mentioned.]

17 Leases, with obligation to renew, registerable
Leases containing an obligation upon the granter to renew the same from time to time at fixed periods, or upon the termination of a life or lives, or otherwise, shall be deemed leases within the meaning of this Act, and registerable as such, provided such leases shall by the terms of such obligation be renewable from time to time so as to endure for a period [exceeding twenty years].

20   Clauses in schedules to be held to import and to have effect as declared by 10 & 11 Vict c 50, ss 2, 3, &c
The several clauses in the schedules to this Act annexed shall be held to import such and the like meaning and to have such and the like effect as is declared by the Act of the tenth and eleventh of Queen Victoria, chapter fifty, sections second and third, to belong to the corresponding clauses in the schedule to the said recited Act annexed; and the procedure thereby prescribed for a sale under a bond and disposition in security shall be applicable to a sale of any such lease as aforesaid under any such assignation in security as is herein-before mentioned.

21   Short title
This Act may be cited for all purposes as 'The Registration of Leases (Scotland) Act, 1857.'

SCHEDULES

SCHEDULE (A)   Sect 3

Form of Assignation of Lease

I, *A.B.*, [*designation*] in consideration of the sum of   now paid to me, [*or otherwise, as the case may be,*] assign to *C.D.* [*designation*] a lease, dated   , and recorded in the   register of sasines at   , of date   , granted by *E.F.* [*designation*] in my favour [*or if not in assigner's favour, name and design grantee*], of [*shortly mention subjects*] in the parish of   and county of   [. . .], [but (*where the lease is assigned in part only*) in so far only as regards the following portion of the subjects leased; viz. (*specify particularly the portion*),] with entry as at (*term of entry*). And [*where sub-lease*] I assign the rents from [*term*]; and I grant warrandice; and I bind myself to free and relieve the said *C.D.* of all rents and burdens due to the landlord or others at and prior to the term of entry in respect of said lease; and I consent to registration for preservation and execution.

[Testing clause †]

[† Note—Subscription of the document by the granter of it will be sufficient for the document to be formally valid, but witnessing of it may be necessary or desirable for other purposes (see the Requirements of Writing (Scotland) Act 1995).]

SCHEDULE (D)   Sect 6

Form of Translation of Assignation in Security

I, *A.B.*, [*designation,*] in consideration of the sum of   now paid to me [*or as the case may be*], assign and transfer to *C.D.* [*designation*] a bond and assignation in security for the principal sum of   [*or as the case may be*], granted by *E.F.* [*designation*] in my favour, [*or, if not in granter's favour, name and design the party in whose favour granted,*] dated   , and recorded [*register and date of recording*] of and over a lease granted by *G.H.* [*designation*] of [*shortly describe subjects leased*] in the parish of   , and county of   , which lease is dated   , and is recorded in the said register of date   [. . .], [but (*where the translation is partial*) only to the extent of (*insert sum*), and to the effect of giving *pari passu* preference to the said *C.D.* over the said lease with me, my heirs and assigns, as regards the remainder of the said principal sum and corresponding interest], with the interest from [*date*].

[Testing clause †]

[† Note—Subscription of the document by the granter of it will be sufficient for the document to be formally valid, but witnessing of it may be necessary or desirable for other purposes (see the Requirements of Writing (Scotland) Act 1995).]

Sect 13   SCHEDULE (G)

Renunciation of Lease

I, *A.B.* [*designation,*] renounce as from the term of   in favour of *C.D.*
[*designation*] a lease granted by the said *C.D.* [*or as the case may be*] of [*shortly set forth
subjects*] in the parish of   , and county of   , which lease
is dated   , and recorded [*register, and date of recording,*] [. . .]

[*Testing clause* †]

[† Note—Subscription of the document by the granter of it will be sufficient for the document
to be formally valid, but witnessing of it may be necessary or desirable for other purposes
(see the Requirements of Writing (Scotland) Act 1995).]

Sect 13   SCHEDULE (H)

Form of Discharge of Bond and Assignation in Security

I, *A.B.*, [*designation*] in consideration of the sum of   , now paid to me by
C.D., [*designation,*] discharge a bond and assignation in security for the sum of
                    , granted by the said *C.D.* in my favour [*or as the case may be*[1]], and
which is dated   , and recorded in the [*register, and date of
recording*]; and I declare to be disburdened thereof a lease granted by *E.F.* [*designation*]
of [*shortly mention subjects leased*] in the parish of   and county
of   , which lease is dated   , and recorded
[*register, and date of recording*].

[*Testing clause* †]

[† Note—Subscription of the document by the granter of it will be sufficient for the document
to be formally valid, but witnessing of it may be necessary or desirable for other purposes
(see the Requirements of Writing (Scotland) Act 1995).]
[1] Note—If granter not original creditor, [name and design original creditor].

LAND REGISTERS (SCOTLAND) ACT 1868
(31 & 32 Vict, c 64)

3   In general register of sasines, writs of each county to be kept separate
The general register of sasines for Scotland shall be so kept that the writs applicable to each county shall be entered in a separate series of presentment books, and
the writs shall be minuted in a separate series of minute books, and engrossed in a
separate series of register volumes, in the order of presentment; and where any
writ shall contain land in more than one county, such writ shall be entered by the
ingiver in the presentment book of such of these counties as may be specified in
the [application for registration] and shall be minuted in the minute book of such
of these counties or county as are specified in [that application], and shall be
engrossed at length in the division of the register applicable to one only of the said
counties; and a memorandum shall be entered in each division of the register
applicable to the other counties or county in the presentment book of which it is
entered as aforesaid, setting forth the volume of the register and the folio or folios
of such volume in which such engrossment is made; and such memorandum shall
be deemed to be equivalent to full engrossment of such writ in the division of the
register wherein such memorandum shall be entered as aforesaid: For the purposes of this Act, the barony and regality of Glasgow, and also the stewartry of
Kirkcudbright, shall each be treated as a county.

6 Provision for writs transmitted by post to general register of sasines
Where [an application for registration of a writ in the general register of sasines is transmitted by post], the keeper of said register shall, upon the receipt of such [application], cause the same to be acknowledged to the sender, and [cause the writ] to be presented [. . .] by a clerk in his office to be appointed by him for that purpose, and who shall be held as the ingiver of the writ; and such clerk shall [enter in the presentment book] the name of the sender; and such writ shall be recorded in the same manner as any writ presented for registration; and on the writ being ready for delivery [. . .], the keeper shall transmit the writs to the sender by post; and where two or more [such applications] shall be received by the keeper at the same time, the entries [. . .] in the presentment book and minute book [for the writs in respect of which such applications are made] shall be of the same year, month [and day,] and such writs shall be deemed and taken to be presented and registered contemporaneously.

TITLES TO LAND CONSOLIDATION (SCOTLAND) ACT 1868
(31 & 32 Vict, c 101)

[Preamble]

1 Short title
This Act may be cited for all purposes as 'The Titles to Land Consolidation (Scotland) Act, 1868.'

2 Commencement of Act
This Act shall take effect from and after the thirty-first day of December one thousand eight hundred and sixty-eight, unless in so far as it is herein appointed to take effect at an earlier date.

3 Interpretation of terms
The following words and expressions in this Act, and in the schedules annexed to this Act, shall have the several meanings hereby assigned to them, unless there be something in the subject or context repugnant to such construction; that is to say,

The words [. . .] 'grantor,' 'grantee,' 'disponer,' 'disponee,' 'legatee,' 'adjudger,' and 'purchaser' shall extend to and include the heirs, successors, and representatives of such [. . .] grantor, grantee, disponer, disponee, legatee, adjudger, or purchaser respectively; and the word 'successors' shall extend to and include heirs, disponees, assignees legal as well as voluntary, executors, and representatives:
[. . .]
The words 'sheriff of Chancery' shall extend to and include the sheriff of Chancery and his substitute under this Act, or under the Act of the tenth and eleventh Victoria, chapter forty-seven, and the word 'sheriff' shall extend to and include the sheriff of any county and his substitute, and the sheriff of Chancery and his substitute:
The words 'sheriff clerk of Chancery' shall extend to and include the sheriff clerk of Chancery acting under this Act, or who acted under the Act of the tenth and eleventh Victoria, chapter forty-seven, and the depute of such sheriff clerk; and the words 'sheriff clerk' shall extend to and include the sheriff clerk of Chancery, and the sheriff clerk of any county and their respective deputes:
[. . .] The word 'Prince' shall extend to and include the Prince and Steward of Scotland and his successors:
[. . .]
The word 'deed' and the word 'conveyance' shall each extend to and include all [. . .] writs, dispositions, [. . .] whether inter vivos or mortis causa, and whether absolute or in trust, [. . .] heritable securities, reversions, assignations, instruments, decrees of constitution relating to land to be afterwards adjudged, decrees of adjudication for debt, and of adjudication in implement, and of constitution and

adjudication combined, whether for debt or implement, decrees of declarator and adjudication, decrees of sale, and decrees of general and of special service [. . .] and the summonses, petitions, or warrants on which any such decrees proceed, warrants to judicial factors, trustees, or beneficiaries of a lapsed trust, to make up titles to lands, and the petitions on which such warrants proceed, writs of acknowledgment, contracts of excambion, deeds of entail [. . .] and all deeds, decrees, and writings by which lands, or rights in lands, are constituted or completed or conveyed, or discharged, whether dated, granted, or obtained before or after the passing of this Act, and official extracts of all deeds and conveyances; and all codicils, deeds of nomination, and other writings annexed to or endorsed on deeds or conveyances or bearing reference to deeds or conveyances separately granted, and decrees of declarator naming or appointing persons to exercise or enjoy the rights or powers conferred by such deeds or conveyances, shall be deemed and taken for the purposes of this Act to be parts of the deeds or conveyances to which they severally relate, and shall have the same effect in all respects as to the persons so named and appointed as if they had been named and appointed in the deeds or conveyances themselves:
  [. . .]
The word 'instrument' shall extend to and include all notarial instruments [. . .] and also all instruments of sasine, instruments of resignation ad remanentiam, instruments of resignation and sasine and instruments of cognition and sasine, and instruments of cognition:
The words 'heritable security' and 'security' shall each extend to and include all heritable bonds, bonds and dispositions in security, bonds of annual rent, bonds of annuity, and all securities authorised to be granted by the seventh section of the Debts Securities (Scotland) Act, 1856, and all deeds and conveyances whatsoever, legal as well as voluntary, which are or may be used for the purpose of constituting or completing or transmitting a security over lands or over the rents and profits thereof, as well as such lands themselves and the rents and profits thereof, and the sums, principal, interest, and penalties, secured by such securities; but shall not include securities by way of ground annual, whether redeemable or irredeemable, or absolute dispositions qualified by back bonds or letters:
The word 'creditor' shall extend to and include the party in whose favour an heritable security is granted, and his successors in right thereof:
The word 'debtor' shall include the debtor and his successors:
The word 'lands' shall extend to and include all heritable subjects, securities, and rights:
The words 'notary public' shall be held to mean a notary public duly admitted to practise in Scotland:
The word 'petitioner' shall extend to and include any person who may have presented or may present a petition within the meaning of this Act, or of any Act hereby repealed:
  [. . .]

8 Import of clauses in Schedule (B) nos 1 and 2
[. . .] The clause of assignation of writs and evidents in [Form No 1] of schedule (B) hereto annexed shall, unless specially qualified, be held to import an absolute and unconditional assignation to such writs and evidents [. . .] therein contained, and to all unrecorded conveyances to which the disponer has right; and the clause of assignation of rents [. . .] shall, unless specially qualified, be held to import an assignation to the rents to become due for the possession following the term of entry, according to the legal and not the conventional terms, unless in the case of forehand rents, in which case it shall be held to import an assignation to the rents payable at the conventional terms subsequent to the date of entry; and the clause of warrandice [. . .] shall, unless specially qualified, be held to imply absolute warrandice as regards the lands and writs and evidents, and warrandice from fact and

deed as regards the rents; and the clause of obligation to free and relieve from [public burdens] shall, unless specially qualified, be held to import an obligation to relieve of all [public] and local burdens due from or on account of the lands conveyed prior to the date of entry; [. . .]; and the clause of consent to registration [shall, unless specially qualified, have the meaning and effect assigned].

12   Clause directing part of conveyance to be recorded
Immediately before the testing clause of any conveyance of lands, it shall be competent to insert a clause of direction, in or as nearly as may be in the form No 1 of schedule (F) hereto annexed, specifying the part or parts of the conveyance which the grantor thereof desires to be recorded in the register of sasines; and when such clause is so inserted in any conveyance, whether dated before or after the commencement of this Act, and [. . .] is presented to the keeper of the appropriate register of sasines for registration, such keeper shall record such part or parts only, together with the clause of direction, and the testing clause [. . .]: Provided, that notwithstanding such clause of direction it shall be competent for the person entitled to present the conveyance for registration to record the whole conveyance. [. . .]

13   Several lands conveyed by the same deed may be comprehended under one general name
Where several lands are comprehended in one conveyance in favour of the same person or persons, it shall be competent to insert a clause in the conveyance, declaring that the whole lands conveyed and therein particularly described shall be designed and known in future by one general name, to be therein specified; and on the conveyance containing such clause, whether dated before or after the commencement of this Act, or on an instrument following thereon, whether dated before or after the commencement of this Act, and containing such particular description and clause, being duly recorded in the appropriate register of sasines, it shall be competent in all subsequent conveyances and deeds and discharges of or relating to such several lands to use the general name specified in such clause as the name of the several lands declared by such clause to be comprehended under it; and such subsequent conveyances and deeds and discharges of or relating to such several lands under the general name so specified shall be as effectual in all respects as if the same contained a particular description of each of such several lands, exactly as the same is set forth in such recorded conveyance or instrument: Provided always, that reference be made in such subsequent conveyances and deeds and discharges to a prior conveyance or instrument recorded as aforesaid, in which such particular description and clause are contained: Provided also, that it shall not be necessary in such clause to comprehend under one general name the whole lands contained in the conveyance in which such clause is inserted, but that it shall be competent to comprehend certain lands under one general name and certain other lands under another general name, it being clearly specified what lands are comprehended under each general name; and such reference shall be in or as nearly as may be in the terms set forth in schedule (G) hereunto annexed. [. . .]

20   De praesenti words, or words of style unnecessary in mortis causa deeds
From and after the commencement of this Act it shall be competent to any owner of lands to settle the succession to the same in the event of his death, not only by conveyances de præsenti, according to the existing law and practice, but likewise by testamentary or mortis causa deeds or writings; and no testamentary or mortis causa deed or writing purporting to convey or bequeath lands which shall have been granted by any person alive at the commencement of this Act, or which shall be granted by any person after the commencement of this Act, shall be held to be invalid as a settlement of the lands to which such deed or writing applies on the ground that the grantor has not used with reference to such lands the word 'dispone,' or other word or words importing a conveyance de præsenti; and where

such deed or writing shall not be expressed in the terms required by the existing law or practice for the conveyance of lands, but shall contain with reference to such lands any word or words which would, if used in a will or testament with reference to moveables, be sufficient to confer upon the executor of the grantor, or upon the grantee or legatee of such moveables, a right to claim and receive the same, such deed or writing, if duly executed in the manner required or permitted in the case of any testamentary writing by the law of Scotland, shall be deemed and taken to be [valid as a settlement on a grantee or legatee of the lands to which it applies; and the executor of the grantor may complete title to such lands by expeding and recording a notarial instrument as aforesaid]: Provided always, that nothing herein contained shall be held to confer any right to such lands on the successors of any such grantee or legatee who shall predecease the grantor, unless the deed or writing shall be so expressed as to give them such right in the event of the predecease of such grantee or legatee.

21   Trustee or executor to apply lands for purposes of trust or will

Where such testamentary or mortis causa deed or writing shall be conceived in favour of a grantee as trustee or executor of the grantor and shall not be expressed to be wholly in favour of such trustee or executor for his own benefit, such trustee or executor shall apply such whole lands for the purposes specified in such deed or writing; and where such purposes cannot, in whole or in part, be carried into effect, or where no purposes with reference to such lands have been or shall be specified in such deed or writing, such trustee or executor shall convey such lands, or so much thereof, or shall apply so much of the proceeds thereof, if such lands shall have been sold and realized by him, as may not be required for the purposes of such deed or writing, to or for behoof of the person or the successors of the person who, but for the passing of this Act and the granting of such deed or writing, would have been entitled to succeed to such lands on the death of such grantor.

24   Mode of completing title by a judicial factor on a trust estate, &c

Where in a petition to the Court of Session for the appointment of a judicial factor authority has been or shall be asked for the completion of a title by such factor to any lands forming the whole or part of the estate to be managed by such judicial factor, or where a judicial factor has applied or shall apply, by petition or note to the said Court, for authority to complete a title to such lands, either in his own person as judicial factor, or in the person of any persons under legal disability by reason of nonage, or mental or other incapacity to whom he may have been appointed judicial factor, and where any petition or note has specified and described or shall specify and describe the lands to which such title is to be completed, or has referred or shall refer to the description of the same, in the form or as nearly as may be in the form [. . .] of schedule (G) hereto annexed, as the case may be, the warrant granted for completing such title shall also so specify and describe the lands to which such title is to be completed, or shall so refer to the description thereof; and such warrant shall be held to be a conveyance in due and common form of the lands therein specified in favour of such judicial factor, granted by the person, whether in life or deceased, whose estate is under judicial management, or where the estate is that of a person under legal disability by reason of nonage, or mental or other incapacity, in whose person a title has not been made up, such warrant shall be held to be such a conveyance in favour of the persons under legal disability by reason of nonage, or mental or other incapacity, or of a judicial factor appointed to such persons under legal disability by reason of nonage, or mental or other incapacity, as the case may be, granted by a predecessor or author having such title, or where such judicial factor has been or shall be appointed on an estate which shall have been vested in a trustee or former judicial factor, such warrant shall be held to be such a conveyance granted by such trustee or former factor, whether in life or deceased, for the purposes of such estate, or trust, or factory, [. . .] to be holden of Her Majesty in free burgage; and such warrant may [. . .] be recorded in the appropriate register of sasines as a conveyance in favour of such judicial factor, or persons under legal disability by reason of nonage, or mental or other incapacity, or of the factor on his estate, and being so recorded shall have the same force and effect as if at the date of such recording such conveyance had been granted to the judicial factor, or persons under legal disability by reason of nonage, or mental or other incapacity, or the judicial factor appointed to such persons under legal disability by reason of nonage, or mental or other incapacity, as the case may be, and recorded in the appropriate register of sasines: Provided always, that for enabling the person in whom such lands were last vested, or his representatives, or other parties interested, to bring forward competent objections against such warrant being granted, or claims upon the estate, the Court shall order such intimation and service of the petition or note as to them shall seem proper: Declaring always, that the whole enactments and provisions herein contained shall extend and apply to all petitions to and warrants by the Court of Session under the Trusts (Scotland) Act, 1867, unless in so far as such provisions and enactments may be inapplicable to the form or objects of such petitions or warrants.]

[25 Deduction of title by liquidator
The liquidator in the winding up of a company shall, for the purposes of sections 3 (disposition etc by person with unrecorded title) and 4 (completion of title) of the Conveyancing (Scotland) Act 1924 (c 27) (including those sections as applied to registered leases by section 24 of that Act), be taken to be a person having right to any land belonging to the company.]

26 Heritable property conveyed for religious or educational purposes to vest in disponees or their successors
Wherever lands have been or may hereafter be acquired by any congregation, society, or body of men associated for religious purposes, or for the promotion of education, including the general assemblies, synods, and presbyteries of the Established Church of Scotland, and of all other Presbyterian churches in Scotland, as a chapel, meeting house, or other place of worship, or as a manse or dwelling house for the minister of such congregation or society or body of men, or offices, garden, or glebe for his use, or as a schoolhouse, or schoolmaster's house, garden, or playground, or as a college, academy, or seminary, or as a hall or rooms for meeting for the transaction of business, or as part of the property belonging to such congregation, society, or body of men, and wherever the conveyance or lease of such lands has been or may be taken in favour of the moderator, minister, kirk session, vestrymen, deacons, managers, or other office bearers or office bearer of such congregation or society or body of men, or any of them, or of trustees appointed or to be from time to time appointed, or of any party or parties named in such conveyance or lease in trust for behoof of the congregation or society or body of men, or of the individuals comprising the same, such conveyance, when recorded [. . .] in terms of this Act, or such lease, shall not only vest the party or parties named therein in the lands thereby [. . .] conveyed, or leased, but shall also, after the death or resignation or removal from office of such party or parties, or any of them, effectually vest their successors in office for the time being chosen and appointed in the manner provided or referred to in such conveyance or lease, or if no mode of appointment be therein set forth or prescribed, then in terms of the rules or regulations of such congregation or society or body of men, in such lands, subject to such and the like trusts, and with and under the same powers and provisions, as are contained or referred to in the conveyance or lease given and granted to the parties disponees or lessees therein, and that without any transmission or renewal of the investiture whatsoever, anything in such conveyance or lease contained to the contrary notwithstanding: And the provisions of this section shall apply also to all trusts for the maintenance, support, or endowment of minis-

ters of religion, missionaries, or schoolmasters, or for the maintenance of the fabric of churches, chapels, meeting houses, or other places of worship, or of manses or dwelling houses or offices for ministers of the gospel, or of schoolhouses or school-master's houses, or other like buildings.

[26A   Application for declarator of succession as heir in general or to specified lands

On an application being made by any person having an interest, the sheriff of Chancery may, if satisfied that—

(a)   such deceased person as may be specified in the application died before 10th September 1964 and that person either—

(i)   was domiciled in Scotland at the date of his death; or

(ii)   was the owner of lands situated in Scotland to which the application relates; and

(b)   the applicant, or as the case may be such person as may be specified in the application, has succeeded as heir to that deceased, and is either—

(i)   heir in general; or

(ii)   heir to such lands as may be specified in the application, grant declarator that the applicant, or as the case may be such person as may be specified in the declarator, is the heir in general or heir to the lands so specified.

26B   Application for declarator of succession as heir to last surviving trustee under a trust

On an application being made under this section, the sheriff of Chancery may, if satisfied that—

(a)   such deceased person as may be specified in the application was the last surviving trustee named in, or assumed under, a trust;

(b)   the trust provides for the heir of such last surviving trustee to be a trustee;

(c)   either—

(i)   the trust is governed by the law of Scotland; or

(ii)   lands subject to the trust and to which the application relates are situated in Scotland; and

(d)   the applicant has succeeded as heir to the deceased.

26C   Construction of reference to service of heir

A reference in any enactment or deed to a decree of service of heir (however expressed) shall include a reference to a declarator granted under section 26A or 26B of this Act.]

51   Power to the Court of Session to pass Acts of Sederunt

It shall be competent to the [. . .] Court of Session, and they are hereby authorized and required, from time to time to pass such acts of sederunt as shall be necessary or proper for regulating in all respects the proceedings under this Act before the sheriff of Chancery [. . .].

59   Unnecessary to libel and conclude for decree of special adjudication

Whereas it is inconvenient in practice to libel and conclude for general adjudication of lands as the alternative only of special adjudication, in terms of an Act of the Parliament of Scotland passed in the year one thousand six hundred and seventy-two: It shall not be necessary to libel or conclude for special adjudication, and it shall be lawful to libel and conclude and decern for general adjudication without such alternative, anything in the said last-recited Act of the Parliament of Scotland, or in any other Act or Acts of the Parliament of Scotland or of Great Britain or of the United Kingdom of Great Britain and Ireland, to the contrary notwithstanding.

62   Effect of a decree of adjudication or of sale

In all cases a decree of adjudication, whether for debt or in implement, or a decree of constitution and adjudication, whether for debt or in implement, if duly obtained in the form prescribed by this Act, or obtained, if prior to the commencement of this Act, in the form then in use, or a decree of declarator and adjudication, or a decree of sale, shall, except in the case where the subjects contained in the decree of adjudication, or of constitution and adjudication, or of declarator and adjudication, are heritable securities, be held equivalent to and shall have the legal operation and effect of a conveyance in ordinary form of the lands therein contained granted in favour of the adjudger or purchaser by the ancestor of such apparent heir, or by the owner or proprietor, in trust or otherwise, and whether in life or deceased, of the lands adjudged, or by the seller of the lands sold, although [under legal disability by reason of nonage] or [mental or other incapacity] [. . .] and it shall be lawful and competent to such adjudger or purchaser to complete [title by recording the decree as a conveyance or by using the decree as a mid-couple or link of title].

[117 Heritable security in succession of creditor in the security
In the succession of the creditor in a heritable security, the security shall be moveable estate; except that in relation to the legal rights of the spouse, or of the descendants, of the deceased it shall be heritable estate.]

120 Securities may be registered during lifetime of grantee, or title completed after his death
Heritable securities [. . .] may be registered in the appropriate register of sasines at any time during the lifetime of the grantee, and shall in competition be preferred according to the date of the registration thereof [. . .].

[129 Adjudgers may complete their title to heritable securities by recording abbreviate of adjudication
In all cases of adjudication, whether for debt or in implement, or of constitution and adjudication, whether for debt or in implement, in which the adjudger has obtained a decree of adjudication, or of constitution and adjudication, in the manner and to the effect provided by this Act, or in cases of declarator and adjudication, where the subjects contained in any such decree are heritable securities, it shall be competent for the adjudger to complete his title to such securities by recording either the abbreviate of adjudication or an extract of such decree in the appropriate register of sasines, in either of which cases he shall be in the same position as if an assignation of such heritable securities had been granted in his favour by the ancestor or person or creditor, in trust or otherwise, and whether in life or deceased, whose estate is adjudged, and as if such assignation had been duly recorded in the appropriate register of sasines at the date of so recording such abbreviate or such extract decree.]

138 Short clauses of consent to registration may be used in any deed
The short clauses of consent to registration for preservation, and for preservation and execution contained in [form No 1] of schedule (B) hereto annexed, when occurring in any deed or conveyance under this Act, or in any deed or writing or document of whatsoever nature, and whether relating to lands or not, shall, unless specially qualified, import a consent to registration and a procuratory of registration in the books of council and session, or other judges books competent, therein to remain for preservation; and also, if for execution, that [, upon the issue of an extract containing a warrant for execution, all lawful execution shall pass thereon].

140 Additional sheets may be added to writs
In all cases where writs or deeds of any description are by this or any other Act permitted or directed to be engrossed on any conveyance or deed, it shall be competent, when necessary, to engross such deeds or writs on a sheet or sheets of paper, or of whatever other material the conveyance itself consists, added to such conveyance, provided that the engrossing of the deed or writ shall be commenced

on some part of the conveyance or deed itself on which it is permitted or directed to be engrossed; and the first of such additional sheets shall be chargeable with the stamp duty applicable to the writ or deed partly engrossed thereon [. . .]

142   Recording of conveyances in the Register of Sasines authorised
All conveyances and deeds [. . .] authorized to be recorded in the register of sasines, may [. . .] be recorded at any time in the life of the person on whose behalf the [application for registration of such conveyance or deed is made and on such application the conveyance or deed] shall be presented for registration [and] when presented for registration shall be forthwith shortly registered in the minute books of the said register in common form, and shall with all due despatch be fully registered in the register books, and thereafter redelivered to the parties with certificates of due registration thereon, which shall specify the date of presentation, and the book and folios in which the engrossment has been made, [. . .] and shall be probative of such registration, and when so registered shall in competition be preferable according to the date of registration, and the date of entry in the minute book shall be held to be the date of registration: Provided, that where two or more [applications for registration of] deeds or conveyances [. . .] shall be received by the keeper of the register of sasines [on the same day], the entries [. . .] in the presentment book and minute book [for the conveyances or deeds in respect of which such applications are made] shall be of the same year, month [and day], and such deeds and conveyances shall be deemed and taken to be presented and registered contemporaneously [. . .].

[143   Recording anew
Where there is an error or defect in recording a deed or conveyance in the Register of Sasines it shall be competent to record it anew.]

155   Inhibitions to take effect from registration of notice etc
It shall be competent, before or after execution of any inhibition, whether by separate letters or contained in a summons before the Court of Session, to register in the general register of inhibitions a notice thereof, setting forth the names and designations of the persons by and against whom the same is raised, and the date of signeting the same, in the form or as nearly as may be in the form of schedule (PP) hereto annexed; and where any such inhibition and the execution thereof shall be duly registered in the general register of inhibitions not later than twenty-one days from the date of the registration therein of such notice thereof, such inhibition shall take effect from the date when such notice was registered as aforesaid, but otherwise only from the date of the registration of such inhibition and the execution thereof; and no inhibition shall have any effect against any act or deed done, committed, or executed prior to the registration of such notice thereof, or of such inhibition and the execution thereof, as the case may be.

157   No inhibition to have effect against acquirenda, unless in case of heir under entail or other indefeasible title
No inhibition to be recorded from and after the thirty-first day of December one thousand eight hundred and sixty-eight shall have any force or effect as against any lands to be acquired by the person or persons against whom such inhibition is used after the date of recording such inhibition, or of recording the previous notice thereof prescribed by this Act, as the case may be: Provided always, that where such inhibition is used against a person or persons who shall thereafter succeed to any lands which, at the date of recording the inhibition or previous notice thereof, as the case may be, were destined to such person or persons by a deed of entail, or by a similar indefeasible title, then and in that case such inhibition shall affect the said person or persons in so far as regards the lands so destined, and to which he or they shall succeed as aforesaid, but no further.

159   Litigiosity not to begin before date of registration of notice of summons
It shall be competent to register in the general register of inhibitions a notice of
any signeted summons of reduction of any conveyance or deed of or relating to
lands, and in the register of adjudications a notice of any signeted summons of
adjudication or of constitution and adjudication combined for debt or in security
or in implement, which notice shall set forth the names and designations of the
pursuer and defender of such action, and the date of signeting such summons,
[and contain a description of the lands to which the summons relates] in the form
or as nearly as may be in the form of schedule (RR) hereto annexed; and no
summons of reduction, constitution, adjudication, or constitution and adjudication
combined, shall have any effect in rendering litigious the lands to which such
summons relates, except from and after the date of the registration of such notice.

SCHEDULES

SCHEDULE (B)   Sects 5–8, 46, 138

No 1

Formal clauses of a disposition of land, &c [. . .]

[*After the inductive and dispositive clauses, the deed may proceed thus:*] With entry
at the term of [*here specify the date of entry*]; [. . .] and I assign the writs, and have
delivered the same according to inventory; and I assign the rents; and I bind
myself to free and relieve the said disponee and his foresaids of all [. . .] public
burdens; and I grant warrandice; and I consent to registration hereof for preservation [*or for preservation and execution*]. [. . .]

[*Testing clause* †]

[† Note—Subscription of the document by the granter of it will be sufficient for the document
to be formally valid, but witnessing of it may be necessary or desirable for other purposes
(see the Requirements of Writing (Scotland) Act 1995).

[. . .]

SCHEDULE (F)   Sect 12

No 1

Clause of direction specifying part of deed which grantor desires to be recorded

And I direct to be recorded in the register of sasines the part of this deed from its
commencement to the words [*insert words*] on the   line of the   page
[and also the part from the words [*insert words*] on the   line of the
page to the words [*insert words*] on the   line of the   page]. [*Or,* I
direct the whole of this deed to be recorded in the register of sasines, with the exception of the part [*or parts, as the case may be, specifying the part or parts excepted, as
above*].]
[. . .]

SCHEDULE (G)   Sects 13, 24

Clause of reference to conveyance, containing general designation of lands

[*After giving the general name or names of the lands, and the name of the county or burgh and county, as the case may be, add*] as particularly described in the disposition [*or other deed, as the case may be,*] granted by C.D., and bearing date [*here insert date*], and recorded in the [*specify the register of sasines*] on the   day of   , in the year   , and in which the lands hereby conveyed are declared to be designed and known by the said name of [*here insert name*] [*or,* 'as particularly described in the instrument (*specify instrument*) recorded, *&c*, and in which the lands hereby conveyed are declared,' *&c*] [*If part only of lands is conveyed, then follow form for similar case given in schedule (E)*]
    [. . .]

Sect 155   SCHEDULE (PP)

Notice of inhibition

Notice of letters of inhibition [*or, of summons containing inhibition, as the case may be*].—A.B. [*insert designation of the inhibitor*] against C.D. [*insert designation of the inhibited*].—Signeted [*insert date of signeting*].

E.F., W.S. [*or* S.S.C.], Agent.

    [. . .]

Sect 159   SCHEDULE (RR)

Notice of summons of reduction, adjudication, &c

Notice of summons of reduction [*or of adjudication, or of constitution and adjudication, as the case may be*].—A.B. [*insert designation of pursuer*] against C.D. [*insert designation of defender*]. Signeted [*insert date of signeting*]. The summons relates to [*insert description of lands*]

E.F., W.S. [*or* S.S.C.], Agent.

CONVEYANCING (SCOTLAND) ACT 1874
(37 & 38 Vict, c 94)

[*Preamble*]

1 Short title
This Act may be cited for all purposes as 'The Conveyancing (Scotland) Act 1874'.

2 Commencement of Act
This Act shall, except where otherwise provided, come into operation on the first day of October one thousand eight hundred and seventy-four, which date is hereinafter referred to as the commencement of this Act.

3 Interpretation
The following words and expressions in this Act shall have the several meanings hereby assigned to them; that is to say,
    'Land' or 'lands' shall include all subjects of heritable property which [prior to the day appointed by order made under section 71 of the Abolition of Feudal Tenure etc (Scotland) Act 2000 (asp 5) were, or might be,] held of a superior according to feudal tenure, or which prior to the commencement of this Act have been or might have been held by burgage tenure, or by tenure of booking:
    [. . .]

'Conveyance' and 'deed' and 'instrument' shall each have the meaning attached thereto by the Titles to Land Consolidation (Scotland) Act, 1868 and the Titles to Land Consolidation (Scotland) (Amendment) Act, 1869, and shall also, when used in this Act, include all the deeds, instruments, decrees, petitions, and writings specified in this Act; and the words 'heritable securities' and 'securities' shall have the meaning attached thereto by the said recited Acts. [. . .]

27 The word 'dispone' unnecessary
It shall not be competent to object to the validity of any deed or writing as a conveyance of heritage coming into operation after the passing of this Act, on the ground that it does not contain the word 'dispone,' provided it contains any other word or words importing conveyance or transference, or present intention to convey or transfer.

28 Date of entry
Where no term of entry is stated in a conveyance of lands, the entry shall be at the first term of Whitsunday or Martinmas after the date or last date of the conveyance, unless it shall appear from the terms of the conveyance that another term of entry was intended.

29 General dispositions forming links of series of titles not objectionable on certain grounds
No decree, instrument, or conveyance [. . .], whether dated before or after the commencement of this Act, shall be deemed to be invalid because the series of titles connecting the person obtaining such decree, or expeding such instrument, or holding such conveyance, with the person [who last held a recorded title contains] as links of the series two or more general dispositions, or because any general disposition forming a part of the series does not contain a clause of assignation of writs.

35 Registration of a decree of division
A decree of division of commonty or of common property or runrig lands, whether pronounced by a court of law, or by arbiters or by an oversman, shall have the effect of a conveyance containing assignations of writs by all the [. . .] proprietors in favour of the several parties participating in the division of the shares severally allotted to them, and the extract decree pronounced by the court, or the decree pronounced by the arbiters or oversman, or an extract thereof from any competent court books, may be recorded in the appropriate register of sasines, in ordinary form on behalf of all or any of the parties, or may be used by all or any of the parties for the purpose of [deducing title] to the shares severally allotted to them, or to any portion thereof [. . .].

36 Effect of decree of sale of glebe
A decree of sale obtained in terms of section seventeen of the Glebe Lands (Scotland) Act 1866, shall have the effect of a conveyance by the minister of the parish at the sight of the heritors of the parish and of the presbytery of the bounds, to the heritor in whose favour it is pronounced, and his heirs and assignees whomsoever, of the glebe or portion of glebe therein contained; and, on an extract of such decree being recorded in the appropriate register of sasines, shall vest in such heritor the glebe or portion of the glebe described therein [. . .].

44 Provisions for the case of a person appointed by the court to administer a trust
When a trust title [to land or to a real right in or over land] has been duly completed and recorded, and any person is subsequently appointed by the Court to administer the trust in whole or in part as a trustee or judicial factor, the interlocutor whereby the appointment is made shall specify the trust deed, and the other title or titles (if any) by which the trust title had been completed as aforesaid, in such manner as to identify the same, and shall refer to the register or registers

of sasines where such deed or title or titles is or are recorded, and also set forth the lands by description or reference; and an extract of such interlocutor, being recorded in the appropriate register of sasines, shall operate [to complete] in favour of the trustee or judicial factor thereby appointed [title to the land or real right,] in the same manner as if he had been a trustee named in the completed and recorded title in conformity always with the nature and terms of the appointment, and to the effect of enabling him to perform the duties of the office to which he is appointed.

45   How title shall be completed when the holder of an office or proprietor is ex officio a trustee and his successor in office takes the trust

When by the tenor of the title to any [land, or any real right in or over land] held in trust duly completed in favour of the trustee or trustees therein named, or any of them, and recorded in the appropriate register of sasines, the office of a trustee has been or shall be conferred upon the holder of any place or office, or proprietor of any estate, and his successors therein, any person subsequently becoming a trustee by appointment or succession to the place or office or estate to which the office of trustee has thus been or shall be annexed shall be deemed and taken to have a valid and complete title [to the land or real right] in the same manner and to the same effect as if he had been named in the completed and recorded title, without the necessity of any deed of conveyance or other procedure.

47   Securities upon land, and relative personal obligations, shall transmit against heirs and disponees [. . .]

An heritable security for money, duly constituted [over land, or over a real right in land,] shall, together with any personal obligation to pay principal, interest, and penalty contained in the deed or instrument whereby the security is constituted, transmit against any person taking [such land or real right] by succession, gift, or bequest, or by conveyance, when an agreement to that effect appears in gremio of the conveyance, and shall be a burden upon his title in the same manner as it was upon that of his ancestor or author, without the necessity of a bond of corroboration or other deed or procedure; and the personal obligation may be enforced against such person by summary diligence or otherwise, in the same manner as against the original debtor. A warrant to charge may be applied for and validly granted in the Bill Chamber or in a Sheriff Court, in the form set forth in Schedule K hereto annexed, or in a similar form, and all diligence may thereafter proceed against the party in common form. A discharge of the personal obligation of the original or any subsequent debtor, whether granted before or after the commencement of this Act, shall not where the debt still exists prejudice the security on [the land or real right] or the obligation as hereby made transmissible against the existing proprietor.

50   Form and effect of assigning right of relief or other right affecting land

An assignation or conveyance of any obligation or right of relief or other right connected with lands, but the title to which does not, according to the present law, pass under the general assignation of writs in the disposition of the lands, may be granted in, or as nearly as may be in, the form of Schedule M hereto annexed, and may either be a separate deed or part of another deed, and shall have the effect of vesting in the person or persons in whose favour it is granted, and his or their successors, a valid and complete right and title to the obligation or right thereby assigned or conveyed, with all the intermediate transmissions thereof, to the same effect in all respects as if an assignation or conveyance in the form at present in use had been granted in his or their favour.

51   Probate equivalent to will or extract for completing title

The [. . .] probate of the will or other testamentary settlement of a person deceased, issued by

[(a)]   any court of probate in England or in Ireland, or in any British colony or dependency, or
    [(b)   a district court in Palestine before 15th May 1948, or
    (c)   the Supreme Court of Aden before 30th November 1967,]
or of [an exemplification of such probate, shall for the purpose of completing a title to any land, or real right in land,] or to any heritable security, be held to be equivalent to and as effectual as [. . .] the will or settlement itself, or of an extract thereof from the books of council and session [. . .].

54   Recorded deed or instrument unchallengeable on certain grounds
No challenge of any deed, instrument, or writing recorded in any register of sasines shall receive effect on the ground that any part of the record of such deed, instrument, or writing is written on erasure, unless such erasure be proved to have been made for the purpose of fraud, or the record is not conformable to the deed, instrument, or writing as presented for registration.

61   Description of lands contained in recorded deeds may be inserted in subsequent writs by reference merely—reference already made in recorded deed not challengeable if certain particulars correctly given
[. . .] In all cases where any lands have been particularly described in any conveyance, deed, or instrument of or relating thereto, recorded in the appropriate register of sasines, it shall not be necessary in any subsequent conveyance, deed, or instrument, conveying or referring to the whole or any part of such lands, to repeat the particular description of the lands at length; but it shall be sufficient to specify the name of the county, and where the lands were held by burgage or by any similar tenure prior to the commencement of this Act, the name of the burgh and county in which the lands are situated, and to refer to the particular description of such lands as contained in such prior conveyance, deed, or instrument so recorded in or as nearly as may be in the form set forth in Schedule O hereto annexed; and the specification and reference so made in any such subsequent conveyance, deed, or instrument, whether dated prior or subsequent to the commencement of this Act, shall be held to be equivalent to the full insertion of the particular description contained in such prior conveyance, deed, or instrument, and shall have the same effect as if the particular description had been inserted in such subsequent conveyance, deed, or instrument exactly as it is contained in such prior conveyance, deed, or instrument; and it shall not be competent . . . to object to any specification and reference to any particular description of lands contained in any conveyance, deed, or instrument recorded prior to the commencement of this Act, provided such specification and reference states correctly the name of the county, and where the lands were held by burgage or by any similar tenure prior to the commencement of this Act, the name of the burgh and county in which the lands are situated, and refers correctly to the prior recorded conveyance, deed, or instrument containing the particular description of such lands; and where any conveyance, deed, or instrument recorded prior to the commencement of this Act contains a specification and reference stating these particulars correctly, the specification and reference so made shall be held to have been equivalent to the full insertion of the particular description contained in the prior conveyance, deed, or instrument referred to, as if the particular description had been inserted in such recorded conveyance, deed, or instrument exactly as it is contained in the prior conveyance, deed, or instrument referred to.

[Note the effect here of the Conveyancing (Scotland) Act 1924, s 8.]

66   Schedules to be part of Act
The schedules annexed to this Act, and the directions therein contained, and notes thereto appended, shall have the same effect as if they were contained in the body of this Act.

67 Repeal of Acts, &c

All statutes, laws, and usages at variance with any of the provisions of this Act are hereby repealed.

SCHEDULES

[. . .]

Sect 47   SCHEDULE K
FORM OF MINUTE TO BE PRESENTED IN BILL CHAMBER OF COURT OF
SESSION, OR IN SHERIFF COURT, FOR WARRANT TO CHARGE AN HEIR
OR DISPONEE UNDER A PERSONAL OBLIGATION BY HIS ANCESTOR
OR AUTHOR

Warrant is craved, in virtue of the Conveyancing (Scotland) Act, 1874, at the instance of *A.B.* [*name and design applicant*], the creditor [*if he is not the original creditor, or only a partial creditor, add*, in virtue of (*or* to the extent and in virtue of) the assignation (*or* general disposition and notarial instrument *or other writ or writs forming the title in the creditor's person*) in his favour after mentioned] under a bond and disposition in security over the lands of [*specify shortly the lands*], for the principal sum of £   with corresponding interest and penalties, granted by *C.D.* [*design him*], then proprietor of the said lands, in favour of the said *A.B.* [*or of G.H.* (*design him*) *as the case may be*], and dated [*state date*] [*and if recorded, say*, and recorded in the register of sasines (*state register and date of recording*), *or* and instrument of sasine thereon recorded, &c, *as the case may be*]: To charge *E.F.* [*design him*], the present proprietor of the said lands, and as such the present debtor in the said bond and disposition in security, to make payment to the said *A.B.* of the said principal sum of £   contained in and due by the said bond and disposition in security [*if A.B. is only a partial creditor, say*, of the principal sum of £   being the extent to which the said *A.B.* is in right of the said bond and disposition in security]: And also of the further sum of £   being the amount of the interest due thereon. Produced herewith the said bond and disposition in security [*or an extract thereof from the books of council and session or from the register of sasines; if the applicant is not the original creditor, the title in his own person to the security will also be stated and produced*].

    Dated the   day of   .

                        (Signed)   *A.B.*, W.S., Edinburgh,
                                       [*or as the case may be*].
        The Clerk of the Bills, or Sheriff Clerk, as the case may be, will subjoin
                            Fiat ut petitur.
                    [*To be dated and signed by the Clerk.*]

Sect 50   SCHEDULE M
                FORM OF ASSIGNATION OF RIGHT OF RELIEF, &c

I [*here insert the name and designation of the granter, and the cause of granting, unless the assignation forms part of another deed*] hereby assign to *C.D.* [*here insert the desig-nation of the grantee, unless already given*], and his heirs and assignees [*or and his foresaids*], a disposition [*or other deed, as the case may be*] granted by [*here insert the names and designations of the persons by and in whose favour the deed to be assigned was granted, with its date and also the date of registration, and the register in which it is recorded, if it has been recorded*], whereby the said [*name of the original granter of the disposition or obligation*] bound and obliged himself, his heirs and successors [*here insert the terms of the obligation in the terms so far as possible of the disposition or other deed. If the right to be assigned was originally granted in favour of some other person than the granter of the assignation, here specify the series of writs by which he acquired right.*]

[*Testing clause* †]

[† Note—Subscription of the document by the granter of it will be sufficient for the document to be formally valid, but witnessing of it may be necessary or desirable for other purposes (see the Requirements of Writing (Scotland) Act 1995).]
[. . .]

SCHEDULE O   Sect 61
CLAUSE OF REFERENCE TO PARTICULAR DESCRIPTION OF LANDS
CONTAINED IN A PRIOR CONVEYANCE, DEED, OR INSTRUMENT

[*Repealed by Conveyancing (Scotland) Act 1924, s 8(1). See Schedule D to that Act.*]

HERITABLE SECURITIES (SCOTLAND) ACT 1894
(57 & 58 Vict, c 44)

1   Short title
This Act may be cited for all purposes as the Heritable Securities (Scotland) Act, 1894.

2   Extent and commencement of Act
This Act shall apply to Scotland only.

3   Tenants need not be parties to actions of maills and duties
The creditor in a heritable security may, without calling the tenants of the lands disponed in security as defenders, raise an action of maills and duties either in the sheriff court, in the form as nearly as may be of Schedule (A) annexed to this Act, or in the Court of Session in common form, with the necessary alterations consequent upon the provisions of this Act, and may give notice of the raising of such action to the tenants by registered letter in the form as nearly as may be of Schedule (B) annexed to this Act, and from and after the date when such notice is received by the tenants they shall be held as interpelled from making payment of the rents due by them, in the same manner and to the same effect as if they were called as defenders in an action of maills and duties according to the present law and practice, and upon intimation of the decree obtained in said action being made to the tenants by registered letter in the form as nearly as may be of Schedule (C) annexed to this Act, the said tenants shall make payment of the rents due by them respectively in the same manner and under the like legal compulsitors as if the same had been decerned for and a charge for payment given in an action of maills and duties according to the existing law and practice, and payment when so made shall be a complete exoneration and discharge to such tenants respectively: Provided always, that no decree in such action shall affect the right of the tenants to refuse payment of such rents on any ground not affecting the title of such creditor or the right of any prior creditor to enter into possession, and nothing herein contained shall prevent an action of maills and duties from being raised in the form heretofore in use, or deprive a creditor of any existing right competent to him of entering into possession without having recourse to an action of maills and duties.

4   Power to interpel security holder
Any person interested may take proceedings to interpel the creditor from entering into possession of the lands disponed in security or collecting the rents thereof.

5   Power to eject proprietor in personal occupation
Where a creditor desires to enter into possession of the lands disponed in security, and the proprietor thereof is in personal occupation of the same, or any part thereof, such proprietor shall be deemed to be an occupant without a title, and the creditor may take proceedings to eject him in all respects in the same way as if he

were such occupant: Provided that this section shall not apply in any case unless such proprietor has made default in the punctual payment of the interest due under the security, or in due payment of the principal after formal requisition.

6   Power to lease security subjects for seven years or under
Any creditor in possession of lands [by virtue of an adjudication] may let such lands held in security, or part thereof, on lease, for a period not exceeding seven years in duration.

7   Sheriff may grant power to lease security subjects for longer periods, not more than 21 years for heritable property in general, and 31 years for minerals
Any creditor in possession of lands [by virtue of an adjudication] may apply to the sheriff for warrant to let the lands [. . .] or part thereof, for a period exceeding seven years, setting forth the name of the proposed tenant or tenants, the duration and conditions of the proposed lease; and the sheriff may, after service on the proprietor and on the other heritable creditors, if any, and after such intimation and inquiry as he may think proper, and if satisfied that a lease for a longer period than seven years is expedient for the beneficial occupation of the lands, approve of the proposed lease on the terms and conditions proposed, or on such other terms and conditions as may appear to him expedient: Provided always, that such lease shall in no case exceed twenty-one years for heritable property in general and thirty-one years for minerals.

11   Sheriff may grant power to *pari passu* security holder to sell *pari passu* security
Any creditor holding a security ranking *pari passu* with another security who desires to sell the lands conveyed in security by his security, and who is unable to obtain the consent of the creditor holding such other *pari passu* security to a sale, may apply to the sheriff for warrant to sell the said lands, calling such other creditor as defender; and the sheriff, after hearing parties and making such inquiry as he thinks fit, may order a sale of the said lands, if in his opinion it is reasonable and expedient that such sale should take place; and in case of difference of opinion, the sheriff may fix the price, authorise both or either of the parties or some other person to carry through the sale, and upon payment or consignation of the price to grant a conveyance and disencumber the lands of the said securities in the same way and as fully as if the creditors therein were by agreement carrying through said sale, and also to fix the times and conditions of sale in conformity with the law and practice relating to premonition and advertisement. And the expenses of and connected with the sale shall be payable preferably out of the price or proceeds of the sale, and the balance of such price or proceeds after providing for such expenses shall be paid to the creditors in the securities charged upon the lands according to their just rights and preferences.

12   Provisions anent procedure
The following provisions shall have effect with regard to applications under sections seven [. . .] and eleven of this Act:—

(1)   The interlocutor of the sheriff who pronounces any order or decree shall be final, and not subject to review, except (1) as to questions of title and (2) where the principal sum due under the heritable security exceeds one thousand pounds.

(2)   The sheriff may award expenses, or may direct that the expenses be treated as part of the expenses of the sale.

13   Provisions of Act to have effect not withstanding incapacity of debtor. Trustees and others to have powers conferred by Act
The rights and powers [under a heritable security] may be exercised by any creditor, although the debtor or any other creditor holding a security over the same lands, or other person to whom intimation may require or be ordered to be given is [subject to any legal disability by reason of nonage or otherwise] and any

action or proceeding [by a creditor in exercise of those rights and powers] shall have the same force and effect as it would have had if [the debtor, proprietor, other] creditor, or other person had been of full age and not subject to any legal incapacity when such action or proceeding was taken; [and

(a) any person entitled, within the meaning of Part I of the Children (Scotland) Act 1995, to act as the legal representative of a child; and

(b) trustees; [and]

(c) the person entitled to act as the legal representative of any such person,] executors, [guardians], judicial factors, and other officers of court may exercise all or any of the powers conferred by this Act.

18 Interpretation clause

In this Act the words 'conveyance,' 'heritable security,' 'security,' 'creditor,' 'debtor,' and 'purchaser' shall have the same meanings respectively as in the Titles to Land Consolidation (Scotland) Act, 1868.

The word 'lands' shall extend to and include all heritable subjects.

19 Saving as to rights of Crown

Nothing in this Act contained shall affect the present law and practice in regard to the preferential character of debts due to the Crown, nor shall anything done under the new procedure by this Act authorised prejudice the rights of the Crown as these exist according to the present law and practice.

SCHEDULES

SCHEDULE (A)   Section 3

In the sheriff court of
at

A.B., Pursuer,
against
C.D., Defender.

The above-named pursuer submits to the court the condescendence and note of plea-in-law hereto annexed, and prays the court—

To grant a decree against the above-named defender, finding and declaring that the pursuer has right to the rents, maills, and duties of the subjects and others specified in the bond and disposition in security for £   , granted by   in favour of   , dated the
and recorded in the
register
or, at least so much of the said rents, maills, and duties as will satisfy and pay the pursuer the principal sum of £   with interest thereon at the rate of   per centum per annum from the   day of   18   , liquidate penalty and termly failures all as specified and contained in the said bond and disposition in security dated and recorded as aforesaid, and to find the said C.D. liable in expenses, and to decern therefor.

Add condescendence and pleas-in-law.

SCHEDULE (B)   Section 3

In the court of session   [or]
In the sheriff court of   shire, at
Notice.

An action has been raised of this date [*specify place and date*] in the above court, at the instance of A.B. [*design him*], pursuer, against C.D. [*design him*], defender, in which the said pursuer asks that it be declared that as holding a bond and disposition in security over the subjects situated at [*here give such description of the subjects,* e.g., *their name or the number of street in which they are situated, as may identify them*], he has right to the rents due, current, and to become due, from the subjects.

Should you, after receiving this notice, pay your rent to the defender, you will do so at the risk of having to pay again to the pursuer should he obtain decree in the action.

[*To be signed by the pursuer or his law agent, or messenger at arms, or sheriff officer.*]

Section 3   SCHEDULE (C)

In the court of session   [*or*]
In the sheriff court of   shire, at

Notice.

Decree having been obtained of this date [*specify place and date*] in the above court, at the instance of *A.B.* [*design him*] pursuer, against *C.D.* [*design him*] defender, finding and declaring that the pursuer has right to the rents, maills, and duties of the subjects and others situated at [*here give such description of the subjects,* e.g., *their name, or the number of street in which they are situated, as may identify them*] specified in a bond and disposition in security for £   granted by   in favour of   dated the   and recorded in the register, you are hereby notified of the same, and desired and required to make payment to the said *A.B.* of the rents, maills, and duties due by you in respect of the occupancy of said subjects or part thereof.

[*To be signed by the pursuer or his law agent, or messenger at arms, or sheriff officer.*]

CONVEYANCING (SCOTLAND) ACT 1924
(1924, 14 & 15 Geo 5, c 27)

1   Short title, extent and commencement of Act
   (1)   This Act may be cited as the Conveyancing (Scotland) Act, 1924.
   [. . .]
   (3)   This Act shall apply to Scotland only.

2   Interpretation clause
The words and expressions after mentioned or referred to shall have the several meanings hereby assigned to them, unless there be something in the subject or context repugnant to such construction (that is to say):—
   (1)   The words and expressions used in this Act and in the schedules annexed to this Act which are interpreted in the Titles to Land Consolidation (Scotland) Act, 1868, and the Conveyancing (Scotland) Act, 1874, shall have the meaning assigned thereto respectively by these Acts, subject to the following qualifications:—
      (a)   'Land' or 'lands' shall not include 'securities';
      (b)   'Heritable securities' and 'securities' shall include [. . .] securities over a lease, but shall not include securities constituted by ex facie absolute disposition; and
      (c)   'Conveyance' and 'deed' and 'instrument' shall include all deeds, notices of title, decrees, petitions and writings specified in this Act; and these words and the words 'writing,' 'writ' and 'decree' occurring in the said Acts and in this Act shall each mean and include an extract or office copy of such 'conveyance,' 'deed,' 'instrument,' 'writing,' 'writ' or 'decree':
   (2)   'Extract' and 'office copy' shall each mean and include a duly authenticated extract of any act, decree or warrant of the Lords of Council and Session, or any inferior court or a duly authenticated extract or office copy from the Register of the

Great Seal, or from the Books of Council and Session, or of any sheriff court, or of any other public authentic register of probative writs, or from the appropriate Register of Sasines, of any conveyance, deed, instrument, writing, writ or decree, and shall also mean and include a probate of the will or testamentary settlement of a person deceased issued by any court of probate in England or Northern Ireland, or in any part of His Majesty's Dominions, or an exemplification of such probate:

(3) 'Deduction of title' shall mean the specification in a deed, decree or instrument of the writ or series of writs (without narration of the contents thereof) by which the person granting such deed or in whose favour such decree is conceived or by whom such instrument is expede, has acquired right from the person from whom such title is deduced, and such specification shall be a compliance with an instruction to 'deduce' a title in terms of this Act:

(4) 'Adjudication' shall include adjudication whether for debt or in implement, and constitution and adjudication whether for debt or in implement, and declarator and adjudication:

(5) 'Lease' shall mean a lease which has been registered or is registrable in the Register of Sasines in virtue of the Registration of Leases (Scotland) Act, 1857, and Acts amending the same:

(6) 'Law agent' shall mean and include writers to the signet, solicitors in the supreme courts, procurators in any sheriff court, and every person entitled to practise as an agent in a court of law in Scotland:

(7) 'Agent' in the Schedules hereto shall mean law agent or notary public:

(8) 'Register of Sasines,' shall mean and include the General Register of Sasines, the Particular Registers of Sasines now discontinued, the Register of Sasines kept for any royal or other burgh and the Register of Booking in the burgh of Paisley.

3 Disposition &c by person uninfeft

If a disposition of land, or an assignation, discharge or deed of restriction of a heritable security duly recorded in the appropriate Register of Sasines, or of any part of such security, is granted by a person having a right to such land, or to such heritable security, or such part thereof, but whose title to such land or heritable security or part thereof has not been completed by being so recorded, and who in such disposition or other deed deduces his title from the person [. . .] having the last recorded title, in or as nearly as may be in the terms of Form No 1 of Schedule A to this Act in the case of land, or in or as nearly as may be in manner prescribed in Note 2 to Schedule K to this Act in the case of a heritable security, then on such disposition or other deed being recorded in the appropriate Register of Sasines, the title of the grantee thereof shall be [completed].

4 Completion of title

Any person having right either to land or to a heritable security by a title which has not been completed by being recorded in the appropriate Register of Sasines, may complete his title in manner following:—

(1) A person having such right to land may complete a title thereto by recording in the appropriate Register of Sasines a notice of title in or as nearly as may be in the terms of Form No 1 of Schedule B to this Act, in which notice of title such person shall deduce his title from the person [having the last recorded title]:

(2) When the writ forming the immediate connection with the person [having the last recorded title] is an unrecorded conveyance, deed or decree, the recording of which in the appropriate Register of Sasines on behalf of the person in whose favour the same is conceived would have completed his title [. . .], the person having such right to the land therein contained or part thereof may complete a title thereto by recording in the appropriate Register of Sasines such conveyance, deed or decree, docqueted in manner prescribed in Note 7 to Schedule B to this Act, along with a notice of title in or as nearly as may be in the terms of Form No 2 of that Schedule, in which notice of title such person shall deduce his title from the person in whose favour such conveyance, deed or decree is conceived:

(3)   A person having such right to a heritable security, or part thereof, which appears in the appropriate Register of Sasines as a burden on land, may complete a title thereto by recording in the appropriate Register of Sasines a notice of title in or as nearly as may be in the terms of Form No 3 of Schedule B to this Act [. . .], in which notice of title such person shall deduce his title from the person [having the last recorded title to the heritable security]:

(4)   A person having such right to an unrecorded heritable security or part thereof contained in a deed the recording of which in the appropriate Register of Sasines on behalf of the original creditor would have [completed his title thereto and to] the land out of which it is payable, or either of them, but which has not been so recorded, may complete a title thereto by recording in the appropriate Register of Sasines such heritable security, which shall be docqueted in manner prescribed in Note 7 to Schedule B to this Act, along with a notice of title in or as nearly as may be in the terms of Form No 5 of that Schedule [. . .], in which notice of title such person shall deduce his title from the original creditor in such heritable security.

[. . .]

5   Deduction of title

(1)   In a deduction of title in terms of this Act it shall be competent to specify as a title or as a midcouple or link of title, any statute, conveyance, deed, instrument, decree or other writing whereby a right to land or to [any real right in] land is vested in or transmitted to any person, or in virtue of which a notarial instrument could [(before the day appointed by order made under section 71 of the Abolition of Feudal Tenure etc (Scotland) Act 2000 (asp 5))] be expede, or which could be used as a midcouple or link of title in expeding such instrument, or any minute of a meeting at which any person is appointed to any place or office, if such appointment involves a right to land or to [a real right in] land; and any copy of or excerpt from such minute of meeting certified as correct by the chairman of such meeting or other person duly authorised to sign such minute or to give extracts therefrom, or by any law agent or notary public shall be primâ facie evidence of the terms of such minute of meeting.

(2)(a)   When the holder of a heritable security [. . .] has died, whether [. . .] with or without a recorded title, and whether testate or intestate, any confirmation in favour of an executor of such deceased which includes such security shall of itself be a valid title to the debt thereby secured, and shall also be a warrant for such executor dealing with such debt and also with such security in terms of the third [section] of this Act, and also for completing a title to such security in terms of the fourth section of this Act.

(b)   For the purposes of this subsection, 'confirmation' shall include any probate or letters of administration or other grant of representation to movable or personal estate of a deceased person [issued—

(a)   by any court in England and Wales or Northern Ireland and noting his domicile in England and Wales or in Northern Ireland, as the case may be, or

(b)   by any court outwith the United Kingdom and sealed in Scotland under section 2 of the Colonial Probates Act 1892

and] the confirmation thereby implied shall operate in favour of the person or the persons or the survivors or survivor of them to whom such probate, letters of administration or other grant of representation were granted; and 'executor' shall include such person or persons; and such implied confirmation shall be deemed to include all heritable securities which belonged to the deceased [. . .].

(3)(a)   It shall be competent in any warrant, interlocutor or decree of court conferring a right to land or to a heritable security, or granting authority to complete a title thereto, and also in the application upon which such warrant, interlocutor or decree proceeds, to insert a deduction of title from the person [. . .] holding the last recorded title, and an extract of such warrant, interlocutor or decree shall be equivalent to a disposition of land or an assignation of a heritable security granted in terms of section three of this Act and on being recorded in the appropriate Register of Sasines shall have the same force and effect as such a disposition or assignation duly recorded in such register.

(b) Section twenty-four of the Titles to Land Consolidation (Scotland) Act, 1868, and section forty-four of the Conveyancing (Scotland) Act, 1874, are hereby amended in accordance with the provisions of this subsection, and the procedure prescribed in section forty-four of the said Act of 1874, as hereby amended, shall be competent irrespective of whether the trust title has or has not been duly completed and recorded, and shall be applicable to all judicial factors within the meaning of section three of the said Act of 1868, and both of such sections hereby amended shall apply to heritable securities, and such heritable security may be referred to in any warrant, interlocutor or decree, or in any application upon which the same proceeds, in the manner prescribed in the forms relative thereto referred to in section four of this Act.

8 Description by reference and short reference to deed bearing more than one date

(1) It shall be no objection to a description by reference to a particular description of land in accordance with section sixty-one of the Conveyancing (Scotland) Act, 1874, that the description referred to contains a description by reference of a larger piece of land of which the land particularly described forms part, and Schedule O annexed to the said Act of 1874 is hereby repealed and Schedule D to this Act is substituted therefor: The provisions of this section shall be retrospective.

[. . .]

(3) In specifying any writ recorded in any Register of Sasines, it shall be competent for the better identification of such writ, to state the number of the volume or book of the register in which, and of the folio on which, the same has been recorded; but it shall be no objection to the specification of any writ that such volume or book and folio or either of them are not stated or are misstated, provided that such specification is sufficient for the identification of such writ.

(4) Where any deed, instrument, or writing bearing more than one date is [. . .] specified or referred to in any other deed, instrument, or writing, it shall be no objection to such specification or reference that only the first date is given with the addition of the words 'and subsequent date' (or 'dates').

[(5) Note 1 to Schedule D to this Act shall apply to a reference competently made to any deed for reservations, real burdens, conditions, provisions, limitations, obligations and stipulations affecting lands and to the form of such reference given in [schedule 1 to the Title Conditions (Scotland) Act 2003 (asp 9)].]

14 Abolition of real warrandice

(1) From and after the commencement of this Act, it shall not be competent to dispone lands in real warrandice of a conveyance of other lands, and such real warrandice shall not arise ex lege from any contract or agreement entered into after the commencement of this Act.

[. . .]

15 Transmission of personal obligation

(1) The personal obligation contained in any deed or writing whereby any heritable security is constituted shall not transmit in terms of section forty-seven of the Conveyancing (Scotland) Act, 1874, against any person taking the estate by conveyance in the sense of that section dated after the commencement of this Act, unless such conveyance be signed by such person.

(2) After the commencement of this Act, summary diligence, in terms of the said section, shall not be competent against any obligant whose obligation is created by succession, gift or bequest, unless in cases in which there shall be an agreement to the transmission of such obligation executed by such obligant.

(3)   An agreement for transmission of a personal obligation pursuant to the said section may be in terms of Form No 2 of Schedule A to this Act, or in any other form sufficiently expressing such agreement.

19   Applicability of forms prescribed by Act

The forms prescribed by this Act for the completion of the titles to and the conveyance, assignation, discharge or restriction of rights of property [. . .] in land or heritable securities shall respectively be applicable to all other rights in or over land or in or over a heritable security the title to which may according to the present law and practice be competently completed by the recording of such title in the appropriate Register of Sasines.

22   Assimilation of law as regards legitim and jus relictæ, &c

(1)   In the case of any person dying after the commencement of this Act, the rules of law which determine what estate belonging to a deceased is subject to claims for legitim shall be applicable in determining what estate belonging to the deceased is subject to the claim for jus relictæ or jus relicti: And the estates of all such persons shall be distributed on the footing that there shall no longer be any distinction between the description of estate subject to claims for legitim and the description of estate subject to claims for jus relictæ and jus relicti.

(2)   All debts which if due to any person dying after the commencement of this Act would, according to the present law and practice or in terms of this section, be subject to legitim and jus relictæ or jus relicti shall, if due by the deceased or out of his or her estate, form, so far as the estate on which such debts are secured may be insufficient to meet the same, deductions from the deceased's moveable estate before ascertaining legitim and jus relictæ or jus relicti.

24   Registered leases. Assimilation of forms

All enabling powers and rights which, by this Act, are conferred upon or implied in favour of a person in right of land or of a security over land [. . .] shall, so far as applicable, be held as conferred upon a person who has right to a lease, or to a security over a lease respectively; and the forms prescribed by this Act may be used in connection with the constitution, transmission, restriction and discharge of securities over leases, and the completion of titles to leases and to securities over the same, and to sales thereof under such securities, [. . .] and the clauses held as implied in any of the forms prescribed by this Act shall, so far as applicable, be held as implied when such forms are used in connection with leases and securities over the same: Provided that in applying this Act and relative schedules to leases and securities over the same the following modifications and such other verbal modifications as may be necessary shall be given effect to:—

(1)   For 'lands,' 'lands and others' or 'subjects' there shall be substituted 'lease,' for 'conveyance' or 'disposition' there shall be substituted 'assignation' [. . .], for 'bond and disposition in security' there shall be substituted 'bond and assignation in security,' for 'assignation of a bond and disposition in security' there shall be substituted 'translation of a bond and assignation in security,' for 'dispone' or 'convey' there shall be substituted 'assign,' for 'proprietor' there shall be substituted 'lessee,' [and] for 'disponee' there shall be substituted 'assignee':

(2)   In an assignation of a lease, or in a bond and assignation in security of a lease, or in a notice of title relating to a lease, there may be substituted for a description of the land a reference to such lease in or as nearly as may be in the terms of Schedule J to this Act:

(3)   In the event of the lease, to which a title is being completed by notice of title under this Act, not having been recorded in the appropriate Register of Sasines, it shall be recorded therein along with such notice of title in which the lease shall be referred to in manner prescribed in Note 5 to Schedule J to this Act, and such lease, before being so recorded, shall be docqueted in manner prescribed in Note 7 to Schedule B to this Act, and, on the same being so recorded, it shall

have the same force and effect as a recorded title under the Registration of Leases (Scotland) Act, 1857, and Acts amending the same:

(4) [. . .]

(5) A renunciation of a lease in terms of Schedule G to the Registration of Leases (Scotland) Act, 1857, may competently be granted by a person not holding a recorded title to such lease, provided that he shall therein deduce his title from the person holding the last recorded title in manner prescribed in Note 4 to Schedule J to this Act, and on such renunciation being recorded in the appropriate Register of Sasines such lease shall be as effectually renounced as if the title of the granter of such renunciation had been completed as at the date of such recording [. . .], and section thirteen of the said Act of 1857, and Schedule G annexed to that Act, are hereby amended accordingly:

(6) Section twenty-four of the Titles to Land Consolidation (Scotland) Act, 1868, and section forty-four of the Conveyancing (Scotland) Act, 1874, as amended by section five of this Act, shall apply to a lease and to a security over a lease, and in the warrant, interlocutor or decree of Court conferring a right to such lease or security over the same or granting authority to complete title thereto, and also in the application upon which such warrant, interlocutor or decree proceeds, such lease may be referred to in or as nearly as may be in the terms of Schedule J hereto:

(7) An adjudger or purchaser of a lease, or an adjudger or assignee of a security over a lease, may complete his title thereto by recording in the appropriate Register of Sasines an extract of the decree of adjudication or of sale (as the case may be) or may use such extract decree as an assignation or one of a series of assignations of an unrecorded lease or of an unrecorded security over a lease, and section ten of the Registration of Leases (Scotland) Act, 1857, is hereby amended accordingly.

27 Restriction of agent's lien

From and after the commencement of this Act it shall be incompetent for any law agent or notary public acting for the proprietor or creditors or others, whose rights in or over land conveyed in security are postponed to those of the creditor in such heritable security, to acquire over the writs and evidents as against such creditor any right of hypothec, lien or retention after the date of recording such heritable security.

40 Exposure in lots and apportionment of feu-duty

[(1) [Land, or any part thereof, sold in exercise of a power of sale under a bond and disposition in security] may be exposed to, or offered for, sale either in whole or in lots, and in the former case at such upset price or prices as the creditor may think proper, and in the latter case at the best price that can be reasonably obtained] subject to such proportion of any existing [. . .] valued rent or land tax, as the creditor may think proper, and, without prejudice to the rights of any third party, the creditor may, in selling the land in lots, provide that the proprietor for the time being of any lot shall be obliged to relieve the proprietor or proprietors of another lot or lots of the whole or such part of an existing [. . .] land tax, as the creditor may think proper, and for that purpose the creditor may create such obligation a real burden on such lot.

[(2) Where there is a sale as aforesaid in lots, the creditor shall have power to create such rights and impose such duties and conditions [(whether or not by creating a real burden)] as he considers may be reasonably required for the proper management, maintenance and use of any part of the land to be held in common by the owners for the time being of the lots.]

41 Purchasers protected

(1) All proceedings [relating to the redemption or calling up of, or a sale under, a bond and disposition in security] shall be valid and effectual notwithstanding

that any person to whom premonition or notice requires to be given in terms of this Act may be [subject to any legal disability by reason of nonage or otherwise] and any sale and disposition in implement thereof shall be as valid to the purchaser as if made by the proprietor of the land not being under disability, and any such disposition shall import an assignation to the purchaser of the warrandice contained or implied in the bond and disposition in security under which the land is sold, and also an obligation by the granter of the security to ratify, approve and confirm the sale and disposition.

[(2) Where a disposition of land is duly recorded in the appropriate Register of Sasines and that disposition bears to be granted in the exercise of a power of sale contained in a deed granting a bond and disposition in security, and the exercise of that power was *ex facie* regular, the title of a *bona fide* purchaser of the land for value shall not be challengeable on the ground that the debt had ceased to exist, unless that fact appeared in the said Register, or was known to the purchaser prior to the payment of the price, or on the ground of any irregularity relating to the sale or in any preliminary procedure thereto; but nothing in the provisions of this subsection shall affect the competency of any claim for damages in respect of the sale of the land against the person exercising the said power.]

44 General register of inhibitions and register of adjudications to be combined; limitation of effect of entries therein

(1) The General Register of Inhibitions and Interdictions and the Register of Adjudications shall be combined, and the Keeper thereof shall keep only one register for inhibitions, interdictions, adjudications, reductions, and notices of litigiosity, and such register shall be called the Register of Inhibitions and Adjudications; and a reference in any public, general or local Act to the General Register of Inhibitions or the Register of Adjudications shall be deemed to mean and include such Register of Inhibitions and Adjudications.

(2)(a) No action whether raised before or after the commencement of this Act relating to land or to a lease or to a heritable security, shall be deemed to have had or shall have the effect of making such land, lease or heritable security litigious, unless and until

[(i)] a notice relative to such action in or as nearly as may be in the form of Schedule RR annexed to the Titles to Land Consolidation (Scotland) Act, 1868, shall have been or shall be registered in the Register of Inhibitions and Adjudications in the manner provided by section one hundred and fifty-nine of that Act [; or

(ii) a notice of an application under section 8 of the Law Reform (Miscellaneous Provisions) (Scotland) Act 1985 has been registered in the said register.]

(b) No decree in any action of adjudication of land or of a lease or of a heritable security, whether pronounced before or after the commencement of this Act, and no abbreviate of any such decree shall be deemed have had or to have any effect in making such land, lease or heritable security litigious.

(3)(a) All inhibitions and all notices of litigiosity registered in terms of section one hundred and fifty-nine of the Titles to Land Consolidation (Scotland) Act, 1868, subsisting at the commencement of this Act shall prescribe and be of no effect on the lapse of five years after such commencement or at such earlier date as they would prescribe according to the present law and practice; and all inhibitions [, notices of litigiosity and notices of applications under section 8 of the Law Reform (Miscellaneous Provisions) (Scotland) Act 1985] which relate to land or to a lease or to a heritable security and which shall be first registered after the commencement of this Act, shall prescribe and be of no effect on the lapse of five years from the date on which the same shall respectively take effect: Provided that in no case shall litigiosity be pleadable or be founded on to any effect after the expiry of six months from and after final decree is pronounced in the action creating such litigiosity.

(b) From and after the commencement of this Act interdiction, whether judicial or voluntary, shall be incompetent, and any interdiction which is legally operative at such commencement shall remain legally operative for not longer than the period of five years thereafter.

(4)(a), (b) [. . .]

(c) No deed, decree, instrument or writing granted or expede by a person whose estates have been sequestrated under the Bankruptcy (Scotland) Act, 1856, or the Bankruptcy (Scotland) Act, 1913 [, or the Bankruptcy (Scotland) Act 1985], or the heirs, executors, successors or assignees of such person relative to any land or lease or heritable security belonging to such person at the date of such sequestration or subsequently acquired by him shall be challengeable or denied effect on the ground of such sequestration if such deed, decree, instrument or writing shall have been granted or expede, or shall come into operation at a date when the effect of recording (a) the abbreviate provided for under section forty-four of the said Act of 1913, as amended by this Act, shall have expired in terms of the said section as amended as aforesaid [; or (b) under subsection (1)(a) of section 14 of the Bankruptcy (Scotland) Act 1985 the certified copy of an order shall have expired by virtue of subsection (3) of that section], unless the trustee in such sequestration shall before the recording of such deed, decree, instrument or writing in the appropriate Register of Sasines have completed his title to such land, lease or heritable security by recording the same in such register [or have recorded a memorandum in such register in the form provided by Schedule O to this Act]: Provided always, in case of sequestrations awarded under the Bankruptcy (Scotland) Act, 1856, that the provisions of this section shall not apply to any deed, decree, instrument or writing dated within five years after the commencement of this Act.

(5) The provisions of this section shall not affect the ranking of adjudgers inter se, or any real right obtained in virtue of a decree of adjudication, or in virtue of a decree pronounced in an action creating litigiosity, or by a trustee in bankruptcy, if such right has been completed by the recording in the appropriate Register of Sasines of any deed, decree, abbreviate, or instrument necessary to effect the completion of such right.

(6) Section one hundred and fifty-nine of the Titles to Land Consolidation (Scotland) Act, 1868, and sections sixteen and seventeen of the Land Registers (Scotland) Act, 1868, [. . .] are hereby amended in accordance with this section, and section forty-two of the Conveyancing (Scotland) Act, 1874, and Schedule J thereto annexed, are hereby repealed.

45 Provision for termination of perpetual trusts of moveables

In any case where the provisions of section nine of the Trusts (Scotland) Act, 1921, would apply to any deed, and to the right of any party thereunder if such deed had been dated after the thirty-first day of July, eighteen hundred and sixty-eight, the provisions of the said section shall, from and after the passing of this Act, apply to such deed and to the right of any party thereunder notwithstanding that the same be dated on or prior to the said thirty-first day of July, eighteen hundred and sixty-eight:

Provided that, in the application of the said provisions to the deeds to which this section refers and to the right of any party thereunder, the date of such deeds shall be deemed to be the date of the passing of this Act.

46 Extract decree of reduction to be recorded

[(1)] In the case of the reduction of a deed, decree or instrument recorded in the Register of Sasines or forming a midcouple or link of title in a title recorded in the said register there shall be recorded in the said register either an extract of the decree of reduction of such deed, decree or instrument, or a title in which such extract decree forms a midcouple or link of title, and such decree of reduction shall not be pleadable against a third party who shall in bonâ fide onerously acquire right to the land, lease or heritable security contained in the deed, decree, or instrument reduced by such decree of reduction prior to an extract of such decree of reduction, or a title, in which it forms a midcouple or link of title, being recorded in the Register of Sasines.

[(2)   This section shall apply to the rectification of a document by an order under section 8 of the Law Reform (Miscellaneous Provisions) (Scotland) Act 1985 as it applies to the reduction of a deed but with the substitution of any reference to the decree of reduction of the deed with a reference to the order rectifying the document.]

47   Re-recording of deeds relative to leasehold subjects

Where in terms of the Registration of Leases (Scotland) Act, 1857, or of section twenty-four of this Act, any deed or extract shall have been recorded in the appropriate Register of Sasines, and where in terms of that Act or of the said section any such deed or extract shall fall to be recorded again, or where any extract from a competent register of any deed the principal of which has already been recorded in the appropriate Register of Sasines falls to be so recorded, it shall not be necessary for the keeper of the Register of Sasines in which such deed or extract falls to be recorded, or in which such extract of any recorded deed falls to be recorded, to engross such deed or extract in the register at length, but the keeper of such Register of Sasines may in place of such engrossment enter in the register a short memorandum specifying the deed or extract and the book and folio in which the same is already engrossed, and in the case of an extract of a deed the principal of which has already been recorded in the appropriate Register of Sasines the book and folio in which the principal is already engrossed, and such memorandum shall have the same effect as if the deed or extract were engrossed in the register at length in place of such memorandum.

48   Duplicate plans may be retained with register

Where any writ which refers to a plan signed as relative thereto is presented or transmitted by post for registration in the General Register of Sasines it shall be competent to ingive to the said register along therewith a duplicate of such plan, docqueted with reference to the said writ and authenticated in the same manner as the principal plan, and such duplicate plan shall be retained in the said register. The ingiving of such duplicate plan shall be noted in the register, and acknowledgement of the receipt thereof shall be marked by the keeper of the register on the plan signed as relative to the writ.

Along with each register volume transmitted to the Keeper of the Records for custody there shall be sent the duplicate plans, if any, relative to any of the writs engrossed in such volume.

Such duplicate plans when transmitted to the Keeper of the Records shall remain in his custody, subject to the same rights on the part of the public to have access thereto as apply to the Record Volumes.

49   Saving clause

(1)   [. . .]

(2)   Nothing in this Act contained shall affect the preparation of the printed minutes and printed indexes of persons and places applicable to each county in Scotland, and the Keeper of the General Register of Sasines shall supply as full information in the printed minute books as hitherto according to the existing law and practice.

SCHEDULES

SCHEDULE A

FORM NO 1
CLAUSE OF DEDUCTION OF TITLE IN A DISPOSITION OF
LAND WHERE THE GRANTER [DOES NOT HAVE A RECORDED TITLE]

Section 3

[To be inserted immediately after the clause specifying the date or term of entry or after the dispositive clause where no date or term of entry is specified.]

Which lands and others (*or* subjects) were last vested [*or* are part of the lands and others (*or* subjects) last vested] in *A.B.*, (*designation of person* [*having last recorded title*]), whose title thereto is recorded in (*specify Register of Sasines and date of recording, or if the last* [*recorded title*] *has already been mentioned say* in the said *A.B.* as aforesaid), and from whom I acquired right by (*here specify shortly the writ or series of writs by which right was so acquired*).

NOTE TO FORM NO 1 OF SCHEDULE A

If any conditions, reservations, provisions, obligations, servitudes or other burdens which affect the land or any part thereof or qualify the granter's right thereto be contained in or imposed by the writ or any of the writs by which the granter acquired right and are proper to be inserted, insert the same at length in the dispositive clause, and if they affect only part of the land specify the part or parts of the land affected thereby, and in case of money burdens specify the amounts thereof and the name and designation or designative description of the creditor therein, all as in the writ containing or imposing such money burdens, and in all cases specify the writ or writs containing or imposing such conditions and others.

FORM NO 2
CLAUSE TRANSMITTING PERSONAL OBLIGATION IN A HERITABLE
SECURITY IN A DISPOSITION OF LAND

Section 15

I, *A.B.* (*designation*), in consideration of (*specify any part of price paid in money*) and in consideration also of *C.D.* (*designation*) undertaking as by his signature hereto he undertakes the personal obligation contained in a bond and disposition in security for the sum of (*insert amount*) granted by me [*or by E.F.* (*original debtor*)] in favour of *G.H.* (*original creditor*), dated (*insert date*), and recorded in (*specify Register of Sasines and date of recording*) do hereby dispone, &c.

SCHEDULE B
NOTICE OF TITLE

FORM NO 1
ON BEHALF OF A PERSON WHO HAS RIGHT TO LAND BY A TITLE WHICH
HAS NOT BEEN RECORDED IN THE APPROPRIATE REGISTER OF SASINES AND
WHICH IS NOT TO BE RECORDED ALONG WITH THE NOTICE OF TITLE

Section 4(1)

Be it known that *A.B.* (*designation*) has right as proprietor (*or* life-renter *or* proprietor in trust *or otherwise, as the case may be*) to all and whole [*here describe the land or refer to description thereof as in Schedule D to this Act or as in Schedule G to the Titles to Land Consolidation (Scotland) Act, 1868; and if* [. . .] *any conditions, reservations, pro-*

visions, obligations, servitudes, or other burdens which affect the land or any part thereof [. . .] or qualify A.B.'s right thereto be contained in or imposed by the writ or any of the writs by which A.B. acquired right and are proper to be inserted, here insert the same at length, and if they affect only part of the land specify the part or parts of the land affected thereby, and in case of money burdens specify the amount thereof and the name and designation or designative description of the creditor therein all as in the writ containing or imposing such money burdens, and in all cases specify the writ or writs containing or imposing such conditions and others]; Which lands and others (*or* subjects) were last vested [*or are part of the lands and others* (*or* subjects) *last vested*] in C.D. (*design person* [*having last recorded title*]), whose title thereto was recorded in (*specify Register of Sasines and date of recording, or if the last* [*recorded title*] *has already been mentioned say* in the said C.D. as aforesaid), and from whom the said A.B. acquired right by (*here specify shortly the writ or series of writs by which he acquired right*); Which last recorded title and subsequent writ (*or* writs) have been presented to me, Y.Z. (*designation*), Notary Public, (*or* Law Agent).

[*Testing clause* †]

Y.Z.

FORM NO 2
ON BEHALF OF A PERSON WHO HAS RIGHT TO LAND CONVEYED BY
AN UNRECORDED SPECIAL CONVEYANCE WHICH IS TO BE RECORDED ALONG
WITH THE NOTICE OF TITLE
Section 4(2)

Be it known that A.B. (*designation*) has right as proprietor (*or* life-renter *or* proprietor in trust *or otherwise, as the case may be*) to all and whole the lands and others (*or* subjects) disponed by (*or contained in*) the disposition (*or feu charter or other special conveyance*) granted by C.D. (*designation*) in favour of E.F. (*designation*) dated (*insert date*), and recorded in (*specify Register of Sasines*) of even date herewith [*if any conditions, reservations, provisions, obligations, servitudes or other burdens affecting the land or any part thereof or qualifying A.B.'s right thereto be contained in or imposed by the writ or any of the writs by which A.B. acquired right other than such special conveyance and are proper to be inserted, here insert the same at length, and if they affect only part of the land specify the part or parts of the land affected thereby, and in case of money burdens specify the amount thereof and the name and designation or designative description of the creditor therein, all as in the writ containing or imposing such money burdens, and in all cases specify the writ or writs containing or imposing such conditions and others*]; To which lands and others (*or* subjects) the said A.B. acquired right by the foresaid disposition (*or as the case may be*) and by (*here specify shortly the subsequent writ or series of writs by which he acquired right*); Which disposition and subsequent writ (*or* writs) have been presented to me (*as in Form No 1 of this Schedule*).

[*Testing clause* †]

FORM NO 3
ON BEHALF OF A PERSON WHO HAS RIGHT TO A RECORDED HERITABLE
SECURITY BY A TITLE WHICH HAS NOT BEEN RECORDED IN THE
APPROPRIATE REGISTER OF SASINES AND WHICH IS NOT TO BE RECORDED
ALONG WITH THE NOTICE OF TITLE
Section 4(3)

Be it known that A.B. (*designation*) has right (*adding if such be the case* to the extent aftermentioned) to a bond and disposition in security (*or as the case may be*) for the sum of (*insert amount*) granted by C.D. (*design original debtor*) in favour of E.F. (*design original creditor*), dated (*insert date*) and recorded in [*specify Register of Sasines and date of recording; adding, if necessary,* but only to the extent of (*insert sum*) of principal]; Which bond and disposition in security was last vested in the said *E.F.* as aforesaid [*or if E.F. is not the person* [. . .] *holding the last recorded title thereto, say* Which bond and disposition in security (*adding, if necessary,* to the extent foresaid *or as the case may be*) was last vested in *G.H.* (*design person holding the last recorded title thereto*), whose title thereto was recorded in said Register of Sasines (*or as the case may be, and give date of recording*)], and from whom the said *A.B.* acquired right (*adding, if necessary,* to the extent foresaid, *or as the case may be*), by (*here specify shortly the writ or series of writs by which he acquired right*); Which last recorded title and subsequent writ (*or* writs) have been presented to me (*as in Form No 1 of this Schedule*).

[*Testing clause* †]

FORM NO 5

ON BEHALF OF A PERSON WHO HAS RIGHT TO AN UNRECORDED HERITABLE SECURITY WHICH IS TO BE RECORDED ALONG WITH THE NOTICE OF TITLE
Section 4(4)

Be it known that *A.B.* (*designation*) has right (*adding if such be the case* to the extent aftermentioned) to a bond and disposition in security (*or as the case may be*) for the sum of (*insert amount*) granted by *C.D.* (*designation*) in favour of *E.F.* (*designation*) dated (*insert date*), and recorded in (*specify Register of Sasines*) of even date herewith [*adding if necessary* but only to the extent of (*insert sum*) of principal]; To which bond and disposition in security (*adding if necessary* to the extent foresaid *or as the case may be*) the said *A.B.* acquired right by (*here specify shortly the writ or series of writs by which he acquired right*); Which bond and disposition in Security (*or as the case may be*) and subsequent writ (*or* writs) have been presented to me (*as in Form No 1 of this Schedule*).

[*Testing clause* †]

NOTES TO SCHEDULE B
Sections 4(2), (4), 24(3)

Note 1.—Where the description in the last [recorded title] is a particular description, the description in Form No 1 of this Schedule should be by reference thereto, unless there is reason to the contrary.

Note 2.—In adapting Form No 2 of this Schedule to the case of a person who has right to only a part of the land contained in an unrecorded conveyance, deed, or decree there shall be inserted immediately before the words 'all and whole' a description of such part of the land, and the form may then proceed *which lands and others* (or *subjects*) *are part of.*

Note 3.—If the original [title to] a bond and disposition in security or other heritable security [has been completed] otherwise than by recording the same in the appropriate Register of Sasines add immediately after the mention of the date thereof *and instrument of sasine* (or *notarial instrument,* or if such be the case *and along with notice of title*) *thereon* (adding if such instrument or notice is not in favour of the original creditor the name and designation of the person in whose favour it is conceived) *recorded in* (specify Register of Sasines and date of recording).

Note 4.—In adapting Forms Nos 3 and 5 of this Schedule to real burdens for capital sums, there shall be substituted for the specification of the bond and disposition in security the following: *A real burden for the sum of* (insert amount) *payable to E.F.* (designation) *in terms of* (specify the disposition or other deed under which the real burden was reserved or constituted, giving the names and designations of the granter and grantee, or of the parties thereto), *dated* (insert date) *and recorded in* (specify Register of Sasines and date of recording); and in specifying the writs by which *A.B.* acquired right to such real burden there shall in Form No. 5 be mentioned as the first of such writs *the said disposition* (or other deed as above), and the same shall along with the other writ or writs be presented to the Agent expeding the notice of title.

Note 5.—*[repealed]*

Note 6.—Where in place of the principal titles or writs on which any notice of title bears to proceed there are presented to the agent expeding such notice extracts or office copies thereof, the statement in the notice as to the presentation of such titles or writs may be varied accordingly; but it shall be no objection to any notice of title that it states that the principal titles or writs were so presented although there were presented only extracts or office copies of such titles or writs.

Note 7.—Where a deed, decree or heritable security is to be recorded along with a notice of title it should be docqueted as follows:—*Docqueted with reference to notice of title in favour of A.B. recorded of even date herewith.*

Y.Z. (*designation*),
Agent

[† Note 8.—Subscription of the document by the notary public (or law agent) on behalf of granter of it will be sufficient for the document to be formally valid, but witnessing of it may be necessary or desirable for other purposes (see the Requirements of Writing (Scotland) Act 1995).]

[. . .]

SCHEDULE D
CLAUSE OF REFERENCE TO A DESCRIPTION OF LAND CONTAINED IN A PRIOR CONVEYANCE, DEED, OR INSTRUMENT
Section 8

All and whole the lands and others (*or* subjects) in the county of
(*or* in the burgh of   and county of   *as the case may be*)
described in (*refer to the conveyance, deed, or instrument in such terms as shall be suffi-cient to identify it, and specify the Register of Sasines in which it is recorded and date of recording, or where the conveyance, deed, or instrument referred to is recorded on the same date as the conveyance, deed, or instrument containing the reference substitute for the date of recording the words* of even date with the recording of these presents):—

NOTES TO SCHEDULE D

Note 1.—In referring to a Deed containing a particular description [or to a Deed containing reservations, real burdens, conditions, provisions, limitations, obligations and stipulations affecting lands] it shall be sufficient to give the names of the granter and grantee or of the parties thereto without adding their designations, and when there are several granters or grantees or several parties acting in the same category it shall be sufficient to give the name of the first mentioned person only with the addition of the words *and others*; and where the granter or granters or grantee or grantees, or the parties or one of the parties thereto acts or act in a fiduciary capacity it shall be sufficient to state such capacity without giving their individual name or names, *e.g.*:

(a)   *Feu Charter granted by A.B. in favour of C.D., dated* (insert date) *and recorded in* (specify Register of Sasines and give date of recording).

(b)   *Disposition granted by C.D. and others in favour of E.F. and others, dated, &c* (as above).

(c)   *Notarial Instrument* (or *Notice of title*) *in favour of the Trustee* (or *Trustees*) *of G.H.* (or *the Judicial Factor of J.K. or the Trustee on the Sequestrated Estates of L.M. or the Liquidator of the N.O. Company, Limited, or* as the case may be) *recorded in* (specify Register of Sasines and date of recording).

Note 2.—Where it is desired to insert a short description of the land or subjects, this may be done as follows:—*All and whole that dwelling-house, number ten, Rosebery Crescent, Edinburgh,* (or *the eastmost half-flat on the second storey of the tenement entering from number fifteen, Lothian Street, Edinburgh,* or otherwise, in the case may be) *in the county of Edinburgh, described in, &c.* (as above).

Note 3.—If part only of the land or subjects described in a former recorded conveyance, deed, instrument, or notice of title is being conveyed or otherwise dealt with for the first time as a separate subject, such part should be described at length, adding *being part of the lands and*

others (or *subjects*) *in the county of*   or *in the burgh of*   *and county*
of   *described in*, &c (as above); or thus: *All and Whole the lands and others* (or *sub-*
jects) *in the county of*   or *in the burgh of*   *and county of*   *de-*
scribed in, &c (as above), *with the exception of* (describe, the part excepted).

Note 4.—If several lands or subjects are described in the conveyance, deed, or instrument
referred to, and it is intended to specify one or more of them, these may be distinguished
from the others thus: *All and Whole the lands and others* (or *subjects*) *first* (or *second and third*)
described in, &c (as above, or otherwise, as the case may be).

[. . .]

SCHEDULE J
REGISTRABLE LEASES

Section 24

A lease (*or* tack) granted by *E.F.* (*designation*) in my favour [*or* in favour of *G.H.*
(*designation*) *or as the case may be*] of the subjects therein described lying in the
county of   (*or* burgh of   and county of   )
dated (*insert date*) and recorded in (*specify Register of Sasines and date of recording*).

NOTES TO SCHEDULE J

Note 1.—If the recording of a lease in the appropriate Register of Sasines has
been effected by a successor of the original lessee, add immediately after the mention of the date thereof *and along with notarial instrument* (or *notice of title*) *thereon in
favour of* (giving the name and designation of the person in whose favour it is conceived) *recorded in* (specify Register of Sasines and date of recording).

Note 2.—Where any deed authorised by this Act relates to part only of the subjects contained in a lease add *but in so far only as regards the following portion of the
subjects leased, viz.* (here describe the portion or refer to description thereof as in
Schedule D hereto).

Note 3.—Where the granter of an assignation of a recorded lease or of a bond
and assignation in security of a recorded lease is not the original lessee but has a
recorded title [no specification of the granter's title is required].

Note 4.—In an assignation or renunciation of a recorded lease the title of the
granter of which assignation or renunciation is not recorded, and in a notice of title
to a recorded lease, insert *which lease* (adding if necessary *to the extent foresaid* or as
the case may be) *was last vested in the said G.H. as aforesaid* [or if *G.H.* is not the
person having such title say *in J.K.* (design person having such title) *whose title
thereto is recorded in said Register of Sasines* (or as the case, may be, and give date of
recording)], *and from whom I* (in the case of an assignation or renunciation) or *the
said A.B.* (in the case of a notice of title) *acquired right by* (here specify shortly the
writ or series of writs by which right was so acquired by the person granting the
assignation or renunciation, or expeding the notice of title.)

Note 5.—Where a title to an unrecorded lease is being completed by notice of
title under this Act the lease shall be referred to in manner above prescribed
except that the Register of Sasines shall be specified, and for the date of recording
of the lease there shall be substituted the words *of even date herewith.*

[SCHEDULE O
FORM OF MEMORANDUM TO BE RECORDED IN THE REGISTER OF
SASINES

Section 44

Memorandum with regard to the subjects after described:
With reference to the subjects (*describe particularly or by reference*) T the trustee in

the sequestration of B has obtained a vesting order under section 98 of the Bankruptcy (Scotland) Act 1913 dated (*insert date of order*).

The memorandum should be signed by the trustee or his law agent, dated, and recorded [. . .] in the appropriate division or divisions of the Register of Sasines.

The form may be adapted in the case of a lease thus:—

Memorandum with regard to the lease after-mentioned:

With reference to the lease granted by C in favour of D of the subjects therein described lying in the county of K, dated (*insert date*), and recorded in [*specify Register of Sasines and date of recording*], T the trustee &c.

And in the case of a heritable security thus:—

Memorandum with regard to the bond and disposition in security after-mentioned:

With reference to the bond and disposition in security for the sum of (*insert sum*) granted by E in favour of F dated (*insert date*) and recorded in (*specify Register of Sasines and date of recording*), T the trustee &c.]

CONVEYANCING AND FEUDAL REFORM (SCOTLAND) ACT 1970
(1970, c 35)

PART II
THE STANDARD SECURITY

9   The standard security

(1)   The provisions of this Part of this Act shall have effect for the purpose of enabling a new form of heritable security to be created to be known as a standard security.

(2)   It shall be competent to grant and record in the Register of Sasines a standard security over any [land or real right in land] to be expressed in conformity with one of the forms prescribed in Schedule 2 to this Act.

[(2B)   It shall not be competent to grant a standard security over a personal preemption burden or personal redemption burden (both within the meaning of Part 4 of the Abolition of Feudal Tenure etc (Scotland) Act 2000 (asp 5)).]

(3)   A grant of any right over [land or a real right] in land for the purpose of securing any debt by way of a heritable security shall only be capable of being effected at law if it is embodied in a standard security.

(4)   Where for the purpose last-mentioned any deed which is not in the form of a standard security contains a disposition or assignation [of land or of a real right] in land, it shall to that extent be void and unenforceable, and where that deed has been duly recorded the creditor in the purported security may be required, by any person having an interest, to grant any deed which may be appropriate to clear the Register of Sasines of that security.

(5)   A standard security may be used for any other purpose for which a heritable security may be used if any of the said forms is appropriate to that purpose, and for the purpose of any enactment affecting heritable securities a standard security, if so used, or if used as is required by this Act instead of a heritable security as defined therein, shall be a heritable security for the purposes of that enactment.

(6)   The Bankruptcy Act 1696, in so far as it renders a heritable security of no effect in relation to a debt contracted after the recording of that security, and any rule of law which requires that a real burden for money may only be created in respect of a sum specified in the deed of creation, shall not apply in relation to a standard security.

(7)   The provisions of this section shall not affect the operation of the Small Dwellings Acquisition (Scotland) Acts 1899 to 1923, except that in section 11(8) of

the Small Dwellings Acquisition Act 1899, in the substitution for section 2(e) of that Act, after the words 'other security' there shall be inserted the words 'not being a security constituted by an *ex facie* absolute disposition or assignation, whether qualified by a back letter or not'.

(8)   For the purposes of this Part of this Act—

(a)   'heritable security' (except in subsection (5) of this section if the context otherwise requires) means any security capable of being constituted over any [land or real right] in land by disposition or assignation of that [land or real right] in security of any debt and of being recorded in the Register of Sasines;

[(b)   'real right in land' means any such right, other than ownership or a real burden, which is capable of being held separately and to which a title may be recorded in the Register of Sasines;]

(c)   'debt' means any obligation due, or which will or may become due, to repay or pay money, including any such obligation arising from a transaction or part of a transaction in the course of any trade, business or profession, and any obligation to pay an annuity or *ad factum praestandum*, but does not include an obligation to pay any [. . .], rent or other periodical sum payable in respect of land, and 'creditor' and 'debtor', in relation to a standard security, shall be construed accordingly.

10   Import of forms of, and certain clauses in, standard security

(1)   The import of the clause relating to the personal obligation contained in Form A of Schedule 2 to this Act expressed in any standard security shall, unless specially qualified, be as follows—

(a)   where the security is for a fixed amount advanced or payable at, or prior to, the delivery of the deed, the clause undertaking to make payment to the creditor shall import an acknowledgment of receipt by the debtor of the principal sum advanced or an acknowledgment by the debtor of liability to pay that sum and a personal obligation undertaken by the debtor to repay or pay to the creditor on demand in writing at any time after the date of delivery of the standard security the said sum, with interest at the rate stated payable on the dates specified, together with all expenses for which the debtor is liable by virtue of the deed or of this Part of this Act;

(b)   where the security is for a fluctuating amount, whether subject to a maximum amount or not and whether advanced or due partly before and partly after delivery of the deed or whether to be advanced or to become due wholly after such delivery, the clause undertaking to make payment to the creditor shall import a personal obligation by the debtor to repay or pay to the creditor on demand in writing the amount, not being greater than the maximum amount, if any, specified in the deed, advanced or due and outstanding at the time of demand, with interest on each advance from the date when it was made until repayment thereof, or on each sum payable from the date on which it became due until payment thereof, and at the rate stated payable on the dates specified, together with all expenses for which the debtor is liable by virtue of the deed or of this Part of this Act.

(2)   The clause of warrandice in the forms of standard security contained in Schedule 2 to this Act expressed in any standard security shall, unless specially qualified, import absolute warrandice as regards the [land or real right] in land over which the security is granted and the title deeds thereof, and warrandice from fact and deed as regards the rents thereof.

(3)   The clause relating to consent to registration for execution contained in Form A of Schedule 2 to this Act expressed in any standard security shall, unless specially qualified, import a consent to registration in the Books of Council and Session, or, as the case may be, in the books of the appropriate sheriff court, for execution.

(4)   The forms of standard security contained in Schedule 2 to this Act shall,

unless specially qualified, import an assignation to the creditor of the title deeds, including searches, and all conveyances not duly recorded, affecting the security subjects or any part thereof, with power to the creditor in the event of a sale under the powers conferred by the security, but subject to the rights of any person holding prior rights to possession of those title deeds, to deliver them, so far as in the creditor's possession, to the purchaser, and to assign to the purchaser any right he may possess to have the title deeds made forthcoming.

11 Effect of recorded standard security, and incorporation of standard conditions

(1) Where a standard security is duly recorded, it shall operate to vest [in the grantee a real right in security] for the performance of the contract to which the security relates.

(2) Subject to the provisions of this Part of this Act, the conditions set out in Schedule 3 to this Act, either as so set out or with such variations as have been agreed by the parties in the exercise of the powers conferred by the said Part (which conditions are hereinafter in this Act referred to as 'the standard conditions'), shall regulate every standard security.

(3) Subject to the provisions of this Part of this Act, the creditor and debtor in a standard security may vary any of the standard conditions, other than [standard condition 11 (procedure on redemption) and] the provisions of Schedule 3 to this Act relating to the powers of sale [. . .] and foreclosure and to the exercise of those powers, but no condition capable of being varied shall be varied in a manner inconsistent with any condition which may not be varied by virtue of this subsection.

(4) In this Part of this Act—

(a) any reference to a variation of the standard conditions shall include a reference to the inclusion of an additional condition and to the exclusion of a standard condition;

(b) any purported variation of a standard condition which contravenes the provisions of subsection (3) of this section shall be void and unenforceable.

12 Standard security may be granted by person uninfeft

(1) Notwithstanding any rule of law, a standard security may be granted over [land or real right] in land by a person [. . .] whose title thereto has not been completed by being duly recorded, if in the deed expressing that security the grantor deduces his title to that [land or real right] from the person who appears in the Register of Sasines as having the last recorded title thereto.

(2) A deduction of title in a deed for the purposes of the foregoing subsection shall be expressed in the form prescribed by Note 2 or 3 of Schedule 2 to this Act, and on such a deed being recorded as aforesaid the title of the grantee shall, for the purposes of the rights and obligations between the grantor and the grantee thereof and those deriving right from them, but for no other purpose, in all respects be of the same effect as if the title of the grantor of the deed to the [land or real right in land] to which he has deduced title therein had been duly completed; and any references to a proprietor or to a person [having the last recorded title] shall in this Part of this Act be construed accordingly.

(3) There may be specified for the purposes of any deduction of title in pursuance of any provision of this Part of this Act any writing which it is competent to specify as a title, midcouple, or link in title for the purposes of section 5 of the Conveyancing (Scotland) Act 1924 (deduction of title).

13 Ranking of standard securities

(1) Where the creditor in a standard security duly recorded has received notice of the creation of a subsequent security over the same [land or real right in land or over any part thereof, or of the subsequent assignation or conveyance of that land or real right,] in whole or in part, being a security, assignation or conveyance so

recorded, the preference in ranking of the security of that creditor shall be restricted to security for

[(a)   the present debt incurred (whenever payable); and

(b)   any future debt which, under the contract to which the security relates, he is required to allow the debtor in the security to incur,]

and interest present or future due thereon (including any such interest which has accrued or may accrue) and for any expenses or outlays (including interest thereon) which may be, or may have been, reasonably incurred in the exercise of any power conferred on any creditor by the deed expressing the existing security.

(2)   For the purposes of the foregoing subsection—

(a)   a creditor in an existing standard security duly recorded shall not be held to have had any notice referred to in that subsection, by reason only of the subsequent recording of the relevant deed in the Register of Sasines;

(b)   any assignation, conveyance or vesting in favour of or in any other person of the interest of the debtor in the security subjects or in any part thereof resulting from any judicial decree, or otherwise by operation of law, shall constitute sufficient notice thereof to the creditor.

(3)   Nothing in the foregoing provisions of this section shall affect—

(a)   any preference in ranking enjoyed by the Crown; and

(b)   any powers of the creditor and debtor in any heritable security to regulate the preference to be enjoyed by creditors in such manner as they may think fit.

14   Assignation of standard security

(1)   Any standard security duly recorded may be transferred, in whole or in part, by the creditor by an assignation in conformity with Form A or B of Schedule 4 to this Act, and upon such an assignation being duly recorded, the security, or, as the case may be, part thereof, shall be vested in the assignee as effectually as if the security or the part had been granted in his favour.

(2)   An assignation of a standard security shall, except so far as otherwise therein stated, be deemed to convey to the grantee all rights competent to the grantor to the writs, and shall have the effect *inter alia* of vesting in the assignee—

(a)   the full benefit of all corroborative or substitutional obligations for the debt, or any part thereof, whether those obligations are contained in any deed or arise by operation of law or otherwise,

(b)   the right to recover payment from the debtor of all expenses properly incurred by the creditor in connection with the security, and

(c)   the entitlement to the benefit of any notices served and of all procedure instituted by the creditor in respect of the security to the effect that the grantee may proceed as if he had originally served or instituted such notices or procedure.

15   Restriction of standard security

(1)   The security constituted by any standard security duly recorded may be restricted, as regards any part of the [land or real right] in land burdened by the security, by a deed of restriction in conformity with Form C of Schedule 4 to this Act, and, upon that deed being duly recorded, the security shall be restricted [to the land or real right contained in the standard security other than the part of that land or real right disburdened by the deed; and the land or real right] thereby disburdened shall be released from the security wholly or to the extent specified in the deed.

(2)   A partial discharge and deed of restriction of a standard security, which has been duly recorded, may be combined in one deed, which shall be in conformity with Form D of the said Schedule 4.

16   Variation of standard security

(1)   Any alteration in the provisions (including any standard condition) of a

standard security duly recorded, other than an alteration which may appropriately be effected by an assignation, discharge or restriction of that standard security, or an alteration which involves an addition to, or an extension of, the [land or real right] in land mentioned therein, may be effected by a variation endorsed on the standard security in conformity with Form E of Schedule 4 to this Act, or by a variation contained in a separate deed in a form appropriate for that purpose, duly recorded in either case.

(2)   Where a standard security has been duly recorded, but the personal obligation or any other provision (including any standard condition) relating to the security has been created or specified in a deed which has not been so recorded, nothing contained in this section shall prevent any alteration in that personal obligation or provision, other than an alteration which may be appropriately effected by an assignation, discharge or restriction of the standard security, or an alteration which involves an addition to, or an extension of, the [land or real right] in land mentioned therein, by a variation contained in any form of deed appropriate for that purpose, and such a variation shall not require to be recorded in the Register of Sasines.

(3)   [. . .]

(4)   Any variation effected in accordance with this section shall not prejudice any other security or right over the same [land or real right in land, or over] any part thereof, effectively constituted before the variation is recorded, or, where the variation is effected by an unrecorded deed, before that deed is executed, as the case may be.

17   Discharge of standard security

A standard security duly recorded may be discharged, and the [land or real right] in land burdened by that security may be disburdened thereof, in whole or in part, by a discharge in conformity with Form F of Schedule 4 to this Act, duly recorded.

18   Redemption of standard security

(1)   [Subject to the provisions of subsection (1A) of this section,] the debtor in a standard security or, where the debtor is not the proprietor, the proprietor of the security subjects shall be entitled to redeem the security [on giving two months' notice of his intention so to do, and] in conformity with the terms of standard condition 11 and the appropriate Forms of Schedule 5 to this Act.

[(1A)   Without prejudice to section 11 of the Land Tenure Reform (Scotland) Act 1974 the provisions of the foregoing subsection shall be subject to any agreement to the contrary, but any right to redeem the security shall be exercisable in conformity with the terms and Forms referred to in that subsection.]

(2)   Where owing to the death or absence of the creditor, or to any other cause, the debtor in a standard security or, as the case may be, the proprietor of the security subjects [(being in either case a person entitled to redeem the security)] is unable to obtain a discharge under the [foregoing provisions of this section], he may—

(a)   where the security was granted in respect of any obligation to repay or pay money, consign in any bank in Scotland, incorporated by or under Act of Parliament or by Royal Charter, the whole amount due to the creditor on redemption, other than any unascertained expenses of the creditor, for the person appearing to have the best right thereto, and

(b)   in any other case, apply to the court for declarator that the whole obligations under the contract to which the security relates have been performed.

(3)   On consignation, or on the court granting declarator as aforesaid, a certificate to that effect may be expede by a solicitor in the appropriate form prescribed by Form D of Schedule 5 to this Act, which on being duly recorded shall disburden the [land or real right] in land, to which the standard security relates, of that security.

(4)   For the purposes of this section, 'whole amount due' means the debt to

which the security relates, so far as outstanding, and any other sums due thereunder by way of interest or otherwise.

19 Calling-up of standard security

(1) Where a creditor in a standard security intends to require discharge of the debt thereby secured and, failing that discharge, to exercise any power conferred by the security to sell any subjects of the security or any other power which he may appropriately exercise on the default of the debtor within the meaning of standard condition 9(1)(a), he shall serve a notice calling-up the security in conformity with Form A of Schedule 6 to this Act (hereinafter in this Act referred to as a 'calling-up notice'), in accordance with the following provisions of this section.

(2) Subject to the following provisions of this section, a calling-up notice shall be served on the person [having the last recorded title to] the security subjects and appearing on the record as the proprietor, and should the proprietor of those subjects, or any part thereof, be dead then on his representative or the person entitled to the subjects in terms of the last recorded title thereto, notwithstanding any alteration of the succession not appearing in the Register of Sasines.

(3) Where the person [having the last recorded title to] the security subjects was an incorporated company which has been removed from the Register of Companies, or a person deceased who has left no representatives, a calling-up notice shall be served on the Lord Advocate and, where the estates of the person [having the last recorded title have] been sequestrated under the Bankruptcy (Scotland) Act 1913, the notice shall be served on the trustee in the sequestration (unless such trustee has been discharged) as well as on the bankrupt.

(4) If the proprietor be a body of trustees, it shall be sufficient if the notice is served on a majority of the trustees [having title to] the security subjects.

(5) It shall be an obligation on the creditor to serve a copy of the calling-up notice on any other person against whom he wishes to preserve any right of recourse in respect of the debt.

(6) For the purposes of the foregoing provisions of this section, the service of a calling-up notice may be made by delivery to the person on whom it is desired to be served or the notice may be sent by registered post or by the recorded delivery service to him at his last known address, or, in the case of the Lord Advocate, at the Crown Office, Edinburgh, and an acknowledgment, signed by the person on whom service has been made, in conformity with Form C of Schedule 6 to this Act, or, as the case may be, a certificate in conformity with Form D of that Schedule, accompanied by the postal receipt shall be sufficient evidence of the service of that notice; and if the address of the person on whom the notice is desired to be served is not known, or if it is not known whether that person is still alive, or if the packet containing a calling-up notice is returned to the creditor with an intimation that it could not be delivered, that notice shall be sent to the Extractor of the Court of Session, and shall be equivalent to the service of a calling-up notice on the person on whom it is desired to be served.

(7) For the purposes of the last foregoing subsection, an acknowledgment of receipt by the said Extractor on a copy of a calling-up notice shall be sufficient evidence of the receipt by him of that notice.

(8) A calling-up notice served by post shall be held to have been served on the next day after the day of posting.

(9) Where a creditor in a standard security has indicated in a calling-up notice that any sum and any interest thereon due under the contract may be subject to adjustment in amount, he shall, if the person on whom notice has been served so requests, furnish the debtor with a statement of the amount as finally determined within a period of one month from the date of service of the calling-up notice, and a failure by the creditor to comply with the provisions of this subsection shall cause the calling-up notice to be of no effect.

(10)   The period of notice mentioned in the calling-up notice may be effectively dispensed with or shortened by the person on whom it is served, with the consent of the creditors, if any, holding securities *pari passu* with, or postponed to, the security held by the creditor serving the calling-up notice, by a minute written or endorsed upon the said notice, or a copy thereof, in conformity with Form C of Schedule 6 to this Act.

[Provided, that without prejudice to the foregoing generality, if the standard security is over a matrimonial home as defined in section 22 of the Matrimonial Homes (Family Protection) (Scotland) Act 1981, the spouse on whom the calling-up notice has been served may not dispense with or shorten the said period without the consent in writing of the other spouse.]

(11)   A calling-up notice shall cease to have effect for the purpose of a sale in the exercise of any power conferred by the security on the expiration of a period of five years, which period shall run—

(a)   in the case where the subjects of the security, or any part thereof, have not been offered for or exposed to sale, from the date of the notice,

(b)   in the case where there has been such an offer or exposure, from the date of the last offer or exposure.

[19A   Notice to occupier of calling-up

(1)   Where a creditor in a standard security over [land or a real right] in land used to any extent for residential purposes serves a calling-up notice, he shall serve a notice in conformity with Form BB (notice to occupier) of Schedule 6 to this Act together with a copy of the calling-up notice.

(2)   Notices under subsection (1) above shall be sent by recorded delivery letter addressed to 'The Occupier' at the security subjects.

(3)   If a creditor fails to comply with subsections (1) and (2) above, the calling-up notice shall be of no effect.

19B   Notice to local authority of calling-up

(1)   Where a creditor in a standard security over an interest in land used to any extent for residential purposes serves a calling-up notice, the creditor shall give notice of that fact to the local authority in whose area the security subjects are situated, unless the creditor is that local authority.

(2)   Notice under subsection (1) shall be given in the form and manner prescribed under section 11(3) of the Homelessness etc (Scotland) Act 2003 (asp 10).]

20   Exercise of rights of creditor on default of debtor in complying with a calling-up notice

(1)   Where the debtor in a standard security is in default within the meaning of standard condition 9(1)(a), the creditor may exercise such of his rights under the security as he may consider appropriate, and any such right shall be in addition to and not in derogation from any other remedy arising from the contract to which the security relates or from any right conferred by any enactment or by any rule of law on the creditor in a heritable security.

(2)   Where the debtor is in default as aforesaid, the creditor shall have the right to sell the security subjects, or any part thereof, in accordance with the provisions of this Part of this Act.

(3)   A creditor in a standard security who is in lawful possession of the security subjects may let the security subjects, or any part thereof, for any period not exceeding seven years, or may make application to the court for warrant to let those subjects, or any part thereof, for a period exceeding seven years, and the application shall state the proposed tenant, and the duration and conditions of the proposed lease, and shall be served on the proprietor of the subjects and on any other heritable creditor having interest as such a creditor in the subjects.

(4)   The court, on such an application as aforesaid and after such inquiry and such further intimation of the application as it may think fit, may grant the appli-

cation as submitted, or subject to such variation as it may consider reasonable in all the circumstances of the case, or may refuse the application.

(5)   There shall be deemed to be assigned to a creditor who is in lawful possession of the security subjects all rights and obligations of the proprietor relating to—

(a)   leases, or any permission or right of occupancy, granted in respect of those subjects or any part thereof, and

(b)   the management and maintenance of the subjects and the effecting of any reconstruction, alteration or improvement reasonably required for the purpose of maintaining the market value of the subjects.

21   Notice of default

(1)   Where the debtor in a standard security is in default within the meaning of standard condition 9(1)(b), and the default is remediable, the creditor may, without prejudice to any other powers he may have by virtue of this Act or otherwise, proceed in accordance with the provisions of this section to call on the debtor and on the proprietor, where he is not the debtor, to purge the default.

(2)   For the aforesaid purpose the creditor may serve on the debtor and, as the case may be, on the proprietor a notice in conformity with Form B of Schedule 6 to this Act (hereinafter in this Act referred to as a 'notice of default') which shall be served in the like manner and with the like requirements as to proof of service as a calling-up notice.

[(2A)   Sections 19A and 19B of this Act apply where the creditor serves a notice of default as it applies where he serves a calling-up notice.]

(3)   For the purpose of dispensing with, or shortening, the period of notice mentioned in a notice of default, section 19(10) of this Act shall apply as it applies in relation to a calling-up notice.

(4)   Notwithstanding the failure to comply with any requirement contained in the notice, a notice of default shall cease to be authority for the exercise of the rights mentioned in section 23(2) of this Act on the expiration of a period of five years from the date of the notice.

22   Objections to notice of default

(1)   Where a person on whom a notice of default has been served considers himself aggrieved by any requirement of that notice he may, within a period of fourteen days of the service of the notice, object to the notice by way of application to the court; and the applicant shall, not later than the lodging of that application, serve a copy of his application on the creditor, and on any other party on whom the notice has been served by the creditor.

(2)   On any such application the court, after hearing the parties and making such inquiry as it may think fit, may order the notice appealed against to be set aside, in whole or in part, or otherwise to be varied, or to be upheld.

(3)   The respondent in any such application may make a counter-application craving for any of the remedies conferred on him by this Act or by any other enactment relating to heritable securities, and the court may grant any such remedy as aforesaid as it may think proper.

(4)   For the purposes of such a counter-application as aforesaid, a certificate which conforms with the requirements of Schedule 7 to this Act may be lodged in court by the creditor, and that certificate shall be *prima facie* evidence of the facts directed by the said Schedule to be contained therein.

23   Rights and duties of parties after service of notice of default to which objection is not taken, or where the notice is not set aside

(1)   Where a person does not object to a notice of default in accordance with the provisions of the last foregoing section, or where he has so objected and the notice has been upheld or varied under that section, it shall be his duty to comply with

any requirement, due to be performed or fulfilled by him, contained in the notice or, as the case may be, in the notice as so varied.

(2)   Subject to the provisions of section 21(4) of this Act, where a person fails to comply as aforesaid, the creditor, subject to the next following subsection, may proceed to exercise such of his rights on default under standard condition 10(2), (6) and (7) as he may consider appropriate.

(3)   At any time after the expiry of the period stated in a notice of default, or in a notice varied as aforesaid, but before the conclusion of any enforceable contract to sell the security subjects, or any part thereof, by virtue of the last foregoing subsection, the debtor or proprietor [(being in either case a person entitled to redeem the security)] may, subject to any agreement to the contrary, redeem the security without the necessity of observance of any requirement as to notice.

24   Application by creditor to court for remedies on default

(1)   Without prejudice to his proceeding by way of notice of default in respect of a default within the meaning of standard condition 9(1)(b), a creditor in a standard security, where the debtor is in default within the meaning of that standard condition or standard condition 9(1)(c), may apply to the court for warrant to exercise any of the remedies which he is entitled to exercise on a default within the meaning of standard condition 9(1)(a).

(2)   For the purposes of such an application as aforesaid in respect of a default within the meaning of standard condition 9(1)(b), a certificate which conforms with the requirements of Schedule 7 to this Act may be lodged in court by the creditor, and that certificate shall be *prima facie* evidence of the facts directed by the said Schedule to be contained therein.

[(3)   Where the creditor applies to the court under subsection (1) above, he shall, if the standard security is over [land or a real right] in land used to any extent for residential purposes—

(a)   serve on the debtor and (where the proprietor is not the debtor) or the proprietor a notice in conformity with Form E of Schedule 6 to this Act,

(b)   serve on the occupier of the security subjects a notice in conformity with Form F of that Schedule, [and

(c)   give notice of the application to the local authority in whose area the security subjects are situated, unless the creditor is that local authority].

(4)   Notices under subsection [(3)(a) or (b)] above shall be sent by recorded delivery letter addressed—

(a)   in the case of a notice under subsection (3)(a), to the debtor or, as the case may be, the proprietor at his last known address,

(b)   in the case of a notice under subsection (3)(b) to 'The Occupier' at the security subjects

(4A)   Notice under subsection (3)(c) above shall be given in the form and manner prescribed under section 11(3) of the Homelessness etc (Scotland) Act 2003 (asp 10).]

25   Exercise of power of sale

A creditor in a standard security having right to sell the security subjects may [, subject to sections 37(5)(e) or 40(1) of the Land Reform (Scotland) Act 2003 (asp 2) (prohibition of transfer of land registered under that Act except in accordance with its provisions),] exercise that right either by private bargain or by exposure to sale, and in either event it shall be the duty of the creditor to advertise the sale and to take all reasonable steps to ensure that the price at which all or any of the subjects are sold is the best that can be reasonably obtained.

26   Disposition by creditor on sale

(1)   Where a creditor in a standard security has effected a sale of the security subjects, or any part thereof, and grants to the purchaser or his nominee a disposition of the subjects sold thereby, which bears to be in implement of the sale, then,

on that disposition being duly recorded, those subjects shall be disburdened of the standard security and of all other heritable securities and diligences ranking *pari passu* with, or postponed to, that security.

(2)   Where on a sale as aforesaid the security subjects remain subject to a prior security, the recording of a disposition under the foregoing subsection shall not affect the rights of the creditor in that security, but the creditor who has effected the sale shall have the like right as the debtor to redeem the security.

27   Application of proceeds of sale

(1)   The money which is received by the creditor in a standard security, arising from any sale by him of the security subjects, shall be held by him in trust to be applied by him in accordance with the following order of priority—

(a)   first, in payment of any expenses properly incurred by him in connection with the sale, or any attempted sale;

(b)   secondly, in payment of the whole amount due under any prior security to which the sale is not made subject;

(c)   thirdly, in payment of the whole amount due under the standard security, and in payment, in due proportion, of the whole amount due under a security, if any, ranking *pari passu* with his own security, which has been duly recorded;

(d)   fourthly, in payment of any amounts due under any securities with a ranking postponed to that of his own security, according to their ranking,

and any residue of the money so received shall be paid to the person entitled to the security subjects at the time of sale, or to any person authorised to give receipts for the proceeds of the sale thereof.

(2)   Where owing to the death or absence of any other creditor, or to any other cause, a creditor is unable to obtain a receipt or discharge for any payment he is required to make under the provisions of the foregoing subsection, he may, without prejudice to his liability to account therefor, consign the amount due (so far as ascertainable) in the sheriff court for the person appearing to have the best right thereto; and where consignation is so made, the creditor shall lodge in court a statement of the amount consigned.

(3)   A consignation made in pursuance of the last foregoing subsection shall operate as a discharge of the payment of the amount due, and a certificate under the hand of the sheriff clerk shall be sufficient evidence thereof.

28   Foreclosure

(1)   Where the creditor in a standard security has exposed the security subjects to sale at a price not exceeding the amount due under the security and under any security ranking prior to, or *pari passu* with, the security, and has failed to find a purchaser, or where, having so failed, he has succeeded in selling only a part of the subjects at a price which is less than the amount due as aforesaid, he may, on the expiration of a period of two months from the date of the first exposure to sale, apply to the court for a decree of foreclosure.

(2)   In any application under the last foregoing subsection the creditor shall lodge a statement setting out the whole amount due under the security but, without prejudice to the right of the debtor or of the proprietor to challenge that statement, it shall be sufficient for the purposes of the application for the creditor to establish to the satisfaction of the court that the amount so stated is not less than the price at which the security subjects have been exposed to sale or sold, where part of the subjects has been sold as aforesaid.

(3)   Any application under subsection (1) of this section shall be served on the debtor in the standard security, the proprietor of the security subjects (if he is a person other than the debtor) and the creditor in any other heritable security affecting the security subjects as disclosed by a search of the Register of Sasines for a period of twenty years immediately preceding the last date to which the appro-

priate Minute Book of the said Register has been completed at the time when the
application is made.

(4) The court may order such intimation and inquiry as it thinks fit and may in
its discretion allow the debtor or the proprietor of the security subjects a period
not exceeding three months in which to pay the whole amount due under the
security and, subject to any such allowance, may—

(a) appoint the security subjects or the unsold part thereof to be re-exposed
to sale at a price to be fixed by the court, in which event the creditor in the
security may bid and purchase at the sale, or

(b) grant a decree of foreclosure in conformity with the provisions of the
next following subsection.

(5) A decree of foreclosure shall contain a declaration that, on the extract of the
decree being duly recorded, [any right to redeem the security] has been extinguished and that the creditor has right to the security subjects or the unsold part
thereof, described by means of a particular description or by reference to a
description thereof as in Schedule D to the Conveyancing (Scotland) Act 1924 or in
Schedule G to the Titles to Land Consolidation (Scotland) Act 1868, including a
reference to any conditions or clauses affecting the subjects or the unsold part
thereof, at the price at which the said subjects were last exposed to sale under
deduction of the price received for any part thereof sold, and shall also contain a
warrant for recording the extract of the decree in the Register of Sasines.

(6) Upon an extract of the decree of foreclosure being duly recorded, the following provisions of this subsection shall have effect in relation to the security
subjects to which the decree relates—

(a) [any right to redeem the security] shall be extinguished, and the creditor
shall have right to, and be vested in, the subjects as if he had received an
irredeemable disposition thereof duly recorded from the proprietor of the
subjects at the date of the recording of the extract of the decree;

(b) the subjects shall be disburdened of the standard security and all
securities and diligences postponed thereto;

(c) the creditor who has obtained the decree shall have the like right as the
debtor to redeem any security prior to, or *pari passu* with, his own security.

(7) Notwithstanding the due recording of an extract of a decree of foreclosure,
any personal obligation of the debtor under the standard security shall remain in
full force and effect so far as not extinguished by the price at which the security
subjects have been acquired and the price for which any part thereof has been
sold.

(8) Where the security subjects or any part thereof have been acquired by a
creditor in the security by virtue of a decree of foreclosure under the provisions of
this section, the title thereto of the creditor shall not be challengeable on the
ground of any irregularity in the proceedings for foreclosure or on calling-up or
default which preceded it; but nothing in the provisions of this subsection shall
affect the competency of any claim for damages in respect of such proceedings
against the creditor.

29 Procedure

(1) The court for the purposes of this Part of this Act, and for the operation of
section 11 of the Heritable Securities (Scotland) Act 1894 (application by *pari passu*
creditor to sell), in relation to a standard security, shall be the sheriff having jurisdiction over any part of the security subjects, and the sheriff shall be deemed to
have such jurisdiction whatever the value of the subjects.

[. . .]

30 Interpretation of Part II

(1) In this Part of this Act, unless the context otherwise requires, the following
expressions have the meanings hereby respectively assigned to them, that is to
say—

'creditor' and 'debtor' shall include any successor in title, assignee or representative of a creditor or debtor;

'debt' and 'creditor' and 'debtor', in relation to a standard security, have the meanings assigned to them by section 9(8) of this Act;

'duly recorded' means recorded in the appropriate division of the General Register of Sasines;

'exposure to sale' means exposure to sale by public roup, and exposed or re-exposed to sale shall be construed accordingly;

'heritable security' has the meaning assigned to it by the said section 9(8);

['real right in land'] has the meaning assigned to it by the said section 9(8);

'Register of Sasines' means the appropriate division of the General Register of Sasines;

'the standard conditions' are the conditions (whether varied or not) referred to in section 11(2) of this Act;

'whole amount due' has the meaning assigned to it by section 18(4) of this Act.

(2) For the purpose of construing this Part of this Act in relation to the creation of a security over a registered lease and to any subsequent transactions connected with that security, the following expressions shall have the meanings hereby respectively assigned to them, that is to say—

'conveyance' or 'disposition' means assignation;

'convey' or 'dispone' means assign;

[. . .]

'proprietor' means lessee;

'security subjects' means a registered lease subject to a security.

31 Saving

Nothing in the provisions of this Part of this Act shall affect the validity of any heritable security within the meaning of this Part which has been duly recorded before the commencement of this Act, and any such security may be dealt with and shall be as capable of being enforced, as if this Part had not been passed.

32 Application of enactments

The provisions of any enactment relating to a bond and disposition or assignation in security shall apply to a standard security, except in so far as such provisions are inconsistent with the provisions of this Part of this Act, but, without prejudice to the generality of that exception, the enactments specified in Schedule 8 to this Act shall not so apply.

40 Discharge of heritable security constituted by *ex facie* absolute conveyance

(1) Where land is held in security by virtue of a heritable security constituted by *ex facie* absolute conveyance, whether qualified by a back letter or not, a discharge by the creditor in security in conformity with Schedule 9 to this Act, either as a separate deed or as a deed endorsed on the conveyance, shall, as from the date on which that discharge is duly recorded, discharge that heritable security, disburden the land to the extent that it is the subject of the security, and vest that land in the person entitled thereto in like manner and to the like effect as if a conveyance containing a clause of warrandice from fact and deed only and all other usual and necessary clauses had been granted by the creditor to that person and duly recorded.

(2) Nothing in the provisions of the foregoing subsection shall affect any method of granting a discharge in existence at the commencement of this Act.

41 Restriction on effect of reduction of certain discharges of securities

(1) Where the discharge, in whole or in part, of a security over land is duly recorded, whether before or after the commencement of this Act, and that discharge bears to be granted by a person entitled so to do, the title of a person [who subsequently acquires the land or a real right in or over it] *bona fide* and for value,

shall not be challengeable, after the expiration of a period of five years commencing with the date of the recording of the discharge, by reason only of the recording of an extract of a decree of reduction of the discharge, whether or not the date of that decree was before or after the date on which the acquisition [. . .] was duly recorded.

(2) Section 46 of the Act of 1924 (which requires extract decrees of reduction of certain deeds to be recorded) shall cease to apply in relation to a decree of reduction of a discharge of a security where that discharge has been duly recorded for a period of five years or more, but the provisions of this subsection shall not preclude the recording of such a decree of reduction as provided for in the said section 46.

(3) Nothing in the provisions of this section shall affect any rights of a creditor in a security as against the debtor therein.

(4) The provisions of this section shall not be pleadable to any effect in any action begun, whether before or after the date of the commencement of this Act, before the expiry of a period of two years beginning with that date.

[(5) This section shall apply to an order under section 8 of the Law Reform (Miscellaneous Provisions) (Scotland) Act 1985 rectifying a discharge as it applies to a decree of reduction of a discharge.]

42   Extension of s 13 to certain existing forms of heritable securities
Section 13 of this Act shall apply, in relation to the effect on the preference in ranking of any heritable security, constituted by *ex facie* absolute disposition or assignation, as it applies to the preference in ranking of a standard security.

43   Interpretation of Part III
(1) In this Part of this Act, unless the context otherwise requires, the following expressions have the meanings hereby respectively assigned to them, that is to say—
   [. . .]
   'the Act of 1924' means the Conveyancing (Scotland) Act 1924;
   'land' has the meaning assigned to it by section 2(1) of the Act of 1924.

(2) For the purpose of construing this Part of this Act in relation to the creation of a security over a registered lease and to any subsequent transactions connected with that security, section 30(2) shall apply as it applies to Part II of this Act, and any reference to a security over land, however expressed, shall be construed as a reference to a registered lease subject to a security, and 'land' shall be construed accordingly.

PART IV
OTHER CONVEYANCING REFORMS

45   Status of sasine extracts
An extract, whether issued before or after the commencement of this Act, of a conveyance, deed instrument or other document bearing to have been recorded in the Register of Sasines shall be accepted for all purposes as sufficient evidence of the contents of the original so recorded and of any matter relating thereto appearing on the extract.

PART VI
GENERAL

51   Application to Crown
This Act shall, subject to any exceptions stated therein, apply to land [owned by the Crown or by] the Prince and Steward of Scotland, and to land in which there is any other interest belonging to Her Majesty in right of the Crown or to a Government department, or held on behalf of Her Majesty for the purposes of a Government department, in like manner as it applies to other land.

52 Saving amendment and repeal

(1) Any procedure, notice, advertisement, certificate or warrant instituted, given or granted, or any other thing done under any enactment amended or disapplied by this Act, shall not be invalidated by the coming into force of that amendment or disapplication, but it and any sale or other proceedings dependent thereon shall have effect as if this Act had not come into operation.

(2), (3) [*Amendments and repeals*]

53 Interpretation

(1) It shall be sufficient compliance with any provisions in this Act which require any deed, notice, certificate or procedure to be in conformity with a Form or Note, or other requirement of this Act, that that deed, notice, certificate or procedure so conforms as closely as may be, and nothing in this Act shall preclude the inclusion of any additional matter which the person granting the deed or giving or serving the notice or giving the certificate or adopting the procedure may consider relevant.

(2) In any Form prescribed by Schedules 2, 4, 5, 6 and 9 to this Act, and in any Note to those Schedules, the expression 'Register for' means the Register of Sasines appropriate for.

(3) Any reference in this Act to any other enactment is a reference thereto as amended, and includes a reference thereto as extended or applied, by or under any other enactment, including this Act.

(4) In this Act, except Part II, unless the context otherwise requires—

'conveyance', 'deed' and 'instrument' have the meanings assigned to them in section 3 of the Titles to Land Consolidation (Scotland) Act 1868, section 3 of the Conveyancing (Scotland) Act 1874, and section 2 of the Conveyancing (Scotland) Act 1924;

'duly recorded' means recorded in the appropriate Register of Sasines;

'Lands Tribunal' means the Lands Tribunal for Scotland;

[. . .]

'Register of Sasines' has the meaning assigned to it in section 2 of the Conveyancing (Scotland) Act 1924.

54 Short title, commencement and extent

(1) This Act may be cited as the Conveyancing and Feudal Reform (Scotland) Act 1970.

(2) This Act shall come into operation—

(a) except as respects sections 1 to 6, section 50, sections 51 to 53 in so far as they relate to those sections, and this section, at the expiration of a period of six months beginning with the date on which it is passed,

(b) as respects sections 1 to 6 and sections 51 to 53 in so far as they relate to those sections, on such date as the Secretary of State may by order made by statutory instrument appoint, and different days may be appointed for different provisions,

(c) as respects section 50, sections 51 to 53 in so far as they relate thereto, and this section, on the passing of this Act;

and any reference in any provision of this Act to the commencement of this Act shall, unless otherwise provided by any such order, be construed as a reference to the date on which that provision comes into operation.

(3) This Act shall extend to Scotland only.

SCHEDULES

[. . .]

Sections 9 and 10   SCHEDULE 2
                    FORMS OF STANDARD SECURITY

FORM A
[To be used where the personal obligation is included in the deed]

I, AB (*designation*), hereby undertake to pay to CD (*designation*), the sum of
£   (*or* a maximum sum of £   ) (*or* all sums due and that may become
due by me to the said CD in respect of .... (*here specify the matter for which the undertaking is granted*)) with interest from .... (*or* from the respective
times of advance) at .... per centum per annum (*or otherwise as the case may be*)
(annually, half-yearly, *or otherwise as the case may be*) on .... in
each year commencing on ....; For which I grant a standard
security in favour of the said CD over ALL and WHOLE (*here describe the security subjects as indicated in Note 1 hereto*): The standard conditions specified in Schedule 3 to
the Conveyancing and Feudal Reform (Scotland) Act 1970, and any lawful variation thereof operative for the time being, shall apply: And I grant warrandice:
And I consent to registration for execution.

[*Testing clause* †]

FORM B
[To be used where the personal obligation is constituted in a separate instrument
or instruments]

I, AB (*designation*) hereby in security of (*here specify the nature of the debt or
obligation in respect of which the security is given and the instrument(s) by which it is
constituted in such manner as will identify these instruments*) grant a standard security
in favour of CD (*designation*) over ALL and WHOLE (*here describe the security subjects
as indicated in Note 1 hereto*): The standard conditions specified in Schedule 3 to the
Conveyancing and Feudal Reform (Scotland) Act 1970, and any lawful variation
thereof operative for the time being, shall apply: And I grant warrandice.

[*Testing clause* †]

NOTES TO SCHEDULE 2

[Note 1.—The security subjects shall be described sufficiently to identify them; but this note
is without prejudice to any additional requirement imposed as respects any register.]
   Note 2.—Where the grantor has not a recorded title to the security subjects, insert after the
description thereof a clause of deduction of title as follows:—*Which subjects ([. . .] lease* (or
tack) or, as the case may be) *were last vested* (or *are part of the subjects last vested*) *in EF whose
title thereto was recorded in the Register for* .... (*or the said Register
of Sasines*) *on* .... (or, if the last [recorded title] has already
been mentioned, say *in the said EF as aforesaid*), *and from whom I acquired right by* (here specify
shortly the writ or writs by which that right was so acquired).
   Note 3.—Where the grantor of a standard security has granted a conveyance *ex facie* absolute of the security subjects, or any part thereof, that conveyance shall be referred to in
accordance with Note 5 to this Schedule. In any such case:—(a) where the grantor [has a
recorded title to] the security subjects, no clause of deduction of title is required in the
standard security, (b) where the grantor [does not have a recorded title to] the security subjects but has right thereto by virtue of an unrecorded title insert in the standard security after
the description of the security subjects a clause of deduction of title as follows.—*Which sub-*

jects (or [. . .] *lease* (or *tack*) or, as the case may be) *were formerly vested in* (or *are part of the subjects formerly vested in*) (give name of person [who last had a recorded title to] the subjects before the grantor acquired right thereto) *whose title thereto was recorded in the Register for* .... (or *the said Register of Sasines*) on .... (or if such [recorded title] has already been mentioned say *in the said* .... *as aforesaid*) *and from whom I acquired right by* (here specify shortly the writ or writs by which that right was so acquired).

Note 4.—Where it is desired to vary any of the standard conditions contained in Schedule 3 to this Act, such variations shall be effected either by an instrument or instruments other than the standard security, and any such instrument shall not require to be recorded in the Register of Sasines or by inserting in the standard security after the description of the security subjects (and after the clause of deduction of title, if any) *And I agree that the standard conditions shall be varied to the effect that* (here insert particulars of the variations desired).

(As regards future variations, see section 16 of, and Form E and Notes 5 and 6 in Schedule 4 to, this Act).

Note 5.—Where the security subjects are burdened by any other standard security or heritable security, or by any security by way of *ex facie* absolute conveyance which ranks prior to the standard security which is being granted, insert immediately before the clause of warrandice the following:—*But the security hereby granted is subject to* (here specify any deed by which such preferable rights were created and any deed modifying or altering such rights), and amend the clause of warrandice to read *And, subject as aforesaid, I grant warrandice*. Where the standard security is to rank prior or postponed to, or *pari passu* with, any other existing heritable security or any other standard security, a ranking clause may be inserted in appropriate terms immediately prior to the warrandice clause, and the warrandice clause shall, where necessary, be qualified accordingly.

Note 6.—Where a standard security is granted in Form A for a fluctuating or uncertain amount, provisions for ascertaining the amount due at any time may be inserted immediately prior to the clause of granting of the security, and the registration clause shall, where necessary, be amended accordingly.

Note 7.—In the case of a standard security for a non-monetary obligation, the forms in this Schedule shall be adapted as appropriate.

[† *Note 8.*—Subscription of the document by the granter of it will be sufficient for the document to be formally valid, but witnessing of it may be necessary or desirable for other purposes (see the Requirements of Writing (Scotland) Act 1995).]

SCHEDULE 3   Section 11

THE STANDARD CONDITIONS

Maintenance and repair

1. It shall be an obligation on the debtor—

(a) to maintain the security subjects in good and sufficient repair to the reasonable satisfaction of the creditor;

(b) to permit, after seven clear days notice in writing, the creditor or his agent to enter upon the security subjects at all reasonable times to examine the condition thereof;

(c) to make all necessary repairs and make good all defects in pursuance of his obligation under head (a) of this condition within such reasonable period as the creditor may require by notice in writing.

Completion of buildings etc and prohibition of alterations etc

2. It shall be an obligation on the debtor—

(a) to complete, as soon as may be practicable, any unfinished buildings and works forming part of the security subjects to the reasonable satisfaction of the creditor;

(b) not to demolish, alter or add to any buildings or works forming part of the security subjects, except in accordance with the terms of a prior written consent of the creditor and in compliance with any consent, licence or approval required by law;

(c) to exhibit to the creditor at his request evidence of that consent, licence or approval.

Observance of conditions in title, payment of duties, charges, etc, and general compliance with requirements of law relating to security subjects

3. It shall be an obligation on the debtor—

(a) to observe any condition or perform any obligation in respect of the security subjects lawfully binding on him in relation to the security subjects;

(b) to make due and punctual payment of any ground burden, teind, stipend, or standard charge, and any rates, taxes and other public burdens, and any other payments exigible in respect of the security subjects;

(c) to comply with any requirement imposed upon him in relation to the security subjects by virtue of any enactment.

Planning notices, etc

4. It shall be an obligation on the debtor—

(a) where he has received any notice or order, issued or made by virtue of the Town and Country Planning (Scotland) Acts 1947 to 1969 or any amendment thereof, or any proposal so made for the making or issuing of any such notice or order, or any other notice or document affecting or likely to affect the security subjects, to give to the creditor, within fourteen days of the receipt of that notice, order or proposal, full particulars thereof;

(b) to take, as soon as practicable, all reasonable or necessary steps to comply with such a notice or order or, as the case may be, duly to object thereto;

(c) in the event of the creditor so requiring, to object or to join with the creditor in objecting to any such notice or order or in making representations against any proposal therefor.

Insurance

5. It shall be an obligation on the debtor—

(a) to insure the security subjects or, at the option of the creditor, to permit the creditor to insure the security subjects in the names of the creditor and the debtor to the extent of the market value thereof against the risk of fire and such other risks as the creditor may reasonably require;

(b) to deposit any policy of insurance effected by the debtor for the aforesaid purpose with the creditor;

(c) to pay any premium due in respect of any such policy, and, where the creditor so requests, to exhibit a receipt therefor not later than the fourteenth day after the renewal date of the policy;

(d) to intimate to the creditor, within fourteen days of the occurrence, any occurrence which may give rise to a claim under the policy, and to authorise the creditor to negotiate the settlement of the claim;

(e) without prejudice to any obligation to the contrary enforceable against him, to comply with any reasonable requirement of the creditor as to the application of any sum received in respect of such a claim;

(f) to refrain from any act or omission which would invalidate the policy.

Restriction on letting

6. It shall be an obligation on the debtor not to let, or agree to let, the security

subjects, or any part thereof, without the prior consent in writing of the creditor, and 'to let' in this condition includes to sub-let.

General power of creditor to perform obligations etc on failure of debtor and power to charge debtor

7.—(1) The creditor shall be entitled to perform any obligation imposed by the standard conditions on the debtor, which the debtor has failed to perform.

(2) Where it is necessary for the performance of any obligation as aforesaid, the creditor may, after giving seven clear days notice in writing to the debtor, enter upon the security subjects at all reasonable times.

(3) All expenses and charges (including any interest thereon), reasonably incurred by the creditor in the exercise of a right conferred by this condition, shall be recoverable from the debtor and shall be deemed to be secured by the security subjects under the standard security, and the rate of any such interest shall be the rate in force at the relevant time in respect of advances secured by the security, or, where no such rate is prescribed, shall be the bank rate in force at the relevant time.

Calling-up

8. The creditor shall be entitled, subject to the terms of the security and to any requirement of law, to call-up a standard security in the manner prescribed by section 19 of this Act.

Default

9.—(1) The debtor shall be held to be in default in any of the following circumstances, that is to say—

(a) where a calling-up notice in respect of the security has been served and has not been complied with;

(b) where there has been a failure to comply with any other requirement arising out of the security;

(c) where the proprietor of the security subjects has become insolvent.

(2) For the purposes of this condition, the proprietor shall be taken to be insolvent if—

(a) he has become notour bankrupt, or he has executed a trust deed for behoof of, or has made a composition contract or arrangement with, his creditors;

(b) he has died and a judicial factor has been appointed under section 163 of the Bankruptcy (Scotland) Act 1913 to divide his insolvent estate among his creditors, or an order has been made for the administration of his estate according to the law of bankruptcy under section 130 of the Bankruptcy Act 1914, or by virtue of an order of the Court his estate is being administered in accordance with the rules set out in Part I of Schedule 1 to the Administration of Estates Act 1925;

(c) where the proprietor is a company, a winding-up order has been made with respect to it, or a resolution for voluntary winding-up (other than a members' voluntary winding-up) has been passed with respect to it, or a receiver or manager of its undertaking has been duly appointed, or possession has been taken, by or on behalf of the holders of any debentures secured by a floating charge, of any property of the company comprised in or subject to the charge.

Rights of creditor on default

10.—(1) Where the debtor is in default, the creditor may, without prejudice to his exercising any other remedy arising from the contract to which the standard security relates, exercise, in accordance with the provisions of Part II of this Act and of any other enactment applying to standard securities, such of the remedies specified in the following sub-paragraphs of this standard condition as he may consider appropriate.

(2)   He may proceed to sell the security subjects or any part thereof.

(3)   He may enter into possession of the security subjects and may receive or recover [. . .] the rents of those subjects or any part thereof.

(4)   Where he has entered into possession as aforesaid, he may let the security subjects or any part thereof.

(5)   Where he has entered into possession as aforesaid there shall be transferred to him all the rights of the debtor in relation to the granting of leases or rights of occupancy over the security subjects and to the management and maintenance of those subjects.

(6)   He may effect all such repairs and may make good such defects as are necessary to maintain the security subjects in good and sufficient repair, and may effect such reconstruction, alteration and improvement on the subjects as would be expected of a prudent proprietor to maintain the market value of the subjects, and for the aforesaid purposes may enter on the subjects at all reasonable times.

(7)   He may apply to the court for a decree of foreclosure.

Exercise of right of redemption

11.—(1)   The debtor shall be entitled to exercise his [right (if any) to redeem the security on giving notice] of his intention so to do, being a notice in writing (hereinafter referred to as a 'notice of redemption').

(2)   Nothing in the provisions of [this Act] shall preclude a creditor from waiving the necessity for a notice of redemption, or from agreeing to a period of notice of less than [that to which he is entitled].

(3)(a)   A notice of redemption may be delivered to the creditor or sent by registered post or recorded delivery to him at his last known address, and an acknowledgment signed by the creditor or his agent or a certificate of postage by the person giving the notice accompanied by the postal receipt shall be sufficient evidence of such notice having been given.

(b)   If the address of the creditor is not known, or if the packet containing the notice of redemption is returned to the sender with intimation that it could not be delivered, a notice of redemption may be sent to the Extractor of the Court of Session and an acknowledgment of receipt by him shall be sufficient evidence of such notice having been given.

(c)   A notice of redemption sent by post shall be held to have been given on the day next after the day of posting.

(4)   When a notice of redemption states that a specified amount will be repaid, and it is subsequently ascertained that the whole amount due to be repaid is more or less than the amount specified in the notice, the notice shall nevertheless be effective as a notice of repayment of the amount due as subsequently ascertained.

(5)   [Where the debtor has exercised a right to redeem, and has made payment] of the whole amount due, or [has performed] the whole obligations of the debtor under the contract to which the security relates, the creditor shall grant a discharge in the terms prescribed in section 17 of this Act.

12.   The debtor shall be personally liable to the creditor for the whole expenses of the preparation and execution of the standard security and any variation, restriction and discharge thereof and, where any of those deeds are recorded, the recording thereof, and all expenses reasonably incurred by the creditor in calling-up the security and realising or attempting to realise the security subjects, or any part thereof, and exercising any other powers conferred upon him by the security.

Interpretation

In this Schedule, where the debtor is not the proprietor of the security subjects, 'debtor' means 'proprietor', except
  (a)   in standard conditions 9(1), 10(1) and 12, and
  (b)   in standard condition 11, where 'debtor' includes the proprietor.

SCHEDULE 4   Sections 14, 15, 16 and 17
FORMS OF DEEDS OF ASSIGNATION, RESTRICTION, &c

FORM A
ASSIGNATION OF STANDARD SECURITY

Separate

I, AB (*designation*), in consideration of £   hereby assign to CD (*designation*) a standard security for £   (*or a maximum sum of £   , to the extent of £   being the amount now due thereunder; in other cases describe as indicated in Note 2 to this Schedule*) by EF in my favour (*or in favour of GH*) recorded in the Register for .... on .... (*adding if necessary, but only to the extent of £   of principal*); With interest from ....

[*Testing clause* †]

FORM B
[To be endorsed on the standard security]

As above save that instead of the words 'a standard security for £   ' (or otherwise, as the case may be) insert 'the foregoing standard security'. Where the security is for a fluctuating amount whether subject to a maximum or not, add 'to the extent of £   being the amount now due thereunder.'.

FORM C
RESTRICTION OF STANDARD SECURITY

I, AB (*designation*), in consideration of (*specify consideration, if any*) hereby disburden of a standard security for £   (*or a maximum sum of £   ; in other cases, describe as indicated in Note 2 to this Schedule*) by CD in my favour (*or in favour of EF*) recorded in the Register for .... on .... (*adding if necessary, but only to the extent of £   of principal*) ALL and WHOLE (*describe the subjects disburdened in the same way as directed in Note 1 to Schedule 2 to this Act in the case of a description of security subjects*).

[*Testing clause* †]

FORM D
COMBINED PARTIAL DISCHARGE AND DEED OF RESTRICTION
OF STANDARD SECURITY

I, AB (*designation*) in consideration of £   paid by CD (*designation*) (*or, as the case may be*), hereby discharge a standard security for £   (*or a maximum sum of £   ; in other cases, describe as indicated in Note 2 to this Schedule*) by the said CD (*or by EF*) in my favour (*or in favour of GH*) recorded in the Register for .... on ...., but only to the extent of £   of principal; And I disburden of the said standard security (*adding if necessary, but only to the extent of £   of principal*) ALL and WHOLE (*describe the subjects disburdened in the same way as directed in Note 1 to Schedule 2 to this Act in the case of a description of security subjects).*

[*Testing clause* †]

FORM E
VARIATION OF STANDARD SECURITY
[To be endorsed on the standard security]

I, AB (*designation*), agree that the foregoing standard security granted by me (*or by CD*) in favour of EF recorded in the Register for .... on .... (*if there have been previous variations insert* 'as varied') shall with effect from .... be varied so that (*here insert particulars of the variation agreed*); *And I, EF* (*designation*) (*or if the creditor is not the person in whose favour the standard security was granted say GH* (*designation*) *the creditor now in right of the said standard security*) consent to the variation hereby effected.

[*Testing clause* †]

FORM F
DISCHARGE OF STANDARD SECURITY

Separate

I, AB (*designation*), in consideration of £   (*where the security is in respect of a maximum sum or of all sums due or to become due or is in respect of a personal obligation constituted in an instrument or instruments other than the standard security add being the whole amount secured by the standard security aftermentioned*) paid by CD, (*designation*) (*or, as the case may be*) hereby discharge a standard security for £   (*or a maximum sum of £   in other cases describe as indicated in Note 2 to this Schedule*) by the said CD (or by EF) in my favour (*or in favour of GH*) recorded in the Register for .... on .... (*adding if necessary, but only to the extent of £   of principal*).

[*Testing clause* †]

[To be endorsed on the standard security]

As above save that instead of the words 'a standard security for £   (*or a maximum sum of £   in other cases describe as indicated in Note 2 to this Schedule*)' *insert* 'the foregoing standard security'.

NOTES TO SCHEDULE 4

General

NOTE 1.—Where the grantor of an assignation, discharge or deed of restriction of a standard security, or the creditor consenting to a variation of a standard security, is not the original creditor and has not a recorded title, insert at the end of the deed a clause of deduction of title as follows: *Which standard security* (adding, if necessary, *to the extent aforesaid* or, as the case may be) *was last vested in the said* (give name of original creditor) *as aforesaid* (or where the last recorded title to the standard security was in favour of a person other than the original creditor say *in JK whose title thereto was recorded in the said Register of Sasines on* ....) *and from whom I acquired right by* (here specify shortly the writ or writs by which right was so acquired).

Where the grantor of an assignation, discharge or deed of restriction of a standard security, or the creditor consenting to a variation of a standard security, although not the original creditor, has a recorded title, no specification of the title of the grantor or creditor is required.

Note 2.—In an assignation, discharge or deed of restriction, (1) a standard security in respect of an uncertain amount may be described by specifying shortly the nature of the debt or obligation (e.g., all sums due or to become due) for which the security was granted, adding in the case of an assignation, *to the extent of £* *being the amount now due thereunder* and (2) a standard security in respect of a personal obligation constituted in an instrument or instruments other than the standard security itself may be described by specifying shortly the nature of the debt or obligation and referring to the other instrument or instruments by which it is constituted in such manner as will be sufficient identification thereof.

Note 3.—If the original [title to a standard security has been completed] otherwise than by recording the security in the Register of Sasines, insert immediately after the word 'recorded' the words *along with notice of title thereon* (adding, if such notice is not in favour of the original creditor, the name of the person in whose favour it is drawn).

Note 4.—If part of the security subjects has already been disburdened, there may be inserted in an assignation, after the specification of the standard security assigned, a reference to the previous partial discharge or deed of restriction.

Note 5.—The variation docket Form E of this Schedule shall be used only when the personal obligation or other matter to which the variation relates was contained in the standard security, or in a variation thereof which has been duly recorded. Variations in a personal obligation or other matter constituted in an instrument or instruments which have not been so recorded may be altered by an instrument in appropriate terms which shall not be required to be recorded in the Register of Sasines.

Note 6.—Where the grantor of a variation docket does not have a recorded title to the security subjects, insert at the end of the variation and immediately before the consent by the creditor a clause of deduction of title as follows: *the security subjects to which the said standard security relates being last vested in* (give the name of the person in whom the security subjects were last vested) *whose title thereto was recorded in the said Register of Sasines on* .... *and from whom I acquired right by* (here specify the writ or writs by which such right was so acquired).

[† Note 7—Subscription of the document by the granter of it, or in the case of form E the granter and the consenter to the variation, will be sufficient for the document to be formally valid, but witnessing of it may be necessary or desirable for other purposes (see the Requirements of Writing (Scotland) Act 1995).]

SCHEDULE 5   Section 18
PROCEDURES AS TO REDEMPTION

FORM A
NOTICE OF REDEMPTION OF STANDARD SECURITY

To AB (*address*)

TAKE NOTICE that on .... (*state date of repayment*) CD (*designation*), will repay the sum of £ (*or the whole amount due*) secured by a standard security by the said CD (*or by EF*) in your favour (*or in favour of GH*) recorded in the Register for .... on .... Dated this .... day of ....

(*To be signed by the debtor, or proprietor, or by his agent, who will add his designation and the words* Agent of the said CD.)

In the case of a standard security for a non-monetary obligation this Form shall be adapted accordingly.

FORM B

I, AB, above named, hereby acknowledge receipt of the Notice of Redemption of which the foregoing is a copy. Dated this .... day of ....

(*To be signed by the creditor, or by his agent, who will add his designation and the words* Agent of the said AB)

FORM C

Notice of Redemption, of which the foregoing is a copy, was posted (*or otherwise, as the case may be*) to AB above named on the .... day of ....

(*To be signed by the debtor, or proprietor, or by his agent, who will add his designation and the words* Agent of the said CD *and if posted the postal receipt to be attached.*)

FORM D

NO. 1

CERTIFICATE OF CONSIGNATION ON REDEMPTION OF STANDARD SECURITY WHERE DISCHARGE CANNOT BE OBTAINED

I, AB (*designation*) (solicitor) certify that consignation of the whole amount due under the standard security aftermentioned was made as after stated and was necessitated by reason of a discharge being unobtainable after due notice of redemption had been given.

STANDARD SECURITY for £   (*or a maximum of £   ; in other cases describe as indicated in Note 2 to Schedule 4 to this Act*) by CD in favour of EF recorded in the Register of Sasines for .... on ....

AMOUNT CONSIGNED £   , being £   of principal, £   of interest and £   in respect of ascertained expenses.

BANK IN WHICH CONSIGNED (*specify bank or branch of bank, with address, in which above amount consigned*) conform to deposit receipt dated .... in name of the person appearing to have the best right thereto (*specifying his name and designation if known*) (*or if he is only a partial creditor say to the extent of £   *).

[*Testing clause †*]

NO. 2

CERTIFICATE OF DECLARATOR OF PERFORMANCE OF DEBTOR'S OBLIGATIONS UNDER STANDARD SECURITY WHERE DISCHARGE CANNOT BE OBTAINED

I, AB (*designation*) (solicitor) certify that a decree of declarator of performance of the obligations of the debtor under the standard security aftermentioned was pronounced as after stated and was necessitated by reason of a discharge being unobtainable after due notice of redemption had been given.

STANDARD SECURITY by CD in favour of EF recorded in the Register for .... on ....

DECREE OF DECLARATOR by the Sheriff of .... at .... in the application of the said CD (*or JK (designation*), who is now the debtor (*or the proprietor of the interest in land contained*) in the said standard security).

[*Testing clause †*]

[† Note—Subscription of the document by the granter of it will be sufficient for the document to be formally valid, but witnessing of it may be necessary or desirable for other purposes (see the Requirements of Writing (Scotland) Act 1995).]

SCHEDULE 6   Sections 19 and 21
PROCEDURES AS TO CALLING-UP AND DEFAULT

FORM A
NOTICE OF CALLING-UP OF STANDARD SECURITY

To AB (*address*)

TAKE NOTICE that CD (*designation*) requires payment of the principal sum of £   with interest thereon at the rate of .... per centum per annum from the .... day of .... (*adding if necessary*, subject to such adjustment of the principal sum and the amount of interest as may subsequently be determined) secured by a standard security by you (*or* by EF) in favour of the said CD (*or* of GH to which the said CD has now right) recorded in the Register for .... on ....; And that failing full payment of the said sum and interest thereon (*adding if necessary*, subject to any adjustment as aforesaid), and expenses within two months after the date of service of this demand, the subjects of the security may be sold.

Dated this .... day of ....

*(To be signed by the creditor, or by his agent, who will add his designation
and the words* Agent of the said CD.)

In the case of a standard security for a non-monetary obligation this Form shall be adapted accordingly.

[Note—The Mortgage Rights (Scotland) Act 2001 gives you the right in certain circumstances to apply to the court to suspend the rights of CD. You have two months (which may be shortened only with your consent) to make an application. The court will have regard in particular to the circumstances giving rise to the service of this notice, your ability to comply with this notice, any action taken by CD to assist the debtor in the standard security to fulfil the obligations under it and the ability of you and anyone else residing at the property to find reasonable alternative accommodation. If you wish to make such an application, you should consult a solicitor. You may be eligible for legal aid depending on your circumstances, and you can get information about legal aid from a solicitor. You may also be able to get advice, including advice about how to manage debt, from any Citizens Advice Bureau or from other advice agencies.]

FORM B
NOTICE OF DEFAULT UNDER STANDARD SECURITY

To AB (*address*)

TAKE NOTICE that CD (*designation*), the creditor in a standard security by you (*or* by EF) in favour of the said CD (*or* of GH to which the said CD has now right) recorded in the Register for .... on ...., requires fulfilment of the obligation(s) specified in the Schedule hereto in respect of which there is default; And that failing such fulfilment within one month after the date of service of this notice, the powers competent to the said CD on default may be exercised.

Dated this .... day of ....

*(To be signed by the creditor, or by his agent, who will add his designation
and the words* Agent of the said CD.)

Schedule of Obligation(s) in respect of which there is default.
To (*specify in detail the obligation(s) in respect of which there is default*).

[Note—The Mortgage Rights (Scotland) Act 2001 gives you the right in certain circumstances to apply to the court to suspend the rights of CD. You have two months (which may be shortened only with your consent) to make an application. The court will have regard in particular to the nature of and reasons for the default, your ability to fulfil the obligations under the standard security, any action taken by the CD to assist the debtor in the standard security to fulfil those obligations and the ability of you and anyone else residing at the property to find reasonable alternative accommodation. If you wish to make such an application, you should consult a solicitor. You may be eligible for legal aid depending on your circumstances, and you can get information about legal aid from a solicitor. You may also be able to get advice, including advice about how to manage debt, from any Citizens Advice Bureau or from other advice agencies.]

[FORM BB
NOTICE TO OCCUPIER

To the Occupier (*address*)

A Notice of Calling-up of a standard security/Default under a standard security (*delete as appropriate*) as been served by CD on AB in relation to (*address of subjects*). A copy of the notice is attached.

If you are a tenant of AB, in certain circumstances CD cannot take possession of the property without a court order. You should obtain legal advice about your rights as a tenant. You may be eligible for legal aid depending on your circumstances, and you can get information about legal aid from a solicitor. You may also be able to get advice from any Citizens Advice Bureau or from other advice agencies.

If you are the spouse or partner of AB the Mortgage Rights (Scotland) Act 2001 gives you the right in certain circumstances to apply to the court to suspend the rights of CD. You have two months (which may be shortened only with your consent) to make an application. The court will have regard in particular to—

(*for a Notice of Calling-up*) the circumstances giving rise to the service of the Notice of Calling-up, your ability to comply with the notice, any action taken by CD to assist the debtor in the standard security to fulfil the obligations under it and the ability of you and anyone else residing at the property to find reasonable alternative accommodation.

(*for a Notice of Default*) the nature of and reasons for the default, your ability to fulfil the obligations under the standard security, any action taken by CD to assist the debtor in the standard security to fulfil those obligations and the ability of you and anyone else residing at the property to find reasonable alternative accommodation.

(*delete as appropriate*)

If you wish to make such an application, you should consult a solicitor. You may be eligible for legal aid depending on your circumstances, and you can get information about legal aid from a solicitor. You may also be able to get advice, including advice about how to manage debt, from any Citizens Advice Bureau or from other advice agencies.

Dated this .... day of ....

(*Signature of CD, or signature and designation of CD's agent followed by the words* Agent of CD.)]

FORM C

I, AB, above named, hereby acknowledge receipt of the foregoing Notice of (Calling-up), (Default) of which the foregoing is a copy of the notice *adding where appropriate* 'and I agree to the period of notice being dispensed with (*or* shortened to ....).'

Dated this .... day of ....

(To be signed by the person on whom notice is served, or by his agent, who will add his designation and the words Agent of the said AB.*)*

FORM D

Notice of (Calling-up) (Default), of which the foregoing is a copy, was posted *(or otherwise, as the case may be)* to AB above named on the .... day of ....

(To be signed by the creditor, or by his agent, who will add his designation and the words Agent of the said CD *and if posted the postal receipt to be attached.)*

[FORM E

To AB *(address)*

CD *(designation)*, the creditor in a standard security by you *(or by EF)* in favour of CD *(or of GH to which CD now has right)* recorded in the Register for .... *(or, as the case may be,* registered in the Land Register for Scotland) on *(date)* as applied to the court under section 24 of the Conveyancing and Feudal Reform (Scotland) Act 1970 for warrant to exercise in relation to *(address of security subjects)* remedies to which he is entitled on the following default—

(specify in detail the default in respect of which the application is made)

A copy of the application is attached.

Dated this .... day of ....

(Signature of CD, or signature and designation of CD's agent followed by the words Agent of CD.*)*

Note—The Mortgage Rights (Scotland) Act 2001 gives you the right in certain circumstances to apply to the court for suspension of the rights of CD. The court will have regard in particular to the nature of and reasons for the default, your ability to fulfil the obligations under the standard security, any action taken by CD to assist the debtor in the standard security to fulfil those obligations and the ability of you and anyone else residing at the property to find reasonable alternative accommodation. If you wish to make such an application, you should consult a solicitor. You may be eligible for legal aid depending on your circumstances, and you can get information about legal aid from a solicitor. You may also be able to get advice, including advice about how to manage debt, from any Citizens Advice Bureau or from other advice agencies.

FORM F

To the Occupier *(address)*

CD *(designation)* has applied to the court under section 24 of the Conveyancing and Feudal Reform (Scotland) Act 1970 for warrant to exercise in relation to *(address of security subjects)* remedies to which he is entitled on the default of AB *(designation)* in the performance of his obligations under a standard security over *(address of subjects)*. A copy of the application is attached.

If you are a tenant of AB *(or, if AB is not the proprietor of the subjects,* of EF *(being the proprietor))*, in certain circumstances CD cannot take possession of the property without a court order. You should obtain legal advice about your rights as a tenant. You may be eligible for legal aid depending on your circumstances, and you can get information about legal aid from a solicitor. You may also be able to get advice from any Citizens Advice Bureau or from other advice agencies.

If you are the spouse or partner of AB, the Mortgage Rights (Scotland) Act 2001 gives you the right in certain circumstances to apply to the court to suspend the rights of CD. The court will have regard in particular to the nature of and reasons for the default, your ability to fulfil the obligations under the standard security, any action taken by CD to assist the debtor in the standard security to fulfil those obligations and the ability of you and anyone else residing at the property to find reasonable alternative accommodation. If you wish to make such an application, you should consult a solicitor. You may be eligible for legal aid depending on your circumstances, and you can get information about legal aid from a solicitor. You may also be able to get advice, including advice about how to manage debt, from any Citizens Advice Bureau or from other advice agencies.

Dated this .... day of ....

(Signature of CD, or signature and designation of CD's agent followed by the words Agent of CD.*)]*

Sections 22 and 24 SCHEDULE 7
CONTENTS OF CERTIFICATE STATING A DEFAULT

1. A certificate which is lodged in court by the creditor for the purposes of section 22 or 24 of this Act shall contain the information required by the following provisions of this Schedule.
2. A certificate shall state—
    (i) the name and address of the creditor and shall specify the standard security in respect of which the default is alleged to have occurred by reference to the original creditor and debtor therein and to the particulars of its registration;
    (ii) the nature of the default with full details thereof.
3. The certificate shall be signed by the creditor or his solicitor, and a certificate which does not comply with the foregoing requirements of this Schedule shall not be received in evidence for the purposes of the said section 22 or 24.

Section 32 SCHEDULE 8
EXCLUDED ENACTMENTS

The Debts Securities (Scotland) Act 1856

1. Section 7 (Securities for cash accounts or credits).

Registration of Long Leases (Scotland) Act 1857

[. . .]
4. Section 6 (Translation of assignations in security and creditor's entry on possession in default of payment), so far as relating to such a translation.
5. Section 13 (Renunciations and discharges to be recorded) so far as affecting discharges.
6. Section 20 (Interpretation of clauses in Schedules).
[. . .]

Section 40 SCHEDULE 9
DISCHARGE OF HERITABLE SECURITY CONSTITUTED
BY *EX FACIE* ABSOLUTE CONVEYANCE

I, AB, *(designation)* hereby acknowledge that [the disposition *(or assignation)* granted by CD, *(designation)* *(or* by EF, *(designation)* with consent of CD, *(designation))* in my favour *(or* in favour of GH, *(designation of original creditor))* recorded in the Register for .... on ....] [*or, where endorsed on the disposition or assignation,* the foregoing disposition *(or assignation)*] [*describe security discharged by reference to the parties thereto and to the details of its recording*] although in its terms *ex facie* absolute was truly in security of an advance of £   (or a maximum amount of £   *in other cases describe as indicated in Note 2 to Schedule 4 to this Act*), and that all moneys intended to be secured thereby have been fully paid.

[*Testing clause* †]

NOTES TO SCHEDULE 9

Note 1.—The discharge may be separate or endorsed on the *ex facie* absolute disposition or assignation.

Note 2.—Where the grantor of the discharge is not the original creditor, the separate form of discharge shall be used.

Note 3.—Where the grantor of the discharge is not the original creditor but has a recorded title, no specification of the grantor's title is required. Where the grantor of the discharge is not the original creditor and has not a recorded title, insert at the end of the discharge a clause of deduction of title as follows:

The subjects conveyed by the said disposition (or otherwise, as the case may be) *were last vested in the said GH as aforesaid* (or, where the last recorded title to the subjects was in favour of a person other than the original creditor, say *in JK whose title thereto was recorded in the said Register of Sasines on* ....) *and from whom I acquired right by* (here specify shortly the writ or writs by which right was so acquired).

[† Note 4—Subscription of the document by the granter of it will be sufficient for the document to be formally valid, but witnessing of it may be necessary or desirable for other purposes (see the Requirements of Writing (Scotland) Act 1995).]

PRESCRIPTION AND LIMITATION (SCOTLAND) ACT 1973
(1973 c 52)

PART I
PRESCRIPTION

Positive prescription

[1 Validity of right

(1) If land has been possessed by any person, or by any person and his successors, for a continuous period of ten years openly, peaceably and without any judicial interruption and the possession was founded on, and followed—

(a) the recording of a deed which is sufficient in respect of its terms to constitute in favour of that person a real right in—

(i) that land; or

(ii) land of a description *habile* to include that land; or

(b) registration of a real right in that land, in favour of that person, in the Land Register of Scotland, subject to an exclusion of indemnity under section 12(2) of the Land Registration (Scotland) Act 1979 (c 33),

then, as from the expiry of that period, the real right so far as relating to that land shall be exempt from challenge.

(2) Subsection (1) above shall not apply where—

(a) possession was founded on the recording of a deed which is invalid *ex facie* or was forged; or

(b) possession was founded on registration in the Land Register of Scotland proceeding on a forged deed and the person appearing from the Register to have the real right in question was aware of the forgery at the time of registration in his favour.

(3) In subsection (1) above, the reference to a real right is to a real right which is registrable in the Land Register of Scotland or a deed relating to which can com-

petently be recorded; but this section does not apply to [real burdens,] servitudes or public rights of way.

(4)   In the computation of a prescriptive period for the purposes of this section in a case where the deed in question is a decree of adjudication for debt, any period before the expiry of the legal shall be disregarded.

(5)   Where, in any question involving any foreshore or any salmon fishings, this section is pled against the Crown as owner of the regalia, subsection (1) above shall have effect as if for the words 'ten years' there were substituted 'twenty years'.

(6)   This section is without prejudice to section 2 of this Act.]

[2   Special cases

(1)   If—

(a)   land has been possessed by any person, or by any person and his successors, for a continuous period of twenty years openly, peaceably and without any judicial interruption; and

(b)   the possession was founded on, and followed the execution of, a deed (whether recorded or not) which is sufficient in respect of its terms to constitute in favour of that person a real right in that land, or in land of a description *habile* to include that land, then, as from the expiry of that period, the real right so far as relating to that land shall be exempt from challenge except on the ground that the deed is invalid *ex facie* or was forged.

(2)   This section applies—

(a)   to the real right of the lessee under a lease; and

(b)   to any other real right in land, being a real right of a kind which, under the law in force immediately before the commencement of this Part of this Act, was sufficient to form a foundation for positive prescription without the deed constituting the title to the real right having been recorded,

but does not apply to servitudes or public rights of way.

(3)   This section is without prejudice to section 1 of this Act or to section 3(3) of the Land Registration (Scotland) Act 1979 (c 33).]

3   Positive servitudes and public rights of way

(1)   If in the case of a positive servitude over land—

(a)   the servitude has been possessed for a continuous period of twenty years openly, peaceably and without any judicial interruption, and

(b)   the possession was founded on, and followed the execution of, a deed which is sufficient in respect of its terms (whether expressly or by implication) to constitute the servitude,

then, as from the expiration of the said period, the validity of the servitude as so constituted shall be exempt from challenge except on the ground that the deed is invalid *ex facie* or was forged.

(2)   If a positive servitude over land has been possessed for a continuous period of twenty years openly, peaceably and without judicial interruption, then, as from the expiration of that period, the existence of the servitude as so possessed shall be exempt from challenge.

(3)   If a public right of way over land has been possessed by the public for a continuous period of twenty years openly, peaceably and without judicial interruption, then, as from the expiration of that period, the existence of the right of way as so possessed shall be exempt from challenge.

(4)   References in subsections (1) and (2) of this section to possession of a servitude are references to possession of the servitude by any person in possession of the relative dominant tenement.

(5)   This section is without prejudice to the operation of section 7 of this Act.

4 Judicial interruption of periods of possession for purposes of sections 1, 2 and 3

(1) In sections 1, 2 and 3 of this Act references to a judicial interruption, in relation to possession, are references to the making in appropriate proceedings, by any person having a proper interest to do so, of a claim which challenges the possession in question.

(2) In this section 'appropriate proceedings' means—

(a) any proceedings in a court of competent jurisdiction in Scotland or elsewhere, except proceedings in the Court of Session initiated by a summons which is not subsequently called;

(b) any arbitration in Scotland;

(c) any arbitration in a country other than Scotland, being an arbitration an award in which would be enforceable in Scotland.

(3) The date of a judicial interruption shall be taken to be—

(a) where the claim has been made in an arbitration and the nature of the claim has been stated in a preliminary notice relating to that arbitration, the date when the preliminary notice was served;

(b) in any other case, the date when the claim was made.

(4) In the foregoing subsection 'preliminary notice' in relation to an arbitration means a notice served by one party to the arbitration on the other party or parties requiring him or them to appoint an arbiter or to agree to the appointment of an arbiter, or, where the arbitration agreement or any relevant enactment provides that the reference shall be to a person therein named or designated, a notice requiring him or them to submit the dispute to the person so named or designated.

5 Further provisions supplementary to sections 1, 2 and 3

(1) In sections 1, 2 and 3 of this Act 'deed' includes a judicial decree; and for the purposes of the said sections any of the following, namely an instrument of sasine, a notarial instrument and a notice of title, which narrates or declares that a person has a [right in land shall be treated as a deed sufficient to constitute that right].

[. . .]

Negative prescription

6 Extinction of obligations by prescriptive periods of five years

(1) If, after the appropriate date, an obligation to which this section applies has subsisted for a continuous period of five years—

(a) without any relevant claim having been made in relation to the obligation, and

(b) without the subsistence of the obligation having been relevantly acknowledged,

then as from the expiration of that period the obligation shall be extinguished:

Provided that in its application to an obligation under a bill of exchange or a promissory note this subsection shall have effect as if paragraph (b) thereof were omitted.

(2) Schedule 1 to this Act shall have effect for defining the obligations to which this section applies.

(3) In subsection (1) above the reference to the appropriate date, in relation to an obligation of any kind specified in Schedule 2 to this Act is a reference to the date specified in that Schedule in relation to obligations of that kind, and in relation to an obligation of any other kind is a reference to the date when the obligation became enforceable.

(4) In the computation of a prescriptive period in relation to any obligation for the purposes of this section—

(a) any period during which by reason of—

(i) fraud on the part of the debtor or any person acting on his behalf, or

(ii) error induced by words or conduct of the debtor or any person acting on his behalf,
the creditor was induced to refrain from making a relevant claim in relation to the obligation, and

(b) any period during which the original creditor (while he is the creditor) was under legal disability,

shall not be reckoned as, or as part of, the prescriptive period:

Provided that any period such as is mentioned in paragraph (a) of this subsection shall not include any time occurring after the creditor could with reasonable diligence have discovered the fraud or error, as the case may be, referred to in that paragraph.

(5) Any period such as is mentioned in paragraph (a) or (b) of subsection (4) of this section shall not be regarded as separating the time immediately before it from the time immediately after it.

7 Extinction of obligations by prescriptive periods of twenty years

(1) If, after the date when any obligation to which this section applies has become enforceable, the obligation has subsisted for a continuous period of twenty years—

(a) without any relevant claim having been made in relation to the obligation, and

(b) without the subsistence of the obligation having been relevantly acknowledged,

then as from the expiration of that period the obligation shall be extinguished:

Provided that in its application to an obligation under a bill of exchange or a promissory note this subsection shall have effect as if paragraph (b) thereof were omitted.

(2) This section applies to an obligation of any kind (including an obligation to which section 6 of this Act applies), not being an obligation [to which section 22A of this Act applies or an obligation] specified in Schedule 3 to this Act as an imprescriptible obligation [or an obligation to make reparation in respect of personal injuries within the meaning of Part II of this Act or in respect of the death of any person as a result of such injuries.]

8 Extinction of other rights relating to property by prescriptive periods of twenty years

(1) If, after the date when any right to which this section applies has become exercisable or enforceable, the right has subsisted for a continuous period of twenty years unexercised by or unenforced, and without any relevant claim in relation to it having been made, then as from the expiration of that period the right shall be extinguished.

(2) This section applies to any right relating to property, whether heritable or moveable, not being a right specified in Schedule 3 to this Act as an imprescriptible right or falling within section 6 or 7 of this Act as being a right correlative to an obligation to which either of those sections applies.

[8A Extinction of obligations to make contribution between wrongdoers

(1) If any obligation to make a contribution by virtue of section 3(2) of the Law Reform (Miscellaneous Provisions) (Scotland) Act 1940 in respect of any damages or expenses has subsisted for a continuous period of 2 years after the date on which the right to recover the contribution became enforceable by the creditor in the obligation—

(a) without any relevant claim having been made in relation to the obligation; and

(b) without the subsistence of the obligation having been relevantly acknowledged;

then as from the expiration of that period the obligation shall be extinguished.

(2)   Subsections (4) and (5) of section 6 of this Act shall apply for the purposes of this section as they apply for the purposes of that section.]

9   Definition of 'relevant claim' for purposes of sections 6, 7 and 8

(1)   In sections 6 [, 7 and 8A] of this Act the expression 'relevant claim', in relation to an obligation, means a claim made by or on behalf of the creditor for implement or part-implement of the obligation, being a claim made—

(a)   in appropriate proceedings, or

[(b)   by the presentation of, or the concurring in, a petition for sequestration or by the submission of a claim under section 22 or 48 of the Bankruptcy (Scotland) Act 1985 [. . .]; or

(c)   by a creditor to the trustee acting under a trust deed as defined in section 5(2)(c) of the Bankruptcy (Scotland) Act 1985; or

(d)   by the presentation of, or the concurring in, a petition for the winding up of a company or by the submission of a claim in a liquidation in accordance with rules made under section 411 of the Insolvency Act 1986;]

and for the purposes of the said sections 6 [, 7 and 8A] the execution by or on behalf of the creditor in an obligation of any form of diligence directed to the enforcement of the obligation shall be deemed to be a relevant claim in relation to the obligation.

(2)   In section 8 of this Act the expression 'relevant claim', in relation to a right, means a claim made in appropriate proceedings by or on behalf of the creditor to establish the right or to contest any claim to a right inconsistent therewith.

(3)   Where a claim which, in accordance with the foregoing provisions of this section, is a relevant claim for the purposes of section 6, 7[, 8 or 8A] of this Act is made in an arbitration, and the nature of the claim has been stated in a preliminary notice relating to that arbitration, the date when the notice was served shall be taken for those purposes to be the date of the making of the claim.

(4)   In this section the expression 'appropriate proceedings' and, in relation to an arbitration, the expression 'preliminary notice' have the same meanings as in section 4 of this Act.

10   Relevant acknowledgement for purposes of sections 6 and 7

(1)   The subsistence of an obligation shall be regarded for the purposes of sections 6 [, 7 and 8A] of this Act as having been relevantly acknowledged if, and only if, either of the following conditions is satisfied, namely—

(a)   that there has been such performance by or on behalf of the debtor towards implement of the obligation as clearly indicates that the obligation still subsists;

(b)   that there has been made by or on behalf of the debtor to the creditor or his agent an unequivocal written admission clearly acknowledging that the obligation still subsists.

(2)   Subject to subsection (3) below, where two or more persons are bound jointly by an obligation so that each is liable for the whole, and the subsistence of the obligation has been relevantly acknowledged by or on behalf of one of those persons then—

(a)   if the acknowledgment is made in the manner specified in paragraph (a) of the foregoing subsection it shall have effect for the purposes of the said sections 6 [, 7 and 8A] as respects the liability of each of those persons, and

(b)   if it is made in the manner specified in paragraph (b) of that subsection it shall have effect for those purposes only as respects the liability of the person who makes it.

(3)   Where the subsistence of an obligation affecting a trust has been relevantly acknowledged by or on behalf of one two or more co-trustees in the manner specified in paragraph (a) or (b) of subsection (1) of this section, the acknowledgment shall have effect for the purposes of the said sections 6 [, 7 and 8A] as respects the liability of the trust estate and any liability of each of the trustees.

(4)   In this section references to performance in relation to an obligation include, where the nature of the obligation so requires, references to refraining from doing something and to permitting or suffering something to be done or maintained.

11   Obligations to make reparation

(1)   Subject to subsections (2) and (3) below, any obligation (whether arising from any enactment, or from any rule of law or from, or by reason of any breach of, a contract or promise) to make reparation for loss, injury or damage caused by an act, neglect or default shall be regarded for the purposes of section 6 of this Act as having become enforceable on the date when the loss, injury or damage occurred.

(2)   Where as a result of a continuing act, neglect or default loss, injury or damage has occurred before the cessation of the act, neglect or default the loss, injury or damage shall be deemed for the purposes of subsection (1) above to have occurred on the date when the act, neglect or default ceased.

(3)   In relation to a case where on the date referred to in subsection (1) above (or, as the case may be, that subsection as modified by subsection (2) above) the creditor was not aware, and could not with reasonable diligence have been aware, that loss, injury or damage caused as aforesaid had occurred, the said subsection (1) shall have effect as if for the reference therein to that date there were substituted a reference to the date when the creditor first became, or could with reasonable diligence have become, so aware.

(4)   Subsections (1) and (2) above (with the omission of any reference therein to subsection (3) above) shall have effect for the purposes of section 7 of this Act as they have effect for the purposes of section 6 of this Act.

12   Savings

(1)   Where by virtue of any enactment passed or made before the passing of this Act a claim to establish a right or enforce implement of an obligation may be made only within a period of limitation specified in or determined under the enactment, and, by the expiration of a prescriptive period determined under section 6, 7 or 8 of this Act the right or obligation would, apart from this subsection, be extinguished before the expiration of the period of limitation, the said section shall have effect as if the relevant prescriptive period were extended so that it expires—

(a)   on the date when the period of limitation expires, or

(b)   if on that date any such claim made within that period has not been finally disposed of, on the date when the claim is so disposed of.

(2)   Nothing in section 6, 7 or 8 of this Act shall be construed so as to exempt any deed from challenge at any time on the ground that it is invalid *ex facie* or was forged.

13   Prohibition of contracting out

Any provision in any agreement purporting to provide in relation to any right or obligation that section 6, 7 [, 8 or 8A] of this Act shall not have effect shall be null.

General

14   Computation of prescriptive periods

(1)   In the computation of a prescriptive period for the purposes of any provision of this Part of this Act—

(a)   time occurring before the commencement of this Part of this Act shall be reckonable towards the prescriptive period in like manner as time occurring thereafter, but subject to the restriction that any time reckoned under this paragraph shall be less than the prescriptive period;

(b)   any time during which any person against whom the provision is pled was under legal disability shall (except so far as otherwise provided by [subsection (4) of section 6 of this Act including that subsection as applied by section 8A of this Act] be reckoned as if the person were free from that disability;

    (c) if the commencement of the prescriptive period would, apart from this paragraph, fall at a time in any day other than the beginning of the day, the period shall be deemed to have commenced at the beginning of the next following day;

    (d) if the last day of the prescriptive period would, apart from this paragraph, be a holiday, the period shall, notwithstanding anything in the said provision, be extended to include any immediately succeeding day which is a holiday, any further immediately succeeding days which are holidays, and the next succeeding day which is not a holiday;

    (e) save as otherwise provided in this Part of this Act regard shall be had to the like principles as immediately before the commencement of this Part of this Act were applicable to the computation of periods of prescription for the purposes of the Prescription Act 1617.

(2) In this section 'holiday' means a day of any of the following descriptions, namely, a Saturday, a Sunday and a day which, in Scotland, is a bank holiday under the Banking and Financial Dealings Act 1971.

15 Interpretation of Part I

(1) In this Part of this Act, unless the context otherwise requires, the following expressions have the meanings hereby assigned to them, namely—

    'bill of exchange' has the same meaning as it has for the purposes of the Bills of Exchange Act 1882;

    'date of execution', in relation to a deed executed on several dates, means the last of those dates;

    'enactment' includes an order, regulation, rule or other instrument having effect by virtue of an Act;

    'holiday' has the meaning assigned to it by section 14 of this Act;

    'land' includes heritable property of any description;

    'lease' includes a sub-lease;

    'legal disability' means legal disability by reason of nonage or unsoundness of mind;

    'possession' includes civil possession, and 'possessed' shall be construed accordingly;

    'prescriptive period' means a period required for the operation of section 1, 2, 3, 6, 7 [, 8 or 8A] of this Act;

    'promissory note' has the same meaning as it has for the purposes of the Bills of Exchange Act 1882;

    'trustee' includes any person holding property in fiduciary capacity for another and, without prejudice to that generality, includes a trustee within the meaning of the Trusts (Scotland) Act 1921; and 'trust' shall be construed accordingly;

and references to the recording of a deed are references to the recording thereof in the General Register of Sasines.

(2) In this Part of this Act, unless the context otherwise requires, any reference to an obligation or to a right includes a reference to the right or, as the case may be, to the obligation (if any), correlative thereto.

(3) In this Part of this Act any reference to an enactment shall, unless the context otherwise requires, be construed as a reference to that enactment as amended or extended, and as including a reference thereto as applied, by or under any other enactment.

16 Amendments and repeals related to Part I

(1) The enactment specified in Part I of Schedule 4 to this Act shall have effect

subject to the amendment there specified, being an amendment related to this Part of this Act.

(2) Subject to the next following subsection, the enactments specified in Part I of Schedule 5 to this Act (which includes certain enactments relating to the limitation of proof) are hereby repealed to the extent specified in column 3 of that Schedule.

(3) Where by virtue of any Act repealed by this section the subsistence of an obligation in force at the date of the commencement of this Part of this Act was immediately before that date, by reason of the passage of time, provable only by the writ or oath of the debtor the subsistence of the obligation shall [(notwithstanding anything in sections 16(1) and 17(2)(a) of the Interpretation Act 1978, which relates to the effect of repeals)] as from that date be provable as if the said repealed Act had not passed.

SCHEDULES

Section 6   SCHEDULE 1
OBLIGATIONS AFFECTED BY PRESCRIPTIVE PERIODS OF FIVE YEARS
UNDER SECTION 6

1.   Subject to paragraph 2 below, section 6 of this Act applies—
     (a)   to any obligation to pay a sum of money due in respect of a particular period—
          (i)   by way of interest;
          (ii) by way of an instalment of an annuity;
          [. . .]
          (v)   by way of rent or other periodical payment under a lease;
          (vi) by way of a periodical payment in respect of the occupancy or use of land, not being an obligation falling within any other provision of this sub-paragraph;
          (vii) by way of a periodical payment under a [title condition], not being an obligation falling within any other provision of this sub-paragraph;
     [(aa)   to any obligation to make a compensatory payment ('compensatory payment' being construed in accordance with section 8(1) of the Abolition of Feudal Tenure etc (Scotland) Act 2000 (asp 5), including that section as read with section 56 of that Act);
     (aa)   to any obligation to pay compensation by virtue of section 2 of the Leasehold Casualties (Scotland) Act 2001 (asp 5);
     (ab)   to any obligation arising by virtue of a right—
          (i)   of reversion under the third proviso to section 2 of the School Sites Act 1841 (4 & 5 Vict c 38) (or of reversion under that proviso as applied by virtue of any other enactment);
          (ii) to petition for a declaration of forfeiture under section 7 of the Entail Sites Act 1840 (3 & 4 Vict c 48);]
     [(ac)   to any obligation to pay a sum of money by way of costs to which section 12 of the Tenements (Scotland) Act 2004 (asp 11) applies;]
     (b)   to any obligation based on redress of unjustified enrichment, including without prejudice to that generality any obligation of restitution, repetition or recompense;
     (c)   to any obligation arising from *negotiorum gestio*;
     (d)   to any obligation arising from liability (whether arising from any enactment or from any rule of law) to make reparation;
     (e)   to any obligation under a bill of exchange or a promissory note;
     (f)   to any obligation of accounting, other than accounting for trust funds;
     (g)   to any obligation arising from, or by reason of any breach of, a contract

or promise, not being an obligation falling within any other provision of this paragraph.

2. Notwithstanding anything in the foregoing paragraph, section 6 of this Act does not apply—

(a) to any obligation to recognise or obtemper a decree of court, an arbitration award or an order of a tribunal or authority exercising jurisdiction under any enactment;

(b) to any obligation arising from the issue of a bank note;

[. . .]

(d) to any obligation under a contract of partnership or of agency, not being an obligation remaining, or becoming prestable on or after the termination of the relationship between the parties under the contract;

(e) except as provided in paragraph 1(a)[, (aa) or (ac)] of this Schedule, to any obligation relating to land (including an obligation to recognise a servitude);

[(ee) so as to extinguish, before the expiry of the continuous period of five years which immediately follows the coming into force of section 88 of the Title Conditions (Scotland) Act 2003 (asp 9) (prescriptive period for obligations arising by virtue of 1841 Act or 1840 Act), an obligation mentioned in sub-paragraph (ab) of paragraph 1 of this Schedule;]

(f) to any obligation to satisfy any claim to [. . .] legitim, jus relicti or jus relictae, or to any prior right of a surviving spouse under section 8 or 9 of the Succession (Scotland) Act 1964;

(g) to any obligation to make reparation in respect of personal injuries within the meaning of Part II of this Act or in respect of the death of any person as a result of such injuries;

[(gg) to any obligation to make reparation or otherwise make good in respect of defamation within the meaning of section 18A of this Act;

(ggg) to any obligation arising from liability under section 2 of the Consumer Protection Act 1987 (to make reparation for damage caused wholly or partly by a defect in a product);]

(h) to any obligation specified in Schedule 3 to this Act as an imprescriptible obligation.

[. . .]

[4. In this Schedule, 'title condition' shall be construed in accordance with section 122(1) of the Title Conditions (Scotland) Act 2003 (asp 9).]

SCHEDULE 2   Section 6
APPROPRIATE DATES FOR CERTAIN OBLIGATIONS FOR PURPOSES OF SECTION 6

1—(1) This paragraph applies to any obligation, not being part of a banking transaction, to pay money in respect of—

(a) goods supplied on sale or hire, or

(b) services rendered,

in a series of transactions between the same parties (whether under a single contract or under several contracts) and charged on continuing account.

(2) In the foregoing sub-paragraph—

(a) any reference to the supply of goods on sale includes a reference to the supply of goods under a hire-purchase agreement, a credit-sale agreement or a conditional sale agreement as defined (in each case) by section 1 of the Hire-Purchase (Scotland) Act 1965; and

(b) any reference to services rendered does not include the work of keeping the account in question.

(3) Where there is a series of transactions between a partnership and another party, the series shall be regarded for the purposes of this paragraph as terminated (without prejudice to any other mode of termination) if the partnership (in the fur-

ther provisions of this sub-paragraph referred to as 'the old partnership') is dissolved and is replaced by a single new partnership having among its partners any person who was a partner in the old partnership, then, for the purposes of this paragraph, the new partnership shall be regarded as if it were identical with the old partnership.

(4)   The appropriate date in relation to an obligation to which this paragraph applies is the date on which payment for the goods last supplied, or, as the case may be, the services last rendered, became due.

2—(1)   This paragraph applies to any obligation to repay the whole, or any part of, a sum of money lent to, or deposited with, the debtor under a contract of loan or, as the case may be, deposit.

(2)   The appropriate date in relation to an obligation to which this paragraph applies is—

(a)   if the contract contains a stipulation which makes provision with respect to the date on or before which repayment of the sum or, as the case may be, the part thereof is to be made, the date on or before which, in terms of that stipulation, the sum or part thereof is to be repaid; and

(b)   if the contract contains no such stipulation, but a written demand for repayment of the sum, or, as the case may be, the part thereof, is made by or on behalf of the creditor to the debtor, the date when such demand is made or first made.

3—(1)   This paragraph applies to any obligation under a contract of partnership or of agency, being an obligation remaining, or becoming, prestable on or after the termination of the relationship between the parties under the contract.

(2)   The appropriate date in relation to an obligation to which this paragraph applies is—

(a)   if the contract contains a stipulation which makes provision with respect to the date on or before which performance on the obligation is to be due, the date on or before which, in terms of that stipulation, the obligation is to be performed; and

(b)   in any other case the date when the said relationship terminated.

4—(1)   This paragraph applies to any obligation—

(a)   to pay an instalment of a sum of money payable by instalments,

(b)   to execute any instalment of work due to be executed by instalments, not being an obligation to which any of the foregoing paragraphs applies.

(2)   The appropriate date in relation to an obligation to which this paragraph applies is the date on which the last of the instalments is due to be paid or, as the case may be, to be executed.

Sections 7 & 8: Schedule 1   SCHEDULE 3
RIGHTS AND OBLIGATIONS WHICH ARE IMPRESCRIPTIBLE FOR THE
PURPOSES OF SECTIONS 7 AND 8 AND SCHEDULE 1

The following are imprescriptible rights and obligations for the purposes of sections 7(2) and 8(2) of, and paragraph 2(h) of Schedule 1 to, this Act, namely—

(a)   any real right of ownership in land;

(b)   the right in land of the lessee under a recorded lease;

(c)   any right exercisable as a *res merae facultatis*;

(d)   any right to recover property *extra commercium*;

(e)   any obligation of a trustee—

(i)   to produce accounts of the trustee's intromissions with any property of the trust;

(ii)   to make reparation or restitution in respect of any fraudulent breach of trust to which the trustee was a party or was privy;

(iii)   to make furthcoming to any person entitled thereto any trust property, or the proceeds of any such property, in the possession of the trustee, or to make good the value of any such property previously received by the trustee and appropriated to his own use;

(f) any obligation of a third party to make furthcoming to any person entitled thereto any trust property received by the third party otherwise then in good faith and in his possession;

(g) any right to recover stolen property from the person by whom it was stolen or from any person privy to the stealing thereof;

(h) any right to be served as heir to an ancestor or to take any steps necessary for making up or completing title to any [real right] in land.

LAND TENURE REFORM (SCOTLAND) ACT 1974
(1974, c 38)

2 Prohibition of new ground annuals and other periodical payments from land

(1) No deed executed after the commencement of this Act shall impose ground annual, skat or any other periodical payment [. . .] in respect of the tenure or use of land or under a [title condition] not being a payment in respect of a lease, liferent or other right of occupancy, [. . .] a payment in defrayal of or contribution towards some continuing cost related to the land, or a payment under a heritable security.

(2) A provision in a deed executed after such commencement which purports to impose any payment to which subsection (1) above applies shall not render the deed void or unenforceable, but the deed shall have effect only to the extent (if any) that it would have had effect under the law in force before such commencement if it had not imposed any such payment.

[(3) In subsection (1) above, 'title condition' has the meaning given by section 122(1) of the Title Conditions (Scotland) Act 2003 (asp 9).]

PART II
LIMITATIONS ON RESIDENTIAL USE OF PROPERTY
LET UNDER FUTURE LONG LEASES

8 Property let under future long lease, etc not to be used as private dwelling-house

(1) It shall be a condition of every long lease executed after the commencement of this Act that, subject to the provisions of this Part of this Act, no part of the property which is subject to the lease shall be used as or as part of a private dwelling-house.

(2) For the purposes of this Part of this Act, any garden, yard, garage, outhouse or pertinent used along with any dwelling-house shall be deemed to form part of a dwelling-house, and use as a dwelling-house shall not include use as the site of a caravan.

(3) The use as or as part of a private dwelling-house of part of a property which is subject to a long lease shall not constitute a breach of the condition contained in subsection (1) above if such use is ancillary to the use of the remainder of the property otherwise than as or as part of a private dwelling-house and it would be detrimental to the efficient exercise of the use last-mentioned if the said ancillary use did not occur on that property.

(4) For the purposes of this Part of this Act—

'lessor' and 'lessee' mean any person holding for the time being the interest of lessor or lessee (as the case may be); and

'long lease' means any grant of—

(a) a lease, or

(b) a liferent or other right of occupancy granted for payment (other than payment in defrayal of or contribution towards some continuing cost related to such liferent use or such occupancy, as the case may be), which is either—

(i) subject to a duration, whether definite or indefinite, which could (in terms of the grant and without any subsequent agreement, express or implied, between the persons holding the interests of the grantor and the grantee) extend for more than 20 years, or

(ii) subject to any provision whereby any person holding the interest of the grantor or the grantee is under a future obligation, if so requested by the other, to renew the grant so that the total duration could so extend for more than 20 years, or whereby, if he does not so renew it, he will be liable to make some payment or to perform some other obligation.

[but, in relation to a lease granted before 1st September 1974, does not include its renewal (whether before or after the commencement of section 1 of the Law Reform (Miscellaneous Provisions) (Scotland) Act 1985) in implement of an obligation in or under it].

(5) This Part of this Act shall not apply in relation to the use of property for the time being forming part or deemed to form part of—

[(a) the land comprised in a lease constituting a 1991 Act tenancy, within the meaning of the Agricultural Holdings (Scotland) Act 2003 (asp 11);

(b) the land comprised in a lease constituting a short limited duration tenancy or a limited duration tenancy within the meaning of that Act;]

(c) a croft, within the meaning of the Crofters (Scotland) Acts 1955 and 1961.

(6) Nothing in this Part of this Act shall affect the right of the lessor to terminate the lease and recover possession of the property subject thereto on the ground of breach of a conventional condition of the lease which has the effect of prohibiting such use of the property as constitutes a breach of the condition contained in subsection (1) above.

(7) Nothing in this Part of this Act shall prevent a tenancy from being or becoming a protected or statutory tenancy within the meaning of the Rent (Scotland) Act [1984 or a Scottish secure tenancy within the meaning of the Housing (Scotland) Act 2001 (asp 10)], but nothing in [either of those Acts] restricting the power of a court to make an order for possession of a dwelling-house shall prevent the granting of a decree of removing under section 9(1) of this Act.

9   Consequences of use as dwelling-house of property subject to long lease

(1) A breach of the condition of a long lease executed after the commencement of this Act, contained in section 8(1) of this Act, shall not render the lease void or unenforceable, but, subject to the provisions of this section and of section 10 of this Act, where such a breach occurs, the lessor shall be entitled to give to the lessee notice to terminate the use constituting the breach within 28 days from the date of the notice; and, if the lessee shall fail to terminate that use within that period, the lessor shall be entitled to raise an action of removing against the lessee concluding for his removal from such part of the property as is subject to the use at the expiry of 28 days after the decree of removing is extracted, and the court may decern for the termination of the lease in respect of such part and the removal of the lessee therefrom and, failing such removal, for his ejection therefrom on expiry of the 28 days last mentioned.

(2) A notice under subsection (1) above shall be in or as nearly as may be in the form contained in Schedule 5 to this Act.

(3) It shall be a defence to an action under subsection (1) above that the breach of condition constituting the ground of action has ceased.

(4) Subject to section 10(3) of this Act, in an action under subsection (1) above, if it is proved that the use of the property constituting the ground of action has at any time been approved by the person holding at that time the interest of the lessor in the lease, either expressly or by his actings, and the said use has not subsequently been discontinued, the court shall not decern in terms of that subsection, but—

(a)   where the lease is subject to a duration expiring in a year more than 20 years after the year in which the notice under subsection (1) above relative to the breach was given, the court shall decern that the lease shall, in respect of such part of the property as is subject to the use, have effect as if for the year of expiry there were substituted the year 20 years after the year in which the said notice was given;

(b)   where the lease is subject to a duration expiring in a year less than 20 years after that year, the lease shall continue in force according to its terms; and the said part of the property subject to the lease (and, during the remaining period of the lease as determined by reference to this subsection, any over-lease, insofar as it relates to that part) shall cease to be subject to the condition contained in section 8(1) of this Act.

(5)   Where the breach of condition constituting the ground of action under subsection (1) above relates to part only of the property subject to the lease, any decree granted to the pursuer in the action under subsection (1) or (4)(a) above shall contain a particular description or a description by reference (in accordance with the provisions of the Conveyancing (Scotland) Act 1874 and the Conveyancing (Scotland) Act 1924) of such part; and in such a case the court shall decern for such adjustment (if any) as it thinks fit (to take effect on the termination of the lease of such part in terms of the decree) in the rent of the remaining part of the property and in the conditions of the lease, including the addition of new conditions, but not including any provision for the payment of money.

(6)   Subject to the provisions of this Part of this Act and of section 37(1) of the Sheriff Courts (Scotland) Act 1971, and notwithstanding section 35(1)(c) of that Act, the procedure in an action of removing under this section shall be that in an ordinary cause; and on the granting of a decree to the pursuer in such an action, or at any time before the decree is extracted, the court may sist extract of the decree for such period or periods as it thinks fit to enable any facts to be established which (if the action were still pending) would constitute a defence thereto, and if the court is satisfied that any such facts are established it may vary or rescind the decree, subject to such conditions (if any) with regard to payment of arrears of rent and otherwise as the court thinks fit.

(7)   Notwithstanding the provisions of section 24 of the Court of Session Act 1868, Rule 63(b) of the Rules of Court 1965 or Rule 25 of Schedule 1 to the Sheriff Courts (Scotland) Act 1907, a decree granted in an action under this section shall, as in a question with third parties who have acted onerously and in good faith in reliance on the records, be final and not subject to challenge when an extract thereof shall have been recorded in the Register of Sasines.

(8)   The provisions of this section and of section 10 of this Act shall apply in relation to a grant (not being a lease) mentioned in section 8(4) of this Act as they apply in relation to a lease, and any reference to a lease, over-lease or sub-lease, to the parties thereto, or to rent, shall be construed accordingly.

10   Modification of s 9 where lease subject to sub-lease or heritable security

(1)   For the avoidance of doubt, it is hereby declared that (subject to the provisions of this section) sections 8 and 9 of this Act shall apply, as between the parties to any over-lease or sub-lease executed after the commencement of this Act, as they apply as between the parties to any other lease so executed.

(2)   The pursuer in an action under section 9 of this Act shall give such intimation thereof as the court may direct—

(a)   to every person appearing, from a search in the Register of Sasines for a period of 20 years immediately prior to the raising of the action, to hold for the time being the interest of creditor in a heritable security over the lease which is the subject of the action; and

(b)   where the said lease is, in relation to any part of the property which is subject to the use constituting the ground of action, subject to any sub-lease, to every person appearing from such a search and from examination of the valuation roll or otherwise to be the lessee in any such sub-lease (of whatever duration) or the creditor in a heritable security over any such sub-lease; and any such creditor or lessee as aforesaid shall, subject to the provisions of this section, be titled to plead in the action any defence which could be pleaded by the defender in the action.

(3)   The defence provided under section 9(4) of this Act shall not be available to the lessee in a lease in respect of the use of property subject to a sub-lease derived from that lease.

(4)   A sub-lessee, provided that he could have pleaded the defence provided by section 9(4) of this Act in an action by the lessor in the sub-lease, may, on being sisted to an action under the said section 9 by the lessor in any over-lease, plead that defence in relation to the approval by the lessor in that over-lease or in any sub-lease under that over-lease of property which is subject to the use constituting the ground of action; and the court, on being satisfied that the defence is established to that effect, shall be entitled to decern in terms of the said section 9(4) as if the action had been brought by the lessor in the sub-least first mentioned.

(5)   The right provided by subsection (4) above shall be available to a sub-lessee whose lease is not a long lease to the same extent as if it had been a long lease.

PART III
MISCELLANEOUS

11   Right to redeem heritable security after 20 years where security subjects used as private dwelling-house

(1)   The provisions of this section shall apply in relation to a heritable security executed after the commencement of this Act, including a heritable security in relation to a debenture described in section 89 of the Companies Act 1948 (perpetual debentures, etc).

(2)   The debtor in a heritable security to which this section applies, or, where the debtor is not the proprietor, the proprietor of the security subjects shall, subject to the provisions of this section, be entitled, on giving two months' notice of his intention so to do, to redeem the security at any time not less than 20 years after the execution thereof, if, at the time when he gives such notice, the security subjects or any part thereof are used as or as part of a private dwelling-house.

In determining for the purposes of this section whether such use has occurred, subsection (2) of section 8 of this Act shall apply as it applies for the purposes of that section, and the ancillary use described in subsection (3) of that section shall not render the security subjects subject to the provisions of this section.

(3)   The right to redeem a heritable security conferred by this section shall not apply where the use of the security subjects which is purported to constitute the ground of the right, in terms of subsection (2) above, was, at the time of the notice aforesaid, in contravention of a conventional condition of or relating to the security, unless the person in right of the creditor at any time had approved that use expressly or by his actings, and the said use had not subsequently been discontinued.

(4)   Subject to the provisions of subsection (5) below, the whole amount due to the creditor in a heritable security on redemption under this section, including any sums due thereunder by way of interest or otherwise, shall not exceed the amount remaining unredeemed of—

(a)   where the security constituted to any extent (whether expressly or otherwise) the consideration for the acquisition of the security subjects by the debtor or proprietor or his predecessor in title, any excess of the value of the security subjects at the date of the execution of the security over the amount of money paid for the subjects, and

(b)   any money advanced under the security to the debtor or proprietor and his predecessors in title, and

(c)   any expense or charge reasonably incurred by the creditor in the exercise of a right to perform any obligation imposed on the debtor, which the debtor has failed to perform, and which was reasonably necessary for the protection of the security,

together with interest outstanding at the date of the said notice of redemption and interest due for the period between the date of that notice and the date of redemption, at the rate applicable in terms of the security immediately before that date.

(5)   In the application of paragraph (a) of subsection (4) above to security subjects which are burdened with two or more heritable securities to which this section applies, the maximum amount determined in accordance with that paragraph shall be apportioned among the securities according to the rights and preferences of the creditors in the securities; and the amount so apportioned in respect of each of the securities shall, on the redemption of any of the securities, be the maximum amount due in terms of that paragraph on the redemption at any time of all such securities.

[. . .]

12   Restriction to 20 years of period within which certain rights of redemption and reversion are exercisable

A right of redemption or reversion of land (other than the right of a lessor to the reversion of a lease), created in a deed executed after the commencement of this Act, which purports to be exercisable on the happening of an event which is bound to occur, or the occurrence of which is within the control of the person for the time being entitled to exercise the right or of a third party, shall be exercisable only within 20 years of the date of its creation.

16   No casualties in future leases

In leases executed after the commencement of this Act, it shall not be lawful to stipulate for the payment of any casualty, but this provision shall be without prejudice to the right to stipulate for review of rent or for a permanent or periodical variation of rent in accordance with any condition of or relating to the lease.

17   Interposed leases

(1)   It shall be competent, and shall be deemed always to have been competent, for the person in right of the lessor of a lease to grant, during the subsistence of that lease, a lease of or including his interest in the whole or part of the land subject to the lease first mentioned, and whether longer or shorter than or of the same duration as that lease, and the said grant shall be effectual (or, as the case may be, shall be deemed to have been effectual) for all purposes as a lease of land; and the grantee or person in his right shall be deemed (whether before or after the commencement of this Act) to have entered into the possession of the land leased under the grant at the date of that grant: Provided that, in the case of a lease which is registrable under the Registration of Leases (Scotland) Act 1857, or which (being a lease granted before the commencement of this Act) would have been so registrable if this Act had been in force, the rights of parties shall be determined by reference to that Act, as amended by any other enactment, including this Act.

(2)   Subject to any agreement to the contrary, as from the date of the grant of a lease in terms of subsection (1) above, the lessee under the lease so granted shall become (or, as the case may be, shall be deemed to have become) the lessor of the lessee in the subsisting lease, on the same terms and conditions as if the subsisting lease had, in respect of the property subject to the lease granted as aforesaid, been assigned to the grantee of the lease so granted; and, on the determination, for any reason, of the lease so granted, any remaining rights and obligations of the person in right of the said grantee, in relation to the said subsisting lease, shall vest (or as the case may be, shall be deemed to have vested) in the person in right of the

grantor of the lease granted as aforesaid, on the same terms and conditions as if that lease had not been granted.

PART IV
GENERAL

21 Provisions for contracting out to be void
Subject to the provisions of sections 8(6) and 11(3) of this Act, any agreement or other provision, however constituted, which is made after the commencement of this Act, shall be void in so far as it purports to exclude or limit the operation of any enactment contained in this Act.

22 Application to Crown
This Act shall apply to land [. . .] belonging to Her Majesty in right of the Crown or to a Government department, or held on behalf of Her Majesty for the purposes of a Government department, in like manner as it applies to other land.

23 Interpretation and repeals
(1)   In this Act, unless the context otherwise requires—
'deed' has the meaning assigned to it in section 3 of the Titles to Land Consolidation (Scotland) Act 1868, section 3 of the Conveyancing (Scotland) Act 1874 and section 2 of the Conveyancing (Scotland) Act 1924;
'heritable security' (except in relation to sections 4(5), 5(10) and 10(2)), does not include any security for the purpose of securing the payment of a periodical sum payable in respect of land, and 'heritable creditors' shall be construed accordingly;
'land' has the meaning assigned to it in section 2 of the said Act of 1924.
(2)   Unless the context otherwise requires, any reference in this Act to any other enactment is a reference thereto as amended, and includes a reference thereto as extended or applied, by or under a any other enactment, including this Act.
(3)   The enactments specified in Schedule 7 to this Act are hereby repealed to the extent specified in relation thereto in that Schedule.

24 Short title, commencement and extent
(1)   This Act may be cited as the Land Tenure Reform Scotland) Act 1974.
(2)   This Act shall come into operation on 1st September 1974.
(3)   This Act shall extend to Scotland only.

SCHEDULES

[. . .]

Section 9   SCHEDULE 5
                 FORM OF NOTICE PRESCRIBED UNDER SECTION 9

'NOTICE

under subsection (1) of section 9 of the Land Tenure Reform (Scotland) Act 1974 (consequences of use as dwelling-house of property subject to long lease, etc)

To Terminate Use as or as part of Private Dwelling-House of
Property subject to [Lease]
[Liferent]
[Right of Occupancy]
                                    [*Address of person sending notice, and Date*]
To [*name and address of addressee*]
   You are required to terminate the use as or as part of a private dwelling-house of [*give sufficient identification of the property by reference to the lease, etc. or otherwise: if the notice relates to the use of part only of the property subject to the lease, etc., the identi-*

fication should be a particular description or a description by reference of that part, in terms of section 9(5) of this Act] within 28 days from the date of this notice, under pain of action of removing in terms of section 9 of the Land Tenure Reform (Scotland) Act 1974.

(*Signed*) AB.
or CD,
Agent for AB.'

Note to be appended to Notice

'The reason for giving this notice is contravention of the condition contained in subsection (1) of section 8 of the Land Tenure Reform (Scotland) Act 1974 (property let under long lease, etc. not to be used as private dwelling-house).

Without prejudice to any other rights, obligations or defences which you may have under section 8, 9 or 10 of the said Act or otherwise, your attention is directed to the following provisions of the Act:—

Section 9(3):

[Here quote the subsection verbatim]

Section 9(4):

[Here quote the subsection verbatim]

Section 10(3):

[Here quote the subsection verbatim]

If you are in doubt about your position in law you should obtain legal advice promptly.'

LAND REGISTRATION (SCOTLAND) ACT 1979
(1979, c 33)

PART I
REGISTRATION OF INTERESTS IN LAND

1 The Land Register of Scotland

(1)   There shall be a public register of interests in land in Scotland to be known as the 'Land Register of Scotland' (in this Act referred to as 'the register').

(2)   The register shall be under the management and control of the Keeper of the Registers of Scotland (in this Act referred to as 'the Keeper') and shall have a seal.

(3)   In this Act 'registered' means registered in the register in accordance with this Act and 'registrable', 'registration' and other cognate expressions shall be construed accordingly.

2 Registration

(1)   Subject to subsection (2) below, an unregistered interest in land other than an overriding interest shall be registrable—

(a)   in any of the following circumstances occurring after the commencement of this Act—

(i)   on a grant of the interest in land in [. . .] long lease [. . .] but only to the extent that the interest has become that of the [. . .] lessee [. . .];

(ii)   on a transfer of the interest for valuable consideration;

(iii)   on a transfer of the interest in consideration of marriage;

(iv)   on a transfer of the interest whereby it is absorbed into a registered interest in land;

(v)   on any transfer of the interest where it is held under a long lease [or udal tenure];

(b)   in any other circumstances in which an application is made for registration of the interest by the person or persons having that interest and the Keeper considers it expedient that the interest should be registered.

(2)   Subsection (1) above does not apply to an unregistered interest which is a

heritable security, liferent or incorporeal heritable right; and subsection (1)(a)(ii) above does not apply where the interest on transference is absorbed into another unregistered interest.

(3)   The creation over a registered interest in land of any of the following interests in land—

    (i)   a heritable security;

    (ii)   a liferent;

    (iii)   an incorporeal heritable right,

shall be registrable; and on registration of its creation such an interest shall become a registered interest in land.

(4)   There shall also be registrable—

    (a)   any transfer of a registered interest in land including any transfer whereby it is absorbed into another registered interest in land;

    (b)   any absorption by a registered interest in land of another registered interest in land;

    (c)   any other transaction or event which (whether by itself or in conjunction with registration) is capable under any enactment or rule of law of affecting the title to a registered interest in land but which is not a transaction or event creating or affecting an overriding interest.

(5)   The Secretary of State may, by order made by statutory instrument, provide that interests in land of a kind or kinds specified in the order, being interests in land which are unregistered at the date of the making of the order other than overriding interests, shall be registered; and the provisions of this Act shall apply for the purposes of such registration with such modifications, which may include provision as to the expenses of such registration, as may be specified in the order.

(6)   In this section, 'enactment' includes section [. . .] 19 of this Act.

3   Effect of registration

(1)   Registration shall have the effect of—

    (a)   vesting in the person registered as entitled to the registered interest in land a real right in and to the interest and in and to any right, pertinent or servitude, express or implied, forming part of the interest, subject only to the effect of any matter entered in the title sheet of that interest under section 6 of this Act so far as adverse to the interest or that person's entitlement to it and to any overriding interest whether noted under that section or not;

    (b)   making any registered right or obligation relating to the registered interest in land a real right or obligation;

    (c)   affecting any registered real right or obligation relating to the registered interest in land,

insofar as the right or obligation is capable, under any enactment or rule of law, of being vested as a real right, of being made real or, as the case may be, of being affected as a real right.

In this subsection, 'enactment' includes section [. . .] 19 of this Act.

(2)   Registration shall supersede the recording of a deed in the Register of Sasines but, subject to subsection (3) below, shall be without prejudice to any other means of creating or affecting real rights or obligations under any enactment or rule of law.

(3)   A—

    (a)   lessee under a long lease;

    (b)   proprietor under udal tenure;

    [. . .]

shall obtain a real right in and to his interest as such only by registration; and registration shall be the only means of making rights or obligations relating to the registered interest in land of such a person real rights or obligations or of affecting such real rights or obligations.

(4)   The date—

(a)   at which a real right or obligation is created or as from which it is affected under this section;

(b)   [. . .]

shall be the date of registration.

(5)   Where an interest in land has been registered, any obligation to assign title deeds and searches relating to that interest in land or to deliver them or make them forthcoming or any related obligation shall be of no effect in relation to that interest or to any other registered interest in land.

This subsection does not apply—

(a)   to a land or charge certificate issued under section 5 of this Act;

(b)   where the Keeper has, under section 12(2) of this Act, excluded indemnity under Part II of this Act.

(6)   It shall not be necessary for [an unregistered holder] of an interest in land which has been registered to expede a notice of title in order to complete his title to that interest if evidence of sufficient midcouples or links between [him] and the person last [registered as entitled to the interest] are produced to the Keeper on any registration in respect of that interest and accordingly [—

(a)   section 4 of the Conveyancing (Scotland) Act 1924 (c 27);

(b)   section 18A(8)(a) of the Abolition of Feudal Tenure etc (Scotland) Act 2000 (asp 5); and

(c)   section 41(a) of the Title Conditions (Scotland) Act 2003 (asp 9),

(each of which relates to completion of title) shall be of no effect in relation to such an interest in land.]

This subsection does not apply to the completion of title under section 74 or 76 of the Lands Clauses Consolidation (Scotland) Act 1845 (procedure on compulsory purchase of lands).

(7)   Nothing in this section affects any question as to the validity or effect of an overriding interest.

4   Applications for registration

(1)   Subject to subsection (2) below, an application for registration shall be accepted by the Keeper if it is accompanied by such documents and other evidence as he may require.

(2)   An application for registration shall not be accepted by the Keeper if—

(a)   it relates to land which is not sufficiently described to enable him to identify it by reference to the Ordnance Map;

[(aa)   it relates in whole or in part to an interest in land which by, under or by virtue of any provision of the Abolition of Feudal Tenure etc (Scotland) Act 2000 (asp 5) is an interest which has ceased to exist;]

(b)   it relates to land which is a souvenir plot, that is a piece of land which, being of inconsiderable size or no practical utility, is unlikely to be wanted in isolation except for the sake of mere ownership or for sentimental reasons or commemorative purposes; or

(c)   it is frivolous or vexatious;

(d)   a, deed which—

(i)   accompanies the application;

(ii)   relates to a registered interest in land; and

(iii)   is executed after that interest has been registered,

does not bear a reference to the number of the title sheet of that interest;

[(e)   payment of the fee payable in respect of such registration under section 25 of the Land Registers (Scotland) Act 1868 has not been tendered.]

(3)   On receipt of an application for registration, the Keeper shall forthwith note the date of such receipt, and that date shall be deemed for the purposes of this Act to be the date of registration either—

(a)   where the application, after examination by the Keeper, is accepted by him, or

(b)   where the application is not accepted by him on the grounds that it does not comply with subsection (1) or (2)(a) or (d) above but, without being rejected by the Keeper or withdrawn by the applicant, is subsequently accepted by the Keeper on his being satisfied that it does so comply, or has been made so to comply.

[(4)   Where an application is not accepted by the Keeper on the ground that he has not been provided with sufficient evidence to confirm that it does not relate to a transfer which is prohibited by section 40(1) of the Land Reform (Scotland) Act 2003 (asp 2), or by virtue of section 37(5)(e) of that Act, the Keeper shall, subject to subsection (5) below, provide the Scottish Ministers with a copy of the application and notify them of the reason for which the application has been rejected.

(5)   Subsection (4) above does not apply where the application has been rejected by reason only of the application not being accompanied by a declaration required under section 43(2) of that Act of 2003.]

5   Completion of registration

(1)   The Keeper shall complete registration—

(a)   in respect of an interest in land which is not a heritable security, liferent or incorporeal heritable right—

(i)   if the interest has not previously been registered, by making up a title sheet for it in the register in accordance with section 6 of this Act, or

(ii)   if the interest has previously been registered, by making such amendment as is necessary to the title sheet of the interest;

(b)   in respect of an interest in land which is a heritable security, liferent or incorporeal heritable right or in respect of the matters registrable under section 2(4) of this Act by making such amendment as is necessary to the title sheet of the interest in land to which the heritable security, liferent, incorporeal heritable right or matter, as the case may be, relates,

and in each case by making such consequential amendments in the register as are necessary.

(2)   Where the Keeper has completed registration under subsection (1)(a) above, he shall issue to the applicant a copy of the title sheet, authenticated by the seal of the register; and such copy shall be known as a land certificate.

(3)   Where the Keeper has completed registration in respect of a heritable security, he shall issue to the applicant a certificate authenticated by the seal of the register; and such certificate shall be known as a charge certificate.

(4)   A land certificate shall be accepted for all purposes as sufficient evidence of the contents of the title sheet of which the land certificate is a copy; and a charge certificate shall be accepted for all purposes as sufficient evidence of the facts stated in it.

(5)   Every land certificate and charge certificate shall contain a statement as to indemnity by the Keeper under Part II of this Act.

6   The title sheet

(1)   Subject to subsection (3) below, the Keeper shall make up and maintain a title sheet of an interest in land in the register by entering therein—

(a)   a description of the land which shall consist of or include a description of it based on the Ordnance Map, and, where the interest is that of the proprietor of the [land] or the lessee under a long lease and the land appears to the Keeper to extend to 2 hectares or more, its area as calculated by the Keeper;

(b)   the name and designation of the person entitled to the interest in the land and the nature of that interest;

(c)   any subsisting entry in the Register of Inhibitions and Adjudications adverse to the interest;

(d)   any heritable security over the interest;

[(e) any subsisting real right pertaining to the interest or subsisting real burden or condition affecting the interest and, where the interest is so affected by virtue of section 18, 18A, 18B, 18C, 19, 20, 27 or 27A of the Abolition of Feudal Tenure etc (Scotland) Act 2000 (asp 5) or section 4(5), 50, 75 or 80 of the Title Conditions (Scotland) Act 2003 (asp 9), the Keeper shall in the entry identify the benefited property, or as the case may be the dominant tenement, (if any) and any person in whose favour the real burden is constituted;

(ee) any subsisting right to a title condition pertaining to the interest by virtue of section 18, 19 or 20 of that Act of 2000 or 4(5), 50, 75 or 80 of that Act of 2003, the Keeper identifying in the entry the burdened property;]

(f)   any exclusion of indemnity under section 12(2) of this Act in respect of the interest;

(g)   such other information as the Keeper thinks fit to enter in the register.

(2) The Keeper shall enter a real right or real burden or condition in the title sheet by entering its terms or a summary of its terms therein; and such a summary shall, unless it contains a reference to a further entry in the title sheet wherein the terms of the real right, burden or condition are set out in full be presumed to be a correct statement of the terms of the right, burden or condition.

(3) The Keeper's duty under subsection (1) above shall not extend to entering in the title sheet any [. . .] over-rent exigible in respect of the interest in land, but he may so enter any such [. . .] over-rent.

(4) Any overriding interest which appears to the Keeper to affect an interest in land—

(a) shall be noted by him in the title sheet of that interest if it has been disclosed in any document accompanying an application for registration in respect of that interest;

(b) may be so noted if—

(i)   application is made to him to do so;.

(ii) the overriding interest is disclosed in any application for registration; or

(iii) the overriding interest otherwise comes to his notice.

In this subsection 'overriding interest' does not include the interest of—

[(i) a lessee under a lease which is not a long lease and

(ii) a non-entitled spouse within the meaning of section 6 of the Matrimonial Homes (Family Protection) (Scotland) Act 1981.]

(5) The Keeper shall issue, to any person applying, a copy, authenticated as the Keeper thinks fit, of any title sheet, part thereof, or of any document referred to in a title sheet; and such copy, which shall be known as an office copy, shall be accepted for all purposes as sufficient evidence of the contents of the original.

[(6) In subsections (1)(e) and (2) above, 'condition' includes a servitude created by a deed registered in accordance with section 75(1) of the Title Conditions (Scotland) Act 2003 (asp 9) and a rule of a development management scheme ('development management scheme' being construed in accordance with section 71 of that Act).]

7 Ranking

(1) Without prejudice to any express provision as to ranking in any deed or any other provision as to ranking in, or having effect by virtue of, any enactment or rule of law, the following provisions of this section shall have effect to determine the ranking of titles to interests in land.

(2) Titles to registered interests in land shall rank according to the date of registration of those interests.

(3) A title to a registered interest and a title governed by a deed recorded in the Register of Sasines shall rank according to the respective dates of registration and recording.

(4) Where the date of registration or recording of the titles to two or more interests in land is the same, the titles to those interests shall rank equally.

8 Continuing effectiveness of recording in Register of Sasines

(1) Subject to subsection (3) below, the only means of creating or affecting a real right or a real obligation relating to anything to which subsection (2) below applies shall be by recording a deed in the Register of Sasines.

(2) This subsection applies to—

(a) an interest in land which is to be transferred or otherwise affected by—

(i) an instrument which, having been recorded before the commencement of this Act in the Register of Sasines with an error or defect; or

(ii) a deed which, having been recorded before the commencement of this Act in the Register of Sasines, with an error or defect in the recording,

has not, before such commencement, been re-presented, corrected as necessary, for the purposes of recording of new under section 143 of the Titles to Land Consolidation (Scotland) Act 1868;

In this paragraph, 'instrument' has the same meaning as in section 3 of the said Act of 1868.

(b) a registered interest in land which has been absorbed, otherwise than by operation of prescription, into another interest in land the title to which is governed by a deed recorded in the Register of Sasines;

(c) anything which is not registrable under subsections (1) to (4) of section 2 of this Act and in respect of which, immediately before the commencement of this Act, a real right or obligation could be created or affected by recording a deed in the Register of Sasines.

(3) Nothing in subsection (1) above shall prejudice any other means, other than by registration, of creating or affecting real rights or obligations under any enactment or rule of law.

(4) Except as provided in this section, the Keeper shall reject any deed submitted for recording in the Register of Sasines.

9 Rectification of the register

(1) Subject to subsection (3) below, the Keeper may, whether on being so requested or not, and shall, on being so ordered by the court or the Lands Tribunal for Scotland, rectify any inaccuracy in the register by inserting, amending or cancelling anything therein.

(2) Subject to subsection (3)(b) below, the powers of the court and of the Lands Tribunal for Scotland to deal with questions of heritable right or title shall include power to make orders for the purposes of subsection (1) above.

(3) [Subject to subsection (3B) below] if rectification under subsection (1) above would prejudice a proprietor in possession—

(a) the Keeper may exercise his power to rectify only where—

(i) the purpose of the rectification is to note an overriding interest or to correct any information in the register relating to an overriding interest;

(ii) all persons whose interests in land are likely to be affected by the rectification have been informed by the Keeper of his intention to rectify and have consented in writing;

(iii) the inaccuracy has been caused wholly or substantially by the fraud or carelessness of the proprietor in possession; or

(iv) the rectification relates to a matter in respect of which indemnity has been excluded under section 12(2) of this Act;

(b) the court or the Lands Tribunal for Scotland may order the Keeper to rectify only where sub-paragraph (i), (iii) or (iv) of paragraph (a) above applies [or the rectification is consequential on the making of an order under section 8 of the Law Reform (Miscellaneous Provisions) (Scotland) Act 1985].

[(3A) Where a rectification of an entry in the register is consequential on the making of an order under section 8 of the said Act of 1985, the entry shall have effect as rectified as from the date when the entry was made:

Provided that the court, for the purpose of protecting the interests of a person to whom section 9 of that Act applies, may order that the rectification shall have effect as from such later date as it may specify.

(3B)　Subject to subsection (3C) below, rectification (whether requisite or in exercise of the Keeper's discretion) to take account of, or of anything done (or purportedly done) under or by virtue of—

[(a)]　any provision of the Abolition of Feudal Tenure etc (Scotland) Act 2000 (asp 5), other than section 4 or 65 [; or

(b)　section 49, 50, 58 or 80 of the Title Conditions (Scotland) Act 2003 (asp 9),] shall, for the purposes of subsection (3) above (and of section 12(3)(cc) of this Act), be deemed not to prejudice a proprietor in possession.

(3C)　For the purposes of subsection (3B) above, rectification does not include entering or reinstating in a title sheet a real burden or a condition affecting an interest in land.]

(4)　In this section—

(a)　'the court' means any court having jurisdiction in questions of heritable right or title;

(b)　'overriding interest' does not include the interest of—

[(i)]　a lessee under a lease which is not a long lease, [and

(ii)　a non-entitled spouse within the meaning of section 6 of the Matrimonial Homes (Family Protection) (Scotland) Act 1981].

11　Transitional provisions for Part I

(1)　If an application for registration relates to land no part of which is in an operational area, the Keeper may nevertheless accept that application as if it related to land wholly within an operational area, and if the Keeper has so accepted such an application, the provisions of this Act relating to registration then in force shall apply in relation to that application.

(2)　An application for registration which relates to land which is partly in an operational area shall be treated as if it related to land wholly in that area, and the provisions of this Act relating to registration in force shall apply in relation to that application.

(3)　In this section an 'operational area' means an area in respect of which the provisions of this Act relating to registration have come into operation.

PART II
INDEMNITY IN RESPECT OF REGISTERED INTERESTS IN LAND

12　Indemnity in respect of loss

(1)　Subject to the provisions of this section, a person who suffers loss as a result of—

(a)　a rectification of the register made under section 9 of this Act;

(b)　the refusal or omission of the Keeper to make such a rectification;

(c)　the loss or destruction of any document, while lodged with the Keeper;

(d)　an error or omission in any land or charge certificate or in any information given by the Keeper in writing or in such other manner as may be prescribed by rules made under section 27 of this Act,

shall be entitled to be indemnified by the Keeper in respect of that loss.

(2)　Subject to section 14 of this Act, the Keeper may on registration in respect of an interest in land exclude, in whole or in part, any right to indemnity under this section in respect of anything appearing in, or omitted from, the title sheet of that interest.

(3)　There shall be no entitlement to indemnity under this section in respect of loss where—

(a)　the loss arises as a result of a title prevailing over that of the claimant in a case where—

(i)　the prevailing title is one in respect of which the right to indemnity has been partially excluded under subsection (2) above, and

(ii)   such exclusion has been cancelled but only on the prevailing title having been fortified by prescription;

(b)   the loss arises in respect of a title which has been reduced[, whether or not under subsection (4) of section 34, or subsection (5) of section 36, of the Bankruptcy (Scotland) Act 1985 (or either of those subsections as applied by sections 615A(4) and 615B of the Companies Act 1985, respectively),] as a gratuitous alienation or fraudulent preference, or has been reduced or varied by an order under section 6(2) of the Divorce (Scotland) Act 1976 [or by an order made by virtue of section 29 of the Matrimonial and Family Proceedings Act 1984] (orders relating to settlements and other dealings) [or has been set aside or varied by an order under section 18(2) (orders relating to avoidance trans-actions) of the Family Law (Scotland) Act 1985];

(c)   the loss arises in consequence of the making of a further order under section 5(2) of the Presumption of Death (Scotland) Act 1977 (effect on property rights of recall or variation of decree of declarator of presumed death);

[(cc)   the loss arises in consequence of—

(i)   a rectification which; or

(ii)   there being, in the register, an inaccuracy the rectification of which,

were there a proprietor in possession, would be deemed, by subsection (3B) of section 9 of this Act, not to prejudice that proprietor;]

(d)   the loss arises as a result of any inaccuracy in the delineation of any boundaries shown in a title sheet, being an inaccuracy which could not have been rectified by reference to the Ordnance Map, unless the Keeper has expressly assumed responsibility for the accuracy of that delineation;

(e)   the loss arises, in the case of land extending to 2 hectares or more the area of which falls to be entered in the title sheet of an interest in that land under section 6(1)(a) of this Act, as a result of the Keeper's failure to enter such area in the title sheet or, where he has so entered such area, as a result of any inaccuracy in the specification of that area in the title sheet;

(f)   the loss arises in respect of an interest in mines and minerals and the title sheet of any interest in land which is or includes the surface land does not expressly disclose that the interest in mines and minerals and is included in that interest in land;

(g)   the loss arises from inability to enforce a real burden or condition entered in the register, unless the Keeper expressly assumes responsibility for the enforceability of that burden or condition;

[(gg)   the loss arises from inability to enforce sporting rights converted into a tenement in land by virtue of section 65A of the Abolition of Feudal Tenure etc (Scotland) Act 2000 (asp 5), unless the Keeper expressly assumes responsibility for the enforceability of those rights;]

(h)   the loss arises in respect of an error or omission in the noting of an overriding interest;

(j)   the loss is suffered by—

(i)   a beneficiary under a trust in respect of any transaction entered into by its trustees or in respect of any title granted by them the validity of which is unchallengeable by virtue of section 2 of the Trusts (Scotland) Act 1961 (validity of certain transactions by trustees), or as the case may be, section 17 of the Succession (Scotland) Act 1964 (protection of persons acquiring title), or

(ii)   a person in respect of any interest transferred to him by trustees in purported implement of trust purposes;

(k)   the loss arises as a result of an error or omission in an office copy as to the effect of any subsisting adverse entry in the Register of Inhibitions and Adjudications affecting any person in respect of any registered interest in land, and that person's entitlement to that interest is neither disclosed in the register nor otherwise known to the Keeper;

[(kk)   the loss is suffered by an adult within the meaning of the Adults with Incapacity (Scotland) Act 2000 (asp 4) because of the operation of sections 24, 53, 67, 77 or 79 of that Act, or by any person who acquires any right, title or interest from that adult;]

(l)   the claimant is the proprietor of the dominant tenement in a servitude, except insofar as the claim may relate to the validity of the constitution of that servitude;

(m)   the claimant is [. . .] a landlord under a long lease and the claim relates to any information—

(i)   contained in [. . .] the lease [. . .] and

(ii)   omitted from the title sheet of the interest of the [. . .] landlord,

(except insofar as the claim may relate to the constitution or amount of the [. . .] rent and adequate information has been made available to the Keeper to enable him to make an entry in the register in respect of such constitution or amount or to the description of the land in respect of which the [. . .] rent is payable);

(n)   the claimant has by his fraudulent or careless act or omission caused the loss;

(o)   the claim relates to the amount due under a heritable security;

(p)   the loss arises from a rectification of the register consequential on the making of an order under section 8 of the Law Reform (Miscellaneous Provisions) (Scotland) Act 1985.]

[(q)   the loss arises in consequence of an inaccuracy in any information contained in a notice of potential liability for costs registered in pursuance of—

(i)   section 10(2A)(a) or 10A(3) of the Title Conditions (Scotland) Act 2003 (asp 9); or

(ii)   section 12(3)(a) or 13(3) of the Tenements (Scotland) Act 2004 (asp 11).]

(4)   A refusal or omission by the Keeper to enter in a title sheet—

(a)   any [. . .] over-rent exigible in respect of a registrable interest;

(b)   any right alleged to be a real right on the ground that by virtue of section 6 of this Act he has no duty to do so since it is unenforceable,

shall not by itself prevent a claim to indemnity under this section.

[(5)   In subsection (3)(g) above, 'condition' includes a rule of a development management scheme ('development management scheme' being construed in accordance with section 71 of the Title Conditions (Scotland) Act 2003 (asp 9)).]

13   Provisions supplementary to section 12

(1)   Subject to any order by the Lands Tribunal for Scotland or the court for the payment of expenses in connection with any claim disposed of by the Lands Tribunal under section 25 of this Act or the court, the Keeper shall reimburse any expenditure reasonably and properly incurred by a person in pursuing a *prima facie* well-founded claim under section 12 of this Act, whether successful or not.

(2)   On settlement of any claim to indemnity under the said section 12, the Keeper shall be subrogated to all rights which would have been available to the claimant to recover the loss indemnified.

(3)   The Keeper may require a claimant, as a condition of payment of his claim, to grant, at the Keeper's expense, a formal assignation to the Keeper of the rights mentioned in subsection (2) above.

(4)   If a claimant to indemnity has by his fraudulent or careless act or omission contributed to the loss in respect of which he claims indemnity, the amount of the indemnity to which he would have been entitled had he not so contributed to his loss shall be reduced proportionately to the extent to which he has so contributed.

14   The foreshore

(1)   If—

(a)   it appears to the Keeper that—

(i)   an interest in land which is registered or in respect of which an application for registration has been made consists, in whole or in part, of foreshore or a right in foreshore, or might so consist, and

(ii) discounting any other deficiencies in his title in respect of that foreshore or right in foreshore, the person registered or, as the case may be, applying to be registered as entitled to the interest will not have an unchallengeable title in respect of the foreshore or the right in foreshore until prescription against the Crown has fortified his title in that respect, and

(b) the Keeper wholly excludes or proposes wholly to exclude rights to indemnity in respect of that person's entitlement to that foreshore or that right in foreshore, and is requested by that person not to do so,

the Keeper shall notify the Crown Estate Commissioners that he has been so requested.

(2) If the Crown Estate Commissioners have—

(a) within one month of receipt of the notification referred to in subsection (1) above, given to the Keeper written notice of their interest, and

(b) within three months of that receipt informed the Keeper in writing that they are taking steps to challenge that title,

the Keeper shall

(i) during the prescriptive period, or

(ii) until such time as it appears to the Keeper that the Commissioners are no longer taking steps to challenge that title or that their challenge has been unsuccessful,

whichever is the shorter, continue wholly to exclude or, as the case may be, wholly exclude right to indemnity in respect of that person's entitlement to that foreshore or that right in foreshore.

(3) This section, or anything done under it, shall be without prejudice to any other right or remedy available to any person in respect of foreshore or any right in foreshore.

PART III
SIMPLICATION AND EFFECT OF DEEDS

15 Simplification of deeds relating to registered interests

(1) Land in respect of which an interest has been registered shall be sufficiently described in any deed relating to that interest if it is described by reference to the number of the title sheet of that interest, and accordingly, section 13 of and Schedule G to the Titles to Land Consolidation (Scotland) Act 1868, section 61 of the Conveyancing (Scotland) Act 1874, sections 8 and 24(2) of and Schedules D and J to the Conveyancing (Scotland) Act 1924 and Note 1 of Schedule 2 to the Conveyancing and Feudal Reform (Scotland) Act 1970 (sufficiency of description by reference) shall not apply to such a deed.

(2) It shall not be necessary in any deed relating to a registered interest in land to insert or refer to any real burden, condition, provision or other matter affecting that interest if that real burden, condition, provision or other matter has been entered in the title sheet of that interest under section 6(1)(e) of this Act, and, accordingly, in such a case such a deed shall import for all purposes a full insertion of the real burden, condition, provision or other matter.

[(3) It shall not be necessary, in any deed relating to a registered interest in land, to deduce title if evidence of sufficient midcouples or links between the unregistered holder and the person last registered as entitled to the interest are produced to the Keeper on registration in respect of that interest in land.]

(4) It shall not be necessary, in connection with any deed relating to a registered interest in land, to include an assignation of any obligation or right of relief or to narrate the series of writs by which the grantor of the deed became entitled to enforce that obligation or exercise that right if the obligation or right has been entered in the title sheet of that interest and, accordingly, in such a case—

(a)   section 50 of and Schedule M to the Conveyancing (Scotland) Act 1874 (form and effect of assigning right of relief or other right affecting land) shall not apply to such a deed; and

(b)   such a deed shall for all purposes import a valid and complete assignation of that obligation or right.

16   Omission of certain clauses in deeds

(1)   It shall not be necessary to insert in any deed executed after the commencement of this Act which conveys an interest in land a clause of assignation of writs and any such deed shall, unless specially qualified, import an assignation to the grantee of the title deeds and searches and all deeds not duly recorded, and shall—

(a)   impose on the grantor or any successor an obligation—

(i)   to deliver to the grantee all title deeds and searches relating exclusively to the interest conveyed;

(ii)   to make forthcoming to the grantee and his successors at his or their expense on all necessary occasions any title deeds and searches which remain in the possession of the grantor or any successor and which relate partly to the interest conveyed; and

(b)   import an assignation to the grantee by the grantor of his right to require any person having custody thereof to exhibit or deliver any title deeds and searches remaining undelivered; and

(c)   impose on the grantee or any successor an obligation to make forthcoming on all necessary occasions to any party having an interest therein any deeds and searches which have been delivered to the grantee but which relate partly to interests other than the interest conveyed to the grantee.

(2)   [. . .]

(3)   It shall not be necessary to insert in any deed conveying an interest in land executed after the commencement of this Act a clause of assignation of rents or a clause of obligation of relief, and any such deed so executed shall, unless specially qualified, import—

(a)   an assignation of the rents payable—

(i)   in the case of backhand rents, at the legal terms following the date of entry, and

(ii)   in the case of forehand rents, at the conventional terms following that date;

(b)   an obligation on the grantor to relieve the grantee of all [. . .] annuities and public, parochial and local burdens exigible in respect of the interest prior to the date of entry [. . .].

19   Agreement as to common boundary

(1)   This section shall apply where the titles to adjoining lands disclose a discrepancy as to the common boundary and the proprietors of those lands have agreed to, and have executed a plan of, that boundary.

(2)   Where one or both of the proprietors holds his interest or their interest in the land or lands by virtue of a deed or, as the case may be, deeds recorded in the Register of Sasines, the agreement and plan may be recorded in the Register of Sasines and on being so recorded shall be binding on the singular successors of that proprietor or, as the case may be, those proprietors and on all other persons having an interest in the land or, as the case may be, the lands.

(3)   Where one or both of the interests in the lands is or are registered interests, the plan with a docquet thereon executed by both proprietors referring to the agreement shall be registrable as affecting that interest or those interests, and on its being so registered its effect shall be binding on the singular successors of the proprietor of that interest or, as the case may be, the proprietors of those interests and on all other persons having an interest in the land or, as the case may be, the lands.

PART IV
MISCELLANEOUS AND GENERAL

20 Tenants-at-will

(1) A tenant-at-will shall be entitled, in accordance with this section, to acquire his landlord's interest as such in the land which is subject to the tenancy-at-will (hereinafter referred to as the 'tenancy land').

(2) Subject to section 21(2) of this Act, a tenant-at-will who wishes to acquire his landlord's interest under this section shall serve notice on him in, or as nearly as may be in, the form set out in Schedule 1 to this Act.

(3) There shall be payable by the tenant-at-will to his landlord by way of compensation in respect of an acquisition of tenancy land such amount as may be agreed between them or, failing agreement, an amount equal to—

(a) the value of the tenancy land, not including any buildings thereon, but assuming that planning permission for residential purposes has been granted in respect of it; or

(b) one twenty-fifth of the value of the tenancy land, including any buildings thereon,

whichever is the lesser, together with—

(i) subject to subsection (4) below, such further amount as may be required to discharge any heritable security over the tenancy land or, where the heritable security is granted over land including the tenancy land, such further amount (being such proportion of the sum secured over the land which includes the tenancy land as may reasonably be regarded as attributable to the tenancy land) as is required to restrict the heritable security so as to disburden the tenancy land [. . .]

(4) In respect of any acquisition under this section, the amount mentioned in paragraph (i) of subsection (3) above shall not exceed ninety per cent of the amount fixed by virtue of paragraph (a) or (b) of that subsection.

(5) The tenant-at-will shall reimburse the expenses reasonably and properly incurred by the landlord in conveying his interest in the tenancy land to the tenant-at-will, including the expenses of any discharge [or restriction] under subsection (3) above.

(6) The landlord shall, on there being tendered to him the compensation and expenses specified in this section, convey his interest in the tenancy land to his tenant-at-will on such terms and conditions (additional to those relating to compensation and expenses under subsections (3), (4) and (5) above) as may be agreed between them or, failing agreement, as may be appropriate to the circumstances of the case and free of all heritable securities [. . .].

(7) A heritable creditor whose security is over the tenancy land or land which includes the tenancy land, on there being tendered to him the amount mentioned in paragraph (i) of subsection (3) above (as read with subsection (4) above) and his reasonable expenses, shall discharge or, as the case may be, restrict the security so as to disburden the tenancy land.

(8) In this section and in sections 21 and 22 of this Act, 'tenant-at-will' means a person—

(a) who, not being—

(i) a tenant under a lease;

[. . .] or

(iii) a tenant or occupier by virtue of any enactment,

is by custom and usage the occupier (actual or constructive) of land on which there is a building or buildings erected or acquired for value by him or any predecessor of his;

(b) who is under an obligation to pay a ground rent to the owner of the land in respect of the said land but not in respect of the building or buildings on it, or would have been under such an obligation if the ground rent had not been redeemed; and

(c)   whose right of occupancy of the land is without ish.

(9)   In subsections (5) and (6) above, references to the conveying of the landlord's interest in tenancy land shall be construed in accordance with section 21(10) of this Act.

21   Provisions supplementary to section 20

(1)   Any question arising under section 20 of this Act as to—

(a)   whether a person is a tenant-at-will;

(b)   the extent or boundaries of any tenancy land;

(c)   the value of any tenancy land or as to what proportion of any sum secured over any land may reasonably be regarded as attributable to any tenancy land included in that land;

(d)   whether any expenses are reasonably and properly incurred;

(e)   what are appropriate terms and conditions,

shall be determined, on the application of the tenant-at-will, a person claiming to be the tenant-at-will or the landlord, by the Lands Tribunal for Scotland.

(2)   The Lands Tribunal for Scotland may, on the application of a tenant-at-will who wishes to acquire his landlord's interest in the tenancy land under section 20 of this Act, if they are satisfied that such landlord is unknown or cannot be found, make an order—

(a)   dispensing with notice under section 20(2) above;

(b)   fixing an amount by way of compensation in accordance with section 20(3) of this Act;

(c)   determining appropriate terms and conditions on which the landlord's interest in the tenancy land should be conveyed,

for the purposes of the acquisition by the tenant-at-will of his landlord's said interest.

(3)   If the landlord—

(a)   fails to convey his interest in accordance with section 20(6) of this Act, or

(b)   is unknown or cannot be found,

the tenant-at-will may apply to the sheriff for an order dispensing with the execution by the landlord of the conveyance in favour of the tenant-at-will and directing the sheriff clerk to execute the conveyance instead of the landlord, and on making such an order the sheriff may require the tenant-at-will to consign in court any sums payable by the tenant-at-will under section 20(3) and (5) of this Act or, as the case may be, any sums specified in an order under subsection (2) above.

(4)   Where, in pursuance of an order made by the sheriff under this section, a conveyance is executed by the sheriff clerk on behalf of the landlord, such conveyance shall have the like force and effect as if it had been executed by such landlord.

(5)   The sheriff may, on the application of any party, order the investment, payment or distribution of any sums consigned in court under subsection (3) above, and in so doing the sheriff shall have regard to the respective interests of any parties appearing to have a claim on such sums.

(6)   Nothing in section 5 of the Sheriff Courts (Scotland) Act 1907 shall entitle any party to an application to the sheriff under this section to require it to be remitted to the Court of Session on the grounds that it relates to a question of heritable right or title.

(7)   A landlord shall have power to execute a valid conveyance in pursuance of this section notwithstanding that he may be under any such disability as is mentioned in section 7 of the Lands Clauses Consolidation (Scotland) Act 1845.

(8)   Where a person other than the landlord is [owner of] the subjects to be conveyed, references in section 20 of this Act and in this section to the landlord shall

be construed as references to the landlord and such other person for their respective rights.

[(9) Any condition or provision to the effect that a person with an interest in land shall be entitled to a right of pre-emption in the event of a sale of the land, or of any part of the land, by the proprietor for the time being, shall not be capable of being enforced where the sale is by a landlord to his tenant-at-will under section 20 of this Act.]

(10) In this section and in section 20(5) and (6) of this Act, references to the conveying of the landlord's interest in the tenancy land shall be construed as references to a [disposition by him] of that land or, where the landlord is a lessee under a lease, an assignation of the lease but only as regards the tenancy land and, in this section, 'conveyance' shall be construed accordingly.

22 Provisions supplementary to section 20: heritable creditors

(1) The provisions of this section shall have effect where a heritable security over tenancy land or over land which includes tenancy land falls to be discharged or restricted under section 20(7) of this Act.

(2) The heritable creditor shall be entitled for his interest to apply, and to be a party to an application, under section 21(1) of this Act.

(3) The Lands Tribunal for Scotland, if they are satisfied that the heritable creditor is unknown or cannot be found, may, on the application of the tenant-at-will or his landlord or both, make an order fixing the amount required to discharge or restrict the heritable security so as to disburden the tenancy land.

(4) If the heritable creditor—

(a) fails to disburden the tenancy land in accordance with section 20(7) of this Act, or

(b) is unknown or cannot be found,

the tenant-at-will or the landlord or both may apply to the sheriff for an order dispensing with the execution by the heritable creditor of the deed of discharge or restriction in favour of the landlord and directing the sheriff clerk to execute the deed instead of the heritable creditor and on making such an order the sheriff may require the landlord to consign in court any amount or expenses which the landlord requires to pay for the purposes of section 20(3)(i), (4) and (5) of this Act to the heritable creditor or, as the case may be, any amount specified in an order under subsection (3) above.

(5) Where, in pursuance of an order made by the sheriff under this section, a deed of discharge or restriction is executed by the sheriff clerk on behalf of the heritable creditor, such deed shall have the like force and effect as if it had been executed by such heritable creditor.

(6) The sheriff may, on the application of any party, order the investment, payment or distribution of any amount consigned in court under subsection (4) above, and in so doing the sheriff shall have regard to the respective interests of any parties appearing to have a claim on such amount.

(7) Nothing in section 5 of the Sheriff Courts (Scotland) Act 1907 shall entitle any party to an application to the sheriff under this section to require it to be remitted to the Court of Session on the grounds that it relates to a question of heritable right or title.

(8) A heritable creditor shall have power to execute a valid deed of discharge or restriction in pursuance of this section notwithstanding that he may be under any such disability as is mentioned in section 7 of the Lands Clauses Consolidation (Scotland) Act 1845.

[22A Power of sheriff to grant renewals of certain long leases

(1) Where a landlord has failed to renew a long lease in implement of an obligation in or under it, the sheriff may, on summary application by the tenant, make an order directing the sheriff clerk to execute a renewal of the lease instead of the landlord.

(2)   On making an order under subsection (1) above, the sheriff may require the tenant to consign in court such amount (whether by way of rent or expenses or otherwise) in respect of the lease and its renewal as appears to the sheriff to be lawfully due and payable or appears to him would have been so due and payable had the landlord duly renewed the lease.

(3)   A renewal executed under this section shall have the like force and effect as if it were executed by the landlord.

(4)   Without prejudice to subsection (7)(a) below, a landlord shall be regarded, for the purposes of subsection (1) above, as having failed to renew a lease in implement of an obligation in or under it if, having been given written notice in accordance with subsection (5) below by the tenant that he requires the landlord, in implement of the obligation, to renew the lease, the landlord has failed to do so when he was obliged to and continues so to fail.

(5)   Notice is in accordance with this subsection if it is given not less than 3 months before the lodging of the summary application.

(6)   Subsection (4) above is subject to subsection (7)(b) below and to any provision in or under the lease for earlier, or a longer period of, notice requiring renewal of the lease than that mentioned in subsection (5) above.

(7)   if the sheriff is satisfied that a landlord is unknown or cannot be found, he may—

   (a)   in a case where the tenant is thereby prevented from bringing the landlord, in accordance with the lease, under an obligation to renew it, order that the landlord shall be regarded, for the purposes of subsection (1) above, as having failed to renew the lease in implement of an obligation under it; and

   (b)   in any other case, dispense with notice under subsection (4) above.

(8)   The sheriff may, on the application of any party, order the investment, payment or distribution of any sums consigned in court under subsection (2) above, and in so doing the sheriff shall have regard to the respective interests of any parties appearing to have a claim on such sums.

(9)   The sheriff's power under subsection (8) above extends to ordering that any award of expenses of the application under this section be paid out of any sums consigned in court under subsection (2) above.]

24   Financial provisions

There shall be defrayed out of money provided by Parliament all expenses incurred by the Keeper in consequence of the provisions of this Act.

25   Appeals

(1)   Subject subsections (3) and (4) below, an appeal shall lie, on any question of fact or law arising from anything done or omitted to be done by the Keeper under this Act, to the Lands Tribunal for Scotland.

(2)   Subject to subsections (3) and (4) below subsection (1) above is without prejudice to any right of recourse under any enactment other than this Act or under any rule of law.

(3)   Nothing in subsection (1) above shall enable the taking of an appeal if it is, under the law relating to *res judicata*, excluded as a result of the exercise of any right of recourse by virtue of subsection (2) above; and nothing in subsection (2) above shall enable the exercise of any right of recourse if it is so excluded as a result of the taking of an appeal under subsection (1) above.

(4)   No appeal shall lie under this section, nor shall there be any right of recourse by virtue of this section in respect of a decision of the Keeper under section 2(1)(b) or 11(1) of this Act.

26   Application to Crown

This Act shall apply to land [owned by the Crown or by] the Prince and Steward of Scotland, and to land in which there is any other interest belonging to Her Majesty in right of the Crown or to a Government department, or held on behalf of

Her Majesty for the purposes of a Government department, in like manner as it applies to other land.

27 Rules

(1) The Secretary of State may, after consultation with the Lord President of the Court of Session, make rules—

(a) regulating the making up and keeping of the register;

(b) prescribing the form of any search, report or other document to be issued or used under or in connection with this Act and regulating the issue of any such document;

(c) regulating the procedure on application for any registration;

(d) prescribing the form of deeds relating to registered interests in land;

(e) concerning such other matters as seem to the Secretary of State to be necessary or proper in order to give full effect to the purposes of this Act.

(2) The power to make rules under this section shall be exerciseable by statutory instrument subject to annulment in pursuance of a resolution of either House of Parliament.

28 Interpretation, etc

(1) In this Act, except where the context otherwise requires—

'deed' has the meaning assigned to it by section 3 of the Titles to Land Consolidation (Scotland) Act 1868, section 3 of the Conveyancing (Scotland) Act 1874 and section 2 of the Conveyancing (Scotland) Act 1922;

'heritable security' has the same meaning as in section 9(8) of the Conveyancing and Feudal Reform (Scotland) Act 1970;

'incorporeal heritable right' does not include [a right of ownership of land, the right of a lessee under a long lease of land, a right to mines or minerals or

(a)] a right to salmon fishings; [or

(b) sporting rights (as defined by section 65A(9) of the Abolition of Feudal Tenure etc (Scotland) Act 2000 (asp 5);]

['interest in land'—

(a) means any right in or over land, including any heritable security or servitude but excluding any lease which is not a long lease; and

(b) where the context admits, includes the land;]

'the Keeper' has the meaning assigned by section 1(2) of this Act;

'land' includes buildings and other structures and land covered with water;

'long lease' means a probative lease—

(a) exceeding 20 years; or

(b) which is subject to any provision whereby any person holding the interest of the grantor is under a future obligation, if so requested by the grantee, to renew the lease so that the total duration could (in terms of the lease, as renewed, and without any subsequent agreement, express or implied, between the persons holding the interests of the grantor and the grantee) extend for more than 20 years;

'overriding interest' means, subject to sections 6(4) and 9(4) of this Act, in relation to any interest in land, the right or interest over it of—

(a) the lessee under a lease which is not a long lease;

(b) the lessee under a long lease who, prior to the commencement of this Act, has acquired a real right to the subjects of the lease by virtue of possession of them;

(c) a crofter or cottar within the meaning of section 3 or 28(4) respectively of the Crofters (Scotland) Act 1955, or a landholder or statutory small tenant within the meaning of section 2(2) or 32(1) respectively of the Small Landholders (Scotland), Act 1911;

(d) the proprietor of the dominant tenement in [any servitude which was not created by registration in accordance with section 75(1) of the Title Conditions (Scotland) Act 2003 (asp 9)];

(e)   the Crown or any Government or other public department, or any public or local authority, under any enactment or rule of law, other than an enactment or rule of law authorising or requiring the recording of a deed in the Register of Sasines or registration in order to complete the right or interest;

[(ee)   the operator having a right conferred in accordance with paragraph 2, 3 or 5 of Schedule 2 to the Telecommunications Act 1984 (agreements for execution of works, obstruction of access, etc);'.

(ef)   a licence holder within the meaning of Part I of the Electricity Act 1989 having such a wayleave as is mentioned in paragraph 6 of Schedule 4 to that Act (wayleaves for electric lines), whether granted under that paragraph or by agreement between the parties;

(eg)   a licence holder within the meaning of Part I of the Electricity Act 1989 who is authorised by virtue of paragraph 1 of Schedule 5 to that Act to abstract, divert and use water for a generating station wholly or mainly driven by water;

(eh)   insofar as it is an interest vesting by virtue of section 7(3) of the Coal Industry Act 1994, the Coal Authority;]

(f)   the holder of a floating charge whether or not the charge has attached to the interest;

(g)   a member of the public in respect of any public right of way or in respect of any right held inalienably by the Crown in trust for the public [or in respect of the exercise of access rights within the meaning of the Land Reform (Scotland) Act 2003 (asp 2) by way of a path delineated in a path order made under section 22 of that Act];

[(gg)   the non-entitled spouse within the meaning of section 6 of the Matrimonial Homes (Family Protection) (Scotland) Act 1981;]

(h)   any person, being a right which has been made real, otherwise than by the recording of a deed in the Register of Sasines or by registration; or

(i)   any other person under any rule of law relating to common interest or joint or common property, not being a right or interest constituting a real right, burden or condition entered in the title sheet of the interest in land under section 6(1)(e) of this Act or having effect by virtue of a deed recorded in the Register of Sasines,

but does not include any subsisting burden or condition enforceable against the interest in land and entered in its title sheet under section 6(1) of this Act;

'the register' and 'registered' have the meanings assigned to them respectively by subsections (1) and (3) of section 1 of this Act;

'Register of Sasines' has the same meaning as in section 2 of the Conveyancing (Scotland) Act 1924;

'transfer' includes transfer by operation of law.

[. . .]

30   Short title, extent and commencement

(1)   This Act may be cited as the Land Registration (Scotland) Act 1979 and extends to Scotland only.

(2)   Sections 1, 16 to 23 of this Act, this section and so much of the remainder of this Part of this Act as relates to the aforesaid provisions of this Act shall come into operation on the passing of this Act, and the other provisions of this Act shall come into operation on the appointed day, being such day as the Secretary of State may by order made by statutory instrument appoint; and different days may be appointed under this subsection for different areas, or for different provisions of this Act.

(3)   Any reference in any provision of this Act to the commencement of this Act shall be construed as a reference to the date on which that provision comes into operation.

SCHEDULES

Section 20   SCHEDULE 1
FORM OF NOTICE TO BE GIVEN BY A TENANT-AT-WILL WHO WISHES TO
ACQUIRE HIS LANDLORD'S INTEREST AS SUCH IN THE TENANCY

To .... (1)
  Take Notice that .... (2), as tenant-at-will of .... (3),
requires you to make over to him your interest as landlord of the tenancy land
in accordance with the provisions of the Land Registration (Scotland) Act
1979.
  Dated this .... of .... 19.....

                                         Signed ....

Notes

(1)   To be addressed to the landlord.
(2)   Insert name and designation of tenant-at-will.
(3)   Give the address or a short identifying description of the property to be
acquired.

SALE OF GOODS ACT 1979
(1979, c 54)

PART II
FORMATION OF THE CONTRACT

Contract of sale

2   Contract of sale
(1)   A contract of sale of goods is a contract by which the seller transfers or
agrees to transfer the property in goods to the buyer for a money consideration,
called the price.
(2)   There may be a contract of sale between one part owner and another.
(3)   A contract of sale may be absolute or conditional.
(4)   Where under a contract of sale the property in the goods is transferred from
the seller to the buyer the contract is called a sale.
(5)   Where under a contract of sale the transfer of the property in the goods is
to take place at a future time or subject to some condition later to be fulfilled the
contract is called an agreement to sell.
(6)   An agreement to sell becomes a sale when the time elapses or the conditions are fulfilled subject to which the property in the goods is to be transferred.

Subject matter of contract

5   Existing or future goods
(1)   The goods which form the subject of a contract of sale may be either existing goods, owned or possessed by the seller, or goods to be manufactured or
acquired by him after the making of the contract of sale, in this Act called future
goods.
(2)   There may be a contract for the sale of goods the acquisition of which by
the seller depends on a contingency which may or may not happen.
(3)   Where by a contract of sale the seller purports to effect a present sale of
future goods, the contract operates as an agreement to sell the goods.

[Implied terms etc]

12   Implied terms about title, etc

(1)   In a contract of sale, other than one to which subsection (3) below applies, there is an implied [term] on the part of the seller that in the case of a sale he has a right to sell the goods, and in the case of an agreement to sell he will have such a right at the time when the property is to pass.

(2)   In a contract of sale, other than one to which subsection (3) below applies, there is also an implied [term] that—

(a)   the goods are free, and will remain free until the time when the property is to pass, from any charge or encumbrance not disclosed or known to the buyer before the contract is made, and

(b)   the buyer will enjoy quiet possession of the goods except so far as it may be disturbed by the owner or other person entitled to the benefit of any charge or encumbrance so disclosed or known.

(3)   This subsection applies to a contract of sale in the case of which there appears from the contract or is to be inferred from its circumstances an intention that the seller should transfer only such title as he or a third person may have.

(4)   In a contract to which subsection (3) above applies there is an implied [term] that all charges or encumbrances known to the seller and not known to the buyer have been disclosed to the buyer before the contract is made.

(5)   In a contract to which subsection (3) above applies there is also an implied [term] that none of the following will disturb the buyer's quiet possession of the goods, namely—

(a)   the seller;

(b)   in a case where the parties to the contract intend that the seller should transfer only such title as a third person may have, that person;

(c)   anyone claiming through or under the seller or that third person otherwise than under a charge or encumbrance disclosed or known to the buyer before the contract is made.

PART III
EFFECTS OF THE CONTRACT

Transfer of property as between seller and buyer

16   Goods must he ascertained

[Subject to section 20A below] where there is a contract for the sale of unascertained goods no property in the goods is transferred to the buyer unless and until the goods are ascertained.

17   Property passes when intended to pass

(1)   Where there is a contract for the sale of specific or ascertained goods the property in them is transferred to the buyer at such time as the parties to the contract intend it to be transferred.

(2)   For the purpose of ascertaining the intention of the parties regard shall be had to the terms of the contract, the conduct of the parties and the circumstances of the case.

18   Rules for ascertaining intention

Unless a different intention appears, the following are rules for ascertaining the intention of the parties as to the time at which the property in the goods is to pass to the buyer.

Rule 1.—Where there is an unconditional contract for the sale of specific goods in a deliverable state the property in the goods passes to the buyer when the contract is made, and it is immaterial whether the time of payment or the time of delivery, or both, be postponed.

Rule 2.—Where there is a contract for the sale of specific goods and the seller is bound to do something to the goods for the purpose of putting them into a deliverable state, the property does not pass until the thing is done and the buyer has notice that it has been done.

Rule 3.—Where there is a contract for the sale of specific goods in a deliverable state but the seller is bound to weigh, measure, test, or do some other act or thing with reference to the goods for the purpose of ascertaining the price, the property does not pass until the act or thing is done and the buyer has notice that it has been done.

Rule 4.—When goods are delivered to the buyer on approval or on sale or return or other similar terms the property in the goods passes to the buyer:—

(a)   when he signifies his approval or acceptance to the seller or does any other act adopting the transaction;

(b)   if he does not signify his approval or acceptance to the seller but retains the goods without giving notice of rejection, then, if a time has been fixed for the return of the goods, on the expiration of that time, and, if no time has been fixed, on the expiration of a reasonable time.

Rule 5.—(1)   Where there is a contract for the sale of unascertained or future goods by description, and goods of that description and in a deliverable state are unconditionally appropriated to the contract, either by the seller with the assent of the buyer or by the buyer with the assent of the seller, the property in the goods then passes to the buyer; and the assent may be express or implied, and may be given either before or after the appropriation is made.

(2)   Where, in pursuance of the contract, the seller delivers the goods to the buyer or to a carrier or other bailee or custodier (whether named by the buyer or not) for the purpose of transmission to the buyer, and does not reserve the right of disposal, he is to be taken to have unconditionally appropriated the goods to the contract.

[(3)   Where there is a contract for the sale of a specified quantity of unascertained goods in a deliverable state forming part of a bulk which is identified either in the contract or by subsequent agreement between the parties and the bulk is reduced to (or to less than) that quantity, then, if the buyer under that contract is the only buyer to whom goods are then due out of the bulk—

(a)   the remaining goods are to be taken as appropriated to that contract at the time when the bulk is so reduced; and

(b)   the property in those goods then passes to that buyer.

(4)   Paragraph (3) above applies also (with the necessary modifications) where a bulk is reduced to (or to less than) the aggregate of the quantities due to a single buyer under separate contracts relating to that bulk and he is the only buyer to whom goods are then due out of that bulk.]

19   Reservation of right of disposal

(1)   Where there is a contract for the sale of specific goods or where goods are subsequently appropriated to the contract, the seller may, by the terms of the contract or appropriation, reserve the right of disposal of the goods until certain conditions are fulfilled; and in such a case, notwithstanding the delivery of the goods to the buyer, or to a carrier or other bailee or custodier for the purpose of transmission to the buyer, the property in the goods does not pass to the buyer until the conditions imposed by the seller are fulfilled.

(2)   Where goods are shipped, and by the bill of lading the goods are deliverable to the order of the seller or his agent, the seller is prima facie to be taken to reserve the right of disposal.

(3)   Where the seller of goods draws on the buyer for the price, and transmits the bill of exchange and bill of lading to the buyer together to secure acceptance or payment of the bill of exchange, the buyer is bound to return the bill of lading if

he does not honour the bill of exchange, and if he wrongfully retains the bill of lading the property in the goods does not pass to him.

20 [Passing of risk]

(1) Unless otherwise agreed, the goods remain at the seller's risk until the property in them is transferred to the buyer, but when the property in them is transferred to the buyer the goods are at the buyer's risk whether delivery has been made or not.

(2) But where delivery has been delayed through the fault of either buyer or seller the goods are at the risk of the party at fault as regards any loss which might not have occurred but for such fault.

(3) Nothing in this section affects the duties or liabilities of either seller or buyer as a bailee or custodier of the goods of the other party.

[(4) In a case where the buyer deals as consumer or, in Scotland, where there is a consumer contract in which the buyer is a consumer, subsections (1) to (3) above must be ignored and the goods remain at the seller's risk until they are delivered to the consumer.]

[20A Undivided shares in goods forming part of a bulk

(1) This section applies to a contract for the sale of a specified quantity of unascertained goods if the following conditions are met—

(a) the goods or some of them form part of a bulk which is identified either in the contract or by subsequent agreement between the parties; and

(b) the buyer has paid the price for some or all of the goods which are the subject of the contract and which form part of the bulk.

(2) Where this section applies, then (unless the parties agree otherwise), as soon as the conditions specified in paragraphs (a) and (b) of subsection (1) above are met or at such later time as the parties may agree—

(a) property in an undivided share in the bulk is transferred to the buyer; and

(b) the buyer becomes an owner in common of the bulk.

(3) Subject to subsection (4) below, for the purposes of this section, the undivided share of a buyer in a bulk at any time shall be such share as the quantity of goods paid for and due to the buyer out of the bulk bears to the quantity of goods in the bulk at that time.

(4) Where the aggregate of the undivided shares of buyers in a bulk determined under subsection (3) above would at any time exceed the whole of the bulk at that time, the undivided share in the bulk of each buyer shall be reduced proportionately so that the aggregate of the undivided shares is equal to the whole bulk.

(5) Where a buyer has paid the price for only some of the goods due to him out of a bulk, any delivery to the buyer out of the bulk shall, for the purposes of this section, be ascribed in the first place to the goods in respect of which payment has been made.

(6) For the purpose of this section payment of part of the price for any goods shall be treated as payment for a corresponding part of the goods.]

[20B Deemed consent by co-owner to dealings in bulk goods

(1) A person who has become an owner in common of a bulk by virtue of section 20A above shall be deemed to have consented to—

(a) any delivery of goods out of the bulk to any other owner in common of the bulk, being goods which are due to him under his contract;

(b) any removal, dealing with, delivery or disposal of goods in the bulk by any other person who is an owner in common of the bulk in so far as the goods fall within that co-owner's undivided share in the bulk at the time of the removal, dealing, delivery or disposal.

(2)   No cause of action shall accrue to anyone against a person by reason of that person having acted in accordance with paragraph (a) or (b) of subsection (1) above in reliance on any consent deemed to have been given under that sub-section.

(3)   Nothing in this section or section 20A above shall—

(a)   impose an obligation on a buyer of goods out of a bulk to compensate any other buyer of goods out of that bulk for any shortfall in the goods received by that other buyer;

(b)   affects any contractual arrangement between buyers of goods out of a bulk for adjustments between themselves; or

(c)   affect the rights of any buyer under his contract.]

Transfer of title

21   Sale by person not the owner

(1)   Subject to this Act, where goods are sold by a person who is not their owner, and who does not sell them under the authority or with the consent of the owner, the buyer acquires no better title to the goods than the seller had, unless the owner of the goods is by his conduct precluded from denying the seller's authority to sell.

(2)   Nothing in this Act affects—

(a)   the provisions of the Factors Acts or any enactment enabling the ap-parent owner of goods to dispose of them as if he were their true owner;

(b)   the validity of any contract of sale under any special common law or statutory power of sale or under the order of a court of competent jurisdiction.

22   [*Does not apply to Scotland.*]

23   Sale under voidable title

When the seller of goods has a voidable title to them, but his title has not been avoided at the time of the sale, the buyer acquires a good title to the goods, pro-vided he buys them in good faith and without notice of the seller's defect of title.

24   Seller in possession after sale

Where a person having sold goods continues or is in possession of the goods, or of the documents of title to the goods, the delivery or transfer by that person, or by a mercantile agent acting for him, of the goods or documents of title under any sale, pledge, or other disposition thereof, to any person receiving the same in good faith and without notice of the previous sale, has the same effect as if the person mak-ing the delivery or transfer were expressly authorised by the owner of the goods to make the same.

25   Buyer in possession after sale

(1)   Where a person having bought or agreed to buy goods obtains, with the consent of the seller, possession of the goods or the documents of title to the goods, the delivery or transfer by that person, or by a mercantile agent acting for him, of the goods or documents of title, under any sale, pledge, or other disposi-tion thereof, to any person receiving the same in good faith and without notice of any lien or other right of the original seller in respect of the goods, has the same effect as if the person making the delivery or transfer were a mercantile agent in possession of the goods or documents of title with the consent of the owner.

(2)   For the purposes of subsection (1) above—

(a)   the buyer under a conditional sale agreement is to be taken not to be a person who has bought or agreed to buy goods, and

(b)   'conditional sale agreement' means an agreement for the sale of goods which is a consumer credit agreement within the meaning of the Consumer

Credit Act 1974 under which the purchase price or part of it is payable by instalments, and the property in the goods is to remain in the seller (notwithstanding that the buyer is to be in possession of the goods) until such conditions as to the payment of instalments or otherwise as may be specified in the agreement are fulfilled.

(3) Paragraph 9 of Schedule 1 below applies in relation to a contract under which a person buys or agrees to buy goods and which is made before the appointed day.

(4) In subsection (3) above and paragraph 9 of Schedule 1 below references to the appointed day are to the day appointed for the purposes of those provisions by an order of the Secretary of State made by statutory instrument.

62 Savings: rules of law etc
(1) The rules in bankruptcy relating to contracts of sale apply to those contracts, notwithstanding anything in this Act.

(2) The rules of the common law, including the law merchant, except in so far as they are inconsistent with the provisions of this Act, and in particular the rules relating to the law of principal and agent and the effect of fraud, misrepresentation, duress or coercion, mistake, or other invalidating cause, apply to contracts for the sale of goods.

(3) Nothing in this Act or the Sale of Goods Act 1893 affects the enactments relating to bills of sale, or any enactment relating to the sale of goods which is not expressly repealed or amended by this Act or that.

(4) The provisions of this Act about contracts of sale do not apply to a transaction in the form of a contract of sale which is intended to operate by way of mortgage, pledge, charge, or other security.

(5) Nothing in this Act prejudices or affects the landlord's right of hypothec or sequestration for rent in Scotland.

MATRIMONIAL HOMES (FAMILY PROTECTION) (SCOTLAND) ACT 1981
(1981, c 59)

Protection of occupancy rights of one spouse against the other

1 Right of spouse without title to occupy matrimonial home
(1) Where, apart from the provisions of this Act, one spouse is entitled, or permitted by a third party, to occupy a matrimonial home (an 'entitled spouse') and the other spouse is not so entitled or permitted (a 'non-entitled spouse'), the non-entitled spouse shall, subject to the provisions of this Act, have the following rights—
    (a) if in occupation, a right [. . .] to [continue to occupy] the matrimonial home or any part of it by the entitled spouse;
    (b) if not in occupation, a right to enter into and occupy the matrimonial home.

[(1A) The rights conferred by subsection (1) above to continue to occupy or, as the case may be, to enter and occupy the matrimonial home include, without prejudice to their generality, the right to do so together with any child of the family.]

(2) In subsection (1) above, an 'entitled spouse' includes a spouse who is entitled, or permitted by a third party, to occupy a matrimonial home along with an individual who is not the other spouse only if that individual has waived his or her right of occupation in favour of the spouse so entitled or permitted.

(3) If the entitled spouse refuses to allow the non-entitled spouse to exercise the right conferred by subsection (1)(b) above, the non-entitled spouse may exercise that right only with the leave of the court under section 3(3) or (4) of this Act.

(4) In this Act, the rights mentioned in paragraphs (a) and (b) of subsection (1) above are referred to as occupancy rights.

(5)   A non-entitled spouse may renounce in writing his or her occupancy rights only—

(a)   in a particular matrimonial home; or

(b)   in a particular property which it is intended by the spouses will become a matrimonial home.

(6)   A renunciation under subsection (5) above shall have effect only if at the time of making the renunciation, the non-entitled spouse has sworn or affirmed before a notary public that it was made freely and without coercion of any kind.

[In this subsection, 'notary public' includes any person duly authorised by the law of the country (other than Scotland) in which the swearing or affirmation takes place to administer oaths or receive affirmations in that other country.]

2   Subsidiary and consequential rights

(1)   For the purpose of securing the occupancy rights of a non-entitled spouse, that spouse shall, in relation to a matrimonial home, be entitled without the consent of the entitled spouse—

(a)   to make any payment due by the entitled spouse in respect of rent, rates, secured loan instalments, interest or other outgoings (not being outgoings on repairs or improvements);

(b)   to perform any other obligation incumbent on the entitled spouse (not being an obligation in respect of non-essential repairs or improvements);

(c)   to enforce performance of an obligation by a third party which that third party has undertaken to the entitled spouse to the extent that the entitled spouse may enforce such performance;

(d)   to carry out such essential repairs as the entitled spouse may carry out;

(e)   to carry out such non-essential repairs or improvements as may be authorised by an order of the court, being such repairs or improvements as the entitled spouse may carry out and which the court considers to be appropriate for the reasonable enjoyment of the occupancy rights;

(f)   to take such other steps, for the purpose of protecting the occupancy rights of the non-entitled spouse, as the entitled spouse may take to protect the occupancy rights of the entitled spouse.

(2)   Any payment made under subsection (1)(a) above or any obligation performed under subsection (1)(b) above shall have effect in relation to the rights of a third party as if the payment were made or the obligation were performed by the entitled spouse; and the performance of an obligation which has been enforced under subsection (1)(c) above shall have effect as if it had been enforced by the entitled spouse.

(3)   Where there is an entitled and a non-entitled spouse, the court, on the application of either of them, may, having regard in particular to the respective financial circumstances of the spouses, make an order apportioning expenditure incurred or to be incurred by either spouse—

(a)   without the consent of the other spouse, on any of the items mentioned in paragraphs (a) and (d) of subsection (1) above;

(b)   with the consent of the other spouse, on anything relating to a matrimonial home.

(4)   Where both spouses are entitled, or permitted by a third party, to occupy a matrimonial home—

(a)   either spouse shall be entitled, without the consent of the other spouse, to carry out such non-essential repairs or improvements as may be authorised by an order of the court, being such repairs or improvements as the court considers to be appropriate for the reasonable enjoyment of the occupancy rights;

(b)   the court, on the application of either spouse, may, having regard in particular to the respective financial circumstances of the spouses, make an order apportioning expenditure incurred or to be incurred by either spouse, with or without the consent of the other spouse, on anything relating to the matrimonial home.

(5) Where one spouse owns or hires, or is acquiring under a hire-purchase or conditional sale agreement, furniture and plenishings in a matrimonial home—

(a) the other spouse may, without the consent of the first mentioned spouse—

(i) make any payment due by the first mentioned spouse which is necessary, or take any other step which the first mentioned spouse is entitled to take to secure the possession or use of any such furniture and plenishings (and any such payment shall have effect in relation to the rights of a third party as if it were made by the first mentioned spouse); or

(ii) carry out such essential repairs to the furniture and plenishings as the first mentioned spouse is entitled to carry out;

(b) the court, on the application of either spouse, may, having regard in particular to the respective financial circumstances of the spouses, make an order apportioning expenditure incurred or to be incurred by either spouse—

(i) without the consent of the other spouse, in making payments under a hire, hire-purchase or conditional sale agreement, or in paying interest charges in respect of the furniture and plenishings, or in carrying out essential repairs to the furniture and plenishings; or

(ii) with the consent of the other spouse, on anything relating to the furniture and plenishings.

(6) An order under subsection (3), (4)(b) or (5)(b) above may require one spouse to make a payment to the other spouse in implementation of the apportionment.

(7) Any application under subsection (3), (4)(b) or (5)(b) above shall be made within five years of the date on which any payment in respect of such incurred expenditure was made.

(8) Where—

(a) the entitled spouse is a tenant of a matrimonial home; and

(b) possession thereof is necessary in order to continue the tenancy; and

(c) the entitled spouse abandons such possession,

the tenancy shall be continued by such possession by the non-entitled spouse.

(9) In this section 'improvements' includes alterations and enlargement.

3 Regulation by court of rights of occupancy of matrimonial home

(1) Where there is an entitled and a non-entitled spouse, or where both spouses are entitled, or permitted by a third party, to occupy a matrimonial home, either spouse may apply to the court for an order—

(a) declaring the occupancy rights of the applicant spouse;

(b) enforcing the occupancy rights of the applicant spouse;

(c) restricting the occupancy rights of the non-applicant spouse;

(d) regulating the exercise by either spouse of his or her occupancy rights;

(e) protecting the occupancy rights of the applicant spouse in relation to the other spouse.

(2) Where one spouse owns or hires, or is acquiring under a hire-purchase or conditional sale agreement, furniture and plenishings in a matrimonial home, the other spouse, if he or she has occupancy rights in that home, may apply to the court for an order granting to the applicant the possession or use in the matrimonial home of any such furniture and plenishings; but, subject to section 2 of this Act, an order under this subsection shall not prejudice the rights of any third party in relation to the non-performance of any obligation under such hire-purchase or conditional sale agreement.

(3) The court shall grant an application under subsection (1)(a) above if it appears to the court that the application relates to a matrimonial home; and, on an

application under any of paragraphs (b) to (e) of subsection (1) or under sub-section (2) above, the court may make such order relating to the application as appears to it to be just and reasonable having regard to all the circumstances of the case including—
    (a)   the conduct of the spouses in relation to each other and otherwise;
    (b)   the respective needs and financial resources of the spouses;
    (c)   the needs of any child of the family;
    (d)   the extent (if any) to which—
        (i) the matrimonial home; and
        (ii) in relation only to an order under subsection (2) above, any item of furniture and plenishings referred to in that subsection,
  is used in connection with a trade, business or profession of either spouse; and
    (e)   whether the entitled spouse offers or has offered to make available to the non-entitled spouse any suitable alternative accommodation.
  (4) Pending the making of an order under subsection (3) above, the court, on the application of either spouse, may make such interim order as it may consider necessary or expedient in relation to—
    (a)   the residence of either spouse in the home to which the application relates;
    (b)   the personal effects of either spouse or of any child of the family; or
    (c)   the furniture and plenishings:
Provided that an interim order may be made only if the non-applicant spouse has been afforded an opportunity of being heard by or represented before the court.
  (5) The court shall not make an order under subsection (3) or (4) above if it appears that the effect of the order would be to exclude the non-applicant spouse from the matrimonial home.
  (6) If the court makes an order under subsection (3) or (4) above which re-quires the delivery to one spouse of anything which has been left in or removed from the matrimonial home, it may also grant a warrant authorising a messenger-at-arms or sheriff officer to enter the matrimonial home or other premises occupied by the other spouse and to search for and take possession of the thing required to be delivered, if need be by opening shut and lockfast places, and to deliver the thing in accordance with the said order:
Provided that a warrant granted under this subsection shall be executed only after expiry of the period of a charge, being such period as the court shall specify in the order for delivery.
  (7) Where it appears to the court—
    (a)   on the application of a non-entitled spouse, that that spouse has suffered a loss of occupancy rights or that the quality of the non-entitled spouse's occupation of a matrimonial home has been impaired; or
    (b)   on the application of a spouse who has been given the possession or use of furniture and plenishings by virtue of an order under subsection (3) above, that the applicant has suffered a loss of such possession or use or that the quality of the applicant's possession or use of the furniture and plenishings has been impaired,
in consequence of any act or default on the part of the other spouse which was intended to result in such loss or impairment, it may order that other spouse to pay to the applicant such compensation as the court in the circumstances considers just and reasonable in respect of that loss or impairment.
  (8) A spouse may renounce in writing the right to apply under subsection (2) above for the possession or use of any item of furniture and plenishings.

4 Exclusion orders

  (1) Where there is an entitled and a non-entitled spouse, or where both spouses are entitled, or permitted by a third party, to occupy a matrimonial home, either

spouse [whether or not that spouse is in occupation at the time of the application] may apply to the court for an order (in this Act referred to as 'an exclusion order') suspending the occupancy rights of the other spouse ('the non-applicant spouse') in a matrimonial home.

(2) Subject to subsection (3) below, the court shall make an exclusion order if it appears to the court that the making of the order is necessary for the protection of the applicant or any child of the family from any conduct or threatened or reasonably apprehended conduct of the non-applicant spouse which is or would be injurious to the physical or mental health of the applicant or child.

(3) The court shall not make an exclusion order if it appears to the court that the making of the order would be unjustified or unreasonable—

(a) having regard to all the circumstances of the case including the matters specified in paragraphs (a) to (e) of section 3(3) of this Act; and

(b) where the matrimonial home—

(i) is or is part of an agricultural holding within the meaning of section 1 of the [Agricultural Holdings (Scotland) Act 1991]; or

(ii) is let, or is a home in respect of which possession is given, to the non-applicant spouse or to both spouses by an employer as an incident of employment,

subject to a requirement that the non-applicant spouse or, as the case may be, both spouses must reside in the matrimonial home, having regard to that requirement and the likely consequences of the exclusion of the non-applicant spouse from the matrimonial home.

(4) In making an exclusion order the court shall, on the application of the applicant spouse,—

(a) grant a warrant for the summary ejection of the non-applicant spouse from the matrimonial home;

(b) grant an interdict prohibiting the non-applicant spouse from entering the matrimonial home without the express permission of the applicant;

(c) grant an interdict prohibiting the removal by the non-applicant spouse, except with the written consent of the applicant or by a further order of the court, of any furniture and plenishings in the matrimonial home;

unless, in relation to paragraph (a) or (c) above, the non-applicant spouse satisfies the court that it is unnecessary for it to grant such a remedy.

(5) In making an exclusion order the court may—

(a) grant an interdict prohibiting the non-applicant spouse from entering or remaining in a specified area in the vicinity of the matrimonial home;

(b) where the warrant for the summary ejection of the non-applicant spouse has been granted in his or her absence, give directions as to the preservation of the non-applicant spouse's goods and effects which remain in the matrimonial home;

(c) on the application of either spouse, make the exclusion order or the warrant or interdict mentioned in paragraph (a), (b) or (c) of subsection (4) above or paragraph (a) of this subsection subject to such terms and conditions as the court may prescribe;

(d) on application as aforesaid, make such other order as it may consider necessary for the proper enforcement of an order made under subsection (4) above or paragraph (a), (b) or (c) of this subsection.

(6) Pending the making of an exclusion order, the court may, on the application of the applicant spouse, make an interim order suspending the occupancy rights of the non-applicant spouse in the matrimonial home to which the application for the exclusion order relates; and subsections (4) and (5) above shall apply to such interim order as they apply to an exclusion order:

Provided that an interim order may be made only if the non-applicant spouse has been afforded an opportunity of being heard by or represented before the court.

(7) Without prejudice to subsections (1) and (6) above, where both spouses are entitled, or permitted by a third party, to occupy a matrimonial home, it shall be incompetent for one spouse to bring an action of ejection from the matrimonial home against the other spouse.

5 Duration of orders under ss 3 and 4

(1) The court may, on the application of either spouse, vary or recall any order made by it under section 3 or 4 of this Act, but, subject to subsection (2) below, any such order shall, unless previously so varied or recalled, cease to have effect—

(a) on the termination of the marriage; or

(b) subject to section 6(1) of this Act, where there is an entitled and a non-entitled spouse, on the entitled spouse ceasing to be an entitled spouse in respect of the matrimonial home to which the order relates; or

(c) where both spouses are entitled, or permitted by a third party, to occupy the matrimonial home, on both spouses ceasing to be so entitled or permitted.

(2) Without prejudice to the generality of subsection (1) above, an order under section 3(3) or (4) of this Act which grants the possession or use of furniture and plenishings shall cease to have effect if the furniture and plenishings cease to be permitted by a third party to be retained in the matrimonial home.

Occupancy rights in relation to dealings with third parties

6 Continued exercise of occupancy rights after dealing

(1) Subject to subsection (3) below—

(a) the continued exercise of the rights conferred on a non-entitled spouse by the provisions of this Act in respect of a matrimonial home shall not be prejudiced by reason only of any dealing of the entitled spouse relating to that home; and

(b) a third party shall not by reason only of such a dealing be entitled to occupy that matrimonial home or any part of it.

(2) In this section and section 7 of this Act—

'dealing' includes the grant of a heritable security and the creation of a trust but does not include a conveyance under section 80 of the Lands Clauses Consolidation (Scotland) Act 1845;

'entitled spouse' does not include a spouse who, apart from the provisions of this Act,—

(a) is permitted by a third party to occupy a matrimonial home; or

(b) is entitled to occupy a matrimonial home along with an individual who is not the other spouse, whether or not that individual has waived his or her right of occupation in favour of the spouse so entitled;

and 'non-entitled spouse' shall be construed accordingly.

(3) This section shall not apply in any case where—

(a) the non-entitled spouse in writing either—

(i) consents or has consented to the dealing, and any consent shall be in such form as the Secretary of State may, by regulations made by statutory instrument, prescribe; or

(ii) renounces or has renounced his or her occupancy rights in relation to the matrimonial home or property to which the dealing relates;

(b) the court has made an order under section 7 of this Act dispensing with the consent of the non-entitled spouse to the dealing;

(c) the dealing occurred, or implements, a binding obligation entered into by the entitled spouse before his or her marriage to the non-entitled spouse;

(d) the dealing occurred, or implements, a binding obligation entered into before the commencement of this Act; . . .

(e) the dealing comprises [a sale to] a third party who has acted in good faith if, . . . there is produced to the third party by the [seller]—

[(i) an affidavit sworn or affirmed by the seller declaring that the subjects of sale are not or were not at the time of the dealing a matrimonial home in relation to which a spouse of the seller has or had occupancy rights.

For the purposes of this paragraph, the time of the dealing, in the case of the sale of an interest in heritable property, is the date of delivery to the purchaser of the deed transferring title to that interest.]

(ii) a renunciation of occupancy rights or consent to the dealing which bears to have been properly made or given by the non-entitled spouse; or

(f) the entitled spouse has permanently ceased to be entitled to occupy the matrimonial home, and at any time thereafter a continuous period of 5 years has elapsed, during which the non-entitled spouse has not occupied the matrimonial home.]

(4) [*Amends Land Registration (Scotland) Act 1979.*]

7 Dispensation by court with spouse's consent to dealing

(1) The court may, on the application of an entitled spouse or any other person having an interest, make an order dispensing with the consent of a non-entitled spouse to a dealing which has taken place or a proposed dealing, if—

(a) such consent is unreasonably withheld;

(b) such consent cannot be given by reason of physical or mental disability;

(c) the non-entitled spouse cannot be found after reasonable steps have been taken to trace him or her; or

(d) the non-entitled spouse is [under legal disability by reason of nonage].

(2) For the purposes of subsection (1)(a) above, a non-entitled spouse shall have unreasonably withheld consent to a dealing which has taken place or a proposed dealing, where it appears to the court—

(a) that the non-entitled spouse has led the entitled spouse to believe that he or she would consent to the dealing and that the non-entitled spouse would not be prejudiced by any change in the circumstances of the case since such apparent consent was given; or

(b) that the entitled spouse has, having taken all reasonable steps to do so, been unable to obtain an answer to a request for consent.

(3) The court, in considering whether to make an order under subsection (1) above, shall have regard to all the circumstances of the case including the matters specified in paragraphs (a) to (e) of section 3(3) of this Act.

(4) Where—

(a) an application is made for an order under this section; and

(b) an action is or has been raised by a non-entitled spouse to enforce occupancy rights,

the action shall be sisted until the conclusion of the proceedings on the application.

(5) [. . .]

8 Interests of heritable creditors

(1) The rights of a third party with an interest in the matrimonial home as a creditor under a secured loan in relation to the non-performance of any obligation under the loan shall not be prejudiced by reason only of the occupancy rights of the non-entitled spouse; but where a non-entitled spouse has or obtains occupation of a matrimonial home and—

(a) the entitled spouse is not in occupation; and

(b) there is a third party with such an interest in the matrimonial home,

the court may, on the application of the third party, make an order requiring the non-entitled spouse to make any payment due by the entitled spouse in respect of the loan.

(2) This section shall not apply [to secured loans in respect of which the security was granted prior to the commencement of section 13 of the Law Reform (Miscellaneous Provisions) (Scotland) Act 1985] unless the third party in granting the secured loan acted in good faith and . . . there was produced to the third party by the entitled spouse—

(a)   an affidavit sworn or affirmed by the entitled spouse declaring that there is no non-entitled spouse; or

(b)   a renunciation of occupancy rights or consent to the taking of the loan which bears to have been properly made or given by the non-entitled spouse.

[(2A)   This section shall not apply to secured loans in respect of which the security was granted after the commencement of section 13 of the Law Reform (Miscellaneous Provisions) (Scotland) Act 1985 unless the third party in granting the secured loan acted in good faith and . . . there was produced to the third party by the grantor—

(a)   an affidavit sworn or affirmed by the grantor declaring that the security subjects are not or were not at the time of the granting of the security a matrimonial home in relation to which a spouse of the grantor has or had occupancy rights; or

(b)   a renunciation of occupancy rights or consent to the granting of the security which bears to have been properly made or given by the non-entitled spouse.

(2B)   for the purposes of subsections (2) and (2A) above, the time of granting a security, in the case of a heritable security, is the date of delivery of the deed creating the security.]

9   Provisions where both spouses have title

(1)   Subject to subsection (2) below, where, apart from the provisions of this Act, both spouses are entitled to occupy a matrimonial home—

(a)   the rights in that home of one spouse shall not be prejudiced by reason only of any dealing of the other spouse; and

(b)   a third party shall not by reason only of such a dealing be entitled to occupy that matrimonial home or any part of it.

(2)   The definition of 'dealing' in section 6(2) of this Act and sections 6(3) and 7 of this Act shall apply for the purposes of subsection (1) above as they apply for the purposes of section 6(1) of this Act subject to the following modifications—

(a)   any reference to the entitled spouse and to the non-entitled spouse shall be construed as a reference to a spouse who has entered into or, as the case may be, proposes to enter into a dealing and to the other spouse respectively; and

(b)   in paragraph (b) of section 7(4) the reference to occupancy rights shall be construed as a reference to any rights in the matrimonial home.

[. . .]

11   Poinding

Where [an attachment] has been executed of furniture and plenishings of which the debtor's spouse has the possession or use by virtue of an order under section 3(3) or (4) of this Act, the sheriff, on the application of that spouse within 40 days of the date of execution of [the attachment], may—

(a)   declare that [the attachment] is null; or

(b)   make such order as he thinks appropriate to protect such possession or use by that spouse,

if he is satisfied that the purpose of the diligence was wholly or mainly to prevent such possession or use.

12   Adjudication

(1)   Where a matrimonial home of which there is an entitled spouse and a non-entitled spouse is adjudged, the Court of Session, on the application of the non-entitled spouse within 40 days of the date of the decree of adjudication, may—

(a)   order the reduction of the decree; or

(b)   make such order as it thinks appropriate to protect the occupancy rights of the non-entitled spouse,

if it is satisfied that the purpose of the diligence was wholly or mainly to defeat the occupancy rights of the non-entitled spouse.

(2) In this section, 'entitled spouse' and 'non-entitled spouse' have the same meanings respectively as in section 6(2) of this Act.

Transfer of tenancy

13 Transfer of tenancy

(1) The court may, on the application of a non-entitled spouse, make an order transferring the tenancy of a matrimonial home to that spouse and providing, subject to subsection (11) below, for the payment by the non-entitled spouse to the entitled spouse of such compensation as seems just and reasonable in all the circumstances of the case.

[(2) In an action—
(a) for divorce, the Court of Session or a sheriff;
(b) for nullity of marriage, the Court of Session,
may, on granting decree or within such period as the court may specify on granting decree, make an order granting an application under subsection (1) above.]

(3) In determining whether to grant an application under subsection (1) above, the court shall have regard to all the circumstances of the case including the matters specified in paragraphs (a) to (e) of section 3(3) of this Act and the suitability of the applicant to become the tenant and the applicant's capacity to perform the obligations under the lease of the matrimonial home.

(4) The non-entitled spouse shall serve a copy of an application under subsection (1) above on the landlord and, before making an order under subsection (1) above, the court shall give the landlord an opportunity of being heard by it.

(5) On the making of an order granting an application under subsection (1) above, the tenancy shall vest in the non-entitled spouse without intimation to the landlord, subject to all the liabilities under the lease (other than any arrears of rent for the period before the making of the order, which shall remain the liability of the original entitled spouse).

(6) The clerk of court shall notify the landlord of the making of an order granting an application under subsection (1) above.

(7) It shall not be competent for a non-entitled spouse to apply for an order under subsection (1) above where the matrimonial home—
(a) is let to the entitled spouse by his or her employer as an incident of employment, and the lease is subject to a requirement that the entitled spouse must reside therein;
(b) [is on or pertains to land comprised in an agricultural lease];
(c) is on or pertains to a croft or the subject of a cottar or the holding of a landholder or a statutory small tenant;
(d) is let on a long lease;
(e) is part of the tenancy land of a tenant-at-will.

(8) In subsection (7) above—
['agricultural lease' means a lease constituting a 1991 Act tenancy within the meaning of the Agricultural Holdings (Scotland) Act 2003 (asp 11) or a lease constituting a limited duration tenancy or a short limited duration tenancy (within the meaning of that Act);]

'cottar' has the same meaning as in section 28(4) of the [Crofters (Scotland) Act 1993];

'croft' has the same meaning as in the [Crofters (Scotland) Act 1993];

'holding', in relation to a landholder and a statutory small tenant, 'landholder' and 'statutory small tenant' have the same meanings respectively as in sections 2(1), 2(2) and 32(1) of the Small Landholders (Scotland) Act 1911;

'long lease' has the same meaning as in section 28(1) of the Land Registration (Scotland) Act 1979;

'tenant-at-will' has the same meaning as in section 20(8) of the Land Registration (Scotland) Act 1979.

(9) Where both spouses are joint or common tenants of a matrimonial home, the court may, on the application of one of the spouses, make an order vesting the tenancy in that spouse solely and providing, subject to subsection (11) below, for the payment by the applicant to the other spouse of such compensation as seems just and reasonable in the circumstances of the case.

(10) Subsections (2) to (8) above shall apply for the purposes of an order under subsection (9) above as they apply for the purposes of an order under subsection (1) above subject to the following modifications—

(a) in subsection (3) for the word 'tenant' there shall substituted the words 'sole tenant';

(b) in subsection (4) for the words 'non-entitled' there should be substituted the word 'applicant';

(c) in subsection (5) for the words 'non-entitled' and 'liability of the original entitled spouse' there shall substituted respectively the words 'applicant' and 'joint and several liability of both spouses';

(d) in subsection (7)—

(i) for the words 'a non-entitled' there shall substituted the words 'an applicant';

(ii) for paragraph (a) there shall be substituted the following paragraph—

'(a) is let to both spouses by their employer as an incident of employment, and the lease is subject to a requirement that both spouses must reside there;';

(iii) paragraphs (c) and (e) shall be omitted.

(11) Where the matrimonial home is a [Scottish secure tenancy within the meaning of the Housing (Scotland) Act 2001 (asp 10)] no account shall be taken, in assessing the amount of any compensation to be awarded under subsection (1) or (9) above, of the loss, by virtue of the transfer of the tenancy of the home, of a right to purchase the home under [Part III of the Housing (Scotland) Act 1987 (c 26)].

(12) In the Tenants' Rights, Etc (Scotland) Act 1980—

(a) paragraph 6 of Part I of Schedule 2 is repealed.

[. . .]

Matrimonial interdicts

14 Interdict competent where spouses live together

(1) It shall not be incompetent for the court to entertain an application by a spouse for a matrimonial interdict by reason only that the spouses are living together as man and wife.

(2) In this section and section 15 of this Act—

'matrimonial interdict' means an interdict including an interim interdict which—

(a) restrains or prohibits any conduct of one spouse towards the other spouse or a child of the family, or

(b) prohibits a spouse from entering or remaining in a matrimonial home or in a specified area in the vicinity of the matrimonial home.

15 Attachment of powers of arrest to matrimonial interdicts

(1) [Subject to subsection (1A) below, the] court shall, on the application of the applicant spouse, attach a power of arrest—

(a) to any matrimonial interdict which is ancillary to an exclusion order, including an interim order under section 4(6) of this Act;

(b) to any other matrimonial interdict where the non-applicant spouse has had the opportunity of being heard by or represented before the court, unless it appears to the court that in all the circumstances of the case such a power is unnecessary.

[(1A) The court may attach a power of arrest to an interdict by virtue of subsection (1) above only if satisfied that attaching the power would not result in the non-applicant spouse being subject, in relation to the interdict, to a power of arrest under both this Act and the Protection from Abuse (Scotland) Act 2001 (asp 14.)

(2)   A power of arrest attached to an interdict by virtue of subsection (1) above shall not have effect until such interdict [together with the attached power of arrest] is served on the non-applicant spouse, and such a power of arrest shall, unless previously recalled, cease to have effect upon the termination of the marriage.

(3)   If, by virtue of subsection (1) above, a power of arrest is attached to an interdict, a constable may arrest without warrant the non-applicant spouse if he has reasonable cause for suspecting that spouse of being in breach of the interdict.

(4)   If, by virtue of subsection (1) above, a power of arrest is attached to an interdict, the applicant spouse shall, as soon as possible after service of the interdict [together with the attached power of arrest] on the non-applicant spouse, ensure that there is delivered—

(a)   to the chief constable of the police area in which the matrimonial home is situated; and

(b)   if the applicant spouse resides in another police area, to the chief constable of that other police area,

a copy of the application for the interdict and of the interlocutor granting the interdict together with a certificate of service of the interdict [and where the application to attach the power of arrest to the interdict was made after the interdict was granted, a copy of that application and of the interlocutor granting it and a certificate of service of the interdict together with the attached power of arrest].

(5)   Where any matrimonial interdict to which, by virtue of subsection (1) above there is attached a power of arrest, is varied or recalled, the spouse who applied for the variation or recall shall ensure that there is delivered—

(a)   to the chief constable of the police area in which the matrimonial home is situated; and

(b)   if the applicant spouse (within the meaning of subsection (6) below) resides in another police area, to the chief constable of that other police area,

a copy of the application for variation or recall and of the interlocutor granting the variation or recall.

(6)   In this section and in sections 16 and 17 of this Act—
'applicant spouse' means the spouse who has applied for the interdict; and
'non-applicant spouse' shall be construed accordingly.

16   Police powers after arrest

(1)   Where a person has been arrested under section 15(3) of this Act, the officer in charge of a police station may—

(a)   if satisfied that there is no likelihood of violence to the applicant spouse or any child of the family, liberate that person unconditionally; or

(b)   refuse to liberate that person; and such refusal and the detention of that person until his or her appearance in court by virtue of—

(i)   section 17(2) of this Act; or

(ii)   any provision of the [Criminal Procedure (Scotland) Act 1995],

shall not subject the officer to any claim whatsoever.

(2)   Where a person arrested under section 15(3) of this Act is liberated under subsection (1) above, the facts and circumstances which gave rise to the arrest shall be reported forthwith to the procurator fiscal who, if he decides to take no criminal proceedings in respect of those facts and circumstances, shall at the earliest opportunity take all reasonable steps to intimate his decision to the persons mentioned in paragraphs (a) and (b) of section 17(4) of this Act.

17   Procedure after arrest

(1)   The provisions of this section shall apply only where—

(a)   the non-applicant spouse has not been liberated under section 16(1) of this Act; and

(b)   the procurator fiscal decides that no criminal proceedings are to be taken in respect of the facts and circumstances which gave rise to the arrest.

(2)   The non-applicant spouse who has been arrested under section 15(3) of this Act shall wherever practicable be brought before the sheriff sitting as a court of summary criminal jurisdiction for the district in which he or she was arrested not later than in the course of the first day after the arrest, such day not being a Saturday, a Sunday or a court holiday prescribed for that court under [section 8 of the Criminal Procedure (Scotland) Act 1995].

Provided that nothing in this subsection shall prevent the non-applicant spouse from being brought before the sheriff on a Saturday, a Sunday or such a court holiday where the sheriff is in pursuance of the said section 10 sitting on such day for the disposal of criminal business.

(3)   [Subsections (1) to (3) of section 15 of the said Act of 1995] (intimation to a named person) shall apply to a non-applicant spouse who has been arrested under section 15(3) of this Act as they apply to a person who has been arrested in respect of any offence.

(4)   The procurator fiscal shall at the earliest opportunity, and in any event prior to the non-applicant spouse being brought before the sheriff under subsection (2) above, take all reasonable steps to intimate—

(a)   to the applicant spouse; and

(b)   to the solicitor who acted for that spouse when the interdict was granted or to any other solicitor who the procurator fiscal has reason to believe acts for the time being for that spouse,

that the criminal proceedings referred to in subsection (1) above will not be taken.

(5)   On the non-applicant spouse being brought before the sheriff under subsection (2) above, the following procedure shall apply—

(a)   the procurator fiscal shall present to the court a petition containing—

(i)   a statement of the particulars of the non-applicant spouse;

(ii)   a statement of the facts and circumstances which gave rise to the arrest; and

(iii)   a request that the non-applicant spouse be detained for a further period not exceeding 2 days;

(b)   if it appears to the sheriff that—

(i)   the statement referred to in paragraph (a)(ii) above discloses a *prima facie* breach of interdict by the non-applicant spouse;

(ii)   proceedings for breach of interdict will be taken; and

(iii)   there is a substantial risk of violence by the non-applicant spouse against the applicant spouse or any child of the family,

he may order the non-applicant spouse to be detained for a further period not exceeding 2 days;

(c)   in any case to which paragraph (b) above does not apply, the non-applicant spouse shall, unless in custody in respect of any other matter, be released from custody;

and in computing the period of two days referred to in paragraphs (a) and (b) above, no account shall be taken of a Saturday or Sunday or of any holiday in the court in which the proceedings for breach of interdict will require to be raised.

Cohabiting couples

18   Occupancy rights of cohabiting couples

(1)   If a man and a woman are living with each other as if they were man and wife ('a cohabiting couple') in a house which, apart from the provisions of this section—

(a)   one of them (an 'entitled partner') is entitled, or permitted by a third party, to occupy; and

(b)   the other (a 'non-entitled partner') is not so entitled or permitted to occupy,
the court may, on the application of the non-entitled partner, if it appears that the man and the woman are a cohabiting couple in that house, grant occupancy rights therein to the applicant for such period, not exceeding [6] months, as the court may specify:
Provided that the court may extend the said period for a further period or periods, no such period exceeding 6 months.

(2)   In determining whether for the purpose of subsection (1) above a man and woman are a cohabiting couple the court shall have regard to all the circumstances of the case including—

(a)   the time for which it appears they have been living together; and

(b)   whether there are any children of the relationship.

(3)   While an order granting an application under subsection (1) above or an extension of such an order is in force, or where both partners of a cohabiting couple are entitled, or permitted by a third party, to occupy the house where they are cohabiting, the following provisions of this Act shall subject to any necessary modifications—

(a)   apply to the cohabiting couple as they apply to parties to a marriage; and

(b)   have effect in relation to any child residing with the cohabiting couple as they have effect in relation to a child of the family,

section 2;

section 3, except subsection (1)(a);

section 4;

in section 5(1), the words from the beginning to 'Act' where it first occurs;

sections 13 and 14;

section 15, except the words in subsection (2) from 'and such a power of arrest' to the end;

sections 16 and 17; and

section 22,

and any reference in these provisions to a matrimonial home shall be construed as a reference to a house.

(4)   Any order under section 3 or 4 of this Act as applied to a cohabiting couple by subsection (3) above shall have effect—

(a)   if one of them is a non-entitled partner, for such a period, not exceeding the period or periods which from time to time may be specified in any order under subsection (1) above for which occupancy rights have been granted under that subsection, as may be specified in the order;

(b)   if they are both entitled, or permitted by a third party, to occupy the house, until a further order of the court.

(5)   Nothing in this section shall prejudice the rights of any third party having an interest in the house referred to in subsection (1) above.

(6)   In this section—

'house' includes a caravan, houseboat or other structure in which the couple are cohabiting and any garden or other ground or building attached to, and usually occupied with, or otherwise required for the amenity or convenience of, the house, caravan, houseboat or other structure;

'occupancy rights' means the following rights of a non-entitled partner—

(a)   if in occupation, a right to [continue to occupy] the house [and, without prejudice to the generality of these rights, includes the right to continue to occupy or, as the case may be, to enter and occupy the house together with any child residing with the cohabiting couple];

(b)   if not in occupation, a right to enter into and occupy the house;

'entitled partner' includes a partner who is entitled, or permitted by a third party, to occupy the house along with an individual who is not the other partner only if that individual has waived his or her right of occupation in favour of the partner so entitled or permitted.

Miscellaneous and general

19 Rights of occupancy in relation to division and sale
Where a spouse brings an action for the division and sale of a matrimonial home which the spouses own in common, the court, after having regard to all the circumstances of the case including—

(a) the matters specified in paragraphs (a) to (d) of section 3(3) of this Act; and

(b) whether the spouse bringing the action offers or has offered to make available to the other spouse any suitable alternative accommodation,

may refuse to grant decree in that action or may postpone the granting of decree for such period as it may consider reasonable in the circumstances or may grant decree subject to such conditions as it may prescribe.

20 Spouse's consent in relation to calling up of standard securities over matrimonial homes
Section 19(10) of the Conveyancing and Feudal Reform (Scotland) Act 1970 shall have effect as if at the end there were added the following proviso—

'Provided that, without prejudice to the foregoing generality, if the standard security is over a matrimonial home as defined in section 22 of the Matrimonial Homes (Family Protection) (Scotland) Act 1981, the spouse on whom the calling-up notice has been served may not dispense with or shorten the said period without the consent in writing of the other spouse.'.

21 Procedural provision
Section 2(2) of the Law Reform (Husband and Wife) Act 1962 (dismissal by court of delictual proceedings between spouses) shall not apply to any proceedings brought before the court in pursuance of any provision of this Act.

22 Interpretation
In this Act—

'caravan' means a caravan which is mobile or affixed to the land;

'child of the family' includes any child or grandchild of either spouse, and any person who has been brought up or [treated] by either spouse as if he or she were a child of that spouse, whatever the age of such a child, grandchild or person may be;

'the court' means the Court of Session or the sheriff;

'furniture and plenishings' means any article situated in a matrimonial home which—

(a) is owned or hired by either spouse or is being acquired by either spouse under a hire-purchase agreement or conditional sale agreement; and

(b) is reasonably necessary to enable the home to be used as a family residence,

but does not include any vehicle, caravan or houseboat, or such other structure as is mentioned in the definition of 'matrimonial home';

'matrimonial home' means any house, caravan, houseboat or other structure which has been provided or has been made available by one or both of the spouses as, or has become, a family residence and includes any garden or other ground or building attached to, and usually occupied with, or otherwise required for the amenity or convenience of, the house, caravan, houseboat or other structure [but does not include a residence provided or made available by one spouse for that spouse to reside in, whether with any child of the family or not, separately from the other spouse];

'occupancy rights' has, subject to section 18(6) of this Act, the meaning assigned by section 1(4) of this Act;

'the sheriff' includes the sheriff having jurisdiction in the district where the matrimonial home is situated;

'tenant' includes sub-tenant and a statutory tenant as defined in section 3 of the Rent (Scotland) Act [1984 and a statutory assured tenant as defined in section 16(1) of the Housing (Scotland) Act 1988] and 'tenancy' shall be construed accordingly;

'entitled spouse' and 'non-entitled spouse', subject to sections 6(2) and 12(2) of this Act, have the meanings respectively assigned to them by section 1 of this Act.

23 Short title, commencement and extent

(1) This Act may be cited as the Matrimonial Homes (Family Protection) (Scotland) Act 1981.

(2) This Act (except this section) shall come into operation on such day as the Secretary of State may by order made by statutory instrument appoint, and different days may be so appointed for different provisions and for different purposes.

(3) This Act extends to Scotland only.

Equivalent provisions for civil partners are contained in the Civil Partnership Act 2004, ss 101–112.

FAMILY LAW (SCOTLAND) ACT 1985

Matrimonial property, etc

24 Marriage not to affect property rights or legal capacity

(1) Subject to the provisions of any enactment (including this Act), marriage [or civil partnership] shall not of itself affect—

    (a) the respective rights of the parties to the marriage [or as the case may be the partners in a civil partnership] in relation to their property;

    (b) the legal capacity of [those parties or partners].

(2) Nothing in subsection (1) above affects the law of succession.

25 Presumption of equal shares in household goods

(1) If any question arises (whether during or after a marriage [or civil partnership]) as to the respective rights of ownership of the parties to a marriage [or the partners in a civil partnership] in any household goods obtained in prospect of or during the marriage [or civil partnership] other than by gift or succession from a third party, it shall be presumed, unless the contrary is proved, that each has a right to an equal share in the goods in question.

(2) For the purposes of subsection (1) above, the contrary shall not be treated as proved by reason only that while [—

    (a)] the parties were married;

    [(b) the partners were in a civil partnership],

and living together the goods in question were purchased from a third party by either party alone or by both in unequal shares.

(3) In this section 'household goods' means any goods (including decorative or ornamental goods) kept or used at any time during the marriage [or civil partnership in any family] home for the joint domestic purposes of the parties to the marriage [or the partners], other than—

    (a) money or securities;

    (b) any motor car, caravan or other road vehicle;

    (c) any domestic animal.

26 Presumption of equal shares in money and property derived from housekeeping allowance

If any question arises (whether during or after a marriage [or civil partnership]) as to the right of a party to a marriage [or as the case may be of a partner in a civil partnership] to money derived from any allowance made by either party [or partner] for their joint household expenses or for similar purposes, or to any property acquired out of such money, the money or property shall, in the absence of any agreement between them to the contrary, be treated as belonging to each party [or partner] in equal shares.

COMPANIES ACT 1985
(1985, c 6)

PART XII
REGISTRATION OF CHARGES

CHAPTER II
REGISTRATION OF CHARGES (SCOTLAND)

410 Charges void unless registered

(1) The following provisions of this Chapter have effect for the purpose of securing the registration in Scotland of charges created by companies.

(2) Every charge created by a company, being a charge to which this section applies, is, so far as any security on the company's property or any part of it is conferred by the charge, void against the liquidator [or administrator] and any creditor of the company unless the prescribed particulars of the charge, together with a copy (certified in the prescribed manner to be a correct copy) of the instrument (if any) by which the charge is created or evidenced, are delivered to or received by the registrar of companies for registration in the manner required by this Chapter within 21 days after the date of the creation of the charge.

(3) Subsection (2) is without prejudice to any contract or obligation for repayment of the money secured by the charge; and when a charge becomes void under this section the money secured by it immediately becomes payable.

(4) This section, applies to the following charges—

(a) a charge on land wherever situated, or any interest in such land (not including a charge for any rent, ground annual or other periodical sum payable in respect of the land, but including a charge created by a heritable security within the meaning of section 9(8) of the Conveyancing and Feudal Reform (Scotland) Act 1970),

(b) a security over the uncalled share capital of the company,

(c) a security over incorporeal moveable property of any of the following categories—

(i) the book debts of the company,

(ii) calls made but not paid,

(iii) goodwill,

(iv) a patent or a licence under a patent,

(v) a trademark,

(vi) a copyright or a licence under a copyright,

[(vii) a registered design or a licence in respect of such a design,

(viii) a design right or a licence under a design right,]

(d) security over a ship or aircraft or any share in a ship, and

(e) a floating charge,

(5) In this Chapter 'company' (except in section 424) means an incorporated company registered in Scotland; 'registrar of companies' means the registrar or other officer per forming under this Act the duty of registration of companies in Scotland; and references to the date of creation of a charge are—

(a) in the case of a floating charge, the date on which the instrument creating the floating charge was executed by the company creating the charge, and

(b)   in any other case, the date on which the right of the person entitled to the benefit of the charge was constituted as a real right.

411   Charges on property outside United Kingdom

(1)   In the case of a charge created out of the United Kingdom comprising property situated outside the United Kingdom, the period of 21 days after the date on which the copy of the instrument creating it could (in due course of post, and if despatched with due diligence) have been received in the United Kingdom is substituted for the period of 21 days after the date of the creation of the charge as the time within which, under section 410(2), the particulars and copy are to be delivered to the registrar.

(2)   Where a charge is created in the United Kingdom but comprises property outside the United Kingdom, the copy of the instrument creating or purporting to create the charge may be sent for registration under section 410 notwithstanding that further proceedings may be necessary to make the charge valid or effectual according to the law of the country in which the property is situated.

412   Negotiable instrument to secure book debts

Where a negotiable instrument has been given to secure the payment of any book debts of a company, the deposit of the instrument for the purpose of securing an advance to the company is not, for purposes of section 410, to be treated as a charge on those book debts.

413   Charges associated with debentures

(1)   The holding of debentures entitling the holder to a charge on land is not, for the purposes of section 410, deemed to be an interest in land.

(2)   Where a series of debentures containing, or giving by reference to any other instrument, any charge to the benefit of which the debenture-holders of that series are entitled *pari passu*, is created by a company, it is sufficient for purposes of section 410 if there are delivered to or received by the registrar of companies within 21 days after the execution of the deed containing the charge or, if there is no such deed, after the execution of any debentures of the series, the following particulars in the prescribed form—

(a)   the total amount secured by the whole series,

(b)   the dates of the resolutions authorising the issue of the series and the date of the covering deed (if any) by which the security is created or defined,

(c)   a general description of the property charged,

(d)   the names of the trustees (if any) for the debenture holders, and

(e)   in the case of a floating charge, a statement of any provisions of the charge and of any instrument relating to it which prohibit or restrict or regulate the power of the company to grant further securities ranking in priority to, or *pari passu* with, the floating charge, or which vary or otherwise regulate the order of ranking of the floating charge in relation to subsisting securities,

together with a copy of the deed containing the charge or, if there is no such deed, of one of the debentures of the series:

Provided that, where more than one issue is made of debentures in the series, there shall be sent to the registrar of companies for entry in the register particulars (in the prescribed form) of the date and amount of each issue of debentures of the series, but any omission to do this does not affect the validity of any of those debentures.

(3)   Where any commission, allowance or discount has been paid or made, either directly or indirectly, by a company to any person in consideration of his subscribing or agreeing to subscribe, whether absolutely or conditionally, for any debentures of the company, or procuring or agreeing to procure subscriptions (whether absolute or conditional) for any such debentures, the particulars required to be sent for registration under section 410 include particulars as to the amount or

rate per cent of the commission, discount or allowance so paid or made; but any omission to do this does not affect the validity of the debentures issued.

The deposit of any debentures as security for any debt of the company is not, for purposes of this subsection, treated as the issue of the debentures at a discount.

414   Charge by way of *ex facie* absolute disposition, etc

(1)   For the avoidance of doubt, it is hereby declared that, in the case of a charge created by way of an *ex facie* absolute disposition or assignation qualified by a back letter or other agreement, or by a standard security qualified by an agreement, compliance with section 410(2) does not of itself render the charge unavailable as security for indebtedness incurred after the date of compliance.

(2)   Where the amount secured by a charge so created is purported to be increased by a further back letter or agreement, a further charge is held to have been created by the *ex facie* absolute disposition or assignation or (as the case may be) by the standard security, as qualified by the further back letter or agreement; and the provisions of this Chapter apply to the further charge as if—

(a)   references in this Chapter (other than in this section) to the charge were references to the further charge, and

(b)   references to the date of the creation of the charge were references to the date on which the further back letter or agreement was executed.

415   Company's duty to register charges created by it

(1)   It is a company's duty to send to the registrar of companies for registration the particulars of every charge created by the company and of the issues of debentures of a series requiring registration under sections 410 to 414; but registration of any such charge may be effected on the application of any person interested in it.

(2)   Where registration is effected on the application of some person other than the company, that person is entitled to recover from the company the amount of any fees properly paid by him to the registrar on the registration.

(3)   If a company makes default in sending to the registrar for registration the particulars of any charge created by the company or of the issues of debentures of a series requiring registration as above mentioned, then, unless the registration has been effected on the application of some other person, the company and every officer of it who is in default is liable to a fine and, for continued contravention, to a daily default fine.

416   Duty to register charges existing on property acquired

(1)   Where a company acquires any property which is subject to a charge of any kind as would, if it had been created by the company after the acquisition of the property, have been required to be registered under this Chapter, the company shall cause the prescribed particulars of the charge, together with a copy (certified in the prescribed manner to be a correct copy) of the instrument (if any) by which the charge was created or is evidenced, to be delivered to the registrar of companies for registration in the manner required by this Chapter within 21 days after the date on which the transaction was settled.

(2)   If, however, the property is situated and the charge was created outside Great Britain, 21 days after the date on which the copy of the instrument could (in due course of post, and if despatched with due diligence) have been received in the United Kingdom are substituted for 21 days after the settlement of the transaction as the time within which the particulars and the copy of the instrument are to be delivered to the registrar.

(3)   If default is made in complying with this section, the company and every officer of it who is in default is liable to a fine and, for continued contravention, to a daily default fine.

417   Register of charges to be kept by registrar of companies

(1)   The registrar of companies shall keep, with respect to each company, a register in the prescribed form of all the charges requiring registration under this

Chapter, and shall enter in the register with respect to such charges the particulars specified below.

(2)   In the case of a charge to the benefit of which the holders of a series of debentures are entitled, there shall be entered in the register the particulars specified in section 413(2).

(3)   In the case of any other charge, there shall be entered—

(a)   if it is a charge created by the company, the date of its creation, and if it was a charge existing on property acquired by the company, the date of the acquisition of the property,

(b)   the amount secured by the charge,

(c)   short particulars of the property charged,

(d)   the persons entitled to the charge, and

(e)   in the case of a floating charge, a statement of any of the provisions of the charge and of any instrument relating to it which prohibit or restrict or regulate the company's power to grant further securities ranking it priority to, or *pari passu* with, the floating charge, or which vary or otherwise regulate the order of ranking of the floating charge in relation to subsisting securities.

(4)   The register kept in pursuance of this section shall be open to inspection by any person.

418   Certificate of registration to be issued

(1)   The registrar of companies shall give a certificate of the registration of any charge registered in pursuance of this Chapter.

(2)   The certificate—

(a)   shall be either signed by the registrar, or authenticated by his official seal,

(b)   shall state the name of the company and the person first-named in the charge among those entitled to the benefit of the charge (or, in the case of a series of debentures, the name of the holder of the first such debenture to be issued) and the amount secured by the charge, and

(c)   is conclusive evidence that the requirements of this Chapter as to registration have been complied with.

419   Entries of satisfaction and relief

(1)   [Subject to subsections (1A) and (1B), the] registrar of companies, on application being made to him in the prescribed form, and on receipt of a statutory declaration in the prescribed form verifying, with respect to any registered charge,—

(a)   that the debt for which the charge was given has been paid or satisfied in whole or in part, or

(b)   that part of the property charged has been released from the charge or has ceased to form part of the company's property,

may enter on the register a memorandum of satisfaction (in whole or in part) regarding that fact.

[(1A)   On an application being made to him in the prescribed form, the registrar of companies may make any such entry as is mentioned in subsection (1) where, instead of receiving such a statutory declaration as is mentioned in that subsection, he receives a statement by a director, secretary, liquidator, receiver or administrator of the company which is contained in an electronic communication and that statement—

(a)   verifies the matters set out in paragraph (a) or (b) of that subsection,

(b)   contains a description of the charge,

(c)   states the date of creation of the charge and the date of its registration under this Chapter,

(d)   states the name and address of the chargee or, in the case of a debenture, trustee, and

(e)   where paragraph (b) of subsection (1) applies, contains short particulars of the property which has been released from the charge, or which has ceased to form part of the company's property (as the case may be).

(1B) Where the statement under subsection (1A) concerns the satisfaction of a floating charge, then there shall be delivered to the registrar a further statement which—

(a) is made by the creditor entitled to the benefit of the floating charge or a person authorised to act on his behalf;

(b) is incorporated into, or logically associated with, the electronic communication containing the statement; and

(c) certifies that the particulars contained in the statement are correct.]

(2) Where the registrar enters a memorandum of satisfaction in whole, he shall, if required, furnish the company with a copy of the memorandum.

(3) Without prejudice to the registrar's duty under this section to require to be satisfied as above mentioned, he shall not be so satisfied unless—

(a) the creditor entitled to the benefit of the floating charge, or a person authorised to do so on his behalf, certifies as correct the particulars submitted to the registrar with respect to the entry on the register of a memorandun under this section, or

(b) the court, on being satisfied that such certification cannot readily be obtained, directs him accordingly.

(4) Nothing in this section requires the company to submit particulars with respect to the entry in the register of a memorandum of satisfaction where the company, having created a floating charge over all or any part of its property, disposes of part of the property subject to the floating charge.

(5) A memorandum or certification required for the purposes of this section shall be in such form as may be prescribed.

[(5A) Any person who makes a false statement under subsection (1A) or (1B) which he knows to be false or does not believe to be true is liable to imprisonment or a fine, or both.]

420   Rectification of register

The court, on being satisfied that the omission to register a charge within the time required by this Act or that the omission or mis-statement of any particular with respect to any such charge or in a memorandum of satisfaction was accidental, or due to inadvertence or to some other sufficient cause, or is not of a nature to prejudice the position of creditors or shareholders of the company, or that it is on other grounds just and equitable to grant relief, may, on the application of the company or any person interested, and on such terms and conditions as seem to the court just and expedient, order that the time for registration shall be extended or (as the case may be) that the omission or mis-statement shall be rectified.

421   Copies of instruments creating charges to be kept by company

(1) Every company shall cause a copy of every instrument creating a charge requiring registration under this Chapter to be kept at the company's registered office.

(2) In the case of a series of uniform debentures, a copy of one debenture of the series is sufficient.

422   Company's register of charges

(1) Every company shall keep at its registered office a register of charges and enter in it all charges specifically affecting property of the company, and all floating charges on any property of the company.

(2) There shall be given in each case a short description of the property charged, the amount of the charge and, except in the case of securities to bearer, the names of the persons entitled to it.

(3) If an officer of the company knowingly and wilfully authorises or permits

the omission of an entry required to be made in pursuance of this section, he is liable to a fine.

423 Right to inspect copies of instruments, and company's register

(1) The copies of instruments creating charges requiring registration under this Chapter with the registrar of companies, and the register of charges kept in pursuance of section 422, shall be open during business hours (but subject to such reasonable restrictions as the company in general meeting may impose, so that not less than 2 hours in each day be allowed for inspection) to the inspection of any creditor or member of the company without fee.

(2) The register of charges shall be open to the inspection of any other person on payment of such fee, not exceeding 5 pence for each inspection, as the company may prescribe.

(3) If inspection of the copies or register is refused, every officer of the company who is in default is liable to a fine and, for continued contravention, to a daily default fine.

(4) If such a refusal occurs in relation to a company, the court may by order compel an immediate inspection of the copies or register.

424 Extension of Chapter II

(1) This Chapter extends to charges on property in Scotland which are created, and to charges on property in Scotland which is acquired, by a company incorporated outside Great Britain which has a place of business in Scotland.

(2) In relation to such a company, sections 421 and 422 apply with the substitution, for the reference to the company's registered office, of a reference to its principal place of business in Scotland.

PART XVIII
FLOATING CHARGES AND RECEIVERS (SCOTLAND)

CHAPTER I
FLOATING CHARGES

462 Power of incorporated company to create floating charge

(1) It is competent under the law of Scotland for an incorporated company (whether a company within the meaning of this Act or not), for the purpose of securing any debt or other obligation (including a cautionary obligation) incurred or to be incurred by, or binding upon, the company or any other person, to create in favour of the creditor in the debt or obligation a charge, in this Part referred to as a floating charge, over all or any part of the property (including uncalled capital) which may from time to time be comprised in its property and undertaking.

[. . .]

(4) References in this Part to the instrument by which a floating charge was created are, in the case of a floating charge created by words in a bond or other written acknowledgment, references to the bond or, as the case may be, the other written acknowledgment.

(5) Subject to this Act, a floating charge has effect in accordance with this Part [and Part III of the Insolvency Act 1986] in relation to any heritable property in Scotland to which it relates, notwithstanding that the instrument creating it is not recorded in the Register of Sasines or, as appropriate, registered in accordance with the Land Registration (Scotland) Act 1979.

463 Effect of floating charge on winding up

(1) [Where a company goes into liquidation within the meaning of section 247(2) of the Insolvency Act 1986], a floating charge created by the company

attaches to the property then comprised in the company's property and under-taking or, as the case may be, in part of that property and undertaking, but does so subject to the rights of any person who—

(a)   has effectually executed diligence on the property or any part of it; or

(b)   holds a fixed security over the property or any part of it ranking in priority to the floating charge; or

(c)   holds over the property or any part of it another floating charge so ranking.

(2)   The provisions of [Part IV of the Insolvency Act (except section 185)] have effect in relation to a floating charge, subject to subsection (1), as if the charge were a fixed security over the property to which it has attached in respect of the principal of the debt or obligation to which it relates and any interest due or to become due thereon.

[(3)   Nothing in this section derogates from the provisions of sections 53(7) and 54(6) of the Insolvency Act (attachment of floating charge on appointment of receiver), or prejudices the operation of sections 175 and 176 of that Act (payment of preferential debts in winding up).]

(4)   Interest accrues, in respect of a floating charge which after 16th November 1972 attaches to the property of the company, until payment of the sum due under the charge is made.

464   Ranking of floating charges

(1)   Subject to subsection (2), the instrument creating a floating charge over all or any part of the company's property under section 462 may contain—

(a)   provisions prohibiting or restricting the creation of any fixed security or any other floating charge having priority over, or ranking *pari passu* with, the floating charge; or

(b)   [with the consent of the holder of any subsisting floating charge or fixed security which would be adversely affected] provisions regulating the order in which the floating charge shall rank with any other subsisting or future floating charges or fixed securities over that property or any part of it.

[(1A)   Where an instrument creating a floating charge contains any such provision as is mentioned in subsection (1)(a), that provision shall be effective to confer priority on the floating charge over any fixed security or floating charge created after the date of the instrument.]

(2)   Where all or any part of the property of a company is subject both to a floating charge and to a fixed security arising by operation of law, the fixed security has priority over the floating charge.

[(3)   The order of ranking of the floating charge with any other subsisting or future floating charges or fixed securities over all or any part of the company's property is determined in accordance with the provisions of subsections (4) and (5) except where it is determined in accordance with any provision such as is mentioned in paragraph (a) or (b) of subsection (1).]

(4)   Subject to the provisions of this section—

(a)   a fixed security, the right to which has been constituted as a real right before a floating charge has attached to all or any part of the property of the company, has priority of ranking over the floating charge;

(b)   floating charges rank with one another according to the time of registration accordance with Chapter II of Part XII;

(c)   floating charges which have been received by the registrar for registration by the same postal delivery rank with one another equally.

(5)   Where the holder of a floating charge over all or any part of the company's property which has been registered in accordance with Chapter II of Part XII has received, intimation in writing of the subsequent registration in accordance with that Chapter of another floating charge over the same property or any part thereof, the preference in ranking of the first-mentioned floating charge is restricted to security for—

(a)   the holder's present advances;

(b)   future advances which he may be required to make under the instrument creating the floating charge or under any ancillary document;

(c)   interest due or to become due on all such advances;

(d)   any expenses or outlays which may reasonably be incurred by the holder [; and]

[(e)   (in the case of a floating charge to secure a contingent liability other than a liability arising under any further advances made from time to time) the maximum sum to which that contingent liability is capable of amounting whether or not it is contractually limited.]

(6)   This section is subject to [Part XII and to sections 175 and 176 of the Insolvency Act].

LAW REFORM (MISCELLANEOUS PROVISIONS) (SCOTLAND) ACT 1985
(1985 c 73)

Provisions relating to other contracts and obligations

8   Rectification of defectively expressed documents

(1)   Subject to section 9 of this Act, where the court is satisfied, on an application made to it, that—

(a)   a document intended to express or to give effect to an agreement fails to express accurately the common intention of the parties to the agreement at the date when it was made; or

(b)   a document intended to create, transfer, vary or renounce a right, not being a document falling within paragraph (a) above, fails to express accurately the intention of the grantor of the document at the date when it was executed,

it may order the document to be rectified in any manner that it may specify in order to give effect to that intention.

(2)   For the purposes of subsection (1) above, the court shall be entitled to have regard to all relevant evidence, whether written or oral.

(3)   Subject to section 9 of this Act, in ordering the rectification of a document under subsection (1) above (in this subsection referred, to as 'the original document'), the court may, at its own instance or on an application made to it, order the rectification of any other document intended for any of the purposes mentioned in paragraph (a) or (b) of subsection (1) above which is defectively expressed by reason of the defect in the original document.

(4)   Subject to section 9(4) of this Act, a document ordered to be rectified under this section shall have effect as if it had always been so rectified.

(5)   Subject to section 9(5) of this Act, where a document recorded in the Register of Sasines is ordered to be rectified under this section and the order is likewise recorded, the document shall be treated as having been always so recorded as rectified.

(6)   Nothing in this section shall apply to a document of a testamentary nature.

(7)   It shall be competent to register in the Register of Inhibitions and Adjudications a notice of an application under this section for the rectification of a deed relating to land, being an application in respect of which authority for service or citation has been granted; and the land to which the application relates shall be rendered litigious as from the date of registration of such a notice.

(8)   A notice under subsection (7) above shall specify the names and designations of the parties to the application and the date when authority for service or citation was granted and contain a description of the land to which the application relates.

(9)   In this section and section 9 of this Act 'the court' means the Court of Session or the sheriff.

9 Provisions supplementary to section 8: protection of other interest

(1) The court shall order a document to be rectified under section 8 of this Act only where it is satisfied—

(a)   that the interests of a person to whom this section applies would not be adversely affected to a material extent by the rectification; or

(b)   that that person has consented to the proposed rectification.

(2)   Subject to subsection (3) below, this section applies to a person (other than a party to the agreement or the grantor of the document) who has acted or refrained from acting in reliance on the terms of the document or on the title sheet of an interest in land registered in the Land Register of Scotland being an interest to which the document relates, with the result that his position has been affected to a material extent.

(3)   This section does not apply to a person—

(a)   who, at the time when he acted or refrained from acting as mentioned in subsection (2) above, knew, or ought in the circumstances known to him at that time to have been aware, that the document or (as the case may be) the title sheet failed accurately to express the common intention of the parties to the agreement or, as the case may be, the intention of the grantor of the document; or

(b)   whose reliance on the terms of the document or on the title sheet was otherwise unreasonable.

(4)   Notwithstanding subsection (4) of section 8 of this Act and without prejudice to subsection (5) below, the court may, for the purpose of protecting the interests of a person to whom this section applies, order that the rectification of a document shall have effect as at such date as it may specify, being a date later than that as at which it would have effect by virtue of the said subsection (4).

(5)   Notwithstanding subsection (5) of section 8 of this Act and without prejudice to subsection (4) above, the court may, for the purpose of protecting the interests of a person to whom this section applies, order that a document as rectified shall be treated as having been recorded as mentioned in the said subsection (5) at such date as it may specify, being a date later than that as at which it would be treated by virtue of that subsection as having been so recorded.

(6)   For the purposes of subsection (1) above, the court may require the Keeper of the Registers of Scotland to produce such information as he has in his possession relating to any persons who have asked him to supply details with regard to a title sheet mentioned in subsection (2) above; and any expense incurred by the Keeper under this subsection shall be borne by the applicant for the order.

(7)   Where a person to whom this section applies was unaware, before a document was ordered to be rectified under section 8 of this Act, that an application had been made under that section for the rectification of the document, the Court of Session, on an application made by that person within the time specified in subsection (8) below, may—

(a)   reduce the rectifying order; or

(b)   order the applicant for the rectifying order to pay such compensation to that person as it thinks fit in respect of his reliance on the terms of the document or on the title sheet.

(8)   The time referred to in subsection (7) above is whichever is the earlier of the following—

(a)   the expiry of 5 years after the making of the rectifying order;

(b)   the expiry of 2 years after the making of that order first came to the notice of the person referred to in that subsection.

INSOLVENCY ACT 1986
(1986, c 45)

53 Mode of appointment by holder of charge

(1)–(6)   [*deal with powers of receivers*]

(7) On the appointment of a receiver under this section, the floating charge by virtue of which he was appointed attaches to the property then subject to the charge; and such attachment has effect as if the charge was a fixed security over the property to which it has attached.

60 Distribution of moneys

(1) Subject to the next section, and to the rights of any of the following categories of persons (which rights shall, except to the extent otherwise provided in any instrument, have the following order of priority), namely—

(a) the holder of any fixed security which is over property subject to the floating charge and which ranks prior to, or *pari passu* with, the floating charge;

(b) all persons who have effectually executed diligence on any part of the property of the company which is subject to the charge by virtue of which the receiver was appointed;

(c) creditors in respect of all liabilities, charges and expenses incurred by or on behalf of the receiver;

(d) the receiver in respect of his liabilities, expenses and remuneration, and any indemnity to which he is entitled out of the property of the company; and

(e) the preferential creditors entitled to payment under section 59,

the receiver shall pay moneys received by him to the holder of the floating charge by virtue of which the receiver was appointed in or towards satisfaction of the debt secured by the floating charge.

(2) Any balance of moneys remaining after the provisions of subsection (1) and section 61 below have been satisfied shall be paid in accordance with their respective rights and interests to the following persons, as the case may require—

(a) any other receiver;

(b) the holder of a fixed security which is over property subject to the floating charge;

(c) the company or its liquidator, as the case may be.

(3) Where any question arises as to the person entitled to a payment under this section, or where a receipt or a discharge of a security cannot be obtained in respect of any such payment, the receiver shall consign the amount of such payment in any joint stock bank of issue in Scotland in name of the Accountant of Court for behoof of the person or persons entitled thereto.

REQUIREMENTS OF WRITING (SCOTLAND) ACT 1995
(1995, c 7)

1 Writing required for certain contracts, obligations, trusts, conveyances and wills

(1) Subject to subsection (2) below and any other enactment, writing shall not be required for the constitution of a contract, unilateral obligation or trust.

(2) Subject to subsection (3) below, a written document complying with section 2 of this Act shall be required for—

(a) the constitution of—

(i) a contract or unilateral obligation for the creation, transfer, variation or extinction of [a real right] in land;

(ii) a gratuitous unilateral obligation except an obligation undertaken in the course of business; and

(iii) a trust whereby a person declares himself to be sole trustee of his own property or any property which he may acquire;

(b) the creation, transfer, variation or extinction of [a real right] in land otherwise than by the operation of a court decree, enactment or rule of law; and

(c) the making of any will, testamentary trust disposition and settlement or codicil.

(3) Where a contract, obligation or trust mentioned in subsection (2)(a) above is

not constituted in a written document complying with section 2 of this Act, but one of the parties to the contract, a creditor in the obligation or a beneficiary under the trust ('the first person') has acted or refrained from acting in reliance on the contract, obligation or trust with the knowledge and acquiescence of the other party to the contract, the debtor in the obligation or the truster ('the second person')—

(a)   the second person shall not be entitled to withdraw from the contract, obligation or trust; and

(b)   the contract, obligation or trust shall not be regarded as invalid, on the ground that it is not so constituted, if the condition set out in subsection (4) below is satisfied.

(4)   The condition referred to in subsection (3) above is that the position of the first person—

(a)   as a result of acting or refraining from acting as mentioned in that subsection has been affected to a material extent; and

(b)   as a result of such a withdrawal as is mentioned in that subsection would be adversely affected to a material extent.

(5)   In relation to the constitution of any contract, obligation or trust mentioned in subsection (2)(a) above, subsections (3) and (4) above replace the rules of law known as *rei interventus* and homologation.

(6)   This section shall apply to the variation of a contract, obligation or trust as it applies to the constitution thereof but as if in subsections (3) and (4) for the references to acting or refraining from acting in reliance on the contract, obligation or trust and withdrawing therefrom there were substituted respectively references to acting or refraining from acting in reliance on the variation of the contract, obligation or trust and withdrawing from the variation.

(7)   In this section ['real right in land' means any real] right in or over land, including any right to occupy or to use land or to restrict the occupation or use of land, but does not include—

(a)   a tenancy;

(b)   a right to occupy or use land; or

(c)   a right to restrict the occupation or use of land,

if the tenancy or right is not granted for more than one year, unless the tenancy or right is for a recurring period or recurring periods and there is a gap of more than one year between the beginning of the first, and the end of the last, such period.

(8)   For the purposes of subsection (7) above 'land' does not include—

(a)   growing crops; or

(b)   a moveable building or other moveable structure.

2   Type of writing required for formal validity of certain documents

(1)   No document required by section 1(2) of this Act shall be valid in respect of the formalities of execution unless it is subscribed by the granter of it or, if there is more than one granter, by each granter, but nothing apart from such subscription shall be required for the document to be valid as aforesaid.

(2)   A contract mentioned in section 1(2)(a)(i) of this Act may be regarded as constituted or varied (as the case may be) if the offer is contained in one or more documents and the acceptance is contained in another document or other documents, and each document is subscribed by the granter or granters thereof.

(3)   Nothing in this section shall prevent a document which has not been subscribed by the granter or granters of it from being used as evidence in relation to any right or obligation to which the document relates.

(4)   This section is without prejudice to any other enactment which makes different provision in respect of the formalities of execution of a document to which this section applies.

3   Presumption as to granter's subscription or date or place of subscription

(1)   Subject to subsections (2) to (7) below, where—

(a)   a document bears to have been subscribed by a granter of it;

(b)   the document bears to have been signed by a person as a witness of that granter's subscription and the document, or the testing clause or its equivalent, bears to state the name and address of the witness; and

(c)   nothing in the document, or in the testing clause or its equivalent, indicates—

(i)   that it was not subscribed by that granter as it bears to have been so subscribed; or

(ii)   that it was not validly witnessed for any reason specified in paragraphs (a) to (e) of subsection (4) below,

the document shall be presumed to have been subscribed by that granter.

(2)   Where a testamentary document consists of more than one sheet, it shall not be presumed to have been subscribed by a granter as mentioned in subsection (1) above unless, in addition to it bearing to have been subscribed by him and otherwise complying with that subsection, it bears to have been signed by him on every sheet.

(3)   For the purposes of subsection (1)(b) above—

(a)   the name and address of a witness may be added at any time before the document is—

(i)   founded on in legal proceedings; or

(ii)   registered for preservation in the Books of Council and Session or in sheriff court books; and

(b)   the name and address of a witness need not be written by the witness himself.

(4)   Where, in any proceedings relating to a document in which a question arises as to a granter's subscription, it is established—

(a)   that a signature bearing to be the signature of the witness of that granter's subscription is not such a signature, whether by reason of forgery or otherwise;

(b)   that the person who signed the document as the witness of that granter's subscription is a person who is named in the document as a granter of it;

(c)   that the person who signed the document as the witness of that granter's subscription, at the time of signing—

(i)   did not know the granter;

(ii)   was under the age of 16 years; or

(iii)   was mentally incapable of acting as a witness;

(d)   that the person who signed the document, purporting to be the witness of that granter's subscription, did not witness such subscription;

(e)   that the person who signed the document as the witness of that granter's subscription did not sign the document after him or that the granter's subscription or, as the case may be, acknowledgement of his subscription and the person's signature as witness of that subscription were not one continuous process;

(f)   that the name or address of the witness of that granter's subscription was added after the document was founded on or registered as mentioned in subsection (3)(a) above or is erroneous in any material respect; or

(g)   in the case of a testamentary document consisting of more than one sheet, that a signature on any sheet bearing to be the signature of the granter is not such a signature, whether by reason of forgery or otherwise,

then, for the purposes of those proceedings, there shall be no presumption that the document has been subscribed by that granter.

(5)   For the purposes of subsection (4)(c)(i) above, the witness shall be regarded as having known the person whose subscription he has witnessed at the time of witnessing if he had credible information at that time of his identity.

(6)   For the purposes of subsection (4)(e) above, where—

(a)   a document is granted by more than one granter; and

(b)   a person is the witness to the subscription of more than one granter, the subscription or acknowledgement of any such granter and the signature of the person witnessing that granter's subscription shall not be regarded as not being one continuous process by reason only that, between the time of that subscription or acknowledgement and that signature, another granter has subscribed the document or acknowledged his subscription.

(7) For the purposes of the foregoing provisions of this section a person witnesses a granter's subscription of a document—

(a) if he sees the granter subscribe it; or

(b) if the granter acknowledges his subscription to that person.

(8) Where—

(a) by virtue of subsection (1) above a document to which this subsection applies is presumed to have been subscribed by a granter of it;

(b) the document, or the testing clause or its equivalent, bears to state the date or place of subscription of the document by that granter; and

(c) nothing in the document, or in the testing clause or its equivalent, indicates that that statement as to date or place is incorrect,

there shall be a presumption that the document was subscribed by that granter on the date or at the place as stated.

(9) Subsection (8) above applies to any document other than a testamentary document.

(10) Where—

(a) a testamentary document bears to have been subscribed and the document, or the testing clause or its equivalent, bears to state the date or place of subscription (whether or not it is presumed under subsections (1) to (7) above to have been subscribed by a granter of it); and

(b) nothing in the document, or in the testing clause or its equivalent, indicates that that statement as to date or place is incorrect,

there shall be a presumption that the statement as to date or place is correct.

4 Presumption as to granter's subscription or date or place of subscription when established in court proceedings

(1) Where a document bears to have been subscribed by a granter of it, but there is no presumption under section 3 of this Act that the document has been subscribed by that granter, then, if the court, on an application being made to it by any person who has an interest in the document, is satisfied that the document was subscribed by that granter, it shall—

(a) cause the document to be endorsed with a certificate to that effect; or

(b) where the document has already been registered in the Books of Council and Session or in sheriff court books, grant decree to that effect.

(2) Where a document bears to have been subscribed by a granter of it, but there is no presumption under section 3 of this Act as to the date or place of subscription, then, if the court, on an application being made to it by any person who has an interest in the document, is satisfied as to the date or place of subscription, it shall—

(a) cause the document to be endorsed with a certificate to that effect; or

(b) where the document has already been registered in the Books of Council and Session or in sheriff court books, grant decree to that effect.

(3) On an application under subsection (1) or (2) above evidence shall, unless the court otherwise directs, be given by affidavit.

(4) An application under subsection (1) or (2) above may be made either as a summary application or as incidental to and in the course of other proceedings.

(5) The effect of a certificate or decree—

(a) under subsection (1) above shall be to establish a presumption that the document has been subscribed by the granter concerned;

(b) under subsection (2) above shall be to establish a presumption that the statement in the certificate or decree as to date or place is correct.

(6)   In this section 'the court' means—
(a)   in the case of a summary application—
(i)   the sheriff in whose sheriffdom the applicant resides; or
(ii)   if the applicant does not reside in Scotland, the sheriff at Edinburgh; and
(b)   in the case of an application made in the course of other proceedings, the court before which those proceedings are pending.

5   Alterations to documents: formal validity and presumptions

(1)   An alteration made to a document required by section 1(2) of this Act—
(a)   before the document is subscribed by the granter or, if there is more than one granter, by the granter first subscribing it, shall form part of the document as so subscribed;
(b)   after the document is so subscribed shall, if the alteration has been signed by the granter or (as the case may be) by all the granters, have effect as a formally valid alteration of the document as so subscribed,
but an alteration made to such a document otherwise than as mentioned in paragraphs (a) and (b) above shall not be formally valid.
(2)   Subsection (1) above is without prejudice to—
(a)   any rule of law enabling any provision in a testamentary document to be revoked by deletion or erasure without authentication of the deletion or erasure by the testator;
(b)   the Erasures in Deeds (Scotland) Act 1836 and section 54 of the Conveyancing (Scotland) Act 1874.
(3)   The fact that an alteration to a document was made before the document was subscribed by the granter of it, or by the granter first subscribing it, may be established by all relevant evidence, whether written or oral.
(4)   Where a document bears to have been subscribed by the granter or, if there is more than one granter, by all the granters of it, then, if subsection (5) or (6) below applies, an alteration made to the document shall be presumed to have been made before the document was subscribed by the granter or, if there is more than one granter, by the granter first subscribing it, and to form part of the document as so subscribed.
(5)   This subsection applies where—
(a)   the document is presumed under section 3 of this Act to have been subscribed by the granter or granters (as the case may be);
(b)   it is stated in the document, or in the testing clause or its equivalent, that the alteration was made before the document was subscribed; and
(c)   nothing in the document, or in the testing clause or its equivalent, indicates that the alteration was made after the document was subscribed.
(6)   This subsection applies where subsection (5) above does not apply, but the court is satisfied, on an application being made to it, that the alteration was made before the document was subscribed by the granter or, if there is more than one granter, by the granter first subscribing it, and causes the document to be endorsed with a certificate to that effect or, where the document has already been registered in the Books of Council and Session or in sheriff court books, grants decree to that effect.
(7)   Subsections (3), (4) and (6) of section 4 of this Act shall apply in relation to an application under subsection (6) above as they apply in relation to an application under subsection (1) of that section.
(8)   Where an alteration is made to a document after the document has been subscribed by a granter, Schedule 1 to this Act (presumptions as to granter's signature and date and place of signing in relation to such alterations) shall have effect.

6   Registration of documents

(1)   Subject to subsection (3) below, it shall not be competent—

(a)   to record a document in the Register of Sasines; or
(b)   to register a document for execution or preservation in the Books of
Council and Session or in sheriff court books,
unless subsection (2) below applies in relation to the document.
(2)   This subsection applies where—
(a)   the document is presumed under section 3 or 4 of this Act to have been
subscribed by the granter; or
(b)   if there is more than one granter, the document is presumed under
section 3 or 4 or partly under the one section and partly under the other to have
been subscribed by at least one of the granters.
(3)   Subsection (1) above shall not apply in relation to—
(a)   the recording of a document in the Register of Sasines or the registration
of a document in the Books of Council and Session or in sheriff court books, if
such recording or registration is required or expressly permitted under any
enactment;
(b)   the recording of a court decree in the Register of Sasines;
(c)   the registration in the Books of Council and Session or in sheriff court
books of—
    (i)   a testamentary document;
    (ii)   a document which is directed by the Court of Session or (as the case
    may be) the sheriff to be so registered;
    (iii)   a document whose formal validity is governed by a law other than
    Scots law, if the Keeper of the Registers of Scotland or (as the case may be) the
    sheriff clerk is satisfied that the document is formally valid according to the
    law governing such validity;
    (iv)   a court decree granted under section 4 or 5 of this Act in relation to a
    document already registered in the Books of Council and Session or in sheriff
    court books (as the case may be); or
(d)   the registration of a court decree in a separate register maintained for
that purpose.
(4)   A document may be registered for preservation in the Books of Council and
Session or in sheriff court books without a clause of consent to registration.

7   Subscription and signing

(1)   Except where an enactment expressly provides otherwise, a document is
subscribed by a granter of it if it is signed by him at the end of the last page
(excluding any annexation, whether or not incorporated in the document as provided for in section 8 of this Act).
(2)   Subject to paragraph 2(2) of Schedule 2 to this Act, a document, or an
alteration to a document, is signed by an individual natural person as a granter or
on behalf of a granter of it if it is signed by him—
(a)   with the full name by which he is identified in the document or in any
testing clause or its equivalent; or
(b)   with his surname, preceded by at least one forename (or an initial or
abbreviation or familiar form of a forename); or
(c)   except for the purposes of section 3(1) to (7) of this Act, with a name (not
in accordance with paragraph (a) or (b) above) or description or an initial or
mark if it is established that the name, description, initial or mark—
    (i)   was his usual method of signing, or his usual method of signing
    documents or alterations of the type in question; or
    (ii)   was intended by him as his signature of the document or alteration.
(3)   Where there is more than one granter, the requirement under subsection (1)
above of signing at the end of the last page of a document shall be regarded as
complied with if at least one granter signs at the end of the last page and any
other granter signs on an additional page.
(4)   Where a person grants a document in more than one capacity, one sub-

scription of the document by him shall be sufficient to bind him in all such capacities.

(5) A document, or an alteration to a document, is signed by a witness if it is signed by him—

(a) with the full name by which he is identified in the document or in any testing clause or its equivalent; or

(b) with his surname, preceded by at least one forename (or an initial or abbreviation or familiar form of a forename),

and if the witness is witnessing the signature of more than one granter, it shall be unnecessary for him to sign the document or alteration more than once.

(6) This section is without prejudice to any rule of law relating to the subscription or signing of documents by members of the Royal Family, by peers or by the wives or the eldest sons of peers.

(7) Schedule 2 to this Act (special rules relating to subscription and signing of documents etc by partnerships, companies, [limited liability partnerships,] local authorities, other bodies corporate and Ministers) shall have effect.

8 Annexations to documents

(1) Subject to subsection (2) below and except where an enactment expressly otherwise provides, any annexation to a document shall be regarded as incorporated in the document if it is—

(a) referred to in the document; and

(b) identified on its face as being the annexation referred to in the document,

without the annexation having to be signed or subscribed.

(2) Where a document relates to land and an annexation to it describes or shows all or any part of the land to which the document relates, the annexation shall be regarded as incorporated in the document if and only if—

(a) it is referred to in the document; and

(b) it is identified on its face as being the annexation referred to in the document; and

(c) it is signed on—

(i) each page, where it is a plan, drawing, photograph or other representation; or

(ii) the last page, where it is an inventory, appendix, schedule or other writing.

(3) Any annexation referred to in subsection (2) above which bears to have been signed by a granter of the document shall be presumed to have been signed by the person who subscribed the document as that granter.

(4) Section 7(2) of this Act shall apply in relation to any annexation referred to in subsection (2) above as it applies in relation to a document as if for any reference to a document (except the reference in paragraph (a)) there were substituted a reference to an annexation.

(5) It shall be competent to sign any annexation to a document at any time before the document is—

(a) founded on in legal proceedings;

(b) registered for preservation in the Books of Council and Session or in sheriff court books;

(c) recorded in the Register of Sasines;

(d) registered in the Land Register of Scotland.

(6) Where there is more than one granter, the requirement under subsection (2)(c)(ii) above of signing on the last page shall be regarded as complied with (provided that at least one granter signs at the end of the last page) if any other granter signs on an additional page.

9 Subscription on behalf of blind granter or granter unable to write

(1) Where a granter of a document makes a declaration to a relevant person that he is blind or unable to write, the relevant person—

    (a)   having read the document to that granter; or
    (b)   if the granter makes a declaration that he does not wish him to do so,
without having read it to the granter,
shall, if authorised by the granter, be entitled to subscribe it and, if it is a
testamentary document, sign it as mentioned in section 3(2) of this Act, on the
granter's behalf.

(2)   Subscription or signing by a relevant person under subsection (1) above
shall take place in the presence of the granter.

(3)   This Act shall have effect in relation to subscription or signing by a relevant
person under subsection (1) above subject to the modifications set out in Schedule
3 to this Act.

(4)   A document subscribed by a relevant person under subsection (1) above
which confers on the relevant person or his spouse, son or daughter a benefit in
money or money's worth (whether directly or indirectly) shall be invalid to the
extent, but only to the extent, that it confers such benefit.

(5)   This section and Schedule 3 to this Act apply in relation to the signing of—
    (a)   an annexation to a document as mentioned in section 8(2) of this Act;
    (b)   an alteration made to a document or to any such annexation to a document,
as they apply in relation to the subscription of a document; and for that purpose,
any reference to reading a document includes a reference to describing a plan,
drawing, photograph or other representation in such an annexation or in an
alteration to such an annexation.

(6)   In this Act 'relevant person' means a solicitor who has in force a practising
certificate as defined in section 4(c) of the Solicitors (Scotland) Act 1980, an advocate, a justice of the peace or a sheriff clerk and, in relation to the execution of
documents outwith Scotland, includes a notary public or any other person with
official authority under the law of the place of execution to execute documents on
behalf of persons who are blind or unable to write.

(7)   Nothing in this section shall prevent the granter of a document who is
blind from subscribing or signing the document as mentioned in section 7 of this
Act.

10   Forms of testing clause

(1)   Without prejudice to the effectiveness of any other means of providing
information relating to the execution of a document, this information may be provided in such form of testing clause as may be prescribed in regulations made by
the Secretary of State.

(2)   Regulations under subsection (1) above shall be made by statutory instrument which shall be subject to annulment in pursuance of a resolution of either
House of Parliament and may prescribe different forms for different cases or
classes of case.

11   Abolition of proof by writ or oath, reference to oath and other common law rules

(1)   Any rule of law and any enactment whereby the proof of any matter is
restricted to proof by writ or by reference to oath shall cease to have effect.

(2)   The procedure of proving any matter in any civil proceedings by reference
to oath is hereby abolished.

(3)   The following rules of law shall cease to have effect—
    (a)   any rule whereby certain contracts and obligations and any variations of
    those contracts and obligations, and assignations of incorporeal moveables, are
    required to be in writing; and
        (b)   any rule which confers any privilege—
            (i)   on a document which is holograph or adopted as holograph; or
            (ii)   on a writ *in re mercatoria*.

(4)   Subsections (1) and (2) above shall not apply in relation to proceedings
commenced before the commencement of this Act.

12 Interpretation

(1) In this Act, except where the context otherwise requires—

'alteration' includes interlineation, marginal addition, deletion, substitution, erasure or anything written on erasure;

'annexation' includes any inventory, appendix, schedule, other writing, plan, drawing, photograph or other representation annexed to a document;

'authorised' means expressly or impliedly authorised and any reference to a person authorised to sign includes a reference to a person authorised to sign generally or in relation to a particular document;

'company' has the same meaning as in section 735(1) of the Companies Act 1985;

'decree' includes a judgment or order, or an official certified copy, abbreviate or extract of a decree;

'director' includes any person occupying the position of director, by whatever name he is called;

'document' includes any annexation which is incorporated in it under section 8 of this Act and any reference, however expressed, to the signing of a document includes a reference to the signing of an annexation;

'enactment' includes an enactment contained in a statutory instrument [and an enactment comprised in, or in an instrument made under, an Act of the Scottish Parliament];

'governing board', in relation to a body corporate to which paragraph 5 of Schedule 2 to this Act applies, means any governing body, however described;

'local authority' means a local authority within the meaning of section 235(1) of the Local Government (Scotland) Act 1973 and a council constituted under section 2 of the Local Government etc. (Scotland) Act 1994;

'Minister' has the same meaning as 'Minister of the Crown' has in section 8 of the Ministers of the Crown Act 1975 [and also includes a Member of the Scottish Executive];

'office-holder' does not include a Minister but, subject to that, means—

(a) the holder of an office created or continued in existence by a public general Act of Parliament;

(b) the holder of an office the remuneration in respect of which is paid out of money provided by Parliament [or out of the Scottish Consolidated Fund];

(c) the registrar of companies within the meaning of the Companies Act 1985;

'officer'—

(a) in relation to a Minister, means any person in the civil service of the Crown who is serving in his Department [or as the case may be, as a member of the staff of the Scottish Ministers or the Lord Advocate];

(b) in relation to an office-holder, means any member of his staff, or any person in the civil service of the Crown who has been assigned or appointed to assist him in the exercise of his functions;

'proper officer', in relation to a local authority, has the same meaning as in section 235(3) of the Local Government (Scotland) Act 1973; and

'secretary' means, if there are two or more joint secretaries, any one of them.

(2) Any reference in this Act to subscription or signing by a granter of a document or an alteration made to a document, in a case where a person is subscribing or signing under a power of attorney on behalf of the granter, shall be construed as a reference to subscription or signing by that person of the document or alteration.

13 Application of Act to Crown

(1) Nothing in this Act shall—

(a) prevent Her Majesty from authenticating—

(i) a document by superscription; or

(ii) a document relating to her private estates situated or arising in Scotland in accordance with section 6 of the Crown Private Estates Act 1862;

(b)   prevent authentication under the Writs Act 1672 of a document passing the seal appointed by the Treaty of Union to be kept and used in Scotland in place of the Great Seal of Scotland formerly in use; or

(c)   prevent any document mentioned in paragraph (a) or (b) above authenticated as aforesaid from being recorded in the Register of Sasines or registered for execution or preservation in the Books of Council and Session or in sheriff court books.

(2)   [. . .]

(3)   Subject to subsections (1) and (2) above, this Act binds the Crown.

14   Minor and consequential amendments, repeals, transitional provisions and savings

(1)   The enactments mentioned in Schedule 4 to this Act shall have effect subject to the minor and consequential amendments specified in that Schedule.

(2)   The enactments mentioned in Schedule 5 to this Act are hereby repealed to the extent specified in the third column of that Schedule.

(3)   Subject to subsection (4) below and without prejudice to subsection (5) below and section 11(4) of this Act, nothing in this Act shall—

(a)   apply to any document executed or anything done before the commencement of this Act; or

(b)   affect the operation, in relation to any document executed before such commencement, of any procedure for establishing the authenticity of such a document.

(4)   In the repeal of the Blank Bonds and Trusts Act 1696 (provided for in Schedule 5 to this Act), the repeal of the words from 'And farder' to the end—

(a)   shall have effect in relation to a deed of trust, whether executed before or after the commencement of this Act; but

(b)   notwithstanding paragraph (a) above, shall not have effect in relation to proceedings commenced before the commencement of this Act in which a question arises as to the deed of trust.

(5)   The repeal of certain provisions of the Lyon King of Arms Act 1672 (provided for in Schedule 5 to this Act) shall not affect any right of a person to add a territorial designation to his signature or the jurisdiction of the Lord Lyon King of Arms in relation to any such designation.

(6)   For the purposes of this Act, if it cannot be ascertained whether a document was executed before or after the commencement of this Act, there shall be a presumption that it was executed after such commencement.

15   Short title, commencement and extent

(1)   This Act may be cited as the Requirements of Writing (Scotland) Act 1995.

(2)   This Act shall come into force at the end of the period of three months beginning with the date on which it is passed.

(3)   This Act extends to Scotland only.

SCHEDULES

Section 5(8)   SCHEDULE 1
ALTERATIONS MADE TO A DOCUMENT AFTER IT HAS BEEN SUBSCRIBED

Presumption as to granter's signature or date or place of signing

1.—(1)   Subject to sub-paragraphs (2) to (7) below, where—

(a)   an alteration to a document bears to have been signed by a granter of the document;

(b)   the alteration bears to have been signed by a person as a witness of that granter's signature and the alteration, or the testing clause or its equivalent, bears to state the name and address of the witness; and

(c)   nothing in the document or alteration, or in the testing clause or its equivalent, indicates—

(i)   that the alteration was not signed by that granter as it bears to have been so signed; or

(ii)   that it was not validly witnessed for any reason specified in paragraphs (a) to (e) of sub-paragraph (4) below,

the alteration shall be presumed to have been signed by that granter.

(2)   Where an alteration to a testamentary document consists of more than one sheet, the alteration shall not be presumed to have been signed by a granter as mentioned in sub-paragraph (1) above unless, in addition to it bearing to have been signed by him on the last sheet and otherwise complying with that sub-paragraph, it bears to have been signed by him on every other sheet.

(3)   For the purposes of sub-paragraph (1)(b) above—

(a)   the name and address of a witness may be added at any time before the alteration is—

(i)   founded on in legal proceedings; or

(ii)   registered for preservation in the Books of Council and Session or in sheriff court books; and

(b)   the name and address of a witness need not be written by the witness himself.

(4)   Where, in any proceedings relating to an alteration to a document in which a question arises as to a granter's signature, it is established—

(a)   that a signature bearing to be the signature of the witness of that granter's signature is not such a signature, whether by reason of forgery or otherwise;

(b)   that the person who signed the alteration as the witness of that granter's signature is a person who is named in the document as a granter of the document;

(c)   that the person who signed the alteration as the witness of that granter's signature, at the time of signing—

(i)   did not know the granter;

(ii)   was under the age of 16 years; or

(iii)   was mentally incapable of acting as a witness;

(d)   that the person who signed the alteration, purporting to be the witness of that granter's signature, did not witness such signature;

(e)   that the person who signed the alteration as the witness of that granter's signature did not sign the alteration after him or that the signing of the alteration by the granter or, as the case may be, the granter's acknowledgement of his signature and the signing by the person as witness were not one continuous process;

(f)   that the name or address of the witness of that granter's signature was added after the alteration was founded on or registered as mentioned in sub-paragraph (3)(a) above or is erroneous in any material respect; or

(g)   in the case of an alteration to a testamentary document consisting of more than one sheet, that a signature on any sheet of the alteration bearing to be the signature of the granter is not such a signature, whether by reason of forgery or otherwise,

then, for the purposes of those proceedings, there shall be no presumption that the alteration has been signed by that granter.

(5)   For the purposes of sub-paragraph (4)(c)(i) above, the witness shall be regarded as having known the person whose signature he has witnessed at the time of witnessing if he had credible information at that time of his identity.

(6)   For the purposes of sub-paragraph (4)(e) above, where—

(a)   an alteration to a document is made by more than one granter; and

(b)   a person is the witness to the signature of more than one granter,

the signing of the alteration by any such granter or the acknowledgement of his signature and the signing by the person witnessing that granter's signature shall not be regarded as not being one continuous process by reason only that, between the time of signing or acknowledgement by that granter and of signing by that witness, another granter has signed the alteration or acknowledged his signature.

(7)   For the purposes of the foregoing provisions of this paragraph a person witnesses a granter's signature of an alteration—

(a)   if he sees the granter sign it; or

(b)   if the granter acknowledges his signature to that person.

(8)   Where—

(a)   by virtue of sub-paragraph (1) above an alteration to a document to which this sub-paragraph applies is presumed to have been signed by a granter of the document;

(b)   the alteration, or the testing clause or its equivalent, bears to state the date or place of signing of the alteration by that granter; and

(c)   nothing in the document or alteration, or in the testing clause or its equivalent, indicates that that statement as to date or place is incorrect,

there shall be a presumption that the alteration was signed by that granter on the date or at the place as stated.

(9)   Sub-paragraph (8) above applies to any document other than a testamentary document.

(10)   Where—

(a)   an alteration to a testamentary document bears to have been signed and the alteration, or the testing clause or its equivalent, bears to state the date or place of signing (whether or not it is presumed under sub-paragraphs (1) to (7) above to have been signed by a granter of the document); and

(b)   nothing in the document or alteration, or in the testing clause or its equivalent, indicates that that statement as to date or place is incorrect,

there shall be a presumption that the statement as to date or place is correct.

Presumption as to granter's signature or date or place of signing when established in court proceedings

2.—(1)   Where an alteration to a document bears to have been signed by a granter of the document, but there is no presumption under paragraph 1 above that the alteration has been signed by that granter, then, if the court, on an application being made to it by any person having an interest in the document, is satisfied that the alteration was signed by that granter, it shall—

(a)   cause the document to be endorsed with a certificate to that effect; or

(b)   where the document has already been registered in the Books of Council and Session or in sheriff court books, grant decree to that effect.

(2)   Where an alteration to a document bears to have been signed by a granter of the document, but there is no presumption under paragraph 1 above as to the date or place of signing, then, if the court, on an application being made to it by any person having an interest in the document, is satisfied as to the date or place of signing, it shall—

(a)   cause the document to be endorsed with a certificate to that effect; or

(b)   where the document has already been registered in the Books of Council and Session or in sheriff court books, grant decree to that effect.

(3)   In relation to an application under sub-paragraph (1) or (2) above evidence shall, unless the court otherwise directs, be given by affidavit.

(4)   An application under sub-paragraph (1) or (2) above may be made either as a summary application or as incidental to and in the course of other proceedings.

(5)   The effect of a certificate or decree—

(a)   under sub-paragraph (1) above shall be to establish a presumption that the alteration has been signed by the granter concerned;

(b)   under sub-paragraph (2) above shall be to establish a presumption that the statement in the certificate or decree as to date or place is correct.

(6)   In this paragraph 'the court' means—

(a)   in the case of a summary application—

(i)   the sheriff in whose sheriffdom the applicant resides; or

(ii)   if the applicant does not reside in Scotland, the sheriff at Edinburgh; and

(b)   in the case of an application made in the course of other proceedings, the court before which those proceedings are pending.

<table>
<tr><td>Section 7(7)</td><td style="text-align:center">SCHEDULE 2
SUBSCRIPTION AND SIGNING: SPECIAL CASES</td></tr>
</table>

General

1.   Any reference in this Act to subscription or signing by a granter of a document or an alteration to a document, in a case where the granter is a person to whom any of paragraphs 2 to 6 of this Schedule applies shall, unless the context otherwise requires, be construed as a reference to subscription or, as the case may be, signing of the document or alteration by a person in accordance with that paragraph.

Partnerships

2.—(1)   Except where an enactment expressly provides otherwise, where a granter of a document is a partnership, the document is signed by the partnership if it is signed on its behalf by a partner or by a person authorised to sign the document on its behalf.

(2)   A person signing on behalf of a partnership under this paragraph may use his own name or the firm name.

(3)   Sub-paragraphs (1) and (2) of this paragraph apply in relation to the signing of an alteration made to a document as they apply in relation to the signing of a document.

(4)   In this paragraph 'partnership' has the same meaning as in section 1 of the Partnership Act 1890.

Companies

3.—(1)   Except where an enactment expressly provides otherwise, where a granter of a document is a company, the document is signed by the company if it is signed on its behalf by a director, or by the secretary, of the company or by a person authorised to sign the document on its behalf.

(2)   This Act is without prejudice to—

(a)   section 283(3) of the Companies Act 1985; and

(b)   paragraph 9 of Schedule 1, paragraph 9 of Schedule 2, and paragraph 7 of Schedule 4, to the Insolvency Act 1986.

(3)   Sub-paragraphs (1) and (2) of this paragraph apply in relation to the signing of an alteration made to a document as they apply in relation to the signing of a document.

(4)   Where a granter of a document is a company, section 3 of and Schedule 1 to this Act shall have effect subject to the modifications set out in sub-paragraphs (5) and (6) below.

(5)   In section 3—

(a)   for subsection (1) there shall be substituted the following subsections—

'(1)   Subject to subsections (1A) to (7) below, where—

(a)   a document bears to have been subscribed on behalf of a company by a director, or by the secretary, of the company or by a person bearing to have been authorised to subscribe the document on its behalf;

(b)   the document bears to have been signed by a person as a witness of the subscription of the director, secretary or other person subscribing on behalf of the company and to state the name and address of the witness; and

(c)   nothing in the document, or in the testing clause or its equivalent, indicates—

(i)   that it was not subscribed on behalf of the company as it bears to have been so subscribed; or

(ii)   that it was not validly witnessed for any reason specified in paragraphs (a) to (e) of subsection (4) below,

the document shall be presumed to have been subscribed by the company.

(1A)   Where a document does not bear to have been signed by a person as a witness of the subscription of the director, secretary or other person subscribing on behalf of the company it shall be presumed to have been subscribed by the company if it bears to have been subscribed on behalf of the company by—

(a)   two directors of the company; or

(b)   a director and secretary of the company; or

(c)   two persons bearing to have been authorised to subscribe the document on its behalf.

(1B)   For the purposes of subsection (1)(b) above, the name and address of the witness may bear to be stated in the document itself or in the testing clause or its equivalent.

(1C)   A presumption under subsection (1) or (1A) above as to subscription of a document does not include a presumption—

(a)   that a person bearing to subscribe the document as a director or the secretary of the company was such director or secretary; or

(b)   that a person subscribing the document on behalf of the company bearing to have been authorised to do so was authorised to do so.';

(b)   in subsection (4) after paragraph (g) there shall be inserted the following paragraph—

'(h)   if the document does not bear to have been witnessed, but bears to have been subscribed on behalf of the company by two of the directors of the company, or by a director and secretary of the company, or by two authorised persons, that a signature bearing to be the signature of a director, secretary or authorised person is not such a signature, whether by reason of forgery or otherwise;'.

(6)   In paragraph 1 of Schedule 1—

(a)   for sub-paragraph (1) there shall be substituted the following sub-paragraphs—

'(1)   Subject to sub-paragraphs (1A) to (7) below, where—

(a)   an alteration to a document bears to have been signed on behalf of a company by a director, or by the secretary, of the company or by a person bearing to have been authorised to sign the alteration on its behalf;

(b)   the alteration bears to have been signed by a person as a witness of the signature of the director, secretary or other person signing on behalf of the company and to state the name and address of the witness; and

(c)   nothing in the document or alteration, or in the testing clause or its equivalent, indicates—

(i)   that the alteration was not signed on behalf of the company as it bears to have been so signed; or

(ii)   that the alteration was not validly witnessed for any reason specified in paragraphs (a) to (e) of sub-paragraph (4) below, the alteration shall be presumed to have been signed by the company.

(1A)   Where an alteration does not bear to have been signed by a person as a witness of the signature of the director, secretary or other person signing on behalf of the company it shall be presumed to have been signed by the company if it bears to have been signed on behalf of the company by—

(a)   two directors of the company; or

(b)   a director and secretary of the company; or

(c)   two persons bearing to have been authorised to sign the alteration on its behalf.

(1B)   For the purposes of sub-paragraph (1)(b) above, the name and address of the witness may bear to be stated in the alteration itself or in the testing clause or its equivalent.

(1C)   A presumption under sub-paragraph (1) or (1A) above as to signing of an alteration to a document does not include a presumption—

(a)   that a person bearing to sign the alteration as a director or the secretary of the company was such director or secretary; or

(b)   that a person signing the alteration on behalf of the company bearing to have been authorised to do so was authorised to do so.';

(b)   in sub-paragraph (4) after paragraph (g) there shall be inserted the following paragraph—

'(h)   if the alteration does not bear to have been witnessed, but bears to have been signed on behalf of the company by two of the directors of the company, or by a director and secretary of the company, or by two authorised persons, that a signature bearing to be the signature of a director, secretary or authorised person is not such a signature, whether by reason of forgery or otherwise;'.

[Limited liability partnerships

3A.   (1)   Except where an enactment expressly provides otherwise, where a granter of a document is a limited liability partnership, the document is signed by the limited liability partnership if it is signed on its behalf by a member of the limited liability partnership.

(2)   This Act is without prejudice to paragraph 9 of Schedule 1, paragraph 9 of Schedule 2, and paragraph 7 of Schedule 4, to the Insolvency Act 1986.

(3)   Sub-paragraphs (1) and (2) of this paragraph apply in relation to the signing of an alteration made to a document as they apply in relation to the signing of a document.

(4)   Where a granter of a document is a limited liability partnership, section 3 of and Schedule 1 to this Act shall have effect subject to the modifications set out in sub-paragraphs (5) and (6) below.

(5)   In section 3—

(a)   for subsection (1) there shall be substituted the following sub-sections—

'(1)   Subject to subsections (1A) to (7) below, where—

(a)   a document bears to have been subscribed on behalf of a limited liability partnership by a member of the limited liability partnership;

(b)   the document bears to have been signed by a person as a witness of the subscription of the member of the limited liability partnership and to state the name and address of the witness; and

(c)   nothing in the document, or in the testing clause or its equivalent, indicates—

(i)   that it was not subscribed on behalf of the limited liability partnership as it bears to have been so subscribed; or

(ii)   that it was not validly witnessed for any reason specified in paragraphs (a) to (e) of subsection (4) below,

the document shall be presumed to have been subscribed by the limited liability partnership.

(1A)   Where a document does not bear to have been signed by a person as a witness of the subscription of the member of the limited liability partnership it shall be presumed to have been subscribed by the limited liability partnership if it bears to have been subscribed on behalf of the limited liability partnership by two members of the limited liability partnership.

(1B)   A presumption under subsection (1) or (1A) above as to subscription of a document does not include a presumption that a person bearing to subscribe the document as a member of the limited liability partnership was such member.'

(b)   in subsection (4) after paragraph (g) there shall be inserted the following paragraph—

'(h)   if the document does not bear to have been witnessed, but bears to have been subscribed on behalf of the limited liability partnership by two of the members of the limited liability partnership, that a signature bearing to be the signature of a member is not such a signature, whether by reason of forgery or otherwise;'

(6)   In paragraph 1 of Schedule 1—

(a)   for sub-paragraph (1) there shall be substituted the following sub-paragraphs—

'(1)   Subject to sub-paragraphs (1A) to (7) below, where—

(a)   an alteration to a document bears to have been signed on behalf of a limited liability partnership by a member of the limited liability partnership;

(b)   the alteration bears to have been signed by a person as a witness of the signature of the member of the limited liability partnership and to state the name and address of the witness; and

(c)   nothing in the document or alteration, or in the testing clause or its equivalent, indicates—

(i)   that the alteration was not signed on behalf of the limited liability partnership as it bears to have been so signed; or

(ii)   that the alteration was not validly witnessed for any reason specified in paragraphs (a) to (e) of sub-paragraph (4) below,

the alteration shall be presumed to have been signed by the limited liability partnership.

(1A)   Where an alteration does not bear to have been signed by a person as a witness of the signature of the member of the limited liability partnership it shall be presumed to have been signed by the limited liability partnership if it bears to have been signed on behalf of the limited liability partnership by two members of the limited liability partnership.

(1B)   For the purposes of sub-paragraph (1)(b) above, the name and address of the witness may bear to be stated in the alteration itself or in the testing clause or its equivalent.

(1C)   A presumption under sub-paragraph (1) or (1A) above as to signing of an alteration to a document does not include a presumption that a person bearing to sign the alteration as a member of the limited liability partnership was such member';

(b)   in sub-paragraph (4) after paragraph (g) there shall be inserted the following—

'; or
    (h)   if the alteration does not bear to have been witnessed, but bears
to have been signed on behalf of the limited liability partnership by two
of the members of the limited liability partnership, that a signature
bearing to be the signature of a member is not such a signature, whether
by reason of forgery or otherwise;']

Local authorities

4.—(1)   Except where an enactment expressly provides otherwise, where a granter
of a document is a local authority, the document is signed by the authority if it is
signed on their behalf by the proper officer of the authority.
    (2)   For the purposes of the signing of a document under this paragraph, a
person purporting to sign on behalf of a local authority as an officer of the authority shall be presumed to be the proper officer of the authority.
    (3)   Sub-paragraphs (1) and (2) of this paragraph apply in relation to the sign-
ing of an alteration made to a document as they apply in relation to the signing of
a document.
    (4)   Where a granter of a document is a local authority, section 3 of and
Schedule 1 to this Act shall have effect subject to the modifications set out in sub-
paragraphs (5) to (8) below.
    (5)   For section 3(1) there shall be substituted the following subsections—
        '(1)   Subject to subsections (1A) to (7) below, where—
        (a)   a document bears to have been subscribed on behalf of a local
    authority by the proper officer of the authority;
        (b)   the document bears—
            (i)   to have been signed by a person as a witness of the proper
        officer's subscription and to state the name and address of the
        witness; or
            (ii)   (if the subscription is not so witnessed), to have been sealed
        with the common seal of the authority; and
        (c)   nothing in the document, or in the testing clause or its equivalent,
    indicates—
            (i)   that it was not subscribed on behalf of the authority as it
        bears to have been so subscribed; or
            (ii)   that it was not validly witnessed for any reason specified in
        paragraphs (a) to (e) of subsection (4) below or that it was not sealed as
        it bears to have been sealed or that it was not validly sealed for the
        reason specified in subsection (4)(h) below,
    the document shall be presumed to have been subscribed by the proper
    officer and by the authority.
        (1A)   For the purposes of subsection (1)(b)(i) above, the name and
    address of the witness may bear to be stated in the document itself or in the
    testing clause or its equivalent.'.
    (6)   In section 3(4) after paragraph (g) there shall be inserted the following
paragraph—
        '(h)   if the document does not bear to have been witnessed, but bears to
    have been sealed with the common seal of the authority, that it was sealed
    by a person without authority to do so or was not sealed on the date on
    which it was subscribed on behalf of the authority;'.
    (7)   For paragraph 1(1) of Schedule 1 there shall be substituted the following
sub-paragraphs—
        '(1)   Subject to sub-paragraphs (1A) to (7) below, where—
        (a)   an alteration to a document bears to have been signed on behalf of
    a local authority by the proper officer of the authority;
        (b)   the alteration bears—

(i)   to have been signed by a person as a witness of the proper officer's signature and to state the name and address of the witness; or

(ii)   (if the signature is not so witnessed), to have been sealed with the common seal of the authority; and

(c)   nothing in the document or alteration, or in the testing clause or its equivalent, indicates—

(i)   that the alteration was not signed on behalf of the authority as it bears to have been so signed; or

(ii)   that the alteration was not validly witnessed for any reason specified in paragraphs (a) to (e) of sub-paragraph (4) below or that it was not sealed as it bears to have been sealed or that it was not validly sealed for the reason specified in sub-paragraph (4)(h) below,

the alteration shall be presumed to have been signed by the proper officer and by the authority.

(1A)   For the purposes of sub-paragraph (1)(b)(i) above, the name and address of the witness may bear to be stated in the alteration itself or in the testing clause or its equivalent.'.

(8)   In paragraph 1(4) of Schedule 1 after paragraph (g) there shall be inserted the following paragraph—

'(h)   if the alteration does not bear to have been witnessed, but bears to have been sealed with the common seal of the authority, that it was sealed by a person without authority to do so or was not sealed on the date on which it was signed on behalf of the authority;'.

Other bodies corporate

5.—(1)   This paragraph applies to any body corporate other than a company or a local authority.

(2)   Except where an enactment expressly provides otherwise, where a granter of a document is a body corporate to which this paragraph applies, the document is signed by the body if it is signed on its behalf by—

(a)   a member of the body's governing board or, if there is no governing board, a member of the body;

(b)   the secretary of the body by whatever name he is called; or

(c)   a person authorised to sign the document on behalf of the body.

(3)   Sub-paragraphs (1) and (2) of this paragraph apply in relation to the signing of an alteration made to a document as they apply in relation to the signing of a document.

(4)   Where a granter of a document is a body corporate to which this paragraph applies, section 3 of and Schedule 1 to this Act shall have effect subject to the modifications set out in sub-paragraphs (5) to (8) below.

(5)   For section 3(1) there shall be substituted the following subsections—

'(1)   Subject to subsections (1A) to (7) below, where—

(a)   a document bears to have been subscribed on behalf of a body corporate to which paragraph 5 of Schedule 2 to this Act applies by—

(i)   a member of the body's governing board or, if there is no governing board, a member of the body;

(ii)   the secretary of the body; or

(iii)   a person bearing to have been authorised to subscribe the document on its behalf;

(b)   the document bears—

(i)   to have been signed by a person as a witness of the subscription of the member, secretary or other person signing on behalf of the body and to state the name and address of the witness; or

(ii)   (if the subscription is not so witnessed), to have been sealed with the common seal of the body; and

(c)   nothing in the document, or in the testing clause or its equivalent, indicates—

(i)   that it was not subscribed on behalf of the body as it bears to have been so subscribed; or

(ii)   that it was not validly witnessed for any reason specified in paragraphs (a) to (e) of subsection (4) below or that it was not sealed as it bears to have been sealed or that it was not validly sealed for the reason specified in subsection (4)(h) below,

the document shall be presumed to have been subscribed by the member, secretary or authorised person (as the case may be) and by the body.

(1A)   For the purposes of subsection (1)(b)(i) above, the name and address of the witness may bear to be stated in the document itself or in the testing clause or its equivalent.

(1B)   A presumption under subsection (1) above as to subscription of a document does not include a presumption—

(a)   that a person bearing to subscribe the document as a member of the body's governing board, a member of the body or the secretary of the body was such member or secretary; or

(b)   that a person subscribing the document on behalf of the body bearing to have been authorised to do so was authorised to do so.'.

(6)   In section 3(4) after paragraph (g) there shall be inserted the following paragraph—

'(h)   if the document does not bear to have been witnessed, but bears to have been sealed with the common seal of the body, that it was sealed by a person without authority to do so or was not sealed on the date on which it was subscribed on behalf of the body;'.

(7)   For paragraph 1(1) of Schedule 1 there shall be substituted the following sub-paragraphs—

'(1) Subject to sub-paragraphs (1A) to (7) below, where—

(a)   an alteration to a document bears to have been signed on behalf of a body corporate to which paragraph 5 of Schedule 2 to this Act applies by—

(i)   a member of the body's governing board or, if there is no governing board, a member of the body;

(ii)   the secretary of the body; or

(iii)   a person bearing to have been authorised to sign the alteration on its behalf,

(b)   the alteration bears—

(i)   to have been signed by a person as a witness of the signature of the member, secretary or other person signing on behalf of the body and to state the name and address of the witness; or

(ii)   (if the signature is not so witnessed), to have been sealed with the common seal of the body; and

(c)   nothing in the document or alteration, or in the testing clause or its equivalent, indicates—

(i)   that the alteration was not signed on behalf of the body as it bears to have been so signed; or

(ii)   that the alteration was not validly witnessed for any reason specified in paragraphs (a) to (e) of sub-paragraph (4) below or that it was not sealed as it bears to have been sealed or that it was not validly sealed for the reason specified in sub-paragraph (4)(h) below,

the alteration shall be presumed to have been signed by the member, secretary or authorised person (as the case may be) and by the body.

(1A)   For the purposes of sub-paragraph (1)(b)(i) above, the name and address of the witness may bear to be stated in the alteration itself or in the testing clause or its equivalent.

(1B)   A presumption under sub-paragraph (1) above as to signing of an alteration to a document does not include a presumption—

(a)   that a person bearing to sign the alteration as a member of the body's governing board, a member of the body or the secretary of the body was such member or secretary; or

(b)   that a person signing the alteration on behalf of the body bearing to have been authorised to do so was authorised to do so.'.

(8)   In paragraph 1(4) of Schedule 1 after paragraph (g) there shall be inserted the following paragraph—

'(h)   if the alteration does not bear to have been witnessed, but bears to have been sealed with the common seal of the body, that it was sealed by a person without authority to do so or was not sealed on the date on which it was signed on behalf of the body;'.

Ministers of the Crown and office-holders

6.—(1)   Except where an enactment expressly provides otherwise, where a granter of a document is a Minister or an office-holder, the document is signed by the Minister or office-holder if it is signed—

(a)   by him personally; or

(b)   in a case where by virtue of any enactment or rule of law a document by a Minister may be signed by an officer of his or by any other Minister, by that officer or by that other Minister as the case may be; or

(c)   in a case where by virtue of any enactment or rule of law a document by an office-holder may be signed by an officer of his, by that officer; or

(d)   by any other person authorised to sign the document on his behalf.

(2)   For the purposes of the signing of a document under this paragraph, a person purporting to sign—

(a)   as an officer as mentioned in sub-paragraph (1)(b) or (1)(c) above;

(b)   as another Minister as mentioned in sub-paragraph (1)(b) above;

(c)   as a person authorised as mentioned in sub-paragraph (1)(d) above,

shall be presumed to be the officer, other Minister or authorised person, as the case may be.

(3)   Sub-paragraphs (1) and (2) of this paragraph are without prejudice to section 3 of and Schedule 1 to the Ministers of the Crown Act 1975.

(4)   Sub-paragraphs (1) to (3) of this paragraph apply in relation to the signing of an alteration made to a document as they apply in relation to the signing of a document.

(5)   Where a granter of a document is a Minister or office-holder, section 3 of and Schedule 1 to this Act shall have effect subject to the modifications set out in sub-paragraphs (6) and (7) below.

(6)   For section 3(1) there shall be substituted the following subsections—

'(1)   Subject to subsections (1A) to (7) below, where—

(a)   a document bears to have been subscribed—

(i)   by a Minister or, in a case where by virtue of any enactment or rule of law a document by a Minister may be signed by an officer of his or by any other Minister, by that officer or by that other Minister; or

(ii)   by an office-holder or, in a case where by virtue of any enactment or rule of law a document by an office-holder may be signed by an officer of his, by that officer; or

(iii)   by any other person bearing to have been authorised to subscribe the document on behalf of the Minister or office-holder;

(b)   the document bears to have been signed by a person as a witness of the subscription mentioned in paragraph (a) above and to state the name and address of the witness; and

(c)   nothing in the document, or in the testing clause or its equivalent, indicates—

(i)   that it was not subscribed as it bears to have been subscribed; or

(ii)   that it was not validly witnessed for any reason specified in paragraphs (a) to (e) of subsection (4) below,

the document shall be presumed to have been subscribed by the officer, other Minister or authorised person and by the Minister or office-holder, as the case may be.

(1A)   For the purposes of subsection (1)(b) above, the name and address of the witness may bear to be stated in the document itself or in the testing clause or its equivalent.'.

(7)   For paragraph 1(1) of Schedule 1 there shall be substituted the following sub-paragraphs—

'(1)   Subject to sub-paragraphs (1A) to (7) below, where—

(a)   an alteration to a document bears to have been signed by—

(i)   a Minister or, in a case where by virtue of any enactment or rule of law a document by a Minister may be signed by an officer of his or by any other Minister, by that officer or by that other Minister; or

(ii)   an office-holder or, in a case where by virtue of any enactment or rule of law a document by an office-holder may be signed by an officer of his, by that officer; or

(iii)   any other person bearing to have been authorised to sign the alteration on behalf of the Minister or office-holder;

(b)   the alteration bears to have been signed by a person as a witness of the signature mentioned in paragraph (a) above and to state the name and address of the witness; and

(c)   nothing in the document or alteration, or in the testing clause or its equivalent, indicates—

(i)   that the alteration was not signed as it bears to have been signed; or

(ii)   that the alteration was not validly witnessed for any reason specified in paragraphs (a) to (e) of sub-paragraph (4) below,

the alteration shall be presumed to have been signed by the officer, other Minister or authorised person and by the Minister or office-holder, as the case may be.

(1A)   For the purposes of sub-paragraph (1)(b) above, the name and address of the witness may bear to be stated in the alteration itself or in the testing clause or its equivalent.'.

SCHEDULE 3   Section 9(3)
MODIFICATIONS OF THIS ACT IN RELATION TO SUBSCRIPTION OR
SIGNING BY RELEVANT PERSON UNDER SECTION 9

1.   For any reference to the subscription or signing of a document by a granter there shall be substituted a reference to such subscription or signing by a relevant person under section 9(1).

2.   For section 3(1) there shall be substituted the following subsection—

'(1)   Subject to subsections (2) to (6) below, where—

(a)   a document bears to have been subscribed by a relevant person with the authority of a granter of it;

(b)   the document, or the testing clause or its equivalent, states that the document was read to that granter by the relevant person before such subscription or states that it was not so read because the granter made a declaration that he did not wish him to do so;

(c)   the document bears to have been signed by a person as a witness of the relevant person's subscription and the document, or the testing clause or its equivalent, bears to state the name and address of the witness; and

(d)   nothing in the document, or in the testing clause or its equivalent, indicates—

(i)   that it was not subscribed by the relevant person as it bears to have been so subscribed;

(ii)   that the statement mentioned in paragraph (b) above is incorrect; or

(iii)   that it was not validly witnessed for any reason specified in paragraphs (a) to (e) of subsection (4) below (as modified by paragraph 4 of Schedule 3 to this Act),

the document shall be presumed to have been subscribed by the relevant person and the statement so mentioned shall be presumed to be correct.'.

3.   In section 3(3) for the words 'subsection (1)(b)' there shall be substituted the words 'subsection (1)(c)'.

4.   For section 3(4) there shall be substituted the following subsection—

'(4)   Where, in any proceedings relating to a document in which a question arises as to a relevant person's subscription on behalf of a granter under section 9(1) of this Act, it is established—

(a)   that a signature bearing to be the signature of the witness of the relevant person's subscription is not such a signature, whether by reason of forgery or otherwise;

(b)   that the person who signed the document as the witness of the relevant person's subscription is a person who is named in the document as a granter of it;

(c)   that the person who signed the document as the witness of the relevant person's subscription, at the time of signing—

(i)   did not know the granter on whose behalf the relevant person had so subscribed;

(ii)   was under the age of 16 years; or

(iii)   was mentally incapable of acting as a witness;

(d)   that the person who signed the document, purporting to be the witness of the relevant person's subscription, did not see him subscribe it;

(dd)   that the person who signed the document as the witness of the relevant person's subscription did not witness the granting of authority by the granter concerned to the relevant person to subscribe the document on his behalf or did not witness the reading of the document to the granter by the relevant person or the declaration that the granter did not wish him to do so;

(e)   that the person who signed the document as the witness of the relevant person's subscription did not sign the document after him or that such subscription and signature were not one continuous process;

(f)   that the name or address of such a witness was added after the document was founded on or registered as mentioned in subsection (3)(a) above or is erroneous in any material respect; or

(g)   in the case of a testamentary document consisting of more than one sheet, that a signature on any sheet bearing to be the signature of the relevant person is not such a signature, whether by reason of forgery or otherwise,

then, for the purposes of those proceedings, there shall be no presumption that the document has been subscribed by the relevant person on behalf of the granter concerned.'.

5. In section 3(6) the words 'or acknowledgement' in both places where they occur shall be omitted.

6. Section 3(7) shall be omitted.

7. For section 4(1) there shall be substituted the following subsection—
    '(1) Where—
        (a) a document bears to have been subscribed by a relevant person under section 9(1) of this Act on behalf of a granter of it; but
        (b) there is no presumption under section 3 of this Act (as modified by paragraph 2 of Schedule 3 to this Act) that the document has been subscribed by that person or that the procedure referred to section 3(1)(b) of this Act as so modified was followed,
then, if the court, on an application being made to it by any person who has an interest in the document, is satisfied that the document was so subscribed by the relevant person with the authority of the granter and that the relevant person read the document to the granter before subscription or did not so read it because the granter declared that he did not wish him to do so, it shall—
        (i) cause the document to be endorsed with a certificate to that effect; or
        (ii) where the document has already been registered in the Books of Council and Session or in sheriff court books, grant decree to that effect.'.

8. At the end of section 4(5)(a) there shall be added the following words—
'and that the procedure referred to in section 3(1)(b) of this Act as modified by paragraph 2 of Schedule 3 to this Act was followed.'.

9. For paragraph 1(1) of Schedule 1 there shall be substituted the following sub-paragraph—
    '(1) Subject to sub-paragraphs (2) to (6) below, where—
        (a) an alteration to a document bears to have been signed by a relevant person with the authority of a granter of the document;
        (b) the document or alteration, or the testing clause or its equivalent, states that the alteration was read to that granter by the relevant person before such signature or states that the alteration was not so read because the granter made a declaration that he did not wish him to do so;
        (c) the alteration bears to have been signed by a person as a witness of the relevant person's signature and the alteration, or the testing clause or its equivalent, bears to state the name and address of the witness; and
        (d) nothing in the document or alteration, or in the testing clause or its equivalent, indicates—
           (i) that the alteration was not signed by the relevant person as it bears to have been so signed;
           (ii) that the statement mentioned in paragraph (b) above is incorrect; or
           (iii) that the alteration was not validly witnessed for any reason specified in paragraphs (a) to (e) of sub-paragraph (4) below (as modified by paragraph 11 of Schedule 3 to this Act),
the alteration shall be presumed to have been signed by the relevant person and the statement so mentioned shall be presumed to be correct.'.

10. In paragraph 1(3) of Schedule 1 for the words 'sub-paragraph (1)(b)' there shall be substituted the words 'sub-paragraph (1)(c)'.

11. For paragraph 1(4) of Schedule 1 there shall be substituted the following sub-paragraph—

'(4) Where, in any proceedings relating to an alteration to a document in which a question arises as to a relevant person's signature on behalf of a granter under section 9(1) of this Act, it is established—

(a) that a signature bearing to be the signature of the witness of the relevant person's signature is not such a signature, whether by reason of forgery or otherwise;

(b) that the person who signed the alteration as the witness of the relevant person's signature is a person who is named in the document as a granter of it;

(c) that the person who signed the alteration as the witness of the relevant person's signature, at the time of signing—

(i) did not know the granter on whose behalf the relevant person had so signed;

(ii) was under the age of 16 years; or

(iii) was mentally incapable of acting as a witness;

(d) that the person who signed the alteration, purporting to be the witness of the relevant person's signature, did not see him sign it;

(dd) that the person who signed the alteration as the witness of the relevant person's signature did not witness the granting of authority by the granter concerned to the relevant person to sign the alteration on his behalf or did not witness the reading of the alteration to the granter by the relevant person or the declaration that the granter did not wish him to do so;

(e) that the person who signed the alteration as the witness of the relevant person's signature did not sign the alteration after him or that the signing of the alteration by the granter and the witness was not one continuous process;

(f) that the name or address of such a witness was added after the alteration was founded on or registered as mentioned in sub-paragraph (3)(a) above or is erroneous in any material respect; or

(g) in the case of an alteration to a testamentary document consisting of more than one sheet, that a signature on any sheet of the alteration bearing to be the signature of the relevant person is not such a signature, whether by reason of forgery or otherwise,

then, for the purposes of those proceedings, there shall be no presumption that the alteration has been signed by the relevant person on behalf of the granter concerned.'.

12. In paragraph 1(6) of Schedule 1 the words 'or the acknowledgement of his signature' and the words 'or acknowledgement' shall be omitted.

13. Paragraph 1(7) of Schedule 1 shall be omitted.

14. For paragraph 2(1) of Schedule 1 there shall be substituted the following sub-paragraph—

'(1) Where—

(a) an alteration to a document bears to have been signed by a relevant person under section 9(1) of this Act on behalf of a granter of the document; but

(b) there is no presumption under paragraph 1 of Schedule 1 to this Act (as modified by paragraph 9 of Schedule 3 to this Act) that the alteration has been signed by that person or that the procedure referred to in paragraph 1(1)(b) of Schedule 1 to this Act as so modified was followed,

then, if the court, on an application being made to it by any person who has an interest in the document, is satisfied that the alteration was so signed by the relevant person with the authority of the granter and that the relevant person read the alteration to the granter before signing or did not so read it because the granter declared that he did not wish him to do so, it shall—

(i)   cause the document to be endorsed with a certificate to that effect; or

(ii)   where the document has already been registered in the Books of Council and Session or in sheriff court books, grant decree to that effect.'.

15.   At the end of paragraph 2(5)(a) of Schedule 1 there shall be added the following words—

'and that the procedure referred to in paragraph 1(1)(b) of Schedule 1 to this Act as modified by paragraph 9 of Schedule 3 to this Act was followed.'.

CONTRACT (SCOTLAND) ACT 1997
(1997, c 34)

1   Extrinsic evidence of additional contract term etc

(1)   Where a document appears (or two or more documents appear) to comprise all the express terms of a contract or unilateral voluntary obligation, it shall be presumed, unless the contrary is proved, that the document does (or the documents do) comprise all the express terms of the contract or unilateral voluntary obligation.

(2)   Extrinsic oral or documentary evidence shall be admissible to prove, for the purposes of subsection (1) above, that the contract or unilateral voluntary obligation includes additional express terms (whether or not written terms).

(3)   Notwithstanding the foregoing provisions of this section, where one of the terms in the document (or in the documents) is to the effect that the document does (or the documents do) comprise all the express terms of the contract or unilateral voluntary obligation, that term shall be conclusive in the matter.

(4)   This section is without prejudice to any enactment which makes provision as respects the constitution, or formalities of execution, of a contract or unilateral voluntary obligation.

2   Supersession

(1)   Where a deed is executed in implement, or purportedly in implement, of a contract, an unimplemented, or otherwise unfulfilled, term of the contract shall not be taken to be superseded by virtue only of that execution or of the delivery and acceptance of the deed.

(2)   Subsection (1) above is without prejudice to any agreement which the parties to a contract may reach (whether or not an agreement incorporated into the contract) as to supersession of the contract.

3   Damages for breach of contract of sale

Any rule of law which precludes the buyer in a contract of sale of property from obtaining damages for breach of that contract by the seller unless the buyer rejects the property and rescinds the contract shall cease to have effect.

4   Short title, extent etc

(1)   This Act may be cited as the Contract (Scotland) Act 1997.

(2)   This Act shall come into force at the end of that period of three months which begins with the day on which the Act is passed.

(3)   Section 1 of this Act applies only for the purposes of proceedings commenced on or after, and sections 2 and 3 only as respects contracts entered into on or after, the date on which this Act comes into force.

(4)   This Act extends to Scotland only.

ABOLITION OF FEUDAL TENURE ETC (SCOTLAND) ACT 2000
(2000, asp 5)

PART 1
ABOLITION OF FEUDAL TENURE

1　Abolition on appointed day
The feudal system of land tenure, that is to say the entire system whereby land is held by a vassal on perpetual tenure from a superior is, on the appointed day, abolished.

2　Consequences of abolition
(1)　An estate of dominium utile of land shall, on the appointed day, cease to exist as a feudal estate but shall forthwith become the ownership of the land and, in so far as is consistent with the provisions of this Act, the land shall be subject to the same subordinate real rights and other encumbrances as was the estate of dominium utile.
(2)　Every other feudal estate in land shall, on that day, cease to exist.
(3)　It shall, on that day, cease to be possible to create a feudal estate in land.

3　[*Amends the Land Registration (Scotland) Act 1979.*]

PART 2
LAND TRANSFERS ETC ON AND AFTER APPOINTED DAY

4　Ownership of land
(1)　Ownership of land shall pass—
(a)　in a case where a transfer is registrable under section 2 of the Land Registration (Scotland) Act 1979 (c 33), on registration in the Land Register of Scotland;
(b)　in any other case, on recording of a conveyance of the land in the Register of Sasines.
(2)　This section is without prejudice to any other enactment, or rule of law, by or under which ownership of land may pass.
(3)　In subsection (1) above—
(a)　'conveyance' includes—
(i)　conveyance by, or under, any enactment, rule of law or decree; and
(ii)　a notice of title deducing title through a conveyance; and
(b)　'registrable' and 'registration' have the meanings respectively assigned to those expressions by section 1(3) of the Land Registration (Scotland) Act 1979 (c 33).

5　Form of application for recording deed in Register of Sasines
(1)　Any application for the recording of a deed in the Register of Sasines shall be made by, or on behalf of, the person in whose favour the deed is granted; and it shall not be necessary to endorse on any deed a warrant of registration.
(2)　The Scottish Ministers may, after consultation with the Lord President of the Court of Session, make rules—
(a)　prescribing the form to be used for the purposes of subsection (1) above; and
(b)　regulating the procedure relating to applications for recording.

6　Deduction of title for unregistered land etc
In respect of any land—
(a)　a real right in which has never been registered in the Land Register of Scotland; and
(b)　title to which has never been constituted by the recording of a deed in the Register of Sasines,
title may be deduced from any person having ownership of the land.

PART 3
FEUDUTIES

Extinction of feuduties

7 Extinction on appointed day

Without prejudice to section 13 of this Act, any feuduty which has not been extinguished before the appointed day is extinguished on that day; and accordingly no payment shall be exigible, in respect of feuduty, for that day or for any period after that day.

8 Requiring compensatory payment

(1) Where a feuduty is extinguished by section 7 of this Act, the person who was the superior in relation to the feu (that person being in the following provisions of this Part of this Act referred to as the 'former superior') may, within two years after the appointed day, duly serve on the person who was the vassal in relation to the feu (that person being in those provisions referred to as the 'former vassal') notice requiring that a payment specified in the notice (being a payment calculated in accordance with section 9 of this Act) be made to him by the former vassal; and any such payment is referred to in this Act as a 'compensatory payment'.

(2) In its application to a feuduty which was, at extinction, a cumulo feuduty, subsection (1) above shall be construed as relating to separate notice being duly served on each former vassal from whom payment is sought; and in that application, notice under that subsection shall be in (or as nearly as may be in) the form, with its Appendix, contained in schedule 1 to this Act.

(3) Except in the application mentioned in subsection (2) above, notice under subsection (1) above shall be in (or as nearly as may be in) the form contained in schedule 2 to this Act.

(4) To any notice served under subsection (1) above shall be attached a copy of the explanatory note which immediately follows, as the case may be—

(a) the Appendix to the form in schedule 1; or

(b) the form in schedule 2,

to this Act.

(5) Subject to section 10 of this Act, if subsections (1) to (4) above are complied with, then within 56 days after due service on him a former vassal shall make the compensatory payment.

(6) The reference in subsection (1) above to a notice being duly served shall be construed in accordance with section 11 of this Act.

9 Calculation of amount of compensatory payment

(1) In calculating the compensatory payment in respect of which notice may be served under section 8(1) of this Act, there shall first be determined the sum of money which would, if invested in two and a half per cent Consolidated Stock at the middle market price at the close of business last preceding the appointed day, produce an annual sum equal to the feuduty.

(2) Unless the feuduty was, at extinction, a cumulo feuduty the sum so determined shall be the compensatory payment.

(3) If the feuduty was, at extinction, a cumulo feuduty the former superior shall, after determining that sum, allocate it among the former vassals in such proportions as are reasonable in all the circumstances; and an amount which is so allocated to a former vassal shall be the compensatory payment for that former vassal.

(4) If the feuduty was, at extinction, a cumulo feuduty wholly or partly apportioned among the former vassals, then for the purposes of subsection (3) above the proportions of an allocation shall be presumed reasonable in so far as they accord with that apportionment.

10   Making compensatory payment by instalments

(1)   Where notice under subsection (1) of section 8 of this Act requires from a former vassal a compensatory payment of not less than £50, the former superior shall serve with it a filled out document (in this section referred to as an 'instalment document'), in (or as nearly as may be in) the form contained in schedule 3 to this Act, for signature and dating by the former vassal (there being appended to the document so sent a copy of the explanatory note which immediately follows that form in the schedule); and if the former superior does not do so then no requirement to make the compensatory payment shall arise under subsection (5) of that section by virtue of that notice.

(2)   Subject to subsection (3) below, a former vassal on whom an instalment document is served shall obtain the option of making the compensatory payment by instalments if (and only if)—

(a)   he signs, dates and returns the document within the period which (but for this section) is allowed for making that payment by section 8(5) of this Act; and

(b)   when so returning the document, he pays to the former superior an amount equivalent to one tenth of the compensatory payment (being an amount thus payable in addition to the compensatory payment and irrespective of how or when the compensatory payment is subsequently made).

(3)   If on or after the date on which an instalment document is served on a former vassal he ceases by virtue of a sale, or transfer for valuable consideration, to have right to the land in respect of which the feuduty was payable or any part of that land (that land or any part of it being in this section referred to as 'the land') then—

(a)   where he has obtained the option mentioned in subsection (2) above, he shall lose that option; and

(b)   where he has not obtained that option, he shall lose the right to obtain it.

(4)   Where the option of making the compensatory payment by instalments is obtained, those instalments shall be equal instalments payable where—

(a)   the compensatory payment is £500 or less, on each of the five;

(b)   it is more than £500 but not more than £1,000, on each of the ten;

(c)   it is more than £1,000 but not more than £1,500, on each of the fifteen; and

(d)   it is more than £1,500, on each of the twenty,

term days of Whitsunday or Martinmas which then next follow; except that—

(i)   in a case where any such instalment remains unpaid for forty-two days after falling due, the outstanding balance of the entire compensatory payment shall immediately fall due;

(ii)   in a case where, by virtue of subsection (3)(a) above, the option is lost, that outstanding balance shall fall due on the seventh day after the day on which the former vassal ceases to have right to the land; and

(iii)   in any other case, the former vassal may pay that outstanding balance at any time.

(5)   In a case where, by virtue of subsection (3)(b) above, the right to obtain the option of making the compensatory payment by instalments is lost, section 8(5) of this Act shall apply accordingly.

11   Service under section 8(1)

(1)   Due service under section 8(11) of this Act is effected by delivering the documents in question to the former vassal or by sending them by registered post, or the recorded delivery service, addressed to him at an appropriate place.

(2)   An acknowledgement, signed by the former vassal, which conforms to Form A of schedule 4 to this Act, or as the case may be a certificate which conforms to Form B of that schedule and is accompanied by the postal receipt, shall be sufficient evidence of such due service; and if the packet containing the docu-

ments in question is, under subsection (1) above, sent by post but is returned to the former superior with an intimation that it could not be delivered, the packet may be delivered or sent by post, with that intimation, to the Extractor of the Court of Session, the delivering or sending to the Extractor being taken to be equivalent to the service of those documents on the former vassal.

(3) For the purposes of subsection (2) above, an acknowledgement of receipt by the Extractor on a copy of those documents shall be sufficient evidence of their receipt by him.

(4) The date on which notice under section 8(1) of this Act is served on a former vassal is the date of delivery, or as the case may be of posting, in compliance with subsection (1) or (2) above.

(5) A reference in this section to an 'appropriate place' is, for any former vassal, to be construed as a reference to—

(a) his place of residence;

(b) his place of business; or

(c) a postal address which he ordinarily uses,

or, if none of those is known at the time of delivery or posting, as a reference to whatever place is at that time his most recently known place of residence or place of business or postal address which he ordinarily used.

12 [*Amends the Prescription and Limitation (Scotland) Act 1973.*]

Arrears

13 Arrears of feuduty etc

(1) Feuduty shall continue to be exigible for any period before the appointed day; and if (in so far as so exigible) it has not fallen due before that day, it shall fall due on that day.

(2) On the appointed day feuduty shall cease to constitute a debitum fundi as shall any amount secured, in favour of a superior, by virtue of section 5 of the Land Tenure Reform (Scotland) Act 1974 (c 38) (redemption on transfer of land).

(3) The superior's hypothec is, on the appointed day, abolished.

(4) Subsections (2) and (3) above are without prejudice to any—

(a) action—

(i) founded on a debitum fundi or superior's hypothec; and

(ii) commenced before the appointed day; or

(b) right or preference—

(i) so founded; and

(ii) claimed in a sequestration, or in some other process in which there is ranking, commenced before that day.

Disclosure

14 Duty of collecting third party to disclose information

For the purposes of section 8(1) of this Act, a superior (or, on or after the appointed day, a former superior) who receives, or has at any time received, from a third party an amount collected in respect of feuduty from and remitted to the superior (or former superior) on behalf of a vassal (or, on or after the appointed day, a former vassal) may require the third party to disclose the identity and address of the vassal (or former vassal) and, in the case of remission as a part of a feuduty, the amount so collected from the vassal (or former vassal); and the third party shall, in so far as it is practicable for him to do so, forthwith comply with that requirement.

15 Duty to disclose identity etc of former vassal

Where the former superior purports duly to serve notice under section 8(1) of this Act but the person on whom it is served, being a person who had right to the feu before the appointed day, is not the former vassal because, immediately before the appointed day, some other person and not he had right to the feu, he shall forthwith disclose to the former superior—

  (a)   the identity and address of that other person; or

  (b)   (if he cannot do that) such other information as he has which might enable the former superior to discover that identity and address.

Interpretation

16   Interpretation of Part 3

(1)   In this Part of this Act, unless the context otherwise requires—

'compensatory payment' shall be construed in accordance with section 8(1) of this Act;

'feuduty' includes blench duty;

'superior', in relation to a feu, means the person who, immediately before the appointed day, has right to the immediate superiority, whether or not he has completed title (and if more than one person comes within that description, then the person who has most recently acquired such right); and 'former superior' shall be construed in accordance with section 8(1) of this Act; and

'vassal', in relation to a feu, means the person who, immediately before the appointed day, has right to the feu, whether or not he has completed title (and if more than one person comes within that description, then the person who has most recently acquired such right); and 'former vassal' shall be construed in accordance with section 8(1) of this Act.

(2)   Where a feu comprises parts each held by a separate vassal, being parts upon which feuduty has not been allocated, the whole of any feuduty exigible in respect of the parts so held is in this Part of this Act referred to as a 'cumulo feuduty'; and any reference in this Part of this Act to a feu is to be construed, in relation to the parts so held, as a reference to those parts collectively.

(3)   Any reference in this Part of this Act to a feu is to be construed as including a reference to any part of a feu if it is a part upon which feuduty has been allocated.

(4)   Where, immediately before the appointed day a feu, or any part of a feu, is held by two or more vassals as common property—

  (a)   they shall be severally liable to make any compensatory payment (but as between, or as the case may be among, themselves they shall be liable in the proportions in which they hold the feu); and

  (b)   subject to section 11 of this Act they shall together be treated for the purposes of this Act as being a single vassal.

PART 4
REAL BURDENS

Extinction of superior's rights

17   Extinction of superior's right

(1)   Subject to sections 18 [to 18C], 19, 20, 23, 27, [27A,] 28, [28A] and 60 of this Act [and to sections 52 to 56 (which make provision as to common schemes, facility burdens and service burdens) and 63 (which makes provision as to manager burdens) of the Title Conditions (Scotland) Act 2003 (asp 9)]—

  (a)   a real burden which, immediately before the appointed day, is enforceable by, and only by, a superior shall on that day be extinguished; and

  (b)   any other real burden shall, on and after that day, not be enforceable by a former superior [other than in that person's capacity as owner of land or as holder of a conservation burden, health care burden or economic development burden].

(2)   Subject to subsection (3) below and to the provision made by section 20 of

this Act for there to be a transitional period during which a real burden shall yet be enforceable—

(a)   on or after the appointed day, no proceedings for such enforcement shall be commenced;

(b)   any proceedings already commenced for such enforcement shall be deemed to have been abandoned on that day and may, without further process and without any requirement that full judicial expenses shall have been paid by the pursuer, be dismissed accordingly; and

(c)   any decree or interlocutor already pronounced in proceedings for such enforcement shall be deemed to have been reduced, or as the case may be re-called, on that day.

(3)   Subsection (2) above shall not affect any proceedings, decree or interlocutor in relation to—

(a)   a right of irritancy held by a superior;

[(aa)   a right of enforcement held by virtue of any of the provisions mentioned in subsection (1) above;] or

(b)   a right to recover damages or to the payment of money.

Reallotment etc

18   Reallotment of real burden by nomination of new dominant tenement

(1)   [Without prejudice to sections 18A to 18C of this Act,] where—

(a)   a feudal estate of dominium utile of land is subject to a real burden enforceable by a superior of the feu or which would be so enforceable were the person in question to complete title to the dominium directum; and

(b)   at least one of the conditions set out in subsection (7) below is met, the superior may, before the appointed day, prospectively nominate other land (being land of which he has right to the sole dominium utile or sole allodial ownership), or any part of that other land, as a dominant tenement by duly executing and registering a notice in, or as nearly as may be in, the form contained in schedule 5 to this Act.

(2)   The notice shall—

(a)   set out the title of the superior;

(b)   describe, sufficiently to enable identification by reference to the Ordnance Map, both the land the dominium utile of which is subject to the real burden (or any part of that land) and the land (or part) nominated;

(c)   specify which of the conditions set out in subsection (7) below is (or are) met;

(d)   set out the terms of the real burden; and

(e)   set out the terms of any counter-obligation to the real burden if it is a counter-obligation enforceable against the superior.

(3)   For the purposes of subsection (1) above a notice is duly registered only when registered against both tenements described in pursuance of subsection (2)(b) above.

(4)   Before submitting any notice for registration under this section, the superior shall swear or affirm before a notary public that to the best of the knowledge and belief of the superior all the information contained in the notice is true.

(5)   For the purposes of subsection (4) above, if the superior is—

(a)   an individual unable by reason of legal disability, or incapacity, to swear or affirm as mentioned in that subsection, then a legal representative of the superior may swear or affirm;

(b)   not an individual, then any person authorised to sign documents on its behalf may swear or affirm;

and any reference in that subsection to a superior shall be construed accordingly.

(6)   [Subject to subsection (6A) below,] if subsections (1) to (5) above are complied with and immediately before the appointed day the real burden is still

enforceable by the superior (or by his successor) or would be so enforceable, or
still so enforceable, were the person in question to complete title to the dominium
directum then, on that day—

(a)   the land (or part) nominated shall become a dominant tenement; and

(b)   the land the dominium utile of which was subject to the real burden (or
if part only of that land is described in pursuance of subsection (2)(b) above, that
part) shall be the servient tenement.

[(6A)   Such compliance as is mentioned in subsection (6) above shall not be
effective to preserve any right to enforce a manager burden ('manager burden'
being construed in accordance with section 63(1) of the Title Conditions (Scotland)
Act 2003 (asp 9)).]

(7)   The conditions are—

(a)   that the land which by virtue of this section would become the dominant
tenement has on it a permanent building which is in use wholly or mainly as a
place of human—

(i)   habitation; or

(ii)   resort,

and that building is, at some point, within one hundred metres (measuring
along a horizontal plane) of the land which would be the servient tenement;

(b)   that the real burden comprises—

(i)   a right [(other than any sporting rights, as defined by section 65A(9) of
this Act)] to enter, or otherwise make use of, the servient tenement; or

(ii)   a right of pre-emption or of redemption; or

(c)   that the land which by virtue of this section would become the dominant
tenement comprises—

(i)   minerals; or

(ii)   salmon fishings or some other incorporeal property, and it is apparent
from the terms of the real burden that it was created for the benefit of such
land.

(8)   This section is subject to sections 41 and 42 of this Act.

[18A   Personal pre-emption burdens and personal redemption burdens

(1)   Without prejudice to section 18 of this Act, where a feudal estate of
dominium utile of land is subject to a real burden which comprises a right of pre-
emption or redemption and is enforceable by a superior of the feu or would be so
enforceable were the person in question to complete title to the dominium directum the superior may, before the appointed day, by duly executing and registering
against the dominium utile a notice in, or as nearly as may be in, the form contained in schedule 5A to this Act, prospectively convert that burden into a
personal pre-emption burden or as the case may be into a personal redemption
burden.

(2)   The notice shall—

(a)   set out the title of the superior;

(b)   describe, sufficiently to enable identification by reference to the
Ordnance Map, the land the dominium utile of which is subject to the real
burden (or any part of that land);

(c)   set out the terms of the real burden; and

(d)   set out the terms of any counter-obligation to the real burden if it is a
counter-obligation enforceable against the superior.

(3)   Before submitting any notice for registration under this section, the superior
shall swear or affirm as is mentioned in subsection (4) of section 18 of this Act.

(4)   Subsection (5) of that section applies for the purposes of subsection (3)
above as it applies for the purposes of subsection (4) of that section.

(5)   If subsections (1) to (3) above are, with subsection (4) of that section, complied with and immediately before the appointed day the real burden is still
enforceable by the superior (or his successor) or would be so enforceable, or still so

enforceable, were the person in question to complete title to the dominium directum then, on that day—

(a)   the real burden shall be converted into a real burden in favour of that person, to be known as a 'personal pre-emption burden' or as the case may be as a 'personal redemption burden'; and

(b)   the land the dominium utile of which was subject to the real burden (or if part only of that land is described in pursuance of subsection (2)(b) above, that part) shall become the servient tenement.

(6)   Title to enforce the burden against the land to which the notice relates shall be subject to any such counter-obligation as was set out by virtue of subsection (2)(d) above.

(7)   The right to a personal pre-emption burden or personal redemption burden may be assigned or otherwise transferred to any person; and any such assignation or transfer shall take effect on registration.

(8)   Where the holder of a personal pre-emption burden or personal redemption burden does not have a completed title—

(a)   title may be completed by the holder registering a notice of title; or

(b)   without completing title, the holder may grant a deed—

(i)   assigning the right to; or

(ii)   discharging, in whole or in part,

the burden; but unless the deed is one to which section 15(3) of the Land Registration (Scotland) Act 1979 (c 33) (circumstances where unnecessary to deduce title) applies, it shall be necessary, in the deed, to deduce title to the burden through the midcouples linking the holder to the person who had the last completed title.

(9)   This section is subject to sections 41 and 42 of this Act.

18B   Conversion into economic development burden

(1)   Without prejudice to section 18 of this Act, where a feudal estate of dominium utile of land is subject to a real burden which is imposed for the purpose of promoting economic development and is enforceable by the Scottish Ministers or a local authority, being in either case the superior of the feu, or would be so enforceable were the Scottish Ministers or as the case may be the local authority to complete title to the dominium directum, the superior may, before the appointed day, by duly executing and registering against the dominium utile a notice in, or as nearly as may be in, the form contained in schedule 5B to this Act, prospectively convert that burden into an economic development burden.

(2)   The notice shall—

(a)   set out the title of the superior;

(b)   describe, sufficiently to enable identification by reference to the Ordnance Map, the land the dominium utile of which is subject to the real burden (or any part of that land);

(c)   set out the terms of the real burden;

(d)   set out the terms of any counter-obligation to the real burden if it is a counter-obligation enforceable against the superior; and

(e)   state that the burden was imposed for the purpose of promoting economic development and provide information in support of that statement.

(3)   If subsections (1) and (2) above are complied with and immediately before the appointed day the real burden is still enforceable by the superior or would be so enforceable were the Scottish Ministers or as the case may be the local authority to complete title to the dominium directum then on that day the real burden shall be converted into an economic development burden and on and after that day the Scottish Ministers or, as the case may be, the authority, shall—

(a)   have title to enforce the burden against the land to which the notice relates; and

(b)   be presumed to have an interest to enforce it.

(4) Title to enforce the burden against the land to which the notice relates shall be subject to any such counter-obligation as was set out by virtue of subsection (2)(d) above.

(5) This section is subject to sections 41 and 42 of this Act.

18C Conversion into health care burden

(1) Without prejudice to section 18 of this Act, where a feudal estate of dominium utile of land is subject to a real burden which is imposed for the purpose of promoting the provision of facilities for health care and is enforceable by a National Health Service trust or the Scottish Ministers, being in either case the superior of the feu, or would be so enforceable were the trust or as the case may be the Scottish Ministers to complete title to the dominium directum, the superior may, before the appointed day, by duly executing and registering against the dominium utile a notice in, or as nearly as may be in, the form contained in schedule 5C to this Act, prospectively convert that burden into a health care burden.

(2) The notice shall—

(a) set out the title of the superior;

(b) describe, sufficiently to enable identification by reference to the Ordnance Map, the land the dominium utile of which is subject to the real burden (or any part of that land);

(c) set out the terms of the real burden;

(d) set out the terms of any counter-obligation to the real burden if it is a counter-obligation enforceable against the superior; and

(e) state that the burden was imposed for the purpose of promoting the provision of facilities for health care and provide information in support of that statement.

(3) If subsections (1) and (2) are complied with and immediately before the appointed day the real burden is still enforceable by the superior or would be so enforceable were the trust or as the case may be the Scottish Ministers to complete title to the dominium directum then on that day the real burden shall be converted into a health care burden and on and after that day the trust or, as the case may be, the Scottish Ministers, shall—

(a) have title to enforce the burden against the land to which the notice in question relates; and

(b) be presumed to have an interest to enforce it.

(4) Title to enforce the burden against the land to which the notice relates shall be subject to any such counter-obligation as was set out by virtue of subsection (2)(d) above.

(5) In subsections (1) and (2) above, 'facilities for health care' includes facilities ancillary to health care; as for example (but without prejudice to that generality) accommodation for staff employed to provide health care.

(6) This section is subject to sections 41 and 42 of this Act.]

19 Reallotment of real burden by agreement

(1) Where a feudal estate of dominium utile of land is subject to a real burden enforceable by a superior of the feu or which would be so enforceable were the person in question to complete title to the dominium directum the superior may, before the appointed day—

(a) serve notice in, or as nearly as may be in, the form contained in schedule 6 to this Act, on the person who has right to the feu that he seeks to enter into an agreement with that person under this section prospectively nominating other land (being land of which the superior has right to the sole dominium utile or sole allodial ownership), or any part of that other land, as a dominant tenement;

(b) enter into such an agreement with that person; and

(c)   duly register that agreement;

but if they think fit they may, by the agreement, modify the real burden or any counter-obligation to the real burden if it is a counter-obligation enforceable against the superior (or both the real burden and any such counter-obligation).

(2)   The notice shall—

(a)   set out the title of the superior;

(b)   describe both the land the dominium utile of which is subject to the real burden (or any part of that land) and the land (or part) nominated;

(c)   set out the terms of the real burden; and

(d)   set out the terms of any such counter-obligation as is mentioned in sub-section (1) above.

(3)   An agreement such as is mentioned in paragraph (b) of subsection (1) above shall be a written agreement—

(a)   which expressly states that it is made under this section; and

(b)   which includes all the information, other than that relating to service, re-quired to be set out in completing the notice the form of which is contained in schedule 6 to this Act.

(4)   For the purposes of subsection (1)(c) above an agreement is duly registered only when registered against both tenements described in pursuance of subsection (2)(b) above.

(5)   If subsections (1)(b) and (c), (3) and (4) above are complied with and im-mediately before the appointed day the real burden is still enforceable by the superior (or by his successor) or would be so enforceable, or still so enforceable, were the person in question to complete title to the dominium directum then on that day—

(a)   the land (or part) nominated shall become a dominant tenement; and

(b)   the land the dominium utile of which was subject to the real burden (or if part only of that land is described in pursuance of subsection (2)(b) above, that part) shall be the servient tenement.

(6)   A person may enter into an agreement under this section even if he has not completed title to the dominium utile of the land subject to the real burden, or as the case may be title to the dominium directum of that land or to the dominium utile of the land nominated (or, if the land nominated is allodial land, to the land nominated), provided that, in any case to which section 15(3) of the Land Regis-tration (Scotland) Act 1979 (c 33) (simplification of deeds relating to registered interests) does not apply, he deduces title, in the agreement, from the person who appears in the Register of Sasines as having the last recorded title to the interest in question.

(7)   This section is subject to section 42 of this Act.

20   Reallotment of real burden by order of Lands Tribunal

(1)   Where but for paragraph (b) of subsection (1) of section 18 of this Act a superior could proceed under that subsection prospectively to nominate land (in this section referred to as the ('prospective dominant tenement') he may, provided that he has first, in pursuance of section 19 of this Act, attempted to reach agree-ment as respects the real burden in question with the person who has right to the feu, apply to the Lands Tribunal for an order under subsection (7) of this section; but such an application is competent only if made [. . .] before the appointed day).

(2)   An applicant under subsection (1) above shall include in his application a description of the requisite attempt to reach agreement.

(3)   After sending or delivering to the Lands Tribunal an application under sub-section (1) above, the superior may, within—

(a)   42 days; or

(b)   such longer period of days (being a period which ends before the ap-pointed day) as the Lands Tribunal may allow if it is satisfied that there is good cause for so allowing, duly execute and register a notice in, or as nearly as may be in, the form contained in schedule 7 to this Act. [. . .]

(4)   The notice shall—

(a)   set out the title of the superior;

(b)   describe, sufficiently to enable identification by reference to the Ordnance Map, both the land the dominium utile of which is subject to the real burden (or any part of that land) and the prospective dominant tenement;

(c)   set out the terms of the real burden; and

(d)   set out the terms of any counter-obligation to the real burden if it is a counter-obligation enforceable against the superior.

(5)   For the purposes of this section, a notice is duly registered only when registered against both tenements described in pursuance of subsection (4)(b) above; and if it is so registered and immediately before the appointed day—

(a)   the real burden is still enforceable by the superior (or by his successor) or would be so enforceable, or still so enforceable, were the person in question to complete title to the dominium directum; and

(b)   no order under subsection (7) below has been registered under subsection (11) below in respect of the application, then on that day the prospective dominant tenement shall, for the transitional period, become the dominant tenement and the land the dominium utile of which is subject to the real burden (or, if part only of that land is described under paragraph (b) of subsection (4) above, that part) shall, for the transitional period, be the servient tenement.

(6)   The reference in subsection (5) above to the transitional period is to the period beginning on the appointed day and ending on—

(a)   the day on which an order under subsection (7) below is registered under subsection (11) below in respect of the application; or

(b)   if no such order is so registered, such day later than the appointed day as the Scottish Ministers may by order specify (that later day being in this Act referred to as the ('specified day'.

(7)   If, on an application under subsection (1) above as respects which a notice has been duly registered—

(a)   the Lands Tribunal is satisfied that, were the real burden to be extinguished, there would be [material detriment to the value or enjoyment of the applicant's ownership (taking him to have ownership)] of the dominant tenement, the Tribunal may order that, subject to subsection (9) of this section—

(i)   if the order can be and is registered before the appointed day, then on that day the prospective dominant tenement shall become the dominant tenement and the land the dominium utile of which is subject to the real burden (or, if part only of that land is described under paragraph (b) of subsection (4) above, that part) shall be the servient tenement; or

(ii)   the dominant tenement for the transitional period shall, after that period, continue to be the dominant tenement and the servient tenement for the transitional period shall, after that period, continue to be the servient tenement; [or

(b)   the Lands Tribunal is not so satisfied, it may make an order refusing the application.]

(8)   Where in respect of the application—

(a)   an order under paragraph (a) of subsection (7) above is registered-

(i)   before the appointed day and immediately before that day the real burden is still enforceable by the superior (or by his successor) or would be so enforceable, or still so enforceable, were the person in question to complete title to the dominium directum, then on that day; or

(ii)   on or after the appointed day and immediately before the day of registration the real burden is still enforceable by the former superior (or by his successor) or would be so enforceable, or still so enforceable, as mentioned in sub-paragraph (i) above, then on the day of registration,

the prospective dominant tenement shall become the dominant tenement and the land the dominium utile of which was subject to the real burden (or, if part only of that land is described under paragraph (b) of subsection (4) above, that part) shall be the servient tenement;
[. . .]

(9)   An order under subsection (7)(a) above may modify the real burden or any counter-obligation to the real burden if it is a counter-obligation enforceable against the applicant (or both the real burden and any such counter-obligation).

(10)   The decision of the Lands Tribunal on an application under subsection (1) above shall be final.

(11)   An order under subsection (7) above shall forthwith be extracted and registered by the Lands Tribunal against both tenements described in pursuance of subsection (4)(b) above; and the expenses of registration shall be borne by the applicant.

(12)   Subsections (2) and (3) of section 17 of this Act shall apply in relation to real burdens extinguished or rendered unenforceable by virtue of this section as they apply in relation to real burdens extinguished or so rendered by subsection (1) of that section with the substitution, if the extinction or rendering is after the appointed day, for each reference in them to that day, of a reference to the day which ends the transitional period.

(13)   A person opposing an application made under subsection (1) above incurs no liability, unless in the opinion of the Lands Tribunal his actings are vexatious or frivolous, in respect of expenses incurred by the applicant.

(14)   This section is subject to sections 41 and 42 of this Act.

(15)   Before submitting any notice for registration under this section, the superior shall swear or affirm before a notary public that to the best of the knowledge and belief of the superior all the information contained in the notice is true.

(16)   For the purposes of subsection (15) above, if the superior is—

(a)   an individual unable by reason of legal disability, or incapacity, to swear or affirm as mentioned in that subsection, then a legal representative of the superior may swear or affirm;

(b)   not an individual, then any person authorised to sign documents on its behalf may swear or affirm;

and the references in that subsection to the superior shall be construed accordingly.

21   Manner of dealing with application under section 20

(1)   On receiving an application under section 20 of this Act the Lands Tribunal shall give such notice of that application, whether by way of advertisement or otherwise, as may be prescribed for the purposes of that section by the Scottish Ministers by rules under section 3 of the Lands Tribunal Act 1949 (c 42) to any person who has right to the feu which is subject to the real burden in question and, if the Lands Tribunal thinks fit, to any other person.

(2)   Any person who, whether or not he has received notice under subsection (1) above, has right to the feu which is subject to the real burden in question (or as the case may be has right to the servient tenement) or is affected by that real burden or by its proposed reallotment shall be entitled, within such time as may be so prescribed, to oppose or make representations in relation to the application; and the Lands Tribunal shall allow any such person, and may allow any other person who appears to it to be affected by that real burden or by its proposed reallotment, to be heard in relation to the application.

(3)   Without prejudice to subsections (1) and (2) above, the Scottish Ministers may, in rules under the said section 3, make special provision in relation to any matter pertaining to proceedings in applications under section 20 of this Act (or in any class of such applications).

22 [*Amends Tribunals and Inquiries Act 1992.*]

[. . .]

24 Interest to enforce real burden
Sections 18 to 20 and 23 of this Act are without prejudice to any requirement that a dominant proprietor have an interest to enforce a real burden (and such interest shall not be presumed).

25 Counter-obligations on reallotment
Where a real burden is reallotted under section 18, 19, [or 20] of this Act [or under section 56 or 63 of the Title Conditions (Scotland) Act 2003 (asp 9) (which makes provision, respectively, as to facility burdens and service burdens and as to manager burdens)], the right to enforce the burden shall be subject to any counter-obligation (modified as the case may be by the agreement or by the order of the Lands Tribunal) enforceable against the superior immediately before [reallotment is effected].

Conservation burdens

[. . .]

27 Notice preserving right to enforce conservation burden
(1) Where a conservation body has, or the Scottish Ministers have, the right as superior to enforce a real burden of the class described in subsection (2) below or would have that right were it or they to complete title to the dominium directum, it or they may, before the appointed day, preserve for the benefit of the public the right to enforce the burden in question after that day by executing and registering against the dominium utile of the land subject to the burden a notice in, or as nearly as may be in, the form contained in schedule 8 to this Act; and [, without prejudice to section 27A(1) of this Act,] any burden as respects which such a right is so preserved shall, on and after the appointed day, be known as a 'conservation burden'.
(2) The class is those real burdens which are enforceable against a feudal estate of dominium utile of land for the purpose of preserving, or protecting—
    (a) the architectural or historical characteristics of the land; or
    (b) any other special characteristics of the land (including, without prejudice to the generality of this paragraph, a special characteristic derived from the flora, fauna or general appearance of the land).
(3) The notice shall—
    (a) state that the superior is a conservation body by virtue of section [38 of the Title Conditions (Scotland) Act 2003 (asp 9) (which makes provision generally as respects conservation burdens)] or that the superior is the Scottish Ministers;
    (b) set out the title of the superior;
    (c) describe, sufficiently to enable identification by reference to the Ordnance Map, the land subject to the real burden (or any part of that land);
    (d) set out the terms of the real burden; and
    (e) set out the terms of any counter-obligation to the real burden if it is a counter-obligation enforceable against the superior.
(4) This section is subject to sections 41 and 42 of this Act.

[27A Nomination of conservation body or Scottish Ministers to have title to enforce conservation burden
(1) Where a person other than a conservation body or the Scottish Ministers has the right as superior to enforce a real burden of the class described in section 27(2) of this Act or would have that right were he to complete title to the dominium directum, he may, subject to subsection (2) below, before the appointed day nominate for the benefit of the public, by executing and registering against the dominium utile of the land subject to the burden a notice in, or as nearly as may

be in, the form contained in schedule 8A to this Act, a conservation body or the Scottish Ministers to have title on or after that day to enforce the burden against that land; and, without prejudice to section 27(1) of this Act, any burden as respects which such title to enforce is by virtue of this subsection so obtained shall, on and after the appointed day, be known as a 'conservation burden'.

(2)   Subsection (1) above applies only where the consent of the nominee to being so nominated is obtained—

(a)   in a case where sending a copy of the notice, in compliance with section 41(3) of this Act, is reasonably practicable, before that copy is so sent; and

(b)   in any other case, before the notice is executed.

(3)   The notice shall—

(a)   state that the nominee is a conservation body (identifying it) or the Scottish Ministers, as the case may be; and

(b)   do as mentioned in paragraphs (b) to (e) of section 27(3) of this Act.

(4)   This section is subject to sections 41 and 42 of this Act except that, in the application of subsection (1)(i) of section 42 for the purposes of this subsection, such discharge as is mentioned in that subsection shall be taken to require the consent of the nominated person.]

28   Enforcement of conservation burden

(1)   If a notice has been executed and registered in accordance with section 27 of this Act and, immediately before the appointed day, the burden to which the notice relates is still enforceable by the conservation body or the Scottish Ministers as superior or would be so enforceable, or still so enforceable, were the body in question or they to complete title to the dominium directum then, on and after the appointed day, the conservation body or as the case may be the Scottish Ministers shall—

(a)   subject to any counter-obligation, have title to enforce the burden against the land to which the notice in question relates; and

(b)   be presumed to have an interest to enforce that burden.

(2)   The references in subsection (1) above to—

(a)   the conservation body include references to—

(i)   any conservation body which is; or

(ii)   the Scottish Ministers where they are, its successor as superior;

(b)   the Scottish Ministers include references to a conservation body which is their successor as superior.

[28A   Effect of section 27A nomination

If a notice has been executed and registered in accordance with section 27A of this Act and, immediately before the appointed day, the burden to which the notice relates is still enforceable by the nominating person as superior (or by such person as is his successor) or would be so enforceable, or still so enforceable, were the person in question to complete title to the dominium directum then, on and after the appointed day, the conservation body or as the case may be the Scottish Ministers shall—

(a)   subject to any counter-obligation, have title to enforce the burden against the land to which the notice in question relates; and

(b)   be presumed to have an interest to enforce that burden.]

[. . .]

Compensation

33   Notice reserving right to claim compensation where land subject to development value burden

(1)   Where—

(a)   before the appointed day, land was feued subject to a real burden enforceable by a superior (or so enforceable if the person in question were to complete title to the dominium directum) which reserved for the superior the benefit (whether wholly or in part) of any development value of the land (such a real burden being referred to in this Part of this Act as a ('development value burden'; and

    (b)   either—

        (i) the consideration paid, or payable, under the grant in feu was significantly lower than it would have been had the feu not been subject to the real burden; or

        (ii) no consideration was paid, or payable, under the grant in feu, the superior may, before that day, reserve the right to claim (in accordance with section 35 of this Act) compensation by executing and registering against the dominium utile of the land subject to the burden a notice in, or as nearly as may be in, the form contained in schedule 9 to this Act.

    (2) A notice under this section shall—

    (a) set out the title of the superior;

    (b) describe, sufficiently to enable identification by reference to the Ordnance Map, the land the dominium utile of which is subject to the development value burden;

    (c) set out the terms of the burden;

    (d) state that the burden reserves development value and set out any information relevant to that statement;

    (e) set out, to the best of the superior's knowledge and belief, the amount by which the consideration was reduced because of the imposition of the burden; and

    (f) the superior reserves the right to claim compensation in accordance with section 35 of this Act.

    (3) Before submitting any notice for registration under this section, the superior shall swear or affirm before a notary public that to the best of the knowledge and belief of the superior all the information contained in the notice is true.

    (4) For the purposes of subsection (3) above, if the superior is—

    (a) an individual unable by reason of legal disability, or incapacity, to swear or affirm as mentioned in that subsection, then a legal representative of the superior may swear or affirm;

    (b) not an individual, then any person authorised to sign documents on its behalf may swear or affirm;

and any reference in that subsection to a superior shall be construed accordingly.

    (5) In this Part of this Act, 'development value' (except in the expression 'development value burden') means any significant increase in the value of the land arising as a result of the land becoming free to be used, or dealt with, in some way not permitted under the grant in feu.

    (6) This section is subject to sections 41 and 42 of this Act.

34 Transmissibility of right to claim compensation

A right to claim compensation reserved in accordance with section 33 of this Act is transmissible.

35 Claiming compensation

    (1) Where the conditions mentioned in subsection (2) below are satisfied, any person who has, by or by virtue of a notice executed and registered in accordance with section 33 of this Act, a reserved right to claim compensation shall be entitled, subject to any order under section 44(2) of this Act, to compensation from the person who is the owner.

    (2) The conditions are that—

    (a) the real burden set out in the notice was, immediately before the appointed day, enforceable by the superior or would have been so enforceable immediately before that day had the person in question completed title to the dominium directum;

(b) on that day the burden, or as the case may be any right (or right on completion of title) of the superior to enforce the burden, was extinguished, or rendered unenforceable, by section 17(1) of this Act; and

(c) at any time—

(i) during the period of five years ending immediately before the appointed day, there was a breach of the burden; or

(ii) during the period of twenty years beginning with the appointed day, there was an occurrence, which, but for the burden becoming extinct, or unenforceable, as mentioned in paragraph (b) above, would have been a breach of the burden.

(3) Where a person is entitled, by virtue of subsection (1) above, to compensation, he shall make any claim for such compensation by notice in writing duly served on the owner; and any such notice shall specify, in accordance with section 37 of this Act, the amount of compensation claimed.

(4) Where, in relation to a claim made under subsection (3) above, the condition mentioned in—

(a) sub-paragraph (i) of subsection (2)(c) above applies, any such claim may not be made more than three years after the appointed day;

(b) sub-paragraph (ii) of subsection (2)(c) above applies, any such claim may not be made more than three years after the date of the occurrence.

(5) For the purposes of this section, if a breach, or occurrence, such as is mentioned in subsection (2)(c) above is continuing, the breach or, as the case may be, occurrence shall be taken to occur when it first happens.

(6) The reference in subsection (3) above to a notice being duly served shall be construed in accordance with section 36 of this Act.

36 Service under section 35(3)

(1) Due service under section 35(33) of this Act is effected by delivering the notice in question to the owner or by sending it by registered post, or the recorded delivery service, addressed to him at an appropriate place.

(2) An acknowledgement, signed by the owner, which conforms to Form A of schedule 10 to this Act, or as the case may be a certificate which conforms to Form B of that schedule and is accompanied by the postal receipt, shall be sufficient evidence of such due service; and if the notice in question is, under subsection (1) above, sent by post but is returned to the person who is entitled to compensation with an intimation that it could not be delivered, the notice may be delivered or sent by post, with that intimation, to the Extractor of the Court of Session, the delivery or sending to the Extractor being taken to be equivalent to the service of that notice on the owner.

(3) For the purposes of subsection (2) above, an acknowledgement of receipt by the Extractor on a copy of that notice shall be sufficient evidence of its receipt by him.

(4) The date on which notice under section 35(3) of this Act is served on an owner is the date of delivery, or as the case may be of posting, in compliance with subsection (1) or (2) above.

(5) A reference in this section to an 'appropriate place' is, for any owner, to be construed as a reference to—

(a) his place of residence;

(b) his place of business; or

(c) a postal address which he ordinarily uses,

or, if none of those is known at the time of delivery or posting, as a reference to whatever place is at that time his most recently known place of residence or place of business or postal address which he ordinarily used.

37 Amount of compensation

(1) The amount of any compensation payable on a claim made under section 35(3) of this Act shall, subject to subsections (2) and (3) below, be such sum as

represents, at the time of the breach or occurrence in question, any development value which would have accrued to the owner had the burden been modified to the extent necessary to permit the land to be used, or dealt with, in the way that constituted the breach or, as the case may be, occurrence on which the claim is based.

(2)   The amount payable as compensation (or, where more than one claim is made in relation to the same development value burden, the total compensation payable) under subsection (1) above shall not exceed such sum as will make up for any effect which the burden produced, at the time when it was imposed, in reducing the consideration then paid or made payable for the feu.

(3)   In assessing for the purposes of subsection (1) above an amount of compensation payable—

(a)   any entitlement of the claimant to recover any part of the development value of the land subject to the development value burden shall be taken into account; and

(b)   a claimant to whom the reserved right was assigned or otherwise transferred shall be entitled to no greater sum than the former superior would have been had there been no such assignation or transfer.

(4)   The reference in subsection (1) above to a burden shall, in relation to an occurrence, be construed as a reference to the burden which would have been breached but for its becoming, by section 17(1) of this Act, extinct or unenforceable.

38   Duty to disclose identity of owner

Where a person ('the claimant') purports duly to serve notice under section 35(3) of this Act and the person on whom it is served, being a person who had right, before the time of the breach (or, as the case may be, occurrence) founded on by the claimant, to the dominium utile (or the ownership) of the land, is not the owner, that person shall forthwith disclose to the claimant—

(a)   the identity and address of the owner; or

(b)   (if he cannot do that) such other information as he has that might enable the claimant to discover the identity and address;

and the notice shall refer to that requirement for disclosure.

39   The expression 'owner' for purposes of sections 35 to 38

(1)   In sections 35 to 38 of this Act, "owner' means the person who, at the time of the breach or, as the case may be, occurrence, mentioned in section 35(2)(c) of this Act, has right to—

(a)   the dominium utile; or

(b)   the ownership,

of the land which, immediately before the appointed day, was subject to the development value burden, whether or not he has completed title; and if more than one person comes within that description, then the owner is the person who has most recently acquired such right.

(2)   Where the land in question is held by two or more such owners as common property, they shall be severally liable to make any compensatory payment (but as between, or as the case may be among, themselves they shall be liable in the proportions in which they hold the land).

40   Assignation, discharge, or restriction, of reserved right to claim compensation

A reserved right to claim, in accordance with section 35 of this Act, compensation may be—

(a)   assigned, whether wholly or to such extent (expressed as a percentage of each claim which may come to be made) as may be specified in the assignation; or

(b)   discharged or restricted,

by execution and registration of an assignation, or as the case may be a discharge, or restriction, in the form, or as nearly as may be in the form, contained in schedule 11 to this Act.

Miscellaneous

41 Notices: pre-registration requirements etc

(1) This section applies in relation to any notice which is to be submitted for registration under this Act.

(2) It shall not be necessary to endorse on the notice a warrant of registration.

(3) Except where it is not reasonably practicable to do so, a superior shall, before he executes the notice, send by post to the person who has the estate of dominium utile of the land to which the burden relates (addressed to 'The Proprietor' where the name of that person is not known) a copy of—

(a) the notice; and

(b) the explanatory note set out in whichever schedule to this Act relates to the notice.

(4) A superior shall, in the notice, state either—

(a) that a copy of the notice has been sent in accordance with subsection (3) above; or

(b) that it was not reasonably practicable for such a copy to be sent.

42 Further provision as respects sections 18 to 20, 27 and 33

(1) Where—

(a) a notice relating to a real burden has been registered under section 18, [18A, 18B, 18C,] 20, 27 [, 27A] or 33 of this Act; or

(b) an agreement relating to a real burden has been registered under section 19 of this Act,

against the dominium utile of any land which is subject to the burden, it shall not be competent to register under any of those sections against that dominium utile another such notice or agreement relating to the same real burden; but nothing in this subsection shall prevent registration where—

(i) the discharge of any earlier such notice has been registered by the person who registered that notice (or by his successor); or

(ii) as the case may be, the discharge of any earlier such agreement has been registered, jointly, by the parties to that agreement (or by their successors).

(2) Where the dominium utile of any land comprises parts each held by a separate vassal, each part shall be taken to be a separate feudal estate of dominium utile.

(3) Where more than one feudal estate of dominium utile is subject to the same real burden enforceable by a superior of the feu, he shall, if he wishes to execute and register a notice under section 18, [18A, 18B, 18C,] 20, 27 [, 27A] or 33 of this Act against those feudal estates in respect of that real burden, require to do so against each separately.

(4) Where a feudal estate of dominium utile is subject to more than one real burden enforceable by a superior of the feu, he may if he wishes to—

(a) execute and register a notice under section 18, [18A, 18B, 18C,] 20, 27 [, 27A] or 33 of this Act against that feudal estate in respect of those real burdens, do so by a single notice; or

(b) enter into and register an agreement under section 19 of this Act against that feudal estate in respect of those real burdens, do so by a single agreement.

[(5) Nothing in this Part requires registration against land prospectively nominated as a dominant tenement but outwith Scotland.]

43 Notices and agreements under certain sections: extent of Keeper's duty

(1) In relation to any notice submitted for registration under section 18, [18A,

18B, 18C,] 20, 27 [, 27A] or 33 of this Act, the Keeper of the Registers of Scotland shall not be required to determine whether the superior has complied with the terms of section 41(3) of this Act.

(2) In relation to any notice, or as the case may be any agreement, submitted for registration under—

(a) section 18, [18A, 18B, 18C,] 19, 20, 27 [, 27A] or 33 of this Act, the Keeper shall not be required to determine whether, for the purposes of subsection (1) of the section in question, a real burden is enforceable by a superior;

(b) section 18 of this Act, the Keeper shall not be required to determine, where, in pursuance of subsection (2)(c) of that section, the condition specified is that mentioned in subsection (7)(a) of that section, whether the terms of that condition are satisfied;

[(bb) section 18B or 18C of this Act, the Keeper shall not be required to determine whether—

(i) the requirements of subsection (1) of the section in question are satisfied; or

(ii) the statement made in pursuance of subsection (2)(e) of the section in question is correct;]

(c) paragraph (c) of subsection (1) of section 19 of this Act, the Keeper shall not be required to determine whether the requirements of paragraph (a) of that subsection are satisfied;

(d) section 20 of this Act, the Keeper shall not be required to determine—

(i) whether the description provided in pursuance of subsection (2) of that section is correct;

(ii) whether the notice has been executed, and is being registered, timeously; or

(iii) any matter as to which the Lands Tribunal must be satisfied before making an order under that section;

(e) section 33 of this Act, the Keeper shall not be required to determine whether—

(i) the requirements of subsection (1)(a) and (b) of that section are satisfied; or

(ii) the statements made or information provided, in pursuance of subsection (2)(d) or (e) of that section, are correct.

(3) The Keeper shall not be required to determine—

(a) for the purposes of section 18(6), [18A(5), 18B(3), 18C(3),] 19(5), 20(5) or (8)(a)(i), 28 [, 28A] or 60(1) of this Act, whether immediately before the appointed day a real burden is, or is still, enforceable, or by whom; or

(b) for the purposes of subsection (8)(a)(ii) of section 20 of this Act, whether immediately before the day of registration of an order of the Lands Tribunal under subsection (7) of that section a real burden is, or is still, enforceable, or by whom.

44 Referral to Lands Tribunal of notice dispute

(1) Any dispute arising in relation to a notice registered under this Act may be referred to the Lands Tribunal; and, in determining the dispute, the Tribunal may make such order as it thinks fit discharging or, to such extent as may be specified in the order, restricting the notice in question.

(2) Any dispute arising in relation to a claim made under section 35(3) of this Act may be referred to the Lands Tribunal; and, in determining the dispute, the Tribunal may make such order as it thinks fit (including an order fixing the amount of any compensation payable under the claim in question).

(3) In any referral under subsection (1) or (2) above, the burden of proving any disputed question of fact shall be on the person relying on the notice or, as the case may be, making the claim.

(4) An extract of any order made under subsection (1) or (2) above may be

registered and the order shall take effect as respects third parties on such registration.

45　Circumstances where certain notices may be registered after appointed day

(1)　Subject to subsection (2) below, where—

(a)　a notice submitted, before the appointed day, for registration under this Act, or an agreement so submitted for registration under section 19 of this Act, is rejected by the Keeper of the Registers of Scotland; but

(b)　a court or the Lands Tribunal then determines that the notice or agreement is registrable,

the notice or agreement may, if not registered before the appointed day, be registered—

(i)　within two months after the determination is made; but

(ii)　before such date after the appointed day as the Scottish Ministers may by order prescribe,

and any notice or agreement registered under this subsection on or after the appointed day shall be treated as if it had been registered before that day.

(2)　For the purposes of subsection (1) above, the application to the court, or to the Lands Tribunal, which has resulted in the determination shall require to have been made within such period as the Scottish Ministers may by order prescribe.

(3)　In subsection (1)(b) above, 'court' means any court having jurisdiction in questions of heritable right or title.

46　Duties of Keeper: amendments relating to the extinction of certain real burdens

(1)　The Keeper of the Registers of Scotland shall not be required to remove from the Land Register of Scotland a real burden extinguished by section 17(1)(a) of this Act unless—

(a)　subject to subsection (3) below, he is requested to do so in an application for registration or rectification; or

(b)　he is, under section 9(1) of the Land Registration (Scotland) Act 1979 (c 33) (rectification of the register), ordered, subject to subsection (3) below, to do so by the court or the Lands Tribunal;

and no such request or order shall be competent during a period which commences with the appointed day and is of such number of years as the Scottish Ministers may by order prescribe.

(2)　During the period mentioned in subsection (1) above a real burden, notwithstanding that it has been so extinguished, may at the discretion of the Keeper, for the purposes of section 6(1)(e) of that Act of 1979 (entering [subsisting] real right in title sheet), be taken to subsist; but this subsection is without prejudice to subsection (3) below.

(3)　The Keeper shall not, before the date mentioned in subsection (4) below, remove from the Land Register of Scotland a real burden which is the subject of a notice or agreement in respect of which application had been made for a determination by—

(a)　a court; or

(b)　the Lands Tribunal,

under section 45(1)(b) of this Act.

(4)　The date is whichever is the earlier of—

(a)　that two months after the final decision on the application; and

(b)　that prescribed under section 45(1)(ii) of this Act.

47　Extinction of counter-obligation

Without prejudice to any other way in which a counter-obligation to a real burden may be extinguished, any such counter-obligation is extinguished on the extinction of the real burden.

48   No implication as to dominant tenement where real burden created in grant in feu

Where a real burden is created (or has at any time been created) in a grant in feu, the superior having the dominium utile, or allodial ownership, of land (the 'superior's land') in the vicinity of the land feued, no implication shall thereby arise that the superior's land is a dominant tenement.

Interpretation

49   Interpretation of Part 4

In this Part of this Act, unless the context otherwise requires—

'conservation body' means a body prescribed [by order under section 38(4) of the Title Conditions (Scotland) Act 2003 (asp 9)];

'conservation burden' shall be construed in accordance with [sections 27(1) and 27A(1)] of this Act;

'development value burden' and 'development value' shall be construed in accordance with section 33 of this Act;

['economic development burden' shall be construed in accordance with section 18B(3) of this Act;

'health care burden' shall be construed in accordance with section 18C(3) of this Act;

'local authority' means a council constituted under section 2 of the Local Government etc (Scotland) Act 1994 (c 39);]

'notary public' includes any person duly authorised by the law of the country (other than Scotland) in which the swearing or affirmation takes place to administer oaths or receive affirmations in that other country;

['personal pre-emption burden' and 'personal redemption burden' shall be construed in accordance with section 18A(5) of the Act;]

'real burden'—

    (a)   includes-

        (i)   a right of pre-emption;

        (ii)   a right of redemption; [. . .] but

    (b)   does not include a pecuniary real burden [or sporting rights (as defined by section 65A(9) of this Act)];

'registering' means registering an interest in land (or information relating to such an interest) in the Land Register of Scotland or, as the case may be, recording a document in the Register of Sasines; and cognate expressions shall be construed accordingly; and

'superior' means a person who has right to the immediate superiority or to any over-superiority, whether or not he has completed title (and if more than one person comes within either of those descriptions then, in relation to that description, the person who has most recently acquired such right) and 'former superior' shall be construed accordingly.

PART 5
ENTAILS

50   Disentailment on appointed day

    (1)   Land which, immediately before the appointed day, is held under an entail is disentailed on that day.

    (2)   Section 32 of the Entail Amendment Act 1848 (c 36) (which makes provision as respects an instrument of disentail executed and recorded under that Act) shall apply to the effect of disentailment by subsection (1) above as that section applies to the effect of such an instrument so executed and recorded.

51 Compensation for expectancy or interest of apparent or other nearest heir in an entailed estate

(1) Where, immediately before the appointed day—

(a) land is held under an entail; and

(b) the consent of a person who is an apparent or other nearest heir is required to any petition for authority of the court for the purpose of presenting an instrument of disentail, the valuation of any expectancy or interest of the person, which on his refusal to give such consent would fall, before the appointed day, to be ascertained under section 13 of the Entail (Scotland) Act 1882 (c 53) may, within two years after the appointed day, be referred by him to, and determined by, the Lands Tribunal.

(2) The Tribunal shall direct that any sum ascertained by them in a valuation by virtue of subsection (1) above shall be secured on the land, for the benefit of the person, in such manner as they think fit.

52 Closure of Register of Entails

The Keeper of the Registers of Scotland shall, immediately before the appointed day, close the Register of Entails; and as soon as is practicable thereafter, he shall transmit that register to the Keeper of the Records of Scotland for preservation.

PART 6

MISCELLANEOUS

Discharge of certain rights and extinction of certain obligations and payments

53 Discharge of rights of irritancy

(1) All rights of irritancy held by a superior are, on the day on which this section comes into force, discharged; and on that day any proceedings already commenced to enforce any such right shall be deemed abandoned and may, without further process and without any requirement that full judicial expenses shall have been paid by the pursuer, be dismissed accordingly.

(2) Subsection (1) above shall not affect any cause in which final decree (that is to say, any decree or interlocutor which disposes of the cause and is not subject to appeal or review) is granted before the coming into force of this section.

54 Extinction of superior's rights and obligations qua superior

(1) Subject to section 13, to Part 4, and to [sections 60(1) and 65A], of this Act, a right or obligation which, immediately before the appointed day, is enforceable by, or as the case may be against, a superior qua superior [(including, without prejudice to that generality, sporting rights as defined by subsection (9) of that section 65A)] shall, on that day, be extinguished.

(2) Subject to subsection (3) below—

(a) on or after the appointed day, no proceedings for such enforcement shall be commenced;

(b) any proceedings already commenced for such enforcement shall be deemed to have been abandoned on that day and may, without further process and without any requirement that full judicial expenses shall have been paid by the pursuer, be dismissed accordingly; and

(c) any decree, or interlocutor, already pronounced in proceedings for such enforcement shall be deemed to have been reduced, or as the case may be recalled, on that day.

(3) Subsection (2) above shall not affect any proceedings, decree or interlocutor in relation to—

(a) a right of irritancy held by a superior;

[(aa) a right of enforcement held by virtue of section 13, 33, 60(1) or 65A of this Act;] or

(b) a right to recover damages or to the payment of money.

55 Abolition of thirlage

Any obligation of thirlage which has not been extinguished before the appointed day is extinguished on that day.

56 Extinction etc of certain payments analogous to feuduty

(1) The provisions of Part 3 of this Act shall apply as regards ground annual, skat, teind, stipend, standard charge, dry multures (including compensation payable in respect of commutation pursuant to the Thirlage Act 1799 (c 55)) and, subject to the exceptions mentioned in subsection (2) below, as regards any other perpetual periodical payment in respect of the tenure, occupancy or use of land or under a [title condition], as those provisions apply as regards feuduty; but for the purposes of that application—

(a) references in the provisions to 'vassal' and 'superior' shall be construed as references to, respectively, the payer and the recipient of the ground annual, skat, teind, stipend, standard charge, dry multures or other payment in question ('former vassal' and 'former superior' being construed accordingly); and

(b) a form (and its explanatory note) contained in a schedule to this Act shall be modified so as to accord with the kind of payment to which it relates.

(2) The exceptions are any payments—

(a) in defrayal of, or as a contribution towards, some continuing cost related to land; or

(b) made under a heritable security.

[(3) The definition of 'title condition' in section 122(1) of the Title Conditions (Scotland) Act 2003 (asp 9) shall apply for the purposes of this section as that definition applies for the purposes of that Act.]

(4) Nothing in subsections (1) to (3) above shall be taken to prejudice the tenure, occupancy or use of land.

57 Extinction by prescription of obligation to pay redemption money for feuduty, ground annual etc

Notwithstanding the terms of Schedule 1 to the Prescription and Limitation (Scotland) Act 1973 (c 52) (which defines obligations affected by prescriptive periods of five years), any obligation under section 5 (redemption of feuduty, ground annual etc on transfer for valuable consideration) or 6 (redemption of feuduty, ground annual etc on compulsory acquisition) of the Land Tenure Reform (Scotland) Act 1974 (c 38) to pay redemption money is an obligation to which section 6 of that Act of 1973 (extinction of obligation by prescriptive period of five years) applies; and for the purposes of that application, the reference in subsection (1) of section 6 of that Act of 1973 to the 'appropriate date' is a reference to the date of redemption within the meaning of—

(a) except in the case mentioned in paragraph (b) below, section 5 (read, as the case may be, with section 6(2)(a)); or

(b) in the case of an obligation arising out of the acquisition of land by means of a general vesting declaration, section 6(4),

of that Act of 1974.

The Crown, the Lord Lyon and Barony

58 Crown application

(1) This Act binds the Crown and accordingly such provision as is made by section 2 of this Act as respects feudal estates of dominium shall apply to the superiority of the Prince and Steward of Scotland and to the ultimate superiority of the Crown; but nothing in this Act shall be taken to supersede or impair any power exercisable by Her Majesty by virtue of Her prerogative.

(2) Without prejudice to the generality of subsection (1) above, in that subsection—

(a) Her Majesty's prerogative includes the prerogative of honour; and

(b)　'any power exercisable by Her Majesty by virtue of Her prerogative' includes—
　　(i)　prerogative rights as respects ownerless or unclaimed property; and
　　(ii)　the regalia majora.

59　Crown may sell or otherwise dispose of land by disposition

It shall be competent for the Crown, in selling or otherwise disposing of any land, to do so by granting a disposition of that land.

60　Preserved right of Crown to maritime burdens

(1)　Where, immediately before the appointed day, the Crown has the right as superior to enforce a real burden against part of the sea bed or part of the foreshore, then, on and after that day, the Crown shall—
　　(a)　subject to any counter-obligation, have title to enforce; and
　　(b)　be presumed to have an interest to enforce,
the burden; and any burden as respects which the Crown has such title and interest shall, on and after the appointed day, be known as a 'maritime burden'.
(2)　[. . .]
(3)　For the purposes of this section—
'sea bed' means the bed of the territorial sea adjacent to Scotland; and
'territorial sea' includes any tidal waters.
(4)　In this section, 'real burden' has the same meaning as in Part 4 of this Act.

61　Mines of gold and silver

The periodical payment to the Crown, in respect of the produce of a mine which by the Royal Mines Act 1424 (c 12) belongs to the Crown, of an amount which is not fixed but is calculated as a proportion of that produce is not—
　　(a)　a payment to the Crown qua superior for the purposes of section 54 of this Act;
　　(b)　a perpetual periodical payment for the purposes of section 56 of this Act; or
　　(c)　a feuduty for the purposes of Part 3 of this Act.

62　Jurisdiction and prerogative of Lord Lyon

Nothing in this Act shall be taken to supersede or impair the jurisdiction or prerogative of the Lord Lyon King of Arms.

63　Baronies and other dignities and offices

(1)　Any jurisdiction of, and any conveyancing privilege incidental to, barony shall on the appointed day cease to exist; but nothing in this Act affects the dignity of baron or any other dignity or office (whether or not of feudal origin).
(2)　When, by this Act, an estate held in barony ceases to exist as a feudal estate, the dignity of baron, though retained, shall not attach to the land; and on and after the appointed day any such dignity shall be, and shall be transferable only as, incorporeal heritable property (and shall not be an interest in land for the purposes of the Land Registration (Scotland) Act 1979 (c 33) or a right as respects which a deed can be recorded in the Register of Sasines).
(3)　Where there is registered, before the appointed day, a heritable security over an estate to which is attached the dignity of baron, the security shall on and after that day (until discharge) affect—
　　(a)　in the case of an estate of dominium utile, both the dignity of baron and the land; and
　　(b)　in any other case, the dignity of baron.
(4)　In this section—
'conveyancing privilege' includes any privilege in relation to prescription;
'dignity' includes any quality or precedence associated with, and any heraldic privilege incidental to, a dignity; and
'registered' has the same meaning as in Part 4 of this Act.

Kindly Tenants of Lochmaben

64 Abolition of Kindly Tenancies

(1) The system of land tenure whereby the persons known as the Kindly Tenants of Lochmaben hold land on perpetual tenure without requiring to procure infeftment is, on the appointed day, abolished.

(2) On the appointed day the interest of a Kindly Tenant shall forthwith become the ownership of the land (which shall be taken to include any right of salmon fishing inseverable from the kindly tenancy); and, in so far as is consistent with the provisions of this Act, the land shall be subject to the same subordinate real rights and other encumbrances as was the kindly tenancy.

(3) A right of salmon fishing inseverable from a kindly tenancy shall on and after the appointed day be inseverable from the ownership of the land in question.

Miscellaneous

65 Creation of proper liferent

(1) A proper liferent over land is created—

(a) in a case where the right is registrable under section 2 of the Land Registration (Scotland) Act 1979 (c 33)—

(i) (unless the deed granting or reserving the right makes provision for some later date) on registration; or

(ii) (where provision is made for such a date and the right has been registered) on that date; or

(b) in any other case—

(i) (unless the deed granting or reserving the right makes provision for some later date) on recording of the deed in the Register of Sasines; or

(ii) (where provision is made for such a date and such deed has been so recorded) on that date.

(2) This section is without prejudice to any other enactment, or rule of law, by or under which a proper liferent over land may be created.

(3) In subsection (1)(a) above, 'registrable' and 'registration' have the meanings respectively assigned to those expressions by section 1(3) of the Land Registration (Scotland) Act 1979 (c 33).

(4) The references, in subsection (1)(b) above, to a deed being recorded include references to a notice of title deducing title through a deed being recorded.

[65A Sporting rights

(1) Where a feudal estate of dominium utile of land is subject to sporting rights which are enforceable by a superior of the feu or which would be so enforceable were the person in question to complete title to the dominium directum the superior may, before the appointed day, by duly executing and registering against the dominium utile a notice in, or as nearly as may be in, the form contained in schedule 11A to this Act, prospectively convert those rights into a tenement in land.

(2) The notice shall—

(a) set out the title of the superior;

(b) describe, sufficiently to enable identification by reference to the Ordnance Map, the land the dominium utile of which is subject to the sporting rights (or any part of that land);

(c) describe those rights; and

(d) set out the terms of any counter-obligation to those rights if it is a counter-obligation enforceable against the superior.

(3) Before submitting any notice for registration under this section, the superior shall swear or affirm as is mentioned in subsection (4) of section 18 of this Act.

(4) Subsection (5) of that section applies for the purposes of subsection (3) above as it applies for the purposes of subsection (4) of that section.

(5) If subsections (1) to (3) above are, with subsection (4) of that section, complied with and immediately before the appointed day the sporting rights are still enforceable by the superior (or his successor) or would be so enforceable, or still so enforceable, were the person in question to complete title to the dominium directum then, on that day, the sporting rights shall be converted into a tenement in land.

(6) No greater, or more exclusive, sporting rights shall be enforceable by virtue of such conversion than were (or would have been) enforceable as mentioned in subsection (5) above.

(7) Where the dominium utile comprises parts each held by a separate vassal, each part shall be taken to be a separate feudal estate of dominium utile.

(8) Where sporting rights become, under subsection (5) above, a tenement in land, the right to enforce those rights shall be subject to any counter-obligation enforceable against the superior immediately before the appointed day; and section 47 of this Act shall apply in relation to any counter-obligation to sporting rights as it applies in relation to any counter-obligation to a real burden.

(9) In this section, 'sporting rights' means a right of fishing or game.

(10) This section is subject to section 41 of this Act.

(11) Subsections (1) and (2)(a) of section 43 of this Act apply in relation to a notice submitted for registration under this section as they apply in relation to a notice so submitted under any of the provisions mentioned in those subsections; and paragraph (a) of subsection (3) of that section applies in relation to a determination for the purposes of subsection (5) of this section as it applies in relation to a determination for the purposes of any of the provisions mentioned in that paragraph.

(12) Subsections (1), (3) and (4) of section 46 of this Act apply in relation to sporting rights extinguished by virtue of section 54 of this Act as they apply in relation to a real burden extinguished by section 17(1)(a) of this Act.]

66 Obligation to make title deeds and searches available
A possessor of title deeds or searches which relate to any land shall make them available to a person who has (or is entitled to acquire) a real right in the land, on all necessary occasions when the person so requests, at the person's expense.

67 Prohibition on leases for periods of more than 175 years
(1) Notwithstanding any provision to the contrary in any lease, no lease of land executed on or after the coming into force of this section (in this section referred to as the 'commencement date') may continue for a period of more than 175 years; and any such lease which is still subsisting at the end of that period shall, by virtue of this subsection, be terminated forthwith.

(2) If a lease of land so executed includes provision (however expressed) requiring the landlord or the tenant to renew the lease then the duration of any such renewed lease shall be added to the duration of the original lease for the purposes of reckoning the period mentioned in subsection (1) above.

(3) Nothing in subsection (1) above shall prevent—

(a) any lease being continued by tacit relocation; or

(b) the duration of any lease being extended by, under or by virtue of any enactment.

(4) Subsections (1) and (2) above do not apply—

(a) to a lease executed on or after the commencement date in implement of an obligation entered into before that date;

(b) to a lease executed after the commencement date in implement of an obligation contained in a lease such as is mentioned in paragraph (a) above; or

(c) where—

(i) a lease for a period of more than 175 years has been executed before the commencement date; or

    (ii)   a lease such as is mentioned in paragraph (a) or (b) above is executed on or after that date,

to a sub-lease executed on or after that date of the whole, or part, of the land subject to the lease in question.

    (5)   For the purposes of this section 'lease' includes sub-lease.

68   [*Amends the Titles to Land Consolidation (Scotland) Act 1868.*]

69   Application of 1970 Act to earlier forms of heritable security

    (1)   Sections 14 to 30 of the Conveyancing and Feudal Reform (Scotland) Act 1970 (c 35) (which provisions relate to the assignation, variation, discharge and calling-up etc of standard securities) shall apply (with the substitution of the word 'heritable' for 'standard' and subject to such other modifications as may be necessary) as respects any heritable security granted before 29th November 1970 as those provisions apply as respects a standard security.

    (2)   For the purposes of the said sections 14 to 30 (as modified by, or by virtue of, subsection (1) above), 'heritable security' shall, with the modification mentioned in subsection (3) below, include a pecuniary real burden but shall not include a security constituted by ex facie absolute disposition.

    (3)   The modification is that the reference to the date in subsection (1) above shall be disregarded.

70   Ownership of land by a firm

A firm may, if it has a legal personality distinct from the persons who compose it, itself own land.

PART 7

GENERAL

71   The appointed day

The Scottish Ministers may, for the purposes of this Act, by order appoint a day (in this Act referred to as the ('appointed day', being a day which—

    (a)   falls not less than six months after the order is made; and

    (b)   is one or other of the terms of Whitsunday and Martinmas.

72   Interpretation

In this Act, unless the context otherwise requires-

    'land' includes all subjects of heritable property which, before the appointed day, are, or of their nature might be, held of a superior according to feudal tenure;

    'Lands Tribunal' means Lands Tribunal for Scotland; and

    'the specified day' and 'the transitional period' shall be construed in accordance with section 20(6) of this Act.

73   Feudal terms in enactments and documents: construction after abolition of feudal system

    (1)   Where a term or expression, which before the appointed day would ordinarily, or in the context in which it is used, depend for its meaning on there being a feudal system of land tenure, requires to be construed, in relation to any period from that day onwards—

    (a)   in an enactment (other than this Act) passed [before that day];

    (b)   in an enactment contained in subordinate legislation made [before that day];

    (c)   in a document executed [before that day; or

    (d)   in the Land Register of Scotland or in—

        (i)   a land certificate;

        (ii)   a charge certificate; or

        (iii)   an office copy,

issued, whether or not before that day, under the Land Registration (Scotland) Act 1979 (c 33), then] in so far as the context admits, where the term or expression is, or contains, a reference to—

(i) the dominium utile of the land, that reference shall be construed either as a reference to the land or as a reference to the ownership of that land;

(ii) an estate in land, that reference shall be construed as a reference to a right in land and as including ownership of land;

(iii) a vassal in relation to land, that reference shall be construed as a reference to the owner of the land;

(iv) feuing, that reference shall be construed as a reference to disponing;

(v) a feu disposition, that reference shall be construed as a reference to a disposition;

(vi) taking infeftment, that reference shall be construed as a reference to completing title,

analogous terms and expressions being construed accordingly.

(2) On and after the appointed day, any reference

[(a)] in any document executed before that day [or

(b) in the Land Register of Scotland or in any certificate or copy such as is mentioned in subsection (1)(d) above (whenever issued),]

to a superior shall, where that reference requires to be construed in relation to a real burden which a person is entitled, by virtue of section [18A, 18B, 18C, 19, 20, 28, 28A or 60 of this Act or section 56 of the Title Conditions (Scotland) Act 2003 (asp 9) (facility burdens and service burdens)] to enforce on and after that day, be construed as a reference to that person.

[(2A) In construing, after the appointed day and in relation to a right enforceable on or after that day, a document, or entry in the Land Register, which—

(a) sets out the terms of a real burden; and

(b) is not a document or entry references in which require to be construed as mentioned in subsection (2) above,

any provision of the document or entry to the effect that a person other than the person entitled to enforce the burden may waive compliance with, or mitigate or otherwise vary a condition of, the burden shall be disregarded].

(3) Subsection (1) above is without prejudice to section 76 of, and schedules 12 and 13 to, this Act or to any order made under subsection (3) of that section.

(4) In subsection (1) above—

(a) in paragraph (a), 'enactment' includes a local and personal or private Act; and

(b) in paragraph (b), 'subordinate legislation' has the same meaning as in the Interpretation Act 1978 (c 30) (but includes subordinate legislation made under an Act of the Scottish Parliament).

74 Orders, regulations and rules

(1) Any power of the Scottish Ministers under this Act to make orders, regulations or rules shall be exercisable by statutory instrument; and a statutory instrument containing any such orders, regulations or rules, other than an order under section 71, 76(3) or 77(4), shall be subject to annulment in pursuance of a resolution of the Scottish Parliament.

(2) A statutory instrument containing an order under section 76(3) of this Act shall not be made unless a draft of the instrument has been—

(a) laid before; and

(b) approved by a resolution of,

the Scottish Parliament.

75 Saving for contractual rights

[(1)] As respects any land granted in feu before the appointed day, nothing in this Act shall affect any right (other than a right to feuduty) included in the grant in so far as that right is contractual as between the parties to the grant (or, as the case may be, as between one of them and a person to whom any such right is assigned).

[(2)   In construing the expression 'parties to the grant' in subsection (1) above, any enactment or rule of law whereby investiture is deemed renewed when the parties change shall be disregarded.]

76   Minor and consequential amendments, repeals and power to amend or repeal enactments

(1)   Schedule 12 to this Act, which contains minor amendments and amendments consequential upon the provisions of this Act, shall have effect.

(2)   The enactments mentioned in schedule 13 to this Act are hereby repealed to the extent specified in the second column of that schedule.

(3)   The Scottish Ministers may by order make such further amendments or repeals, in such enactments as may be specified in the order, as appear to them to be necessary or expedient in consequence of any provision of this Act.

(4)   In this section 'enactment' has the same meaning as in section 73(1)(a) of this Act.

77   Short title and commencement

(1)   This Act—

(a)   may be cited as the Abolition of Feudal Tenure etc (Scotland) Act 2000; and

(b)   subject to subsections (2) and (4) below, comes into force on Royal Assent.

(2)   [. . .] There shall come into force on the appointed day—

(a)   sections 1 and 2, 4 to 13, 32, 35 to 37, 46, 50 and 51, 54 to 57, 59 to 61, [64, 65,] 66, 68 to 70, 73, 75 and 76(1) (except in so far as relating to paragraph 30(23)(a) of schedule 12) and (2);

(b)   schedules 1 to 3;

(c)   subject to paragraph 46(3) of schedule 12, that schedule, except paragraph 30(23)(a); and

(d)   schedule 13.

(3)   Note 1 to Schedule 2 to the Conveyancing and Feudal Reform (Scotland) Act 1970 (c 35) shall be deemed to have been originally enacted as amended by the said paragraph 30(23)(a).

(4)   There shall come into force on such day as the Scottish Ministers may by order appoint—

(a)   sections 17 to 31, 33, 34, 38 to 45[, 47 to 49, 63 and 65A];

(b)   schedules 5 to 11.

[. . .]

SCHEDULES

SCHEDULE 1
FORM OF NOTICE REQUIRING COMPENSATORY PAYMENT ETC: CUMULO FEUDUTY

'NOTICE UNDER SECTION 8(1) OF THE ABOLITION OF FEUDAL TENURE ETC (SCOTLAND) ACT 2000 (CUMULO FEUDUTY)

To: [*name and address of former vassal*].

This notice is sent by [*name and address of former superior*]. You are required to pay the sum of £ [*amount*] as a compensatory payment for the extinction of the cumulo feuduty of £ [*amount*] per annum due in respect of [*give sufficient identification of the land in respect of which the cumulo feuduty was due*].

The attached appendix shows the total sum due as compensation for the extinction of the feuduty and the compensatory payment due by each owner.

(If arrears of the feuduty are also sought, then add:

You are also required to pay the sum of £ [*amount*] as arrears of the feuduty.)

Signed: [*signature either of the former superior or of his agent; and if an agent signs he should put the word 'Agent' after his signature*]

Date:

(If payment is to be made to an agent of the former superior then add:

Payment should be made to: [*name and address of agent*].).'

Appendix referred to in the Notice:

Total compensation payable is £ [*amount*], allocated as follows:

Owner (see note for completion1)	Property (see note for completion 2)	Compensatory payment (see note for completion 3)

Explanatory Note

(This explanation, and the 'Notes for completion of the Appendix' which immediately follows it, have no legal effect)

The feudal system was abolished on [*insert date of abolition*]. By this notice your former feudal superior is claiming compensation from you for the extinction of the cumulo feuduty which affected your property. A cumulo feuduty is one which affects two or more properties in separate ownership. This notice must have been sent within two years after the date of abolition.

The appendix sets out the total sum due as compensation for the extinction of the cumulo feuduty and divides that sum among the owners of the affected properties.

The total compensation payable is that sum which would, if invested in 2½ per-cent, Consolidated Stock at the middle market price at the close of business last preceding the date of abolition, produce an annual sum equal to the cumulo feuduty. In practice the sum is arrived at by multiplying the feuduty by a factor known as the 'compensation factor'. This factor is [*insert factor*].

If the amount of the compensatory payment allocated to you is £50 or more you can choose to pay the sum due by instalments. You may do this by signing, dating and returning, within eight weeks, the enclosed instalment document.

If, having received the instalment document, you sell, or transfer for valuable consideration, the property or any part of it you will lose the option of paying by instalments.

Unless you are paying by instalments you must pay the compensatory payment allocated to you within eight weeks.

Your former feudal superior may also be claiming arrears of feuduty for the period before the date of abolition.

If at one time you had right to the property in question but, immediately before the feudal system was abolished, you no longer had that right (because, for example, you had sold that property to someone else) then this notice has been served on you in error and no payment will be due; but you nevertheless have to provide the person who sent you the notice, if you can, with such information as you have which might enable him to identify the person who should have received notice instead of you.

If you think that the amount required from you is not due for that or any other reason, you are advised to consult your solicitor or other adviser.

Notes for completion of the Appendix

1   Insert the name of each owner.
2   Give sufficient identification of each part of the land held in separate owner-ship (including, where appropriate, the postal address) which was subject to the cumulo feuduty.
3   Insert the amount of the compensation allocated to each owner.

SCHEDULE 2
FORM OF NOTICE REQUIRING COMPENSATORY PAYMENT ETC:
ORDINARY CASE

'NOTICE UNDER SECTION 8(1) OF THE ABOLITION OF FEUDAL TENURE ETC (SCOTLAND) ACT 2000 (ORDINARY CASE)

To: [*name and address of former vassal*].

This notice is sent by [*name and address of former superior*]. You are required to pay the sum of £ [*amount*] as a compensatory payment for the extinction of the feuduty of £ [*amount*] per annum due in respect of [*give sufficient identification of the land in respect of which the feuduty was due*].

(*If arrears of the feuduty are also sought, then add:*

You are also required to pay the sum of £ [*amount*] as arrears of the feuduty.)

Signed: [*signature either of the former superior or of his agent; and if an agent signs he should put the word 'Agent' after his signature*]

Date:

(*If payment is to be made to an agent of the former superior then add:*

Payment should be made to: [*name and address of agent*].)'.

Explanatory Note

(*This explanation has no legal effect*)

The feudal system was abolished on [*insert date of abolition*]. By this notice your former feudal superior is claiming compensation from you for the extinction of the feuduty which affected your property. This notice must have been sent within two years after the date of abolition.

The compensatory payment is that sum which would, if invested in 2½ percent; Consolidated Stock at the middle market price at the close of business last preceding the date of abolition, produce an annual sum equal to the feuduty. In practice the sum is arrived at by multiplying the feuduty by a factor known as the 'compensation factor'. This factor is [*insert factor*].

If the compensatory payment is £50 or more you can choose to pay the sum by instalments. You may do this by signing, dating and returning, within eight weeks, the enclosed instalment document.

If, having received the instalment document, you sell, or transfer for valuable consideration, the property or any part of it you will lose the option of paying by instalments.

Unless you are paying by instalments you must pay the compensatory payment within eight weeks.

Your former feudal superior may also be claiming arrears of feuduty for the period before the date of abolition.

If at one time you had right to the property in question but, immediately before the feudal system was abolished, you no longer had that right (because, for example, you had transferred that property to someone else) then this notice has been served on you in error and no payment will be due in terms of the notice; but you nevertheless have to provide the person who sent you the notice, if you can, with such information as you have which might enable him to identify the person who ostensibly (that is to say, disregarding questions such as whether the feuduty has already been redeemed in the case of a transfer by conveyance for valuable consideration) should have received notice instead of you.

If you think that the amount required from you is not due for whatever reason, you are advised to consult your solicitor or other adviser.

SCHEDULE 3
FORM OF INSTALMENT DOCUMENT

'INSTALMENT DOCUMENT

To: [*name and address of former superior or of his agent*].

I [*name and address of former vassal*] opt to make the compensatory payment of £ [*amount*] due under the notice dated [*date*] by [*number of instalments: see note for completion*] equal half-yearly instalments of £ [*amount*] on 28 May and 28 November each year, commencing on [28 May *or* 28 November] [*year*].

I enclose payment of £ [*amount*] as an amount payable in addition to the compensatory payment.

Signed:

Date: .'.

Explanatory Note

(This explanation has no legal effect)

You can choose to pay by instalments by signing, dating and returning this form within eight weeks, but if you do so you must enclose the additional amount (10 percent; over and above the compensatory payment) mentioned in this notice.

The compensatory payment will be payable in 5, 10, 15, or 20 equal instalments (depending on the total amount). The first payment will be made at the first term day of Whitsunday (28 May) and Martinmas (28 November) which follows the return of the instalment document. Payments will be due half-yearly thereafter on 28 May and 28 November until payment in full has been made.

If you fail to pay an instalment within 42 days after the day on which it is due, the whole balance of the compensatory payment will be due at once.

If, having chosen to pay by instalments, you sell, or transfer for valuable consideration, the property or any part of it the whole balance of the compensatory payment will be due seven days after the sale or transfer.

If, after you receive this document, you sell, or so transfer, the property or any part of it without having signed, dated and returned this form, you will lose the right to obtain the option to pay by instalments and the entire compensatory payment will be payable in accordance with the notice which accompanied this document.

If you have difficulty in making the compensatory payment you may be able to make arrangements with your former superior different from those you would obtain by signing, dating and completing this form; but that is a matter on which you are advised to consult your solicitor or other adviser without delay.

Note for completion of the form by the former superior

(This note has no legal effect)

Insert the number of instalments in accordance with the following table:

Compensatory payment	*Number of instalments*
£50 but not exceeding £500	5
exceeding £500 but not exceeding £1,000	10
exceeding £1,000 but not exceeding £1,500	15
exceeding £1,500	20

SCHEDULE 4
PROCEDURES AS TO SERVICE UNDER SECTION 8(1)

FORM A

'I, [*name of former vassal*], acknowledge receipt of a notice under section 8(1) of the Abolition of Feudal Tenure etc (Scotland) Act 2000 requiring a compensatory payment [*add if applicable,* of an instalment document] and of an explanatory note relating to the notice.

Signed: [*signature of former vassal*]

Date: .'.

FORM B

'Notice under section 8(1) of the Abolition of Feudal Tenure etc (Scotland) Act 2000 requiring a compensatory payment was posted to [*name of former vassal*], together with [*add if applicable* an instalment document and] the requisite explanatory note relating to the notice, on [*date*].

Signature: [*signature either of the former superior or of his agent; and if an agent signs he should put the word 'Agent' after his signature*]

Date: .'.

SCHEDULE 5
FORM OF NOTICE PROSPECTIVELY NOMINATING DOMINANT TENEMENT

'NOTICE PROSPECTIVELY NOMINATING DOMINANT TENEMENT

Superior:
(see note for completion 1)

Description of land which is to be the servient tenement:
(see note for completion 2)

Description of land nominated as dominant tenement:
(see note for completion 2)

Specification of condition met:
(see note for completion 3)

Terms of real burden:
(see note for completion 4)

Any counter-obligation:
(see note for completion 4)

Title to the superiority:
(see note for completion 5)

Title to land nominated as dominant tenement:
(see note for completion 5)

Service:
(see note for completion 6)

I swear [*or* affirm] that the information contained in the notice is, to the best of my knowledge and belief, true.

Signature of superior:
(see note for completion 7)

Signature of notary public:

Date: .'.

Explanatory Note

(This explanation has no legal effect)

This notice is sent by your feudal superior, who is also a neighbour. In this notice your property (or some part of it) is referred to (prospectively) as the 'servient tenement' and neighbouring property belonging to the superior is referred to (again prospectively) as the 'dominant tenement'.

By this notice the feudal superior asserts that at present the use of your property is subject to certain burdens and conditions enforceable by him and claims the right to continue to enforce the burdens and conditions, not as superior but in his capacity of owner of neighbouring property. The notice, if it is registered in the Land Register or Register of Sasines under section 18 of the Abolition of Feudal Tenure etc (Scotland) Act 2000, will allow him and his successors, as such owners, to enforce the burdens and conditions after the feudal system is abolished (which will be shortly).

Normally, for the notice to be valid, there must, on the dominant tenement, be a permanent building which is within 100 metres of the servient tenement. That building must be in use as a place of human habitation or of human resort. However, the presence of a building is not required if the burden gives a right to enter or otherwise make use of the servient tenement, or if it gives a right of preemption or redemption, or if the dominant tenement comprises, and the real burden was created for the benefit of, minerals, salmon fishings or some other incorporeal property.

If you think that there is a mistake in this notice or if you wish to challenge it, you are advised to contact your solicitor or other adviser.

Notes for completion of the notice

(These notes have no legal effect)

1   Insert name and address of superior.

2   Describe the land in a way that is sufficient to enable the Keeper to identify it by reference to the Ordnance Map. Where the title to the land has been registered in the Land Register the description should refer to the title number of the land or of the larger subjects of which the land forms part. Otherwise it should normally refer to and identify a deed recorded in a specified division of the Register of Sasines.

3   Insert one or more of the following:

'The dominant tenement has on it a [specify type of building] at [specify address of building] which is within 100 metres of the servient tenement.';

'The real burden comprises a right to enter, or otherwise make use of, the servient tenement.';

'The real burden comprises a right of [specify pre-emption or redemption (or both)].'.

'The dominant tenement comprises, and (as is apparent from the terms of the real burden) that burden was created for the benefit of, [specify minerals or salmon fishings or some other incorporeal property].'.

4   Specify by reference to the appropriate Register the deed or deeds in which the real burden or counter-obligation was imposed. Set out the real burden or counter-obligation in full or refer to the deed in such a way as to identify the real burden or counter-obligation.

5   Where the title has been registered in the Land Register of Scotland and the superior is—

(a)   registered as proprietor, specify the title number;

(b)   not registered as proprietor, specify the title number and set out the midcouples or links between the person last registered and the superior so as sufficiently to identify them.

Where the title has not been registered in the Land Register and the superior—

(a)   has a recorded title, specify by reference to the Register of Sasines the deed constituting the immediate title;

(b)   does not have a recorded title, either—

(i)   specify by reference to the Register of Sasines the deed constituting the immediate title of the person with the last recorded title and set out the midcouples or links between that person and the superior so as sufficiently to identify them; or

(ii)   if there is no such deed, specify the nature of the superior's title.

6   Do not complete until a copy of the notice has been sent to the owner of the prospective servient tenement (except in a case where this is not reasonably practicable). Then insert whichever is applicable of the following:

'The superior has sent a copy of this notice by [specify whether by recorded delivery or registered post or by ordinary post] on [date of posting] to the owner of the prospective servient tenement at [state address].'; or

'It has not been reasonably practicable to send a copy of this notice to the owner of the prospective servient tenement for the following reason: [specify the reason].'.

7   The superior should not swear or affirm, or sign, until a copy of the notice has been sent (or otherwise) as mentioned in note 6. Before signing the superior should swear or affirm before a notary public (or, if the notice is being completed outwith Scotland, before a person duly authorised under the local law to administer oaths or receive affirmations) that, to the best of the superior's knowledge and belief, all the information contained in the notice is true. The notary public should also sign. Swearing or affirming a statement which is known to be false or which is

believed not to be true is a criminal offence under the False Oaths (Scotland) Act 1933. Normally the superior should swear or affirm, and sign, personally. If, however, the superior is legally disabled or incapable (for example, because of mental disorder) his legal representative should swear or affirm and sign. If the superior is not an individual (for example, if it is a company) a person entitled by law to sign formal documents on its behalf should swear or affirm and sign.

Section 18A(1)   [SCHEDULE 5A
FORM OF NOTICE PROSPECTIVELY CONVERTING REAL BURDEN INTO PERSONAL PRE-EMPTION BURDEN OR PERSONAL REDEMPTION BURDEN

'NOTICE PROSPECTIVELY CONVERTING REAL BURDEN INTO PERSONAL PRE-EMPTION BURDEN OR PERSONAL REDEMPTION BURDEN

Superior:
(see note for completion 1)

Description of land which is to be servient tenement:
(see note for completion 2)

Terms of real burden:
(see note for completion 3)

Any counter obligation:
(see note for completion 3)

Title to the superiority:
(see note for completion 4)

Service:
(see note for completion 5)

I swear [*or* affirm] that the information contained in the notice is, to the best of my knowledge and belief, true.

Signature of superior:
(see note for completion 6)

Signature of notary public:

Date: .'

Explanatory Note

(This explanation has no legal effect)

This notice is sent by your feudal superior. In this notice your property (or some part of it) is referred to (prospectively) as the 'servient tenement'.

By this notice the feudal superior asserts that at present your property is subject to a right of pre-emption [or of redemption] enforceable by him and claims the right to continue to enforce it not as superior but in a personal capacity. The notice, if it is registered in the Land Register or Register of Sasines under section 18A of the Abolition of Feudal Tenure etc (Scotland) Act 2000, will allow him to enforce the right after the feudal system is abolished (which will be shortly).

If you think that there is a mistake in this notice or if you wish to challenge it, you are advised to contact your solicitor or other adviser.

Notes for completion of the notice

(These notes have no legal effect)

1   Insert name and address of superior.

2   Describe the land in a way that is sufficient to enable the Keeper to identify it by reference to the Ordnance Map. Where the title to the land has been registered in the Land Register the description should refer to the title number of the land or of the larger subjects of which the land forms part. Otherwise it should normally refer to and identify a deed recorded in a specified division of the Register of Sasines.

3   Specify by reference to the appropriate Register the deed or deeds in which the real burden or counter-obligation was imposed. Set out the real burden or counter-obligation in full or refer to the deed in such a way as to identify the real burden or counter-obligation.

4   Where the title has been registered in the Land Register of Scotland and the superior is—

(a)   registered as proprietor, specify the title number;

(b)   not so registered, specify the title number and set out the midcouples or links between the person last registered and the superior so as sufficiently to identify them.

Where the title has not been registered in the Land Register and the superior—

(a)   has a recorded title, specify by reference to the Register of Sasines the deed constituting the immediate title;

(b)   does not have a recorded title, either—

(i)   specify by reference to the Register of Sasines the deed constituting the immediate title of the person with the last recorded title and set out the midcouples or links between that person and the superior so as sufficiently to identify them; or

(ii)   if there is no such deed, specify the nature of the superior's title.

5   Do not complete until a copy of the notice has been sent to the owner of the prospective servient tenement (except in a case where this is not reasonably practicable). Then insert whichever is applicable of the following:

'The superior has sent a copy of this notice by [*specify whether by recorded delivery or registered post or by ordinary post*] on [*date of posting*] to the owner of the prospective servient tenement at [*state address*].'; or

'It has not been reasonably practicable to send a copy of this notice to the owner of the prospective servient tenement for the following reason: [*specify the reason*]'.

6   The superior should not swear or affirm, or sign, until a copy of the notice has been sent (or otherwise) as mentioned in note 5. Before signing, the superior should swear or affirm before a notary public (or, if the notice is being completed outwith Scotland, before a person duly authorised under the local law to administer oaths or receive affirmations) that, to the best of the superior's knowledge and belief, all the information contained in the notice is true. The notary public should also sign. Swearing or affirming a statement which is known to be false or which is believed not to be true is a criminal offence under the False Oaths (Scotland) Act 1933. Normally the superior should swear or affirm, and sign, personally. If, however, the superior is legally disabled or incapable (for example, because of mental disorder) his legal representative should swear or affirm and sign. If the superior is not an individual (for example, if it is a company) a person entitled by law to sign formal documents on its behalf should swear or affirm and sign.

Section 18B(1)   SCHEDULE 5B
FORM OF NOTICE PROSPECTIVELY CONVERTING REAL BURDEN INTO
                    ECONOMIC DEVELOPMENT BURDEN

'NOTICE PROSPECTIVELY CONVERTING REAL BURDEN INTO ECONOMIC
                         DEVELOPMENT BURDEN

Superior:
(see note for completion 1)

Description of land which is to be servient tenement:
(see note for completion 2)

Terms of real burden:
(see note for completion 3)

Statement that purpose was to promote economic development:
(with supporting evidence: see note for completion 3)

Any counter obligation:
(see note for completion 3)

Title to the superiority:
(see note for completion 4)

Service:
(see note for completion 5)

Signature on behalf of superior:

Date: .'

Explanatory Note

(This explanation has no legal effect)

This notice is sent by your feudal superior; that is to say by [the Scottish Ministers]
or [specify local authority].

By this notice the feudal superior asserts that at present your property is subject
to a real burden enforceable by the superior and claims both the right to continue
to enforce it, not as superior but in a personal capacity, and that the real burden is
for the purpose of promoting economic development. The notice, if it is registered
in the Land Register or Register of Sasines under section 18B of the Abolition of
Feudal Tenure etc (Scotland) Act 2000, will allow the superior to enforce that right
after the feudal system is abolished (which will be shortly).

If you think that there is a mistake in this notice or if you wish to challenge it,
you are advised to contact your solicitor or other adviser.

Notes for completion of the notice

(These notes have no legal effect)

1   Insert 'the Scottish Ministers' or as the case may be the name and address of
the local authority.

2   Describe the land in a way that is sufficient to enable the Keeper to identify it
by reference to the Ordnance Map. Where the title to the land has been registered
in the Land Register the description should refer to the title number of the land or
of the larger subjects of which the land forms part. Otherwise it should normally
refer to and identify a deed recorded in a specified division of the Register of
Sasines.

3   Specify by reference to the appropriate Register the deed or deeds in which

the real burden or counter-obligation was imposed. Set out the terms of the real burden, or as the case may be the terms of the counter-obligation, in full or refer to the deed in such a way as to identify the real burden or counter-obligation. Provide the statement specified and set out any information which supports it.

4   Where the title has been registered in the Land Register of Scotland and the superior is—

    (a)   registered as proprietor, specify the title number;

    (b)   not so registered, specify the title number and set out the midcouples or links between the person last registered and the superior so as sufficiently to identify them.

Where the title has not been registered in the Land Register and the superior—

    (a)   has a recorded title, specify by reference to the Register of Sasines the deed constituting the immediate title;

    (b)   does not have a recorded title, either—

        (i)   specify by reference to the Register of Sasines the deed constituting the immediate title of the person with the last recorded title and set out the midcouples or links between that person and the superior so as sufficiently to identify them; or

        (ii)   if there is no such deed, specify the nature of the superior's title.

5   Do not complete until a copy of the notice has been sent to the owner of the prospective servient tenement (except in a case where such sending is not reasonably practicable). Then insert whichever is applicable of the following:

'The superior has sent a copy of this notice by [*specify whether by recorded delivery or registered post or by ordinary post*] on [*date of posting*] to the owner of the prospective servient tenement at [state address].'; or

'It has not been reasonably practicable to send a copy of this notice to the owner of the prospective servient tenement and the reason is that: [*specify the reason*].'

SCHEDULE 5C   Section 18C(1)

FORM OF NOTICE PROSPECTIVELY CONVERTING REAL BURDEN INTO HEALTH CARE BURDEN

'NOTICE PROSPECTIVELY CONVERTING REAL BURDEN INTO HEALTH CARE BURDEN

Superior:
(see note for completion 1)

Description of land which is to be servient tenement:
(see note for completion 2)

Terms of real burden:
(see note for completion 3)

Statement that purpose was to promote the provision of facilities for health care:
(with supporting evidence: see note for completion 3)

Any counter obligation:
(see note for completion 3)

Title to the superiority:
(see note for completion 4)

Service:
(see note for completion 5)

Signature on behalf of superior:

Date: .'

Explanatory Note

(This explanation has no legal effect)

This notice is sent by your feudal superior; that is to say by [*the Scottish Ministers*] or [*specify National Health Service trust*].

By this notice the feudal superior asserts that at present your property is subject to a real burden enforceable by the superior and claims both the right to continue to enforce it, not as superior but in a personal capacity, and that the real burden is for the purpose of promoting the provision of facilities for health care. The notice, if it is registered in the Land Register or Register of Sasines under section 18C of the Abolition of Feudal Tenure etc (Scotland) Act 2000, will allow the superior to enforce that right after the feudal system is abolished (which will be shortly).

If you think that there is a mistake in this notice or if you wish to challenge it, you are advised to contact your solicitor or other adviser.

Notes for completion of the notice

(These notes have no legal effect)

1   Insert 'the Scottish Ministers' or as the case may be the name and address of the National Health Service trust.

2   Describe the land in a way that is sufficient to enable the Keeper to identify it by reference to the Ordnance Map. Where the title to the land has been registered in the Land Register the description should refer to the title number of the land or of the larger subjects of which the land forms part. Otherwise it should normally refer to and identify a deed recorded in a specified division of the Register of Sasines.

3   Specify by reference to the appropriate Register the deed or deeds in which the real burden or counter-obligation was imposed. Set out the terms of the real burden, or as the case may be the terms of the counter-obligation, in full or refer to the deed in such a way as to identify the real burden or counter-obligation. Provide the statement specified and set out any information which supports it.

4   Where the title has been registered in the Land Register of Scotland and the superior is—

(a)   registered as proprietor, specify the title number;

(b)   not so registered, specify the title number and set out the midcouples or links between the person last registered and the superior so as sufficiently to identify them.

Where the title has not been registered in the Land Register and the superior—

(a)   has a recorded title, specify by reference to the Register of Sasines the deed constituting the immediate title;

(b)   does not have a recorded title, either—

(i)   specify by reference to the Register of Sasines the deed constituting the immediate title of the person with the last recorded title and set out the midcouples or links between that person and the superior so as sufficiently to identify them; or

(ii)   if there is no such deed, specify the nature of the superior's title.

5   Do not complete until a copy of the notice has been sent to the owner of the prospective servient tenement (except in a case where such sending is not reasonably practicable). Then insert whichever is applicable of the following:

'The superior has sent a copy of this notice by [*specify whether by recorded delivery or registered post or by ordinary post*] on [*date of posting*] to the owner of the prospective servient tenement at [*state address*].'; or

'It has not been reasonably practicable to send a copy of this notice to the owner of the prospective servient tenement and the reason is that: [*specify the reason*].'.]

SCHEDULE 6
FORM OF NOTICE SEEKING AGREEMENT TO THE PROSPECTIVE
NOMINATION OF A DOMINANT TENEMENT
'NOTICE SEEKING AGREEMENT TO PROSPECTIVE NOMINATION OF DOMINANT
TENEMENT

Superior:
(see note for completion 1)

Person who has the feudal estate of dominium utile:
(see note for completion 2)

Description of land which, if agreement is reached and the agreement is registered, shall be the prospective servient tenement:

Description of land which, if agreement is reached and the agreement is registered, shall be the prospective dominant tenement:

Terms of real burden:
(see note for completion 3)

Any counter-obligation:
(see note for completion 3)

Title to the superiority:
(see note for completion 4)

Title to land which would be the prospective dominant tenement:
(see note for completion 4)

Service:
(see note for completion 5)

Signature of superior:

Date: .'.

Explanatory Note

(This explanation has no legal effect)

This notice is sent by your feudal superior. In this notice your property (or some part of it) is referred to (prospectively) as the 'servient tenement' and property belonging to the superior is referred to (again prospectively) as the 'dominant tenement'.

By this notice the feudal superior asserts that at present the use of your property is subject to certain burdens and conditions enforceable by him. He wishes to be able to continue to enforce the burdens and conditions, not as superior but in his capacity of owner of the prospective dominant tenement. If you agree and if the agreement is registered in the Land Register or Register of Sasines under section 19 of the Abolition of Feudal Tenure etc (Scotland) Act 2000, he and his successors, as such owners, will be able to enforce the burdens and conditions after the feudal system is abolished (which will be shortly).

In the absence of agreement the superior may yet be able to enforce the burdens and conditions provided that he can meet certain statutory conditions or if he applies to the Lands Tribunal for Scotland and the Tribunal grants an appropriate order on being satisfied by him that there would be substantial loss or disadvantage to him as owner of the prospective dominant tenement were the real burden to be extinguished or to cease to be enforceable by him.

If the superior does apply to the Tribunal you may oppose the application and in doing so may be eligible for Legal Aid. You would not ordinarily have to meet the superior's expenses. You are advised to consult your solicitor or other adviser if you wish to consider opposing the application or if you are uncertain about what is said in this notice.

Notes for completion of the notice

(These notes have no legal effect)

1   Insert name and address of superior.

2   Insert name and address of person who has the feudal estate of dominium utile.

3   Specify by reference to the appropriate Register the deed or deeds in which the real burden or counter-obligation was imposed. Set out the real burden or counter-obligation in full or refer to the deed in such a way as to identify the real burden or counter-obligation. You may if you wish propose and set out a modification to either the real burden or to the counter-obligation (or modifications to both).

4   Where the title has been registered in the Land Register of Scotland and the superior is—

(a)   registered as proprietor, specify the title number;

(b)   not registered as proprietor, specify the title number and set out the mid-couples or links between the person last registered and the superior so as sufficiently to identify them.

Where the title has not been registered in the Land Register and the superior—

(a)   has a recorded title, specify by reference to the Register of Sasines the deed constituting the immediate title;

(b)   does not have a recorded title, either—

(i)   specify by reference to the Register of Sasines the deed constituting the immediate title of the person with the last recorded title and set out the midcouples or links between that person and the superior so as sufficiently to identify them; or

(ii)   if there is no such deed, specify the nature of the superior's title.

5   Do not complete until a copy of the notice has been delivered or sent to the person with right to the feu. Then insert the following:

'The superior has served this notice by [*specify whether by delivery, by recorded delivery, by registered post or by ordinary post*] on [*date of posting*] to the person with right to the feu at [*state address*].'.

The notice should not be signed until a copy of it has been so delivered or sent.

SCHEDULE 7
FORM OF NOTICE INTIMATING APPLICATION TO LANDS TRIBUNAL UNDER SECTION 20(1)

'NOTICE INTIMATING APPLICATION TO LANDS TRIBUNAL UNDER SECTION 20(1) OF THE ABOLITION OF FEUDAL TENURE ETC (SCOTLAND) ACT 2000

Superior:
(see note for completion 1)

Description of land which is the prospective servient tenement:
(see note for completion 2)

Description of land which is the prospective dominant tenement:
(see note for completion 2)

Terms of real burden:
(see note for completion 3)

Any counter-obligation:
(see note for completion 3)

Title to the superiority:
(see note for completion 4)

Title to the dominium utile of the prospective dominant tenement:
(see note for completion 4)

Terms of description given, in application to Lands Tribunal, of attempt to reach agreement:
(see note for completion 5)

Service:
(see note for completion 6)
I swear [*or* affirm] that the information contained in the notice is, to the best of my knowledge and belief, true.

Signature of superior:
(see note for completion 7)

Signature of notary public:

Date: .'.

Explanatory Note

(This explanation has no legal effect)

This notice is sent by your feudal superior. In this notice your property (or some part of it) is referred to as the 'prospective servient tenement' and the superior's property is referred to as the 'prospective dominant tenement'.

At present the use of your property is subject to certain burdens and conditions enforceable by the feudal superior. The feudal system is shortly to be abolished. The feudal superior cannot satisfy any of the conditions in section 18(7) of the Abolition of Feudal Tenure etc (Scotland) Act 2000 but is applying to the Lands Tribunal for Scotland to be allowed the right to continue to enforce the burdens and conditions, not as superior but in his capacity of owner of the prospective dominant tenement. The Lands Tribunal's order, if it is registered in the Land Register or Register of Sasines under section 20 of the 2000 Act, would allow him and his successors, as such owners, to enforce the burdens and conditions after the feudal system is abolished. He claims that there would be substantial loss or disadvantage to him as owner of the prospective dominant tenement were the real burden to be extinguished or no longer to be enforceable by him.

You may oppose his application to the Tribunal and in doing so may be eligible for Legal Aid. You would not ordinarily have to meet the superior's expenses. You are advised to consult your solicitor or other adviser if you wish to consider opposing the application or if you think that there is a mistake in this notice.

The effect of the superior registering this notice will be that the burdens and conditions to which the notice relates will continue to be burdens and conditions (though, after the feudal system is abolished, non-feudal burdens and conditions) until the order made by the Lands Tribunal in respect of the application is registered as mentioned above unless the order is registered before the feudal system is abolished in which case until the feudal system is abolished (or, if there is no such registration at all, until a date specified by the Scottish Ministers) at which time the burdens and conditions would either be saved as non-feudal burdens and conditions or would be extinguished because the superior had been unsuccessful in his application.

Notes for completion of the notice

(These notes have no legal effect)

1   Insert name and address of superior.

2   Describe the land in a way that is sufficient to enable the Keeper to identify it by reference to the Ordnance Map. Where the title to the land has been registered in the Land Register the description should refer to the relevant title number of the land or of the larger subjects of which the land forms part. Otherwise it should normally refer to and identify a deed recorded in a specified division of the Register of Sasines.

3   Specify by reference to the Register the deed or deeds in which the real burden or counter-obligation was imposed. Set out the real burden or counter-obligation in full or so as sufficiently to identify it.

4   The superiority referred to in the box 'Title to the superiority' is the superiority of land which comprises the prospective servient tenement.
Where the title—

(a)   has been registered in the Land Register and the applicant is infeft, specify the title number or if he is uninfeft specify the title number and set out the midcouples or links between the person last infeft and the applicant in such terms as are sufficient to identify them;

(b)   has not been registered in the Land Register and the applicant is infeft, specify by reference to the Register the deed constituting the title or if he is uninfeft specify the deed constituting the title of the person last infeft and the date of recording and set out the midcouples or links as in paragraph (a).

5   Set out in full the description which was, in pursuance of section 20(2) of the Abolition of Feudal Tenure etc (Scotland) Act 2000, included in the application.

6   Insert either: 'The applicant has sent a copy of this notice by [*specify recorded delivery mail or registered post*] to the owner of the prospective servient tenement at [*specify the address of the prospective servient tenement, or the place of residence or place of business, or the most recently known place of residence or place of business, of the owner of the servient tenement*].' or 'It has not been reasonably practicable to serve a copy of this notice on the owner of the prospective servient tenement for the following reasons: [*specify the reasons*].'.

7   The superior should not swear or affirm, or sign, until a copy of the notice has been sent (or otherwise) as mentioned in note 6. Before signing the superior should swear or affirm before a notary public (or, if the notice is being completed outwith Scotland, before a person duly authorised under the local law to administer oaths or receive affirmations) that, to the best of the superior's knowledge and belief, all the information contained in the notice is true. The notary public should also sign. Swearing or affirming a statement which is known to be false or which is believed not to be true is a criminal offence under the False Oaths (Scotland) Act 1933. Normally the superior should swear or affirm, and sign, personally. If, however, the superior is legally disabled or incapable (for example, because of mental disorder) his legal representative should swear or affirm and sign. If the superior is not an individual (for example, if it is a company) a person entitled by law to sign formal documents on its behalf should swear or affirm and sign.

SCHEDULE 8
FORM OF NOTICE PRESERVING CONSERVATION BODY'S OR SCOTTISH
MINISTERS' RIGHT TO REAL BURDEN

'NOTICE PRESERVING CONSERVATION BODY'S OR SCOTTISH MINISTERS'
RIGHT TO REAL BURDEN

Superior (being a conservation body or the Scottish Ministers):
(see note for completion 1)

Description of land subject to the real burden:
(see note for completion 2)

Terms of real burden:
(see note for completion 3)

Any counter-obligation:
(see note for completion 3)

Title to the superiority:
(see note for completion 4)

Service:
(see note for completion 5)

Signature of superior:
(see note for completion 6)

Signature of witness:

Name and address of witness:

Date: .'.

Explanatory Note

(This explanation has no legal effect)

This notice is sent by your feudal superior.

At present the use of your property is subject to certain burdens and conditions enforceable by the feudal superior. The feudal system is shortly to be abolished. [By the regulations mentioned in the notice, the Scottish Ministers have prescribed that your superior should be a conservation body. Such a body is entitled to enforce certain real burdens (referred to prospectively as 'conservation burdens').] *or* [The feudal superior is the Scottish Ministers and it is intended that they shall enforce certain real burdens (referred to prospectively as 'conservation burdens').] These are burdens which have been imposed in the public interest for the pre-servation or protection either of architectural or historic characteristics of land or of some other special characteristic of land derived from the flora, fauna, or general appearance of the land. By this notice [the conservation body is] [the Scottish Ministers are] claiming the right to continue to enforce a conservation burden, not as superior but [in its capacity as a conservation body] [in their capacity as the Scottish Ministers]. The notice, if it is registered in the Land Register of Scotland or recorded in the Register of Sasines under section 27 of the Abolition of Feudal Tenure etc (Scotland) Act 2000, will allow the burden and conditions to be so enforced after the feudal system has been abolished.

If you think that there is a mistake in this notice or if you wish to challenge it, you are advised to consult your solicitor or other adviser.

Notes for completion of the notice

(These notes have no legal effect)

1   [In the case of a conservation body] insert the year and number of the relevant statutory instrument and the name and address of [that] body.

2   Describe the land in a way that is sufficient to enable the Keeper to identify it by reference to the Ordnance Map. Where the title to the land has been registered in the Land Register the description should refer to the title number of the land or of the larger subjects of which the land forms part. Otherwise it should normally refer to and identify a deed recorded in a specified division of the Register of Sasines.

3   Specify by reference to the appropriate Register the deed or deeds in which the real burden or counter-obligation was imposed. Set out the real burden or counter-obligation in full or refer to the deed in such a way as to identify the real burden or counter-obligation.

4   Where the title has been registered in the Land Register of Scotland and the superior is—

   (a)   infeft, specify the title number;

   (b)   uninfeft, specify the title number and set out the midcouples or links between the person last infeft and the superior so as sufficiently to identify them.

Where the title has not been registered in the Land Register and the superior—

   (a)   has a recorded title, specify by reference to the Register of Sasines the deed constituting the immediate title;

   (b)   does not have a recorded title, either—

      (i)   specify by reference to the Register of Sasines the deed constituting the immediate title of the person last infeft and set out the midcouples or links between the person last infeft and the superior so as sufficiently to identify them; or

      (ii)   if there is no such deed, specify the nature of the superior's title.

5   Do not complete until a copy of the notice has been sent to the owner of the land subject to the burden (except in a case where this is not reasonably practicable). Then insert whichever is applicable of the following:

   'The superior has sent a copy of this notice by [*specify whether by recorded delivery or registered post or by ordinary post*] on [*date of posting*] to the owner of the land subject to the real burden at [*state address*].'; or

   'It has not been reasonably practicable to send a copy of this notice to the owner of the land subject to the real burden for the following reason: [*specify the reason*].'.

6   The notice should not be signed until a copy of it has been sent (or otherwise) as mentioned in note 5. The conservation body or the Scottish Ministers should sign.

Section 27A(1)   [SCHEDULE 8A
FORM OF NOTICE NOMINATING CONSERVATION BODY OR SCOTTISH MINISTERS TO HAVE TITLE TO ENFORCE REAL BURDEN

'NOTICE NOMINATING CONSERVATION BODY OR SCOTTISH MINISTERS TO HAVE TITLE TO ENFORCE REAL BURDEN

Superior:

Nominee (being a conservation body or the Scottish Ministers):
(see note for completion 1)

Description of land subject to the real burden:
(see note for completion 2)

Terms of real burden:
(see note for completion 3)

Any counter-obligation:
(see note for completion 3)

Title to the superiority:
(see notes for completion 4 and 5)

Service:
(see note for completion 6)

Signature of superior: Signature of consenting nominee:
(see note for completion 7) (see note for completion 8)

Signature of superior's witness: Signature of nominee's witness:

Name and address of witness: Name and address of witness:

Date: .'

Explanatory note

(This explanation has no legal effect)

This notice is sent by your feudal superior.

At present the use of your property is subject to certain burdens and conditions enforceable by the feudal superior. The feudal system is shortly to be abolished. The feudal superior intends to nominate a conservation body or the Scottish Ministers to have title to enforce certain of those burdens (referred to prospectively as 'conservation burdens') when he ceases to have such title. These are burdens which have been imposed in the public interest for the preservation or protection either of architectural or historic characteristics of land or of some other special characteristic of land derived from the flora, fauna or general appearance of the land. By virtue of this notice the nominee would have the right to enforce a conservation burden in the capacity of conservation body or of the Scottish Ministers, as the case may be. The notice, if it is registered in the Land Register of Scotland or recorded in the Register of Sasines under section 27A of the Abolition of Feudal Tenure etc (Scotland) Act 2000, will allow the burden to be so enforced after the feudal system has been abolished.

If you think there is a mistake in this notice or if you wish to challenge it, you are advised to consult your solicitor or other adviser.

Notes for completion of the notice

(These notes have no legal effect)

1   In the case of a conservation body, insert the year and number of the relevant statutory instrument and the name and address of that body.

2   Describe the land in a way that is sufficient to enable the Keeper to identify it by reference to the Ordnance Map. Where the title to the land has been registered in the Land Register the description should refer to the title number of the land or of the larger subjects of which the land forms part. Otherwise it should normally refer to and identify a deed recorded in a specified division of the Register of Sasines.

3   Specify by reference to the appropriate Register the deed or deeds in which the real burden or counter-obligation was imposed. Set out the real burden or counter-obligation in full or refer to the deed in such a way as to identify the real burden or counter-obligation.

4   Where the title has been registered in the Land Register of Scotland and the superior is-
   (a)   infeft, specify the title number;
   (b)   uninfeft, specify the title number and set out the midcouples or links between the person last infeft and the superior so as sufficiently to identify them.
5   Where the title has not been registered in the Land Register and the superior—
   (a)   has a recorded title, specify by reference to the Register of Sasines the deed constituting the immediate title;
   (b)   does not have a recorded title, either—
      (i)   specify by reference to the Register of Sasines the deed constituting the immediate title of the person last infeft and set out the midcouples or links between the person last infeft and the superior so as sufficiently to identify them; or
      (ii)   if there is no such deed, specify the nature of the superior's title.
6   Do not complete until a copy of the notice has been sent to the owner of the land subject to the burden (except in a case where this is not reasonably practicable). Then insert whichever is applicable of the following:
   'The superior has sent a copy of this notice by [specify whether by recorded delivery or registered post or by ordinary post] on [date of posting] to the owner of the land subject to the real burden at [state address].'; or
   'It has not been reasonably practicable to send a copy of this notice to the owner of the land subject to the real burden for the following reason: [specify the reason].'
7   The notice should not be signed by the superior until a copy of it has been sent (or otherwise) as mentioned in note 6.
8   The nominee should sign, so as to indicate consent, before that copy is sent (or otherwise) as so mentioned.]

SCHEDULE 9

FORM OF NOTICE RESERVING RIGHT TO COMPENSATION IN RESPECT OF EXTINCTION OF DEVELOPMENT VALUE BURDEN

'NOTICE RESERVING RIGHT TO COMPENSATION IN RESPECT OF EXTINCTION OF DEVELOPMENT VALUE BURDEN

Superior:
(see note for completion 1)

Description of land (or part) subject to the real burden:
(see note for completion 2)

Terms of real burden:
(see note for completion 3)

Statement that burden reserves development value:
(see note for completion 4)

Title to the superiority:
(see note for completion 5)

Details of feu grant:
(see note for completion 6)

Amount by which consideration reduced:
(see note for completion 7)

Service:
(see note for completion 8)

By this notice I [AB] (*superior*) reserve the right to claim compensation in respect of the extinction of the development value burden(s) set out in this form.

I swear [*or* affirm] that the information contained in the notice is, to the best of my knowledge and belief, true.

Signature of superior:
(see note for completion 9)

Signature of notary public:

Date: .'.

Explanatory Note

(This explanation has no legal effect)

This notice is sent by your feudal superior.

The feudal system is shortly to be abolished. By this notice the feudal superior is claiming that your property is subject to a development value burden. He is reserving the right to claim compensation for the loss of the burden. Compensation so claimed is payable if either during the five year period ending on [insert date of appointed day] or during the twenty year period starting on that date something happens which, had the feudal system not been abolished, would have been a breach of the burden.

A development value burden is a special type of real burden designed to reserve for the superior the benefit of any increase in the value of the land arising from the land being freed to be used or dealt with in a way prohibited by the burden. Burdens of this type were typically inserted in feudal grants where the superior gave away land, or sold it very cheaply, on condition that it was used only for some charitable or community purposes (for example, for use only as a community hall or sports field).

For the superior to be entitled to reserve the right to claim compensation, the burden must have led to the price paid for your property when it was first sold by the superior being significantly lower than it would otherwise have been.

This notice will be registered in the Land Register of Scotland, or recorded in the Register of Sasines, under section 33 of the Abolition of Feudal Tenure etc (Scotland) Act 2000.

If you think that there is a mistake in this notice or if you wish to challenge it, you are advised to consult your solicitor or other adviser.

Notes for completion of notice

(These notes have no legal effect)

1   Insert name and address of superior.

2   Describe the land in a way that is sufficient to enable the Keeper to identify it by reference to the Ordnance Map. Where the title to the land has been registered in the Land Register the description should refer to the title number of the land or of the larger subjects of which the land forms part. Otherwise it should normally refer to and identify a deed recorded in a specified division of the Register of Sasines.

3   Specify by reference to the appropriate Register the deed or deeds in which the development value burden was imposed. Set out the burden in full or refer to the deed in such a way as to identify the burden. If the notice is used to reserve rights in relation to more than one development value burden, details of each burden should be set out separately, in numbered paragraphs.

4   State that the burden reserves the development value. Section 33(5) of the Abolition of Feudal Tenure etc (Scotland) Act 2000 defines 'development value' as

'any significant increase in the value of the land arising as a result of the land becoming free to be used, or dealt with, in some way not permitted under the grant in feu'. Set out any information (additional to that provided in the other boxes) which supports that statement.

5   Where the title has been registered in the Land Register of Scotland and the superior is—

(a)   infeft, specify the title number;

(b)   uninfeft, specify the title number and set out the midcouples or links between the person last infeft and the superior so as sufficiently to identify them.

Where the title has not been registered in the Land Register and the superior—

(a)   has a recorded title, specify by reference to the Register of Sasines the deed constituting the immediate title;

(b)   does not have a recorded title, either—

(i)   specify by reference to the Register of Sasines the deed constituting the immediate title of the person last infeft and set out the midcouples or links between the person last infeft and the superior so as sufficiently to identify them; or

(ii)   if there is no such deed, specify the nature of the superior's title.

6   Specify by reference to the appropriate Register the writ granting the relevant land in feu.

7   State the amount by which the consideration was reduced because of the imposition of the burden. (If the notice relates to more than one burden, the amounts should be shown separately for each burden.) The statement should be made to the best of the superior's knowledge and belief.

8   Do not complete until a copy of the notice has been sent to the owner of the land subject to the burden (except in a case where this is not reasonably practicable). Then insert whichever is applicable of the following:

'The superior has sent a copy of this notice by [specify whether by recorded delivery or registered post or by ordinary post] on [date of posting] to the owner of the land subject to the burden at [state address].'; or

'It has not been reasonably practicable to send a copy of this notice to the owner of the land subject to the burden for the following reason: [specify the reason].'.

9   The superior should not swear or affirm, or sign, until a copy of the notice has been sent (or otherwise) as mentioned in note 8. Before signing the superior should swear or affirm before a notary public (or, if the notice is being completed outwith Scotland, before a person duly authorised under the local law to administer oaths or receive affirmations) that, to the best of the superior's knowledge and belief, all the information contained in the notice is true. The notary public should also sign. Swearing or affirming a statement which is known to be false or which is believed not to be true is a criminal offence under the False Oaths (Scotland) Act 1933. Normally the superior should swear or affirm, and sign, personally. If, however, the superior is legally disabled or incapable (for example, because of mental disorder) his legal representative should swear or affirm and sign. If the superior is not an individual (for example, if it is a company) a person entitled by law to sign formal documents on its behalf should swear or affirm and sign.

SCHEDULE 10
PROCEDURES AS TO SERVICE UNDER SECTION 35(3)

FORM A

'I [name of owner] acknowledge receipt of a notice under section 35(3) of the Abolition of Feudal Tenure etc (Scotland) Act 2000 claiming compensation of [amount].

Signed: [*signature of owner*]

Date: .'.

FORM B

'Notice under section 35(3) of the Abolition of Feudal Tenure etc (Scotland) Act 2000 claiming compensation was posted to [*name of owner*] on [*date*].

Signature: [*signature either of the owner or his agent; and if an agent signs he should put the word 'Agent' after his signature*]

Date: .'.

SCHEDULE 11
FORM OF ASSIGNATION, DISCHARGE OR RESTRICTION OF RESERVED RIGHT TO CLAIM COMPENSATION

'ASSIGNATION [OR DISCHARGE OR RESTRICTION] OF RESERVED RIGHT TO CLAIM COMPENSATION

I, [AB] (*designation*), hereby [assign to CD (*designation*)] or [*discharge*] the right to claim compensation reserved by a notice dated (*specify date*) and [recorded in the Register of Sasines for (*specify county*) on (*specify date*) under (*specify fiche and frame*) or registered in the Land Register of Scotland on (*specify date*) against the subjects in title number (*specify number*)] [*add if applicable* but only to the extent of (*specify percentage*) of each claim which may come to be made] or [add if applicable but only to the extent of (specify restriction) or but only in relation to (specify restriction)]. [*Where the person assigning or as the case may be discharging or restricting the right to claim compensation is not registered as having that right, add a note setting out the midcouples or links between that person and the person last so registered so as sufficiently to identify them.*]'.

(*Execute in accordance with section 3 of the Requirements of Writing (Scotland) Act 1995.*)

[SCHEDULE 11A   Section 65A(1)
FORM OF NOTICE PROSPECTIVELY CONVERTING SPORTING RIGHTS INTO TENEMENT IN LAND

'NOTICE PROSPECTIVELY CONVERTING SPORTING RIGHTS INTO TENEMENT IN LAND

Superior:
(*see note for completion 1*)

Description of land subject to sporting rights:
(*see note for completion 2*)

Description of sporting rights:
(*see note for completion 3*)

Any counter-obligation:
(*see note for completion 3*)

Title to the superiority:
(*see note for completion 4*)

Service:
(*see note for completion 5*)

I swear [*or* affirm] that the information contained in this notice is, to the best of my knowledge and belief, true.

Signature of superior:
(see note for completion 6)

Signature of notary public:

Date: .'.

Explanatory note

(This explanation has no legal effect)

This notice is sent by your feudal superior.

By it the feudal superior asserts that at present your property is subject to certain sporting rights (that is to say, to rights of fishing or game) enforceable by him as superior and he seeks to continue to enjoy those rights on a different basis: that is to say, as a tenement in land.

The notice, if it is registered in the Land Register of Scotland or recorded in the Register of Sasines under section 65A of the Abolition of Feudal Tenure etc (Scotland) Act 2000, will have that effect when (shortly) the feudal system is abolished.

If you think there is a mistake in this notice or if you wish to challenge it, you are advised to consult your solicitor or other adviser.

Notes for completion of the notice

(These notes have no legal effect)

1   Insert name and address of superior.

2   Describe the land in a way that is sufficient to enable the Keeper to identify it by reference to the Ordnance Map. Where the title to the land has been registered in the Land Register the description should refer to the title number of the land or of the larger subjects of which the land forms part. Otherwise it should normally refer to and identify a deed recorded in a specified division of the Register of Sasines.

3   Specify by reference to the appropriate Register the deed or deeds in which the sporting rights were reserved or the counter-obligation was imposed. Describe the sporting rights or set out the counter-obligation in full or refer to the deed in such a way as to identify those rights or that counter-obligation.

4   Where the title has been registered in the Land Register of Scotland and the superior is—

(a)   infeft, specify the title number;

(b)   uninfeft, specify the title number and set out the midcouples or links between the person last infeft and the superior so as sufficiently to identify them.

Where the title has not been registered in the Land Register and the superior—

(a)   has a recorded title, specify by reference to the Register of Sasines the deed constituting the immediate title;

(b)   does not have a recorded title, either—

(i)   specify by reference to the Register of Sasines the deed constituting the immediate title of the person last infeft and set out the midcouples or links between the person last infeft and the superior so as sufficiently to identify them; or

(ii)   if there is no such deed, specify the nature of the superior's title.

5   Do not complete until a copy of the notice has been sent to the owner of the land subject to the sporting rights (except in a case where this is not reasonably practicable). Then insert whichever is applicable of the following:

'The superior has sent a copy of this notice by [*specify whether by recorded delivery or registered post or by ordinary post*] on [*date of posting*] to the owner of the land subject to the sporting rights at [state address]'.; or

'It has not been reasonably practicable to send a copy of this notice to the owner of the land subject to the sporting rights for the following reason: [*specify the reason*]'.

6   The notice should not be signed by the superior until a copy of it has been sent (or otherwise) as mentioned in note 5. Before signing, the superior should swear or affirm before a notary public (or, if the notice is being completed outwith Scotland, before a person duly authorised under the local law to administer oaths or receive affirmations) that, to the best of the superior's knowledge and belief, all the information contained in the notice is true. The notary public should also sign. Swearing or affirming a statement which is known to be false or which is believed not to be true is a criminal offence under the False Oaths (Scotland) Act 1933. Normally the superior should swear or affirm, and sign, personally. If, however, the superior is legally disabled or incapable (for example, because of mental disorder) his legal representative should swear or affirm and sign. If the superior is not an individual (for example, if it is a company) a person entitled by law to sign formal documents on its behalf should swear or affirm and sign.]

MORTGAGE RIGHTS (SCOTLAND) ACT 2001
(2001, asp 11)

1   Application to suspend enforcement of standard security

(1)   This section applies where a creditor in a standard security over [land or a real right] in land used to any extent for residential purposes has—

(a)   served—

(i)   a calling-up notice under section 19 (calling-up of standard security), or

(ii)   a notice of default under section 21 (notice of default),

(b)   made an application to the court under section 24 (application to court for remedies on default) of that Act, or

(c)   commenced proceedings under section 5 (power to eject proprietor in personal occupancy) of the Heritable Securities (Scotland) Act 1894 (c 44) (in this Act referred to as 'the 1894 Act').

(2)   The following persons may apply to the court for an order under section 2 of this Act—

(a)   the debtor in the standard security or the proprietor of the security subjects (where the proprietor is not the debtor), if the security subjects (in whole or in part) are that person's sole or main residence,

(b)   the non-entitled spouse of the debtor or the proprietor, where the security subjects (in whole or in part) are a matrimonial home and the sole or main residence of the non-entitled spouse,

(c)   a person living together with the debtor or the proprietor as husband or wife or in a relationship which has the characteristics of the relationship between husband and wife except that the persons are of the same sex, if the security subjects (in whole or in part) are that person's sole or main residence,

(d)   a person who has lived together with the debtor or the proprietor as mentioned in paragraph (c), if—

(i)   the security subjects (in whole or in part) are the sole or main residence of that person but not of the debtor or, as the case may be, the proprietor,

(ii)   that person lived together with the debtor or the proprietor as mentioned in that paragraph throughout the period of 6 months ending with the date on which the security subjects ceased to be the sole or main residence of the debtor or the proprietor, and

(iii)   the security subjects (in whole or in part) are the sole or main residence of a child under the age of 16 years who is a child of that person and of the debtor or the proprietor.

(3) In paragraph (d)(iii) of subsection (2), 'child' includes a stepchild and any person brought up or treated by the person mentioned in that paragraph and the debtor or the proprietor as their child.

(4) An application under subsection (2) must be made—

(a) in the case mentioned in subsection (1)(a)(i), before the expiry of the period of notice in relation to the calling-up notice,

(b) in the case mentioned in subsection (1)(a)(ii), not later than one month after the expiry of the period of notice specified in the notice of default,

(c) in a case mentioned in subsection (1)(b) or (c), before the conclusion of the proceedings.

(5) The period of one month mentioned in subsection (4)(b) may be dispensed with or shortened by the person on whom the notice of default has been served, but only with the consent in writing of—

(a) any other person on whom the notice of default has been served,

(b) if the standard security is over a matrimonial home, the spouse of each person on whom the notice of default has been served, and

(c) any person entitled to make an application under subsection (2) by virtue of paragraph (c) or (d) of that subsection.

(6) An application under subsection (2) in a case mentioned in subsection (1)(a) must be made by summary application.

(7) Any rights which the creditor has, or acquires, by virtue of the enactments mentioned in subsection (1)(a) to (c) may not be exercised—

(a) at any time when an application under subsection (2) is competent,

(b) at any time when such an application has been made but has not been determined.

(8) In a case mentioned in subsection (1)(a)—

(a) section 19 (calling-up of standard security) of the 1970 Act has effect as if—

(i) in subsection (10), the words 'effectively dispensed with or' and 'dispense with or' were omitted,

(ii) after subsection (10) there were inserted—

'(10A) Subsection (10) above does not permit the period of notice mentioned in the calling-up notice to be shortened to a period of less than one month.

(10B) The period of notice mentioned in the calling-up notice may be shortened under subsection (10) above only with the consent in writing (in addition to any consent required by that subsection) of—

(a) any person entitled to make an application under subsection (2) of section 1 (application to suspend enforcement of standard security) of the Mortgage Rights (Scotland) Act 2001 (asp 11) by virtue of paragraph (c) or (d) of that subsection, and

(b) where the debtor in the standard security is not the proprietor—

(i) the debtor, and

(ii) if the standard security is over a matrimonial home (within the definition referred to in that subsection), the debtor's spouse.',

(b) section 21 (notice of default) of that Act has effect as if subsection (3) of that section were omitted, and

(c) Form C in Schedule 6 (procedures as to calling up and default) to that Act has effect as if the words 'dispensed with or' were omitted.

2 Disposal of application

(1) On an application under section 1(2) the court may—

(a) suspend the exercise of the rights which the creditor has, or may acquire, by virtue of the enactments mentioned in subsection (1)(a) to (c) of that section—

     (i)   to such extent,
     (ii) for such period, and
     (iii) subject to such conditions,
as the court thinks fit,
     (b) if the application is made in proceedings under section 24 of the 1970 Act or section 5 of the 1894 Act, continue those proceedings to such date as the court thinks fit.

(2)   The court may make an order under this section only where it considers it reasonable in all the circumstances to do so; and the court, in considering whether to make such an order and what its terms should be, is to have regard in particular to—

     (a)   the nature of and reasons for the default,
     (b)   the applicant's ability to fulfil within a reasonable period the obligations under the standard security in respect of which the debtor is in default,
     (c)   any action taken by the creditor to assist the debtor to fulfil those obligations, and
     (d)   the ability of the applicant and any other person residing at the security subjects to secure reasonable alternative accommodation.

(3)   If, while an order under this section is in force, the obligations under the standard security in respect of which the debtor is in default are fulfilled, the standard security has effect as if the default had not occurred.

(4)   In relation to an application under section 1(2) in the case mentioned in subsection (1)(a)(i) of that section, the preceding provisions of this section have effect with the following modifications—

     (a)   the power to specify a period in pursuance of subsection (1)(a) includes, without prejudice to the generality of that provision, power to specify the period which expires on the calling-up notice ceasing to have effect by virtue of section 19(11) of the 1970 Act,
     (b)   subsection (2)(a) is to be read as referring to the circumstances giving rise to the service of the calling-up notice,
     (c)   subsection (2)(b) is to be read as referring to the ability of the applicant to comply with the notice within a reasonable period,
     (d)   subsection (2)(c) is to be read as referring to any action taken by the creditor to assist the debtor to fulfil the debtor's obligations under the standard security, and
     (e)   subsection (3) does not apply.

(5)   The court may, if requested to do so by the creditor or the applicant—
     (a)   vary or revoke an order made under subsection (1)(a),
     (b)   further continue proceedings continued under subsection (1)(b).

(6)   Section 1 and this section are without prejudice to any rights which a debtor, proprietor or non-entitled spouse may have under any other enactment or rule of law.

(7)   In section 1 and this section—
'applicant' means the person who makes an application under section 1(2),
'court' means the sheriff court,
'matrimonial home' and 'non-entitled spouse' are to be construed in accordance with the Matrimonial Homes (Family Protection) (Scotland) Act 1981 (c 59).

3 Registration of order under section 2

(1)   Where the court makes an order under section 2 the clerk of court must, as soon as possible, send to the Keeper of the Register of Inhibitions and Adjudications, for recording in that Register—

     (a)   a certified copy of the order, and
     (b)   a notice complying with subsection (2).

(2)   A notice referred to in subsection (1)(b)—
     (a)   must be in such form, and

(b)   must contain such particulars of the order, the proceedings in which it was made and the standard security,

as may be prescribed by the Scottish Ministers by order made by statutory instrument.

(3)   A statutory instrument containing an order under subsection (2) is subject to annulment in pursuance of a resolution of the Scottish Parliament.

4   Notices to debtors, proprietors and occupiers

(1)–(3)   *[Amend the Conveyancing and Feudal Reform (Scotland) Act 1970.]*

(4)   Where a creditor in a standard security over [land or a real right] in land used to any extent for residential purposes commences proceedings under section 5 (power to eject proprietor in personal occupancy) of the 1894 Act, the creditor must—

(a)   serve on the proprietor a notice in conformity with Form 1 in Part 2 of the schedule to this Act, and

(b)   serve on the occupier of the security subjects a notice in conformity with Form 2 in that Part of that schedule.

(5)   Notices under subsection (4) must be sent by recorded delivery letter addressed—

(a)   in the case of a notice under subsection (4)(a), to the proprietor at the proprietor's last known address,

(b)   in the case of a notice under subsection (4)(b), to 'The Occupier' at the security subjects.

(6)   The schedule to this Act, Part 1 of which amends Schedule 6 to the 1970 Act (forms to be used in relation to calling-up and default) and Part 2 of which sets out the Forms referred to in subsection (4), has effect.

(7)   The Scottish Ministers may, by order made by statutory instrument, amend—

(a)   the Notes inserted in Forms A and B in Schedule 6 to the 1970 Act by Part 1 of the schedule to this Act,

(b)   Forms BB, E and F in Schedule 6 to the 1970 Act,

(c)   the Forms set out in Part 2 of the schedule to this Act.

(8)   A statutory instrument containing an order under subsection (7) is subject to annulment in pursuance of a resolution of the Scottish Parliament.

5   Crown application

This Act binds the Crown.

6   Interpretation

Except so far as the context otherwise requires, expressions used in this Act and in Part II of the 1970 Act have the same meanings in this Act as they have in that Part.

7   Commencement and short title

(1)   The preceding provisions of this Act come into force on such day as the Scottish Ministers may by order made by statutory instrument appoint.

(2)   An order under subsection (1) may include such transitional and transitory provisions and savings as the Scottish Ministers think expedient.

(3)   This Act may be cited as the Mortgage Rights (Scotland) Act 2001.

Section 4   SCHEDULE
                    NOTICES TO DEBTORS, PROPRIETORS AND OCCUPIERS

[Part 1 amends Conveyancing and Feudal Reform (Scotland) Act 1970, Sch 6.]

PART 2
FORMS RELATING TO PROCEEDINGS UNDER SECTION 5 OF THE
1894 ACT

FORM 1

To AB (*address*)

CD (*designation*), the creditor in a standard security by you (*or* by EF) in favour of
CD (*or* of GH to which CD now has right) recorded in the Register for (or, as the
case may be, registered in the Land Register for Scotland) on (*date*) has commenced proceedings against you under section 5 of the Heritable Securities
(Scotland) Act 1894 to eject you from (*address of security subjects*). A copy of the
initial writ is attached.

Dated

(*Signature of CD, or signature and designation of CD's agent followed by the words*
Agent of CD.)

   NOTE: The Mortgage Rights (Scotland) Act 2001 gives you the right in certain circumstances to apply to the court for suspension of the rights of CD. The court will have regard in
particular to the nature of and reasons for the default, your ability to fulfil the obligations
under the standard security, any action taken by CD. to assist the debtor in the standard
security to fulfil those obligations and the ability of you and anyone else residing at the property to find reasonable alternative accommodation. If you wish to make such an application,
you should consult a solicitor. You may be eligible for legal aid depending on your circumstances, and you can get information about legal aid from a solicitor. You may also be able to
get advice, including advice about how to manage debt, from any Citizens Advice Bureau or
from other advice agencies.

FORM 2

To the Occupier (*address*)

CD (*designation*) has commenced proceedings under section 5 of the Heritable
Securities (Scotland) Act 1894 to eject AB from (*address of security subjects*). A copy
of the initial writ is attached.
   If you are a tenant of AB, in certain circumstances CD cannot take possession of
the property without a court order. You should obtain legal advice about your
rights as a tenant. You may be eligible for legal aid depending on your circumstances, and you can get information about legal aid from a solicitor. You may also
be able to get advice from any Citizens Advice Bureau or from other advice
agencies.
   If you are the spouse or partner of AB, the Mortgage Rights (Scotland) Act 2001
gives you the right in certain circumstances to apply to the court to suspend the
rights of CD. The court will have regard in particular to the nature of and reasons
for the default, your ability to fulfil the obligations under the standard security,
any action taken by CD to assist the debtor in the standard security to fulfil those
obligations and the ability of you and anyone else residing at the property to find
reasonable alternative accommodation. If you wish to make such an application,
you should consult a solicitor. You may be eligible for legal aid depending on your
circumstances, and you can get information about legal aid from a solicitor. You
may also be able to get advice, including advice about how to manage debt, from
any Citizens Advice Bureau or from other advice agencies.

Dated

(*Signature of CD, or signature and designation of CD's agent followed by the words*
Agent of CD.)

LAND REFORM (SCOTLAND) ACT 2003
(2003, asp 2)

PART 1
ACCESS RIGHTS

CHAPTER 1
NATURE AND EXTENT OF ACCESS RIGHTS

1 Access rights

(1) Everyone has the statutory rights established by this Part of this Act.

(2) Those rights (in this Part of this Act called 'access rights') are—

(a) the right to be, for any of the purposes set out in subsection (3) below, on land; and

(b) the right to cross land.

(3) The right set out in subsection (2)(a) above may be exercised only—

(a) for recreational purposes;

(b) for the purposes of carrying on a relevant educational activity; or

(c) for the purposes of carrying on, commercially or for profit, an activity which the person exercising the right could carry on otherwise than commercially or for profit.

(4) The reference—

(a) in subsection (2)(a) above to being on land for any of the purposes set out in subsection (3) above is a reference to—

(i) going into, passing over and remaining on it for any of those purposes and then leaving it; or

(ii) any combination of those;

(b) in subsection (2)(b) above to crossing land is a reference to going into it, passing over it and leaving it all for the purpose of getting from one place outside the land to another such place.

(5) A 'relevant educational activity' is, for the purposes of subsection (3) above, an activity which is carried on by a person for the purposes of—

(a) furthering the person's understanding of natural or cultural heritage; or

(b) enabling or assisting other persons to further their understanding of natural or cultural heritage.

(6) Access rights are exercisable above and below (as well as on) the surface of the land.

(7) The land in respect of which access rights are exercisable is all land except that specified in or under section 6 below.

2 Access rights to be exercised responsibly

(1) A person has access rights only if they are exercised responsibly.

(2) In determining whether access rights are exercised responsibly a person is to be presumed to be exercising access rights responsibly if they are exercised so as not to cause unreasonable interference with any of the rights (whether access rights, rights associated with the ownership of land or any others) of any other person, but—

(a) a person purporting to exercise access rights who, at the same time—

(i) engages in any of the conduct within section 9 below or within any byelaw made under section 12(1)(a)(i) below; or

(ii) does anything which undoes anything done by Scottish Natural Heritage under section 29 below,

is to be taken as not exercising those rights responsibly; and

(b) regard is to be had to whether the person exercising or purporting to exercise access rights is, at the same time—

(i) disregarding the guidance on responsible conduct set out in the Access Code and incumbent on persons exercising access rights; or

(ii) disregarding any request included or which might reasonably be implied in anything done by Scottish Natural Heritage under section 29 below.

(3)   In this section the references to the responsible exercise of access rights are references to the exercise of these rights in a way which is lawful and reasonable and takes proper account of the interests of others and of the features of the land in respect of which the rights are exercised.

3   Reciprocal obligations of owners

(1)   It is the duty of every owner of land in respect of which access rights are exercisable—

(a)   to use and manage the land; and

(b)   otherwise to conduct the ownership of it,

in a way which, as respects those rights, is responsible.

(2)   In determining whether the way in which land is used, managed or the ownership of it is conducted is responsible an owner is to be presumed to be using, managing and conducting the ownership of land in a way which is responsible if it does not cause unreasonable interference with the access rights of any person exercising or seeking to exercise them, but—

(a)   an owner who contravenes section 14(1) or (3) or 23(2) of this Act or any byelaw made under section 12(1)(a)(ii) below is to be taken as not using, managing or conducting the ownership of the land in a responsible way;

(b)   regard is to be had to whether any act or omission occurring in the use, management or conduct of the ownership of the land disregards the guidance on responsible conduct set out in the Access Code and incumbent on the owners of land.

(3)   In this section the references to the use, management and conduct of the ownership of land in a way which is responsible are references to the use, management and conduct of the ownership of it in a way which is lawful and reasonable and takes proper account of the interests of persons exercising or seeking to exercise access rights.

4   Modification of sections 9, 14 and 23

(1)   Ministers may by order modify, for the purposes of sections 2 and 3 above, any of the provisions of sections 9, 14 and 23 below.

(2)   They may do so generally (that is to say in terms similar to those in sections 2 and 3 above as enacted) or by making provision which relates to particular areas, locations or classes of land or to particular access rights or particular activities which may take place in the exercise of access rights or to particular ways of using, managing or conducting the ownership of land or any combination of those.

(3)   Before doing so, they shall consult such persons whom they consider to have a particular interest in the effect of the proposed modification (or associations representing such persons) and such other persons as they think fit.

5   Access rights, reciprocal obligations and other rules and rights

(1)   The exercise of access rights does not of itself constitute trespass.

(2)   The extent of the duty of care owed by an occupier of land to another person present on the land is not, subject to section 22(4) below, affected by this Part of this Act or by its operation.

(3)   The existence or exercise of access rights does not diminish or displace any other rights (whether public or private) of entry, way, passage or access.

(4)   The existence or exercise of access rights does not diminish or displace any public rights under the guardianship of the Crown in relation to the foreshore.

(5)   The exercise of access rights does not of itself amount to the exercise or possession of any right for the purpose of any enactment or rule of law relating to the circumstances in which a right of way or servitude or right of public navigation may be constituted.

(6) Access rights do not constitute a public right of passage for the purposes of the definition of 'road' in section 151(1) (interpretation) of the Roads (Scotland) Act 1984 (c 54).

(7) A person exercising access rights is to be regarded as being in a public place for the purposes of section 53 (obstruction by pedestrians) of the Civic Government (Scotland) Act 1982 (c 45).

CHAPTER 2
NATURE AND EXTENT OF ACCESS RIGHTS: FURTHER PROVISIONS

6 Land over which access rights not exercisable
(1) The land in respect of which access rights are not exercisable is land—
    (a) to the extent that there is on it—
        (i) a building or other structure or works, plant or fixed machinery;
        (ii) a caravan, tent or other place affording a person privacy or shelter;
    (b) which—
        (i) forms the curtilage of a building which is not a house or of a group of buildings none of which is a house;
        (ii) forms a compound or other enclosure containing any such structure, works, plant or fixed machinery as is referred to in paragraph (a)(i) above;
        (iii) consists of land contiguous to and used for the purposes of a school; or
        (iv) comprises, in relation to a house or any of the places mentioned in paragraph (a)(ii) above, sufficient adjacent land to enable persons living there to have reasonable measures of privacy in that house or place and to ensure that their enjoyment of that house or place is not unreasonably disturbed;
    (c) to which, not being land within paragraph (b)(iv) above, two or more persons have rights in common and which is used by those persons as a private garden;
    (d) to which public access is, by or under any enactment other than this Act, prohibited, excluded or restricted;
    (e) which has been developed or set out—
        (i) as a sports or playing field; or
        (ii) for a particular recreational purpose;
    (f) to which—
        (i) for not fewer than 90 days in the year ending on 31st January 2001, members of the public were admitted only on payment; and
        (ii) after that date, and for not fewer than 90 days in each year beginning on 1st February 2001, members of the public are, or are to be, so admitted;
    (g) on which—
        (i) building, civil engineering or demolition works; or
        (ii) works being carried out by a statutory undertaker for the purposes of the undertaking,
are being carried out;
    (h) which is used for the working of minerals by surface workings (including quarrying);
    (i) in which crops have been sown or are growing;
    (j) which has been specified in an order under section 11 or in byelaws under section 12 below as land in respect of which access rights are not exercisable.

(2) For the purposes of subsection (1)(a)(i) above, a bridge, tunnel, causeway, launching site, groyne, weir, boulder weir, embankment of a canalised waterway, fence, wall or anything designed to facilitate passage is not to be regarded as a structure.

7 Provisions supplementing and qualifying section 6
(1) Section 6 above does not prevent or restrict the exercise of access rights over any land which is a core path.

(2) Land which bears to be within section 6 above by virtue of a development or change of use for which planning permission was or is required under the Town and Country Planning (Scotland) Act 1997 (c 8) shall, if—

(a) such planning permission has not been granted; or

(b) such permission was granted subject to a condition which has not been complied with,

be regarded, for the purposes of that section, as if that development or change of use had not occurred.

(3) Where planning permission for such a development or change of use of land has been granted, the land shall, for the purposes of section 6 above, be regarded, while that development or change of use is taking place in accordance with the permission, as having been developed or having had its use changed accordingly.

(4) In section 6(1)(b)(iii) above, 'school' means not only a school within the meaning of section 135(1) of the Education (Scotland) Act 1980 (c 44) but also any other institution which provides education for children below school age within the meaning of that provision.

(5) There are included among the factors which go to determine what extent of land is sufficient for the purposes mentioned in section 6(1)(b)(iv) above, the location and other characteristics of the house or other place.

(6) For the purposes of section 6(1)(d) above, access rights do not extend to the land to which public access is prohibited, excluded or restricted only to the extent of the prohibition, exclusion or restriction.

(7) Section 6(1)(e) above prevents the exercise of access rights over land to which it applies only if—

(a) the land is being used for the purpose for which it has been developed or set out and, in the case of land which is not a sports or playing field, the exercise of those rights would interfere with the recreational use to which the land is being put;

(b) the land is a golf green, bowling green, cricket square, lawn tennis court or other similar area on which grass is grown and prepared for a particular recreational purpose; or

(c) in the case of land which is a sports or playing field, the surface of the land is comprised of synthetic grass, acrylic, resin or rubber granule.

(8) For the purposes of section 6(1)(e) above, land which has been developed or set out for a particular recreational purpose does not include land on which groynes have been constructed, deepening of pools has been undertaken, fishing platforms have been erected, or where other works for the purposes of fishing have taken place.

(9) Section 6(1)(f) above does not prevent or restrict the exercise of access rights over land to which it applies by any person who forms part of a class of persons who are not, on the days taken into account for the purposes of determining whether that provision applies in relation to the land, required to pay to gain admittance to the land.

(10) For the purposes of section 6(1)(i) above land on which crops are growing—

(a) includes land on which grass is being grown for hay and silage which is at such a late stage of growth that it is likely to be damaged by the exercise of access rights in respect of the land in which it is growing, but otherwise does not include grassland;

(b) does not include headrigs, endrigs or other margins of fields in which crops are growing,

[(c) does not include land used wholly or mainly—

(i) as woodland or an orchard, or

(ii) for the growing or trees;

but does include land used wholly for the cultivation of tree seedlings in beds,] and 'crops' means plants which are cultivated for agricultural [. . .] or commercial purposes.

8   Adjustment of land excluded from access rights

(1)   Ministers may by order modify any of the provisions of sections 6 and 7 above.

(2)   They may do so generally (that is to say, in terms similar to those in sections 6 and 7 above as enacted) or by making provision which relates to particular areas, locations or classes of land.

(3)   Before doing so, they shall consult such persons whom they consider to have a particular interest in the effect of the proposed modification (or associations representing such persons) and such other persons as they think fit.

9   Conduct excluded from access rights

The conduct which is within this section is—

(a)   being on or crossing land in breach of an interdict or other order of a court;

(b)   being on or crossing land for the purpose of doing anything which is an offence or a breach of an interdict or other order of a court;

(c)   hunting, shooting or fishing;

(d)   being on or crossing land while responsible for a dog or other animal which is not under proper control;

(e)   being on or crossing land for the purpose of taking away, for commercial purposes or for profit, anything in or on the land;

(f)   being on or crossing land in or with a motorised vehicle or vessel (other than a vehicle or vessel which has been constructed or adapted for use by a person who has a disability and which is being used by such a person);

(g)   being, for any of the purposes set out in section 1(3) above, on land which is a golf course.

CHAPTER 3

THE SCOTTISH OUTDOOR ACCESS CODE

10   The Scottish Outdoor Access Code

(1)   It is the duty of Scottish Natural Heritage to draw up and issue a code, to be known as the Scottish Outdoor Access Code, setting out, in relation to access rights, guidance as to the circumstances in which—

(a)   those exercising these rights are to be regarded as doing so in a way which is or is not responsible;

(b)   persons are to be regarded as carrying on activities, otherwise than in the course of exercising access rights, in a way which is likely to affect the exercise of these rights by other persons;

(c)   owners of land in respect of which these rights are exercisable are to be regarded as using and managing, or otherwise conducting the ownership of it, in a way which is or is not responsible;

(d)   owners of land in respect of which these rights are not exercisable are to be regarded as using and managing, or otherwise conducting the ownership of it, in a way which is likely to affect the exercise of these rights on land which is contiguous to that land.

(2)   Scottish Natural Heritage shall consult local authorities and such other persons or bodies as they think appropriate about the proposed Access Code and then submit it (with or without modifications) to Ministers together with copies of any objections or representations made in response to that consultation.

(3)   On receiving a proposed Access Code, Ministers may—

(a)   approve it, with or without modifications; or

(b)   reject it.

(4)   Where Ministers reject a proposed Access Code under subsection (3)(b)

above they may either instruct Scottish Natural Heritage to submit a new Code or they may substitute a Code of their own devising.

(5)   Where Ministers approve an Access Code with or without modification under subsection (3)(a) above or devise a Code themselves under subsection (4) above, they shall lay the proposed Code before the Scottish Parliament and Scottish Natural Heritage shall not issue the Code unless it has been approved by resolution of the Parliament.

(6)   The Access Code comes into operation on such date as Ministers fix.

(7)   It is the duty of—

(a)   Scottish Natural Heritage and local authorities to publicise the Access Code;

(b)   Scottish Natural Heritage to promote understanding of it.

(8)   Scottish Natural Heritage shall keep the Access Code under review and may modify it from time to time.

(9)   In reviewing the Access Code, Scottish Natural Heritage shall consult such persons or bodies as they think appropriate about the operation of the Code.

(10)   Subsections (2) to (6) above apply to modifications of the Access Code as they apply to the Code.

CHAPTER 4
REGULATION AND PROTECTION OF ACCESS RIGHTS

11   Power to exempt particular land from access rights

(1)   The local authority may (whether on application made to them or not) by order under this section made in respect of a particular area of land specified in the order exempt it for a particular purpose specified in the order from the access rights which would otherwise be exercisable in respect of it during such times as may be specified in the order.

(2)   Before making an order under this section which would have effect for a period of six or more days, the local authority shall—

(a)   consult the owner of the land to which it would relate, the local access forum established by them and such other persons as they think appropriate; and

(b)   give public notice of the intended purpose and effect of the proposed order,

inviting objections to be sent to them within such reasonable time as is specified in the notice; and shall consider any such objections and any other representations made to them.

(3)   An order under this section which would have effect for such a period requires confirmation by Ministers.

(4)   It is the duty of the local authority to send to Ministers—

(a)   copies of any objections made in response to the invitation under subsection (2) above; and

(b)   any other representations made to them,

in relation to an order requiring such confirmation.

(5)   Ministers—

(a)   shall not confirm such an order without considering any objections or representations sent to them under subsection (4) above; and

(b)   may cause an inquiry to be held for the purposes of enabling them to decide whether to confirm the order.

(6)   Subsections (2) to (13) of section 265 (local inquiries) of the Town and Country Planning (Scotland) Act 1997 (c 8) apply to an inquiry held under subsection (5)(b) above as they apply to one held under that section.

(7)   Ministers may—

(a)   confirm the order, with or without modifications; or

(b)   refuse to confirm it.

(8)   An order under this section takes effect—

(a)   where the order does not require to be confirmed by Ministers, from the date on which it is made or such other date as may be specified in it for the purpose; or

(b)   where the order requires to be so confirmed, from such date as is specified in it for the purpose or such other date as Ministers may direct when confirming it.

(9)   The local authority shall give public notice of their making an order under this section as soon as practicable after it is made or, where the order requires to be confirmed by Ministers, the authority receive notice of such confirmation.

(10)   The power of a local authority to make an order under this section includes power to revoke, amend or re-enact any such order.

(11)   Where a revoked, amended or re-enacted order would—

(a)   but for the revocation or amendment; or, as the case may be

(b)   by virtue of the amendment or re-enactment,

have effect for a period of six or more days beginning on or after the date on which it is revoked, amended or re-enacted, subsections (2) to (9) above apply in relation to the revocation, amendment or, as the case may be, re-enactment.

(12)   An order under this section has effect, subject to subsection (13) below—

(a)   for the period of two years beginning on the day on which the order takes effect;

(b)   where the order specifies that it is to cease to have effect for such shorter period as may be specified in the order, for that shorter period; or

(c)   where the order is revoked with effect from a day which falls before the end of that period or, as the case may be, that shorter period, until that day.

(13)   If, at any time before an order under this section ceases to have effect, the local authority which made the order re-enacts it, the order continues to have effect—

(a)   for the period of two years beginning on the day on which the order would otherwise have ceased to have effect under subsection (12)(a) or (b) above (or, as the case may be, under this paragraph or paragraph (b) below);

(b)   where the order (as amended or re-enacted) specifies that it is to cease to have effect for such shorter period as may be specified in the order, for that shorter period; or

(c)   where the order is revoked with effect from a day which falls before the end of that period or, as the case may be, that shorter period, until that day.

12   Byelaws in relation to land over which access rights are exercisable

(1)   The local authority may, in relation to land in respect of which access rights are exercisable, make byelaws—

(a)   making provision further or supplementary to that made—

(i)   by sections 2 and 9 and under section 4 above as to the responsible exercise of access rights; and

(ii)   by section 3(2) and under section 4 above as to the responsible use, management and conduct of the ownership of the land;

(b)   specifying land for the purposes of section 6(j) above;

(c)   providing for—

(i)   the preservation of public order and safety;

(ii)   the prevention of damage;

(iii)   the prevention of nuisance or danger;

(iv)   the conservation or enhancement of natural or cultural heritage.

(2)   Byelaws made under section (1)(c) above may, in particular—

(a)   prohibit, restrict or regulate the exercise of access rights;

(b)   facilitate their exercise;

(c)   so as to protect and further the interests of persons who are exercising or who might exercise access rights, prohibit or regulate—

    (i) the use of vehicles or vessels;

    (ii) the taking place of sporting and recreational activities;

    (iii) the conduct of any trade or business;

    (iv) the depositing or leaving of rubbish or litter; and

    (v) the lighting of fires and the doing of anything likely to cause a fire,

on the land.

(3) Byelaws made under this section shall not interfere with the exercise of—

    (a) any public right of way or navigation; or

    (b) the functions of a statutory undertaker.

(4) Sections 202 to 204 (byelaws) of the Local Government (Scotland) Act 1973 (c 65) apply to byelaws made under this section as they apply to byelaws made under that Act, but with the following modifications and further provisions.

(5) The references to one month in subsections (4), (5) and (7) of section 202 shall be read as references to such period of not less than 12 weeks as the local authority determine.

(6) The local authority shall, at the same time as they first make the proposed byelaws open to public inspection, consult the persons and bodies mentioned in subsection (7) below on the proposed byelaws.

(7) Those persons and bodies are—

    (a) every community council whose area includes an area to which the proposed byelaws would apply;

    (b) the owners of land to which the proposed byelaws would apply;

    (c) such persons as appear to them to be representative of the interests of those who live, work, carry on business or engage in recreational activities on any land affected by the proposed byelaws;

    (d) the local access forum established by them;

    (e) every statutory undertaker which carries on its undertaking on land to which the proposed byelaws would apply;

    (f) Scottish Natural Heritage; and

    (g) such other persons as they think fit.

(8) The local authority are, for the purposes of subsection (6) above, to be taken as having consulted a person of whom or a body of which they have no knowledge or whom or which they cannot find if they have taken reasonable measures to ascertain whether the person or body exists or, as the case may be, the person's or body's whereabouts.

CHAPTER 5
LOCAL AUTHORITY FUNCTIONS: ACCESS AND OTHER RIGHTS

13 Duty of local authority to uphold access rights

(1) It is the duty of the local authority to assert, protect and keep open and free from obstruction or encroachment any route, waterway or other means by which access rights may reasonably be exercised.

(2) A local authority is not required to do anything in pursuance of the duty imposed by subsection (1) above which would be inconsistent with the carrying on of any of the authority's other functions.

(3) The local authority may, for the purposes set out in subsection (1) above, institute and defend legal proceedings and generally take such steps as they think expedient.

14 Prohibition signs, obstructions, dangerous impediments etc

(1) The owner of land in respect of which access rights are exercisable shall not, for the purpose or for the main purpose of preventing or deterring any person entitled to exercise these rights from doing so—

    (a) put up any sign or notice;

    (b) put up any fence or wall, or plant, grow or permit to grow any hedge, tree or other vegetation;

(c)   position or leave at large any animal;

(d)   carry out any agricultural or other operation on the land; or

(e)   take, or fail to take, any other action.

(2)   Where the local authority consider that anything has been done in contravention of subsection (1) above they may, by written notice served on the owner of the land, require that such remedial action as is specified in the notice be taken by the owner of the land within such reasonable time as is so specified.

(3)   If the owner fails to comply with such a notice, the local authority may—

(a)   remove the sign or notice; or, as the case may be,

(b)   take the remedial action specified in the notice served under subsection (2) above,

and, in either case, may recover from the owner such reasonable costs as they have incurred by acting under this subsection.

(4)   An owner on whom a notice has been so served may, by summary application made to the sheriff, appeal against it.

(5)   Rules of Court shall provide—

(a)   for public notice of the making of summary applications for the purposes of this section;

(b)   for enabling persons interested in the exercise of access rights over the land to which a summary application relates, and persons or bodies representative of such persons, to be parties to the proceedings;

(c)   for limiting the number of persons and bodies who may be such parties.

15   Measures for safety, protection, guidance and assistance

(1)   The local authority may take such steps (which may include the putting up and maintenance of notices and fences) as appear to them appropriate—

(a)   to warn the public of and protect the public from danger on any land in respect of which access rights are exercisable;

(b)   to indicate or enclose, or to give directions to, any such land.

(2)   Where the local authority consider that a fence, wall or other erection is so constructed or adapted (whether by the use of barbed wire or other sharp material or by being electrified or otherwise) as to be likely to injure a person exercising access rights, they may by written notice served on the owner of the land on which it is placed, require the owner to take, within such reasonable time as is specified in the notice, such reasonable action as is so specified, being action calculated to remove the risk of injury.

(3)   Subsections (3)(b), (4) and (5) of section 14 above apply in respect of a notice served under subsection (2) above as they apply to a notice served under those subsections.

(4)   The local authority may install and maintain, in any land in respect of which access rights are exercisable, gates, stiles, moorings, launching sites or other means of facilitating the exercise of these rights, and seats, lavatories and other means of contributing to the comfort and convenience of persons exercising them.

(5)   The local authority may, in relation to inland waters in respect of which access rights are exercisable, provide staff for life saving and any boats or equipment which are appropriate for life saving.

(6)   In exercising their powers under this section, the local authority shall—

(a)   have regard to the extent to which there are existing facilities in their area for the purposes of assisting persons to exercise access rights; and

(b)   have regard to the needs of persons with disabilities.

(7)   The local authority may carry out the operations authorised by subsections (4) and (5) above within the land over which the access rights are exercisable only with the consent of the owner.

16   Acquisition by local authority of land to enable or facilitate exercise of access rights

(1)   Where it appears to the local authority to be necessary or expedient for the

purpose of enabling or facilitating the exercise of access rights in respect of any land to which this section applies that the land be acquired by them, the authority may—

(a)   acquire it by agreement (whether by purchase, feu, lease or excambion); or

(b)   with the consent of Ministers, acquire it compulsorily.

(2)   The land to which this section applies is land other than—

(a)   land in respect of which access rights do not extend by virtue of section 6(1)(a)(ii), (d), (e) or (f) above;

(b)   land which has been exempted by order made by the local authority under section 11(1) of this Act.

(3)   A local authority shall hold and manage any land acquired by them under this section so as best to facilitate the exercise of access rights.

(4)   The Acquisition of Land (Authorisation Procedure) (Scotland) Act 1947 (c 42) shall apply in relation to a compulsory purchase under this section as if this section had been in force immediately before that Act.

17   Core paths plan

(1)   It is the duty of the local authority, not later than 3 years after the coming into force of this section, to draw up a plan for a system of paths ('core paths') sufficient for the purpose of giving the public reasonable access throughout their area.

(2)   Such a system of paths may include—

(a)   rights of way by foot, horseback, pedal cycle or any combination of those, being rights which are or may be established by or under any enactment or rule of law;

(b)   paths, footways, footpaths, cycle tracks or other means of access (however described but not falling within paragraph (a) above) which are or may be provided by or under any enactment other than this Act;

(c)   paths which are or may be delineated by a path agreement under section 21 or a path order under section 22 below;

(d)   other routes, waterways or other means by which persons may cross land.

(3)   In drawing up the plan, the local authority shall have regard to—

(a)   the likelihood that persons exercising rights of way and access rights will do so by using core paths;

(b)   the desirability of encouraging such persons to use core paths; and

(c)   the need to balance the exercise of those rights and the interests of the owner of the land in respect of which those rights are exercisable.

(4)   The plan may consist of or include maps showing core paths and, where it does not, shall refer to such maps.

18   Core paths plan: further procedure

(1)   The local authority shall—

(a)   give public notice of the plan drawn up by them under section 17 above and any maps it refers to;

(b)   make the plan and any such maps available thereafter for public inspection for a period of not less than 12 weeks; and

(c)   consult—

(i)   the local access forum for their area;

(ii)   persons representative of those who live, work, carry on business or engage (or would be likely to engage) in recreational activities on the land on which it is proposed that there be core paths;

(iii)   Scottish Natural Heritage; and

(iv)   such other persons as the local authority think fit,

in each case inviting objections and representations to be made to them within such period as they specify.

(2)   If no objections are made or any made are withdrawn, the local authority shall adopt the plan.

(3)   If an objection is made and not withdrawn, the local authority shall not adopt the plan unless Ministers direct them to do so.

(4)   Where an objection remains unwithdrawn, Ministers shall not make such a direction without first causing a local inquiry to be held into whether the plan will, if adopted, fulfil the purpose mentioned in section 17(1) above.

(5)   Ministers may, in any other case, cause such an inquiry to be held.

(6)   Subsections (2) to (13) of section 265 (local inquiries) of the Town and Country Planning (Scotland) Act 1997 (c 8) apply to an inquiry held under subsection (4) or (5) above as they apply to one held under that section.

(7)   Following the publication of the report by the person appointed to hold the inquiry, Ministers may (but need not) direct the local authority to adopt the plan either as drawn up under section 17 above or with such modification as Ministers specify in the direction.

(8)   On adopting the plan, the local authority shall—
  (a)   give public notice of its adoption;
  (b)   compile a list of core paths;
  (c)   keep the plan, any maps it refers to and the list available for public inspection and for sale at a reasonable price; and
  (d)   send a copy of each of those documents to Ministers.

(9)   Where Ministers decline to make a direction under subsection (3) or (7) above, the local authority shall draw up a revised plan and shall do so in accordance with such procedure and within such time limits as Ministers specify.

(10)   Such specification shall include provision under which Ministers may (but need not) direct the local authority to confirm the revised plan.

19   Power to maintain core paths etc

The local authority may do anything which they consider appropriate for the purposes of—
  (a)   maintaining a core path;
  (b)   keeping a core path free from obstruction or encroachment;
  (c)   providing the public with directions to, or with an indication of the extent of, a core path.

20   Review and amendment of core paths plan

(1)   The local authority shall—
  (a)   at such times as they consider appropriate; and
  (b)   on Ministers requiring them to do so,
review the plan adopted under section 18 above (or that plan as amended under this section).

(2)   Where, following a review of a plan under subsection (1) above, the local authority consider that—
  (a)   a core path should be removed from the plan; or
  (b)   the line of a core path, or part of that line, should be diverted,
the authority may amend the plan by removing the core path from the plan or, as the case may be, by diverting the line of the core path on the plan.

(3)   The local authority may not amend the plan under subsection (2) above unless they are satisfied that it is expedient so to do having regard to—
  (a)   the extent to which it appears to them that persons would, but for the amendment, be likely to exercise access rights using the core path; and
  (b)   the effect which the amendment of the plan would have as respects land served by the core path.

(4)   Where the local authority stop up, or divert, a core path by order under section 208 of the Town and Country Planning (Scotland) Act 1997 (c 8) they shall amend their plan accordingly.

(5)   Subsection (8) of section 18 above applies in relation to the amendment of a

plan under subsection (2) or (4) above as it applies in relation to the adoption of a plan under that section.

(6)   Where, following a review of a plan under subsection (1) above, the local authority consider that the plan should be amended so as to include a further path, waterway or other means of crossing land such as is mentioned in section 17(2) above, the authority shall draw up an amended plan.

(7)   Sections 17(3) and (4) and 18 above apply in relation to a plan drawn up under subsection (6) above as they apply to a plan drawn up under section 17(1) above.

21 Delineation by agreement of paths in land in respect of which access rights exercisable

(1)   The local authority may enter an agreement (a 'path agreement') with a person having the necessary power for the delineation and maintenance or, as the case may be, for the delineation, creation and maintenance of a path within land in respect of which access rights are exercisable.

(2)   A path agreement shall be on such terms and conditions as to payment or otherwise as may be specified in it.

22 Compulsory powers to delineate paths in land in respect of which access rights exercisable

(1)   Where, in the circumstances set out in subsection (2) below, it appears to the local authority that, having regard to the rights and interests of the owner of land in respect of which access rights are exercisable and persons likely to exercise these rights, it is expedient to delineate a path within that land, the authority may, by order (a 'path order'), do so.

(2)   These circumstances are that it appears to the local authority to be impracticable to delineate the path by means of a path agreement.

(3)   Where the local authority make a path order—

    (a)   delineating an existing path, they have the duty of maintaining it;

    (b)   delineating a new path, they have the duty of creating and maintaining it.

(4)   Regard may be had, in determining whether a local authority has control of a path for the purposes of the Occupiers' Liability (Scotland) Act 1960 (c 30), to the duties imposed by subsection (3) above.

(5)   A path order may be revoked by the local authority.

(6)   A path order shall be in such form as is prescribed but shall contain a map showing the delineation of the path.

(7)   Where access rights—

    (a)   have, by virtue of any provision of this Part of this Act, not been exercisable over any land consisting of a public path created under sections 30 to 36 of the Countryside (Scotland) Act 1967 (c 86); but

    (b)   become exercisable over that land,

the public path creation agreement or the public path creation order or public path diversion order by which the public path was created shall, for the purposes of the exercise of access rights, be treated as a path agreement or, as the case may be, a path order.

(8)   Schedule 1 to this Act has effect for the purposes of providing further as to path orders.

    [. . .]

23 Ploughing etc

(1)   Where land is, in accordance with good husbandry, being ploughed or having its surface otherwise disturbed and it is convenient to plough, or otherwise disturb the surface of, a core path or a right of way which forms part of the land, nothing in this Part of this Act prevents that path or, as the case may be, right of way from being ploughed or from having its surface otherwise disturbed.

(2) The owner of land being a path or, as the case may be, right of way which has been ploughed or which has had its surface otherwise disturbed in accordance with subsection (1) above shall, however, within the period of 14 days beginning on the day on which the path or, as the case may be, right of way is ploughed or has its surface otherwise disturbed or such longer period as the local authority may allow, reinstate the path or, as the case may be, right of way.

(3) An owner who fails to comply with subsection (2) above shall be guilty of an offence and liable on summary conviction to a fine not exceeding level 3 on the standard scale.

(4) If the owner fails to comply with subsection (2) above, the local authority may, after giving the owner 14 days' notice of their intention to do so—

(a) take all necessary steps to reinstate the path or, as the case may be, right of way; and

(b) recover from the owner their reasonable expenses in doing so.

(5) Nothing in this section prejudices any limitation or condition having effect otherwise.

24 Rangers

(1) The local authority may appoint persons to act as rangers in relation to any land in respect of which access rights are exercisable.

(2) The purposes for which such rangers may be so appointed are—

(a) to advise and assist the owner of the land and other members of the public as to any matter relating to the exercise of access rights in respect of the land; and

(b) to perform such other duties in relation to the exercise of those rights in respect of that land as the local authority determine.

(3) A person appointed under this section as a ranger may, for the purpose of exercising any function conferred by or under subsection (2) above, enter any land in respect of which access rights are exercisable.

25 Local access forums

(1) Each local authority shall establish for its area a body, to be known as the 'local access forum', to carry out the functions set out in subsection (2) below.

(2) Those functions are—

(a) to advise the local authority and any other person or body consulting the forum on matters having to do with the exercise of access rights, the existence and delineation of rights of way or the drawing up and adoption of a plan for a system of core paths under sections 17 and 18 above;

(b) to offer and, where the offer is accepted, to give assistance to the parties to any dispute about—

(i) the exercise of access rights;

(ii) the existence and delineation of rights of way;

(iii) the drawing up and adoption of the plan referred to in paragraph (a) above; or

(iv) the use of core paths,

towards the resolution of the dispute.

(3) A local access forum consists of such persons as are appointed to it by the local authority.

(4) The matters to which the local authority have regard when making appointments to the local access forum shall include—

(a) ensuring reasonable representation in the forum of—

(i) bodies representative of persons with an interest in any of the matters mentioned in subsection (2)(b)(i) to (iv) above;

(ii) persons having such an interest;

(iii) bodies representative of the owners of land in respect of which access rights are exercisable or in which there is a core path; and

(iv) owners of such land, and

(b)   ensuring a reasonable balance among those mentioned in sub-paragraphs (i) to (iv) of paragraph (a) above.

(5)   The local authority may appoint one or more of its own members to a local access forum.

(6)   More than one local access forum may be established for the area of a local authority.

(7)   The local authority may pay to members of the local access forum such expenses and allowances as the local authority determine.

(8)   Ministers may give guidance to local authorities to assist them in the performance of their functions under this section.

26   Power of entry

(1)   Any person authorised by the local authority to do so may enter any land for a purpose connected with the exercise or proposed exercise of any of the authority's functions under this Part of this Act.

(2)   A person so authorised may, subject to subsection (3) below, enter land only—

(a)   at a reasonable time; and

(b)   on giving reasonable notice to the owner of the land.

(3)   Subsection (2) above does not apply—

(a)   in case of emergency; or

(b)   in relation to the exercise by a local authority of any of their powers under sections 15(1)(a) and (4) and 19 above in relation to land which is a core path.

(4)   A person may, on entering any land by virtue of subsection (1) above, take onto the land any machinery, other equipment or materials required for the purpose for which the power of entry is being exercised.

27   Guidance

(1)   Ministers may give guidance to local authorities on the performance of any of their functions under this Part of this Act.

(2)   Such guidance may be given generally or to a particular local authority.

(3)   A local authority to which such guidance is given shall have regard to it.

(4)   Before giving such guidance, Ministers shall—

(a)   consult each (or the) local authority to whom they propose to give it; and

(b)   lay a draft of the proposed guidance before the Scottish Parliament;

and the guidance shall not be given until after a period of 40 days beginning with the day on which the draft was so laid.

(5)   If, within that period, the Parliament resolves that the guidance proposed should not be given, Ministers shall not give it.

(6)   In calculating any period of 40 days for the purposes of subsection (4) or (5) above, no account is to be taken of any time during which the Parliament is dissolved or is in recess for more than 4 days.

CHAPTER 6

GENERAL AND MISCELLANEOUS PROVISIONS

28   Judicial determination of existence and extent of access rights and rights of way

(1)   It is competent, on summary application made to the sheriff, for the sheriff—

(a)   to declare that the land specified in the application is or, as the case may be, is not land in respect of which access rights are exercisable;

(b)   to declare—

(i)   whether a person who has exercised or purported to exercise access rights has exercised those rights responsibly for the purposes of section 2 above;

(ii) whether the owner of land in respect of which access rights are exercisable is using, managing or conducting the ownership of the land in a way which is, for the purposes of section 3 above, responsible.

(2) It is competent, on summary application made to the sheriff, for the sheriff to declare whether a path, bridleway or other means of crossing land specified in the application is, or is not, a right of way by foot, horseback, pedal cycle or any combination of those.

(3) The proceedings for a declaration under subsection (1) or (2) above are those for an action of declarator initiated by summary application to the sheriff.

(4) A summary application for a declaration shall be served on the local authority.

(5) The local authority are entitled to be a party to proceedings for a declaration.

(6) Where the person seeking a declaration is the owner of the land, it is not necessary to serve the application on any person but the local authority.

(7) In any other case, the person seeking the declaration shall serve the application on the owner of the land.

(8) Rules of court shall provide—

(a) for the circumstances in which (including any time periods within which) a summary application may be made for the purposes of this section;

(b) for public notice of the making of summary applications for the purposes of this section;

(c) for enabling persons interested in the exercise of access rights over specific land or, as the case may be, in the existence of a right of way over specific land and persons or bodies representative of such persons to be parties to the proceedings;

(d) for limiting the number of persons and bodies who may be such parties.

(9) This section is without prejudice to any remedy otherwise available in respect of rights conferred and duties imposed by or under this Part of this Act.

29 Powers to protect natural and cultural heritage etc

(1) Scottish Natural Heritage may put up and maintain notices for the purposes of protecting the natural heritage of land in respect of which access rights are exercisable.

(2) The Scottish Ministers may put up and maintain notices for the purposes of protecting the cultural heritage of land in respect of which access rights are exercisable.

(3) Any notice put up under subsection (1) or (2) above may warn persons of any adverse effect that their presence on the land or any activities they might conduct there might have on the natural or, as the case may be, cultural heritage sought to be protected.

30 Existing byelaws providing for public access to land

It is the duty of every person, body or authority having power under any enactment to make byelaws which may provide for or relate to public access to land in respect of which access rights are exercisable and which is owned or managed by that person, body or authority—

(a) within 2 years of the coming into force of this section, to review those of its byelaws which so provide or relate and are in force at the time of the review; and

(b) to modify any of those byelaws which are inconsistent with the provisions of this Act (including any made under it) as they apply to that land so as to make them consistent.

31 Application of sections 14 and 15 to rights of way

Sections 14 and 15 above apply in relation to rights of way by foot, horseback, pedal cycle or any combination of those as they apply in relation to access rights.

32 Interpretation of Part 1
In this Part of this Act—
'Access Code' means the Scottish Outdoor Access Code issued by Scottish Natural Heritage under section 10 above;
'canals' means inland waterways within the meaning of section 92 (interpretation) of the Transport Act 1962 (c 46);
'core path' means a path, waterway or any other means of crossing land such as is mentioned in section 17(2) above which is set out in a plan adopted under section 18 above or, as the case may be, such a plan as amended under section 20 above;
'cultural heritage' includes structures and other remains resulting from human activity of all periods, traditions, ways of life and the historic, artistic and literary associations of people, places and landscapes;
'inland waters' means any inland, non-tidal loch, river (to the extent that it is non-tidal), lake or reservoir, whether natural or artificial and whether navigable or not, and includes the bed and the shores or banks thereof;
'land' includes—
    (a) bridges and other structures built on or over land;
    (b) inland waters;
    (c) canals; and
    (d) the foreshore, that is to say, the land between the high and low water marks of ordinary spring tides;
'local authority' in relation to specific land in respect of which access rights are or would, but for a provision of or order made under this Act, be exercisable means—
    (a) where the land is, on the day on which this section comes into force, within an area designated as a National Park under the National Parks (Scotland) Act 2000 (asp 10), the National Park authority for that National Park; and
    (b) in any other case, the council (being a council constituted under section 2 of the Local Government etc (Scotland) Act 1994 (c 39)) whose area includes that land;
'natural heritage' includes the flora and fauna of land, its geological and physiographical features and its natural beauty and amenity;
'owner', in relation to land, means—
    (a) the owner of the land; and
    (b) where the owner is not in natural possession of the land, the person who is entitled to such natural possession;
'statutory undertaker' means—
    (a) a person authorised by any enactment to carry on any railway, light railway, tramway, road transport, water transport, canal, inland navigation, dock, harbour, pier or lighthouse undertaking or any undertaking for the supply of hydraulic power;
    (b) the operator of a telecommunications code system;
    (c) an airport operator (within the meaning of the Airports Act 1986 (c 31)) operating an airport to which Part V of that Act applies;
    (d) a gas transporter, within the meaning of Part I of the Gas Act 1986 (c 44);
    (e) Scottish Water;
    (f) a holder of a licence under section 6(1) of the Electricity Act 1989 (c 29);
    (g) the Civil Aviation Authority or a holder of a licence under Chapter I of Part I of the Transport Act 2000 (c 38) (to the extent that the person holding the licence is carrying out activities authorised by it);
    (h) the Scottish Environment Protection Agency; or
    (i) a universal postal service provider within the meaning of the Postal Services Act 2000 (c 26);
and 'undertaking' means the undertaking of such a statutory undertaker; and

'telecommunications code system' and 'operator', in relation to such a system, have the same meanings in this Part of this Act as they have in the Telecommunications Act 1984 (c 12).

TITLE CONDITIONS (SCOTLAND) ACT 2003
(2003, asp 9)

PART 1
REAL BURDENS: GENERAL

Meaning and creation

1   The expression 'real burden'

(1)   A real burden is an encumbrance on land constituted in favour of the owner of other land in that person's capacity as owner of that other land.

(2)   In relation to a real burden—

(a)   the encumbered land is known as the 'burdened property'; and

(b)   the other land is known as the 'benefited property'.

(3)   Notwithstanding subsections (1) and (2) above, the expression 'real burden' includes a personal real burden; that is to say a conservation burden, a rural housing burden, a maritime burden, an economic development burden, a health care burden, a manager burden, a personal pre-emption burden and a personal redemption burden (being burdens constituted in favour of a person other than by reference to the person's capacity as owner of any land).

2   Affirmative, negative and ancillary burdens

(1)   Subject to subsection (3) below, a real burden may be created only as—

(a)   an obligation to do something (including an obligation to defray, or contribute towards, some cost); or

(b)   an obligation to refrain from doing something.

(2)   An obligation created as is described in—

(a)   paragraph (a) of subsection (1) above is known as an 'affirmative burden'; and

(b)   paragraph (b) of that subsection is known as a 'negative burden'.

(3)   A real burden may be created which—

(a)   consists of a right to enter, or otherwise make use of, property; or

(b)   makes provision for management or administration,

but only for a purpose ancillary to those of an affirmative burden or a negative burden.

(4)   A real burden created as is described in subsection (3) above is known as an 'ancillary burden'.

(5)   In determining whether a real burden is created as is described in subsection (1) or (3) above, regard shall be had to the effect of a provision rather than to the way in which the provision is expressed.

3   Other characteristics

(1)   A real burden must relate in some way to the burdened property.

(2)   The relationship may be direct or indirect but shall not merely be that the obligated person is the owner of the burdened property.

(3)   In a case in which there is a benefited property, a real burden must, unless it is a community burden, be for the benefit of that property.

(4)   A community burden may be for the benefit of the community to which it relates or of some part of that community.

(5)   A real burden may consist of a right of pre-emption; but a real burden created on or after the appointed day must not consist of—

(a)   a right of redemption or reversion; or

(b)   any other type of option to acquire the burdened property.

(6)   A real burden must not be contrary to public policy as for example an unreasonable restraint of trade and must not be repugnant with ownership (nor must it be illegal).

(7)   Except in so far as expressly permitted by this Act, a real burden must not have the effect of creating a monopoly (as for example, by providing for a particular person to be or to appoint—

(a)   the manager of property; or

(b)   the supplier of any services in relation to property).

(8)   It shall not be competent—

(a)   to make in the constitutive deed provision; or

(b)   to import under section 6(1) of this Act terms which include provision,

to the effect that a person other than [a holder] of the burden may waive compliance with, or mitigate or otherwise vary, a condition of the burden.

(9)   Subsection (8) above is without prejudice to section 33(1)(a) of this Act.

4   Creation

(1)   A real burden is created by duly registering the constitutive deed except that, notwithstanding section 3(4) of the 1979 Act (creation of real right or obligation on date of registration etc), the constitutive deed may provide for the postponement of the effectiveness of the real burden to—

(a)   a date specified in that deed (the specification being of a fixed date and not, for example, of a date determinable by reference to the occurrence of an event); or

(b)   the date of registration of some other deed so specified.

(2)   The reference in subsection (1) above to the constitutive deed is to a deed which—

(a)   sets out (employing, unless subsection (3) below is invoked, the expression 'real burden') the terms of the prospective real burden;

(b)   is granted by or on behalf of the owner of the land which is to be the burdened property; and

(c)   except in the case mentioned in subsection (4) below, nominates and identifies—

(i)   that land;

(ii)   the land (if any) which is to be the benefited property; and

(iii)   any person in whose favour the real burden is to be constituted (if it is to be constituted other than by reference to the person's capacity as owner of any land).

(3)   Where the constitutive deed relates, or purports to relate, to the creation of a nameable type of real burden (such as, for example, a community burden), that deed may, instead of employing the expression 'real burden', employ the expression appropriate to that type.

(4)   Where the constitutive deed relates to the creation of a community burden, that deed shall nominate and identify the community.

(5)   For the purposes of this section, a constitutive deed is duly registered in relation to a real burden only when registered against the land which is to be the burdened property and (except where there will be no benefited property or the land in question is outwith Scotland) the land which is to be the benefited property.

(6)   A right of ownership held pro indiviso shall not in itself constitute a property against which a constitutive deed can be duly registered.

(7)   This section is subject to sections [53(3A),] 73(2) and 90(8) [and (8A)] of this Act and is without prejudice to section 6 of this Act.

5   Further provision as respects constitutive deed

(1)   It shall not be an objection to the validity of a real burden (whenever created) that—

(a)   an amount payable in respect of an obligation to defray some cost is not specified in the constitutive deed; or

(b)   a proportion or share payable in respect of an obligation to contribute towards some cost is not so specified provided that the way in which that proportion or share can be arrived at is so specified.

(2)   Without prejudice to the generality of subsection (1) above, such specification may be by making reference to another document the terms of which are not reproduced in the deed; but for reference to be so made the other document must be a public document (that is to say, an enactment or a public register or some record or roll to which the public readily has access).

6   Further provision as respects creation

(1)   A real burden is created by registering against the land which is to be the burdened property a deed which—

(a)   is granted by or on behalf of the owner of that land; and

(b)   imports the terms of the prospective burden.

(2)   'Imports' in subsection (1)(b) above means imports into itself from a deed of conditions; and importation in, or as near as may be in, the form set out in schedule 1 to this Act shall suffice in that regard.

(3)   A right of ownership held pro indiviso shall not in itself constitute a property against which a deed such as is mentioned in subsection (1) above can be duly registered.

(4)   This section is without prejudice to section 4 of this Act.

Duration, enforceability and liability

7   Duration

Subject to any enactment (including this Act) or to any rule of law, the duration of a real burden is perpetual unless the constitutive deed provides for a duration of a specific period.

8   Right to enforce

(1)   A real burden is enforceable by any person who has both title and interest to enforce it.

(2)   A person has such title if an owner of the benefited property; but the following persons also have such title—

(a)   a person who has a real right of lease or proper liferent in the benefited property (or has a pro indiviso share in such right);

(b)   a person who—

(i)   is the non-entitled spouse of an owner of the benefited property or of a person mentioned in paragraph (a) above; and

(ii)   has occupancy rights in that property; and

(c)   if the real burden was created as mentioned in subsection (3)(b) below, a person who was, at the time the cost in question was incurred—

(i)   an owner of the benefited property; or

(ii)   a person having such title by virtue of paragraph (a) or (b) above.

(3)   A person has such interest if—

(a)   in the circumstances of any case, failure to comply with the real burden is resulting in, or will result in, material detriment to the value or enjoyment of the person's ownership of, or right in, the benefited property; or

(b)   the real burden being an affirmative burden created as an obligation to defray, or contribute towards, some cost, that person seeks (and has grounds to seek) payment of, or as respects, that cost.

(4)   A person has title to enforce a real burden consisting of—

(a)   a right of pre-emption, redemption or reversion; or

(b)   any other type of option to acquire the burdened property,

only if the owner of the benefited property.

(5)   In subsection (2)(b) above, 'non-entitled spouse' and 'occupancy rights' shall be construed in accordance with section 1 of the Matrimonial Homes (Family

Protection) (Scotland) Act 1981 (c 59) (right of spouse without title to occupy matrimonial home).

(6) Subsections (2) to (5) above do not apply in relation to a personal real burden.

9 Persons against whom burdens are enforceable

(1) An affirmative burden is enforceable against the owner of the burdened property.

(2) A negative burden or an ancillary burden is enforceable against—

    (a) the owner, or tenant, of the burdened property; or

    (b) any other person having the use of that property.

10 Affirmative burdens: continuing liability of former owner

(1) An owner of burdened property shall not, by virtue only of ceasing to be such an owner, cease to be liable for the performance of any relevant obligation.

(2) [Subject to subsection (2A) below,] a person who becomes an owner of burdened property (any such person being referred to in this section as a 'new owner') shall be severally liable with any former owner of the property for any relevant obligation for which the former owner is liable.

[(2A) A new owner shall be liable as mentioned in subsection (2) above for any relevant obligation consisting of an obligation to pay a share of costs relating to maintenance or work (other than local authority work) carried out before the acquisition date only if—

    (a) notice of the maintenance or work—

        (i) in, or as near as may be in, the form set out in schedule 1A to this Act; and

        (ii) containing the information required by the notes for completion set out in that schedule,

(such a notice being referred to in this section and section 10A of this Act as a 'notice of potential liability for costs') was registered in relation to the burdened property at least 14 days before the acquisition date; and

    (b) the notice had not expired before the acquisition date.

(2B) In subsection (2A) above—

'acquisition date' means the date on which the new owner acquired right to the burdened property; and

'local authority work' means work carried out by a local authority by virtue of any enactment.']

(3) A new owner who incurs expenditure in the performance of any relevant obligation for which a former owner of the property is liable may recover an amount equal to such expenditure from that former owner.

(4) For the purposes of subsections (1) to (3) above, 'relevant obligation' means any obligation under an affirmative burden which is due for performance; and such an obligation becomes due—

    (a) in a case where—

        (i) the burden is a community burden; and

        (ii) a binding decision to incur expenditure is made,

on the date on which that decision is made; or

    (b) in any other case, on—

        (i) such date; or

        (ii) the occurrence of such event,

as may be stipulated for its performance (whether in the constitutive deed or otherwise).

[(5) This section does not apply in any case where section 12 of the Tenements (Scotland) Act 2004 (asp 11) applies.]

[10A Notice of potential liability for costs: further provision

(1) A notice of potential liability for costs—

(a)   may be registered in relation to burdened property only on the application of—

(i)   an owner of the burdened property;

(ii)   an owner of the benefited property; or

(iii)   any manager; and

(b)   shall not be registered unless it is signed by or on behalf of the applicant.

(2)   A notice of potential liability for costs may be registered—

(a)   in relation to more than one burdened property in respect of the same maintenance or work; and

(b)   in relation to any one burdened property, in respect of different maintenance or work.

(3)   A notice of potential liability for costs expires at the end of the period of 3 years beginning with the date of its registration, unless it is renewed by being registered again before the end of that period.

(4)   This section applies to a renewed notice of potential liability for costs as it applies to any other such notice.

(5)   The Keeper of the Registers of Scotland shall not be required to investigate or determine whether the information contained in any notice of potential liability for costs submitted for registration is accurate.

(6)   The Scottish Ministers may by order amend schedule 1A to this Act.]

11   Affirmative burdens: shared liability

(1)   If a burdened property as respects which an affirmative burden is created is divided (whether before or after the appointed day) into two or more parts then, subject to subsections (2) and (4) below, the owners of the parts—

(a)   are severally liable in respect of the burden; and

(b)   as between (or among) themselves, are liable in the proportions which the areas of their respective parts bear to the area of the burdened property.

(2)   'Part' in subsection (1) above does not include a part to which the affirmative burden cannot relate.

(3)   In the application of subsection (1) above to parts which are flats in a tenement, the reference in paragraph (b) of that subsection to the areas of the respective parts shall be construed as a reference to the floor areas of the respective flats.

[(3A)   For the purposes of subsection (3) above, the floor area of a flat is calculated by measuring the total floor area (including the area occupied by any internal wall or other internal dividing structure) within its boundaries; but no account shall be taken of any pertinents or any of the following parts of a flat—

(a)   a balcony; and

(b)   except where it is used for any purpose other than storage, a loft or basement.]

(4)   Paragraph (a) of subsection (1) above shall not apply if, in the constitutive deed, it is provided that liability as between (or among) the owners of the parts shall be otherwise than is provided for in that paragraph; and paragraph (b) of that subsection shall not apply if, in the constitutive deed or in the conveyance effecting the division, it is provided that liability as between (or among) them shall be otherwise than is provided for in that paragraph.

(5)   If two or more persons own in common a burdened property as respects which an affirmative burden is created then, unless the constitutive deed otherwise provides—

(a)   they are severally liable in respect of the burden; and

(b)   as between (or among) themselves, they are liable in the proportions in which they own the property.

Division of benefited or burdened property

12 Division of a benefited property

(1) Where part of a benefited property is conveyed, then on registration of the conveyance the part conveyed shall cease to be a benefited property unless in the conveyance some other provision is made, as for example—

(a)   that the part retained and the part conveyed are separately to constitute benefited properties; or

(b)   that it is the part retained which is to cease to be a benefited property.

(2) Different provision may, under subsection (1) above, be made in respect of different real burdens.

(3) For the purposes of subsection (1) above, any such provision as is referred to in that subsection shall—

(a)   identify the constitutive deed, say where it is registered and give the date of registration;

(b)   identify the real burdens; and

(c)   be of no effect in so far as it relates to—

(i)   a right of pre-emption, redemption or reversion; or

(ii) any other type of option to acquire the burdened property,

if it is other than such provision as is mentioned in paragraph (b) of that subsection.

(4) Subsection (1) above does not apply where—

(a)   the property, part of which is conveyed, is a benefited property only by virtue of any of sections 52 to 56 of this Act;

(b)   the real burdens are community burdens; or

(c)   the real burdens are set out in a common deed of conditions, that is to say in a deed which sets out the terms of the burdens imposed on the part conveyed, that part being one of two or more properties on which they are or will be imposed under a common scheme.

13 Division of a burdened property

Where part of a burdened property is conveyed (whether before or after the appointed day), then on registration of the conveyance the part retained and the part conveyed shall separately constitute burdened properties unless the real burden cannot relate to one of the parts, in which case that part shall, on that registration, cease to be a burdened property.

Construction

14 Construction

Real burdens shall be construed in the same manner as other provisions of deeds which relate to land and are intended for registration.

Extinction

15 Discharge

(1) A real burden is discharged as respects a benefited property by registering against the burdened property a deed of discharge granted by or on behalf of the owner of the benefited property.

(2) In subsection (1) above, 'discharged' means discharged—

(a)   wholly; or

(b)   to such extent as may be specified in the deed of discharge.

16 Acquiescence

(1) Where—

(a)   a real burden is breached in such a way that material expenditure is incurred;

(b) any benefit arising from such expenditure would be substantially lost were the burden to be enforced; and

(c) in the case of—

(i) a burden other than a conservation burden, economic development burden or health care burden, the owner of the benefited property (if any) has an interest to enforce the burden in respect of the breach and consents to the carrying on of the activity which results in that breach, or every person by whom the burden is enforceable and who has such an interest, either so consents or, being aware of the carrying on of that activity (or, because of its nature, being in a position where that person ought to be aware of it), has not, by the expiry of such period as is in all the circumstances reasonable (being in any event a period which does not exceed that of twelve weeks beginning with the day by which that activity has been substantially completed), objected to its being carried on; or

(ii) a conservation burden, economic development burden or health care burden, the person by whom the burden is enforceable consents to the carrying on of that activity,

the burden shall, to the extent of the breach, be extinguished.

(2) Where the period of twelve weeks following the substantial completion of an activity has expired as mentioned in sub-paragraph (i) of subsection (1)(c) above, it shall be presumed, unless the contrary is shown, that the person by whom the real burden was, at the time in question, enforceable (or where a burden is enforceable by more than one person, each of those persons) was, or ought to have been, aware of the carrying on of the activity and did not object as mentioned in that sub-paragraph.

17 Further provision as regards extinction where no interest to enforce
Where at any time a real burden is breached but at that time no person has an interest to enforce it in respect of the breach, the burden shall, to the extent of the breach, be extinguished.

18 Negative prescription
(1) Subject to subsection (5) below, if—

(a) a real burden is breached to any extent; and

(b) during the period of five years beginning with the breach neither—

(i) a relevant claim; nor

(ii) a relevant acknowledgement,

is made,

then, subject to subsection (2) below, the burden shall, to the extent of the breach, be extinguished on the expiry of that period.

(2) Subject to subsections (5) and (6) below, where, in relation to a real burden which consists of—

(a) a right of pre-emption, redemption or reversion; or

(b) any other type of option to acquire the burdened property,

the owner of the burdened property fails to comply with an obligation to convey (or, as the case may be, to offer to convey) the property (or part of the property) and paragraph (b) of subsection (1) above is satisfied, the burden shall be extinguished in relation to the property (or part) on the expiry of the period mentioned in the said paragraph (b).

(3) Sections 9 and 10 of the Prescription and Limitation (Scotland) Act 1973 (c 52) (which define the expressions 'relevant claim' and 'relevant acknowledgement' for the purposes of sections 6, 7 and 8A of that Act) shall apply for the purposes of subsections (1) and (2) above as those sections apply for the purposes of sections 6, 7 and 8A of that Act but subject to the following modifications—

(a) in each of sections 9 and 10 of that Act—

(i) subsection (2) shall not apply;

(ii) for any reference to an obligation there shall be substituted a reference to a real burden; and

(iii) for any reference to a creditor there shall be substituted a reference to any person by whom a real burden is enforceable;

(b) in section 9 of that Act, for the reference to a creditor in an obligation there shall be substituted a reference to any person by whom a real burden is enforceable; and

(c) in section 10 of that Act, for any reference to a debtor there shall be substituted a reference to any person against whom the real burden is enforceable.

(4) Section 14 of the said Act of 1973 (which makes provision as respects the computation of prescriptive periods) shall apply for the purposes of subsections (1) and (2) above as that section applies for the purposes of Part I of that Act except that paragraph (a) of subsection (1) of that section shall for the purposes of those subsections be disregarded.

(5) In relation to a breach occurring before the appointed day, subsections (1) and (2) above apply with the substitution in paragraph (b) of subsection (1), for the words 'period of five years beginning with the breach', of the words 'appropriate period'.

(6) In the case of a right of pre-emption constituted as a rural housing burden, subsection (2) above shall apply with the modification that for the words 'the burden shall be extinguished in relation to the property (or part) on' there shall be substituted 'it shall not be competent to commence any action in respect of that failure after'.

(7) The reference, in subsection (5) above, to the 'appropriate period' is to whichever first expires of—

(a) the period of five years beginning with the appointed day; and

(b) the period of twenty years beginning with the breach.

19 Confusio not to extinguish real burden

A real burden is not extinguished by reason only that—

(a) the same person is the owner of the benefited property and the burdened property; or

(b) in a case in which there is no benefited property, the person in whose favour the real burden is constituted is the owner of the burdened property.

Termination

20 Notice of termination

(1) Subject to section 23 of this Act, if at least one hundred years have elapsed since the date of registration of the constitutive deed (whether or not the real burden has been varied or renewed since that date), an owner of the burdened property, or any other person against whom the burden is enforceable, may, after intimation under section 21(1) of this Act, execute and register, in (or as nearly as may be in) the form contained in schedule 2 to this Act, a notice of termination as respects the real burden.

(2) It shall be no objection to the validity of a notice of termination that it is executed or registered by a successor in title of the person who has given such intimation; and any reference in this Act to the 'terminator' shall be construed as a reference to—

(a) except where paragraph (b) below applies, the person who has given such intimation; or

(b) where that person no longer has the right or obligation by virtue of which intimation was given, the person who has most recently acquired that right or obligation.

(3) Subsections (1) and (2) above do not apply in relation to—

(a) a conservation burden;

(b) a maritime burden;

   (c)   a facility burden;

   (d)   a service burden; or

   (e)   a real burden which is a title condition of a kind specified in schedule 11 to this Act.

(4)   The notice of termination shall—

   (a)   identify the land which is the burdened property;

   (b)   describe the terminator's connection with the property (as for example by identifying the terminator as an owner or as a tenant);

   (c)   set out the terms of the real burden and (if it is not wholly to be terminated) specify the extent of the termination;

   (d)   specify a date on or before which any application under paragraph (b) of section 90(1) of this Act will require to be made if the real burden is to be renewed or varied under that paragraph (that date being referred to in this Act as the 'renewal date');

   (e)   specify the date on which, and the means by which, intimation was given under subsection (1) of section 21 of this Act; and

   (f)   set out the name (in so far as known) and the address of each person to whom intimation is sent under subsection (2)(a) of that section.

(5)   Any date may be specified under paragraph (d) of subsection (4) above provided that it is a date not less than eight weeks after intimation is last given under subsection (1) of the said section 21 (intimation by affixing being taken, for the purposes of this subsection, to be given when first the notice is affixed).

(6)   Where a property is subject to two or more real burdens, it shall be competent to execute and register a single notice of termination in respect of both (or all) the real burdens.

21 Intimation

(1)   A proposal to execute and register a notice of termination shall be intimated—

   (a)   to the owner of each benefited property;

   (b)   in the case of a personal real burden, to the holder; and

   (c)   to the owner (or, if the terminator is an owner, to any other owner) of the burdened property.

(2)   Subject to subsection (3) below, such intimation may be given—

   (a)   by sending a copy of the proposed notice of termination, completed as respects all the matters which must, in pursuance of paragraphs (a) to (d) and (f) of section 20(4) of this Act, be identified, described, set out or specified in the notice and with the explanatory note which immediately follows the form of notice of termination in schedule 2 to this Act;

   (b)   by affixing to the burdened property and to—

      (i)   in a case (not being one mentioned in paragraph (c)(ii) below) where there exists one, and only one, lamp post which is situated within one hundred metres of that property, that lamp post; or

      (ii)   in a case (not being one so mentioned) where there exists more than one lamp post so situated, each of at least two such lamp posts,

a conspicuous notice in the form set out in schedule 3 to this Act; or

   (c)   in a case where—

      (i)   it is not possible to comply with paragraph (b) above; or

      (ii)   the burdened property is minerals or salmon fishings,

by advertisement in a newspaper circulating in the area of the burdened property.

(3)   Such intimation shall, except where it is impossible to do so, be given by the means described in subsection (2)(a) above if it is given—

   (a)   under subsection (1)(b) or (c) above; or

   (b)   under subsection (1)(a) above in relation to a benefited property which is at some point within four metres of the burdened property.

(4)   An advertisement giving intimation under subsection (2)(c) above shall—

(a)   identify the land which is the burdened property;

(b)   set out the terms of the real burden either in full or by reference to the constitutive deed;

(c)   specify the name and address of a person from whom a copy of the proposed notice of termination may be obtained; and

(d)   state that any owner of a benefited property, or as the case may be any holder of a personal real burden, may apply to the Lands Tribunal for Scotland for the real burden to be renewed or varied but that if no such application is received by a specified date (being the renewal date) the consequence may be that the real burden is extinguished.

(5)   The terminator shall provide a person with a copy of the proposed notice of termination (completed as is mentioned in subsection (2)(a) above and with the explanatory note referred to in that subsection) if so requested by that person.

(6)   A person—

(a)   is entitled to affix a notice to a lamp post in compliance with subsection (2)(b) above regardless of who owns the lamp post but must—

(i)   take all reasonable care not to damage the lamp post in doing so; and

(ii)   remove the notice no later than one week after the date specified in it as the renewal date; and

(b)   must, until the day immediately following the date so specified, take all reasonable steps to ensure that the notice continues to be displayed and remains conspicuous and readily legible.

(7)   Section 184 of the Town and Country Planning (Scotland) Act 1997 (c 8) (planning permission not needed for advertisements complying with regulations) applies in relation to a notice affixed in compliance with subsection (2)(b) above as that section applies in relation to an advertisement displayed in accordance with regulations made under section 182 of that Act (regulations controlling display of advertisements).

22   Oath or affirmation before notary public

(1)   Before submitting a notice of termination for registration, the terminator shall swear or affirm before a notary public that, to the best of the terminator's knowledge and belief, all the information contained in the notice is true and that section 21 of this Act has been complied with.

(2)   For the purposes of subsection (1) above, if the terminator is—

(a)   an individual unable by reason of legal disability, or incapacity, to swear or affirm as mentioned in that subsection, then a legal representative of the terminator may swear or affirm;

(b)   not an individual, then any person authorised to sign documents on its behalf may swear or affirm;

and any reference in that subsection to a terminator shall be construed accordingly.

23   Prerequisite certificate for registration of notice of termination

(1)   A notice of termination shall not be registrable unless, after the renewal date, there is endorsed on the notice (or on an annexation to it referred to in an endorsement on it and identified, on the face of the annexation, as being the annexation so referred to) a certificate executed by a member of the Lands Tribunal, or by their clerk, to the effect that no application in relation to the proposal to execute and register the notice has been received under section 90(1)(b) (and (4)) of this Act or that any such application which has been received—

(a)   has been withdrawn; or

(b)   relates (either or both)—

(i)   to one or more but not to all of the real burdens the terms of which are set out in the notice (any real burden to which it relates being described in the certificate);

(ii)   to one or more but not to all (or probably or possibly not to all) of the

benefited properties (any benefited property to which it relates being
    described in the certificate),
and where more than one such application has been received the certificate shall
relate to both (or as the case may be all) applications.
    (2)   At any time before endorsement under subsection (1) above, a notice of ter-
mination, whether or not it has been submitted for such endorsement, may be
withdrawn, by intimation in writing to the Lands Tribunal, by the terminator; and
it shall not be competent to endorse under that subsection a notice in respect of
which such intimation is given.

24   Effect of registration of notice of termination

    (1)   Subject to subsection (2) below, a notice of termination, when registered
against the burdened property, extinguishes the real burden in question wholly or
as the case may be to such extent as may be described in that notice.
    (2)   A notice of termination registrable by virtue of a certificate under para-
graph (b) of section 23(1) of this Act shall not, on being registered, extinguish a
real burden which is the subject of an application disclosed by the certificate in so
far as that burden—
    (a)   is constituted in favour of the property of which the applicant is owner;
or
    (b)   is a personal real burden of which the applicant is holder,
but if under that section a further certificate is endorsed on the notice (or on an
annexation to the notice) the notice may be registered again, the effect of the later
registration being determined by reference to the further certificate rather than to
the certificate by virtue of which the notice was previously registered.

PART 2
COMMUNITY BURDENS

Meaning, creation etc

25   The expression 'community burdens'

    (1)   Subject to subsection (2) below, where—
    (a)   real burdens are imposed under a common scheme on [two] or more
units; and
    (b)   each of those units is, in relation to some or all of those burdens, both a
benefited property and a burdened property,
the burdens shall, in relation to the units, be known as 'community burdens'.
    (2)   Any real burdens such as are mentioned in section 54(1) of this Act are
community burdens.

26   Creation of community burdens: supplementary provision

    (1)   Without prejudice to section 2 of this Act, community burdens may make
provision as respects any of the following—
    (a)   the appointment by the owners of a manager;
    (b)   the dismissal by the owners of a manager;
    (c)   the powers and duties of a manager;
    (d)   the nomination of a person to be the first manager;
    (e)   the procedures to be followed by the owners in making decisions about
matters affecting the community;
    (f)   the matters on which such decisions may be made; and
    (g)   the resolution of disputes relating to community burdens.
    (2)   In this Act 'community' means—
    (a)   the units subject to community burdens; and
    (b)   any unit in a sheltered or retirement housing development which is used
in some special way as mentioned in section 54(1) of this Act.

27 Effect on units of statement that burdens are community burdens

Where, in relation to any real burdens, the constitutive deed states that the burdens are to be community burdens, each unit shall, in relation to those burdens, be both a benefited property and a burdened property.

Management of community

28 Power of majority to appoint manager etc

(1) Subject to sections 54(5)(a) and 63(8)(a) of this Act and to any provision made by community burdens, the owners of a majority of the units in a community may—

(a) appoint a person to be the manager of the community on such terms as they may specify;

(b) confer on any such manager the right to exercise such of their powers as they may specify;

(c) revoke, or vary, the right to exercise such of the powers conferred under paragraph (b) above as they may specify; and

(d) dismiss any such manager.

(2) Without prejudice to the generality of subsection (1)(b) above, the powers mentioned there include—

(a) power to carry out maintenance;

(b) power to enforce community burdens; and

(c) power to vary or discharge such burdens.

(3) If a unit is owned by two or more persons in common, then, for the purposes of voting on any proposal to exercise a power conferred by subsection (1) above, the vote allocated as respects the unit shall only be counted for or against the proposal if it is the agreed vote of those of them who together own more than a half share of the unit.

(4) The powers conferred by paragraphs (b) to (d) of subsection (1) above may be exercised whether or not the manager was appointed by virtue of paragraph (a) of that subsection.

29 Power of majority to instruct common maintenance

(1) This section applies where—

(a) community burdens impose an obligation on the owners of all or some of the units to maintain, or contribute towards the cost of maintaining, particular property; and

(b) the obligation so imposed accounts for the entire liability for the maintenance of such property.

(2) Subject to any provision made by community burdens, the owners of a majority of the units subject to the obligation may—

(a) decide that maintenance should be carried out;

(b) [subject to subsection (3A) below, require each] owner to deposit—

(i) by such date as they may specify (being a date not less than twenty-eight days after the requirement is made of that owner); and

(ii) [with such person as they may nominate for the purpose,]

a sum of money (being a sum not exceeding that owner's apportioned share, in accordance with the terms of the community burdens, of a reasonable estimate of the cost of maintenance);

[. . .]

(d) instruct or carry out such maintenance; and

(e) modify or revoke anything done by them by virtue of paragraphs (a) to (d) above.

(3) If a unit is owned by two or more persons in common, then, for the purposes of voting on any proposal to exercise a power conferred by subsection (2) above, the vote allocated as respects the unit shall only be counted for or against

the proposal if it is the agreed vote of those of them who together own more than a half share of the unit.

[(3A)   A requirement under subsection (2)(b) above that each owner deposit a sum of money—

(a)   exceeding £100; or

(b)   of £100 or less where the aggregate of that sum taken together with any other sum or sums required (otherwise than by a previous notice under this sub-section) in the preceding 12 months to be deposited under that subsection by each owner exceeds £200,

shall be made by written notice to each owner and shall require the sum to be deposited into such account (the 'maintenance account') as the owners may nomi-nate for the purpose.

(3B)   The owners may authorise a manager or at least two other persons (whether or not owners) to operate the maintenance account on their behalf.]

(4)   Any notice given under subsection [(3A)] above shall contain, or to it shall be attached, a note comprising a summary of the nature and extent of the main-tenance to be carried out together with the following information—

(a)   the estimated cost of carrying out that maintenance;

(b)   why the estimate is considered a reasonable estimate;

(c)   how—

(i)   the sum required from the owner in question; and

(ii)   the apportionment among the owners,

have been arrived at;

(d)   what the apportioned shares of the other owners are;

(e)   the date on which the decision to carry out the maintenance was taken and the names of those by whom it was taken;

(f)   a timetable for the carrying out of the maintenance, including the dates by which it is proposed the maintenance will be—

(i)   commenced; and

(ii)   completed;

(g)   the location and number of the maintenance account; and

(h)   the names and addresses of the persons who will be authorised to oper-ate that account on behalf of the community.

(5)   The maintenance account shall be a bank or building society account which is interest bearing; and the authority of at least two persons, or of a manager on whom has been conferred the right to give authority, shall be required for any payment from it.

(6)   If modification or revocation under paragraph (e) of subsection (2) above affects the information contained in a notice or note under subsection (4) above, that information shall forthwith be sent again, modified accordingly, to the owners.

[(6A)   The notice given under subsection (2)(b) above may specify a date as a refund date for the purposes of subsection (7)(b)(i) below.]

(7)   An owner shall be entitled—

(a)   to inspect, at any reasonable time, any tender received in connection with the maintenance to be carried out;

(b)   if—

(i)   that maintenance is not commenced by [—

(A) where the notice under subsection (2)(b) above specifies a refund date, that date; or

(B) where that notice does not specify such a date, the twenty-eighth] day after the date specified by virtue of subsection (4)(f)(i) above; and

(ii)   the owner demands, by written notice, from the persons authorised under subsection [(3B)] above repayment (with accrued interest) of such sum as has been deposited by that owner in compliance with the requirement under subsection (2)(b) above, to be repayed accordingly; except that no requirement to make repayment in compliance with a notice under paragraph (b)(ii) above shall arise if the persons so authorised do not receive that notice before the maintenance is commenced.

[(7A) A former owner who, before ceasing to be an owner, deposited sums in compliance with a requirement under subsection (2)(b) above, shall have the same entitlement as an owner has under subsection (7)(b) above.]

(8) Such sums as are held in the maintenance account by virtue of subsection [(3A)] above are held in trust for all the depositors, for the purpose of being used by the persons authorised to make payments from the account as payment for the maintenance.

(9) Any sums held in the maintenance account after all sums payable in respect of the maintenance carried out have been paid shall be shared among the owners—

(a) by repaying each depositor, with any accrued interest and after deduction of that person's apportioned share of the actual cost of the maintenance, the sum which the person deposited; or

(b) in such other way as the depositors agree in writing.

[(10) The Scottish Ministers may by order substitute for the sums for the time being specified in subsection (3A) above such other sums as appear to them to be justified by a change in the value of money appearing to them to have occurred since the last occasion on which the sums were fixed.]

30 Owners' decision binding
Anything done (including any decision made) by—

(a) the owners in accordance with such provision as is made in community burdens; or

(b) a majority of them, in accordance with section 28 or 29 of this Act,

is binding on all the owners and their successors as owners.

31 Remuneration of manager
Subject to any provision made by community burdens, liability for any remuneration due to a manager of the community (however appointed) shall be shared equally among the units in a community and each owner shall be liable accordingly; but if two or more persons have common ownership of a unit then—

(a) they are severally liable for any share payable in respect of that unit; and

(b) as between (or among) themselves, they are liable in the proportions in which they own the unit.

[31A Disapplication of provisions of sections 28, 29 and 31 in certain cases
(1) Sections 28(1)(a) and (d) and (2)(a), 29 and 31 of this Act shall not apply in relation to a community consisting of one tenement.

(2) Sections 28(1)(a) and (d) and 31 of this Act shall not apply to a community in any period during which the development management scheme applies to the community.]

Variation, discharge etc

32 The expressions 'affected unit' and 'adjacent unit'
In this Part of this Act a unit in respect of which a community burden is to be varied ('varied' including imposed), or discharged, is referred to as an 'affected unit'; and 'adjacent unit' means, in relation to an affected unit, any unit which is at some point within four metres of the unit.

33 Majority etc variation and discharge of community burdens
(1) A community burden may be varied ('varied' including imposed), or discharged, by registering against each affected unit a deed of variation, or discharge, granted—

(a) where provision is made in the constitutive deed for it to be granted by the owners of such units in the community as may be specified, by or on behalf of the owners of those units; or

(b)   [. . .] in accordance with subsection (2) below.

(2)   A deed is granted in accordance with this subsection if granted—

(a)   [where no such provision as is mentioned in subsection (1)(a) above is made,] by or on behalf of the owners of a majority of the units in the community (except that, where one person owns a majority of those units, the deed must also be granted by at least one other owner); or

(b)   where the manager of the community is authorised to do so (whether in the constitutive deed or otherwise), by that manager.

(3)   An affected unit may, for the purposes of subsection (1)(a) or (2)(a) above, be included in any calculation of the number of units.

(4)   For the purposes of this section, where a unit is owned by two or more persons in common a deed is granted by or on behalf of the owners of the unit if—

(a)   granted in accordance with such provision as is made in that regard in the constitutive deed; or

(b)   where no such provision is made, granted by or on behalf of those of them who together own more than a half share of the unit.

(5)   This section is subject to section 54(5)(b) and (c) of this Act.

34   Variation or discharge under section 33: intimation

(1)   Where a deed of variation or discharge is granted under section 33(2) of this Act, a proposal to register that deed shall be intimated to such other owners of the units in the community as have not granted the deed.

(2)   Such intimation shall be given by sending a copy of the deed, together with—

(a)   a notice in, or as near as may be in, the form set out in schedule 4 to this Act; and

(b)   the explanatory note which immediately follows that form in that schedule.

(3)   Where a deed has been granted as mentioned in subsection (1) above, any person to whom intimation is given under subsection (2) above may, during the period of eight weeks beginning with the latest date on which intimation of the proposal to register the deed is so given, apply to the Lands Tribunal for preservation, unvaried, of the community burden in so far as constituted in favour of, or against, any unit not all of whose owners have granted the deed.

(4)   Subsections (2) to (4) of section 37 of this Act apply to a deed granted as mentioned in subsection (1) above as they apply in relation to a deed granted as mentioned in section 35 of this Act but with the modifications specified in subsection (5) below.

(5)   The modifications are that—

(a)   references in the said subsections (2) and (4) to subsection (1) of that section are to be construed as references to subsection (3) above;

(b)   the reference in the former of those said subsections to no application having been received under section 37 is to be construed as a reference to none having been received under this section; and

(c)   the reference in the latter of those said subsections to section 36 of this Act is to be construed as a reference to subsections (1) and (2) above.

(6)   For the purposes of subsection (4) of section 37 of this Act as so applied, if the person proposing to submit for registration a deed granted as mentioned in subsection (1) above is—

(a)   an individual unable by reason of legal disability, or incapacity, to swear or affirm as mentioned in the said subsection (4), then a legal representative of that person may swear or affirm;

(b)   not an individual, then any person authorised to sign documents on its behalf may swear or affirm, and any reference in the said subsection (4) to the person so proposing shall be construed accordingly.

35 Variation and discharge of community burdens by owners of adjacent units

(1)   A community burden may be varied or discharged by registering against each affected unit a deed of variation, or discharge, granted, [. . .] by or on behalf of the owners of the affected units and by or on behalf of the owners of all units (if any) which in relation to any of the affected units are adjacent units, except that this subsection—

(a)   shall not apply where the burden is a facility burden or a service burden or where the units constitute a sheltered or retirement housing development;

(b)   may expressly be disapplied by the constitutive deed; and

(c)   is subject to sections 36 and 37 of this Act and to any determination of the Lands Tribunal.

(2)   Subsection (4) of section 33 of this Act applies for the purposes of this section as it applies for the purposes of that section.

36 Variation and discharge under section 35: intimation

(1)   A proposal to register under section 35 of this Act a deed of variation or discharge shall be intimated to such owners of the units in the community as have not granted the deed.

(2)   Such intimation may be given—

(a)   by sending a copy of the deed together with—

(i)   a notice in, or as near as may be in, the form set out in schedule 5 to this Act; and

(ii)   the explanatory note which immediately follows that form in that schedule;

(b)   by affixing to each affected unit and to—

(i)   in a case where there exists one, and only one, lamp post which is situated within one hundred metres of that unit, that lamp post; or

(ii)   in a case where there exists more than one lamp post so situated, each of at least two such lamp posts,

a conspicuous notice in the form set out in schedule 6 to this Act; or

(c)   in a case where it is not possible to comply with paragraph (b) above, by advertisement in a newspaper circulating in the area of the affected unit.

(3)   An advertisement giving intimation under subsection (2)(c) above shall—

(a)   identify the land which is the affected unit;

(b)   set out the terms of the community burden either in full or by reference to the constitutive deed;

(c)   specify the name and address of the person who proposes to register the deed and state that from that person (or from some other person whose name and address are specified in the advertisement) a copy of that deed may be obtained;

(d)   state that any owner of a unit who has not granted the deed may apply to the Lands Tribunal for Scotland for the community burden to be preserved but that if no such application is received by a specified date (being the date on which the period mentioned in section 37(1) of this Act expires) the consequence may be that the community burden is varied or discharged in relation to the affected unit.

(4)   The person proposing to register the deed shall provide any other person with a copy of that deed if so requested by that other person.

(5)   Subsections (6) and (7) of section 21 of this Act apply in relation to affixing, and to a notice affixed, under subsection (2)(b) above as they apply in relation to affixing, and to a notice affixed, under subsection (2)(b) of that section (the reference in paragraph (a)(ii) of the said subsection (6) to the date specified in the

notice as the renewal date being construed as a reference to the date so specified by virtue of subsection (2)(b) above).

37   Preservation of community burden in respect of which deed of variation or discharge has been granted as mentioned in section 35(1)

(1)   Where a deed of variation or, as the case may be, of discharge has been granted as mentioned in section 35(1) of this Act, any owner of a unit in the community who has not granted the deed may, during the period of eight weeks beginning with the latest date on which intimation of the proposal to register that deed is given under section 36(2) of this Act, apply to the Lands Tribunal for preservation, unvaried, of the community burden in so far as constituted in favour of, or against, any unit not all of whose owners have granted the deed.

(2)   A deed of variation or discharge granted as so mentioned shall not, on registration, vary or discharge a community burden in so far as constituted in favour of, or against, any unit not all of whose owners have granted the deed unless, after the expiry of the period mentioned in subsection (1) above, there is endorsed on it (or on an annexation to it referred to in an endorsement on it and identified, on the face of the annexation, as being the annexation so referred to) a certificate executed by a member of the Lands Tribunal, or by their clerk, to the effect that no application in relation to the proposal to register the deed has been received under this section or that any such application which has been received—

(a)   has been withdrawn; or

(b)   relates to one or more but not to all of the community burdens the terms of which are set out [or referred to] in the deed (any community burden to which it relates being described in the certificate),

and where more than one such application has been received the certificate shall relate to both (or as the case may be all) applications.

(3)   A deed of variation or discharge granted as so mentioned does not vary or discharge, in so far as constituted in favour of, or against, any unit not all of whose owners have granted the deed, a burden described by virtue of subsection (2)(b) above.

(4)   A person who proposes to submit a deed of variation or discharge granted as so mentioned for registration shall, before doing so, swear or affirm before a notary public (the deed being endorsed accordingly)—

(a)   that section 36 of this Act has been complied with; and

(b)   as to the date on which the period mentioned in subsection (1) above expires,

but if more than one person so proposes only one of them need so swear or affirm.

(5)   Subsection (2) of section 22 of this Act applies in relation to such a person and for the purposes of subsection (4) above as it applies in relation to a terminator and for the purposes of subsection (1) of that section.

(6)   For the purposes of subsection (1) above, intimation by affixing shall be taken to be given when first the notice is affixed.

PART 3
CONSERVATION AND OTHER PERSONAL REAL BURDENS

Conservation burdens

38   Conservation burdens

(1)   On and after the day on which this section comes into force it shall, subject to subsection (2) below, be competent to create a real burden in favour of a conservation body, or of the Scottish Ministers, for the purpose of preserving, or protecting, for the benefit of the public—

(a)   the architectural or historical characteristics of any land; or

(b)   any other special characteristics of any land (including, without prejudice

to the generality of this paragraph, a special characteristic derived from the flora, fauna or general appearance of the land);
and any such burden shall be known as a 'conservation burden'.

(2)   If under subsection (1) above the conservation burden is to be created other than by the conservation body or the Scottish Ministers, the consent of—

(a)   that body to the creation of the burden in its favour; or

(b)   those Ministers to the creation of the burden in their favour,

must be obtained before the constitutive deed is registered.

(3)   It shall not be competent to grant a standard security over a conservation burden.

(4)   The Scottish Ministers may, subject to subsection (5) below, by order, prescribe such body as they think fit to be a conservation body.*

(5)   The power conferred by subsection (4) above may be exercised in relation to a body only if the object, or function, of the body (or, as the case may be, one of its objects or functions) is to preserve, or protect, for the benefit of the public such characteristics of any land as are mentioned in paragraph (a) or (b) of subsection (1) above.

(6)   Where the power conferred by subsection (4) above is exercised in relation to a trust, the conservation body shall be the trustees of the trust.

(7)   The Scottish Ministers may, by order, determine that such conservation body as may be specified in the order shall cease to be a conservation body.

39   Assignation
The right to a conservation burden may be assigned or otherwise transferred to any conservation body or to the Scottish Ministers; and any such assignation or transfer takes effect on registration.

40   Enforcement where no completed title
A conservation burden is enforceable by the holder of the burden irrespective of whether the holder has completed title to the burden.

41   Completion of title
Where the holder of a conservation burden does not have a completed title—

(a)   title may be completed by the holder registering a notice of title; or

(b)   without completing title, the holder may grant—

(i)   under section 39 of this Act, a deed assigning the right to the burden; or

(ii)   under section 48 of this Act, a deed discharging, in whole or in part, the burden,

but unless the deed is one to which section 15(3) of the 1979 Act (circumstances where unnecessary to deduce title) applies, it shall be necessary, in the deed, to deduce title to the burden through the midcouples linking the holder to the person who had the last completed title.

42   Extinction of burden on body ceasing to be conservation body
Where—

(a)   the holder of a conservation burden is a conservation body or, as the case may be, two or more such bodies; and

(b)   that body ceases to be such a body, or those bodies cease to be such bodies (whether because an order under section 38(7) of this Act so provides or because the body in question has ceased to exist),

the conservation burden shall, on the body or bodies so ceasing, forthwith be extinguished.

---

*Prescribed conservation bodies are listed in the Title Conditions (Scotland) Act 2003 (Conservation Bodies) Order 2003 (SSI 2003/453): see p 356 below.

Rural housing burdens

43   Rural housing burdens

(1)   On and after the day on which this section comes into force it shall, subject to subsections (2) and (3) below, be competent to create a real burden [over rural land] which comprises a right of pre-emption in favour of a rural housing body other than by reference to the body's capacity as owner of any land; and any such burden shall be known as a 'rural housing burden'.

(2)   If under subsection (1) above the rural housing burden is to be created other than by the rural housing body, the consent of that body to the creation of the burden in its favour must be obtained before the constitutive deed is registered.

(3)   It shall not be competent to create a rural housing burden on the sale of a property by virtue of section 61 of the Housing (Scotland) Act 1987 (c 26) (secure tenant's right to purchase).

(4)   It shall not be competent to grant a standard security over a rural housing burden.

(5)   The Scottish Ministers may, subject to subsection (6) below, by order, prescribe such body as they think fit to be a rural housing body.*

(6)   The power conferred by subsection (5) above may be exercised in relation to a body only if the object, or function, of the body (or, as the case may be one of its principal objects or functions) is to provide housing [or] land for housing.

(7)   Where the power conferred by subsection (5) above is exercised in relation to a trust, the rural housing body shall be the trustees of the trust.

(8)   The Scottish Ministers may, by order, determine that such rural housing body as may be specified in the order shall cease to be a rural housing body.

(9)   In this section, 'rural land' means land other than excluded land ('excluded land' having the same meaning as in Part 2 of the Land Reform (Scotland) Act 2003 (asp 2)).

(10)   Sections 39 to 42 of this Act apply in relation to a rural housing burden and a rural housing body as they apply in relation to a conservation burden and a conservation body but with the modifications that in section 39 the words 'or to the Scottish Ministers' shall be disregarded and in section 42(b) the reference to an order under section 38(7) of this Act shall be construed as a reference to an order under subsection (8) above.

Maritime burdens

44   Maritime burdens

(1)   On and after the day on which this section comes into force, it shall be competent to create a real burden over the sea bed or foreshore in favour of the Crown for the benefit of the public; and any such burden shall be known as a 'maritime burden'.

(2)   The right of the Crown to a maritime burden may not be assigned or otherwise transferred.

(3)   For the purposes of this section—

(a)   'sea bed' means the bed of the territorial sea adjacent to Scotland; and

(b)   'territorial sea' includes any tidal waters.

Economic development burdens

45   Economic development burdens

(1)   On and after the day on which this section comes into force it shall, subject

---

*Prescribed rural housing bodies are listed in the Title Conditions (Scotland) Act 2003 (Rural Housing Bodies) Order 2004 (SSI 2004/477): see p 357 below.

to subsection (2) below, be competent to create a real burden in favour of a local authority, or of the Scottish Ministers, for the purpose of promoting economic development; and any such burden shall be known as an 'economic development burden'.

(2)   If under subsection (1) above the economic development burden is to be created other than by the local authority or the Scottish Ministers, the consent of that body or those Ministers to the creation of the burden in their favour must be obtained before the constitutive deed is registered.

(3)   An economic development burden may comprise an obligation to pay a sum of money (the sum or the method of determining it being specified in the constitutive deed) to the local authority or the Scottish Ministers as the case may be.

(4)   It shall not be competent—
  (a)   to grant a standard security over; or
  (b)   to assign the right to,
an economic development burden.

(5)   Sections 40 and 41(a) and (b)(ii) of this Act apply in relation to an economic development burden as they apply in relation to a conservation burden.
  [. . .]

Health care burdens

46   Health care burdens

(1)   On and after the day on which this section comes into force it shall, subject to subsection (2) below, be competent to create a real burden in favour of a National Health Service trust, or of the Scottish Ministers, for the purpose of promoting the provision of facilities for health care; and any such burden shall be known as a 'health care burden'.

(2)   If under subsection (1) above the health care burden is to be created other than by the trust or the Scottish Ministers, the consent of the trust or those Ministers to the creation of the burden in its or their favour must be obtained before the constitutive deed is registered.

(3)   A health care burden may comprise an obligation to pay a sum of money (the sum or the method of determining it being specified in the constitutive deed) to the trust or the Scottish Ministers as the case may be.

(4)   It shall not be competent—
  (a)   to grant a standard security over; or
  (b)   to assign the right to,
a health care burden.

(5)   Sections 40 and 41(a) and (b)(ii) of this Act apply in relation to a health care burden as they apply in relation to a conservation burden.

(6)   In subsection (1) above, 'facilities for health care' includes facilities ancillary to health care; as for example (but without prejudice to that generality) accommodation for staff employed to provide health care.

General

47   Interest to enforce
The holder of a personal real burden is presumed to have an interest to enforce the burden.

48   Discharge
(1)   A personal real burden is discharged by registering against the burdened property a deed of discharge granted by or on behalf of the holder of the burden.

(2)   In subsection (1) above, 'discharged' means discharged—
  (a)   wholly; or
  (b)   to such extent as may be specified in the deed of discharge.

PART 4

TRANSITIONAL: IMPLIED RIGHTS OF ENFORCEMENT

Extinction of implied rights of enforcement

49 Extinction

(1) Any rule of law whereby land may be the benefited property, in relation to a real burden, by implication (that is to say, without being nominated in the constitutive deed as the benefited property and without being so nominated in any deed into which the constitutive deed is incorporated) shall cease to have effect on the appointed day and a real burden shall not, on and after that day, be enforceable by virtue of such rule; but this subsection is subject to subsection (2) below.

(2) In relation to a benefited property as respects which, on the appointed day, it is competent (taking such rule of law as is mentioned in subsection (1) above still to be in effect) to register a notice of preservation or of converted servitude, subsection (1) above shall apply with the substitution, for the reference to the appointed day, of a reference to the day immediately following the expiry of the period of ten years beginning with the appointed day.

50 Preservation

(1) Subject to subsection (6) below, an owner of land which is a benefited property by virtue of such rule of law as is mentioned in section 49(1) of this Act may, during the period of ten years beginning with the appointed day, execute and duly register, in (or as nearly as may be in) the form contained in schedule 7 to this Act, a notice of preservation as respects the land; and if the owner does so then the land shall continue to be a benefited property after the expiry of that period (in so far as the burdened property, the benefited property and the real burden are the burdened property, the benefited property, and the real burden identified in the notice of preservation).

(2) The notice of preservation shall—

(a) identify the land which is the burdened property (or any part of that land);

(b) identify the land which is the benefited property (or any part of that land);

(c) where the person registering the notice does not have a completed title to the benefited property, set out the midcouples linking that person to the person who last had such completed title;

(d) set out the terms of the real burden; and

(e) set out the grounds, both factual and legal, for describing as a benefited property the land identified in pursuance of paragraph (b) above.

(3) For the purposes of subsection (1) above, a notice is, subject to section 116 of this Act, duly registered only when registered against both properties identified in pursuance of subsection (2)(a) and (b) above.

(4) A person submitting any notice for registration under this section shall, before doing so, swear or affirm before a notary public that to the best of the knowledge and belief of the person all the information contained in the notice is true.

(5) For the purposes of subsection (4) above, if the person is—

(a) an individual unable by reason of legal disability, or incapacity, to swear or affirm as mentioned in that subsection, then a legal representative of the person may swear or affirm;

(b) not an individual, then any person authorised to sign documents on its behalf may swear or affirm;

and any reference in that subsection to a person shall be construed accordingly.

(6) Subsection (1) above does not apply as respects a real burden which has been imposed under a common scheme affecting both the burdened and the benefited property.

(7) This section is subject to section 115 of this Act.

51 Duties of Keeper: amendments relating to unenforceable real burdens

(1) Unless one of the circumstances mentioned in subsection (2) below arises, the Keeper of the Registers of Scotland shall not be required to remove from the Land Register of Scotland a real burden which section 49 of this Act makes unenforceable.

(2) The circumstances are that the Keeper—

(a) is requested, in an application for registration or rectification, to remove the real burden; or

(b) is, under section 9(1) of the 1979 Act (rectification of the register), ordered to do so by the court or the Lands Tribunal,

and no such request or order shall be competent during that period of ten years which commences with the appointed day.

(3) During the period mentioned in subsection (2) above a real burden, notwithstanding that it has been so made unenforceable, may at the discretion of the Keeper, for the purposes of section 6(1)(e) of the 1979 Act (entering subsisting real right in title sheet), be taken to subsist; but this subsection is without prejudice to subsection (4) below.

(4) The Keeper shall not, before the date mentioned in subsection (5) below, remove from the Land Register of Scotland a real burden which is the subject of a notice in respect of which application has been made for a determination by—

(a) a court; or

(b) the Lands Tribunal,

under section 115(6)(b) of this Act.

(5) The date is whichever is the earlier of—

(a) that two months after the final decision on the application; and

(b) that prescribed under section 115(6)(ii) of this Act.

New implied rights of enforcement

52 Common schemes: general

(1) Where real burdens are imposed under a common scheme and the deed by which they are imposed on any unit, being a deed registered before the appointed day, expressly refers to the common scheme or is so worded that the existence of the common scheme is to be implied (or a constitutive deed incorporated into that deed so refers or is so worded) then, subject to subsection (2) below, any unit subject to the common scheme by virtue of—

(a) that deed; or

(b) any other deed so registered,

shall be a benefited property in relation to the real burdens.

(2) Subsection (1) above applies only in so far as no provision to the contrary is impliedly (as for example by reservation of a right to vary or waive the real burdens) or expressly made in the deed mentioned in paragraph (a) of that subsection (or in any such constitutive deed as is mentioned in that subsection).

(3) This section confers no right of pre-emption, redemption or reversion.

(4) This section is subject to sections 57(1) and 122(2)(ii) of this Act.

53 Common schemes: related properties

(1) Where real burdens are imposed under a common scheme, the deed by which they are imposed on any unit comprised within a group of related properties being a deed registered before the appointed day, then all units comprised within that group and subject to the common scheme (whether or not by virtue of a deed registered before the appointed day) shall be benefited properties in relation to the real burdens.

(2) Whether properties are related properties for the purposes of subsection (1) above is to be inferred from all the circumstances; and without prejudice to the generality of this subsection, circumstances giving rise to such an inference might include—

(a)   the convenience of managing the properties together because they share—
  (i)   some common feature; or
  (ii)   an obligation for common maintenance of some facility;
(b)   there being shared ownership of common property;
(c)   their being subject to the common scheme by virtue of the same deed of conditions; or
(d)   the properties each being a flat in the same tenement.
(3)   This section confers no right of pre-emption, redemption or reversion.
[(3A)   Section 4 of this Act shall apply in relation to any real burden to which subsection (1) above applies as if—
(a)   in subsection (2), paragraph (c)(ii);
(b)   subsection (4); and
(c)   in subsection (5),
the words from 'and' to the end, were omitted.]
(4)   This section is subject to sections 57 and 122(2)(ii) of this Act.

54   Sheltered housing

(1)   Where by a deed (or deeds) registered before the appointed day real burdens are imposed under a common scheme on all the units in a sheltered or retirement housing development or on all such units except a unit which is used in some special way, each unit shall be a benefited property in relation to the real burdens.
(2)   Subsection (1) above is subject to section 122(2)(ii) of this Act.
(3)   In this section, 'sheltered or retirement housing development' means a group of dwelling-houses which, having regard to their design, size and other features, are particularly suitable for occupation by elderly people (or by people who are disabled or infirm or in some other way vulnerable) and which, for the purposes of such occupation, are provided with facilities substantially different from those of ordinary dwelling-houses.
(4)   Any real burden which regulates the use, maintenance, reinstatement or management—
(a)   of—
  (i)   a facility; or
  (ii)   a service,
which is one of those which make a sheltered or retirement housing development particularly suitable for such occupation as is mentioned in subsection (3) above; or
(b)   of any other facility if it is a facility such as is mentioned in that subsection,
is in this section referred to as a 'core burden'.
(5)   In relation to a sheltered or retirement housing development—
(a)   section 28 of this Act applies with the following modifications—
  (i)   in subsection (1), the reference to the owners of a majority of the units in a community shall, for the purposes of paragraphs (b) and (c) of that subsection, be construed as a reference to the owners of at least two thirds of the units in the development; and
  (ii)   in paragraph (c) of subsection (2), the reference to varying or discharging shall be construed as a reference only to varying and that to community burdens as a reference only to real burdens which are not core burdens (the words 'Without prejudice to the generality of subsection (1)(b) above,' which begin the subsection being, for the purposes of that modification, disregarded except in so far as they give meaning to the words 'the powers mentioned there' which immediately follow them);
(b)   section 33 of this Act, in relation to core burdens, applies with the following modifications—
  (i)   in subsection (1), the reference to varying or discharging shall, in re-

lation to a deed granted in accordance with subsection (2) of the section, be construed as a reference only to varying; and

(ii) in subsection (2)(a) the reference to the owners of a majority of the units shall be construed as a reference to the owners of at least two thirds of the units of the development; and

(c) no real burden relating to a restriction as to any person's age may be varied or discharged by virtue of section 33(2) of this Act.

(6) This section confers no right of pre-emption, redemption or reversion and is subject to section 57 of this Act.

55 Grant of deed of variation or discharge of community burdens relating to sheltered or retirement housing: community consultation notice

(1) Where in relation to a sheltered or retirement housing development it is proposed to grant, under section 33(1)(a) or (2) of this Act, a deed of variation or discharge, the proposal shall be intimated to all the owners of the units of the community.

(2) Such intimation shall be given by sending a notice (a 'community consultation notice') in, or as near as may be in, the form set out in schedule 8 to this Act together with the explanatory note which immediately follows that form in that schedule.

(3) The deed of variation or discharge shall not be granted before the date specified in the community consultation notice as that by which any comments are to be made, being a date no earlier than that on which expires the period of three weeks beginning with the latest date on which such intimation is given.

(4) Subsection (4) of section 37 of this Act shall apply in relation to a deed of variation or discharge granted as mentioned in subsection (1) above and to the person giving intimation as it applies in relation to such a deed granted as mentioned in section 35(1) of this Act and to the person proposing to submit the deed but with the modifications that the reference—

(a) in paragraph (a) of the said subsection (4), to section 36 of this Act is to be construed as a reference to this section; and

(b) in paragraph (b) of that subsection, to subsection (1) of section 37 of this Act is to be construed as a reference to subsection (3) above.

(5) For the purposes of subsection (4) of section 37 as so applied, if the person giving intimation is—

(a) an individual unable by reason of legal disability, or incapacity, to swear or affirm as mentioned in the said subsection (4), then a legal representative of that person may swear or affirm;

(b) not an individual, then any person authorised to sign documents on its behalf may swear or affirm,

and any reference in the said subsection (4) (as so applied) to the person giving intimation shall be construed accordingly.

56 Facility burdens and service burdens

(1) Where by a deed registered before the appointed day—

(a) a facility burden is imposed on land, then—

(i) any land to which the facility is (and is intended to be) of benefit; and

(ii) the heritable property which constitutes the facility,

shall be benefited properties in relation to the facility burden;

(b) a service burden is imposed on land, then any land to which the services are provided shall be a benefited property in relation to the service burden.

(2) Subsection (1) above is subject to section 57 of this Act; and in paragraph (a) of that subsection 'facility burden' does not include a manager burden.

57 Further provisions as respects rights of enforcement

(1) Nothing in sections 52 to 56 revives a right of enforcement waived or otherwise lost as at the day immediately preceding the appointed day.

(2)   Where there is a common scheme, and a deed, had it nominated and identified a benefited property, would have imposed under that scheme the real burdens whose terms the deed sets out, the deed shall, for the purposes of sections 25 and 53 to 56 of this Act, be deemed so to have imposed them.

(3)   Sections 53 to 56 do not confer a right of enforcement in respect of anything done, or omitted to be done, in contravention of the terms of a real burden before the appointed day.

58   Duty of Keeper to enter on title sheet statement concerning enforcement rights

The Keeper of the Registers of Scotland—
    (a)   during that period of ten years which commences with the appointed day, may; and
    (b)   after the expiry of that period, shall,
where satisfied that a real burden subsists by virtue of any of sections 52 to 56 of this Act or section 60 of the 2000 Act (preserved right of Crown to maritime burdens), enter on the title sheet of the burdened property—
    (i)   a statement that the real burden subsists by virtue of the section in question; and
    (ii)   where there is sufficient information to enable the Keeper to describe the benefited property, a description of that property,
and where there is that sufficient information the Keeper shall enter that statement on the title sheet of the benefited property also, together with a description of the burdened property.

PART 5
REAL BURDENS: MISCELLANEOUS

59   Effect of extinction etc on court proceedings

Where by virtue of this Act, a real burden is to any extent discharged, extinguished or made unenforceable, then on and after the day on which that happens (but only to the extent in question)—
    (a)   no proceedings for enforcement shall be commenced;
    (b)   any such proceedings already commenced shall, in so far as they do not relate to the payment of money, be deemed to have been abandoned on that day and may, without further process and without any requirement that full judicial expenses shall have been paid by the pursuer, be dismissed accordingly; and
    (c)   any decree or interlocutor already pronounced in proceedings for such enforcement shall, in so far as it does not relate to the payment of money, be deemed to have been reduced, or as the case may be recalled, on that day.

60   Grant of deed where title not completed: requirements

(1)   Subject to subsection (2) below, where an owner who does not have a completed title to land is to grant, as respects a real burden—
    (a)   a constitutive deed;
    (b)   a deed of discharge; or
    (c)   a deed of variation,
then unless the deed is one to which section 15(3) of the 1979 Act (circumstances where unnecessary to deduce title) applies, it shall be necessary in the deed to deduce title to the land through the midcouples linking the owner to the person who had the last completed title to the land.

(2)   Where, under section 33 of this Act, a manager is to grant a deed of variation or discharge, it shall not be necessary to comply with subsection (1) above or with section 15(3) of the 1979 Act.

61   Contractual liability incidental to creation of real burden

Incidental contractual liability which a constitutive deed (or a deed into which a constitutive deed is incorporated) gives rise to as respects a prospective real burden, ends when the deed has been duly registered and the real burden has become effective.

62 Real burdens of combined type

(1) Where an obligation is constituted both as a nameable type of real burden (such as, for example, a community burden) and as a real burden which is not of that nameable type, then in so far as a provision of this Act relates specifically to real burdens of the nameable type the obligation shall be taken, for the purpose of determining the effect of that provision, to be constituted as two distinct real burdens.

(2) The owner of a benefited property which is a unit of a community shall not be entitled to enforce that obligation against the community constituted other than as a community burden or as a burden mentioned in section 1(3) of this Act.

63 Manager burdens

(1) A real burden (whenever created) may make provision conferring on such person as may be specified in the burden power to—

(a) act as the manager of related properties;

(b) appoint some other person to be such manager; and

(c) dismiss any person appointed by virtue of paragraph (b) above,

a real burden making any such provision being referred to in this Act as a 'manager burden'.

(2) A power conferred by a manager burden is exercisable only if the person on whom the power is conferred is the owner of one of the related properties.

(3) The right to a manager burden may be assigned or otherwise transferred; and any such assignation or transfer shall take effect on the sending of written intimation to the owners of the related properties.

(4) A manager burden shall be extinguished on the earliest of the following dates—

(a) the date on which such period as may be specified in the burden expires;

(b) the relevant date;

(c) the ninetieth day of any continuous period throughout which, by virtue of subsection (2) above, the burden is not exerciseable; and

(d) if a manager is dismissed under section 64 of this Act (in the case mentioned in subsection (6) below), the date of dismissal.

(5) In this section, the 'relevant date'—

(a) in the case so mentioned means the date thirty years after the day specified in subsection (7) below;

(b) in a case where the manager burden is imposed under a common scheme on any unit of a sheltered or retirement housing development, means the date three years after the day so specified; and

(c) in any other case, means the date five years after the day so specified.

(6) The case is where the manager burden is imposed on the sale, by virtue of section 61 of the Housing (Scotland) Act 1987 (c 26) (secure tenant's right to purchase), of a property by—

(a) a person such as is mentioned in any of the sub-paragraphs of subsection (2)(a) of that section; or

(b) a predecessor of any such person,

to a tenant of such a person.

(7) The day is that on which the constitutive deed setting out the terms of the burden is registered (and if there is more than one day on which such a constitutive deed is registered in respect of the related properties, then the first such day).

(8) Where a power conferred by a manager burden is exercisable, any person who is, by virtue of that burden, a manager may not be dismissed—

(a) under section 28(1)(d) of this Act; or

(b)   in a case other than that mentioned in subsection (6) above, under section 64 of this Act.

(9)   Section 17(1) of the 2000 Act (extinction on appointed day of certain rights of superior) shall not apply to manager burdens.

64   Overriding power to dismiss and appoint manager

(1)   Where a person is the manager of related properties, the owners of two thirds of those properties may—

(a)   dismiss that person; and

(b)   where they do so, appoint some other person to be such manager,

and such actings shall be effective notwithstanding the terms of any real burden affecting those properties; but this section is subject to section 63(8)(b) of this Act.

(2)   If a property is owned by two or more persons in common, then, for the purposes of voting on any proposal to exercise a power conferred by subsection (1) above, the vote allocated as respects the property shall only be counted for or against the proposal if it is the agreed vote of those of them who together own more than a half share of the property.

65   Manager: transitory provisions

Where, immediately before the appointed day, any person is, by virtue of any real burden or purported real burden, ostensibly the manager of related properties that person shall be deemed to have been validly appointed as such.

66   The expression 'related properties'

(1)   Whether properties are related properties for the purposes of sections 63 to 65 of this Act is, subject to subsection (2) below, to be inferred from all the circumstances; and without prejudice to the generality of this section circumstances giving rise to such an inference might include—

(a)   the convenience of managing the properties together because they share—

(i)   some common feature; or

(ii)   an obligation for common maintenance of some facility;

(b)   it being evident that the properties constitute a group of properties on which real burdens are imposed under a common scheme; or

(c)   there being shared ownership of common property.

(2)   For the purposes of section 63(2) of this Act, the following are not related properties—

(a)   any property which, being a unit in a sheltered or retirement housing development, is used in some special way (that is to say, is the unit mentioned as an exception in section 54(1) of this Act);

(b)   any property to which a development management scheme applies; or

(c)   any facility which benefits two or more properties (examples of such a facility being, without prejudice to the generality of this paragraph, a private road and a common area for recreation).

67   Discharge of rights of irritancy

(1)   All rights of irritancy in respect of a breach of a real burden are, on the day on which this section comes into force, discharged; and on and after that day—

(a)   it shall not be competent to create any such right; and

(b)   any proceedings already commenced to enforce any such right shall be deemed abandoned and may, without further process and without any requirement that full judicial expenses shall have been paid by the pursuer, be dismissed accordingly.

(2)   Subsection (1)(b) above shall not affect any cause in which final decree (that is to say, any decree or interlocutor which disposes of the cause and is not subject to appeal or review) is granted before the coming into force of this section.

68 Requirement for repetition etc of terms of real burden in future deed

In any deed (whenever executed) a requirement to the effect that the terms of a real burden shall be repeated or referred to in any subsequent deed shall be of no effect.

69 Further provision as respects deeds of variation and of discharge

(1) Where a deed of variation or deed of discharge is granted under this Act, it is not requisite that there be a grantee.

(2) Any such deed so granted may be registered by an owner of the burdened property or by any other person against whom the real burden is enforceable.

(3) Without prejudice to subsection (2) above, a deed of variation or deed of discharge granted under section 33 or 35 of this Act may be registered by a granter.

70 Duty to disclose identity of owner

A person who has title to enforce a real burden (the 'entitled person') may require any person who, at any time, was an owner of the burdened property (the 'second person') to disclose to the entitled person—

(a)   the name and address of the owner, for the time being, of such property; or

(b)   (if the second person cannot do that) such other information as the second person has which might enable the entitled person to discover that name and address.

PART 6
DEVELOPMENT MANAGEMENT SCHEME

71 Development management scheme

(1) The development management scheme may be applied to any land by registering against the land (in this Part of this Act referred to as 'the development') a deed of application granted by, or on behalf of, the owner of the land or, if and in so far as the terms of the order mentioned in subsection (3) below so admit, may be thus applied with such variations as may be specified in the deed; and the scheme shall take effect in relation to the development on the date of registration or, notwithstanding section 3(4) of the 1979 Act (creation of real right or obligation on date of registration etc)—

(a)   on such later date as may be so specified (the specification being of a fixed date and not, for example, of a date determinable by reference to the occurrence of an event); or

(b)   on the date of registration of such other deed as may be so specified,

and different provision for the taking effect of the scheme may be made for different parts of the development.

(2) The deed of application shall include specification or description of the matters which the scheme requires shall be specified or described and shall in any event include—

(a)   the meaning, in the scheme, of such expressions as 'the development', 'scheme property' and 'unit';

(b)   the name by which any owners' association established by the scheme is to be known, being a name which either ends with the words 'Owners Association' or begins with those words preceded by the definite article;

(c)   the name and address of the first manager of any association so established.

(3) In this Act, 'the development management scheme' means such scheme of rules for the management of land as is set out in an order made, in consequence of this section, under section 104 of the Scotland Act 1998 (c 46) (power to make provision consequential on legislation of, or scrutinised by, the Scottish Parliament) or,

in relation to a particular development, that scheme as applied to the development.

72 Application of other provisions of this Act to rules of scheme

In so far as the terms of the order mentioned in section 71(3) of this Act so admit, sections 2, 3, 5, 10 (except subsection (4)(a)), 11, 13, 14, 16, 18, 59 to 61, 67 to 70, 98, 100, 104 and 105 of this Act apply in relation to the rules of the development management scheme as those sections apply in relation to community burdens; except that, for the purposes of that application, in those sections any reference—

(a)   to an owner of a benefited property shall be construed as to the manager of any owners' association established by the scheme;

(b)   to a benefited property shall be construed as to a unit of the development in so far as advantaged by those rules;

(c)   to a burdened property shall be construed as to a unit of the development in so far as constrained by those rules;

(d)   to a community shall be construed as to the development; and

(e)   to a constitutive deed shall be construed as to the deed of application.

73 Disapplication

(1)   The development management scheme may be disapplied to the development, or to any part of the development, by an owners' association established by the scheme registering against the development or as the case may be the part, a deed of disapplication granted by that association in accordance with the scheme; and subject to subsection (3) below the disapplication shall take effect—

(a)   on the date of registration; or

(b)   notwithstanding section 3(4) of the 1979 Act (creation of real right or obligation on date of registration etc), on such later date as may be specified in the deed (the specification being of a fixed date and not, for example, of a date determinable by reference to the occurrence of an event).

(2)   The deed of disapplication may by means of real burdens provide for the future management and regulation—

(a)   in the case of disapplication to the development, of the development or of any part of the development; or

(b)   in the case of disapplication to a part of the development, of that part or of any part of that part,

and section 4 of this Act shall apply accordingly except that paragraph (b) of subsection (2) of that section shall, for the purposes of this subsection, apply with the substitution, for the reference to the owner of the land which is to be the burdened property, of a reference to the owners' association.

(3)   The deed of disapplication shall not, on registration, disapply the development management scheme or impose a real burden unless, after the expiry of the period mentioned in subsection (3) of section 74 of this Act, there is endorsed on the deed (or on an annexation to it referred to in an endorsement on it and identified, on the face of the annexation, as being the annexation so referred to) a certificate executed by a member of the Lands Tribunal, or by their clerk, to the effect that no application for preservation of the scheme has been received under that subsection or that any such application which has been received has been withdrawn; and where more than one such application has been received the certificate shall relate to both (or as the case may be all) applications.

(4)   An owners' association proposing to submit a deed of disapplication granted as mentioned in subsection (1) above for registration shall, before doing so, swear or affirm before a notary public (the deed being endorsed accordingly)—

(a)   that section 74 of this Act has been complied with; and

(b)   as to the date on which the period mentioned in subsection (3) of that section expires.

(5)   Subsection (2)(b) of section 22 of this Act applies in relation to the owners'

association and for the purposes of subsection (4) above as it applies in relation to a terminator and for the purposes of subsection (1) of that section.

74 Intimation of proposal to register deed of disapplication

(1) Where a deed of disapplication is granted as mentioned in section 73(1) of this Act, any proposal to register that deed shall be intimated by the owners' association to every person who is the owner of a unit of the development.

(2) Such intimation to an owner shall be given by sending a copy of the deed, together with a notice stating—

(a) what the effect of registering the deed would be; and

(b) that an owner who has not agreed to the granting of the deed and who wishes to apply to the Lands Tribunal for preservation of the development management scheme must do so by a date specified in the notice (being the date on which the period mentioned in subsection (3) below expires).

(3) A person to whom intimation is given under subsection (2) and who has not so agreed may, during the period of eight weeks beginning with the date by which subsection (1) above has been complied with fully, apply to the Lands Tribunal for preservation of the scheme.

PART 7
SERVITUDES

Positive servitudes

75 Creation of positive servitude by writing: deed to be registered

(1) A deed is not effective to create a positive servitude by express provision unless it is registered against both the benefited property and the burdened property.

(2) It shall be no objection to the validity of a positive servitude that, at the time when the deed was registered as mentioned in subsection (1) above, the same person owned the benefited property and the burdened property; but, notwithstanding section 3(4) of the 1979 Act (creation of real right or obligation on date of registration etc), the servitude shall not be created while that person remains owner of both those properties.

(3) Subsection (1) above—

(a) is subject to section 3(1) of the Prescription and Limitation (Scotland) Act 1973 (c 52) (creation of positive servitude by 20 years' possession following execution of deed); and

(b) does not apply to servitudes such as are mentioned in section 77(1) of this Act.

76 Disapplication of requirement that positive servitude created in writing be of a known type

(1) Any rule of law that requires that a positive servitude be of a type known to the law shall not apply in relation to any servitude created in accordance with section 75(1) of this Act.

(2) Nothing in subsection (1) above permits the creation of a servitude that is repugnant with ownership.

77 Positive servitude of leading pipes etc over or under land

(1) A right to lead a pipe, cable, wire or other such enclosed unit over or under land for any purpose may be constituted as a positive servitude.

(2) It shall be deemed always to have been competent to constitute a right such as is mentioned in subsection (1) above as a servitude.

78 Discharge of positive servitude

A positive servitude—

(a) which has been registered against the burdened property; or

(b)   which has been noted in, or otherwise appears in, the title sheet of that property,
is discharged by deed only on registration of the deed against the burdened property.

Negative servitudes

79   Prohibition on creation of negative servitude
On the appointed day it shall cease to be competent to create a negative servitude.

Transitional

80   Negative servitudes to become real burdens
(1)   A negative servitude shall, on the appointed day, cease to exist as such but shall forthwith become a real burden (such a real burden being, for the purposes of this section, referred to as a 'converted servitude').
(2)   Subject to subsections (3) and (4) below, a converted servitude shall be extinguished on the expiry of the period of ten years beginning with the appointed day.
(3)   If, before the appointed day, a negative servitude was registered against the burdened property or was noted in, or otherwise appeared in, the title sheet of that property the converted servitude shall not be extinguished as mentioned in subsection (2) above.
(4)   If, during the period mentioned in subsection (2) above, an owner of the benefited property executes and duly registers, in (or as nearly as may be in) the form contained in schedule 9 to this Act, a notice of converted servitude, the converted servitude shall not be extinguished as mentioned in subsection (2) above (in so far as the burdened property, the benefited property and the converted servitude are, respectively, the burdened property, the benefited property, and the converted servitude identified in the notice of converted servitude).
(5)   The notice of converted servitude shall—
(a)   identify the land which is the burdened property (or any part of that land);
(b)   identify the land which is the benefited property (or any part of that land);
(c)   where the person registering the notice does not have a completed title to the benefited property, set out the midcouples linking that person to the person who last had such completed title;
(d)   set out the terms of the converted servitude;
(e)   include as an annexation the constitutive deed, if any (or a copy of such deed); and
(f)   if the land identified for the purposes of paragraph (b) above is not nominated in the constitutive deed, set out the grounds, both factual and legal, for describing that land as a benefited property.
(6)   For the purposes of subsection (4) above, a notice is, subject to section 116 of this Act, duly registered only when registered against both properties identified in pursuance of subsection (5)(a) and (b) above.
(7)   Subsections (4) and (5) of section 50 of this Act shall apply in respect of a notice of converted servitude as they apply in respect of a notice of preservation.
(8)   This section is subject to section 115 of this Act.

81   Certain real burdens to become positive servitudes
(1)   A real burden consisting of a right to enter, or otherwise make use of, the burdened property shall, on the appointed day, cease to exist as such but shall forthwith become a positive servitude.
(2)   Subsection (1) above—

(a)　is subject to section 17(1) of the 2000 Act (extinction on appointed day of certain rights of superior);

(b)　does not apply to real burdens such as are mentioned in section 2(3)(a) of this Act.

PART 8
PRE-EMPTION AND REVERSION

Pre-emption

82　Application and interpretation of sections 83 and 84

Sections 83 and 84 of this Act apply to any subsisting right of pre-emption con-stituted as a title condition which—

(a)　was originally created in favour of a feudal superior; or

(b)　was created in a deed executed after 1st September 1974,

and for the purposes of sections 83(1)(a) and 84(1)(b) of this Act the person last registered as having title to a personal pre-emption burden or rural housing burden shall be taken to be the holder for a right of pre-emption which that burden comprises.

83　Extinction following pre-sale undertaking

(1)　Where, in relation to any burdened property (or, as the case may be, part of such property)—

(a)　the holder of a right of pre-emption to which this section applies gives an undertaking (in the form, or as nearly as may be in the form, contained in schedule 10 to this Act) that, subject to such conditions (if any) as the holder may specify in the undertaking, the holder will not exercise that right during such period as may be so specified;

(b)　a conveyance in implement of the sale of the burdened property (or part) is registered before the end of that period; and

(c)　any conditions specified under paragraph (a) above have been satisfied,

such right shall, on registration of such a conveyance, be extinguished unless the right is constituted as a rural housing burden in which case the title condition shall be taken to have been complied with as respects that sale only.

(2)　Any undertaking given under subsection (1) above—

(a)　is binding on the holder of the right of pre-emption; and

(b)　if registered is binding on any successor as holder provided that the undertaking was registered before the successor completed title.

84　Extinction following offer to sell

(1)　If in relation to a right of pre-emption to which this section applies—

(a)　an event specified in the constitutive deed as an event on the occurrence of which such right may be exercised occurs; and

(b)　the owner of the burdened property makes, in accordance with sub-sections (2) to (6) below, an offer to sell that property (or, as the case may be, part of that property) to the holder of such right,

then such right shall, in relation to that property (or part), be extinguished unless it is constituted as a rural housing burden in which case the title condition shall be taken to have been complied with as respects that event only.

(2)　An offer shall be in writing and shall comply with section 2 of the Require-ments of Writing (Scotland) Act 1995 (c 7) (requirements for formal validity of certain documents).

(3)　An offer shall be open for acceptance during whichever is the shorter of—

(a)　the period of 21 days, or where the right is constituted as a rural housing burden 42 days, beginning with the day on which the offer is sent;

(b)　such number of days beginning with that day as may be specified in the constitutive deed.

(4)   An offer shall be made on such terms as may be set out, or provided for, in the constitutive deed; but in so far as no such terms are set out, an offer shall be made on such terms (including any terms so provided for) as are reasonable in the circumstances.

(5)   Where—

(a)   an offer is sent in accordance with this section; and

(b)   the holder of the right does not, within the time allowed by virtue of subsection (3) above for acceptance of the offer, inform (in writing, whether or not transmitted by electronic means) the owner of the burdened property that the holder considers, giving reasons for so considering, that the terms on which the offer is made are unreasonable,

the terms of the offer shall, for the purposes of subsection (4) above, be deemed to be reasonable.

(6)   If the holder of a right cannot by reasonable inquiry be identified or found, an offer may be sent to the Extractor of the Court of Session; and for the purposes of this section an offer so sent shall be deemed to have been sent to the holder.

85   Ending of council's right of pre-emption as respects certain churches

In a scheme framed under subsection (1) of section 22 of the Church of Scotland (Property and Endowments) Act 1925 (c 33) (schemes for the ownership, maintenance and administration of churches etc), any provision made in accordance with subsection (2)(h) of that section (council's right of pre-emption) shall cease to have effect.

Reversion

86   Reversions under School Sites Act 1841

(1)   In a case where—

(a)   land would, under the third proviso to section 2 of the School Sites Act 1841 (4 & 5 Vict c 38) (the '1841 Act') revert (but for this section) to any person or has so reverted; but

(b)   the person has not, before the day on which this section comes into force, completed title to the land, subsections (2) to (9) below shall (to the extent that subsection (9) admits) apply in place of that proviso and be deemed always to have applied and nothing shall be void or challengeable by virtue of that proviso.

(2)   If the circumstances are that a contract of sale of the land has been concluded by, or on behalf of, the education authority, the authority shall pay to the person, where the cessation of use by virtue of which the land would (but for this section) revert, or has reverted, occurred—

(a)   before the day on which this section comes into force, an amount equal to the open market value of the land as at that day;

(b)   on or after that day, an amount equal to the open market value of the land as at the date of cessation less any improvement value as at that date.

(3)   If the circumstances are other than is mentioned in subsection (2) above—

(a)   the person may specify an obligation mentioned in paragraph (a), or as the case may be (b), of subsection (4) below and require the authority to comply therewith, which subject to paragraph (b) below the authority shall do;

(b)   the authority may, if the person requires under paragraph (a) above performance of the obligation mentioned in paragraph (a)(i), or as the case may be (b)(i), of that subsection, instead elect to make payment to the person of such amount as is mentioned in paragraph (a)(ii), or as the case may be (b)(ii), of that subsection provided that such election is timeous.

(4)   The obligations are, where the cessation of use by virtue of which the ownership of the land would (but for this section) revert, or has reverted, occurred—

(a)   before the day on which this section comes into force—

    (i)   to convey the land to the person;

    (ii)   to make a payment to the person of an amount equal to the open market value of the land as at that day; or

  (b)   on or after that day—

    (i)   on payment by the person of any improvement value as at the date of cessation, to convey the land to the person;

    (ii)   to make a payment to the person of an amount equal to the open market value of the land as at the date of cessation less any improvement value as at that date.

(5)   Any dispute arising in relation to the assessment of the value for the purposes of this section of any land, buildings or structures may be referred to, and determined by, the Lands Tribunal.

(6)   For the purposes of this section—

'education authority' has the meaning given by section 135(1) of the Education (Scotland) Act 1980 (c 44) except that if title to the land has been transferred to any person by any enactment it means that person; and

'improvement value' means such part of the value of the land as is attributable to any building (or other structure) on the land other than any such building (or other structure) erected by or at the expense of—

  (a)   the person who made the gift, sale or exchange of the land under section 2 of the 1841 Act; or

  (b)   any predecessor, as owner of such land, of that person.

(7)   References in subsection (1) above to the third proviso to section 2 of the 1841 Act shall be construed as including references to that proviso as applied by virtue of any other enactment; and for the purposes of that construction, the reference in paragraph (a) of the definition of 'improvement value' in subsection (6) above to the said section 2 shall be construed as a reference to the provision corresponding to that section in such other enactment.

(8)   The reference in subsection (3)(b) above to an election being timeous is to its being notified to the person within three months after the requirement in question is made.

(9)   Subsections (2) to (8) above do not apply where the person has, before the day on which this section comes into force, accepted an offer of compensation in respect of the land or concluded a contract for, or accepted, a conveyance of the land.

(10)   Subsections (1)(b) and (2) of section 67 of this Act shall apply in relation to any proceedings already commenced by virtue of the proviso mentioned in subsection (1)(a) above as they apply in relation to any proceedings already commenced as mentioned in the said subsection (1)(b).

87   Right to petition under section 7 of Entail Sites Act 1840

(1)   In a case where—

  (a)   it would be competent but for this section, section 50(1) of the 2000 Act (disentailment on appointed day) and the repeal of the Entail Sites Act 1840 by that Act for a person to apply by petition under section 7 of that Act of 1840 (petition praying to have feu charter or other right or lease declared to be forfeited etc); but

  (b)   the person has not, before the day on which this section comes into force, accepted an offer of compensation in respect of the right so to apply,

subsections (2) to (6) and (8) of section 86 of this Act shall, in place of the said section 7 but with the modifications specified in subsection (2) below, apply.

(2)   The modifications are that—

  (a)   for any reference to the education authority there shall be substituted a reference to the parties in whose favour the feu charter or lease was granted, or the successors other than by purchase for value of those parties;

  (b)   in each of subsections (2) and (4), for the word 'revert' there shall be substituted 'be forfeit' and for the word 'reverted' there shall be substituted 'have been forfeit'; and

(c)   in subsection (6), for paragraph (a) of the definition of 'improvement value' there shall be substituted—

'(a)   the person who granted the feu or lease under section 1 of the Entail Sites Act 1840 (3 & 4 Vict c 48) (grants for sites of churches etc);'.

(3)   After such obligations as arise by virtue of this section are met or prescribe, the purposes for which the land in question was feued or leased under the said Act of 1840 need no longer be given effect.

(4)   Subsections (1)(b) and (2) of section 67 of this Act shall apply in relation to any application already made by petition as mentioned in subsection (1)(a) above as they apply in relation to any proceedings already commenced as mentioned in the said subsection (1)(b).

88–89   *[Amendment provisions]*

PART 9
TITLE CONDITIONS: POWERS OF LANDS TRIBUNAL

90   Powers of Lands Tribunal as respects title conditions
(1)   Subject to sections 97, 98 and 104 of this Act and to subsections (3) to (5) below, the Lands Tribunal may by order, on the application of—

(a)   an owner of a burdened property or any other person against whom a title condition (or purported title condition) is enforceable (or bears to be enforceable)—

(i)   discharge it, or vary it, in relation to that property; or

(ii)   if the title condition is a real burden or a rule of a development management scheme, determine any question as to its validity, applicability or enforceability or as to how it is to be construed;

(b)   an owner of a benefited property, renew or vary, in relation to that property, a title condition which is—

(i)   a real burden in respect of which intimation of a proposal to execute and register a notice of termination has been given under section 21 of this Act; or

(ii)   a real burden or servitude affected by a proposal to register a conveyance, being a proposal of which notice has been given under section 107(4) of this Act; or

(c)   an owner of a unit in a community, preserve as mentioned in section 34(3) or 37(1) of this Act, a community burden in respect of which intimation of a proposal to register a deed of variation or discharge has been given under section 34(1) or 36(1) of this Act;

(d)   an owner of a unit of the development to which applies a development management scheme in respect of which intimation of a proposal to register a deed of disapplication has been given under subsection (1) of section 74 of this Act, preserve the scheme;

(e)   the owners' association of a development to which applies a development management scheme in respect of which intimation of a proposal to register a conveyance, being a proposal of which notice has been given as mentioned in subsection (b)(ii) above, preserve the scheme;

but where the Lands Tribunal refuse an application under paragraph (b) or (c) above wholly, or an application under paragraph (b) partly, they shall in relation to the benefited property discharge the title condition, wholly or partly, accordingly or as the case may be shall in relation to the units not all of whose owners have granted the deed vary or discharge the community burden accordingly and where they refuse an application under paragraph (d) or (e) above, they shall disapply the development management scheme.

(2)   Paragraph (b) of subsection (1) above applies in relation to the application

of a holder of a personal real burden as it applies to the application of an owner of a benefited property except that, for the purposes of any application made by virtue of this subsection, the words 'in relation to that property' in paragraph (b) shall be disregarded as shall the words 'in relation to the benefited property' in what follows paragraph (e) in that subsection.

(3)   It shall not be competent to make an application under subsection (1) above in relation to a title condition of a kind specified in schedule 11 to this Act.

(4)   It shall not be competent to make an application under subsection (1)(b), (c), (d) or (e) above—

(a)   after the renewal date, or as the case may be the date specified by virtue of section 107(6)(d)(ii) of, or the expiry of the period mentioned in section 34(3), 37(1) or 74(3) of, this Act, except with the consent of the terminator or as the case may be of—

(i)   the person proposing to register the conveyance or the deed of variation or discharge, or

(ii)   the owners' association; or

(b)   after there has been, in relation to the proposal, endorsement under section 23(1) or, as the case may be, execution of a relevant certificate applied for by virtue of section 107(1)(b), or endorsement under section 37(2) or 73(3), of this Act.

(5)   Variation which would impose a new obligation or would result in a property becoming a benefited property shall not be competent on an application—

(a)   under subsection (1)(a)(i) above unless the owner of the burdened property consents; or

(b)   under subsection (1)(b) above.

(6)   Subject to section 97(1) of this Act and to subsections (9) and (10) below, an order discharging [. . .] or varying a title condition may—

(a)   where made under paragraph (a)(i) of subsection (1) above, direct the applicant; or

(b)   where made by virtue of the refusal of an application under paragraph (b) or (c) of that subsection, direct the terminator or, as the case may be, the person proposing to register the conveyance or deed of variation or discharge,

to pay to any person who in relation to the title condition was an owner of the benefited property or, where there is no benefited property, to any holder of the title condition, such sum as the Lands Tribunal may think it just to award under one, but not both, of the heads mentioned in subsection (7) below.

(7)   The heads are—

(a)   a sum to compensate for any substantial loss or disadvantage suffered by, as the case may be—

(i)   the owner, as owner of the benefited property; or

(ii)   the holder of the title condition,

in consequence of the discharge [or variation];

(b)   a sum to make up for any effect which the title condition produced, at the time when it was created, in reducing the consideration then paid or made payable for the burdened property.

(8)   Subject to section 97(1) of this Act and to subsection (11) below, an order discharging, renewing or varying a title condition may impose on the burdened property a new title condition or vary a title condition extant at the time the order is made.

[(8A)   An order disapplying the development management scheme shall, where the deed of [disapplication] makes such provision as is mentioned in section 73(2) of this Act, impose the real burdens in question.]

(9)   A direction under subsection (6) above shall be made only if the person directed consents.

(10)   Where an application under subsection (1)(b)(ii) above is refused, wholly

or partly, any direction under subsection (6) above for payment to that person may be made only if that application was made by virtue of subsection (2) above.

(11)   An imposition under subsection (8) above shall be made only if the owner of the burdened property consents.

(12)   The jurisdiction conferred by subsection (1) above includes power, in relation to an application under paragraph (a)(ii) only of that subsection, to decline (with reason stated) to proceed to determine the question.

91   Special provision as to variation or discharge of community burdens

(1)   Without prejudice to section 90(1)(a)(i) of this Act, an application may be made to the Lands Tribunal under this section by owners of at least one quarter of the units in a community for the variation ('variation' including imposition) or discharge of a community burden as it affects, or as the case may be would affect, all or some of the units in the community.

(2)   In the case of an application made by owners of some only of the units in the community, the units affected need not be the units which they own.

(3)   Subsections (6), (7) and (9) of section 90 of this Act shall apply in relation to an order made by virtue of subsection (1) above varying or discharging a community burden as they apply to an order under subsection (1)(a)(i) of that section discharging a title condition.

92   Early application for discharge: restrictive provisions

In the constitutive deed, provision may be made to the effect that there shall be no application under section 90(1)(a)(i) or 91(1) of this Act in respect of a title condition before such date as may be specified in the deed (being a date not more than five years after the creation of the title condition); and if such provision is so made it shall not be competent to make an application under the section in question before that date.

93   Notification of application

(1)   The Lands Tribunal shall, on receipt of an application under—

(a)   section 90(1)(a) or 91(1) of this Act, give notice of that application to any person who, not being the applicant, appears to them to fall within any of the following descriptions—

    (i)   an owner of the burdened property;

    (ii)   an owner of any benefited property;

    (iii)   a holder of the title condition;

(b)   section 90(1)(b) of this Act, give such notice to any person who appears to them to fall within any of the following descriptions—

    (i)   in the case mentioned in sub-paragraph (i) of that provision, the terminator;

    (ii)   an owner of the burdened property; or

    (iii)   in the case mentioned in sub-paragraph (ii) of that provision,

the person proposing to register the conveyance;

(c)   section 90(1)(c) of this Act, give such notice to the person proposing to register the deed of variation or discharge;

(d)   section 90(1)(d) of this Act, give such notice to the owners' association; or

(e)   section 90(1)(e) of this Act, give notice to the person proposing to register the conveyance,

and subject to subsection (2) below shall do so by sending the notice.

(2)   Notice under subsection (1) above may be given by advertisement, or by such other method as the Lands Tribunal think fit, if—

(a)   given to a person who cannot, by reasonable inquiry, be identified or found;

(b)   the person to whom it is given, being a person given notice by virtue of paragraph (a)(ii) of that subsection, does not appear to them to have any interest to enforce the title condition; or

(c)   so many people require to be given notice that, in the opinion of the Lands Tribunal, it is not reasonably practicable to send it.

(3)   The Lands Tribunal may also give notice of the application, by such means as they think fit, to any other person.

94   Content of notice

The Lands Tribunal shall—

(a)   in any notice given by them under section 93 of this Act—

(i)   summarise or reproduce the application;

(ii)   set a date (being a date no earlier than twenty-one days after the notice is given) by which representations to them as respects the application may be made;

(iii)   state the fee which must accompany any such representations; and

(iv)   in the case of an application for the discharge, renewal or variation of a real burden, or for the preservation of a real burden or development management scheme, state that if the application is not opposed it may be granted without further inquiry; and

(b)   in any notice so given (other than by advertisement) in respect of an application under section 90(1)(a) or 91(1) of this Act, also set out the name and address of every person to whom the notice is being sent.

95   Persons entitled to make representations

The persons entitled to make representations as respects an application under section 90(1) or 91(1) of this Act are—

(a)   any person who has title to enforce the title condition;

(b)   any person against whom the title condition is enforceable;

(c)   in the case mentioned in paragraph (b)(ii) or (e) of section 90(1), the person proposing to register the conveyance; and

(d)   in the case mentioned in paragraph (d) of that section, the owners' association and the owner of any unit of the development.

96   Representations

(1)   Representations made by any person to the Lands Tribunal as respects an application under section 90(1) or 91(1) of this Act shall be in writing and shall comprise a statement of the facts and contentions upon which the person proposes to rely.

(2)   For the purposes of this Act, representations are made when they are received by the Lands Tribunal with the requisite fee; and a person sending such representations shall forthwith send a copy of them to the applicant.

(3)   Notwithstanding section 94(a)(ii) of this Act, the Lands Tribunal may if they think fit accept representations made after the date set under that section.

97   Granting unopposed application for discharge or renewal of real burden

(1)   Subject to subsection (2) below, an unopposed application duly made for—

(a)   the discharge or variation;

(b)   the renewal or variation; or

(c)   the preservation,

of a real burden shall be granted as of right; and as respects an application under paragraph (a) above neither subsection (6)(a) nor subsection (8) of section 90 of this Act shall apply in relation to the order discharging or as the case may be varying the real burden.

(2)   Subsection (1) above does not apply as respects an application—

(a)   for the discharge or variation of a facility burden;

(b)   for the discharge or variation of a service burden; or

(c)   under section 91(1) of this Act for the discharge or variation of a community burden imposed on any unit of a sheltered or retirement housing development.

(3)   An application is unopposed for the purposes of—

(a)   subsection (1)(a) above if, as at the date on which the application falls to be determined, no representations opposing it have been made under section 96 of this Act either by an owner of any benefited property or by a holder of a personal real burden;

(b)   subsection (1)(b) above if, as at that date, no representations opposing the application have been made under that section by the terminator or as the case may be the person proposing to register the conveyance; or

(c)   subsection (1)(c) above if, as at that date, no representations opposing the application have been made under that section by the person proposing to register the deed of variation or discharge, or all such representations which have been so made have been withdrawn.

(4)   In granting an application under subsection (1)(b) or (c) above, the Lands Tribunal may, as they think fit, order either—

(a)   the person who intimated the proposal to execute and register the notice of termination or as the case may be the deed of variation or discharge or the conveyance; or

(b)   any other person who succeeded that person as terminator or proposer, to pay to the applicant a specific sum in respect of the expenses incurred by the applicant or such proportion of those expenses as the Tribunal think fit.

98   Granting other applications for variation, discharge, renewal or preservation of title condition

An application for the variation, discharge, renewal or preservation, of a title condition shall, unless it falls to be granted as of right under section 97(1) of this Act, be granted by the Lands Tribunal only if they are satisfied, having regard to the factors set out in section 100 of this Act, that—

(a)   except in the case of an application under subsection (3) of section 34 or, in respect of a deed of variation or discharge granted by the owner of an adjacent unit, subsection (1) of section 37 of this Act, it is reasonable to grant the application; or

(b)   in such a case, the variation or discharge in question—

   (i)   is not in the best interests of [all the owners (taken as a group) of] the units in the community; or

   (ii)   is unfairly prejudicial to one or more of those owners.

99   Granting applications as respects development management schemes

(1)   An unopposed application for preservation of a development management scheme shall be granted as of right.

(2)   An application is unopposed for the purposes of subsection (1) above if, as at the date on which the application falls to be determined, no representations opposing it have been made under section 96 of this Act by the owners' association or, as the case may be, by the person proposing to register the conveyance.

(3)   In granting an application under subsection (1) above, the Lands Tribunal may order the owners' association to pay to the applicant a specific sum in respect of the expenses incurred by the applicant or such proportion of those expenses as the Tribunal think fit.

(4)   An application for the preservation of a development management scheme shall, unless it falls to be granted as of right under subsection (1) above, be granted by the Lands Tribunal only if they are satisfied, in the case of an application—

(a)   under paragraph (d) of section 90(1) of this Act, that the disapplication of the development management scheme [or a real burden imposed by the deed of disapplication] is not in the best interests of [all the owners (taken as a group)] of the units of the development or is unfairly prejudicial to one or more of those owners; or

(b)   under paragraph (e) of that section, that having regard to the purpose for which the land is being acquired by the person proposing to register the conveyance it is reasonable to grant the application.

100 Factors to which the Lands Tribunal are to have regard in determining applications etc

The factors mentioned in section 98 of this Act are—

(a) any change in circumstances since the title condition was created (including, without prejudice to that generality, any change in the character of the benefited property, of the burdened property or of the neighbourhood of the properties);

(b) the extent to which the condition—

(i) confers benefit on the benefited property; or

(ii) where there is no benefited property, confers benefit on the public;

(c) the extent to which the condition impedes enjoyment of the burdened property;

(d) if the condition is an obligation to do something, how—

(i) practicable; or

(ii) costly,

it is to comply with the condition;

(e) the length of time which has elapsed since the condition was created;

(f) the purpose of the title condition;

(g) whether in relation to the burdened property there is the consent, or deemed consent, of a planning authority, or the consent of some other regulatory authority, for a use which the condition prevents;

(h) whether the owner of the burdened property is willing to pay compensation;

(i) if the application is under section 90(1)(b)(ii) of this Act, the purpose for which the land is being acquired by the person proposing to register the conveyance; and

(j) any other factor which the Lands Tribunal consider to be material.

101 Regulation of applications to Lands Tribunal

The Scottish Ministers may make rules regulating any application under this Act to the Lands Tribunal and may in particular make provision, in those rules, as to the evidence which may be required for such an application.

102 Referral to Lands Tribunal of notice dispute

(1) Any dispute arising in relation to a notice registered under section 50 or 80 of this Act may be referred to the Lands Tribunal; and in determining the dispute the Tribunal may make such order as they think fit discharging or, to such extent as may be specified in the order, restricting the notice in question.

(2) In any referral under subsection (1) above, the burden of proving any disputed question of fact shall be on the person relying on the notice.

(3) An extract of any order made under subsection (1) above may be registered and the order shall take effect as respects third parties on such registration.

103 Expenses

(1) The Lands Tribunal may, in determining an application made under this Part of this Act, make such order as to expenses as they think fit but shall have regard, in particular, to the extent to which the application, or any opposition to the application, is successful.

(2) Subsection (1) above is without prejudice to sections 97(4) and 99(3) of this Act.

104 Taking effect of orders of Lands Tribunal etc

(1) The Scottish Ministers may, after consultation with the Scottish Committee of the Council on Tribunals, make rules as to when an order of the Lands Tribunal on an application under section 90(1) or 91(1) of this Act shall take effect.

(2) An order under subsection (1)(a)(i), (b) or (c) of section 90, under subsection (1) of that section on the refusal (wholly or partly as the case may be) of an application under paragraph (b) or (c) of that subsection or under section 91(1) of this

Act which has taken effect in accordance with rules made under subsection (1) above may be registered against the burdened property by any person who was a party to the application or who was, under section 95 of this Act, entitled to make representations as respects the application; and on the order being so registered the title condition to which it relates is discharged (wholly or partly), renewed (wholly or partly), imposed, preserved or varied according to the terms of the order.

(3) An order—

(a) which disapplies a development management scheme, being an order under subsection (1) of section 90 of this Act, or preserves it under paragraph (d) or (e) of that subsection; and

(b) which has taken effect in accordance with rules so made,

may be registered against the units of the development by the owners' association or as the case may be by an owner of a unit of the development or the person proposing to register the conveyance; and on the order being so registered the scheme [whether or not it imposes new burdens] is disapplied or preserved [and the burdens imposed] as the case may be.

(4) Any enforceability which the obligation in question has as a contractual obligation shall be unaffected by such an order.

PART 10

MISCELLANEOUS

Consequential alterations to Land Register

105 Alterations to Land Register consequential upon registering certain deeds

(1) Subject to subsection (2) below, in registering in the Register of Sasines a document mentioned in subsection (3) below the Keeper of the Registers of Scotland may make such consequential alterations to the Land Register of Scotland as the Keeper considers requisite.

(2) In so registering such a document, or in registering it in the Land Register, by virtue of section 18, 19 or 20 of the 2000 Act or section 4(5), 50, 75 or 80 of this Act, the Keeper shall make such consequential alterations as are mentioned in subsection (1) above.

(3) The documents are—

(a) any decree, deed or other document which varies, discharges, renews, reallots, preserves or imposes a real burden or servitude; and

(b) any deed which comprises a conveyance of part of—

(i) the benefited property; or

(ii) the burdened property.

Compulsory acquisition of land

106 Extinction of real burdens and servitudes etc on compulsory acquisition of land

(1) If land is acquired compulsorily by virtue of a compulsory purchase order [to which this section applies] then, except in so far as the terms of—

(a) the order; or

(b) the conveyance in implement of such acquisition,

provide otherwise, on registration of the conveyance, any real burden, or servitude, over the land shall be extinguished and any development management scheme applying as respects the land disapplied.

(2) Without prejudice to the generality of the exception in subsection (1) above, such terms as are mentioned in that exception may provide—

(a) for the variation of any of the real burdens or servitudes;

(b) that there shall be such extinction only—

(i) of certain of the real burdens and servitudes;

(ii) in relation to certain parts of the burdened property; or

(iii)   in respect of the enforcement rights of the owners of certain of the benefited properties.

(3)   If the compulsory purchase order provides for an exception such as is mentioned in subsection (1) above, the conveyance in implement of the acquisition shall not, unless the owners of the benefited properties consent, or as the case may be the owners' association or the holder of any personal real burden consents, be registrable if its terms do not conform in that regard.

(4)   Where a personal real burden is extinguished by virtue of subsection (1) above, such person as immediately before the extinction held the right to enforce the burden shall be entitled to receive compensation from the acquiring authority in question for any loss thereby occasioned that person.

[4A)   This section applies to a compulsory purchase order in respect of which notice is given under—

(a)   paragraph 3 of the First Schedule to the Acquisition of Land (Authorisation Procedure) (Scotland) Act 1947 (c 42) on or after the day of which section 109; or

(b)   paragraph 2 of Schedule 5 to the Forestry Act 1967 (c 10) on or after the day on which section 110,
of this Act comes into force.]

(5)   In this section—
'compulsory purchase order' has the meaning given by section 1(1) of the Acquisition of Land (Authorisation Procedure) (Scotland) Act 1947 (c 42) (procedure for compulsory purchase of land by local authorities etc) except that it includes a compulsory purchase order made under the Forestry Act 1967 (c 10); and
'conveyance' means—

(a)   a—
    (i)   disposition;
    (ii)   notice of title; or
    (iii)   notarial instrument,
which includes a reference to the application of subsection (1) above;

(b)   a conveyance in the form set out in Schedule A to the Lands Clauses Consolidation (Scotland) Act 1845 (c 19); or

(c)   a general vesting declaration (as defined in paragraph 1(1) of Schedule 15 to the Town and Country Planning (Scotland) Act 1997 (c 8)).

107   Extinction of real burdens and servitudes etc where land acquired by agreement

(1)   If—

(a)   land acquired by a person by agreement could have been so acquired by that person compulsorily by virtue of any enactment; and

(b)   the person, having complied with subsection (4) below, registers a conveyance in implement of such acquisition together with a relevant certificate,
then, except in so far as the terms of the conveyance provide otherwise, on such registration any real burden, or servitude, over the land shall be extinguished and any development management scheme applying as respects the land disapplied.

(2)   Registration under subsection (1) above shall not vary or extinguish a title condition which is the subject of an application disclosed by the certificate in so far as that title condition—

(a)   is constituted in favour of the property of which the applicant is owner; or

(b)   is a personal real burden of which the applicant is holder,or disapply a development management scheme, described in the certificate; but the conveyance may be registered again, together with a further such certificate, under that subsection, the effect of the later registration being determined by reference to the further certificate rather than to the earlier certificate.

(3)   Subsection (2) of section 106 of this Act shall apply in relation to the excep-

tion in subsection (1) above as it applies in relation to the exception in subsection (1) of that section.

(4)   The person proposing to register the conveyance shall, before doing so in accordance with subsection (1)(b) above—

(a)   if such registration would extinguish a title condition, give notice to the owner of the benefited property (or in the case of a personal real burden to the holder of that burden); and

(b)   if it would disapply a development management scheme, give notice to the owners' association,

of the matters mentioned in subsection (6) below.

(5)   Any person to whom notice is given under subsection (4) above may, on or before the date specified by virtue of subsection (6)(d)(ii) below, apply to the Lands Tribunal for renewal or variation of the title condition or as the case may be preservation of the development management scheme.

(6)   The matters are—

(a)   a description of the land;

(b)   the name and address of the person proposing to register the conveyance;

(c)   the fact that, by virtue of this section (and subject to the terms of the conveyance), real burdens and servitudes over the land may be extinguished and any development management scheme disapplied;

(d)   that the person given notice—

(i)   may obtain information from the person acquiring the land about any entitlement to compensation; and

(ii)   will require to apply to the Lands Tribunal for Scotland, by a date specified in the notice, if the title condition is to be renewed or varied under paragraph (b) of section 90(1) of this Act or as the case may be the development management scheme preserved under paragraph (e) of that section.

(7)   The date so specified may be any date which is not fewer than twenty-one days after the notice is given (intimation by affixing being taken, for the purposes of this subsection, to be given when first the notice is affixed).

(8)   Notice under subsection (4)(a) above may be given—

(a)   by sending;

(b)   by advertisement;

(c)   by affixing a conspicuous notice to the burdened property and to—

(i)   in a case where there exists one, and only one, lamp post within one hundred metres of that property, that lamp post; or

(ii)   in a case where there exists more than one lamp post so situated, each of at least two such lamp posts; or

(d)   by such other method as the person acquiring the land thinks fit,

and notice under subsection (4)(b) above may be given by sending or by such other means as that person thinks fit.

(9)   Subsections (6) and (7) of section 21 of this Act apply in relation to affixing, and to a notice affixed, under subsection (8)(c) above as they apply in relation to affixing, and to a notice affixed, under subsection (2)(b) of that section (the reference in paragraph (a)(ii) of the said subsection (6) to the date specified in the notice as the renewal date being construed as a reference to the date specified by virtue of subsection (6)(d)(ii) above).

(10)   In this section—

'conveyance' has the same meaning as in section 106(5) of this Act except that the reference, in paragraph (a) of the definition of that expression in that section, to subsection (1) of that section shall be read as a reference to that subsection of this section and paragraph (c) of that definition shall be disregarded; and

'relevant certificate' means a certificate executed, on or after the date specified by virtue of subsection (6)(d)(ii) above, by a member of the Lands Tribunal, or by their clerk, to the effect that no application in relation to the proposal to register the conveyance has been received under section 90(1)(b)(ii) or (e) of this Act or that any such application which has been received—

    (a)   has been withdrawn; or

    (b)   relates, in the case of an application under section 90(1)(b)(ii), (either or both)—

        (i)   to one or more but not to all of the title conditions over the land (any title condition to which it relates being described in the certificate);

        (ii)   to one or more but not to all (or probably or possibly not to all) of the benefited properties (any benefited property to which it relates being described in the certificate),

and where more than one such application has been received the certificate shall relate to both (or as the case may be to all) applications.

(11)   Any application for a relevant certificate shall be made in the form set out in schedule 12 to this Act.

Amendments

108–114   [*Amendment provisions*]

Miscellaneous

115 Further provision as respects notices of preservation or of converted servitude

(1)   This section applies in relation to a notice of preservation or of converted servitude.

(2)   Except where it is not reasonably practicable to do so, the owner of the benefited property shall, before executing the notice, send to the owner of the burdened property a copy of—

    (a)   the notice;

    (b)   the explanatory note set out in whichever schedule to this Act relates to the notice; and

    (c)   in the case of a notice of converted servitude, the constitutive deed (if any).

(3)   The owner of the benefited property shall, in the notice, state either—

    (a)   that a copy of the notice has been sent in accordance with subsection (2) above; or

    (b)   that it was not reasonably practicable for such a notice to be so sent.

(4)   However many the benefited or burdened properties may be, if the terms of the real burdens or converted servitudes are set out in a single constitutive deed, execution and registration may be accomplished in a single notice.

(5)   The Keeper of the Registers of Scotland shall not be required to determine whether a person submitting a notice for registration has complied with subsection (2) above.

(6)   Where—

    (a)   a notice submitted before the expiry of the period of ten years which commences immediately after the appointed day is rejected by the Keeper; but

    (b)   a court or the Lands Tribunal then determines that the notice is registrable, the notice may, if not registered before that expiry, be registered—

        (i)   within two months after the determination is made; but

        (ii)   before such date after that expiry as the Scottish Ministers may by order prescribe;

and any notice registered under this subsection shall be treated as if it had been registered before that expiry.

(7)   For the purposes of subsection (6) above, the application to the court, or to the Lands Tribunal, which has resulted in the determination shall require to have been made within such period as the Scottish Ministers may by order prescribe.

(8)   In subsection (6)(b) above, 'court' means Court of Session or sheriff.

116 Benefited property outwith Scotland

As respects a real burden or servitude, the benefited property need not be in Scotland; but where it is not then nothing in this Act requires registration against that property.

117 Pecuniary real burdens

On and after the day on which this section comes into force, it shall not be competent to create a pecuniary real burden (that is to say, to constitute a heritable security by reservation in a conveyance).

118 Common interest

On and after the day on which this section comes into force—
   (a)   it shall not be competent to create a right of common interest; and
   (b)   no such right shall arise otherwise than by implication of law.

PART 11
SAVINGS, TRANSITIONAL AND GENERAL

Savings and transitional provisions etc

119 Savings and transitional provisions etc

(1)   Nothing in this Act shall be taken to impair the validity of creating, varying or discharging a real burden by the registering of a deed before the appointed day.

(2)   This Act is without prejudice to section 3(1) of the 1979 Act (effect of registration).

(3)   The repeal by this Act of section 32 of the Conveyancing (Scotland) Act 1874 (c 94) does not affect the construction of the expression 'deed of conditions' provided for in section 122(1) of this Act.

(4)   Sections 8 and 14 of this Act do not affect proceedings commenced before the appointed day.

(5)   Section 10 of this Act does not apply where a person ceases to be, or becomes, an owner before the appointed day.

(6)   Section 16 of this Act does not apply as respects a breach of a real burden which occurs before the appointed day.

(7)   Section 61 of this Act does not apply as respects a constitutive deed (or a deed into which the constitutive deed is incorporated) registered before the appointed day except in so far as a real burden the terms of which are set out in the constitutive deed is a community burden.

(8)   Sections 75 and 78 of this Act do not apply as respects a deed executed before the appointed day.

[. . .]

(10)   Except where the contrary intention appears, this Act applies to all real burdens, whenever created.

General

120 Requirement for dual registration

A deed which, to be duly registered for the purposes of any provision of this Act, requires to be registered against both a benefited property and a burdened property, shall not be registrable against one only of the properties; nor shall a document which includes but does not wholly consist of such a deed.

121 Crown application

This Act binds the Crown.

122 Interpretation

(1)   In this Act, unless the context otherwise requires—
'the 1979 Act' means the Land Registration (Scotland) Act 1979 (c 33);

'the 2000 Act' means the Abolition of Feudal Tenure etc (Scotland) Act 2000 (asp 5);

'affirmative burden' shall be construed in accordance with section 2(2)(a) of this Act;

'ancillary burden' shall be construed in accordance with section 2(4) of this Act;

'appointed day' means the day appointed under section 71 of the 2000 Act;

'benefited property'—

(a)   in relation to a real burden, shall be construed in accordance with section 1(2)(b) of this Act; and

(b)   in relation to a title condition other than a real burden, means the land, or real right in land, to which the right to enforce the title condition is attached;

'burdened property'—

(a)   in relation to a real burden, shall be construed in accordance with section 1(2)(a) of this Act; and

(b)   in relation to a title condition other than a real burden, means the land, or real right in land, which is subject to the title condition;

'community' has the meaning given by section 26(2) of this Act;

'community burdens' shall be construed in accordance with section 25 of this Act;

'conservation body' means any body prescribed by order under subsection (4) of section 38 of this Act;

'conservation burden' shall be construed in accordance with subsection (1) of that section and includes (other than in subsections (1) and (2) of that section) a reference to a real burden the right to enforce which was—

(a)   preserved by virtue of section 27(1) of the 2000 Act (preservation of right to enforce conservation burden); or

(b)   obtained by virtue of section 27A(1) of that Act (nomination of conservation body or Scottish Ministers to have title to enforce conservation burden);

'constitutive deed' is the deed which sets out the terms of a title condition (or of a prospective title condition) but the expression includes any document in which the terms of the title condition in question are varied;

'deed of conditions' means a deed mentioned in section 32 of the Conveyancing (Scotland) Act 1874 (c 94) (importation by reference) and registered before the appointed day having been executed in accordance with that section;

'the development management scheme' has the meaning given by section 71(3) of this Act;

'economic development burden' shall be construed in accordance with subsection (1) of section 45 of this Act and includes (other than in subsections (1) to (3) of that section) a reference to a real burden which was converted under section 18B of the 2000 Act (conversion into economic development burden);

'enactment' includes a local and personal or private Act;

'facility burden' means, subject to subsection (2) below, a real burden which regulates the maintenance, management, reinstatement or use of heritable property which constitutes, and is intended to constitute, a facility of benefit to other land (examples of property which might constitute such a facility being without prejudice to the generality of this definition, set out in subsection (3) below);

[. . .]

'health care burden' shall be construed in accordance with subsection (1) of section 46 of this Act and includes (other than in subsections (1) to (3) of that section) a reference to a real burden which was converted under section 18C of the 2000 Act (conversion into health care burden);

'holder', in relation to a title condition, means the person who has right to the title condition [but does not include a person who has title to enforce it only by virtue of any of the paragraphs (a), (b) and (c) of section 8(2) of this Act];

'land' includes—

(a)   heritable property, whether corporeal or incorporeal, held as a separate tenement; and

(b)   land covered with water,

but does not include any estate of dominium directum;

'Lands Tribunal' means Lands Tribunal for Scotland;

['local authority' means a council constituted under section 2 of the Local Government etc (Scotland) Act 1994 (c 39);]

'maintenance' includes (cognate expressions being construed accordingly)—

(a)   repair or replacement; and

(b)   such demolition, alteration or improvement as is reasonably incidental to maintenance;

'manager', in relation to related properties, means any person (including an owner of one of those properties or a firm) who is authorised (whether by virtue of this Act or otherwise) to act generally, or for such purposes as may be applicable in relation to a particular authorisation, in respect of those properties;

'manager burden' shall be construed in accordance with section 63(1) of this Act;

'maritime burden' shall be construed in accordance with subsection (1) of section 44 of this Act and includes (other than in that subsection) a reference to any real burden in relation to which the Crown has title and interest under section 60(1) of the 2000 Act (preserved right of Crown to maritime burdens);

'midcouple' means such midcouple or link in title as it is competent to specify, under section 5(1) of the Conveyancing (Scotland) Act 1924 (14 & 15 Geo 5, c 27), in a deduction of title in terms of that Act;

'negative burden' shall be construed in accordance with section 2(2)(b) of this Act;

'notary public' includes, in a case where swearing or affirmation is to take place outwith Scotland, any person duly authorised by the law of the country or territory in question to administer oaths or receive affirmations in that country or territory;

'notice of converted servitude' shall be construed in accordance with section 80(4) and (5) of this Act;

'notice of preservation' shall be construed in accordance with section 50 of this Act;

'notice of termination' shall be construed in accordance with section 20 of this Act;

'owner' shall be construed in accordance with section 123 of this Act;

'personal pre-emption burden' and 'personal redemption burden' shall be construed in accordance with section 18A(5) of the 2000 Act;

'personal real burden' shall be construed in accordance with section 1(3) of this Act;

'property' includes unit;

'real burden' has the meaning given by section 1 of this Act except that in construing that section for the purposes of this definition 'land' shall be taken to include an estate of dominium directum;

'registering', in relation to any document, means registering an interest in land or information relating to an interest in land (being an interest or information for which that document provides) in the Land Register of Scotland or, as the case may be, recording the document in the Register of Sasines (cognate expressions being construed accordingly);

'renewal date' has the meaning given by section 20(4)(d) of this Act;

'road' has the meaning given by section 151(1) of the Roads (Scotland) Act 1984 (c 54) (interpretation);

'rural housing body' means any body prescribed by order under subsection (5) of section 43 of this Act;

'rural housing burden' shall be construed in accordance with subsection (1) of that section and includes a personal pre-emption burden the holder of which is a rural housing body;

'send' shall be construed in accordance with section 124 of this Act (cognate expressions being construed accordingly);

'service burden' means a real burden which relates to the provision of services to land other than the burdened property;

'sheltered or retirement housing development' has the meaning given by section 54(3) of this Act;

['tenement' has the meaning given by section 26 of the Tenements (Scotland) Act 2004 (asp 11); and references to a flat in a tenement shall be construed accordingly;]

'terminator' shall be construed in accordance with section 20(2) of this Act;

'title condition' means—

    (a)   a real burden;

    (b)   a servitude;

    (c)   an affirmative obligation imposed, in a servitude, on the person who is in right of the servitude;

    (d)   a condition in a registrable lease if it is a condition which relates to the land (but not a condition which imposes either an obligation to pay rent or an obligation of relief relating to the payment of rent);

    (e)   a condition or stipulation—

        (i)   imposed under subsection (2) of section 3 of the Registration of Leases (Scotland) Act 1857 (c 26) (assignation of recorded leases) in an assignation which has been duly registered; or

        (ii)   contained in a deed registered under subsection (2A) or (5) of that section;

    (f)   a condition in an agreement entered into under section 7 of the National Trust for Scotland Order Confirmation Act 1938 (c iv); or

    (g)   such other condition relating to land as the Scottish Ministers may, for the purposes of this paragraph, prescribe by order;

'unit' means any land which is designed to be held in separate ownership (whether it is so held or not); and

'variation', in relation to a title condition, includes both—

    (a)   imposition of a new obligation; and

    (b)   provision that a property becomes a benefited property,

(cognate expressions being construed accordingly).

    (2)   In so far as it constitutes an obligation to maintain or reinstate which has been assumed—

    (a)   by a local or other public authority; or

    (b)   by virtue of any enactment, by a successor body to any such authority,

a real burden is neither—

        (i)   a facility burden; nor

        (ii)   for the purposes of sections 52 to 54(1) of this Act, to be regarded as imposed as mentioned in any of those sections.

    (3)   The examples referred to in the definition of 'facility burden' in subsection (1) above are—

    (a)   a common part of a tenement;

    (b)   a common area for recreation;

    (c)   a private road;

    (d)   private sewerage; and

    (e)   a boundary wall.

123   The expression 'owner'

    (1)   Subject to subsections (2) and (3) below, in this Act 'owner', in relation to any property, means a person who has right to the property whether or not that person has completed title; but if, in relation to the property (or, if the property is

held pro indiviso, any pro indiviso share in the property) more than one person comes within that description of owner, then 'owner'—

(a) for the purposes of sections 4(2)(b), 6(1)(a), 15, 16, 19, 33(1) and (2) and 35 of this Act, means any person having such right; and

(b) for any other purposes means such person as has most recently acquired such right.

(2) Where a heritable creditor is in lawful possession of security subjects which comprise the property, then 'owner'—

(a) for the purposes of the sections mentioned in paragraph (a) of subsection (1) above includes, in addition to any such person as is there mentioned, that heritable creditor; and

(b) for any other purposes (other than of construing section 1 of this Act) means the heritable creditor.

(3) In section 60(1) of this Act, 'owner' in relation to any property has the meaning given by subsection (1) above except that, for the purposes of this subsection, in that subsection—

(a) the words 'Subject to subsections (2) and (3) below, in this Act' shall be disregarded; and

(b) paragraph (a) shall be construed as if section 60(1) were one of the sections mentioned.

124 Sending

(1) Where a provision of this Act requires that a thing be sent—

(a) to a person it shall suffice, for the purposes of that provision, that the thing be sent to an agent of the person;

(b) to an owner of property but only the property is known and not the name of the owner, it shall suffice, for the purposes of that provision, that the thing be sent there addressed to 'The Owner' (or using some other such expression, as for example 'The Proprietor').

(2) Except in subsection (3) below, in this Act any reference to a thing being sent shall be construed as a reference to its being—

(a) posted;

(b) delivered; or

(c) transmitted by electronic means.

(3) For the purposes of any provision of this Act, a thing posted shall be taken to be sent on the day of posting; and a thing transmitted by electronic means, to be sent on the day of transmission.

125 References to distance

Where a provision of this Act refers to a property being within a certain distance of another property, the reference is to distance along a horizontal plane, there being disregarded—

(a) the width of any intervening road if of less than twenty metres; and

(b) any pertinent of either property.

126 Fees chargeable by Lands Tribunal in relation to functions under this Act

The Scottish Ministers may, after consultation with the Scottish Committee of the Council on Tribunals, make rules as to the fees chargeable by the Lands Tribunal in respect of that tribunal's functions under this Act.

127 Orders, regulations and rules

(1) Any power of the Scottish Ministers under this Act to make orders, regulations or rules shall be exercisable by statutory instrument; and a statutory instrument containing any such orders, regulations or rules, other than an order under section 128(4) or 129(4), shall be subject to annulment in pursuance of a resolution of the Scottish Parliament.

(2)   A statutory instrument containing an order under section 128(4) of this Act shall not be made unless a draft of the instrument has been—
  (a)   laid before; and
  (b)   approved by a resolution of,
the Scottish Parliament.

128   Minor and consequential amendments, repeals and power to amend forms
  (1)   Schedule 14 to this Act, which contains minor amendments and amendments consequential upon the provisions of this Act, shall have effect.
  (2)   The enactments mentioned in schedule 15 to this Act are repealed to the extent specified.
  (3)   The Scottish Ministers may by order amend any of schedules—
  (a)   [1A] to 10 and 12 to this Act; and
  (b)   1 to 11A to the 2000 Act.
  (4)   The Scottish Ministers may by order make such incidental, supplemental, consequential, transitional, transitory or saving provision as they consider necessary or expedient for the purposes, or in consequence, of this Act or of any order, regulations or rules made under this Act.
  (5)   An order under subsection (4) above may amend or repeal any enactment (including any provision of this Act).

129   Short title and commencement
  (1)   This Act may be cited as the Title Conditions (Scotland) Act 2003.
  (2)   Subject to subsections (3) to (5) below, this Act, except this section, shall come into force on the appointed day.
  (3)   Sections 63, 66, 67, 86 and 88, except in so far as it inserts a sub-paragraph (ab)(ii) into paragraph 1 of Schedule 1 to the Prescription and Limitation (Scotland) Act 1973 (c 52), Part 9 for the purposes of any application under section 107(5) of this Act, sections 111, 113, 114, 117, 118, 122 to 124, 126, 127, 128(3) to (5), schedules 12 and 13 and, in schedule 14, paragraph 7(1), (3) and (6) come into force on the day after Royal Assent.
  (4)   There shall come into force on such day as the Scottish Ministers may by order appoint, Parts 3 and 6 and sections 106 to 110; and different days may be so appointed for different provisions.
  (5)   In so far as—
  (a)   it relates to paragraph 7(1), (3) and (6) of schedule 14, section 128(1);
  (b)   it relates to the 2000 Act, section 128(2);
  (c)   it relates to the 2000 Act, schedule 15;
  (d)   is necessary for the purposes of Part 3 and section 63, Part 1,
shall come into force on the day after Royal Assent.

SCHEDULES

Section 6(2)   SCHEDULE 1
                        FORM IMPORTING TERMS OF TITLE CONDITIONS

There are imported the terms of the title conditions specified in [*refer to the deed of conditions in such terms as shall be sufficient to identify it and specify the register in which it is registered and the date of registration*].

[SCHEDULE 1A
FORM OF NOTICE OF POTENTIAL LIABILITY FOR COSTS
(introduced by section 10(2A))

'NOTICE OF POTENTIAL LIABILITY FOR COSTS

This notice gives details of certain maintenance or work carried out [or to be carried out] in relation to the property specified in the notice. The effect of the notice is that a person may, on becoming the owner of the property, be liable by virtue of section 10(2A) of the Title Conditions (Scotland) Act 2003 (asp 9) for any outstanding costs relating to the maintenance or work.

Property to which the notice relates:
(see note 1 below)

Description of the maintenance or work to which notice relates:
(see note 2 below)

Person giving notice:
(see note 3 below)

Signature:
(see note 4 below)

Date of signing:'

Notes for completion

(These notes are not part of the notice)

    1   Describe the property in a way that is sufficient to identify it. Where the property has a postal address, the description must include that address. Where title to the property has been registered in the Land Register of Scotland, the description must refer to the title number of the property or of the larger subjects of which it forms part. Otherwise, the description should normally refer to and identify a deed recorded in a specified division of the Register of Sasines.
    2   Describe the maintenance or work in general terms.
    3   Give the name and address of the person applying for registration of the notice ('the applicant') or the applicant's name and the name and address of the applicant's agent.
    4   The notice must be signed by or on behalf of the applicant.]

Section 20(1)   SCHEDULE 2
                    FORM OF NOTICE OF TERMINATION

'NOTICE OF TERMINATION

Name and address of terminator:
(see note for completion 1)

Description of burdened property:
(see note for completion 2)

Terminator's connection with burdened property:
(see note for completion 3)

Terms of real burden(s):
(see note for completion 4)

Extent of termination:
(see note for completion 5)

Renewal date:
(see note for completion 6)

An application to the Lands Tribunal for Scotland for renewal or variation of the real burden(s) must be made by not later than the renewal date.

Persons to whom a copy of the notice sent:
(see note for completion 7)

Date and method of intimation:
(see note for completion 8

I swear [*or* affirm] that the information contained in this notice is, to the best of my knowledge and belief, true, and that this notice has been duly intimated.

Signature of person so swearing [*or* affirming]:
(see note for completion 9)

Signature of notary public:

Date:

Certificate by Lands Tribunal for Scotland
(see note for completion 10).'

Explanatory note

(This explanation has no legal effect)

This notice, given under section 20(1) of the Title Conditions (Scotland) Act 2003, concerns real burdens which affect a [*neighbouring*] property (referred to in the notice as the 'burdened property'), and is sent to you by the owner of that property or by some other person affected by the burdens. The sender (who is referred to in the notice and in these notes as the 'terminator') wishes to free the property of the real burdens listed in the notice.

The burdens are more than 100 years old.

If you are opposed to the freeing, you can apply to the Lands Tribunal for Scotland for the burdens to be renewed or varied. The address of the Lands Tribunal is [*insert address*] and their telephone number is [*insert telephone number*]. However, you can only apply if you are an owner of a property which, in a legal sense, takes benefit from the burden and which carries enforcement rights or if the burden is a personal real burden. For further guidance you may wish to consult a solicitor or other adviser.

[A list of other people who have been sent this notice is given in the notice itself. It is possible to make an application to the Lands Tribunal jointly with other people.]

An application to the Lands Tribunal must be made by the renewal date stated in the notice. If no application is made by then, you may lose any right which you may currently hold to enforce the burdens.

Notes for completion of the notice

(These notes have no legal effect)

1 The 'terminator' is the person who, at any time, is seeking to terminate the real burden. Where the person who proposes to execute and register the notice of termination and so intimates is not the terminator when the notice comes to be executed, the name and address of the person executing should be appended after the name and address of the person who so intimated.

2 Describe the property in a way that is sufficient to identify it. Where the property has a postal address the description should include that address. Where the title has been registered in the Land Register the description should refer to the

title number of the property or of the larger subjects of which the property forms part. Otherwise it should normally refer to and identify a deed recorded in a specified division of the Register of Sasines.

3 Describe the terminator's connection with the burdened property, as for example by identification as owner or tenant or by setting out the midcouple which links (or midcouples which link) the terminator to the person who last had a completed title as owner. Where the circumstances mentioned in note for completion 1 arise, the description should be extended accordingly.

4 Identify the constitutive deed by reference to the appropriate Register, and set out the real burden in full. A single notice may be used for two or more real burdens.

5 If the real burden is wholly to be terminated say so; otherwise describe the extent of termination.

6 Insert the date by which applications for renewal or variation must be made. This can be any date, provided that it is not less than 8 weeks after the last date on which this notice is intimated (intimation by affixing being taken to be given when first the notice is affixed).

7 This notice (and the explanatory note) must be intimated to (a) the owner of any benefited property, (b) the holder of any personal real burden and (c) the owner of the burdened property (or, if the terminator is such an owner, any other owner of that property). Intimation can be by sending (or delivering) the notice, by affixing a conspicuous notice to the burdened property and also to a lamp post within 100 metres of that property (or to at least two lamp posts if there is more than one within that distance of that property) or by newspaper advertisement. However, affixing or advertisement cannot be used for the owner of a benefited property which lies within 4 metres of the burdened property (disregarding roads less than 20 metres wide) or for the owner of the burdened property or for any such person as is mentioned in paragraph (b) of this note and advertisement cannot be used where affixing can. Where sending or delivery is used, state (i) the name of the person concerned (if known) (ii) the address to which the notice is sent or delivered, and (iii) the address of the benefited (or burdened) property owned by that person, if different from (ii). Since evidence of sending may be required at the time of registration in the Land Register, it is recommended that the notice be sent by recorded delivery or registered post.

8 State the date and method of intimation. By way of example—

(a) if notices were posted, to the persons listed in the previous note, on 25th March 2003 and advertised in the Inverness Courier on 4th April 2003, insert: '(a) Intimation by post on 25th March 2003; (b) Advertisement in the Inverness Courier on 4th April 2003.'; or

(b) if on 12th July a notice was posted to the owner of the burdened property and otherwise intimation was given by affixing notices on that date, insert: '(a) Intimation by post on 12th July 2005; (b) Notices affixed to the burdened property and to each of two lamp posts within 100 metres of that property on 12th July 2005.'.

9 The terminator should not swear or affirm, or sign, until the notice has been completed (except for the certificate by the Lands Tribunal for Scotland) and duly intimated. Before signing, the terminator should swear or affirm before a notary public (or, if the notice is being completed outwith Scotland, before a person duly authorised under the local law to administer oaths or receive affirmations) that, to the best of the terminator's knowledge and belief, all the information contained in the notice is true and that the notice has been duly intimated. The notary public should also sign. Swearing or affirming a statement which is known to be false or which is believed not to be true is a criminal offence under the False Oaths (Scotland) Act 1933 (c 20). Normally the terminator should swear or affirm, and sign, personally. If, however, the terminator is legally disabled or incapable (for example because of mental disorder) a legal representative should swear or affirm,

and sign. If the terminator is not an individual (for example, if it is a company) a person entitled by law to sign formal documents on its behalf should swear or affirm, and sign.

10   There is to be endorsed before registration the certificate required by section 23(1) of the Title Conditions (Scotland) Act 2003 (asp 9).

Section 21(2)(b)   SCHEDULE 3
FORM OF AFFIXED NOTICE RELATING TO TERMINATION

'TERMINATION OF REAL BURDEN

This notice is intimation that the person who is described below as terminator wishes to free the property which is described below as the burdened property from a real burden which affects that property. The terminator proposes to register a notice of termination so as to extinguish the real burden. A copy of that notice of termination (which among other things describes the real burden fully) is available from the terminator on request.

Name and address of terminator:
(see note for completion 1)

Description of burdened property:
(see note for completion 2)

The real burden and the extent of termination:
(see note for completion 3)

Renewal date:
(see note for completion 4)

If you wish to apply to the Lands Tribunal for Scotland for renewal or variation of the real burden you must do so by not later than the renewal date. If no application is made by then, you may lose any right which you may currently hold to enforce the burden. For further guidance you may wish to consult a solicitor or other adviser.

Signature of terminator:

Date affixed: ʹ

Notes for completion of the notice

(These notes have no legal effect)

1   The 'terminator' is the person who, at any time, is seeking to terminate the real burden. Give the terminator's name and address (or the terminator's name and the name and address of the terminator's agent).

2   Describe the property in a way that is sufficient to identify it. Where the property has a postal address the description should include that address. Where the title has been registered in the Land Register the description should refer to the title number of the property or of the larger subjects of which the property forms part. Otherwise it should normally refer to and identify a deed recorded in a specified division of the Register of Sasines.

3   Provide briefly a description of the real burden. If the burden is wholly to be terminated say so; otherwise describe the extent of termination.

4   Insert the date by which applications for renewal or variation must be made. This can be any date, provided that it is not less than 8 weeks after the last date on which the notice of termination is intimated (intimation by affixing being taken to be given when first the notice is affixed).

SCHEDULE 4   Section 34(2)(a)
FORM OF NOTICE OF PROPOSAL TO REGISTER DEED OF VARIATION OR
DISCHARGE

'NOTICE OF PROPOSAL TO REGISTER DEED OF VARIATION OR
DISCHARGE

Proposer:
(see note for completion 1)

Description of affected unit(s):
(see note for completion 2)

Terms of community burden(s):
(see note for completion 3)

Effect of registration of deed on burden(s):
(see note for completion 4)

An application to the Lands Tribunal for Scotland for preservation of the community burden(s) must be made not later than [specify the date on which the period mentioned in section 34(3) of this Act expires].

Signature of proposer:
Date: .'

Explanatory note

(This explanation has no legal effect)

This notice is given under section 34(2)(a) of the Title Conditions (Scotland) Act 2003. The sender (who is referred to in the notice and in these notes as the 'proposer') wishes [to free a property of a community burden] or [to vary a community burden].

A deed of [discharge] or [variation] has already been granted. A copy of the deed in question is attached. If the deed is duly registered the burden will be [discharged] or [varied] in relation to the affected unit.

If you want to preserve such rights as you may have, you can apply to the Lands Tribunal for Scotland in that regard. The address of the Lands Tribunal is [*insert address*] and their telephone number is [*insert telephone number*]. For further guidance you may wish to consult a solicitor or other adviser.

An application to the Lands Tribunal must be made by the date stated in the notice. If no application is made by then, you may lose any right which you may currently hold to enforce the burdens.

Notes for completion of the notice

(These notes have no legal effect)

1   The 'proposer' is the person who is seeking to discharge or vary the community burden. Give the proposer's name and address (or the proposer's name and the name and address of the proposer's agent).

2   Describe the unit in a way that is sufficient to identify it. Where the unit has a postal address the description should include that address. Where the title has been registered in the Land Register the description should refer to the title number of the property or of the larger subjects of which the unit forms part. Otherwise it should normally refer to and identify a deed recorded in a specified division of the Register of Sasines.

3 Identify the constitutive deed by reference to the appropriate Register, and set out the community burden in full.

4 State whether the deed is of variation or of discharge. If the community burden is wholly to be discharged say so; otherwise describe the extent of variation or discharge.

5 Intimation is by sending (or delivering) the notice. Since evidence of sending may be required at the time of registration in the Land Register, it is recommended that the notice be sent by recorded delivery or registered post.

6 There is to be endorsed on the deed before registration the certificate required by subsection (2) of section 37 of the Title Conditions (Scotland) Act 2003 (asp 9) (as applied by section 34 of that Act).

Section 36(2)(a)   SCHEDULE 5
FURTHER FORM OF NOTICE OF PROPOSAL TO REGISTER DEED OF
VARIATION OR DISCHARGE OF COMMUNITY BURDEN: SENT VERSION

'NOTICE OF PROPOSAL TO REGISTER DEED OF VARIATION OR
DISCHARGE OF COMMUNITY BURDEN

Proposer:
(see note for completion 1)

Description of affected unit:
(see note for completion 2)

Terms of community burden(s):
(see note for completion 3)

Nature of deed:
(see note for completion 4)

An application to the Lands Tribunal for Scotland for preservation of the community burden(s) must be made not later than [specify the date on which the period mentioned in section 37(1) of this Act expires].

Signature of proposer:
Date: ʹ

Explanatory note

(This explanation has no legal effect)
This notice is given under section 36(2)(a) of the Title Conditions (Scotland) Act 2003. The sender (who is referred to in the notice and in these notes as the 'proposer') wishes [to free a property of a community burden] or [to vary a community burden].

A deed of [discharge] or [variation] has already been granted by the owners of adjacent properties and a copy of it is attached. If the deed is duly registered the burden will be [discharged] or [varied] in relation to the affected property.

If you want to preserve such rights as you may have, you can apply to the Lands Tribunal for Scotland in that regard. The address of the Lands Tribunal is [*insert address*] and their telephone number is [*insert telephone number*]. However, you can only apply if you are an owner of a property which, in a legal sense, takes benefit from the burden and which carries enforcement rights. For further guidance you may wish to consult a solicitor or other adviser.

An application to the Lands Tribunal must be made by the date stated in the notice. If no application is made by then, you may lose any right which you may currently hold to enforce the burdens.

Notes for completion of the notice

(These notes have no legal effect)

1   The 'proposer' is the person who is seeking to discharge or vary the community burden. Give the proposer's name and address (or the proposer's name and the name and address of the proposer's agent.)

2   Describe the affected unit in a way that is sufficient to identify it. Where the unit has a postal address the description should include that address. Where the title has been registered in the Land Register the description should refer to the title number of the property or of the larger subjects of which the unit forms part. Otherwise it should normally refer to and identify a deed recorded in a specified division of the Register of Sasines.

3   Identify the constitutive deed by reference to the appropriate Register and set out the community burden in full.

4   State whether the deed is of variation or of discharge. If the community burden is wholly to be discharged say so; otherwise describe the extent of variation or discharge.

5   This notice requires to be sent. Since evidence of sending may be required at the time of registration in the Land Register, it is recommended that the notice be sent by recorded delivery or registered post.

6   There is to be endorsed on the deed before registration the certificate required by subsection (2) of section 37 of the Title Conditions (Scotland) Act 2003 (asp 9).

Section 36(2)(b)   SCHEDULE 6
FURTHER FORM OF NOTICE OF PROPOSAL TO REGISTER DEED OF
VARIATION OR DISCHARGE OF COMMUNITY BURDEN: AFFIXED VERSION

'NOTICE OF PROPOSAL TO REGISTER DEED OF VARIATION OR
DISCHARGE OF COMMUNITY BURDEN

This notice is intimation that the person who is described below as proposer wishes to vary or discharge a community burden which affects a property described below as the affected unit. The proposer intends to register a deed already granted by certain other owners of units. A copy of the deed in question can be obtained from the proposer on request as can a description of the community burden. If the deed is registered the community burden will be varied or discharged in so far as it affects the property.

Proposer:
(see note for completion 1)

Description of affected unit:
(see note for completion 2)

The community burden and the extent of termination:
(see note for completion 3)

An application to the Lands Tribunal for Scotland for preservation of the community burden(s) must be made not later than [specify the date on which the period mentioned in section 37(1) of this Act expires]. If no application is made by then, you may lose any right you may currently hold to enforce the community burden. For further guidance you may wish to consult a solicitor or other adviser.

Signature of proposer:

Date affixed:

Notes for completion of the notice

(These notes have no legal effect)

1 The 'proposer' is the person who is seeking to discharge or vary the community burden. Give the proposer's name and address (or the proposer's name and the name and address of the proposer's agent).

2 Describe the affected unit in a way that is sufficient to identify it. Where the unit has a postal address the description should include that address. Where the title has been registered in the Land Register the description should refer to the title number of the property or of the larger subjects of which the unit forms part. Otherwise it should normally refer to and identify a deed recorded in a specified division of the Register of Sasines.

3 Provide a brief description of the community burden. If the burden is wholly to be discharged say so; otherwise describe the extent of variation or discharge.

4 This notice requires to be affixed conspicuously to the affected unit and also to a lamp post within 100 metres of that unit (or to at least two lamp posts if there is more than one within that distance of that unit).

5 There is to be endorsed on the deed before registration the statement required by subsection (2) of section 37 of the Title Conditions (Scotland) Act 2003 (asp 9).

SCHEDULE 7   Section 50(1)
FORM OF NOTICE OF PRESERVATION

'NOTICE OF PRESERVATION

Name and address of person sending notice:

Description of burdened property:
(see note for completion 1)

Description of benefited property:
(see note for completion 1)

[Links in title:]
(see note for completion 2)

Terms of real burden(s):
(see note for completion 3)

Explanation of why the property described as a benefited property is such a property:
(see note for completion 4)

Service:
(see note for completion 5)

I swear [or affirm] that the information contained in this notice is, to the best of my knowledge and belief, true.

Signature of person sending notice:
(see note for completion 6)

Signature of notary public:

Date: .'

Explanatory note for owner of burdened property

(This explanation has no legal effect)

This notice is sent by a person who asserts that the use of your property is affected by the real burden [or real burdens] whose terms are described in the notice and that that person is one of the people entitled to the benefit of the real burden [or real burdens] and can, if necessary, enforce it [or them] against you. In this notice your property (or some part of it) is referred to as the 'burdened property' and the property belonging to that person is referred to as the 'benefited property'.

The grounds for the assertion are given in the notice. By section 50 of the Title Conditions (Scotland) Act 2003 (asp 9) that person's rights will be lost unless this notice is registered in the Land Register or Register of Sasines by not later than [insert date ten years after the appointed day]. Registration preserves the rights and means that the burden [or burdens] can continue to be enforced by that person and by anyone succeeding as owner of that person's property.

This notice does not require you to take any action; but if you think there is a mistake in it, or if you wish to challenge it, you are advised to contact your solicitor or other adviser. A notice can be challenged even after it has been registered.

Notes for completion of the notice

(These notes have no legal effect)

1   A single notice may be used for any properties covered by the same constitutive deed. Describe the property in a way that is sufficient to identify it. Where the title has been registered in the Land Register the description should refer to the title number of the property or of the larger subjects of which the property forms part. Otherwise it should normally refer to and identify a deed recorded in a specified division of the Register of Sasines.

2   Include the section 'Links in Title' only if the person sending the notice does not have a completed title to the benefited property. Set out the midcouple (or midcouples) linking that person with the person who had the last completed title.

3   A single notice may be used for any real burdens created in the same constitutive deed. Identify the constitutive deed by reference to the appropriate Register, and set out the real burden in full or refer to the deed in such a way as to identify the real burden.

4   Explain the legal and factual grounds on which the land described as a benefited property is a benefited property in relation to the burdened property and the burden described in the notice.

5   Do not complete until a copy of the notice, together with the explanatory note, has been sent (or delivered) to the owner of the burdened property (except in a case where that is not reasonably practicable). Then insert whichever is applicable of the following:

'A copy of this notice has been sent by [state method and if by post specify whether by recorded delivery, by registered post or by ordinary post] on [date] to the owner of the burdened property at [address].'; or

'It has not been reasonably practicable to send a copy of this notice to the owner of the burdened property for the following reason: [specify the reason]'.

6   The person sending the notice should not swear or affirm, or sign, until a copy of the notice has been sent (or otherwise) as mentioned in note 5. Before signing, the sender should swear or affirm before a notary public (or, if the notice is being completed outwith Scotland, before a person duly authorised under the local law to administer oaths or receive affirmations) that, to the best of the sender's knowledge and belief, all the information contained in the notice is true. The notary public should also sign. Swearing or affirming a statement which is known to be false or which is believed not to be true is a criminal offence under the False

Oaths (Scotland) Act 1933 (c 20). Normally the sender should swear or affirm, and sign, personally. If, however, the sender is legally disabled or incapable (for example because of mental disorder) a legal representative should swear or affirm, and sign. If the sender is not an individual (for example, if it is a company) a person entitled by law to sign formal documents on its behalf should swear or affirm, and sign.

Section 55(2)   SCHEDULE 8
                         COMMUNITY CONSULTATION NOTICE

'NOTICE INVITING COMMENTS IN RELATION TO PROPOSAL TO VARY OR
     DISCHARGE COMMUNITY BURDEN AFFECTING SHELTERED OR
                           RETIREMENT HOUSING

Person to whom comments should be sent:
(see note for completion 1)

Description of development:
(see note for completion 2)

Terms of community burden to be varied or discharged:
(see note for completion 3)

Effect of registration of proposed deed on that burden:
(see note for completion 4)

Date by which any comments are to be made:
(see note for completion 5)

Date of intimation:
(see notes for completion 6)

Signature of a person who proposes to grant the deed:

Date: .'

Explanatory note

(This explanation has no legal effect)

This notice, which is sent under section 55 of the Title Conditions (Scotland) Act 2003, concerns a community burden which affects the sheltered or retirement housing development of which your property is part. The sender is intimating to you a proposal to grant a deed of [variation] or [discharge] in respect of the burden and invites your comments.

If such a deed is granted and duly registered (which cannot be before the date specified, in the notice, as that by which any comments are to be made) the burden [may be varied] or [may be discharged] as described in the notice.

For further guidance you may wish to consult a solicitor or other adviser.

Notes for completion of the notice

(These notes have no legal effect)

1   This should ordinarily be a person who proposes to grant the deed. Give the person's name and address.

2   Describe the sheltered or retirement housing development in a way that is sufficient to identify it.

3   Set out the community burden in question in full.

4   State whether the proposed deed is of variation or of discharge. If the community burden is wholly to be discharged say so; otherwise describe the extent of variation or discharge.

5 Specify a date no earlier than three weeks after the latest date mentioned in section 55(3) of the Title Conditions (Scotland) Act 2003 (asp 9).

6 Intimation is by sending (or delivering) the notice. Since evidence of sending may be required at the time of registration in the Land Register of any deed granted, it is recommended that the notice be sent by recorded delivery or registered post.

SCHEDULE 9   Section 80(4)

FORM OF NOTICE OF CONVERTED SERVITUDE

'NOTICE OF CONVERTED SERVITUDE

Name and address of person sending notice:

Description of burdened property:
(see note for completion 1)

Description of benefited property:
(see note for completion 1)

[Links in title:]
(see note for completion 2)

Terms of converted servitude:
(see note for completion 3)

Explanation of why the property described as a benefited property is such a property:
(see note for completion 4)

Service:
(see note for completion 5)

I swear [or affirm] that the information contained in this notice is, to the best of my knowledge and belief, true. The constitutive deed [or A copy of the constitutive deed] is annexed to the notice.
(see note for completion 6)

Signature of person sending notice:
(see note for completion 7)

Signature of notary public:

Date: .'

Explanatory note for owner of burdened property

(This explanation has no legal effect)

This notice is sent by a person who asserts that the use of your property is affected by a converted servitude which the sender is entitled to enforce. In this notice your property (or some part of it) is referred to as the 'burdened property' and the property belonging to the sender is referred to as the 'benefited property'. The 'converted servitude' is a condition which may affect the use of your property. Formerly a servitude, the condition was converted into a real burden by subsection (1) of section 80 of the Title Conditions (Scotland) Act 2003 (asp 9).

At the moment the converted servitude is not disclosed against your title on the property registers. By subsection (2) of that section the sender's right will be lost unless this notice is registered in the Land Register of Scotland or the Register of Sasines by not later than [insert date ten years after the appointed day]. Registration preserves the right and means that the converted servitude can continue to be enforced by the sender, and by anyone succeeding the sender as owner of that property.

This notice does not require you to take any action; but if you think there is a mistake in it, or if you wish to challenge it, you are advised to contact your solicitor or other adviser. A notice can be challenged even after it has been registered.

Notes for completion of the notice

(These notes have no legal effect)

1   A single notice may be used for any properties covered by the same constitutive deed. Describe the property in a way that is sufficient to identify it. Where the title has been registered in the Land Register the description should refer to the title number of the property or of the larger subjects of which the property forms part. Otherwise it should normally refer to and identify a deed recorded in a specified division of the Register of Sasines.

2   Include the section 'Links in Title' only if the person sending the notice does not have a completed title to the benefited property. List the midcouple (or midcouples) linking that person with the person who had the last completed title.

3   A single notice may be used for any converted servitudes created in the same constitutive deed. Set out the converted servitude in full or refer to the constitutive deed in such a way as to identify the servitude. If there is no such deed, explain the factual and legal circumstances in which the servitude was created.

4   Complete this part only if the land described as the benefited property is not nominated as such by the constitutive deed. Explain the legal and factual grounds on which that land is a benefited property in relation to the burdened property and the converted servitude described in the notice.

5   Do not complete until a copy of the notice, together with the constitutive deed and the explanatory note, has been sent (or delivered) to the owner of the burdened property (except in a case where that is not reasonably practicable). Then insert whichever is applicable of the following:

'A copy of this notice has been sent by [state method and if by post specify whether by recorded delivery, by registered post or by ordinary post] on [date] to the owner of the burdened property at [address].'; or

'It has not been reasonably practicable to send a copy of this notice to the owner of the burdened property for the following reason: [specify the reason]'.

6   Endorse on the constitutive deed (or copy) words to the effect of:

'This is the constitutive deed referred to in the notice of converted servitude by [give name of person sending the notice] dated [give date].'

The endorsement need not be signed.

7   The person sending the notice should not swear or affirm, or sign, until a copy of the notice has been sent (or otherwise) as mentioned in note 5. Before signing, the sender should swear or affirm before a notary public (or, if the notice is being completed outwith Scotland, before a person duly authorised under the local law to administer oaths or receive affirmations) that, to the best of the sender's knowledge and belief, all the information contained in the notice is true. The notary public should also sign. Swearing or affirming a statement which is known to be false or which is believed not to be true is a criminal offence under the False Oaths (Scotland) Act 1933 (c 20). Normally the sender should swear or affirm, and sign, personally. If, however, the sender is legally disabled or incapable (for example because of mental disorder) a legal representative should swear or affirm, and sign. If the sender is not an individual (for example, if it is a company) a person entitled by law to sign formal documents on its behalf should swear or affirm, and sign.

SCHEDULE 10   Section 83(1)(a)
FORM OF UNDERTAKING

'UNDERTAKING NOT TO EXERCISE RIGHT OF PRE-EMPTION

Property benefited by right of pre-emption:
(see note for completion 1)

Holder of right of pre-emption:
(see note for completion 2)

Property subject to right of pre-emption:
(see note for completion 3)

Deed in which right of pre-emption imposed:
(see note for completion 4)

I hereby undertake that I will not exercise my right of pre-emption in respect of a sale occurring before (insert date) [if (insert any conditions to be satisfied)— see note for completion 5]

Signature by or on behalf of holder of right of pre-emption:

Signature of witness:

Date: .'

Notes for completion of the undertaking

(These notes have no legal effect)

1   Describe the property in a way that is sufficient to enable it to be identified. Where the title has been registered in the Land Register the description should refer to the title number. Otherwise it should normally refer to and identify a deed recorded in a specified division of the Register of Sasines.
   Where the right of pre-emption is a personal pre-emption burden or rural housing burden, insert (only) 'Personal pre-emption burden' or 'Rural housing burden'.
2   Insert the holder's name and address. The holder is the owner of the benefited property or, in the case of a personal pre-emption burden or rural housing burden, the person in whose favour the burden is constituted. (The person last registered as having title to such a burden is taken to be the holder of the right of pre-emption which the burden comprises.)
3   Describe the property in a way that is sufficient to enable it to be identified. Where the title has been registered in the Land Register the description should refer to the title number. Otherwise it should normally refer to and identify a deed recorded in a specified division of the Register of Sasines. If part only of the burdened property is to be sold, describe that part only.
4   Give the name of the deed and the particulars of its registration or recording.
5   Insert any conditions concerning the type of sale in respect of which the right of pre-emption will not be exercised (for example, 'if the consideration for the sale is £100,000 or more').

Section 90(3)   SCHEDULE 11
TITLE CONDITIONS NOT SUBJECT TO DISCHARGE BY LANDS TRIBUNAL

1   An obligation, however constituted, relating to the right to work minerals or to any ancillary rights in relation to minerals ('minerals' and 'ancillary rights' having the same meanings as in the Mines (Working Facilities and Support) Act 1966 (c 4)).

2   In so far as enforceable by or on behalf of—
   (a)   the Crown, an obligation created or imposed for naval, military or air force purposes; or
   (b)   the Crown or any public or international authority, an obligation created or imposed—
          (i)   for civil aviation purposes; or
          (ii)   in connection with the use of land as an aerodrome.
3   An obligation created or imposed in or in relation to a lease of—
   (a)   an agricultural holding (as defined in section 1(1) of the Agricultural Holdings (Scotland) Act 1991 (c 55));
   (b)   a holding (within the meaning of the Small Landholders (Scotland) Acts 1886 to 1931); or
   (c)   a croft (within the meaning of the Crofters (Scotland) Act 1993 (c 44)).

Section 107(11)   SCHEDULE 12
                    FORM OF APPLICATION FOR RELEVANT CERTIFICATE

'APPLICATION BY ACQUIRING AUTHORITY FOR RELEVANT CERTIFICATE

Acquiring authority:

Description of land acquired:
(see note for completion 1)

Proposed effect of registering conveyance:
(see note for completion 2)

Date and method of intimation:
(see note for completion 3)

Date by which any application to Lands Tribunal must be made:
(see note for completion 4)

Signature:
(see note for completion 5)

Date: .'

Notes for completion of the application

(These notes have no legal effect)

   1   Give the postal address if there is one, then describe the land in a way that is sufficient to enable the Keeper to identify it by reference to the Ordnance Map. Where the title to the land has been registered in the Land Register the description should refer to the title number of the land or the larger subjects of which the land forms part. Otherwise it should normally refer to and identify a deed recorded in a specified division of the Register of Sasines.
   2   If it is proposed that all real burdens and servitudes be extinguished, and any development management scheme disapplied, say so. If the terms of the conveyance are to provide otherwise, annex a copy of the draft conveyance to the application.
   3   Intimation can be by sending, by advertisement or by such other method as the acquiring authority thinks fit.
   4   Specify a date no fewer than 21 days after the date of intimation.
   5   The signature is to be that of a person entitled by law to sign formal documents on behalf of the acquiring authority.

TENEMENTS (SCOTLAND) ACT 2004
(2004, asp 11)

Boundaries and pertinents

1   Determination of boundaries and pertinents

(1)   Except in so far as any different boundaries or pertinents are constituted by virtue of the title to the tenement, or any enactment, the boundaries and pertinents of sectors of a tenement shall be determined in accordance with sections 2 and 3 of this Act.

(2)   In this Act, 'title to the tenement' means—
 (a)   any conveyance, or reservation, of property which affects—
  (i)   the tenement; or
  (ii)   any sector in the tenement; and
 (b)   where an interest in—
  (i)   the tenement; or
  (ii)   any sector in the tenement,
has been registered in the Land Register of Scotland, the title sheet of that interest.

2   Tenement boundaries

(1)   Subject to subsections (3) to (7) below, the boundary between any two contiguous sectors is the median of the structure that separates them; and a sector—
 (a)   extends in any direction to such a boundary; or
 (b)   if it does not first meet such a boundary—
  (i)   extends to and includes the solum or any structure which is an outer surface of the tenement building; or
  (ii)   extends to the boundary that separates the sector from a contiguous building which is not part of the tenement building.

(2)   For the purposes of subsection (1) above, where the structure separating two contiguous sectors is or includes something (as for example, but without prejudice to the generality of this subsection, a door or window) which wholly or mainly serves only one of those sectors, the thing is in its entire thickness part of that sector.

(3)   A top flat extends to and includes the roof over that flat.

(4)   A bottom flat extends to and includes the solum under that flat.

(5)   A close extends to and includes the roof over, and the solum under, the close.

(6)   Where a sector includes the solum (or any part of it) the sector shall also include, subject to subsection (7) below, the airspace above the tenement building and directly over the solum (or part).

(7)   Where the roof of the tenement building slopes, a sector which includes the roof (or any part of it) shall also include the airspace above the slope of the roof (or part) up to the level of the highest point of the roof.

3   Pertinents

(1)   Subject to subsection (2) below, there shall attach to each of the flats, as a pertinent, a right of common property in (and in the whole of) the following parts of a tenement—
 (a)   a close;
 (b)   a lift by means of which access can be obtained to more than one of the flats.

(2)   If a close or lift does not afford a means of access to a flat then there shall not attach to that flat, as a pertinent, a right of common property in the close or, as the case may be, lift.

(3)   Any land (other than the solum of the tenement building) pertaining to a tenement shall attach as a pertinent to the bottom flat most nearly adjacent to the

land (or part of the land); but this subsection shall not apply to any part which constitutes a path, outside stair or other way affording access to any sector other than that flat.

(4) If a tenement includes any part (such as, for example, a path, outside stair, fire escape, rhone, pipe, flue, conduit, cable, tank or chimney stack) that does not fall within subsection (1) or (3) above and that part—

(a) wholly serves one flat, then it shall attach as a pertinent to that flat;

(b) serves two or more flats, then there shall attach to each of the flats served, as a pertinent, a right of common property in (and in the whole of) the part.

(5) For the purposes of this section, references to rights of common property being attached to flats as pertinents are references to there attaching to each flat equal rights of common property; except that where the common property is a chimney stack the share allocated to a flat shall be determined in direct accordance with the ratio which the number of flues serving it in the stack bears to the total number of flues in the stack.

Tenement Management Scheme

4 Application of the Tenement Management Scheme

(1) The Tenement Management Scheme (referred to in this section as 'the Scheme'), which is set out in schedule 1 to this Act, shall apply in relation to a tenement to the extent provided by the following provisions of this section.

(2) The Scheme shall not apply in any period during which the development management scheme applies to the tenement by virtue of section 71 of the Title Conditions (Scotland) Act 2003 (asp 9).

(3) The provisions of rule 1 of the Scheme shall apply, so far as relevant, for the purpose of interpreting any other provision of the Scheme which applies to the tenement.

(4) Rule 2 of the Scheme shall apply unless—

(a) a tenement burden provides procedures for the making of decisions by the owners; and

(b) the same such procedures apply as respects each flat.

(5) The provisions of rule 3 of the Scheme shall apply to the extent that there is no tenement burden enabling the owners to make scheme decisions on any matter on which a scheme decision may be made by them under that rule.

(6) Rule 4 of the Scheme shall apply in relation to any scheme costs incurred in relation to any part of the tenement unless a tenement burden provides that the entire liability for those scheme costs (in so far as liability for those costs is not to be met by someone other than an owner) is to be met by one or more of the owners.

(7) The provisions of rule 5 of the Scheme shall apply to the extent that there is no tenement burden making provision as to the liability of the owners in the circumstances covered by the provisions of that rule.

(8) The provisions of rule 6 of the Scheme shall apply to the extent that there is no tenement burden making provision as to the effect of any procedural irregularity in the making of a scheme decision on—

(a) the validity of the decision; or

(b) the liability of any owner affected by the decision.

(9) Rule 7 of the Scheme shall apply to the extent that there is no tenement burden making provision—

(a) for an owner to instruct or carry out any emergency work as defined in that rule; or

(b) as to the liability of the owners for the cost of any emergency work as so defined.

(10) The provisions of—

(a)   rule 8; and

(b)   subject to subsection (11) below, rule 9,

of the Scheme shall apply, so far as relevant, for the purpose of supplementing any other provision of the Scheme which applies to the tenement.

(11)   The provisions of rule 9 are subject to any different provision in any tenement burden.

(12)   The Scottish Ministers may by order substitute for the sums for the time being specified in rule 3.3 of the Scheme such other sums as appear to them to be justified by a change in the value of money appearing to them to have occurred since the last occasion on which the sums were fixed.

(13)   Where some but not all of the provisions of the Scheme apply, references in the Scheme to 'the scheme' shall be read as references only to those provisions of the Scheme which apply.

(14)   In this section, 'scheme costs' and 'scheme decision' have the same meanings as they have in the Scheme.

Resolution of disputes

5   Application to sheriff for annulment of certain decisions

(1)   Where a decision is made by the owners in accordance with the management scheme which applies as respects the tenement (except where that management scheme is the development management scheme), an owner mentioned in subsection (2) below may, by summary application, apply to the sheriff for an order annulling the decision.

(2)   That owner is—

(a)   any owner who, at the time the decision referred to in subsection (1) above was made, was not in favour of the decision; or

(b)   any new owner, that is to say, any person who was not an owner at that time but who has since become an owner.

(3)   For the purposes of any such application, the defender shall be all the other owners.

(4)   An application under subsection (1) above shall be made—

(a)   in a case where the decision was made at a meeting attended by the owner making the application, not later than 28 days after the date of that meeting; or

(b)   in any other case, not later than 28 days after the date on which notice of the making of the decision was given to the owner for the time being of the flat in question.

(5)   The sheriff may, if satisfied that the decision—

(a)   is not in the best interests of all (or both) the owners taken as a group; or

(b)   is unfairly prejudicial to one or more of the owners,

make an order annulling the decision (in whole or in part).

(6)   Where such an application is made as respects a decision to carry out maintenance, improvements or alterations, the sheriff shall, in considering whether to make an order under subsection (5) above, have regard to—

(a)   the age of the property which is to be maintained, improved or, as the case may be, altered;

(b)   its condition;

(c)   the likely cost of any such maintenance, improvements or alterations; and

(d)   the reasonableness of that cost.

(7)   Where the sheriff makes an order under subsection (5) above annulling a decision (in whole or in part), the sheriff may make such other, consequential, order as the sheriff thinks fit (as, for example, an order as respects the liability of owners for any costs already incurred).

(8)   A party may not later than fourteen days after the date of—

    (a)   an order under subsection (5) above; or

    (b)   an interlocutor dismissing such an application,

appeal to the Court of Session on a point of law.

    (9)   A decision of the Court of Session on an appeal under subsection (8) above shall be final.

    (10)   Where an owner is entitled to make an application under subsection (1) above in relation to any decision, no step shall be taken to implement that decision unless—

    (a)   the period specified in subsection (4) above within which such an application is to be made has expired without such an application having been made and notified to the owners; or

    (b)   where such an application has been so made and notified—

      (i) the application has been disposed of and either the period specified in subsection (8) above within which an appeal against the sheriff's decision may be made has expired without such an appeal having been made or such an appeal has been made and disposed of; or

      (ii) the application has been abandoned.

    (11)   Subsection (10) above does not apply to a decision relating to work which requires to be carried out urgently.

6 Application to sheriff for order resolving certain disputes

    (1)   Any owner may by summary application apply to the sheriff for an order relating to any matter concerning the operation of—

    (a)   the management scheme which applies as respects the tenement (except where that management scheme is the development management scheme); or

    (b)   any provision of this Act in its application as respects the tenement.

    (2)   Where an application is made under subsection (1) above the sheriff may, subject to such conditions (if any) as the sheriff thinks fit—

    (a)   grant the order craved; or

    (b)   make such other order under this section as the sheriff considers necessary or expedient.

    (3)   A party may not later than fourteen days after the date of—

    (a)   an order under subsection (2) above; or

    (b)   an interlocutor dismissing such an application,

appeal to the Court of Session on a point of law.

    (4)   A decision of the Court of Session on an appeal under subsection (3) above shall be final.

Support and shelter

7 Abolition as respects tenements of common law rules of common interest

Any rule of law relating to common interest shall, to the extent that it applies as respects a tenement, cease to have effect; but nothing in this section shall affect the operation of any such rule of law in its application to a question affecting both a tenement and—

    (a)   some other building or former building (whether or not a tenement); or

    (b)   any land not pertaining to the tenement.

8 Duty to maintain so as to provide support and shelter etc

    (1)   Subject to subsection (2) below, the owner of any part of a tenement building, being a part that provides, or is intended to provide, support or shelter to any other part, shall maintain the supporting or sheltering part so as to ensure that it provides support or shelter.

    (2)   An owner shall not by virtue of subsection (1) above be obliged to maintain any part of a tenement building if it would not be reasonable to do so, having regard to all the circumstances (and including, in particular, the age of the tenement building, its condition and the likely cost of any maintenance).

(3) The duty imposed by subsection (1) above on an owner of a part of a tenement building may be enforced by any other such owner who is, or would be, directly affected by any breach of the duty.

(4) Where two or more persons own any such part of a tenement building as is referred to in subsection (1) above in common, any of them may, without the need for the agreement of the others, do anything that is necessary for the purpose of complying with the duty imposed by that subsection.

9 Prohibition on interference with support or shelter etc

(1) No owner or occupier of any part of a tenement shall be entitled to do anything in relation to that part which would, or would be reasonably likely to, impair to a material extent—

    (a) the support or shelter provided to any part of the tenement building; or

    (b) the natural light enjoyed by any part of the tenement building.

(2) The prohibition imposed by subsection (1) above on an owner or occupier of a part of a tenement may be enforced by any other such owner who is, or would be, directly affected by any breach of the prohibition.

10 Recovery of costs incurred by virtue of section 8

Where—

    (a) by virtue of section 8 of this Act an owner carries out maintenance to any part of a tenement; and

    (b) the management scheme which applies as respects the tenement provides for the maintenance of that part,

the owner shall be entitled to recover from any other owner any share of the cost of the maintenance for which that other owner would have been liable had the maintenance been carried out by virtue of the management scheme in question.

Repairs: costs and access

11 Determination of when an owner's liability for certain costs arise

(1) An owner is liable for any relevant costs (other than accumulating relevant costs) arising from a scheme decision from the date when the scheme decision to incur those costs is made.

(2) For the purposes of subsection (1) above, a scheme decision is, in relation to an owner, taken to be made on—

    (a) where the decision is made at a meeting, the date of the meeting; or

    (b) in any other case, the date on which notice of the making of the decision is given to the owner.

(3) An owner is liable for any relevant costs arising from any emergency work from the date on which the work is instructed.

(4) An owner is liable for any relevant costs of the kind mentioned in rule 4.1(d) of the Tenement Management Scheme from the date of any statutory notice requiring the carrying out of the work to which those costs relate.

(5) An owner is liable for any accumulating relevant costs (such as the cost of an insurance premium) on a daily basis.

(6) Except where subsection (1) above applies in relation to the costs, an owner is liable for any relevant costs arising from work instructed by a manager from the date on which the work is instructed.

(7) An owner is liable in accordance with section 10 of this Act for any relevant costs arising from maintenance carried out by virtue of section 8 of this Act from the date on which the maintenance is completed.

(8) An owner is liable for any relevant costs other than those to which subsections (1) to (7) above apply from—

    (a) such date; or

    (b) the occurrence of such event,

as may be stipulated as the date on, or event in, which the costs become due.

(9)   For the purposes of this section and section 12 of this Act, 'relevant costs' means, as respects a flat—
    (a)   the share of any costs for which the owner is liable by virtue of the management scheme which applies as respects the tenement (except where that management scheme is the development management scheme); and
    (b)   any costs for which the owner is liable by virtue of this Act.
(10)   In this section, 'emergency work', 'manager' and 'scheme decision' have the same meanings as they have in the Tenement Management Scheme.

12   Liability of owner and successors for certain costs

(1)   Any owner who is liable for any relevant costs shall not, by virtue only of ceasing to be such an owner, cease to be liable for those costs.
(2)   Subject to subsection (3) below, where a person becomes an owner (any such person being referred to in this section as a 'new owner'), that person shall be severally liable with any former owner of the flat for any relevant costs for which the former owner is liable.
(3)   A new owner shall be liable as mentioned in subsection (2) above for relevant costs relating to any maintenance or work (other than local authority work) carried out before the acquisition date only if—
    (a)   notice of the maintenance or work—
        (i)   in, or as near as may be in, the form set out in schedule 2 to this Act; and
        (ii)   containing the information required by the notes for completion set out in that schedule,
(such a notice being referred to in this section and section 13 of this Act as a 'notice of potential liability for costs') was registered in relation to the new owner's flat at least 14 days before the acquisition date; and
    (b)   the notice had not expired before the acquisition date.
(4)   In subsection (3) above—
    'acquisition date' means the date on which the new owner acquired right to the flat; and
    'local authority work' means work carried out by a local authority by virtue of any enactment.
(5)   Where a new owner pays any relevant costs for which a former owner of the flat is liable, the new owner may recover the amount so paid from the former owner.
(6)   This section applies as respects any relevant costs for which an owner becomes liable on or after the day on which this section comes into force.

13   Notice of potential liability for costs: further provision

(1)   A notice of potential liability for costs—
    (a)   may be registered in relation to a flat only on the application of—
        (i)   the owner of the flat;
        (ii)   the owner of any other flat in the same tenement; or
        (iii)   any manager (within the meaning of the Tenement Management Scheme) of the tenement; and
    (b)   shall not be registered unless it is signed by or on behalf of the applicant.
(2)   A notice of potential liability for costs may be registered—
    (a)   in relation to more than one flat in respect of the same maintenance or work; and
    (b)   in relation to any one flat, in respect of different maintenance or work.
(3)   A notice of potential liability for costs expires at the end of the period of 3 years beginning with the date of its registration, unless the notice is renewed by being registered again before the end of that period.
(4)   This section applies to a renewed notice of potential liability for costs as it applies to any other such notice.
(5)   The Keeper of the Registers of Scotland shall not be required to investigate

or determine whether the information contained in any notice of potential liability
for costs submitted for registration is accurate.

(6)   The Scottish Ministers may by order amend schedule 2 to this Act.

(7)   *[Amends Land Registration (Scotland) Act 1979.]*

14   Former owner's right to recover costs

An owner who is entitled, by virtue of the Tenement Management Scheme or any
other provision of this Act, to recover any costs or a share of any costs from any
other owner shall not, by virtue only of ceasing to be an owner, cease to be entitled
to recover those costs or that share.

15   *[Amends Prescription and Limitation (Scotland) Act 1973.]*

16   Common property: disapplication of common law right of recovery

Any rule of law which enables an owner of common property to recover the cost
of necessary maintenance from the other owners of the property shall not apply in
relation to any common property in a tenement where the maintenance of that
property is provided for in the management scheme which applies as respects the
tenement.

17   Access for maintenance and other purposes

(1)   Where an owner gives reasonable notice to the owner or occupier of any
other part of the tenement that access is required to, or through, that part for any
of the purposes mentioned in subsection (3) below, the person given notice shall,
subject to subsection (5) below, allow access for that purpose.

(2)   Without prejudice to subsection (1) above, where the development management scheme applies, notice under that subsection may be given by any owners'
association established by the scheme to the owner or occupier of any part of the
tenement.

(3)   The purposes are—

(a)   carrying out maintenance or other work by virtue of the management
scheme which applies as respects the tenement;

(b)   carrying out maintenance to any part of the tenement owned (whether
solely or in common) by the person requiring access;

(c)   carrying out an inspection to determine whether it is necessary to carry
out maintenance;

(d)   determining whether the owner of the part is fulfilling the duty imposed
by section 8(1) of this Act;

(e)   determining whether the owner or occupier of the part is complying
with the prohibition imposed by section 9(1) of this Act;

(f)   doing anything which the owner giving notice is entitled to do by virtue
of section 19(1) of this Act;

(g)   where floor area is relevant for the purposes of determining any liability
of owners, measuring floor area; and

(h)   where a power of sale order has been granted in relation to the tenement
building or its site, doing anything necessary for the purpose of or in connection
with any sale in pursuance of the order (other than complying with paragraph
4(3) of schedule 3 to this Act).

(4)   Reasonable notice need not be given as mentioned in subsection (1) above
where access is required for the purpose specified in subsection (3)(a) above and
the maintenance or other work requires to be carried out urgently.

(5)   An owner or occupier may refuse to allow—

(a)   access under subsection (1) above; or

(b)   such access at a particular time,

if, having regard to all the circumstances (and, in particular, whether the requirement for access is reasonable), it is reasonable to refuse access.

(6)   Where access is allowed under subsection (1) above for any purpose, such
right of access may be exercised by—

(a)   the owner who or owners' association which gave notice that access was required; or

(b)   such person as the owner or, as the case may be, owners' association may authorise for the purpose (any such person being referred to in this section as an 'authorised person').

(7)   Where an authorised person acting in accordance with subsection (6) above is liable by virtue of any enactment or rule of law for damage caused to any part of a tenement, the owner who or owners' association which authorised that person shall be severally liable with the authorised person for the cost of remedying the damage; but an owner or, as the case may be, owners' association making any payment as respects that cost shall have a right of relief against the authorised person.

(8)   Where access is allowed under subsection (1) above for any purpose, the owner who or owners' association which gave notice that access was required (referred to as the 'accessing owner or association') shall, so far as reasonably practicable, ensure that the part of the tenement to or through which access is allowed is left substantially in no worse a condition than that which it was in when access was taken.

(9)   If the accessing owner or association fails to comply with the duty in subsection (8) above, the owner of the part to or through which access is allowed may—

(a)   carry out, or arrange for the carrying out of, such work as is reasonably necessary to restore the part so that it is substantially in no worse a condition than that which it was in when access was taken; and

(b)   recover from the accessing owner or association any expenses reasonably incurred in doing so.

Insurance

18   Obligation of owner to insure

(1)   It shall be the duty of each owner to effect and keep in force a contract of insurance against the prescribed risks for the reinstatement value of that owner's flat and any part of the tenement building attaching to that flat as a pertinent.

(2)   The duty imposed by subsection (1) above may be satisfied, in whole or in part, by way of a common policy of insurance arranged for the entire tenement building.

(3)   The Scottish Ministers may by order prescribe risks against which an owner shall require to insure (in this section referred to as the 'prescribed risks').

(4)   Where, whether because of the location of the tenement or otherwise, an owner—

(a)   having made reasonable efforts to do so, is unable to obtain insurance against a particular prescribed risk; or

(b)   would be able to obtain such insurance but only at a cost which is unreasonably high,

the duty imposed by subsection (1) above shall not require an owner to insure against that particular risk.

(5)   Any owner may by notice in writing request the owner of any other flat in the tenement to produce evidence of—

(a)   the policy in respect of any contract of insurance which the owner of that other flat is required to have or to effect; and

(b)   payment of the premium for any such policy,

and not later than 14 days after that notice is given the recipient shall produce to the owner giving the notice the evidence requested.

(6)   The duty imposed by subsection (1) above on an owner may be enforced by any other owner.

Installation of service pipes etc

19 Installation of service pipes etc

(1) Subject to subsections (2) and (3) below and to section 17 of this Act, an owner shall be entitled—

(a) to lead through any part of the tenement such pipe, cable or other equipment; and

(b) to fix to any part of the tenement, and keep there, such equipment,

as is necessary for the provision to that owner's flat of such service or services as the Scottish Ministers may by regulations prescribe.

(2) The right conferred by subsection (1) above is exercisable only in accordance with such procedure as the Scottish Ministers may by regulations prescribe; and different procedures may be so prescribed in relation to different services.

(3) An owner is not entitled by virtue of subsection (1) above to lead anything through or fix anything to any part which is wholly within another owner's flat.

(4) This section is without prejudice to any obligation imposed by virtue of any enactment relating to—

(a) planning;

(b) building; or

(c) any service prescribed under subsection (1) above.

Demolition and abandonment of tenement building

20 Demolition of tenement building not to affect ownership

(1) The demolition of a tenement building shall not alone effect any change as respects any right of ownership.

(2) In particular, the fact that, as a consequence of demolition of a tenement building, any land pertaining to the building no longer serves, or affords access to, any flat or other sector shall not alone effect any change of ownership of the land as a pertinent.

21 Cost of demolishing tenement building

(1) Except where a tenement burden otherwise provides, the cost of demolishing a tenement building shall, subject to subsection (2) below, be shared equally among all (or both) the flats in the tenement, and each owner is liable accordingly.

(2) Where the floor area of the largest (or larger) flat in the tenement is more than one and a half times that of the smallest (or smaller) flat the owner of each flat shall be liable to contribute towards the cost of demolition of the tenement building in the proportion which the floor area of that owner's flat bears to the total floor area of all (or both) the flats.

(3) An owner is liable under this section for the cost of demolishing a tenement building—

(a) in the case where the owner agrees to the proposal that the tenement building be demolished, from the date of the agreement; or

(b) in any other case, from the date on which the carrying out of the demolition is instructed.

(4) This section applies as respects the demolition of part of a tenement building as it applies as respects the demolition of an entire tenement building but with any reference to a flat in the tenement being construed as a reference to a flat in the part.

(5) In this section references to flats in a tenement include references to flats which were comprehended by the tenement before its demolition.

(6) This section is subject to section 123 of the Housing (Scotland) Act 1987 (c 26) (which makes provision as respects demolition of buildings in pursuance of local authority demolition orders and recovery of expenses by local authorities etc).

22   Use and disposal of site where tenement building demolished

(1)   This section applies where a tenement building is demolished and after the demolition two or more flats which were comprehended by the tenement building before its demolition (any such flat being referred to in this section as a 'former flat') are owned by different persons.

(2)   Except in so far as—

(a)   the owners of all (or both) the former flats otherwise agree; or

(b)   those owners are subject to a requirement (whether imposed by a tenement burden or otherwise) to erect a building on the site or to rebuild the tenement,

no owner may build on, or otherwise develop, the site.

(3)   Except where the owners have agreed, or are required, to build on or develop the site as mentioned in paragraphs (a) and (b) of subsection (2) above, any owner of a former flat shall be entitled to apply for power to sell the entire site in accordance with schedule 3.

(4)   Except where a tenement burden otherwise provides, the net proceeds of any sale in pursuance of subsection (3) above shall, subject to subsection (5) below, be shared equally among all (or both) the former flats and the owner of each former flat shall be entitled to the share allocated to that flat.

(5)   Where—

(a)   evidence of the floor area of each of the former flats is readily available; and

(b)   the floor area of the largest (or larger) former flat was more than one and a half times that of the smallest (or smaller) former flat,

the net proceeds of any sale shall be shared among (or between) the flats in the proportion which the floor area of each flat bore to the total floor area of all (or both) the flats and the owner of each former flat shall be entitled to the share allocated to that flat.

(6)   The prohibition imposed by subsection (2) above on an owner of a former flat may be enforced by any other such owner.

(7)   In subsections (4) and (5) above, 'net proceeds of any sale' means the proceeds of the sale less any expenses properly incurred in connection with the sale.

(8)   In this section references to the site are references to the solum of the tenement building that occupied the site together with the airspace that is directly above the solum and any land pertaining, as a means of access, to the tenement building immediately before its demolition.

23   Sale of abandoned tenement building

(1)   Where—

(a)   because of its poor condition a tenement building has been entirely unoccupied by any owner or person authorised by an owner for a period of more than six months; and

(b)   it is unlikely that any such owner or other person will occupy any part of the tenement building,

any owner shall be entitled to apply for power to sell the tenement building in accordance with schedule 3.

(2)   Subsections (4) and (5) of section 22 of this Act shall apply as respects a sale in pursuance of subsection (1) above as those subsections apply as respects a sale in pursuance of subsection (3) of that section.

(3)   In this section any reference to a tenement building includes a reference to its solum and any land pertaining, as a means of access, to the tenement building.

Liability for certain costs

24   Liability to non owner for certain damage costs

(1)   Where—

(a)   any part of a tenement is damaged as the result of the fault of any person (that person being in this subsection referred to as 'A'); and

(b)   the management scheme which applies as respects the tenement makes provision for the maintenance of that part,

any owner of a flat in the tenement (that owner being in this subsection referred to as 'B') who is required by virtue of that provision to contribute to any extent to the cost of maintenance of the damaged part but who at the time when the damage was done was not an owner of the part shall be treated, for the purpose of determining whether A is liable to B as respects the cost of maintenance arising from the damage, as having been such an owner at that time.

(2)   In this section 'fault' means any wrongful act, breach of statutory duty or negligent act or omission which gives rise to liability in damages.

Miscellaneous and general

26   Meaning of 'tenement'

(1)   In this Act, 'tenement' means a building or a part of a building which comprises two related flats which, or more than two such flats at least two of which—

(a)   are, or are designed to be, in separate ownership; and

(b)   are divided from each other horizontally,

and, except where the context otherwise requires, includes the solum and any other land pertaining to that building or, as the case may be, part of the building; and the expression 'tenement building' shall be construed accordingly.

(2)   In determining whether flats comprised in a building or part of a building are related for the purposes of subsection (1), regard shall be had, among other things, to—

(a)   the title to the tenement; and

(b)   any tenement burdens,

treating the building or part for that purpose as if it were a tenement.

27   Meaning of 'management scheme'

References in this Act to the management scheme which applies as respects any tenement are references to—

(a)   if the Tenement Management Scheme applies in its entirety as respects the tenement, that Scheme;

(b)   if the development management scheme applies as respects the tenement, that scheme; or

(c)   in any other case, any tenement burdens relating to maintenance, management or improvement of the tenement together with any provisions of the Tenement Management Scheme which apply as respects the tenement.

28   Meaning of 'owner', determination of liability etc

(1)   In this Act, references to 'owner' without further qualification are, in relation to any tenement, references to the owner of a flat in the tenement.

(2)   Subject to subsection (3) below, in this Act 'owner' means, in relation to a flat in a tenement, a person who has right to the flat whether or not that person has completed title; but if, in relation to the flat (or, if the flat is held pro indiviso, any pro indiviso share in it) more than one person comes within that description of owner, then 'owner' means such person as has most recently acquired such right.

(3)   Where a heritable security has been granted over a flat and the heritable creditor has entered into lawful possession, 'owner' means the heritable creditor in possession of the flat.

(4)   Subject to subsection (5) below, if two or more persons own a flat in common, any reference in this Act to an owner is a reference to both or, as the case may be, all of them.

(5)   Any reference to an owner in sections 5(1) and (2), 6(1), 8(3), 9, 10, 12 to 14, 17(1), (6) and (7), 18(5) and (6), 19, 22, 23 and 24 of, and schedule 3 to, this Act shall be construed as a reference to any person who owns a flat either solely or in common with another.

(6)   Subsections (2) to (5) above apply to references in this Act to the owner of a part of a tenement as they apply to references to the owner of a flat, but as if references in them to a flat were to the part of the tenement.

(7)   Where two or more persons own a flat in common—

(a)   they are severally liable for the performance of any obligation imposed by virtue of this Act on the owner of that flat; and

(b)   as between (or among) themselves they are liable in the proportions in which they own the flat.

29   Interpretation

(1)   In this Act, unless the content otherwise requires—

'chimney stack' does not include flue or chimney pot;

'close' means a connected passage, stairs and landings within a tenement building which together constitute a common access to two or more of the flats;

'demolition' includes destruction and cognate expressions shall be construed accordingly; and demolition may occur on one occasion or over any period of time;

'the development management scheme' has the meaning given by section 71(3) of the Title Conditions (Scotland) Act 2003 (asp 9);

'door' includes its frame;

'flat' includes any premises whether or not—

(a)   used or intended to be used for residential purposes; or

(b)   on the one floor;

'lift' includes its shaft and operating machinery;

'local authority' means a council constituted under section 2 of the Local Government etc. (Scotland) Act 1994 (c 39);

'owner' shall be construed in accordance with section 28 of this Act;

'power of sale order' means an order granted under paragraph 1 of schedule 3 to this Act;

'register', in relation to a notice of potential liability for costs or power of sale order, means register the information contained in the notice or order in the Land Register of Scotland or, as appropriate, record the notice or order in the Register of Sasines, and 'registered' and other related expressions shall be construed accordingly;

'sector' means—

(a)   a flat;

(b)   any close or lift; or

(c)   any other three dimensional space not comprehended by a flat, close or lift,

and the tenement building shall be taken to be entirely divided into sectors;

'solum' means the ground on which a building is erected;

'tenement' shall be construed in accordance with section 26 of this Act;

'tenement burden' means, in relation to a tenement, any real burden (within the meaning of the Title Conditions (Scotland) Act 2003 (asp 9)) which affects—

(a)   the tenement; or

(b)   any sector in the tenement;

'Tenement Management Scheme' means the scheme set out in schedule 1 to this Act;

'title to the tenement' shall be construed in accordance with section 1(2) of this Act; and

'window' includes its frame.

(2)   The floor area of a flat is calculated for the purposes of this Act by measuring the total floor area (including the area occupied by any internal wall or other

internal dividing structure) within its boundaries; but no account shall be taken of any pertinents or any of the following parts of a flat—

(a)   a balcony; and

(b)   except where it is used for any purpose other than storage, a loft or basement.

30   Giving of notice to owners

(1)   Any notice which is to be given to an owner under or in connection with this Act (other than under or in connection with the Tenement Management Scheme) may be given in writing by sending the notice to—

(a)   the owner; or

(b)   the owner's agent.

(2)   The reference in subsection (1) above to sending a notice is to its being—

(a)   posted;

(b)   delivered; or

(c)   transmitted by electronic means.

(3)   Where an owner cannot by reasonable inquiry be identified or found, a notice shall be taken for the purposes of subsection (1)(a) above to be sent to the owner if it is posted or delivered to the owner's flat addressed to 'The Owner' or using some similar expression such as 'The Proprietor'.

(4)   For the purposes of this Act—

(a)   a notice posted shall be taken to be given on the day of posting; and

(b)   a notice transmitted by electronic means shall be taken to be given on the day of transmission.

31   Ancillary provision

(1)   The Scottish Ministers may by order make such incidental, supplemental, consequential, transitional, transitory or saving provision as they consider necessary or expedient for the purposes, or in consequence, of this Act.

(2)   An order under this section may modify any enactment (including this Act), instrument or document.

32   Orders and regulations

(1)   Any power of the Scottish Ministers to make orders or regulations under this Act shall be exercisable by statutory instrument.

(2)   A statutory instrument containing an order or regulations under this Act (except an order under section 34(2) or, where subsection (3) applies, section 31) shall be subject to annulment in pursuance of a resolution of the Scottish Parliament.

(3)   Where an order under section 31 contains provisions which add to, replace or omit any part of the text of an Act, the order shall not be made unless a draft of the statutory instrument containing the order has been laid before, and approved by a resolution of, the Parliament.

33   Crown application

This Act, except section 18, binds the Crown.

34   Short title and commencement

(1)   This Act may be cited as the Tenements (Scotland) Act 2004.

(2)   This Act (other than this section, section 25 and schedule 4) shall come into force on such day as the Scottish Ministers may by order appoint; and different days may be appointed for different purposes.

(3)   Section 25 and schedule 4 shall come into force on the day after Royal Assent.

SCHEDULES

RULE 1—SCOPE AND INTERPRETATION

1.1 Scope of scheme
This scheme provides for the management and maintenance of the scheme property of a tenement.

1.2 Meaning of 'scheme property'
For the purposes of this scheme, 'scheme property' means, in relation to a tenement, all or any of the following—

(a) any part of the tenement that is the common property of two or more of the owners,

(b) any part of the tenement (not being common property of the type mentioned in paragraph (a) above) the maintenance of which, or the cost of maintaining which, is, by virtue of a tenement burden, the responsibility of two or more of the owners,

(c) with the exceptions mentioned in rule 1.3, the following parts of the tenement building (so far as not scheme property by virtue of paragraph (a) or (b) above)—

(i) the ground on which it is built,

(ii) its foundations,

(iii) its external walls,

(iv) its roof (including any rafter or other structure supporting the roof),

(v) if it is separated from another building by a gable wall, the part of the gable wall that is part of the tenement building, and

(vi) any wall (not being one falling within the preceding sub-paragraphs), beam or column that is load bearing.

1.3 Parts not included in rule 1.2(c)
The following parts of a tenement building are the exceptions referred to in rule 1.2(c)—

(a) any extension which forms part of only one flat,

(b) any—

(i) door,

(ii) window,

(iii) skylight,

(iv) vent, or

(v) other opening,

which serves only one flat,

(c) any chimney stack or chimney flue.

1.4 Meaning of 'scheme decision'
A decision is a 'scheme decision' for the purposes of this scheme if it is made in accordance with—

(a) rule 2, or

(b) where that rule does not apply, the tenement burden or burdens providing the procedure for the making of decisions by the owners.

1.5 Other definitions
In this scheme—

'maintenance' includes repairs and replacement, cleaning, painting and other routine works, gardening, the day to day running of a tenement and the reinstate-

ment of a part (but not most) of the tenement building, but does not include demolition, alteration or improvement unless reasonably incidental to the maintenance,

'manager' means, in relation to a tenement, a person appointed (whether or not
by virtue of rule 3.1(c)(i)) to manage the tenement, and

'scheme costs' has the meaning given by rule 4.1.

1.6   Rights of co owners
If a flat is owned by two or more persons, then one of them may do anything that
the owner is by virtue of this scheme entitled to do.

RULE 2—PROCEDURE FOR MAKING SCHEME DECISIONS

2.1   Making scheme decisions
Any decision to be made by the owners shall be made in accordance with the
following provisions of this rule.

2.2   Allocation and exercise of votes
Except as mentioned in rule 2.3, for the purpose of voting on any proposed
scheme decision one vote is allocated as respects each flat, and any right to vote is
exercisable by the owner of that flat or by someone nominated by the owner to
vote as respects the flat.

2.3   Qualification on allocation of votes
No vote is allocated as respects a flat if—
  (a)   the scheme decision relates to the maintenance of scheme property, and
  (b)   the owner of that flat is not liable for maintenance of, or the cost of maintaining, the property concerned.

2.4   Exercise of vote where two or more persons own flat
If a flat is owned by two or more persons the vote allocated as respects that flat
may be exercised in relation to any proposal by either (or any) of them, but if
those persons disagree as to how the vote should be cast then the vote is not to be
counted unless—
  (a)   where one of those persons owns more than a half share of the flat, the
  vote is exercised by that person, or
  (b)   in any other case, the vote is the agreed vote of those who together own
  more than a half share of the flat.

2.5   Decision by majority
A scheme decision is made by majority vote of all the votes allocated.

2.6   Notice of meeting
If any owner wishes to call a meeting of the owners with a view to making a
scheme decision at that meeting that owner must give the other owners at least 48
hours' notice of the date and time of the meeting, its purpose and the place where
it is to be held.

2.7   Consultation of owners if scheme decision not made at meeting
If an owner wishes to propose that a scheme decision be made but does not wish
to call a meeting for the purpose that owner must instead—
  (a)   unless it is impracticable to do so (whether because of absence of any
  owner or for other good reason) consult on the proposal each of the other
  owners of flats as respects which votes are allocated, and
  (b)   count the votes cast by them.

2.8   Consultation where two or more persons own flat
For the purposes of rule 2.7, the requirement to consult each owner is satisfied as
respects any flat which is owned by more than one person if one of those persons
is consulted.

2.9 Notification of scheme decisions
A scheme decision must, as soon as practicable, be notified—

(a) if it was made at a meeting, to all the owners who were not present when the decision was made, by such person as may be nominated for the purpose by the persons who made the decision, or

(b) in any other case, to each of the other owners, by the owner who proposed that the decision be made.

2.10 Case where decision may be annulled by notice
Any owner (or owners) who did not vote in favour of a scheme decision to carry out, or authorise, maintenance to scheme property and who would be liable for not less than 75 per cent. of the scheme costs arising from that decision may, within the time mentioned in rule 2.11, annul that decision by giving notice that the decision is annulled to each of the other owners.

2.11 Time limits for rule 2.10
The time within which a notice under rule 2.10 must be given is—

(a) if the scheme decision was made at a meeting attended by the owner (or any of the owners), not later than 21 days after the date of that meeting, or

(b) in any other case, not later than 21 days after the date on which notification of the making of the decision was given to the owner or owners (that date being, where notification was given to owners on different dates, the date on which it was given to the last of them).

RULE 3—MATTERS ON WHICH SCHEME DECISIONS MAY BE MADE

3.1 Basic scheme decisions
The owners may make a scheme decision on any of the following matters—

(a) to carry out maintenance to scheme property,

(b) to arrange for an inspection of scheme property to determine whether or to what extent it is necessary to carry out maintenance to the property,

(c) except where a power conferred by a manager burden (within the meaning of the Title Conditions (Scotland) Act 2003 (asp 9)) is exercisable in relation to the tenement—

(i) to appoint on such terms as they may determine a person (who may be an owner or a firm) to manage the tenement,

(ii) to dismiss any manager,

(d) to delegate to a manager power to exercise such of their powers as they may specify, including, without prejudice to that generality, any power to decide to carry out maintenance and to instruct it,

(e) to arrange for the tenement a common policy of insurance complying with section 18 of this Act and against such other risks (if any) as the owners may determine and to determine on an equitable basis the liability of each owner to contribute to the premium,

(f) to install a system enabling entry to the tenement to be controlled from each flat,

(g) to determine that an owner is not required to pay a share (or some part of a share) of such scheme costs as may be specified by them,

(h) to authorise any maintenance of scheme property already carried out,

(i) to modify or revoke any scheme decision.

3.2 Scheme decisions relating to maintenance
If the owners make a scheme decision to carry out maintenance to scheme property or if a manager decides, by virtue of a scheme decision, that maintenance needs to be carried out to scheme property, the owners may make a scheme decision on any of the following matters—

(a)   to appoint on such terms as they may determine a person (who may be an owner or a firm) to manage the carrying out of the maintenance,

(b)   to instruct or arrange for the carrying out of the maintenance,

(c)   subject to rule 3.3, to require each owner to deposit—

(i)   by such date as they may decide (being a date not less than 28 days after the requirement is made of that owner), and

(ii)   with such person as they may nominate for the purpose,

a sum of money (being a sum not exceeding that owner's apportioned share of a reasonable estimate of the cost of the maintenance),

(d)   to take such other steps as are necessary to ensure that the maintenance is carried out to a satisfactory standard and completed in good time.

3.3   Scheme decisions under rule 3.2(c) requiring deposits exceeding certain amounts

A requirement, in pursuance of a scheme decision under rule 3.2(c), that each owner deposit a sum of money—

(a)   exceeding £100, or

(b)   of £100 or less where the aggregate of that sum taken together with any other sum or sums required (otherwise than by a previous notice under this rule) in the preceding 12 months to be deposited by each owner by virtue any scheme decision under rule 3.2(c) exceeds £200,

shall be made by written notice to each owner and shall require the sum to be deposited into such account (the 'maintenance account') as the owners may nominate for the purpose.

3.4   Provision supplementary to rule 3.3

Where a requirement is, or is to be, made in accordance with rule 3.3—

(a)   the owners may make a scheme decision authorising a manager or at least two other persons (whether or not owners) to operate the maintenance account on behalf of the owners,

(b)   there must be contained in or attached to the notice to be given under rule 3.3 a note comprising a summary of the nature and extent of the maintenance to be carried out together with the following information—

(i)   the estimated cost of carrying out that maintenance,

(ii)   why the estimate is considered a reasonable estimate,

(iii)   how the sum required from the owner in question and the apportionment among the owners have been arrived at,

(iv)   what the apportioned shares of the other owners are,

(v)   the date on which the decision to carry out the maintenance was made and the names of those by whom it was made,

(vi)   a timetable for the carrying out of the maintenance, including the dates by which it is proposed the maintenance will be commenced and completed,

(vii)   the location and number of the maintenance account, and

(viii)   the names and addresses of the persons who will be authorised to operate that account on behalf of the owners,

(c)   the maintenance account to be nominated under rule 3.3 must be a bank or building society account which is interest bearing, and the authority of at least two persons or of a manager on whom has been conferred the right to give authority, must be required for any payment from it,

(d)   if a modification or revocation under rule 3.1(i) affects the information contained in the notice or the note referred to in paragraph (b) above, the information must be sent again, modified accordingly, to the owners,

(e)   an owner is entitled to inspect, at any reasonable time, any tender received in connection with the maintenance to be carried out,

(f)   the notice to be given under rule 3.3 may specify a date as a refund date for the purposes of paragraph (g)(i) below,

(g)   if—
    (i)   the maintenance is not commenced by—
        (A) where the notice under rule 3.3 specifies a refund date, that date, or
        (B) where that notice does not specify such a date, the twenty-eighth day after the proposed date for its commencement as specified in the notice by virtue of paragraph (b)(vi) above, and
    (ii) a depositor demands, by written notice, from the persons authorised under paragraph (a) above repayment (with accrued interest) of such sum as has been deposited by that person in compliance with the scheme decision under rule 3.2(c),

the depositor is entitled to be repaid accordingly, except that no requirement to make repayment in compliance with a notice under sub-paragraph (ii) arises if the persons so authorised do not receive that notice before the maintenance is commenced,

(h)   such sums as are held in the maintenance account by virtue of rule 3.3 are held in trust for all the depositors, for the purpose of being used by the persons authorised to make payments from the account as payment for the maintenance,

(i)   any sums held in the maintenance account after all sums payable in respect of the maintenance carried out have been paid shall be shared among the depositors—
    (i)   by repaying each depositor, with any accrued interest and after deduction of that person's apportioned share of the actual cost of the maintenance, the sum which the person deposited, or
    (ii) in such other way as the depositors agree in writing.

3.5   Scheme decisions under rule 3.1(g): votes of persons standing to benefit not to be counted

A vote in favour of a scheme decision under rule 3.1(g) is not to be counted if—
    (a)   the owner exercising the vote, or
    (b)   where the vote is exercised by a person nominated by an owner—
        (i)   that person, or
        (ii) the owner who nominated that person,
is the owner or an owner who, by virtue of the decision, would not be required to pay as mentioned in that rule.

RULE 4—SCHEME COSTS: LIABILITY AND APPORTIONMENT

4.1   Meaning of 'scheme costs'

Except in so far as rule 5 applies, this rule provides for the apportionment of liability among the owners for any of the following costs—
    (a)   any costs arising from any maintenance or inspection of scheme property where the maintenance or inspection is in pursuance of, or authorised by, a scheme decision,
    (b)   any remuneration payable to a person appointed to manage the carrying out of such maintenance as is mentioned in paragraph (a),
    (c)   running costs relating to any scheme property (other than costs incurred solely for the benefit of one flat),
    (d)   any costs recoverable by a local authority in respect of work relating to any scheme property carried out by them by virtue of any enactment,
    (e)   any remuneration payable to any manager,
    (f)   the cost of any common insurance to cover the tenement,
    (g)   the cost of installing a system enabling entry to the tenement to be controlled from each flat,

(h)   any costs relating to the calculation of the floor area of any flat, where such calculation is necessary for the purpose of determining the share of any other costs for which each owner is liable,

(i)   any other costs relating to the management of scheme property, and a reference in this scheme to 'scheme costs' is a reference to any of the costs mentioned in paragraphs (a) to (i).

4.2   Maintenance and running costs

Except as provided in rule 4.3, if any scheme costs mentioned in rule 4.1(a) to (d) relate to—

(a)   the scheme property mentioned in rule 1.2(a), then those costs are shared among the owners in the proportions in which the owners share ownership of that property,

(b)   the scheme property mentioned in rule 1.2(b) or (c), then—

(i)   in any case where the floor area of the largest (or larger) flat is more than one and a half times that of the smallest (or smaller) flat, each owner is liable to contribute towards those costs in the proportion which the floor area of that owner's flat bears to the total floor area of all (or both) the flats,

(ii)   in any other case, those costs are shared equally among the flats, and each owner is liable accordingly.

4.3   Scheme costs relating to roof over the close

Where—

(a)   any scheme costs mentioned in rule 4.1(a) to (d) relate to the roof over the close, and

(b)   that roof is common property by virtue of section 3(1)(a) of this Act, then, despite the fact that the roof is scheme property mentioned in rule 1.2(a), paragraph (b) of rule 4.2 shall apply for the purpose of apportioning liability for those costs.

4.4   Insurance premium

Any scheme costs mentioned in rule 4.1(f) are shared among the flats—

(a)   where the costs relate to common insurance arranged by virtue of rule 3.1(e), in such proportions as may be determined by the owners by virtue of that rule, or

(b)   where the costs relate to common insurance arranged by virtue of a tenement burden, equally, and each owner is liable accordingly.

4.5   Other scheme costs

Any scheme costs mentioned in rule 4.1(e), (g), (h) or (i) are shared equally among the flats, and each owner is liable accordingly.

RULE 5—REDISTRIBUTION OF SHARE OF COSTS

Where an owner is liable for a share of any scheme costs but—

(a)   a scheme decision has been made determining that the share (or a portion of it) should not be paid by that owner, or

(b)   the share cannot be recovered for some other reason such as that—

(i)   the estate of that owner has been sequestrated, or

(ii)   that owner cannot, by reasonable inquiry, be identified or found, then that share must be paid by the other owners who are liable for a share of the same costs (the share being divided equally among the flats of those other owners), but where paragraph (b) applies that owner is liable to each of those other owners for the amount paid by each of them.

RULE 6—PROCEDURAL IRREGULARITIES

6.1 Validity of scheme decisions
Any procedural irregularity in the making of a scheme decision does not affect the validity of the decision.

6.2 Liability for scheme costs where procedural irregularity
If any owner is directly affected by a procedural irregularity in the making of a scheme decision and that owner—
    (a) was not aware that any scheme costs relating to that decision were being incurred, or
    (b) on becoming aware as mentioned in paragraph (a), immediately objected to the incurring of those costs,
that owner is not liable for any such costs (whether incurred before or after the date of objection), and, for the purposes of determining the share of those scheme costs due by each of the other owners, that owner is left out of account.

RULE 7—EMERGENCY WORK

7.1 Power to instruct or carry out
Any owner may instruct or carry out emergency work

7.2 Liability for cost
The owners are liable for the cost of any emergency work instructed or carried out as if the cost of that work were scheme costs mentioned in rule 4.1(a).

7.3 Meaning of 'emergency work'
For the purposes of this rule, 'emergency work' means work which, before a scheme decision can be obtained, requires to be carried out to scheme property—
    (a) to prevent damage to any part of the tenement, or
    (b) in the interests of health or safety.

RULE 8—ENFORCEMENT

8.1 Scheme binding on owners
This scheme binds the owners.

8.2 Scheme decision to be binding
A scheme decision is binding on the owners and their successors as owners.

8.3 Enforceability of scheme decisions
Any obligation imposed by this scheme or arising from a scheme decision may be enforced by any owner.

8.4 Enforcement by third party
Any person authorised in writing for the purpose by the owner or owners concerned may—
    (a) enforce an obligation such as is mentioned in rule 8.3 on behalf of one or more owners, and
    (b) in doing so, may bring any claim or action in that person's own name.

RULE 9—GIVING OF NOTICE

9.1 Giving of notice
Any notice which requires to be given to an owner under or in connection with this scheme may be given in writing by sending the notice to—
    (a) the owner, or
    (b) the owner's agent.

9.2 Methods of 'sending' for the purposes of rule 9.1
The reference in rule 9.1 to sending a notice is to its being—
    (a)   posted,
    (b)   delivered, or
    (c)   transmitted by electronic means.

9.3 Giving of notice to owner where owner's name is not known
Where an owner cannot by reasonable inquiry be identified or found, a notice shall be taken for the purposes of rule 9.1(a) to be sent to the owner if it is posted or delivered to the owner's flat addressed to 'The Owner' or using some other similar expression such as 'The Proprietor'.

9.4 Day on which notice is to be taken to be given
For the purposes of this scheme—
    (a)   a notice posted shall be taken to be given on the day of posting, and
    (b)   a notice transmitted by electronic means shall be taken to be given on the day of transmission.

SCHEDULE 2

FORM OF NOTICE OF POTENTIAL LIABILITY FOR COSTS

(introduced by section 12(3))

'NOTICE OF POTENTIAL LIABILITY FOR COSTS

This notice gives details of certain maintenance or work carried out [or to be carried out] in relation to the flat specified in the notice. The effect of the notice is that a person may, on becoming the owner of the flat, be liable by virtue of section 12(3) of the Tenements (Scotland) Act 2004 (asp 11) for any outstanding costs relating to the maintenance or work.

Flat to which notice relates:
(see note 1 below)

Description of the maintenance or work to which notice relates:
(see note 2 below)

Person giving notice:
(see note 3 below)

Signature:
(see note 4 below)

Date of signing:'

Notes for completion

(These notes are not part of the notice)
    1   Describe the flat in a way that is sufficient to identify it. Where the flat has a postal address, the description must include that address. Where title to the flat has been registered in the Land Register of Scotland, the description must refer to the title number of the flat or of the larger subjects of which it forms part. Otherwise, the description should normally refer to and identify a deed recorded in a specified division of the Register of Sasines.
    2   Describe the maintenance or work in general terms.
    3   Give the name and address of the person applying for registration of the notice ('the applicant') or the applicant's name and the name and address of the applicant's agent.
    4   The notice must be signed by or on behalf of the applicant.

SCHEDULE 3
SALE UNDER SECTION 22(3) OR 23(1)
(introduced by sections 22(3) and 23(1)

1 Application to sheriff for power to sell

(1) Where an owner is entitled to apply—

(a) under section 22(3), for power to sell the site; or

(b) under section 23(1), for power to sell the tenement building, the owner may make a summary application to the sheriff seeking an order (referred to in this Act as a 'power of sale order') conferring such power on the owner.

(2) The site or tenement building in relation to which an application or order is made under sub-paragraph (1) is referred to in this schedule as the 'sale subjects'.

(3) An owner making an application under sub-paragraph (1) shall give notice of it to each of the other owners of the sale subjects.

(4) The sheriff shall, on an application under sub-paragraph (1)—

(a) grant the power of sale order sought unless satisfied that to do so would—

(i) not be in the best interests of all (or both) the owners taken as a group; or

(ii) be unfairly prejudicial to one or more of the owners; and

(b) if a power of sale order has previously been granted in respect of the same sale subjects, revoke that previous order.

(5) A power of sale order shall contain—

(a) the name and address of the owner in whose favour it is granted;

(b) the postal address of each flat or, as the case may be, former flat comprised in the sale subjects to which the order relates; and

(c) a sufficient conveyancing description of each of those flats or former flats.

(6) A description of a flat or former flat is a sufficient conveyancing description for the purposes of sub-paragraph (5)(c) if—

(a) where the interest of the proprietor of the land comprising the flat or former flat has been registered in the Land Register of Scotland, the description refers to the number of the title sheet of that interest; or

(b) in relation to any other flat or former flat, the description is by reference to a deed recorded in the Register of Sasines.

(7) An application under sub-paragraph (1) shall state the applicant's conclusions as to—

(a) which of subsections (4) and (5) of section 22 applies for the purpose of determining how the net proceeds of any sale of the sale subjects in pursuance of a power of sale order are to be shared among the owners of those subjects; and

(b) if subsection (5) of that section is stated as applying for that purpose—

(i) the floor area of each of the flats or former flats comprised in the sale subjects; and

(ii) the proportion of the net proceeds of sale allocated to that flat.

2 Appeal against grant or refusal of power of sale order

(1) A party may, not later than 14 days after the date of—

(a) making of a power of sale order; or

(b) an interlocutor refusing an application for such an order, appeal to the Court of Session on a point of law.

(2) The decision of the Court of Session on any such appeal shall be final.

3 Registration of power of sale order

(1) A power of sale order has no effect—

(a) unless it is registered within the period of 14 days after the relevant day; and

(b)   until the beginning of the forty-second day after the day on which it is so registered.

(2)   In sub-paragraph (1)(a) above, 'the relevant day' means, in relation to a power of sale order—

(a)   the last day of the period of 14 days within which an appeal against the order may be lodged under paragraph 2(1) of this schedule; or

(b)   if such an appeal is duly lodged, the day on which the appeal is abandoned or determined.

4   Exercise of power of sale

(1)   An owner in whose favour a power of sale order is granted may exercise the power conferred by the order by private bargain or by exposure to sale.

(2)   However, in either case, the owner shall—

(a)   advertise the sale; and

(b)   take all reasonable steps to ensure that the price at which the sale subjects are sold is the best that can reasonably be obtained.

(3)   In advertising the sale in pursuance of sub-paragraph (2)(a) above, the owner shall, in particular, ensure that there is placed and maintained on the sale subjects a conspicuous sign—

(a)   advertising the fact that the sale subjects are for sale; and

(b)   giving the name and contact details of the owner or of any agent acting on the owner's behalf in connection with the sale.

(4)   So far as may be necessary for the purpose of complying with sub-paragraph (3) above, the owner or any person authorised by the owner shall be entitled to enter any part of the sale subjects not owned, or not owned exclusively, by that owner.

5   Distribution of proceeds of sale

(1)   An owner selling the sale subjects (referred to in this paragraph as the 'selling owner') shall, within seven days of completion of the sale—

(a)   calculate each owner's share; and

(b)   apply that share in accordance with sub-paragraph (2) below.

(2)   An owner's share shall be applied—

(a)   first, to repay any amounts due under any heritable security affecting that owner's flat or former flat;

(b)   next, to defray any expenses properly incurred in complying with paragraph (a) above; and

(c)   finally, to pay to the owner the remainder (if any) of that owner's share.

(3)   If there is more than one heritable security affecting an owner's flat or former flat, the owner's share shall be applied under paragraph (2)(a) above in relation to each security in the order in which they rank.

(4)   If any owner cannot by reasonable inquiry be identified or found, the selling owner shall consign the remainder of that owner's share in the sheriff court.

(5)   On paying to another owner the remainder of that owner's share, the selling owner shall also give to that other owner—

(a)   a written statement showing—

(i)   the amount of that owner's share and of the remainder of it; and

(ii)   how that share and remainder were calculated; and

(b)   evidence of—

(i)   the total amount of the proceeds of sale; and

(ii)   any expenses properly incurred in connection with the sale and in complying with sub-paragraph (2)(a) above.

(6)   In this paragraph—

'remainder', in relation to an owner's share, means the amount of that share remaining after complying with sub-paragraph (2)(a) and (b) above;

'share', in relation to an owner, means the share of the net proceeds of sale to which that owner is entitled in accordance with subsection (4) or, as the case may be, subsection (5) of section 22.

6 Automatic discharge of heritable securities

Where—

    (a) an owner—

        (i) sells the sale subjects in pursuance of a power of sale order; and

        (ii) grants a disposition of those subjects to the purchaser or the purchaser's nominee; and

    (b) that disposition is duly registered in the Land Register of Scotland or recorded in the Register of Sasines,

all heritable securities affecting the sale subjects or any part of them shall, by virtue of this paragraph, be to that extent discharged.

OTHER MATERIALS

MATRIMONIAL HOMES (FORM OF CONSENT) (SCOTLAND) REGULATIONS 1982
(SI 1982/129)

1—(1) These regulations may be cited as the Matrimonial Homes (Form of Consent) (Scotland) Regulations 1982 and shall come into operation on 1st September 1982.

(2) In these regulations—

'the Act' means the Matrimonial Homes (Family Protection) (Scotland) Act 1981, and, in a case where section 9(1) of the Act applies, any references in these regulations to the entitled spouse and to the non-entitled spouse shall be construed in accordance with section 9(2)(a) of the Act.

2   The consent of the non-entitled spouse to any dealing of the entitled spouse relating to a matrimonial home shall be—

(a)   where the consent is given in a deed effecting the dealing, in or as nearly as may be in the form set out in Schedule 1 to these regulation; or

(b)   where the consent is given in a separate document, in or as nearly as may be in the form set out in Schedule 2 to these regulations.

SCHEDULE 1
CONSENT TO BE INSERTED IN THE DEED EFFECTING THE DEALING

(The following words should be inserted where appropriate in the deed. The consenter should sign as a party to the deed.)

. . . with the consent of AB (*designation*), the spouse of the said CD, for the purposes of the Matrimonial Homes (Family Protection) (Scotland) Act 1981 . . . [To be attested]

SCHEDULE 2
CONSENT IN A SEPARATE DOCUMENT

I, AB (*designation*), spouse of CD (*designation*), hereby consent, for the purposes of the Matrimonial Homes (Family Protection) (Scotland) Act 1981, to the undernoted dealing of the said CD relating to (*here describe the matrimonial home or the part of it to which the dealer relates: see Note 1*).

Dealing referred to:—

(*Here describe the dealing: see Note 2.*)

[To be attested].

Note 1

The expression 'matrimonial home' is defined in section 22 of the Matrimonial Homes (Family Protection) (Scotland) Act 1981 as follows:—

'"matrimonial home" means any house, caravan, houseboat or other structure which has been provided or has been made available by one or both of the spouses as, or has become, a family residence and includes any garden or other ground or building attached to, and usually occupied with, or otherwise required for the amenity or convenience of, the house, caravan, houseboat or other structure.'

Note 2

The expression 'dealing' is defined in section 6(2) of the Matrimonial Homes (Family Protection) (Scotland) Act 1981 as follows:—

'"dealing" includes the grant of a heritable security and the creation of a trust but does not include a conveyance under section 80 of the Lands Clauses Consolidation (Scotland) Act 1845.'

LAND REGISTRATION (SCOTLAND) RULES 1980
(SI 1980/1413)

(as amended by Land Registration (Scotland) (Amendment) Rules SI 1982/974,
SI 1995/248, SI 1998/3100 and SSI 2004/476)

PART I
GENERAL

1 Citation and commencement
These rules may be cited as the Land Registration (Scotland) Rules 1980 and shall
come into operation on 6th April 1981.

2 Interpretation
(1) In these rules—
  'the Act' means the Land Registration (Scotland) Act 1979;
  ['the 2000 Act' means the Abolition of Feudal Tenure etc (Scotland) Act 2000;
  'the 2003 Act' means the Title Conditions (Scotland) Act 2003;
  'application for dual registration' means an application made for—
    (a) registration of a constitutive deed under section 4(5) of the 2003 Act;
    (b) registration of a notice of preservation under section 50 of the 2003
Act;
    (c) registration of a deed creating a positive servitude under section 75(1)
of the 2003 Act;
    (d) registration of a notice of converted servitude under section 80 of the
2003 Act;
  'benefited' means in relation to a title condition, the interest in land to which
the right to enforce the title is attached;
  'burdened property' means in relation to a title condition, the interest in land
which is affected by the title condition;]
  'certificate of title' includes a land certificate and a charge certificate;
  ['community burden' has the meaning given in section 25 of the 2003 Act;]
  'constitutive deed' means the deed which sets out the terms of a title
condition;]
  'dealing' means a transaction or event capable of affecting the title to a
registered interest in land:
  'debt' has the meaning assigned to it by section 9(8)(c) of the Conveyancing
and Feudal Reform (Scotland) Act 1970;
  ['holder' in relation to a title condition means the person who has right to the
title condition;
  'personal real burden' has the meaning given in section 1(3) of the 2003 Act;]
  ['Registers Direct service' means the service provided by the Keeper which
allows remote direct access by computer for the purpose of searching and
retrieving information in respect of the register.]
(2) In these rules any reference to a numbered rule or to a numbered form is a
reference to, respectively, the rule bearing that number in these rules or the form
bearing that number in Schedule A to these rules.
(3) In a rule, any reference to a numbered paragraph is a reference to the paragraph in that rule bearing that number.

PART II
THE TITLE SHEET

3 Contents and distinguishing number of title sheet
(1) A title sheet shall consist of the following sections: a Property Section, a
Proprietorship Section, a Charges Section and a Burdens Section.

(2)   Each title sheet of a registered interest in land shall be distinguished by a title number, consisting either of numbers or of letters and numbers.

4   Property Section
(1)   The following matters shall be entered in the Property Section—
    (a)   the description of the land in accordance with section 6(l)(a) of the Act;
    (b)   the nature of the interest in the land;
    (c)   particulars of any [subsisting] real right pertaining to the interest;
    [(cc)   particulars of any subsisting right to a title condition pertaining to the interest by virtue of section 18, 19 or 20 of the 2000 Act or section 4(5), 50, 75 or 80 of the 2003 Act and the identity of the burdened property affected by such title condition;]
    (d)   particulars of any exclusion of indemnity under section 12(2) of the Act which the Keeper considers is appropriate to the Property Section; and
    (e)   such other information as the Keeper thinks fit to enter in the Property Section.
(2)   The Property Section shall include a plan of the land to which the interest relates.
[(3)   An entry in the Property Section in respect of particulars of a right to be entered in accordance with paragraph (1)(cc) shall set out the terms of the title condition either—
    (a)   by setting out the terms of the title condition as set out in the constitutive deed in full or by entering a summary of such terms in the Property Section; or
    (b)   by setting out such terms by means of a reference to an entry in the Burdens Section of the same title sheet wherein such terms are set out in full.]

5   Proprietorship Section
The following matters shall be entered in the Proprietorship Section
    (a)   the name and designation of the person entitled to the interest in land,
    (b)   the extent of that person's entitlement to the interest in land;
    (c)   the capacity in which that person is entitled to the interest in land, if he is not so entitled as an individual
    (d)   the destination, if any, to which the interest in land is subject;
    (e)   the date, if any, stated as the date of entry of that person to the interest in land;
    (f)   the date of registration of that person's entitlement to the interest in land;
    (g)   any consideration stated for the transfer of the interest in land;
    (h)   any subsisting entry in the Register of Inhibitions and Adjudications adverse to the interest;
    (i)   particulars of any exclusion of indemnity under section 12(2) of the Act which the Keeper considers is appropriate to the Proprietorship Section;
    (j)   a statement that there are in respect of the interest in land no subsisting occupancy rights, in terms of the Matrimonial Homes (Family Protection) (Scotland) Act 1981, of spouses of persons who were formerly entitled to the interest in land, if the Keeper is satisfied that there are no such subsisting rights; and
    (k)   such other information as the Keeper thinks fit to enter in the Proprietorship Section.

6   Charges Section
(1)   The following matters shall be entered in the Charges Section—
    (a)   particulars of any heritable security over the interest;
    (b)   particulars of any debt, including a pecuniary real burden, affecting the interest;
    (c)   particulars of any exclusion of indemnity under section 12(2) of the Act which the Keeper considers is appropriate to the Charges Section; and
    (d)   such other information as the Keeper thinks fit to enter in the Charges Section.

(2)   There shall be noted in the Charges Section particulars of a floating charges which, as an overriding interest, may fall to be noted in terms of section 6(4) of the Act.

7   Burdens Section

(1)   The following matters should be entered in the burdens section—

(a)   particulars of any subsisting real burden, other than a real burden which falls to be entered in the Charges Section, and of any subsisting condition affecting the interest;

[(aa)   the identity of the benefited property or of the holder of a personal real burden in respect of any subsisting real burden or condition affecting the interest by virtue of section 18, 18A, 18B, 18C, 19, 20, 27 or 27A of the 2000 Act or section 4(5), 38, 43, 44, 45, 46, 50, 75 or 80 of the 2003 Act;

(ab)   any statement which the Keeper is entitled or required to enter on the title sheet by virtue of section 58 of the 2003 Act;]

(b)   particulars of any exclusion of indemnity under section 12(2) of the Act which the Keeper considers is appropriate to the burdens section; and

(c)   such other information as the Keeper thinks fit to enter in the Burdens Section.

[(1A)   where particulars of any subsisting right to a title condition are to be entered in the Property Section in accordance with rule 4(3)(b), there shall be entered in the Burdens Section the terms of such title conditions as set out in the constitutive deed;]

(2)   There shall be noted in the Burdens Section particulars of any overriding interest, other than a floating charge, which may fall to be noted in terms of section 6(4) of the Act.

(3)   There shall be entered in the Burdens Section

(a)   particulars of a probative discharge of an overriding interest, other than a floating charge or the right of the proprietor of the dominant tenement in a servitude, but only where (i) the overriding interest has been either recorded in the Register of Sasines or noted in the Burdens Section and (ii) the applicant has requested that the particulars be noted; and

(b)   particulars of a probative discharge of the right to the proprietor of the dominant tenement in a servitude.

8   Combination and division of Title Sheets

When it appears to the Keeper to be desirable to do so he may—

(a)   enter the particulars of an interest in land in the title sheet of another interest in land and cancel the title sheet in which the interest was previously entered, or

(b)   enter in another title sheet or in other title sheets a part or parts of the interest in land which was previously entered as a single interest and amend appropriately the title sheet in which the whole interest was previously entered.

PART III
REGISTRATION OF INTERESTS IN LAND AND NOTING OF OVERRIDING INTERESTS AND ENTRY OF ADDITIONAL INFORMATION

9   Application for registration of interest in land

(1)   [Subject to paragraphs (4) and (5),] any application for registration shall be made by the person in whose favour a real right will be created or affected by registration and such an application shall be on the following forms—

(a)   Form 1, where the application is for first registration;

(b)   Form 2, where the application is for registration of a dealing (other than the transfer of part of a registered interest in land); and

(c)   Form 3, where the application is for registration of a transfer of part of a registered interest in land.

(2)   An application for registration shall be accompanied by an inventory of the writs relevant to the application on Form 4.

(3)   Subject to rule 18, an application for registration on Form 2 or on Form 3 shall be accompanied by the certificate of title of the relevant interest in land.

[(4)   Where the application for registration is an application for dual registration the application may be made by any person who has right to the land which in terms of the application is to become a burdened or benefited property.

(5)   Where an enactment permits an application for registration to be made by a person that person may make such application.

(6)   Paragraph (1) shall apply to an application made by virtue of paragraphs (4) or (5) for the purposes of determining on which form the application shall be made.]

10   Withdrawal by applicant of application for registration

An application for registration may be withdrawn by the applicant before the completion of registration.

11   Return by Keeper of document for amendment

Subject to rule 12, where an application for registration is not accepted by the Keeper on the grounds that it does not comply with subsection (1) or (2) (a) or (d) of section 4 of the Act, but has not been rejected by the Keeper or withdrawn by the applicant, the Keeper may return any document relating to the application to the applicant for amendment in order that the application may be made so to comply.

12   Failure by applicant to respond to Keeper's request

Where the applicant, having been requested by the Keeper to supply documents and evidence in accordance with section 4(1) of the Act or to amend a document in accordance with rule 11, fails to do so, the Keeper after the expiry of such reasonable period of time as may be fixed by him and intimated to the applicant, being not less than 60 days, may either complete registration, subject to exclusion of indemnity, or reject the application.

13   Application for noting of overriding interest or for entry of discharge of overriding interest or of additional information

An application for—

    (a)   the noting of an overriding interest in terms of section 6(4) of the Act; or

    (b)   the entering of-

        (i)   the discharge of an overriding interest in terms of rule 7(3); or

        (ii)   additional information entered in terms of section 6(1)(g) of the Act; or

    (c)   the deletion of a note or an entry made, respectively, under paragraph (a) or paragraph (b) of this rule shall be on Form 5.

PART IV
CERTIFICATE OF TITLE

14   Form of land certificate

A land certificate issued by the Keeper in terms of section 5(2) of the Act shall be in, or as nearly as may be in, Form 6 and shall be authenticated by the seal of the register.

15   Form of charge certificate

A charge certificate issued by the Keeper in terms of section 5(3) of the Act shall be in, or as nearly as may be in, Form 7 and shall be authenticated by the seal of the register.

16   Application for certificate of title to be made to correspond with title sheet

(1)   An application may be made to the Keeper for a certificate of title to be made to correspond with the relevant title sheet.

(2)   Such an application shall be Form 8.

17 Amendment or cancellation of certificate of title by Keeper

(1) The Keeper shall have power to amend or cancel a certificate of title in order to make the certificate correspond with the relevant title sheet.

(2) Subject to rule 18, a certificate of title shall be produced to the Keeper for amendment or cancellation if the Keeper requests production.

(3) The Keeper shall not request production of a certificate of title in terms of the preceding paragraph where amendment of the certificate would inform the person entitled to the interest in land of the existence of a recorded deed or a registration upon which possession adverse to him may be founded in terms of section 1 of the Prescription and Limitation (Scotland) Act 1973.

(4) On being requested to do so, the Keeper shall make payment of such expenses occasioned by compliance with paragraph (2), as the Keeper considers to be reasonable.

18 Circumstances where certificate of title need not be produced to Keeper

(1) There shall be no obligation to produce the certificate of title to the Keeper, in terms of rule 9(3) or rule 17(2), where the Keeper is satisfied of the existence of good cause for the failure to produce the certificate.

(2) For the purpose of the preceding paragraph, good cause will include—

(a) with reference to a land certificate or a charge certificate, the fact that the certificate has been lost or destroyed or is otherwise unobtainable; and

(b) with reference to a land certificate, the fact that the land certificate is held by a creditor.

19 Issue by Keeper of substitute certificate of title

Where the Keeper is satisfied that a certificate of title has been lost or destroyed he shall issue a substitute certificate, marked 'substitute' and shall note on the title sheet that a substitute certificate has been issued.

PART V
MISCELLANEOUS

20 Rectification of register

(1) An application to the Keeper, under section 9(1) of the Act, for the rectification of the register shall be on Form 9.

(2) Where it appears to the Keeper that proceedings in the court or the Lands Tribunal for Scotland may result in an order for rectification of the register under section 9(l) of the Act, the Keeper shall note the existence of such proceedings on the title sheet of the interest in land to which the proceedings relate.

21 Notifications by Keeper

(1) The Keeper shall notify his decision on any matter affecting registration to any person whose interest appears from the register to be affected by that decision.

(2) Notification shall not be made under the foregoing paragraph where notification would have the effect of informing the person entitled to the interest in land of the existence of a recorded deed or a registration upon which possession adverse to his interest may be founded in terms of section 1 of the Prescription and Limitation (Scotland) Act 1973.

(3) A notification under paragraph (1) shall be made in such form as the Keeper shall think fit and shall be sufficiently made if sent by post to the person's last address shown on the register.

22 Affidavits to accompany applications for registration

Affidavits intended to accompany an application for registration may be made before a notary public.

23 Maps of registered interests and index of proprietors

The Keeper shall make up and maintain—

(a)   an index map, based on the Ordnance Map, of registered interests in land; and

(b)   an index of the names of all persons currently entered in the proprietorship section of title sheets.

[24   Application to Keeper for report or office copy

(1)   Subject to paragraphs (2) and (3) below, an application to the Keeper for a report or office copy in terms of section 6(5) of the Act mentioned in column 1 of the following table shall be in the appropriate form as referred to in column 2 of the said table.

	Report or office copy applied for	Form
(1)	Report prior to registration	10
(2)	Continuation of report prior to registration	11
(3)	Report over registered subjects	12
(4)	Continuation of report over registered subjects	13
(5)	Report to ascertain whether or not subjects have been registered	14
(6)	Office copy (in terms of section 6(5) of the Act)	15

(2)   An application for a report or office copy in terms of section 6(5) of the Act may be made by telephone provided the information which would have been included under an equivalent application under paragraph (1) above is supplied, together with such additional information as may be required by the Keeper.

(3)   An application for a report or office copy in terms of section 6(5) of the Act may be made by facsimile or electronic mail provided the information which would have been included under an equivalent application under paragraph (1) above is supplied.]

[24A   Application for Registers Direct service

(1)   An application may be made to the Keeper for use of the Registers Direct service.

(2)   On making an application, an applicant shall submit such information as will enable the Keeper to be satisfied that suitable arrangements have been made for payment of any fees incurred by the applicant.

(3)   Any user of the Registers Direct service shall, on being required to do so by the Keeper submit such information as will enable the Keeper to be satisfied that the requirements of paragraph (2) above continue to be met.]

25   Description of a registered interest in land

Land in respect of which an interest has been registered shall be sufficiently described in any deed relating to that interest if it is described by reference to the number of the title sheet of that interest, in or as nearly as may be in, the manner prescribed by Schedule B to these rules.

[SCHEDULE A
LIST OF FORMS TO BE USED IN CONNECTION WITH REGISTRATION

Form	Purpose	Reference to Act
1	Application for first registration	section 4
2	Application for registration of a dealing (other than the transfer of part of a registered interest in land)	section 4

3	Application for registration of a transfer of part of a registered interest in land	section 4
4	Inventory of writs	section 4
5	Application for noting of overriding interest of for entry of other information in terms of section 6(1)(g)	section 6(4)
6	Land certificate	section 5(2)
7	Charge certificate	section 5(3)
8	Application for certificate of title to be made to correspond with title sheet	–
9	Application for rectification of the register	section 9(1)
10	Application for report prior to registration	–
11	Application for continuation of report prior to registration	–
12	Application for report over registered subjects	–
13	Application for continuation of report over registered subjects	–
14	Application for report to ascertain whether or not subjects have been registered	–
15	Application for office copy	section 6(5)

REGISTERS OF SCOTLAND EXECUTIVE AGENCY	FORM 1	Please complete in BLACK TYPE
(Land Registration (Scotland) Rules 1980 Rule 9(1)(a))	VERSION 28/11/2004	No covering letter is required
APPLICATION FOR FIRST REGISTRATION		

1. Presenting Agent. Name and Address (see Note 1)

Keeper of the Registers of Scotland
Meadowbank House
153 London Road
Edinburgh EH8 7AU
Telephone: 0131 659 6111

Part A

2.FAS No. (see Note 2)	3. Agent's Tel No.(include STD Code)	4. Agent's Reference

5. Name of Deed in respect of which registration is required	6. County (see Note 3)	Mark X in box if more than one county

7. Subjects (see Note 4)

Street No.	Street Name	
Town		Post code
Other		

8. Name and Address of Applicant (see Note 5)

1. Surname	Forename(s)
Address	

2. Surname	Forename(s)
Address	

and/ or company/ firm or council, etc.	Mark X in box if more than 2 applicants
Address	

9. Granter/Last recorded title holder (see Note 6)

1. Surname	Forename(s)
2. Surname	Forename(s)

and/ or company/ firm or council, etc.	Mark X in box if more than 2 granters

10. Consideration

(see Note 7)	Value (see Note 8)	Fee (see Note 9) A	Method of Payment	Date of Entry

11. If a Form 10 Report has been issued in connection with this Application, please quote Report No.

12. I/ We apply for registration in respect of Deed(s) No in the Inventory of Writs (Form 4). I/ We certify that the information supplied in this application is correct to the best of my/our knowledge and belief.

FOR OFFICIAL USE

Signature	Date

Notes 1-9 referred to are contained in Notes and Directions for completion of Applications for First Registration

PART B

Delete **YES** or **NO** as appropriate

N.B. If more space is required for any section of this form, a separate sheet, or separate sheets, may be added.

---

1.   Do the deeds submitted in support of this application include a plan illustrating the   **YES/NO**
     extent of the subjects to be registered?
     If **YES**, please specify the deed and its Form 4 Inventory number :

     If **NO**, have you submitted a deed containing a full bounding description with   **YES/NO**
     measurements?

     If **YES**, please specify the deed and its Form 4 Inventory number :

     N.B. If the answer to both the above questions is NO then, unless the property is
     part of a tenement or flatted building, you must submit a plan of the subjects
     properly drawn to a stated scale and showing sufficient surrounding features to
     enable it to be located on the Ordnance Map. The plan should bear a docquet,
     signed by the person signing the Application Form, to the effect that it is a plan of
     the subjects sought to be registered under the attached application.

---

2.   Is a Form P16 Report issued by the Keeper confirming that the boundaries of the   **YES/NO**
     subjects coincide with the Ordnance Map being submitted in support of this
     Application?

     If **NO**, does the legal extent depicted in the plans or descriptions in the deeds   **YES/NO**
     submitted in support of the Application cohere with the occupational extent?

     If **NO**, please advise:-

     (a)   the approximate age and nature of the occupational boundaries, or

     (b)   whether, if the extent of the subjects as defined in the deeds is larger than   **YES/NO**
           the occupational extent, the applicant is prepared to accept the
           occupational extent as viewed, or

     (c)   whether, if the extent of the subjects as defined in the deeds is smaller than   **YES/NO**
           the occupational extent, any remedial action has been taken.

---

3.   Is there any person in possession or occupation of the subjects or any part of   **YES/NO**
     them adversely to the interest of the applicant?
     If **YES**, please give details:

---

4.   If the subjects were acquired by the applicant under any statutory provision, does
     the statutory provision restrict the applicant's power of disposal of the subjects?   **YES/NO**
     If **YES**, please indicate the statute:

---

5.   (a)   Are there any charges affecting the subjects or any part of them, except   **YES/NO**
           as stated in the Schedule of Heritable Securities etc. on page 4 of this
           application?
           If **YES**, please give details:

     (b)   Apart from overriding interests are there any burdens affecting the subjects   **YES/NO**
           or any part of them, except as stated in the Schedule of Burdens on page
           4 of this application?
           If **YES**, please give details:

<table>
<tr><td>(c)</td><td>Are there any overriding interests affecting the subjects or any part of them which you wish noted on the Title Sheet?
If YES, please give details:</td><td>YES/NO</td></tr>
<tr><td>(d)</td><td>Are there any recurrent monetary payments (e.g. leasehold casualties) exigible from the subjects or any part of them?
If YES, please give details:</td><td>YES/NO</td></tr>
</table>

6.   Where any party to the deed inducing registration is a company registered under the Companies Acts

        Has a receiver or liquidator been appointed?   **YES/NO**
        If **YES**, please give details:

        If **NO**, has any resolution been passed or court order made for the winding   **YES/NO**
        up of the company or petition presented for its liquidation?
        If **YES**, please give details:

7.   Where any party to the deed inducing registration is a company registered under the Companies Acts can you confirm

    (a)   that it is not a charity as defined in section 112 of the Companies Act 1989   **YES/NO**
          and
    (b)   that the transaction to which the deed gives effect is not one to which   **YES/NO**
          section 322A of the Companies Act 1985 (as inserted by section 109 of the
          Companies Act 1989) applies?

        Where the answer to either part of the question is **NO**, please give details:

8.   Where any party to the deed inducing registration is a corporate body other than a company registered under the Companies Acts

    (a)   Is it acting *intra vires* ?   **YES/NO**
          If **NO**, please give details:

    (b)   Has any arrangement been put in hand for the dissolution of any such   **YES/NO**
          corporate body?
          If **YES**, please give details:

9.   Are *all* the necessary consents, renunciations or affidavits in terms of section 6 of   **YES/NO**
    the Matrimonial Homes (Family Protection)(Scotland) Act 1981 being submitted in
    connection with this application?

    N.B. If sufficient evidence to satisfy the Keeper that there are no subsisting occupancy rights in the subjects of this application is not submitted with the application then the statement by the Keeper in terms of rule 5 (j) of the Land Registration (Scotland) Rules 1980 will not be inserted in the Title Sheet or will be qualified as appropriate without further enquiry by the Keeper.

10.   Where the deed inducing registration is in implement of the exercise of a power of
               sale under a heritable security

               Have the statutory procedures necessary for the proper exercise of such power   **YES/NO**
               been complied with?

---

11.   Where the deed inducing registration is pursuant on a Compulsory Purchase Order

               Have the necessary statutory procedures been complied with?   **YES/NO**

---

12.   Is any party to the deed inducing registration subject to any legal incapacity or   **YES/NO**
               disability?
               If **YES**, please give details:

---

13.   Are the deeds and documents detailed in the Inventory (Form 4) all the deeds and   **YES/NO**
               documents relevant to the title?
               If **NO**, please give details:

---

14.   Are there any facts and circumstances material to the right or title of the applicant   **YES/NO**
               which have not already been disclosed in this application or its accompanying
               documents?
               If **YES**, please give details:

SCHEDULE OF HERITABLE SECURITIES ETC.
N.B. New Charges granted by the applicant should not be included

---

SCHEDULE OF BURDENS

REGISTERS OF SCOTLAND EXECUTIVE AGENCY
(Land Registration (Scotland) Rules 1980 Rule 9(1)(b))
APPLICATION FOR REGISTRATION OF A DEALING

FORM 2
VERSION 28/11/2004

Please complete in BLACK TYPE
No covering letter is required

1. Presenting Agent. Name and Address (see Note 1)

Keeper of the Registers of Scotland
Meadowbank House
153 London Road
Edinburgh EH8 7AU
Telephone: 0131 659 6111

Part A

2. FAS No. (see Note 2)

3. Agent's Tel No. (include STD Code)

4. Agent's Reference

5. Name of Deed in respect of which registration is required (see Note 3)

6. County (see Note 4)

Mark X in box if more than one county

7. Title No(s) of registered interest(s) affected by this application (see Note 5)

Mark X in box if more than 3 Title Numbers

8. Subjects (see Note 6)

Street No.

Street Name

Town

Post code

Other

9. Name and Address of Applicant (see Note 7)

1. Surname

Forename(s)

Address

2. Surname

Forename(s)

Address

and/ or company/ firm or council, etc.

Mark X in box if more than 2 applicants

Address

10. Consideration -
or amount of loan (see Note 8)

Value - or amount of loan (see Note 9)

Fee (see Note 10)
A/B/C

Method of Payment

Date of Entry

11. I/ We apply for registration in respect of Deed(s) No in the Inventory of Writs (Form 4). I/ We certify that the information supplied in this application is correct to the best of my/our knowledge and belief.

FOR OFFICIAL USE

Signature

Date

Notes 1-10 referred to are contained in Notes and Directions for completion of Applications for Registration of a Dealing

PART B

Delete **YES** or **NO** as appropriate
N.B. If more space is required for any section of this form, a separate sheet, or separate sheets, may be added.

---

1.   Where the dealing in respect of which registration is sought transfers the interest
            specified in the Property Section of the Title Sheet

       (a) Is there any person in possession or occupation of the subjects or any part   **YES/NO**
            of them adversely to the interest of the applicant?
            If **YES**, please give details:

       (b) If the subjects were acquired by the applicant under any statutory provision,   **YES/NO**
            does the statutory provision restrict the applicant's power of disposal of the
            subjects?
            If **YES**, please indicate the statute:

       (c) Apart from overriding interests are there any burdens affecting the subjects   **YES/NO**
            or any part of them, except as already disclosed in the Land Certificate and
            in the documents produced with this application?
            If **YES**, please give details:

       (d) Are there any overriding interests affecting the subjects or any part of them   **YES/NO**
            which you wish noted on the Title Sheet?
            If **YES**, please give details:

       (e) Are there any recurrent monetary payments (e.g. leasehold casualties)   **YES/NO**
            exigible from the subjects or any part of them?
            If **YES**, please give details:

---

2.   Where any party to the dealing is a company registered under the Companies Acts

            Has a receiver or liquidator been appointed?   **YES/NO**
            If **YES**, please give details:

            If **NO**, has any resolution been passed or court order made for the winding   **YES/NO**
            up of the company or petition presented for its liquidation?
            If **YES**, please give details:

---

3.   Where any party to the dealing is a company registered under the Companies Acts
            can you confirm

       (a) that it is not a charity as defined in section 112 of the Companies Act 1989   **YES/NO**
            and

       (b) that the transaction to which the deed gives effect is not one to which   **YES/NO**
            section 322A of the Companies Act 1985 (as inserted by section 109 of the
            Companies Act 1989) applies?

            Where the answer to either part of the question is **NO**, please give
            details:

---

4.   Where any party to the dealing is a corporate body other than a company registered under the Companies Acts

    (a)   Is it acting *intra vires?*   **YES/NO**
           If **NO**, please give details:

    (b)   Has any arrangement been put in hand for the dissolution of any such   **YES/NO**
           corporate body?
           If **YES**, please give details:

5.   Are *all* the necessary consents, renunciations or affidavits in terms of section 6 of   **YES/NO**
    the Matrimonial Homes (Family Protection)(Scotland) Act 1981 being submitted in connection with this application?

    N.B.   If sufficient evidence to satisfy the Keeper that there are no subsisting occupancy rights in the subjects of this application is not submitted with the application then the statement by the Keeper in terms of rule 5 (j) of the Land Registration (Scotland) Rules 1980 will not be inserted in the Title Sheet or will be qualified as appropriate without further enquiry by the Keeper.

6.   Where the dealing is in implement of the exercise of a power of sale under a heritable security

    Have the statutory procedures necessary for the proper exercise of such   **YES/NO**
    power been complied with?

7.   Where the dealing is pursuant on a Compulsory Purchase Order

    Have the necessary statutory procedures been complied with?   **YES/NO**

8.   In all cases

    (a)   Is any party to the dealing subject to any legal incapacity or disability not   **YES/NO**
           already disclosed on the Land Certificate?
           If **YES**, please give details:

    (b)   Are the deeds and documents detailed in the Inventory (Form 4) all the   **YES/NO**
           deeds and documents relevant to the application?
           If **NO**, please give details:

    (c)   Are there any facts and circumstances material to the right or title of the   **YES/NO**
           applicant which have not already been disclosed in this application or its accompanying documents?
           If **YES**, please give details:

REGISTERS OF SCOTLAND EXECUTIVE AGENCY
(Land Registration (Scotland) Rules 1980 Rule 9(1)(c))
**APPLICATION FOR REGISTRATION OF A
TRANSFER OF PART**

FORM 3
VERSION 28/11/2004

Please complete in BLACK TYPE
No covering letter is required

1. Presenting Agent. Name and Address (see Note 1)

Keeper of the Registers of Scotland
Meadowbank House
153 London Road
Edinburgh EH8 7AU
Telephone: 0131 659 6111

Part A

2. FAS No. (see Note 2)

3. Agent's Tel No. (include STD Code)

4. Agent's Reference

5. Name of Deed in respect of which registration is required

6. County (see Note 3)   Mark X in box if more than one county

7. Title No(s) of registered interest(s) affected by this application (see Note 4)

Mark X in box if more
than 3 Title Numbers

8. Subjects (see Note 5)

Street No.   Plot No.   Street Name

Town   Post code

Other

9. Name and Address of Applicant (see Note 6)

1. Surname   Forename(s)

Address

2. Surname   Forename(s)

Address

and/ or company/ firm or council, etc.   Mark X in box if more than 2 applicants

Address

10. Consideration
(see Note 7)   **Value** (see Note 8)   **Fee** (see Note 9)   **Method of Payment**   **Date of Entry**
                                          A

**11. I/ We apply for registration in respect of Deed(s) No   in the Inventory
of Writs (Form 4). I/ We certify that the information supplied in this
application is correct to the best of my/our knowledge and belief.**

FOR OFFICIAL USE

Signature   Date

Notes 1-9 referred to are contained in Notes and Directions for completion of
Applications for Registration of a Transfer of Part.

PART B

Delete **YES** or **NO** as appropriate
N.B. If more space is required for any section of this form, a separate sheet, or separate sheets, may be added.

1.		Is there any person in possession or occupation of the subjects or any part of them adversely to the interest of the applicant? If **YES**, please give details:	**YES/NO**
2.		If the subjects were acquired by the applicant under any statutory provision, does the statutory provision restrict the applicant's power of disposal of the subjects? If **YES**, please indicate the statute:	**YES/NO**
3.	(a)	Apart from overriding interests are there any burdens affecting the subjects or any part of them, except as already disclosed in the Land Certificate and in the documents produced with this application? If **YES**, please give details:	**YES/NO**
	(b)	Are there any overriding interests affecting the subjects or any part of them which you wish noted on the Title Sheet? If **YES**, please give details:	**YES/NO**
	(c)	Are there any recurrent monetary payments (e.g. leasehold casualties) exigible from the subjects or any part of them? If **YES**, please give details:	**YES/NO**
4.		Where any party to the dealing is a company registered under the Companies Acts	
		Has a receiver or liquidator been appointed? If **YES**, please give details:	**YES/NO**
		If **NO**, has any resolution been passed or court order made for the winding up of the company or petition presented for its liquidation? If **YES**, please give details:	**YES/NO**
5.		Where any party to the dealing is a company registered under the Companies Acts can you confirm	
	(a)	that it is not a charity as defined in section 112 of the Companies Act 1989 and	**YES/NO**
	(b)	that the transaction to which the deed gives effect is not one to which section 322A of the Companies Act 1985 (as inserted by section 109 of the Companies Act 1989) applies? Where the answer to either part of the question is **NO**, please give details:	**YES/NO**

6.   Where any party to the dealing is a corporate body other than a company registered under the Companies Acts

        (a)   Is it acting *intra vires*?   **YES/NO**
                  If **NO**, please give details:

        (b)   Has any arrangement been put in hand for the dissolution of any such   **YES/NO**
                  corporate body?
                  If **YES**, please give details:

7.   Are *all* the necessary consents, renunciations or affidavits in terms of section 6 of   **YES/NO**
the Matrimonial Homes (Family Protection)(Scotland) Act 1981 being submitted in connection with this application?

        N.B.   If sufficient evidence to satisfy the Keeper that there are no subsisting occupancy rights in the subjects of this application is not submitted with the application then the statement by the Keeper in terms of rule 5(j) of the Land Registration (Scotland) Rules 1980 will not be inserted in the Title Sheet or will be qualified as appropriate without further enquiry by the Keeper.

8.   Where the dealing is in implement of the exercise of a power of sale under a heritable security

Have the statutory procedures necessary for the proper exercise of such   **YES/NO**
power been complied with?

9.   Where the dealing is pursuant on a Compulsory Purchase Order

        Have the necessary statutory procedures been complied with?   **YES/NO**

10.   Is any party to the dealing subject to any legal incapacity or disability not already   **YES/NO**
disclosed on the Land Certificate?
If **YES**, please give details:

11.   Are the boundaries of the subjects defined on the ground by fencing or other type   **YES/NO**
of enclosure?

12.   Are the deeds and documents detailed in the Inventory (Form 4) all the deeds and   **YES/NO**
documents relevant to the application?
If **NO**, please give details:

13.   Are there any facts and circumstances material to the right or title of the applicant   **YES/NO**
which have not already been disclosed in this application or its accompanying documents?
If **YES**, please give details:

Typewriter Alignment Box
Type XXX in centre

REGISTERS OF SCOTLAND EXECUTIVE AGENCY
(Land Registration (Scotland) Rules 1980 Rule 9(2))

FORM 4

INVENTORY OF WRITS RELEVANT TO APPLICATION FOR REGISTRATION (see Note 1)
(to be completed in duplicate)

(see Note 2)

Title Number(s)
(to be completed for a dealing with registered interests in land.)

Subjects (see Note 3)

Registration County

Applicant's Reference

Please complete Inventory overleaf as in this specimen

Item No.	Please mark "S" against writs submitted	Writ	Grantee	Date of Recording

Particulars of Writs (see Note 4)

* Delete if inapplicable

Notes 1-4 referred to are contained in Notes and Directions for Completion of Inventory of Writs Relevant to Application for Registration.

FOR OFFICIAL USE ONLY

APPLICATION NUMBER	DATE OF RECEIPT	TITLE NUMBER

The writs marked "S" on this inventory were received on the Date of Receipt stamped on this page.

		INVENTORY		Typewriter Alignment Box Type XXX in centre
		Particulars of Writs *(see Note 4)*		
Item No.	**Please mark "S" against writs submitted**	**Writ**	**Grantee**	**Date of Recording**

* delete if inapplicable

FORM 5

REGISTERS OF SCOTLAND EXECUTIVE AGENCY
(Land Registration (Scotland) Rules 1980 Rule 13)

Typewriter Alignment Box
Type XXX in centre

APPLICATION FOR NOTING OR ENTERING ON THE REGISTER

Note: No covering letter is required

Please complete in BLACK TYPE

FOR OFFICIAL USE

DATE OF RECEIPT

TO

Keeper of the Registers of Scotland

Meadowbank House
153 London Road
EDINBURGH EH8 7AU

Telephone: 0131 659 6111

APPLICATION NUMBER

Title No(s)

Mark X in the box if more
than 3 Title Numbers

Short description
of subjects

*I/We apply to have the information set out below noted or entered on the Title Sheet(s) of the above Title(s) viz.
*I/We apply to have the information set out below deleted from the Title Sheet(s) of the above Title(s) viz.

The appropriate fee is enclosed   please place a cross here.

To support this application, I/We*enclose the documents listed on the Inventory (Form 4).

Signature of Applicant or
Applicant's Solicitor

Full Name of Applicant

Address of Applicant

Name of Solicitor

Address of Solicitor

Reference

Telephone No.

Date of Application

FAS No.

1. Please list additional Title Numbers on a separate sheet.
*Delete whichever is inapplicable

(Land Registration (Scotland) Rules 1980, Rule 14)

LAND REGISTER OF SCOTLAND

LAND CERTIFICATE

TITLE NUMBER

SUBJECTS

This Land Certificate, issued pursuant to section 5(2) of the Land Registration (Scotland) Act 1979, is a copy of the Title Sheet relating to the above subjects.

STATEMENT OF INDEMNITY

Subject to any specific qualifications entered in the Title Sheet of which this Land Certificate is a copy, a person who suffers loss as a result of the events specified in section 12(1) of the above Act shall be entitled to be indemnified in respect of that loss by the Keeper of the Registers of Scotland in terms of that Act.

ATTENTION IS DRAWN TO THE NOTICE AND GENERAL INFORMATION OVERLEAF.

NOTICE

This Land Certificate was made to agree with the Title Sheet of which it is a copy on the most recent date entered below.

This Land Certificate may be made to agree with the Title Sheet at any time on payment of the appropriate fee. Application should be made on Form 8.

GENERAL INFORMATION

1. **OVERRIDING INTERESTS** A registered interest in land is in terms of section 3(I) of the Land Registration (Scotland) Act 1979 subject to overriding interests defined in section 28 of that Act (hereinafter referred to as 'the 1979 Act') as amended by the Matrimonial Homes (Family Protection) (Scotland) Act 1981, the Telecommunication Act 1984, the Electricity Act 1989 and the Coal Industry Act 1994 as:

    in relation to any interest in land, the right or interest over it of

    (a) the lessee under a lease which is not a long lease;

    (b) the lessee under a long lease who, prior to the commencement of the 1979 Act, has acquired a real right to the subjects of the lease by virtue of possession of them;

Continued on inside back cover.

(c) a crofter or cottar within the meaning of section 3 or 28(4) respectively of the Crofters (Scotland) Act 1955, or a landholder or statutory small tenant within the meaning of section 2(2) or 32(1) respectively of the Small Landholders (Scotland) Act 1911;

(d) the proprietor of the dominant tenement in a servitude;

(e) the Crown or any Government or other public department, or any public or local authority, under any enactment or rule of law, other than an enactment or rule of law authorising or requiring the recording of a deed in the Register of Sasines or registration in order to complete the right of interest;

(ee) the operator having a right conferred in accordance with paragraph 2, 3 or 5 of schedule 2 to the Telecommunications Act 1984 (agreements for execution of works, obstruction of access, etc.);

(ef) a licence holder within the meaning of Part I of the Electricity Act 1919 having such a wayleave as is mentioned in paragraph 6 of Schedule 4 to that Act (wayleaves for electric lines), whether granted under that paragraph or by agreement between the parties;

(eg) a licence holder within the meaning of Part I of the Electricity Act 1989 who is authorised by virtue of paragraph I of Schedule 5 to that Act to abstract, divert and use water for a generating station wholly or mainly driven by water;

(eh) insofar as it is an interest vesting by virtue of section 7(3) of the Coal Industry Act 1994, the Coal Authority;

(f) the holder of a floating charge whether or not the charge has attached to the interest;

(g) a member of the public in respect of any public right of way or in respect of any right held inalienably by the Crown in trust for the public;

(gg) the non-entitled spouse within the meaning of section 6 of the Matrimonial Homes (Family Protection) (Scotland) Act 1981;

(h) any person, being a right which has been made real, otherwise than by the recording of a deed in the Register of Sasines or by registration; or

(i) any other person under any rule of law relating to common interest or joint or common property, not being a right or interest constituting a real right, burden or condition entered in the title sheet of the interest in land under section 6(1)(e) of the 1979 Act or having effect by virtue of a deed recorded in the Register of Sasines,

but does not include any subsisting burden or condition enforceable against the interest in land and entered in its title sheet under section 6(1) of the 1979 Act.

2. THE USE OF ARROWS ON TITLE PLANS

(a) Where a deed states the line of a boundary in relation to a physical object, e.g. the centre line, that line is indicated on the Title Plan, either by means of a black arrow or verbally.

(b) An arrow across the object indicates that the boundary is stated to be the centre line.

(c) An arrow pointing to the object indicates that the boundary is stated to be the face of the object to which the arrow points.

(d) The physical object presently shown on the Plan may not be the one referred to in the deed. Indemnity is therefore excluded in respect of information as to the line of the boundary.

3. Lineal measurements shown in figures on title plans are subject to the qualification 'or thereby'. Indemnity is excluded in respect of such measurements.

4. SUBMISSION OF LAND CERTIFICATE WITH SUBSEQUENT APPLICATIONS FOR REGISTRATION

In terms of Rule 9(3), this Land Certificate should be submitted to the Keeper of the Registers of Scotland with any application for registration.

5. CAUTION. No unauthorized alteration to this Land Certificate should be made.

(Land Registration (Scotland) Rules 1980, Rule 15)

LAND REGISTER OF SCOTLAND

CHARGE CERTIFICATE

TITLE NUMBER

SUBJECTS

The within-mentioned Charge has been registered against the subjects in the above Title

STATEMENT OF INDEMNITY

Subject to any specific qualifications entered in the Title Sheet of which this Charge Certificate relates a person who suffers loss as a result of the events specified in section 12(1) of the Land Registration (Scotland) Act 1979 shall be entitled to be indemnified in respect of that loss by the Keeper of the Registers of Scotland in terms of that Act.

NOTICE

1. This Certificate must be presented to the Keeper on every transaction affecting the interest of the within-mentioned Registered Creditor.

2. The relative Title Sheet contains a specification of the reservations and burdens affecting the subjects in the above title. An Office Copy of the Title Sheet may be obtained on application to the Keeper.

3. No authorised alterations to this Charge Certificate should be made.

NOTICE

This Charge Certificate was made to agree with the Title Sheet of which it relates on the most recent date entered below.

This Charge Certificate may be made to agree with the Title Sheet at any time on payment of the appropriate fee. Application should be made on Form 8.

LAND REGISTER OF SCOTLAND

CHARGE CERTIFICATE

TITLE NO:

SUBJECTS:

Registered Proprietor of subjects:

THIS IS TO CERTIFY that

Is the Registered Creditor in the heritable security attached
registered on
to the extent of

NOTE
There are no heritable securities ranking prior to or *pari passu* with the above mentioned heritable
security appearing on the Register affecting the subjects (except as stated in the schedule annexed).

REGISTERS OF SCOTLAND EXECUTIVE AGENCY   **FORM 8**
(Land Registration (Scotland) Rules 1980 Rule 16 (2))

Typewriter Alignment Box
Type XXX in centre

APPLICATION FOR LAND OR CHARGE CERTIFICATE TO BE MADE TO CORRESPOND WITH THE TITLE SHEET

Note: No covering letter is required

Please complete in BLACK TYPE

TO

Keeper of the Registers of Scotland

Meadowbank House
153 London Road
EDINBURGH EH8 7AU

Telephone: 0131 659 6111

FOR OFFICIAL USE

DATE OF RECEIPT

APPLICATION NUMBER

Title Number

Short description
of subjects

I/We apply for the accompanying Land Certificate/ Charge Certificate to be made to correspond with the Title Sheet.

To assist the Keeper to disclose in the Land Certificate any relevant entries from the Register of Inhibitions and Adjudications, the full name and designation of any party *who has acquired an interest in the subjects in the title since the Land Certificate was last made to correspond with the Title Sheet* should be inserted.

1. Surname(s)   Forename(s)

    Address(es)

2. Surname(s)   Forename(s)

    Address(es)

3. Surname(s)   Forename(s)

    Address(es)

The appropriate fee is enclosed   please place a cross here.

Signature of Applicant or
Applicant's Solicitor

Full Name of Applicant

Address of Applicant

Reference   Telephone No.

Date of Application   FAS No.

Delete whichever is inapplicable

FORM 9

REGISTERS OF SCOTLAND EXECUTIVE AGENCY
(Land Registration (Scotland) Rules 1980 Rule 20)

APPLICATION FOR RECTIFICATION OF THE REGISTER
Note: No covering letter is required

Please complete in BLACK TYPE

Typewriter Alignment Box
Type XXX in centre

TO

Keeper of the Registers of Scotland

Meadowbank House
153 London Road
EDINBURGH EH8 7AU

Telephone: 0131 659 6111

FOR OFFICIAL USE

DATE OF RECEIPT

APPLICATION NUMBER

Title No

Short description
of subjects

*I/We apply for rectification of the Title Sheet for the above Title No. as follows:

To support this application, I/We*enclose the documents listed on the Inventory (Form 4).

The appropriate fee is enclosed   please place a cross here.

Signature of Applicant or
Applicant's Solicitor

Full Name of Applicant

Address of Applicant

Name of Solicitor

Address of Solicitor

Reference   Telephone No.

Date of Application   FAS No.

Delete whichever is inapplicable

REGISTERS OF SCOTLAND
Executive Agency

· property REPORTS service ·

FORM 10

(Land Registration (Scotland) Rules 1980 Rule 24(1))

APPLICATION FOR A REPORT PRIOR TO REGISTRATION OF THE SUBJECTS DESCRIBED BELOW

Note: No covering letter is required and an existing Search should not be submitted.
VAT Reg No. GD 410 GB 888 8410 64

Please complete in DUPLICATE and in BLACK TYPE   Typewriter Alignment Box. Type XXX in centre

From	FOR OFFICIAL USE
	Report Number
	Date of Receipt
	Search Sheet Nos.
	Fee

County		**FAS No.**	

Applicant's Reference		**FAX No.**	

Telephone No.		**FAX response required (X here)**	

POSTAL ADDRESS OF SUBJECTS

Street No.	**House Name**		**Street Name**	

Town		**Postcode**	

OTHER:

Description of Subjects	

The above subjects being	edged red on the accompanying plan, [2]
	being (part of) [1] the subjects described in [3]

I/We apply for a report

(1) on the subjects described above, for which an application for registration in the Land Register is to be made, from

(a) the **REGISTER OF SASINES** and

(b) the **LAND REGISTER** stating whether or not registration of the said subjects has been effected [4]

1. Delete if inapplicable
2. A plan need not be attached if a verbal description will sufficiently identify the subjects
3. Describe by reference to a writ recorded in the Register of Sasines
4. If the subjects have been registered, the Keeper will supply an Office Copy of the Title Sheet only on specific request.

Faxed applications should not be followed up by a written request and may not be accepted if a plan is included.

DIARY SERVICE:

Please state date and time you require report

Date ——————— Time ———————

NOTE: If you do not state we will assume a 48 hour turnaround

Meadowbank House, 153 London Road, Edinburgh EH8 7AU
www.ros.gov.uk DX 555338 EDINBURGH 15 reports@ros.gov.uk
Tel: 0845 6070162 Fax: 0131 479 3651/3683/3667

· p r o p e r t y **REPORTS** s e r v i c e ·

FORM 10

and (2) from the Registers of Inhibitions and Adjudications for 5 years prior to the date of Certificate against in the Register of Inhibitions and Adjudications, viz.

Typewriter Alignment Box. Type XXX in centre

1.Surname(s)		Forename(s)	

Address(es)	

2.Surname(s)		Forename(s)	

Address(es)	

3.Surname(s)		Forename(s)	

Address(es)	

4.Surname(s)		Forename(s)	

Address(es)	

5.Company/ Firm/ Corporate body	

Address(es)	

6.Company/ Firm/ Corporate body	

Address(es)	

NOTE: Insert full names and addresses of the persons on whom a Report is required.

Signature: ———————————————————   **Date:** ———————————————————

REGISTERS OF SCOTLAND
Executive Agency

• property REPORTS service •
FORM 11

(Land Registration (Scotland) Rules 1980 Rule 24(2))

APPLICATION FOR CONTINUATION OF REPORT PRIOR TO THE REGISTRATION OF THE SUBJECTS DESCRIBED BELOW

Note: No covering letter is required and an existing Search should not be submitted.
VAT Reg No. GD 410 GB 888 8410 64

Please complete in DUPLICATE and in BLACK TYPE   Typewriter Alignment Box. Type XXX in centre

From	FOR OFFICIAL USE
	Report Number
	Date of Receipt
	Fee

County		Previous Report No.	

Search Sheet No. [1]		FAS No.	

Applicant's Reference		FAX No.	

Telephone No.		FAX response required (X here)	

POSTAL ADDRESS OF SUBJECTS

Street No.	House Name		Street Name	

Town		Postcode	

OTHER:

Description of Subjects	

I/We apply for the Report to .... [2] against the above subjects to be brought down to date.

1. Number obtainable from previous Report.
2. Date obtainable from previous Report.

Faxed applications should not be followed up by a written request and may not be accepted if a plan is included.

DIARY SERVICE:

Please state date and time you require report

Date .... Time ....

NOTE: If you do not state we will assume a 48 hour turnaround

Meadowbank House, 153 London Road, Edinburgh EH8 7AU
www.ros.gov.uk DX 555338 EDINBURGH 15 reports@ros.gov.uk
Tel: 0845 6070162 Fax: 0131 479 3651/3683/3667

The following parties (in addition to those noted on the previous report) should be searched against in the Register of Inhibitions and Adjudications, viz.

Typewriter Alignment Box. Type XXX in centre

1. Surname(s)	Forename(s)

Address(es)

2. Surname(s)	Forename(s)

Address(es)

3. Surname(s)	Forename(s)

Address(es)

4. Surname(s)	Forename(s)

Address(es)

5. Company/ Firm/ Corporate body

Address(es)

6. Company/ Firm/ Corporate body

Address(es)

NOTE: Insert full names and addresses of the persons on whom a Report is required.

Signature: ――――――――――――――――――――――― Date: ―――――――――――――――――――――――

REGISTERS OF SCOTLAND
Executive Agency

· property **REPORTS** service ·

FORM 12

(Land Registration (Scotland) Rules 1980 Rule 24(3))

APPLICATION FOR A REPORT OVER REGISTERED SUBJECTS

Note: No covering letter is required.
VAT Reg No. GD 410 GB 888 8410 64

Please complete in DUPLICATE and in BLACK TYPE   Typewriter Alignment Box. Type XXX in centre

From	**FOR OFFICIAL USE**
	Title Number
	Date of Receipt
	Report Number
	Fee

Applicant's Reference	**FAX No.**

Telephone No.	**FAX response required (X here)**

FAS No.

Title number(s)	**Title number(s)**

Title number(s)	**Mark X in box if more than 3 Title Numbers** [1]

I/We apply for a report (1) from the Land Register against:

Short Description of Subjects [2]	

Please cross appropriate box

(a) ☐ being the whole subjects in the above Title

(b) ☐ being part of the subjects in the above Title and edged red on the attached plan [3]

(c) ☐ being part of the subjects in the above Title and comprising the plot numbered _____ on the estate plan
       approved by the Keeper

From the date to which the Land Certificate was last brought down to the date of the Certificate.

1. Please list additional Title Numbers on a separate sheet.
2. If (a) applies, take the description from the title page of the Land Certificate; if (b) or (c) applies, the description must be sufficient to allow the subjects to be identified.
3. A plan need not be attached if a verbal description will sufficiently identify the subjects.

Faxed applications should not be followed up by a written request and may not be accepted if a plan is included.

DIARY SERVICE:

Please state date and time you require report

Date _____ Time _____

NOTE: If you do not state we will assume a 48 hour turnaround

Meadowbank House, 153 London Road, Edinburgh EH8 7AU
www.ros.gov.uk DX 555338 EDINBURGH 15 reports@ros.gov.uk
Tel: 0845 6070162 Fax: 0131 479 3651/3683/3667

· p r o p e r t y REPORTS s e r v i c e ·

FORM 12

and (2) from the Registers of Inhibitions and Adjudications for 5 years prior to the date of Certificate against

Typewriter Alignment Box. Type XXX in centre ☐ ☐ ☐

1. Surname(s)		Forename(s)	

Address(es)	

2. Surname(s)		Forename(s)	

Address(es)	

3. Surname(s)		Forename(s)	

Address(es)	

4. Surname(s)		Forename(s)	

Address(es)	

5. Company/ Firm/ Corporate body	

Address(es)	

6. Company/ Firm/ Corporate body	

Address(es)	

NOTE: Insert full names and addresses of the persons on whom a Report is required.

Signature: ———————————————   **Date:** ————————————————

REGISTERS OF SCOTLAND
Executive Agency

· property **REPORTS** service ·

FORM 13

(Land Registration (Scotland) Rules 1980 Rule 24(4))

APPLICATION FOR CONTINUATION OF REPORT OVER REGISTERED SUBJECTS

Note: No covering letter is required.
VAT Reg No. GD 410 GB 888 8410 64

Please complete in DUPLICATE and in BLACK TYPE   Typewriter Alignment Box. Type XXX in centre

From	FOR OFFICIAL USE
	Title Number
	Date of Receipt
	Report Number
	Fee

Previous Report No. [1]		FAS No.	

Applicant's Reference		FAX No.	

Telephone No.		FAX response required (X here)	

1. Title number		2. Title number	

3. Title number		Mark X in box if more than 3 Title Numbers [2]	

Description of Subjects	

I/We apply for the Report from the Land Register to _____ [3] against the above subjects to be brought down to date.

1. *Number obtainable from previous Report.*
2. *Please list additional Title Numbers on a separate sheet.*
3. *Date obtainable from previous Report.*

Faxed applications should not be followed up by a written request and may not be accepted if a plan is included.

DIARY SERVICE:
Please state date and time you require report
Date _____ Time _____
NOTE: If you do not state we will assume a 48 hour turnaround

Meadowbank House, 153 London Road, Edinburgh EH8 7AU
www.ros.gov.uk DX 555338 EDINBURGH 15 reports@ros.gov.uk
Tel: 0845 6070162 Fax: 0131 479 3651/3683/3667

· p r o p e r t y **REPORTS** s e r v i c e ·

FORM 13

The following parties (in addition to those noted on the previous report) should be searched against in the Register of Inhibitions and Adjudications, viz.

Typewriter Alignment Box. Type XXX in centre

1. Surname(s)   **Forename(s)**

Address(es)

2. Surname(s)   **Forename(s)**

Address(es)

3. Surname(s)   **Forename(s)**

Address(es)

4. Surname(s)   **Forename(s)**

Address(es)

5. Company/ Firm/ Corporate body

Address(es)

6. Company/ Firm/ Corporate body

Address(es)

NOTE: Insert full names and addresses of the persons on whom a Report is required.

Signature: ....   **Date:** ....

REGISTERS OF SCOTLAND
Executive Agency

· property **REPORTS** service ·

FORM 14

(Land Registration (Scotland) Rules 1980 Rule 24(5))

APPLICATION FOR A REPORT TO ASCERTAIN WHETHER OR NOT SUBJECTS HAVE BEEN REGISTERED

Note: No covering letter is required.
VAT Reg No. GD 410 GB 888 8410 64

Please complete in DUPLICATE and in BLACK TYPE   Typewriter Alignment Box. Type XXX in centre [| |]

From	FOR OFFICIAL USE
	Report Number
	Date of Receipt
	Fee

County		FAS No.	

Applicant's Reference		FAX No.	

Telephone No.		FAX response required (X here)	

Postal Address of Subjects

Street No.	House Name		Street Name	

Town		Postcode	

Other:

Description of Subjects	

The above subjects being	edged red on the accompanying plan,[3]
	being (part of [1]) the subjects described in [2]

I/We apply for a report from

(I) **the Land Register** stating whether or not registration of the said subjects has been effected

1. Delete if inapplicable
2. Describe by reference to a writ recorded in the Register of Sasines
3. A Plan need not be attached if a verbal description will sufficiently identify the subjects

Faxed applications should not be followed up by a written request and may not be accepted if a plan is included.

DIARY SERVICE:
Please state date and time you require report
Date ——————— Time ———————————

NOTE: If you do not state we will assume a 48 hour turnaround

Meadowbank House, 153 London Road, Edinburgh EH8 7AU
www.ros.gov.uk DX 555338 EDINBURGH 15 reports@ros.gov.uk
Tel: 0845 6070162 Fax: 0131 479 3651/3683/3667

· p r o p e r t y **REPORTS** s e r v i c e ·

FORM 14

---

and (2) from the Registers of Inhibitions and Adjudications for 5 years prior to the date of Certificate against

Typewriter Alignment Box. Type XXX in centre [ ] [ ] [ ]

1. Surname(s)	Forename(s)

Address(es)

2. Surname(s)	Forename(s)

Address(es)

3. Surname(s)	Forename(s)

Address(es)

4. Surname(s)	Forename(s)

Address(es)

5. Company/ Firm/ Corporate body

Address(es)

6. Company/ Firm/ Corporate body

Address(es)

NOTE: Insert full names and addresses of the persons on whom a Report is required.

Signature: ....   Date: ....

REGISTERS OF SCOTLAND
Executive Agency

FORM 15

(Land Registration (Scotland) Rules 1980 Rule 24(0))

APPLICATION FOR AN OFFICE COPY

Note: No covering letter is required.
VAT Reg No. GD 410 GB 888 8410 64

Please complete in DUPLICATE and in BLACK TYPE   Typewriter Alignment Box. Type XXX in centre

From	FOR OFFICIAL USE
	Application Number
	Date of Receipt
	Fee

Applicant's Reference	Telephone No.

FAS No.	Title No.

Short description of subjects	

I/We apply for
(1) An Office Copy of
Cross appropriate box(es)

☐ Full Title Sheet with Plan   ☐ Proprietorship Section only

☐ Full Title Sheet excluding Plan   ☐ Charges Section only

☐ Title Plan only   ☐ Burdens Section only

☐ Property Section only   ☐ The undernoted documents

Meadowbank House, 153 London Road, Edinburgh EH8 7AU
www.ros.gov.uk DX 555338 EDINBURGH 15 reports@ros.gov.uk
Tel: 0845 6070162 Fax: 0131 479 3651/3683/3667

and (2) A search in the Register of Inhibitions and Adjudications for 5 years prior to the date of the Office Copy against any party who has acquired an interest in the subjects since the last date on which the Land Certificate was made to correspond with the Register,

Typewriter Alignment Box. Type XXX in centre [ ][ ]

1.Surname(s)		Forename(s)	

Address(es)	

2.Surname(s)		Forename(s)	

Address(es)	

3.Surname(s)		Forename(s)	

Address(es)	

4.Surname(s)		Forename(s)	

Address(es)	

5.Company/ Firm/ Corporate body	

Address(es)	

6.Company/ Firm/ Corporate body	

Address(es)	

NOTE: Insert full names and addresses of the persons on whom a Report is required.

Signature: ———————————————————— Date: ————————————————————

TITLE CONDITIONS (SCOTLAND) ACT 2003 (CONSERVATION BODIES) ORDER 2003
(SSI 2003/453)

(amended by SSI 2004/400 and SSI 2004/477)

Citation and commencement

1   This Order may be cited as the Title Conditions (Scotland) Act 2003 (Conservation Bodies) Order 2003 and shall come into force on 1st November 2003.

Prescribed conservation bodies

2   The bodies listed in Parts I and II of the Schedule to this Order are prescribed to be conservation bodies under section 38(4) (conservation burdens) of the Title Conditions (Scotland) Act 2003.

SCHEDULE
CONSERVATION BODIES PRESCRIBED UNDER SECTION 38(4) OF THE
TITLE CONDITIONS (SCOTLAND) ACT 2003

PART I   LOCAL AUTHORITIES

Aberdeen City Council
Aberdeenshire Council
Angus Council
Argyll and Bute Council
City of Edinburgh Council
Clackmannanshire Council
Comhairle nan Eilean Siar
Dumfries and Galloway Council
Dundee City Council
East Ayrshire Council
East Dunbartonshire Council
East Lothian Council
East Renfrewshire Council
Falkirk Council
Fife Council
Glasgow City Council
Highland Council
Inverclyde Council
Midlothian Council
Moray Council
North Ayrshire Council
North Lanarkshire Council
Orkney Islands Council
Perth and Kinross Council
Renfrewshire Council
Scottish Borders Council
Shetland Islands Council
South Ayrshire Council
South Lanarkshire Council
Stirling Council
West Dunbartonshire Council
West Lothian Council

PART II   OTHER BODIES

[Alba Conservation Trust]
Castles of Scotland Preservation Trust
Edinburgh World Heritage Trust
Glasgow Building Preservation Trust
[Glasgow Conservation Trust West]
Highland Buildings Preservation Trust
Plantlife – The Wild-Plant Conservation Charity
Scottish Natural Heritage
Solway Heritage
St Vincent Crescent Preservation Trust
Strathclyde Building Preservation Trust
[Tayside Building Preservation Trust]
The John Muir Trust
The National Trust [for Scotland] for Places of Historic Interest and Natural Beauty
The Royal Society for the Protection of Birds
[The Scottish Wildlife Trust]
The Trustees of The Landmark Trust
The Trustees of the New Lanark Conservation Trust
The Woodland Trust
[United Kingdom Historic Building Preservation Trust]

TITLE CONDITIONS (SCOTLAND) ACT 2003 (RURAL HOUSING BODIES) ORDER 2004 (SSI 2004/477)

Citation and commencement
   1   This Order may be cited as the Title Conditions (Scotland) Act 2003 (Rural Housing Bodies) Order 2004 and shall come into force on 28th November 2004.

Prescribed rural housing bodies
   2   The bodies listed in the Schedule to this Order are prescribed to be rural housing bodies under section 43(5) (rural housing burdens) of the Title Conditions (Scotland) Act 2003.

SCHEDULE
RURAL HOUSING BODIES PRESCRIBED UNDER SECTION 43(5) OF THE TITLE CONDITIONS (SCOTLAND) ACT 2003

Albyn Housing Society Limited
Barra and Vatersay Housing Association Limited
Berneray Housing Association Limited
Buidheann Taigheadais na Meadhanan Limited
Cairn Housing Association Limited
Comhairle nan Eilean Siar
Dunbritton Housing Association Limited
Fyne Homes Limited
Isle of Jura Development Trust
Lochaber Housing Association Limited
Muirneag Housing Association Limited
Orkney Islands Council
Pentland Housing Association Limited
Taighean Ceann a Tuath na'Hearadh Limited
The Highlands Small Communities' Housing Trust
The Isle of Eigg Heritage Trust
The Isle of Gigha Heritage Trust
The North Harris Trust
Tighean Innse Gall Limited

EUROPEAN CONVENTION ON HUMAN RIGHTS

Article 6
Right to a fair trial

1. In the determination of his civil rights and obligations or of any criminal charge against him, everyone is entitled to a fair and public hearing within a reasonable time by an independent and impartial tribunal established by law. Judgment shall be pronounced publicly but the press and public may be excluded from all or part of the trial in the interests of morals, public order or national security in a democratic society, where the interests of juveniles or the protection of the private life of the parties so require, or to the extent strictly necessary in the opinion of the court in special circumstances where publicity would prejudice the interests of justice.

2. Everyone charged with a criminal offence shall be presumed innocent until proved guilty according to law.

3. Everyone charged with a criminal offence has the following minimum rights:

(a)   to be informed promptly, in a language which he understands and in detail, of the nature and cause of the accusation against him;

(b)   to have adequate time and facilities for the preparation of his defence;

(c)   to defend himself in person or through legal assistance of his own choosing or, if he has not sufficient means to pay for legal assistance, to be given it free when the interests of justice so require;

(d)   to examine or have examined witnesses against him and to obtain the attendance and examination of witnesses on his behalf under the same conditions as witnesses against him;

(e)   to have the free assistance of an interpreter if he cannot understand or speak the language used in court.

Article 8
Right to respect for private and family life

1. Everyone has the right to respect for his private and family life, his home and his correspondence.

2. There shall be no interference by a public authority with the exercise of this right except such as is in accordance with the law and is necessary in a democratic society in the interests of national security, public safety or the economic well-being of the country, for the prevention of disorder or crime, for the protection of health or morals, or for the protection of the rights and freedoms of others.

PROTOCOL 1

Article 1
Protection of property

Every natural or legal person is entitled to the peaceful enjoyment of his possessions. No one shall be deprived of his possessions except in the public interest and subject to the conditions provided for by law and by the general principles of international law.

The preceding provisions shall not, however, in any way impair the right of a State to enforce such laws as it deems necessary to control the use of property in accordance with the general interest or to secure the payment of taxes or other contributions or penalties.

PART II
TRUSTS AND SUCCESSION

TRUSTS (SCOTLAND) ACT 1921
(1921, 11 & 12 Geo 5, c 58)

1   Citation
This Act may be cited as the Trusts (Scotland) Act 1921.

2   Definitions
In the construction of this Act unless the context otherwise requires—
'Trust' shall mean and include—
(a)   any trust constituted by any deed or other writing, or by private or local Act of Parliament, or by Royal Charter, or by resolution of any corporation or public or ecclesiastical body, and
(b)   the appointment of any tutor, curator, [guardian] or judicial factor by deed, decree, or otherwise;
'Trust deed' shall mean and include—
(a)   any deed or other writing, private or local Act of Parliament, Royal Charter, or resolution of any corporation or ecclesiastical body, constituting any trust, and
(b)   any decree, deed, or other writing appointing a tutor, curator, [guardian] or judicial factor;
'Trustee' shall mean and include any trustee under any trust whether nominated, appointed, judicially or otherwise, or assumed, whether sole or joint, and whether entitled or not to receive any benefit under the trust or any remuneration as trustee for his services, and shall include any trustee *ex officio*, executor nominate, tutor, curator, [guardian] and judicial factor;
['Curator' and 'tutor' shall have respectively the meanings assigned to these expressions by section 1 of the Judicial Factors Act 1849;
'Guardian' shall not include any person who, within the meaning of Part 1 of the Children (Scotland) Act 1995, is entitled to act as the legal representative of a child;
'Judicial factor' shall mean any person holding a judicial appointment as a factor or curator on another person's estate;]
'Local authority' and 'rate' shall have respectively the meanings assigned to these expressions by the Local Authorities Loans (Scotland) Act 1891;
'The court' shall mean the Court of Session.

3   What trusts shall be held to include
All trusts shall be held to include the following powers and provisions unless the contrary be expressed (that is to say):—
(a)   Power to any trustee to resign the office of trustee;
(b)   Power to the trustee, if there be only one, or to the trustees, if there be more than one, or to a quorum of the trustees, if there be more than two, to assume new trustees;
(c)   A provision that a majority of the trustees accepting and surviving shall be a quorum;
(d)   A provision that each trustee shall be liable only for his own acts and

intromissions and shall not be liable for the acts and intromissions of co-trustees and shall not be liable for omissions:

Provided that—

(1)   A sole trustee shall not be entitled to resign his office by virtue of this Act unless either (1) he has assumed new trustees and they have declared their acceptance of office, or (2) the court shall have appointed new trustees or a judicial factor as hereinafter in this Act provided; and

(2)   A trustee who has accepted any legacy or bequest or annuity expressly given on condition of the recipient thereof accepting the office of trustee under the trust shall not be entitled to resign the office of trustee by virtue of this Act, unless otherwise expressly declared in the trust deed, nor shall any trustee appointed to the office of trustee on the footing of receiving remuneration for his services be entitled so to resign that office in the absence of an express power to resign; but it shall be competent to the court, on the petition of any trustee to whom the foregoing provisions of this proviso apply, to grant authority to such trustee to resign the office of trustee on such conditions (if any) with respect to repayment or otherwise of his legacy as the court may think just; and

(3)   A judicial factor shall not, by virtue of this Act, have the power of assumption, nor shall he have the power by virtue of this Act to resign his office without judicial authority.

Nothing in this section shall affect any liability incurred by any trustee prior to the date of any resignation or assumption under the provisions of this Act or of any Act repealed by this Act.

4   General powers of trustees

(1)   In all trusts the trustees shall have power to do the following acts, where such acts are not at variance with the terms or purposes of the trust, and such acts when done shall be as effectual as if such powers had been contained in the trust deed, *viz:*—

(a)   To sell the trust estate or any part thereof, heritable as well as moveable.

[. . .]

(c)   To grant leases of any duration (including mineral leases) of the heritable estate or any part thereof and to remove tenants.

(d)   To borrow money on the security of the trust estate or any part thereof, heritable as well as moveable.

(e)   To excamb any part of the trust estate which is heritable.

[(ea) To make any kind of investment.

(eb) To acquire heritable property for any other reason.]

(f)   To appoint factors and law agents and to pay them suitable remuneration.

(g)   To discharge trustees who have resigned and the representatives of trustees who have died.

(h)   To uplift, discharge, or assign debts due to the trust estate.

(i)   To compromise or to submit and refer all claims connected with the trust estate.

(j)   To refrain from doing diligence for the recovery of any debt due to the truster which the trustees may reasonably deem irrecoverable.

(k)   To grant all deeds necessary for carrying into effect the powers vested in the trustees.

(l)   To pay debts due by the truster or by the trust estate without requiring the creditors to constitute such debts where the trustees are satisfied that the debts are proper debts of the trust.

(m)   To make abatement or reduction, either temporary or permanent, of the rent, lordship, royalty, or other consideration stipulated in any lease of land, houses, tenements, minerals, metals, or other subjects, and to accept renunciations of leases of any such subjects.

(n)   To apply the whole or any part of trust funds which the trustees are empowered or directed by the trust deed to invest in the purchase of heritable property in the payment or redemption of any debt or burden affecting heritable property which may be destined to the same series of heirs and subject to the same conditions as are by the trust deed made applicable to heritable property directed to be purchased.

[(o)   To concur, in respect of any securities of a company (being securities comprised in the trust estate), in any scheme or arrangement—

(i)   for the reconstruction of the company,

(ii)   for the sale of all or any part of the property and undertaking of the company to another company,

(iii)   for the acquisition of the securities of the company, or of control thereof, by another company,

(iv)   for the amalgamation of the company with another company, or

(v)   for the release, modification, or variation of any rights, privileges or liabilities attached to the securities or any of them,

in like manner as if the trustees were entitled to such securities beneficially; to accept any securities of any denomination or description of the reconstructed or purchasing or new company in lieu of, or in exchange for, all or any of the first mentioned securities; and to retain any securities so accepted as aforesaid for any period for which the trustees could have properly retained the original securities,

(p)   To exercise, to such extent as the trustees think fit, any conditional or preferential right to subscribe for any securities in a company (being a right offered to them in respect of any holding in the company), to apply capital money of the trust estate in payment of the consideration, and to retain any such securities for which they have subscribed for any period for which they have power to retain the holding in respect of which the right to subscribe for the securities was offered (but subject to any conditions subject to which they have that power); to renounce, to such extent as they think fit, any such right; or to assign, to such extent as they think fit and for the best consideration that can reasonably be obtained, the benefit of such right or the title thereto to any person, including any beneficiary under the trust.]

[(1A)   The power to act under subsection (1)(ea) or (eb) above is subject to any restriction or exclusion imposed by or under any enactment.

(1B)   The power to act under subsection (1)(ea) or (eb) above is not conferred on any trustees who are—

(a)   the trustees of a pension scheme,

(b)   the trustees of an authorised unit trust, or

(c)   trustees under any other trust who are entitled by or under any other enactment to make investments of the trust estate.

(1C)   No term relating to the powers of a trustee contained in a trust deed executed before 3rd August 1961 is to be treated as restricting or excluding the power to act under subsection (1)(ea) above.

(1D)   No term restricting the powers of investment of a trustee to those conferred by the Trustee Investments Act 1961 (c 62) contained in a trust deed executed on or after 3rd August 1961 is to be treated as restricting or excluding the power to act under subsection (1)(ea) above.

(1E)   The reference in subsection (1D) above to a trustee does not include a reference to a trustee under a trust constituted by a private or local Act of Parliament or a private Act of the Scottish Parliament; and 'trust deed' shall be construed accordingly.

(1F)   In this section—

'authorised unit trust' means a unit trust scheme in the case of which an order under section 243 of the Financial Services and Markets Act 2000 (c 8) is in force, 'enactment' has the same meaning as in the Scotland Act 1998 (c 46),

'pension scheme' means an occupational pension scheme (within the meaning of the Pension Schemes Act 1993 (c 48)) established under a trust and subject to the law of Scotland.]

(2) This section shall apply to acts done before as well as after the passing of this Act, but shall not apply so as to affect any question relating to an act enumerated in head (a), (b), (c), (d), or (e) of this section which may, at the passing of this Act, be the subject of a depending action.

[4A   Exercise of power of investment: duties of trustee

(1) Before exercising the power of investment under section 4(1)(ea) of this Act, a trustee shall have regard to—

(a)   the suitability to the trust of the proposed investment, and

(b)   the need for diversification of investments.

(2) Before exercising that power of investment, a trustee shall (except where subsection (4) applies) obtain and consider proper advice about the way in which the power should be exercised.

(3) When reviewing the investments of the trust, a trustee shall (except where subsection (4) applies) obtain and consider proper advice about whether the investments should be varied.

(4) If a trustee reasonably concludes that in all the circumstances it is unnecessary or inappropriate to obtain such advice, the trustee need not obtain it.

(5) In this section, 'proper advice' means the advice of a person who is reasonably believed by the trustee to be qualified by the person's ability and practical experience of financial and other matters relating to the proposed investment.]

5   Powers which may be granted to trustees by the court

It shall be competent to the court, on the petition of the trustees under any trust, to grant authority to the trustees to do any of the acts mentioned in the section of this Act relating to general powers of trustees, notwithstanding that such act is at variance with the terms or purposes of the trust, on being satisfied that such act is in all the circumstances expedient for the execution of the trust.

In this section the expression 'trust' shall not include any trust constituted by private or local Act of Parliament, and the expression 'trustees' shall be construed accordingly.

6   Method of sale by trustees

All powers of sale conferred on trustees by the trust deed or by virtue of this Act may be exercised either by public roup or private bargain unless otherwise directed in the trust deed or in the authority given by the court, and when the estate is heritable it shall be lawful in the exercise of such powers to [. . .] reserve the mines and minerals.

7   Deeds granted by trustees

Any deed bearing to be granted by the trustees under any trust, and in fact executed by a quorum of such trustees in favour of any person other than a beneficiary or a co-trustee under the trust where such person has dealt onerously and in good faith shall not be void or challengeable on the ground that any trustee or trustees under the trust was or were not consulted in the matter, or was or were not present, at any meeting of trustees where the same was considered, or did not consent to or concur in the granting of the deed, or on the ground of any other omission or irregularity of procedure on the part of the trustees or any of them in relation to the granting of the deed.

Nothing in this section shall affect any question of liability or otherwise between any trustee under any trust on the one hand and any co-trustee or beneficiary under such trust on the other hand. This section shall apply to deeds granted before as well as after the passing of this Act, but shall not apply so as to affect any question which may, at the passing of this Act, be the subject of a depending action.

In this section the expression 'quorum' means a quorum of the trustees under any trust entitled to act in terms of the trust deed or in virtue of this Act, or of any Act repealed by this Act, as the case may be.

8 Conveyances to non-existing or unidentifiable persons

(1) Where in any deed, whether *inter vivos* or *mortis causa*, heritable or moveable property is conveyed to any person in liferent, and in fee to persons who, when such conveyance comes into operation, are unborn or incapable of ascertainment, the person to whom the property is conveyed in liferent shall not be deemed to be beneficially entitled to the property in fee by reason only that the liferent is not expressed in the deed to be a liferent allenarly; and all such conveyances as aforesaid shall, unless a contrary intention appears in the deed, take effect in the same manner and in all respects as if the liferent were declared to be a liferent allenarly; provided always that this subsection shall not apply to any conveyance which has come into operation before the passing of this Act.

For the purposes of this subsection, the date at which any conveyance in liferent and fee as aforesaid comes into operation shall be deemed to be the date at which the person to whom the liferent is conveyed first becomes entitled to receive the rents or income of the property.

(2) Where under any conveyance, whether coming into operation before or after the passing of this Act, any property is conveyed to one person in liferent and in fee to persons who, when such conveyance comes into operation, are unborn or incapable of ascertainment, it shall be competent to the court, on the application of the liferenter, whether or not he would, according to the existing law, be deemed to be fiduciary fiar, or of any person to whom the fee or any part thereof bears to be presumptively destined, or who may have an interest under such conveyance notwithstanding that such interest is prospective or contingent, or of the accountant of court:—

(a) To grant authority to the fiduciary fiar to exercise all or such of the powers, or to do all or such of the acts, competent to a trustee at common law or under this Act, as to the court may seem fit:

(b) To appoint a trustee or trustees (of whom the liferenter or fiduciary fiar may be one) with all the powers of trustees at common law and under this Act, or a judicial factor, to hold the said property in trust in place of the liferenter or fiduciary fiar; and to authorise and ordain the fiduciary fiar to execute and deliver all such deeds as may be necessary for the completion of title to the said property by such trustee or trustees or judicial factor; or otherwise, to grant warrant to such trustee or trustees or judicial factor to complete a title to the said property in the same manner and to the same effect as under a warrant in favour of a trustee or trustees granted in terms of the section of this Act relating to the appointment of new trustees by the court, or a warrant in favour of a judicial factor granted in terms of section 24 of the Titles to Land Consolidation (Scotland) Act 1868 or section 44 of the Conveyancing (Scotland) Act 1874, as the case may be. The expense of completing the title as aforesaid shall, unless the court otherwise directs, be a charge against the capital of the estate.

(3) For the purposes of this section, all references to a trust deed in this Act contained shall be read and construed as a reference to the conveyance of the property in liferent and fee as aforesaid.

9 Liferents of personal estate beyond certain limits prohibited

It shall be competent to constitute or reserve by means of a trust or otherwise a liferent interest in moveable and personal estate in Scotland in favour only of a person in life at the date of the deed constituting or reserving such liferent, and, where any moveable or personal estate in Scotland shall, by virtue of any deed dated after the 31st day of July 1868 (the date of any testamentary or *mortis causa* deed being taken to be the date of the death of the granter, and the date of any contract of marriage being taken to be the date of the dissolution of the marriage) be held in liferent by or for behoof of a person of full age born after the date of such deed, such moveable or personal estate shall belong absolutely to such person, and, where such estate stands invested in the name of any trustees, such trustees shall be bound to deliver, make over, or convey such estate to such person:

Provided always that, where more persons than one are interested in the moveable or personal estate held by trustees as hereinbefore mentioned, all the expenses connected with the transference of a portion of such estate to any of the beneficiaries in terms of this section shall be borne by the beneficiary in whose favour the transference is made.

[. . .]

15   Trustees not to hold certificates or bonds payable to bearer

(1)   A trustee, unless authorised by the terms of his trust, shall not apply for purchase, acquire, or hold beyond a reasonable time for realisation or conversion into registered or inscribed stock any certificate to bearer or debenture or other bond or document payable to bearer.

(2)   Nothing in this section shall impose on the Bank of England or the Bank of Ireland or on any person authorised by or under any Act of Parliament to issue any such certificate, bond, or document any obligation to inquire whether a person applying for such a certificate, bond, or document is or is not a trustee, or subject them to any liability in the event of their granting any such certificate, bond or document to a trustee, nor invalidate any such certificate, bond or document if granted.

16   The court may authorise the advance of part of the capital of a trust fund

The court may, from time to time under such conditions as they see fit, authorise trustees to advance any part of the capital of a fund destined either absolutely or contingently to beneficiaries who at the date of the application to the court are not of full age, if it shall appear that the income of the fund is insufficient or not applicable to, and that such advance is necessary for, the maintenance or education of such beneficiaries or any of them, and that it is not expressly prohibited by the trust deed, and that the rights of such beneficiaries, if contingent, are contingent only on their survivance.

17   Trustees may apply to court for superintendence order as to investment and distribution of estate

It shall be competent for the trustees under any trust deed or one or more of them to apply to the court for an order of the accountant of court to superintend their administration of the trust insofar as it relates to the investment of the trust funds and the distribution thereof among the creditors interested and the beneficiaries under the trust, and the court may grant such order accordingly, and if such order be granted the accountant of court shall annually examine and audit the accounts of such trustees, and at any time, if he thinks fit, he may report to the court upon any question that may arise in the administration of the trust with regard to any of the foresaid matters and obtain the directions of the court thereupon.

18   Discharge of trustees resigning and heirs of trustees dying during the subsistence of the trust

When a trustee who resigns or the representatives of a trustee who has died or resigned cannot obtain a discharge of his acts and intromissions from the remaining trustees, and when the beneficiaries of the trust refuse or are unable from absence, incapacity or otherwise to grant a discharge, the court may on petition to that effect at the instance of such trustee or representative and after such intimation and inquiry as may be thought necessary, grant such discharge.

19 Form of resignation of trustees

(1) Subject to the provisions of subsection (2) of this section, any trustee entitled to resign his office may do so by minute of the trust entered in the sederunt book of the trust and signed in such sederunt book by such trustee and by the other trustee or trustees acting at the time, or he may do so by signing a minute of resignation in the form of Schedule A to this Act annexed or to the like effect, and may register the same in the books of council and session, and in such case he shall be bound to intimate the same to his co-trustee or trustees, and the resignation shall be held to take effect from and after the date of the receipt of such intimation, or the last date thereof if more than one, and in case after inquiry the residence of any trustee to whom intimation should be given under this provision cannot be found, such intimation shall be sent by post in a registered letter addressed to the Keeper of the Register of Edictal Citations.

(2) A sole trustee desiring to resign his office may apply to the court stating such desire and praying for the appointment of new trustees or of a judicial factor to administer the trust, and the court, after intimation to the beneficiaries under the trust, or such of them as the court may direct, may thereafter appoint either a judicial factor or new trustees, and if the court appoint new trustees the court may grant warrant to complete title as provided in the section of this Act relating to appointment of new trustees by the court.

20 Effect of resignation

Where a trustee entitled to resign his office shall have resigned in either of the modes provided by the immediately preceding section or otherwise, and his resignation shall have been duly completed, such trustee shall be thereby divested of the whole property and estate of the trust, which shall accrue to or devolve upon the continuing trustees or trustee without the necessity of any conveyance or other transfer by the resigning trustee, but without prejudice to the right of the continuing trustee or trustees to require the resigning trustee to execute and deliver to the continuing trustees or trustee at the expense of the trust a conveyance or transfer (or conveyances or transfers) of the property or estate belonging to the trust, or any part thereof if the continuing trustees or trustee shall consider this expedient, and the resigning trustee when so required shall be bound at the expense of the trust to execute and deliver such conveyance or conveyances, transfer or transfers accordingly.

21 Appointment of new or additional trustees by deed of assumption

When trustees have the power of assuming new trustees, such new trustees may be assumed by deed of assumption executed by the trustee or trustees acting under the trust deed or by a quorum of such trustees, if more than two, in the form of Schedule B to this Act annexed or to the like effect, and a deed of assumption so executed, in addition to a general conveyance of the trust estate, may contain a special conveyance of heritable property belonging to the trust estate, and in such case shall be effectual as a conveyance of such heritable property in favour of the existing trustees and the trustees so to be assumed, and such deed of assumption shall also be effectual as an assignation in favour of such existing and assumed trustees of the whole personal property belonging to the trust estate, and in the event of any trustee acting under any trust deed being insane or incapable of acting by reason of physical or mental disability or by continuous absence from the United Kingdom for a period of six months or upwards, such deed of assumption may be executed by the remaining trustee or trustees acting under such trust deed: Provided that, when the signatures of a quorum of trustees cannot be obtained, it shall be necessary to obtain the consent of the court to such deed of assumption on application either by the acting trustee or trustees or by any one or more of the beneficiaries under the trust deed.

22 Appointment of new trustees by the court

When trustees cannot be assumed under any trust deed, or when any person who is the sole trustee appointed in or acting under any trust deed is or has become insane or is or has become incapable of acting by reason of physical or mental disability, or by being absent continuously from the United Kingdom for a period of at least six months, or by having disappeared for a like period, the [Court of Session or an appropriate sheriff court] may, upon the application of any party having interest in the trust estate, after such intimation and inquiry as may be thought necessary, appoint a trustee or trustees under such trust deed with all the powers incident to that office, and, on such appointment being made in the case of any person becoming insane or incapable of acting as aforesaid, such person shall cease to be a trustee under such trust deed, and the court [to which application is made] may, on such application, grant a warrant to complete a title to any heritable property forming part of the trust estate in favour of the trustee or trustees so appointed, which warrant shall specify and describe the heritable property to which it is applicable, or refer in terms of law to a recorded deed containing a description thereof, and shall also specify the moveable or personal property, or bear reference to an inventory appended to the petition to the court in which such moveable or personal property is specified, and such warrant shall be effectual as a conveyance of such heritable property in favour of the trustee or trustees so appointed in like manner and to the same effect as a warrant in favour of a judicial factor granted under the authority of section 24 of the Titles to Land Consolidation (Scotland) Act 1868, or section 44 of the Conveyancing (Scotland) Act 1874, and shall also be effectual as an assignation of such moveable or personal property in favour of the trustee or trustees so appointed.

23 Court may remove trustees in certain cases

In the event of any trustee being or becoming insane or incapable of acting by reason of physical or mental disability or being absent from the United Kingdom continuously for a period of at least six months, or having disappeared for a like period, such trustee, in the case of insanity or incapacity of acting by reason of physical or mental disability, shall, and in the case of continuous absence from the United Kingdom or disappearance for a period of six months or upwards, may, on application in manner in this section provided by any co-trustee or any beneficiary or other person interested in the trust estate, be removed from office upon such evidence as shall satisfy the court to which the application is made of the insanity, incapacity or continuous absence or disappearance of such trustee. Such application [may be made either to the Court of Session or to an appropriate sheriff court.]

24 Completion of title by the beneficiary of a lapsed trust

Any person who shall be entitled to the possession for his own absolute use of any heritable property or moveable or personal property the title to which has been taken in the name of any trustee who has died or become incapable of acting without having executed a conveyance of such property, or any other person deriving right whether immediately or otherwise from the person entitled as aforesaid, may apply by petition to the [Court of Session or an appropriate sheriff court] for authority to complete a title to such property in his own name, and such petition shall specify and describe the heritable property, or refer to a description thereof in terms of law, and refer to an inventory to which the moveable or personal property is specified to which such title is to be completed and after such intimation and inquiry as may be thought necessary it shall be lawful for the court [to which application is made] to grant a warrant for completing such title as aforesaid, which warrant shall specify and describe the heritable property to which it is applicable, or refer in terms of law to a description thereof, and shall also specify the moveable or personal property or shall bear reference to an inventory appended to the petition in which such moveable or personal property is specified, and such warrant shall be effectual as a conveyance of such heritable property in favour of the petitioner in like manner and to the same effect as a warrant in favour of a judicial factor granted under the authority of section 24 of the Titles to Land Consolidation (Scotland) Act 1868, or section 44 of the Conveyancing (Scotland) Act 1874, and shall also be effectual as an assignation of such moveable or personal property in favour of the petitioner.

[24A   Interpretation of sections 22–24

In sections 22 to 24 of this Act the expression 'appropriate sheriff court' means—
  (a)   in the case of a trust other than a marriage contract—
    (i)   where the truster, or any of the trusters, was at the date of the coming into operation of the trust domiciled in a sheriffdom, a sheriff court of that sheriffdom; or
    (ii)   where sub-paragraph (i) of this paragraph does not apply, or where the applicant does not possess sufficient information to enable him to determine which sheriff court, if any, would by virtue of that sub-paragraph be an appropriate sheriff court, the sheriff court at Edinburgh;
  (b)   in the case of a marriage contract—
    (i)   where either spouse is, or was when he died, domiciled in a sheriffdom, a sheriff court of that sheriffdom; or
    (ii)   where sub-paragraph (i) of this paragraph does not apply, or where the applicant does not possess sufficient information to enable him to determine which sheriff court, if any, would by virtue of that sub-paragraph be an appropriate sheriff court, the sheriff court at Edinburgh.]

25   Completion of title of judicial factors

Application for authority to complete the title of a judicial factor to any trust property or estate may be contained in the petition for the appointment of such factor, and such application may include moveable or personal property.

26   Powers of court under this Act to be exercised by Lord Ordinary

Applications to the court under the authority of this Act shall be by petition addressed to the court, and shall be brought in the first instance before one of the Lords Ordinary officiating in the Outer House, who may direct such intimation and service thereof and such investigation or inquiry as he may think fit, and the power of the Lord Ordinary before whom the petition is enrolled may be exercised by the Lord Ordinary on the Bills during vacation, and all such petitions shall, as respects procedure, disposal and review, be subject to the same rules and regulations as are enacted with respect to petitions coming before the Junior Lord Ordinary in virtue of the Court of Session Act 1857: Provided that, when in the exercise of the powers pertaining to the court of appointing trustees and regulating trusts, it shall be necessary to settle a scheme for the administration of any charitable or other permanent endowment, the Lord Ordinary shall, after preparing such scheme, report to one of the divisions of the court, by whom the same shall be finally adjusted and settled, and in all cases where it shall be necessary to settle any such scheme, intimation shall be made to His Majesty's Advocate, who shall be entitled to appear and intervene for the interests of the charity or any object of the trust or the public interest.

27   Court may pass Acts of Sederunt

The court shall be and is hereby empowered from time to time to make such regulations by Act or Acts of Sederunt as may be requisite for carrying into effect the purposes of this Act. [. . .]

28   Resignation of trustee who is also executor to infer resignation as executor
In all cases where a trust deed appoints the trustees to be also executors the resignation of any such trustee shall infer, unless where otherwise expressly declared, his resignation also as an executor under such trust deed.

29   Extent of liability of trustee
Where a trustee shall have improperly advanced trust money on a heritable security which would, at the time of the investment, have been a proper investment in all respects for a less sum than was actually advanced thereon, the security shall be deemed an authorised investment for such less sum, and the trustee shall only be liable to make good the sum advanced in excess thereof with interest.

30   Trustee not to be chargeable with breach of trust for lending money on security of any property on certain conditions
(1)   Any trustee lending money on the security of any property shall not be chargeable with breach of trust by reason only of the proportion borne by the amount of the loan to the value of such property at the time when the loan was made, provided that it shall appear to the court that in making such loan the trustee was acting upon a report as to the value of the property made by a person whom the trustee reasonably believed to be an able practical valuator instructed and employed independently of any owner of the property, whether such valuator carried on business in the locality where the property is situated or elsewhere, and that the amount of the loan by itself or in combination with any other loan or loans upon the property ranking prior to or *pari passu* with the loan in question does not exceed two equal third parts of the value of the property as stated in such report, and this section shall apply to a loan upon any property on which the trustees can lawfully lend.

(2)   This section shall apply to transfers of existing securities as well as to new securities, and in its application to a partial transfer of an existing security the expression 'the amount of the loan' shall include the amount of any other loan or loans upon the property ranking prior to or *pari passu* with the loan in question.

31   Power of court to make orders in case of breach of trust
Where a trustee shall have committed a breach of trust at the instigation or request or with the consent in writing of a beneficiary, the court may, if it shall think fit, make such order as to the court shall seem just for applying all or any part of the interest of the beneficiary in the trust estate by way of indemnity to the trustee or person claiming through him.

32   Court may relieve trustee from personal liability
(1)   If it appears to the court that a trustee is or may be personally liable for any breach of trust, whether the transaction alleged to be a breach of trust occurred before or after the passing of this Act, but has acted honestly and reasonably, and ought fairly to be excused for the breach of trust, then the court may relieve the trustee either wholly or partly from personal liability for the same.

(2)   In this section and in the two immediately preceding sections the expression 'the court' shall mean any court of competent jurisdiction in which a question relative to the actings, liability, or removal of a trustee comes to be tried.

33   Investment ceasing to be an authorised investment
A trustee shall not be liable for breach of trust by reason only of his continuing to hold an investment which has ceased to be an investment authorised by the trust deed or by or under this Act.

34 Expenses of applications under this Act
(1) The court shall determine all questions of expenses in relation to any application made under this Act, and may direct that any such expenses shall be paid out of the trust estate where the court considers this reasonable.
(2) In this section the expression 'the court' shall include any court to which an application may be made under this Act.

35 Application of Act
Save as in this Act expressly otherwise provided—
(1) This Act shall apply to trusts which have come into operation before as well as to trusts coming into operation after the passing of this Act.
(2) Nothing in this Act contained shall be held to extend the liability of trustees.

[. . .]

SCHEDULES

SCHEDULE A   Section 19

FORM OF MINUTE OF RESIGNATION

I, *AB*, do hereby resign the office of trustee under the trust disposition and settlement (*or other deed*) granted by *CD* dated the   day of   ,* (*If the trustee was assumed add*, and to which office of trustee I was assumed by deed of assumption granted by *EF* and *GH*, dated   day of   .*). [Testing clause†]

*If recorded specify register and date of recording.
[† Note—Subscription of the document by the granter of it will be sufficient for the document to be formally valid, but witnessing of it may be necessary or desirable for other purposes (see the Requirements of Writing (Scotland) Act 1995).]

SCHEDULE B   Section 21

FORM OF DEED OF ASSUMPTION

I, *AB* (*or we, AB and CD*), the accepting and surviving (*or remaining*) trustee (*or trustees, or a majority and quorum of the accepting and surviving trustees*), acting under a trust disposition and settlement (*or other deed*) granted by *EF*, dated the   day of   (*if recorded, specify register and date of recording*), do hereby assume *GH* (*or GH and IK*) as a trustee (*or trustees*) under the said trust disposition and settlement (*or other deed*); and I (*or we*) dispone and convey to myself (*or ourselves*) and the said *GH* (*or GH and IK*) as trustees under the said trust disposition and settlement (*or other deed*), and the survivors or survivor, and the heir of the last survivor, the majority, while more than two are acting, being a quorum (*or otherwise in accordance with the terms of the trust deed*), all and sundry the whole trust, estate and effects, heritable and moveable, real and personal, of every description and wherever situated, at present belonging to me (*or us*) or under my (*or our*) control as trustee (*or surviving trustees, or otherwise as the case may be*), under the said trust disposition and settlement (*or other deed*), together with the whole vouchers, titles, and instructions thereof. (*Then may follow, if wished, special conveyances of heritable or personal property, with the usual clauses of a conveyance applicable to such property, and as the case may require.*) [Testing clause†]

[† Note—Subscription of the document by the granter or granters of it will be sufficient for the document to be formally valid, but witnessing of it may be necessary or desirable for other purposes (see the Requirements of Writing (Scotland) Act 1995).]

[. . .]

TRUSTS (SCOTLAND) ACT 1961
(1961, 9 & 10 Eliz 2, c 57)

1 Jurisdiction of court in relation to variation of trust purposes

(1)   In relation to any trust taking effect, whether before or after the commence-ment of this Act, under any will, settlement or other disposition, the court may if it thinks fit, on the petition of the trustees or any of the beneficiaries, approve on behalf of—

(a)   any of the beneficiaries who [because of any legal disability] by reason of nonage or other incapacity is incapable of assenting, or

(b)   any person (whether ascertained or not) who may become one of the beneficiaries as being at a future date or on the happening of a future event a person of any specified description or a member of any specified class of persons, so however that this paragraph shall not include any person who is capable of assenting and would be of that description, or a member of that class, as the case may be, if the said date had fallen or the said event had happened at the date of the presentation of the petition to the court, or

(c)   any person unborn,

any arrangement (by whomsoever proposed, and whether or not there is any other person beneficially interested who is capable of assenting thereto) varying or revoking all or any of the trust purposes or enlarging the powers of the trustees of managing or administering the trust estate:

Provided that the court shall not approve an arrangement under this subsection on behalf of any person unless it is of the opinion that the carrying out thereof would not be prejudicial to that person.

(2)   For the purposes of the foregoing subsection a person who is [of or over the age of 16 years] but has not attained the age of [18 years] shall be deemed to be incapable of assenting: but before approving an arrangement under that subsection on behalf of any such person the court shall take such account as it thinks appro-priate of his attitude to the arrangement.

(3)   [. . .]

(4)   Where under any trust such as is mentioned in subsection (1) of this section a trust purpose entitles any of the beneficiaries (in this subsection referred to as 'the alimentary beneficiary') to an alimentary liferent of, or any alimentary income from the trust estate or any part thereof, the court may if it thinks fit, on the petition of the trustees or any of the beneficiaries, authorise any arrangement vary-ing or revoking that trust purpose and making new provisions in lieu thereof, including, if the court thinks fit, new provision for the disposal of the fee or capital of the trust estate or, as the case may be, of such part thereof as was burdened with the liferent or the payment of the income:

Provided that the court shall not authorise an arrangement under this subsection unless—

(a)   it considers that the carrying out of the arrangement would be reason-able, having regard to the income of the alimentary beneficiary from all sources, and to such other factors, if any, as the court considers material, and

(b)   the arrangement is approved by the alimentary beneficiary, or, where the alimentary beneficiary is a person on whose behalf the court is empowered by subsection (1) of this section or that subsection as extended by subsection (2) of this section to approve the arrangement, the arrangement is so approved by the court under that subsection.

(5)   Nothing in the foregoing provisions of this section shall be taken to limit or restrict any power possessed by the court apart from this section under any Act of Parliament or rule of law.

(6)   In this section the expression 'beneficiary' in relation to a trust includes any person having, directly or indirectly, an interest, whether vested or contingent, under the trust.

2 Validity of certain transactions by trustees

(1) Where, after the commencement of this Act, the trustees under any trust enter into a transaction with any person (in this section referred to as 'the second party'), being a transaction under which the trustees purport to do in relation to the trust estate or any part thereof an act of any of the descriptions specified in paragraphs (a) to [(eb)] of subsection (1) of section 4 of the Act of 1921 (which empowers trustees to do certain acts where such acts are not at variance with the terms or purposes of the trust) the validity of the transaction and of any title acquired by the second party under the transaction shall not be challengeable by the second party or any other person on the ground that the act in question is at variance with the terms or purposes of the trust:

Provided that in relation to a transaction [other than a transaction such as is specified in paragraph (ea) of that subsection] entered into by trustees who are acting under the supervision of the accountant of court this section shall have effect only if the said accountant consents to the transaction.

[(2) Nothing in subsection (1) of this section shall affect any question of liability between any of the trustees on the one hand and any co-trustee or any of the beneficiaries on the other hand.

(3) Without prejudice to the operation of subsection (1) of this section, where in relation to the trust estate or any part thereof a judicial factor thinks it expedient to do any of the acts mentioned in that subsection but the act in question might be at variance with the terms or purposes of the trust, he may, subject to the following provisions of this section, apply to the accountant of court for his consent to the doing of the act.

(4) Where an application is made under subsection (3) of this section to the accountant of court for his consent to the doing of an act to which that subsection applies, he may grant the application subject to such conditions (including conditions as to price) as he thinks fit if—

(a) he considers that the doing of the act is in the best interests of the owner of the trust estate to which the judicial factor's appointment relates or of any person to whom the owner owes a duty of support; and

(b) he is satisfied—

(i) that the judicial factor is not expressly prohibited by the terms of his appointment from doing the act; and

(ii) that there has been compliance with the provisions of subsection (5) of this section and of any rules made thereunder; and

(c) no objection is made to the doing of the act under subsection (5) of this section.

(5) A judicial factor proposing to make an application under subsection (3) of this section to the accountant of court shall notify such persons or such class or classes of persons as may be specified in rules of court in such manner as may be so specified of the proposed application, the act to which it relates, and of their right to object to him doing that act within such time and in such manner as the rules may specify; and the rules may make different provision in respect of different classes of judicial factors, and may make provision exempting a judicial factor or a class of judicial factors from giving notification under this subsection in such circumstances as the rules may specify.

(6) Where a judicial factor does any act in accordance with the consent of the accountant of court granted under subsection (4) of this section and in compliance with the provisions of this section and of any rules made thereunder, it shall be treated as being not at variance with the terms or purposes of the trust.]

3–4 [*Amend Trusts (Scotland) Act 1921.*]

5 Accumulations of income

(1) The following provisions of this section shall have effect in substitution for the provisions of the Accumulations Act 1800, and that Act is hereby repealed.

(2)   No person may by any will, settlement or other disposition dispose of any property in such manner that the income thereof shall be wholly or partially accumulated for any longer period than one of the following, that is to say—

(a)   the life of the grantor; or

(b)   a term of twenty-one years from the death of the grantor; or

(c)   the duration of the minority or respective minorities of any person or persons living or *in utero* at the death of the grantor; or

(d)   the duration of the minority or respective minorities of any person or persons who, under the terms of the will, settlement or other disposition directing the accumulation, would for the time being, if of full age, be entitled to the income directed to be accumulated.

(3)   In every case where any accumulation is directed otherwise than as aforesaid, the direction shall, save as hereinafter provided, be void, and the income directed to be accumulated shall, so long as the same is directed to be accumulated contrary to this section, go to and be received by the person or persons who would have been entitled thereto if such accumulation had not been directed.

(4)   For avoidance of doubt it is hereby declared that, in the case of a settlement or other disposition *inter vivos*, a direction to accumulate income during a period specified in paragraph (d) of subsection (2) of this section shall not be void, nor shall the accumulation of the income be contrary to this section, solely by reason of the fact that the period begins during the life of the grantor and ends after his death.

(5)   The restrictions imposed by this section apply to wills, settlements and other dispositions made on or after the twenty-eighth day of July, 1800, but, in the case of wills, only where the testator was living and of testamentary capacity after the end of one year from that date.

(6)   In this section 'minority' in relation to any person means the period beginning with the birth of the person and ending with his attainment of the age of twenty-one years, and 'grantor' includes settlor and, in relation to a will, the testator.

6   Interpretation

(1)   In this Act, unless the context otherwise requires,—

'Act of 1921' means the Trusts (Scotland) Act 1921;

'the court' means the Court of Session; and

'trust' and 'trustee' have the same meanings respectively as in the Act of 1921.

(2)   Unless the context otherwise requires references in this Act to any other Act are references to that Act as amended, modified or extended by any Act including this Act.

7   Short title, citation, application and commencement

(1)   This Act may be cited as the Trusts (Scotland) Act 1961, and this Act and the Act of 1921 may be cited together as the Trusts (Scotland) Acts 1921 and 1961.

(2)   This Act shall apply to trusts which have come into operation before, as well as to trusts coming into operation after, the commencement of this Act.

(3)   This Act shall come into operation on the expiration of the period of one month beginning with the date of the passing thereof.

SUCCESSION (SCOTLAND) ACT 1964
(1964, c 41)

PART I
INTESTATE SUCCESSION

1   Assimilation of heritage to moveables for purpose of devolution on intestacy

(1)   The whole of the intestate estate of any person dying after the commencement of this Act (so far as it is estate the succession to which falls to be regulated

by the law of Scotland) shall devolve, without distinction as between heritable and moveable property, in accordance with—

(a) the provisions of this Part of this Act, and

(b) any enactment or rule of law in force immediately before the commencement of this Act which is not inconsistent with those provisions and which, apart from this section, would apply to that person's moveable intestate estate, if any;

and, subject to section 37 of this Act, any enactment or rule of law in force immediately before the commencement of this Act with respect to the succession to intestate estates shall, in so far as it is inconsistent with the provisions of this Part of this Act, cease to have effect.

(2) Nothing in this Part of this Act shall affect legal rights or the prior rights of a surviving spouse [or civil partner]; and accordingly any reference in this Part of this Act to an intestate estate shall be construed as a reference to so much of the net intestate estate as remains after the satisfaction of those rights, or the proportion thereof properly attributable to the intestate estate.

2 Rights of succession to intestate estate

(1) Subject to the following provisions of this Part of this Act—

(a) where an intestate is survived by children, they shall have right to the whole of the intestate estate;

(b) where an intestate is survived by either of, or both, his parents and is also survived by brothers or sisters, but is not survived by any prior relative, the surviving parent or parents shall have right to one half of the intestate estate and the surviving brothers and sisters to the other half thereof;

(c) where an intestate is survived by brothers or sisters, but is not survived by any prior relative, the surviving brothers and sisters shall have right to the whole of the intestate estate;

(d) where an intestate is survived by either of, or both, his parents, but is not survived by any prior relative, the surviving parent or parents shall have right to the whole of the intestate estate;

(e) where an intestate is survived by a husband [, wife or civil partner], but is not survived by any prior relative, the surviving spouse [or civil partner] shall have right to the whole of the intestate estate;

(f) where an intestate is survived by uncles or aunts (being brothers or sisters of either parent of the intestate), but is not survived by any prior relative, the surviving uncles and aunts shall have right to the whole of the intestate estate;

(g) where an intestate is survived by a grandparent or grandparents (being a parent or parents of either parent of the intestate), but is not survived by any prior relative, the surviving grandparent or grandparents shall have right to the whole of the intestate estate;

(h) where an intestate is survived by brothers or sisters of any of his grandparents (being a parent or parents of either parent of the intestate), but is not survived by any prior relative, those surviving brothers and sisters shall have right to the whole of the intestate estate;

(i) where an intestate is not survived by any prior relative, the ancestors of the intestate (being remoter than grandparents) generation by generation successively, without distinction between the paternal and maternal lines, shall have right to the whole of the intestate estate; so however that, failing ancestors of any generation, the brothers and sisters of any of those ancestors shall have right thereto before ancestors of the next more remote generation.

(2) References in the foregoing subsection to brothers or sisters include respectively brothers and sisters of the half blood as well as of the whole blood; and in the said subsection 'prior relative', in relation to any class of person mentioned in any paragraph of that subsection, means a person of any other class who, if he had

survived the intestate, would have had right to the intestate estate or any of it by virtue of an earlier paragraph of that subsection or by virtue of any such paragraph and section 5 of this Act.

3 Succession of collaterals

Subject to section 5 of this Act, where brothers and sisters of an intestate or of an ancestor of an intestate (in this section referred to as 'collaterals') have right to the whole, or, in a case to which subsection (1)(b) of the last foregoing section applies, to a half, of the intestate estate, the collaterals of the whole blood shall be entitled to succeed thereto in preference to the collaterals of the half blood; but where the collaterals of the half blood have right as aforesaid they shall rank without distinction as between those related to the intestate, or, as the case may be, the ancestor, through their father and those so related through their mother.

[. . .]

5 Representation

(1)   Subject to section 6 of this Act, where a person who, if he had survived an intestate, would, by virtue of any of the foregoing provisions of this Part of this Act, have had right (otherwise than as a parent [, spouse or civil partner] of the intestate) to the whole or to any part of the intestate estate has predeceased the intestate, but has left issue who survive the intestate, such issue shall have the like right to the whole or to that part of the intestate estate as the said person would have had if he had survived the intestate.

(2)   The right of any issue entitled to share in an intestate estate by virtue of the foregoing subsection to be appointed to the office of executor on the intestate estate shall be postponed to the right thereto of any person who succeeds to the whole or part of the intestate estate by virtue of the foregoing provisions of this Act apart from this section and who applies for appointment to that office.

6 Division of intestate estate among those having right thereto

If, by virtue of the foregoing provisions of this Part of this Act, there are two or more persons having right among them to the whole, or, in a case to which section 2(1)(b) of this Act relates, to a half, of an intestate estate, then the said estate, or, as the case may be, that half thereof, shall—

(a)   if all of those persons are in the same degree of relationship to the intestate, be divided among them equally, and

(b)   in any other case, be divided equally into a number of parts equal to the aggregate of—

(i)   those of the said persons who are nearest in degree of relationship to the intestate (in this section referred to as 'the nearest surviving relatives') and

(ii)   any other persons who were related to the intestate in that degree, but who have predeceased him leaving issue who survive him;

and, of those parts, one shall be taken by each of the nearest surviving relatives, and one shall be taken *per stirpes* by the issue of each of the said predeceased persons.

7 Saving of right of Crown as *ultimus haeres*

Nothing in this Part of this Act shall be held to affect the right of the Crown as *ultimus haeres* to any estate to which no person is entitled by virtue of this Act to succeed.

PART II
LEGAL AND OTHER PRIOR RIGHTS IN ESTATES OF DECEASED PERSONS

8   Prior rights of surviving spouse, on intestacy, in dwelling house and furniture

(1)   Where a person dies intestate leaving a spouse [or civil partner], and the intestate estate includes a relevant interest in a dwelling house to which this

section applies, the surviving spouse [or civil partner] shall be entitled to receive out of the intestate estate—

    (a)   where the value of the relevant interest does not exceed [£300,000 or such larger amount as may from time to time be fixed by order of the Secretary of State:]

        (i)   if subsection (2) of this section does not apply, the relevant interest;

        (ii) if the said subsection (2) applies, a sum equal to the value of the relevant interest;

    (b)   in any other case, the sum of [£300,000]:

Provided that, if the intestate estate comprises a relevant interest in two or more dwelling houses to which this section applies, this subsection shall have effect only in relation to such one of them as the surviving spouse may elect for the purposes of this subsection within six months of the date of death of the intestate.

(2)   This subsection shall apply for the purposes of paragraph (a) of the foregoing subsection if—

    (a)   the dwelling house forms part only of the subjects comprised in one tenancy or lease under which the intestate was the tenant; or

    (b)   the dwelling house forms the whole or part of subjects an interest in which is comprised in the intestate estate and which were used by the intestate for carrying on a trade, profession or occupation, and the value of the estate as a whole would be likely to be substantially diminished if the dwelling house were disposed of otherwise than with the assets of the trade, profession or occupation.

(3)   Where a person dies intestate leaving a spouse [or civil partner], and the intestate estate includes the furniture and plenishings of a dwelling house to which this section applies (whether or not the dwelling house is comprised in the intestate estate), the surviving spouse [or civil partner] shall be entitled to receive out of the intestate estate—

    (a)   where the value of the furniture and plenishings does not exceed [£24,000] the whole thereof;

    (b)   in any other case, such part of the furniture and plenishings, to a value not exceeding [£24,000 or such larger amount as may from time to time be fixed by order of the Secretary of State] as may be chosen by the surviving spouse:

Provided that, if the intestate estate comprises the furniture and plenishings of two or more such dwelling houses, this subsection shall have effect only in relation to the furniture and plenishings of such one of them as the surviving spouse [or civil partner] may elect for the purposes of this subsection within six months of the date of death of the intestate.

(4)   This section applies, in the case of any intestate, to any dwelling house in which the surviving spouse [or civil partner] of the intestate was ordinarily resident at the date of death of the intestate

(5)   Where any question arises as to the value of any furniture or plenishings, or of any interest in a dwelling house, for the purposes of any provision of this section the question shall be determined by arbitration by a single arbiter appointed, in default of agreement, by the sheriff of the county in which the intestate was domiciled at the date of his death or, if that county is uncertain or the intestate was domiciled furth of Scotland, the sheriff of the Lothians and Peebles at Edinburgh.

(6)   In this section—

    (a)   'dwelling house' includes a part of a building occupied (at the date of death of the intestate) as a separate dwelling; and any reference to a dwelling house shall be construed as including any garden or portion of ground attached to, and usually occupied with, the dwelling house or otherwise required for the amenity or convenience of the dwelling house;

    (b)   'furniture and plenishings' includes garden effects, domestic animals, plate, plated articles, linen, china, glass, books, pictures, prints, articles of household use and consumable stores; but does not include any article or animal used

at the date of death of the intestate for business purposes, or money or securities
for money, or any heirloom;

    (c) 'heirloom', in relation to an intestate estate, means any article which
has associations with the intestate's family of such nature and extent that it
ought to pass to some member of that family other than the surviving spouse of
the intestate;

    (d) 'relevant interest', in relation to a dwelling house, means the interest
therein of an owner, or the interest therein of a tenant, subject in either case to
any heritable debt secured over the interest; and for the purposes of this definition 'tenant' means a tenant under a tenancy or lease (whether of the dwelling
house alone or of the dwelling house together with other subjects) which is not a
tenancy to which the Rent and Mortgage Interest Restrictions Acts 1920 to 1939
apply.

9 Prior right of surviving spouse to financial provision on intestacy

    (1) Where a person dies intestate and is survived by a husband [, wife or civil
partner, the survivor] shall be entitled to receive out of the intestate estate—

    (a) if the intestate is survived by issue the sum of [£42,000 or such larger
amount as may from time to time be fixed by order of the Secretary of State;
or]

    (b) if the intestate is not survived by issue the sum of [£75,000 or such larger
amount as may from time to time be fixed by order of the Secretary of State,]
together with, in either case, interest at the rate of 4 per cent per annum [or at such
rate as may from time to time be fixed by order of the Secretary of State} on such
sum from the date of the intestate's death until payment:

Provided that where the surviving spouse [or civil partner] is entitled to receive
a legacy out of the estate of the intestate (other than a legacy of any dwelling
house to which the last foregoing section applies or of any furniture and plenishings of any such dwelling house), he or she shall, unless he or she renounces the
legacy, be entitled under this subsection to receive only such sum, if any, as
remains after deducting from the sum [fixed by virtue of paragraph (a) of this subsection or the sum fixed by virtue of paragraph (b) of this subsection], as the case
may be, the amount or value of the legacy.

    (2) Where the intestate estate is less than the amount which the surviving
spouse [or civil partner] is entitled to receive by virtue of subsection (1) of this
section the right conferred by the said subsection on the surviving spouse [or civil
partner] shall be satisfied by the transfer to him or her of the whole of the intestate
estate.

    (3) The amount which the surviving spouse [or civil partner] is entitled to
receive by virtue of subsection (1) of this section shall be borne by, and paid out
of, the parts of the intestate estate consisting of heritable and moveable property
respectively in proportion to the respective amounts of those parts.

    (4) Where by virtue of subsection (2) of this section a surviving spouse [or civil
partner] has right to the whole of the intestate estate, he or she shall have the right
to be appointed executor.

    (5) The rights conferred by the Intestate Husband's Estate (Scotland) Acts 1911
to 1959 on a surviving spouse in his or her deceased spouse's estate shall not be
exigible out of the estate of any person dying after the commencement of this Act.

    (6) For the purposes of this section—

    (a) the expression 'intestate estate' means so much of the net intestate estate
as remains after the satisfaction of any claims under the last foregoing section;
and

    (b) the expression 'legacy' includes any payment or benefit to which a sur-
viving spouse [or civil partner] becomes entitled by virtue of any testamentary
disposition; and the amount or value of any legacy shall be ascertained as at the
date of the intestate's death.

[9A **Provisions supplementary to ss 8 and 9**

Any order of the Secretary of State, under section 8 or 9 of this Act, fixing an amount or rate—

(a) shall be made by statutory instrument which shall be subject to annulment in pursuance of a resolution of either House of Parliament; and

(b) shall have effect in relation to the estate of any person dying after the coming into force of the order.]

10 Abolition of terce and courtesy, and calculation of legal rights

(1) The right of courtesy of a surviving husband in his deceased wife's estate and the right of terce of a surviving wife in her deceased husband's estate shall not be exigible out of the estate of a person dying after the commencement of this Act.

(2) The amount of any claim to [legal rights] out of an estate shall be calculated by reference to so much of the net moveable estate as remains after the satisfaction of any claims thereon under the two last foregoing sections.

11 Representation in, and division of, legitim

(1) Subject to the next following subsection, where a person (hereinafter in this section referred to as 'the deceased') dies predeceased by a child who has left issue who survive the deceased, and the child would, if he had survived the deceased, have been entitled under any rule of law to legitim out of the deceased's estate, such issue shall have the like right to legitim as the child would have had if he had survived the deceased.

(2) If, by virtue of the foregoing subsection or otherwise, there are two or more persons having right among them to legitim, then the legitim shall—

(a) if all of those persons are in the same degree of relationship to the deceased, be divided among them equally, and

(b) in any other case, be divided equally into a number of parts equal to the aggregate of—

(i) those of the said persons who are nearest in degree of relationship to the deceased (in this paragraph referred to as 'the nearest surviving relatives') and

(ii) any other persons who were related to the deceased in that degree and who (if they had survived him) would have been entitled to legitim out of his estate, but who have predeceased him leaving issue who survive him and are entitled to legitim out of his estate;

and, of those parts, one shall be taken by each of the nearest surviving relatives, and one shall be taken *per stirpes* by the issue of each of the said predeceased persons, being issue who are entitled as aforesaid.

(3) Nothing in the last foregoing subsection shall be construed as altering any rule of law as to collation of advances; and where any person is entitled to claim legitim out of the estate of a deceased person by virtue of subsection (1) of this section he shall be under the like duty to collate any advances made by the deceased to him, and the proportion appropriate to him of any advances so made to any person through whom he derives such entitlement, as if he had been entitled to claim such legitim otherwise than by virtue of the said subsection (1).

(4) For the avoidance of doubt it is hereby declared that where any person is entitled by virtue of subsection (1) of this section to legitim out of the estate of the deceased, and the deceased is not survived by any child, the proportion of the estate due to any surviving spouse in respect of *jus relicti* or *jus relictae* shall be ascertained as if the deceased had been survived by a child.

12 Legitim not to be discharged by ante-nuptial marriage contract

Nothing in any ante-nuptial contract of marriage executed after the commencement of this Act shall operate so as to exclude, on the occurrence of the death of either party to the marriage, the right of any child of the marriage (or of any issue of his coming in his place by virtue of the last foregoing section) to legitim out of the estate of that party unless such child or issue shall elect to accept in lieu of legitim the provision made in his favour under the contract.

13 Equitable compensation

Every testamentary disposition executed after the commencement of this Act by which provision is made in favour of the spouse or of any issue of the testator and which does not contain a declaration that the provision so made is in full and final satisfaction of the right to any share in the testator's estate to which the spouse or the issue, as the case may be, is entitled by virtue of *jus relicti, jus relictae* or legitim, shall (unless the disposition contains an express provision to the contrary) have effect as if it contained such a declaration.

PART III
ADMINISTRATION AND WINDING UP OF ESTATES

14 Assimilation for purposes of administration, etc, of heritage to moveables

(1) Subject to subsection (3) of this section the enactments and rules of law in force immediately before the commencement of this Act with respect to the administration and winding up of the estate of a deceased person so far as consisting of moveable property shall have effect (as modified by the provisions of this Act) in relation to the whole of the estate without distinction between moveable property and heritable property; and accordingly on the death of any person (whether testate or intestate) every part of his estate (whether consisting of moveable property or heritable property) falling to be administered under the law of Scotland shall, by virtue of confirmation thereto, vest for the purposes of administration in the executor thereby confirmed and shall be administered and disposed of according to law by such executor.

(2) Provision shall be made by the Court of Session by act of sederunt made under the enactments mentioned in section 22 of this Act (as extended by that section) for the inclusion in the confirmation of an executor, by reference to an appended inventory or otherwise, of a description, in such form as may be so provided, of any heritable property forming part of the estate.

(3) Nothing in this section shall be taken to alter any rule of law whereby any particular debt of a deceased person falls to be paid out of any particular part of his estate.

15 Provisions as to transfer of heritage

(1) Section 5(2) of the Conveyancing (Scotland) Act 1924 (which provides that a confirmation which includes a heritable security shall be a valid title to the debt thereby secured) shall have effect as if any reference therein to a heritable security, or to a debt secured by a heritable security, included a reference to any interest in heritable property which has vested in an executor in pursuance of the last foregoing section by virtue of a confirmation

Provided that a confirmation [(other than an implied confirmation within the meaning of the said section 5(2))] shall not be deemed for the purposes of the said section 5(2) to include any such interest unless a description of the property, in accordance with any act of sederunt such as is mentioned in subsection (2) of the last foregoing section, is included or referred to in the confirmation.

(2) Where in pursuance of the last foregoing section any heritable property has vested in an executor by virtue of a confirmation, and it is necessary for him in distributing the estate to transfer that property—

    (a) to any person in satisfaction of a claim to legal rights or the prior rights of a surviving spouse [or civil partner] out of the estate, or

    (b) to any person entitled to share in the estate by virtue of this Act, or

    (c) to any person entitled to take the said property under any testamentary disposition of the deceased,

the executor may effect such transfer by endorsing on the confirmation (or where a certificate of confirmation relating to the property has been issued in pursuance of any act of sederunt, on the certificate) a docket in favour of that person in the form set out in Schedule 1 to this Act, or in a form as nearly as may be to the like effect, and any such docket may be specified as a midcouple or link in title in any deduction of title; but this section shall not be construed as prejudicing the competence of any other mode of transfer.

16 Provisions relating to leases

(1) This section applies to any interest, being the interest of a tenant under a lease, which is comprised in the estate of a deceased person and has accordingly vested in the deceased's executor by virtue of section 14 of this Act; and in the following provisions of this section 'interest' means an interest to which this section applies.

(2) [Subject to subsection (4A)] where an interest—

(a) is not the subject of a valid bequest by the deceased, or

(b) is the subject of such a bequest, but the bequest is not accepted by the legatee, or

(c) being an interest under an agricultural lease, is the subject of such a bequest, but the bequest is declared null and void in pursuance of section 16 of the Act of 1886 or [section 11 of the 1991 Act or becomes null and void under section 10 of the Act of 1955],

and there is among the conditions of the lease (whether expressly or by implication) a condition prohibiting assignation of the interest, the executor shall be entitled, notwithstanding that condition, to transfer the interest to any one of the persons entitled to succeed to the deceased's intestate estate, or to claim legal rights or the prior rights of a surviving spouse [or civil partner] out of the estate, in or towards satisfaction of that person's entitlement or claim; but shall not be entitled to transfer the interest to any other person without the consent—

[(i) in the case of an interest under an agricultural lease, being a lease of a croft within the meaning of section 3(1) of the Act of 1955, of the Crofters Commission;

(ii) in any other case, of the landlord.]

(3) [Subject to subsection (4C)] if in the case of any interest—

(a) at any time the executor is satisfied that the interest cannot be disposed of according to law and so informs the landlord, or

(b) the interest is not so disposed of within a period of one year or such longer period as may be fixed by agreement between the landlord and the executor or, failing agreement, by the [relevant court on the application of] the executor—

(i) in the case of an interest under an agricultural lease which is the subject of a petition to the Land Court under section 16 of the Act of 1886 or an application to that court under [section 11 of the 1991 Act] from the date of the determination or withdrawal of the petition or, as the case may be, the application,

[(ia) in the case of an interest under an agricultural lease which is the subject of an application by the legatee to the Crofters Commission under section 10(1) of the Act of 1955, from the date of any refusal by the Commission to determine that the bequest shall not be null and void,

(ib) in the case of an interest under an agricultural lease which is the subject of an intimation of objection by the landlord to the legatee and the Crofters Commission under section 10(3) of the Act of 1955, from the date of any decision of the Commission upholding the objection,]

(ii) in any other case, from the date of death of the deceased,

either the landlord or the executor may, on giving notice in accordance with the next following subsection to the other, terminate the lease (in so far as it relates to the interest) notwithstanding any provision therein, or any enactment or rule of law, to the contrary effect.

(4) The period of notice given under the last foregoing subsection shall be—

(a) in the case of an agricultural lease, such period as may be agreed, or, failing agreement, a period of not less than one year and not more than two years ending with such term of Whitsunday or Martinmas as may be specified in the notice; and

(b) in the case of any other lease, a period of six months:

Provided that paragraph (b) of this subsection shall be without prejudice to any enactment prescribing a shorter period of notice in relation to the lease in question.

[(4A) Where an interest, being an interest under a lease constituting a short limited duration tenancy or a limited duration tenancy—

(a) is not the subject of a valid bequest by the deceased; or

(b) is the subject of such a bequest, but the bequest is not accepted by the legatee; or

(c) is the subject of such a bequest, but the bequest is declared null and void by virtue of section 21 of the 2003 Act,

and there is among the conditions of the lease (whether expressly or by implication) a condition prohibiting assignation of the interest, the executor shall be entitled, notwithstanding that condition, to transfer the interest to a person to whom subsection (4B) below applies; and the executor shall be entitled so to transfer the interest without the consent of the landlord.

(4B) This subsection applies to—

(a) any one of the persons entitled to succeed to the deceased's intestate estate, or to claim legal rights or the prior rights of a surviving spouse out of the estate, in or towards satisfaction of that person's entitlement or claim; or

(b) any other person.

(4C) In the case of any interest under a lease constituting a short limited duration tenancy or a limited duration tenancy—

(a) if at any time the executor is satisfied that the interest cannot be disposed of according to law and so informs the landlord, the executor may terminate the tenancy (in so far as it relates to the interest); and

(b) if the interest is not so disposed of within the period referred to in subsection (4D) below, the lease shall (in so far as it relates to the interest) terminate at the expiry of the period, notwithstanding any provision in the lease, or any enactment or rule of law, to the contrary effect.

(4D) The period is one year or such longer period as may be fixed by agreement or, failing agreement, by the Land Court on the application of the executor—

(a) in the case of an interest which is the subject of an application to that court by virtue of section 21 of the 2003 Act, from the date of the determination or withdrawal of the application; and

(b) in any other case, from the date of death of the deceased.

(4E) The—

(a) interest may be transferred under subsections (4A) and (4B) above; or

(b) tenancy may be terminated under subsection (4C)(a) above,

only if the transfer, or as the case may be, termination is in the best interests of the deceased's estate.]

(5) Subsection (3) of this section shall not prejudice any claim by any party to the lease for compensation or damages in respect of the termination of the lease (or any rights under it) in pursuance of that subsection; but any award of compensation or damages in respect of such termination at the instance of the executor shall be enforceable only against the estate of the deceased and not against the executor personally.

(6) Where an interest is an interest under an agricultural lease, and—

(a)   an application is made under section 3 of the Act of 1931 [or section 13 of the Act of 1955] to the Land Court for an order for removal, or

(b)   a reference is made under [section 23(2) and (3) of the 1991 Act for the determination of] any question which has arisen under [section 22(2)(e)] of that Act in connection with a notice to quit,

the [order or determination shall not be] in favour of the landlord, unless [. . .] it is reasonable, having regard to the fact that the interest is vested in the executor in his capacity as executor, that it should be made.

(7)   Where an interest is not an interest under an agricultural lease, and the landlord brings an action of removing against the executor in respect of a breach of a condition of the lease, the court shall not grant decree in the action unless it is satisfied that the condition alleged to have been breached is one which it is reasonable to expect the executor to have observed, having regard to the fact that the interest is vested in him in his capacity as an executor.

(8)   Where an interest is an interest under an agricultural lease and is the subject of a valid bequest by the deceased, the fact that the interest is vested in the executor under the said section 14 shall not prevent the operation, in relation to the legatee, of paragraphs (a) to (h) of section 16 of the Act of 1886, or, as the case may be, [section 11(2) to (8) of the 1991 Act or, as the case may be, section 21(2) and (3) of the 2003 Act, or, as the case may be, subsections (2) to (7) of section 10 of the Act of 1955].

[(8A)   For the purposes of subsection (3)(b) above the 'relevant court' is—

(a)   in the case of an interest under a lease constituting a 1991 Act tenancy, the Land Court; and

(b)   in any other case, the sheriff,

and an application to the sheriff in any such other case shall be by summary application.]

(9)   In this section—

'agricultural lease' means a lease of a holding within the meaning of the Small Landholders (Scotland) Acts 1886 to 1931 [or the [. . .] lease of a croft within the meaning of section 3(1) of the Act of 1955];

'the Act of 1886' means the Crofters Holdings (Scotland) Act 1886;

'the Act of 1931' means the Small Landholders and Agricultural Holdings (Scotland) Act 1931;

['the 1991 Act' means the Agricultural Holdings (Scotland) Act 1991];

['1991 Act tenancy', 'short limited duration tenancy' and 'limited duration tenancy' shall be construed in accordance with the 2003 Act.]

['the 2003 Act' means the Agricultural Holdings (Scotland) Act 2003 (asp 11);]

['the Act of 1955' means the Crofters (Scotland) Act 1955];

'lease' includes tenancy.

17   Protection of persons acquiring title

Where any person has in good faith and for value acquired title to any interest in or security over heritable property which has vested in an executor as aforesaid directly or indirectly from—

(a)   the executor, or

(b)   a person deriving title directly from the executor,

the title so acquired shall not be challengeable on the ground that the confirmation was reducible or has in fact been reduced, or, in a case falling under paragraph (b) above, that the title should not have been transferred to the person mentioned in that paragraph.

18   Provisions as to entails and special destinations

(1)   [. . .]

(2)   On the death of a person entitled to any heritable property subject to a special destination in favour of some other person, being a destination which the

deceased could not competently have, or in fact has not, evacuated by testamentary disposition or otherwise, the property shall, if the executor of the deceased is confirmed thereto, vest in the executor for the purpose of enabling it to be conveyed to the person next entitled thereto under the destination (if such conveyance is necessary) and for that purpose only.

(3) Section 14(2) of this Act shall apply in relation to property to which this section refers as it applies to property to which the said section 14(2) refers.

(4) Sections 15 and 17 of this Act shall apply to property which has vested in an executor by virtue of this section as they apply to property which has vested in an executor by virtue of section 14 of this Act, as if the person next entitled to the first mentioned property were a person entitled to share in the estate of the deceased.

[. . .]

20 Executor dative to have powers of a trustee
An executor dative appointed to administer the estate of a deceased person shall have in his administration of such estate the whole powers, privileges and immunities, and be subject to the same obligations, limitations and restrictions, which gratuitous trustees have, or are subject to, under any enactment or under common law, and the Trusts (Scotland) Acts 1921 and 1961 shall have effect as if any reference therein to a trustee included a reference to such an executor dative:

Provided that nothing in this section shall exempt an executor dative from finding caution for his intromissions or confer upon him any power to resign or to assume new trustees.

21 Evidence as to holograph wills in commissary proceedings
(1) Notwithstanding any rule of law or practice to the contrary, confirmation of an executor to property disposed of in a holograph testamentary disposition shall not be granted unless the court is satisfied by evidence consisting at least of an affidavit by each of two persons that the writing and signature of the disposition are in the handwriting of the testator.

[(2) This section shall not apply to a testamentary document executed after the commencement of the Requirements of Writing (Scotland) Act 1995.]

[21A Evidence as to testamentary documents in commissary proceedings
Confirmation of an executor to property disposed of in a testamentary document executed after the commencement of the Requirements of Writing (Scotland) Act 1995 shall not be granted unless the formal validity of the document is governed—

(a) by Scots law and the document is presumed under section 3 or 4 of that Act to have been subscribed by the granter so disposing of that property; or

(b) by a law other than Scots law and the court is satisfied that the document is formally valid according to the law governing such validity.]

22 Court of Session may regulate procedure in commissary proceedings
(1) The powers exercisable by the Court of Session by act of sederunt under section 18 of the Confirmation of Executors (Scotland) Act 1858, section 16 of the Sheriff Courts and Legal Officers (Scotland) Act 1927 and section 34 of the Administration of Justice (Scotland) Act 1933 (which empower the court to regulate inter alia procedure in proceedings in the sheriff court and in proceedings for the confirmation of executors) shall include power to regulate the procedure to be followed, and to prescribe the form and content of any petition, writ or other document to be used, in connection with the confirmation of executors in cases where, by virtue of this Act, heritable property devolves upon the executor.

(2) Without prejudice to the generality of the powers conferred on the court by the said sections and by this section, the power conferred by the said section 34 to modify, amend or repeal by act of sederunt enactments relating to certain matters

shall include power so to modify, amend or repeal any enactment relating to the procedure to be followed in proceedings for the confirmation of executors in such cases as aforesaid.

[. . .]

PART IV
ADOPTED PERSONS

23   Adopted person to be treated for purposes of succession etc as child of adopter

(1)   For all purposes relating to—

(a)   the succession to a deceased person (whether testate or intestate), and

(b)   the disposal of property by virtue of any *inter vivos* deed,

an adopted person shall be treated as the child of the adopter and not as the child of any other person.

In this subsection and in the following provisions of this Part of this Act any reference to succession to a deceased person shall be construed as including a reference to the distribution of any property in consequence of the death of the deceased person and any claim to legal rights or the prior rights of a surviving spouse out of his estate.

(2)   In any deed whereby property is conveyed or under which a succession arises, being a deed executed after the making of an adoption order, unless the contrary intention appears, any reference (whether express or implied)—

(a)   to the child or children of the adopter shall be construed as, or as including, a reference to the adopted person;

(b)   to the child or children of the adopted person's natural parents or either of them shall be construed as not being, or as not including, a reference to the adopted person; and

(c)   to a person related to the adopted person in any particular degree shall be construed as a reference to the person who would be related to him in that degree if he were the child of the adopter and were not the child of any other person:

Provided that for the purposes of this subsection a deed containing a provision taking effect on the death of any person shall be deemed to have been executed on the date of death of that person.

(3)   Where the terms of any deed provide that any property or interest in property shall devolve along with a title, honour or dignity, nothing in this section [or in the Children Act 1975 or in the Adoption (Scotland) Act 1978] shall prevent that property or interest from so devolving.

(4)   Nothing in this section shall affect any deed executed, or the devolution of any property on, or in consequence of, the death of a person who dies, before the commencement of this Act.

(5)   In this Part of this Act the expression 'adoption order' [has the same meaning as in section 38 of the Adoption (Scotland) Act 1978 (whether the order took effect before or after the commencement of this Act),] and 'adopted' means adopted in pursuance of an adoption order.

24   Provisions supplementary to s 23

(1)   For the purposes of the law regulating the succession to any property and for the purposes of the construction of any such deed as is mentioned in the last foregoing section, an adopted person shall be deemed to be related to any other person, being the child or the adopted child of the adopter or (in the case of a joint adoption) of either of the adopters,

(a)   where he or she was adopted by two spouses jointly and that other person is the child or adopted child of both of them, as a brother or sister of the whole blood;

(b)   in any other case, as a brother or sister of the half blood.

[(1A)   Where, in relation to any purpose specified in section 23(1) of this Act, any right is conferred or any obligation is imposed, whether by operation of law or under any deed coming into operation after the commencement of the Children Act 1975, by reference to the relative seniority of the members of a class of persons, then, without prejudice to any entitlement under Part I of the Law Reform (Miscellaneous Provisions) (Scotland) Act 1968 of an illegitimate child who is adopted by one of his parents,

(a)   any member of that class who is an adopted person shall rank as if he had been born on the date of his adoption, and

(b)   if two or more members of the class are adopted persons whose dates of adoption are the same, they shall rank as between themselves in accordance with their respective times of birth.]

(2)   Notwithstanding anything in the last foregoing section, a trustee or an executor may distribute any property for the distribution of which he is responsible without having ascertained that no adoption order has been made by virtue of which any person is or may be entitled to any interest therein, and shall not be liable to any such person of whose claim he has not had notice at the time of the distribution; but (without prejudice to section 17 of this Act) nothing in this subsection shall affect any right of any such person to recover the property, or any property representing it, from any person who may have received it.

(3)   Where an adoption order is made in respect of a person who has been previously adopted, the previous adoption shall be disregarded for the purposes of the last foregoing section in relation to the devolution of any property on the death of any person dying after the date of the subsequent adoption order, and in relation to any deed executed after that date whereby property is conveyed or under which a succession arises.

(4)   [. . .]

PART VI
MISCELLANEOUS AND SUPPLEMENTARY

29   Right of tenant to bequeath interest under lease

(1)   A bequest by a tenant of his interest under a tenancy or lease to any one of the persons who, if the tenant had died intestate, would be, or would in any circumstances have been, entitled to succeed to his intestate estate by virtue of this Act shall not be treated as invalid by reason only that there is among the conditions of the tenancy or lease an implied condition prohibiting assignation.

(2)   This section shall not prejudice the operation of section 16 of the Crofters Holdings (Scotland) Act 1886 or [section 11 of the Agricultural Holdings (Scotland) Act 1991 or section 21 of the Agricultural Holdings (Scotland) Act 2003 (asp 11)] (which relate to bequests in the case of agricultural leases) [or of section 10 of the Crofters (Scotland) Act 1955 (which makes similar provision in relation to crofts).]

30   Effect of testamentary dispositions on special destinations

A testamentary disposition executed after the commencement of this Act shall not have effect so as to evacuate a special destination (being a destination which could competently be evacuated by the testamentary disposition) unless it contains a specific reference to the destination and a declared intention on the part of the testator to evacuate it.

31   Presumption of survivorship in respect of claims to property

(1)   Where two persons have died in circumstances indicating that they died simultaneously or rendering it uncertain which, if either, of them survived the other, then, for all purposes affecting title or succession to property or claims to legal rights or the prior rights of a surviving spouse [or civil partner],

(a)   where the persons were husband and wife [or civil partners to each other], it shall be presumed that neither survived the other; and

(b)   in any other case, it shall be presumed that the younger person survived the elder unless the next following subsection applies.

(2)   If, in a case to which paragraph (b) of the foregoing subsection would (apart from this subsection) apply, the elder person has left a testamentary disposition containing a provision, however expressed, in favour of the younger if he survives the elder and, failing the younger, in favour of a third person, and the younger person has died intestate, then it shall be presumed for the purposes of that provision that the elder person survived the younger.

[32   Certain testamentary dispositions to be formally valid

(1)   For the purpose of any question arising as to entitlement, by virtue of a testamentary disposition, to any relevant property or to any interest therein, the disposition shall be treated as valid in respect of the formalities of execution.

(2)   Subsection (1) above is without prejudice to any right to challenge the validity of the testamentary disposition on the ground of forgery or on any other ground of essential invalidity.

(3)   In this section 'relevant property' means property disposed of in the testamentary disposition in respect of which—

   (a)   confirmation has been granted; or

   (b)   probate, letters of administration or other grant of representation—

      (i)   has been issued, and has noted the domicile of the deceased to be, in England and Wales or Northern Ireland; or

      (ii)   has been issued outwith the United Kingdom and had been sealed in Scotland under section 2 of the Colonial Probates Act 1892.]

33   Construction of existing deeds

(1)   Subject to subsection (2) of this section, any reference in any deed taking effect after the commencement of this Act to *jus relicti, jus relictae* or legitim shall be construed as a reference to the right to *jus relicti, jus relictae* or legitim, as the case may be, as modified by Part II of this Act; and any reference in any such deed to courtesy or terce shall be of no effect.

(2)   Any reference to legal rights in a marriage contract made before the commencement of this Act and taking effect in consequence of a decree of divorce granted in an action commenced after the commencement of this Act shall be construed as a reference to any right which the husband or the wife, as the case may be, might obtain by virtue of the provisions of section 26 of this Act [or section 5 of the Divorce (Scotland) Act 1976, or section 29 of the Matrimonial and Family Proceedings Act 1984, or section 8 of the Family Law (Scotland) Act 1985].

34   Modification of enactments and repeals

(1)   Subject to the provisions of section 37 of this Act, the enactments mentioned in Schedule 2 to this Act shall have effect subject to the modifications specified in that Schedule, being modifications consequential on the provisions of this Act.

(2)   [. . .]

35   Transfer of certain jurisdiction to Sheriff of Chancery

(1)   If at any time it appears to the Secretary of State expedient to do so he may by order transfer to the Sheriff of Chancery the jurisdiction of any other sheriff in relation to the service of heirs.

(2)   An order made under this section may contain such consequential provisions as appears to the Secretary of State to be necessary, including provisions for the consequential repeal or consequential modification of any enactment relating to the matters dealt with in the order.

(3)   Any order made under this section shall be made by statutory instrument.

36 Interpretation

(1) In this Act the following expressions shall, unless the context otherwise requires, have the meanings hereby respectively assigned to them, that is to say—

'deed' includes any disposition, contract, instrument or writing, whether *inter vivos* or *mortis causa*;

'an intestate' means a person who has died leaving undisposed of by testamentary disposition the whole or any part of his estate, and 'intestate' shall be construed accordingly;

'intestate estate', in relation to an intestate, means (subject to sections 1(2) and 9(6)(a) of this Act) so much of his estate as is undisposed of by testamentary disposition;

'issue' means issue however remote;

'Land Court' means the Scottish Land Court;

'lease' and 'tenancy' include sub-lease and sub-tenancy, and tenant shall be construed accordingly;

'legal rights' means *jus relicti, jus relictae,* and legitim;

'net estate' and 'net intestate estate' mean respectively so much of an estate or an intestate estate as remains after provision for the satisfaction of estate duty and other liabilities of the estate having priority over legal rights, the prior rights of a surviving spouse and rights of succession, or, as the case may be, the proportion thereof properly attributable to the intestate estate;

'owner' in relation to any heritable property means the person entitled to receive the rents thereof (other than rents under a sub-lease or sub-tenancy);

'prior rights', in relation to a surviving spouse [or civil partner], means the rights conferred by sections 8 and 9 of this Act;

'testamentary disposition', in relation to a deceased, includes any deed taking effect on his death whereby any part of his estate is disposed of or under which a succession thereto arises.

(2) Any reference in this Act to the estate of a deceased person shall, unless the context otherwise requires, be construed as a reference to the whole estate, whether heritable or moveable, or partly heritable and partly moveable, belonging to the deceased at the time of his death or over which the deceased had a power of appointment and, where the deceased immediately before his death held the interest of a tenant under a tenancy or lease which was not expressed to expire on his death, includes that interest:

Provided that—

(a) where any heritable property belonging to a deceased person at the date of his death is subject to a special destination in favour of any person, the property shall not be treated for the purposes of this Act as part of the estate of the deceased unless the destination is one which could competently be, and has in fact been, evacuated by the deceased by testamentary disposition or otherwise; and in that case the property shall be treated for the purposes of this Act as if it were part of the deceased's estate on which he has tested; and

(b) where any heritable property over which a deceased person had a power of appointment has not been disposed of in exercise of that power and is in those circumstances subject to a power of appointment by some other person, that property shall not be treated for the purposes of this Act as part of the estate of the deceased.

(3) Without prejudice to the proviso to section 23(2) of this Act, references in this Act to the date of execution of a testamentary disposition shall be construed as references to the date on which the disposition was actually executed and not to the date of death of the testator.

(4) References in this Act to any enactment shall, except where the context otherwise requires, be construed as references to that enactment as amended by or under any other enactment, including this Act.

[(5) Section 1(1) (legal equality of children) of the Law Reform (Parent and

Child) (Scotland) Act 1986 shall apply to this Act; and any reference (however expressed) in this Act to a relative shall be construed accordingly.]

37 Exclusion of certain matters from operation of Act

(1) Save as otherwise expressly provided, nothing in this Act [or (as respects paragraph (a) of this subsection) in the Children Act 1975] shall—

(a) apply to any title, coat of arms, honour or dignity transmissible on the death of the holder thereof or affect the succession thereto or the devolution thereof;

(b) [. . .]

(c) affect any right on the part of a surviving spouse to claim from the representatives of his or her deceased spouse payment of aliment out of the estate of that spouse;

(d) affect the administration, winding up or distribution of or the making up of title to any part of the estate of any person who died before the commencement of this Act or the rights of succession to such an estate or any claim for legal rights or terce or courtesy or any rights arising under the Intestate Husband's Estate (Scotland) Acts 1911 to 1959 out of such an estate or the right to take any legal proceedings with respect to any such matters;

(e) affect any claim for legal rights arising out of an action of divorce commenced before the commencement of this Act;

and in relation to the matters aforesaid the law in force immediately before the commencement of this Act shall continue to have effect as if this Act had not passed.

(2) Nothing in this Act shall be construed as affecting the operation of any rule of law applicable immediately before the commencement of this Act to the choice of the system of law governing the administration, winding up or distribution of the estate, or any part of the estate, of any deceased person.

38 Citation, extent and commencement

(1) This Act may be cited as the Succession (Scotland) Act 1964.

(2) This Act shall extend to Scotland only.

(3) This Act shall come into operation on the expiration of the period of three months beginning with the date on which it is passed.

SCHEDULES

Section 15   SCHEDULE 1
                                      FORM OF DOCKET

I, AB, being by virtue of the within confirmation [*or certificate of confirmation*] the executor on the estate of the deceased CD so far as specified in the confirmation [*or certificate or inventory attached hereto*] hereby nominate EF [*design*] as the person entitled—

(a) in [part] satisfaction of his claim to prior rights, as a surviving spouse, on the death of the deceased,

(b) in [part] satisfaction of his claim to legal rights on the death of the deceased,

(c) in [part] satisfaction of his share in the said estate,

(d) in [part] implement of a trust disposition and settlement, [*or will, or as the case may be*] of the deceased dated   and registered in the Books of Council and Session   ,

to the following item of estate, that is to say, [*short description*] being number   of the items of the estate specified in the said confirmation [*or certificate or inventory*].

[Testing clause†

†Note—Subscription of the document by the granter of it will be sufficient for the document to be formally valid, but witnessing of it may be necessary or desirable for other purposes (see the Requirements of Writing (Scotland) Act 1995).]

SCHEDULE 2   Section 34
MODIFICATION OF ENACTMENTS

General modifications

1.   Subject to the specific modifications made by the following provisions of this Schedule, references in any enactment to the heir-at-law of a deceased person in relation to any heritable property shall be construed as references to the persons who by virtue of this Act are entitled to succeed to such property on intestacy.

2.   Subject as aforesaid references in general terms in any enactment to the heirs of a deceased person shall include—

(a)   the persons entitled by virtue of this Act to succeed on intestacy to any part of the estate of the deceased; and

(b)   so far as is necessary for the purposes of Part III of this Act, the executor of the deceased.

3.   References in any enactment relating to the confirmation of executors or the administration of the moveable estates of deceased persons to the moveable or personal property or estate of a deceased person shall, except where the context otherwise requires, be construed as references to the whole estate of the deceased person.

4.   References in any enactment (other than in this Act) to courtesy or terce shall be of no effect.

PRESUMPTION OF DEATH (SCOTLAND) ACT 1977
(1977, c 27)

1   Action of declarator

(1)   Where a person who is missing is thought to have died or has not been known to be alive for a period of at least seven years, any person having an interest may raise an action of declarator of the death of that person (hereafter in this Act referred to as the 'missing person') in the Court of Session or the sheriff court in accordance with the provisions of this section.

(2)   An action such as is mentioned in subsection (1) above is, in this Act, referred to as an 'action of declarator'.

(3)   The Court of Session shall have jurisdiction to entertain an action of declarator if and only if—

(a)   the missing person was domiciled in Scotland on the date on which he was last known to be alive or had been habitually resident there throughout the period of one year ending with that date; or

(b)   the pursuer in the action—

(i)   is the spouse [or civil partner] of the missing person, and

(ii)   is domiciled in Scotland at the date of raising the action or was habitually resident there throughout the period of one year ending with that date [;

(c)   in a case where the pursuer in the action is the civil partner of the missing person, the following conditions are met—

(i)   the two people concerned registered as civil partners of each other in Scotland; and

(ii) it appears to the court to be in the interests of justice to assume jurisdiction in the case.]

(4) The sheriff court shall have jurisdiction to entertain an action of declarator if and only if—

(a) the provisions of subsection (3)(a) above are satisfied and the missing person's last known place of residence in Scotland is in the sheriffdom; or

(b) the provisions of subsection (3)(b) above are satisfied and the pursuer was resident in the sheriffdom for a period of not less than forty days ending with the date of raising the action.

(5) Any person having an interest may, in an action of declarator, lodge a minute seeking the making by the court under section 2 of this Act of any determination or appointment not sought by the pursuer.

(6) At any stage of the proceedings the sheriff may, of his own accord or on the application of any party to the action, and shall, if so directed by the Court of Session (which direction may be given on the application of any party to the action), remit to the Court of Session an action of declarator raised in the sheriff court where he or, as the case may be, the Court of Session considers such remit desirable because of the importance or complexity of the matters at issue.

2 Decree in action of declarator and determination of incidental questions in other proceedings

(1) In an action of declarator, the court, having heard proof and being satisfied on a balance of probabilities that the missing person—

(a) has died, shall grant decree accordingly and shall include in the decree a finding as to the date and time of death:

Provided that where it is uncertain when, within any period of time, the missing person died, the court shall find that he died at the end of that period;

(b) has not been known to be alive for a period of at least seven years, shall find that the missing person died at the end of the day occurring seven years after the date on which he was last known to be alive and shall grant decree accordingly.

(2) The court, in granting decree under subsection (1) above, shall have power to—

(a) determine the domicile of the missing person at the date of his death;

(b) determine any question relating to any interest in property which arises as a consequence of the death of the missing person;

(c) appoint a judicial factor on the estate of the missing person notwithstanding (in relation to such an appointment by the sheriff) what the value of the estate may be.

(3) Where, for the purpose of deciding any issue before it, a court or statutory tribunal has to determine any incidental question as to the death of a person, the court or tribunal may, if it thinks fit, determine that question (but for the purpose only of deciding that issue); and in the determination of that question the court or tribunal shall apply the criteria set out in subsection (1) above.

3 Effect of decree

(1) Subject to the provisions of this section and sections 4 and 5 of this Act, where no appeal is made against decree in an action of declarator within the time allowed for appeal, or where an appeal against such a decree has been made and refused or withdrawn, the decree shall be conclusive of the matters contained in the decree and shall, without any special form of words, be effective against any person and for all purposes including the dissolution of a marriage [or of a civil partnership] to which the missing person is a party and the acquisition of rights to or in property belonging to any person.

(2) A decree under section 2(1)(b) of this Act or a determination as mentioned in section 2(3) of this Act shall not determine a substantive question which is properly referable to a foreign law otherwise than in accordance with that law.

(3)   Where a marriage [or civil partnership] to which the missing person is a party has been dissolved by virtue of decree in an action of declarator, [its dissolution] shall not be invalidated by the circumstance that the missing person was in fact alive at the date specified in the decree as the date of death.

(4)   Where the missing person or any other person has committed any crime or offence, the responsibility of that person therefor shall not be affected by the circumstance that decree in an action of declarator has been granted if the missing person was in fact alive at the date specified in the decree as the date of death.

4   Recall or variation of decree

(1)   Decree in an action of declarator may, on application made at any time by any person having an interest, be varied or recalled by an order of the court which granted the decree or, in a case to which subsection (4) below applies, by an order of the Court of Session.

An order of the court pronounced under this subsection is hereafter in this Act referred to as a 'variation order'.

(2)   By a variation order the court may make any determination or appointment referred to in section 2 of this Act.

(3)   Any person having an interest may, in an application for a variation order, [make an application to the court] seeking the making by the court of any determination or appointment referred to in section 2 of this Act, which has not been sought by the person making the application for the variation order.

(4)   At any stage of the proceedings the sheriff may, of his own accord or on the application of any party to the proceedings, and shall, if so directed by the Court of Session (which direction may be given on the application of any party to the proceedings), remit to the Court of Session an application made in the sheriff court for a variation order where he or, as the case may be, the Court of Session considers such remit desirable because of the importance or complexity of the matters at issue.

(5)   Nothing in this section shall operate so as to revive a marriage of the missing person dissolved by virtue of decree in an action of declarator.

5   Effect on property rights of recall or variation of decree

(1)   Subject to the following provisions of this section, a variation order shall have no effect on rights to or in any property acquired as a result of a decree under section 2 of this Act.

(2)   Notwithstanding the generality of subsection (1) above, where a decree under section 2 of this Act has been varied or recalled by a variation order, the court shall make such further order, if any, in relation to any rights to or in any property acquired as a result of that decree as it considers fair and reasonable in all the circumstances of the case; but no such further order shall affect any income accruing between the date of that decree and the date of the variation order.

(3)   In considering what order shall be made under subsection (2) above, the court shall, so far as practicable in the circumstances, have regard to the following considerations, namely:—

(a)   that, in the case of any property which is being or has been administered under a trust, any person who on account of the variation order would, apart from subsection (1) above, have been entitled to rights to or in any such property, or any person deriving right from him, shall be entitled to have made over to him by the trustee in full satisfaction of these rights only—

(i)   the said rights to or in any such property or other property for the time being representing it which is still in the hands of the trustee at the date of the variation order, and

(ii)   the value, as at the date of distribution, of the said rights to or in any such property which has been distributed;

(b)   that any capital sum paid by an insurer as a result of the said decree (other than a capital sum which has been distributed by way of an annuity or other periodical payment) or any part of such sum should be repaid to the insurer if the facts in respect of which the variation order was pronounced justify such repayment.

(4) The court shall not make an order under subsection (2) above unless application for the variation order has been made to the court within the period of five years beginning with the date of the decree under section 2 of this Act.

(5) Where any person who has acquired rights to or in any property as a result of a decree under section 2 of this Act, or any person deriving right from him, enters into a transaction with another person whereby that other person acquires in good faith and for value any right to or in that property or any part of it, the transaction and any title acquired under it by that other person shall not be challengeable on the ground that an order under subsection (2) above has been made in relation to that property.

(6) A trustee shall be liable to any person having entitlement by virtue of an order under subsection (2) above for any loss suffered by that person on account of any breach of trust by the trustee in the administration or distribution of the whole or any part of the property, except in so far as the liability of the trustee may be restricted under any enactment or by any provision in any deed regulating the administration of the trust.

(7) Nothing in this section shall apply to estate duty or capital transfer tax which falls to be repaid as a result of a variation order having been pronounced.

6 Insurance against claims

(1) Where decree has been granted under section 2 of this Act then, unless the court otherwise directs, the trustee, if any, shall as soon as may be effect a policy of insurance in respect of any claim which may arise by virtue of an order under section 5(2) of this Act.

(2) Any premium payable by the trustee in respect of a policy of insurance effected under subsection (1) above shall be a proper charge on the estate being administered by the trustee.

(3) Where decree has been granted under section 2 of this Act, an insurer may, before making payment of any capital sum (other than in respect of an annuity or other periodical payment) to any person as a result of that decree, require that person to effect in his own name for the benefit of that insurer a policy of insurance to satisfy any claim which that insurer may establish in the event of a variation order being pronounced.

7 Value of certain rights may be declared irrecoverable

Where decree has been granted under section 2 of this Act, the court may—

(a) on the application of—

(i) any person whom the missing person would, at the time of the making of the said application (apart from the said decree), have had a duty (other than a contractual duty) to aliment, or

(ii) the trustee, and

(b) subject to such conditions, if any, as it thinks fit,

then or at any time thereafter, make an order directing that the value of any rights to or in any property acquired as a result of the said decree shall not be recoverable by virtue of an order under section 5(2) of this Act.

8 Repayment of estate duty

Where estate duty or capital transfer tax falls to be repaid as a result of a variation order having been pronounced—

(a) the court which pronounced the variation order may order the duty or tax to be repaid to the person entitled to receive repayment;

(b) nothing in this Act shall affect the obligation of any person to whom the duty or tax is repaid to account for the amount of the duty or tax to any other person.

9 Disclosure of information

(1)   Any person (including the Secretary of State for Social Services) who possesses information relating to the survival or death of the missing person, and who is aware that an action of declarator has been raised or an application for a variation order has been made, shall have a duty to disclose that information—

(a)   by means of written communication to the Principal Clerk of Session or, as the case may require, the appropriate sheriff clerk; or

(b)   in such other manner as may be prescribed by act of sederunt.

(2)   Nothing in this section shall impose any duty to disclose information where the person possessing the information would, if cited as a witness or haver, have been entitled to refuse to disclose such information under any rule of law or practice relating to the privilege of witnesses and havers, confidentiality of communications and withholding or non-disclosure of information on the grounds of public interest.

(3)   A statement purporting to be an instrument made or issued by or on behalf of any Minister of the Crown and disclosing to the court facts relating to an action of declarator which has been raised or an application for a variation order which has been made in that court shall be sufficient evidence of those facts.

10 Decree of court furth of Scotland to be sufficient evidence

Where a court in any country furth of Scotland in which a person was domiciled or habitually resident on the date on which he was last known to be alive issues a decree or judgment declaring that that person has died or is presumed to have died, or has died or is presumed to have died on a specified date or within a specified period, that decree or judgment shall, in any proceedings in Scotland, be sufficient evidence of the facts so declared.

11 Appointment or confirmation of executor

(1)   Where, in proceedings for the appointment or confirmation of an executor of any person, a document to which subsection (2) below refers is produced, an oath or affirmation that to the best of the deponent's knowledge and belief that person is dead shall, for the purposes of those proceedings, be equivalent to an oath or affirmation that that person has died or died at any place or on any date appearing in such document as the place or date at or on which he died or was presumed to have died or was lost or missing.

(2)   This subsection refers to the following documents, that is to say—

(a)   a duly certified copy of a decree or judgment such as is referred to in section 10 of this Act;

(b)   a certificate or intimation issued by or on behalf of a competent authority within the United Kingdom that the person—

(i)   has died.

(ii)   is presumed to have died, or

(iii)   is lost or missing in circumstances affording reasonable ground for the belief that he has died as a result of an incident in or in connection with a ship, aircraft, hovercraft or off-shore installation.

(3)   Notwithstanding any provision in or under any enactment, it shall not be necessary, in any petition for appointment as executor of any person in regard to whom a duly certified copy of such a decree or judgment as aforesaid or such a certificate or intimation as aforesaid is produced with the petition, to aver that the person died at any specified place or on any specified date, but it shall be sufficient to aver that the duly certified copy of the decree or judgment or (as the case may be) the certificate or intimation is produced and that to the best of the petitioner's knowledge and belief the person is dead.

12 Particulars of decree or variation order to be intimated to Registrar General

(1)   Where a decree under section 2 of this Act or a variation order has been granted by any court, the clerk of court shall, where no appeal has been made against such decree or order, on the expiration of the time within which such an

appeal may be made, or where an appeal has been made against such a decree or order, on the conclusion of any appellate proceedings, notify the prescribed particulars in connection with such decree or order to the Registrar General of Births, Deaths and Marriages for Scotland, who shall thereupon cause to be made such entry, if any, as appears to him to be appropriate, in a register kept for that purpose.

(2) In this section, 'prescribed' means prescribed by regulations made under section 54 of the Registration of Births, Deaths and Marriages (Scotland) Act 1965.

13 Defence to charge of bigamy
It shall be a defence against a charge of bigamy for the accused to prove that at no time within the period of seven years immediately preceding the date of the purported marriage forming the substance of the charge had he any reason to believe that his spouse was alive.

14 Report of proceedings
For the avoidance of doubt, it is hereby declared that section 1(1)(b) of the Judicial Proceedings (Regulation of Reports) Act 1926 does not apply to an action of declarator.

15 Rules of procedure
(1) Without prejudice to the generality of the powers conferred on the Court of Session by section 16 of the Administration of Justice (Scotland) Act 1933 and section 32 of the Sheriff Courts (Scotland) Act 1971 to regulate procedure by act of sederant, the said powers shall include power to make rules of procedure for the purpose of giving effect to the provisions of this Act.

(2) Such rules of procedure shall include provisions—

(a) specifying the persons (including the Lord Advocate) upon or to whom service or intimation of the summons or initial writ in an action of declarator or of an application for a variation order is to be made; and

(b) relating to the advertisement of the raising of the said action or the making of the said application.

16 Entailed estates
(1) The following provisions of this section shall apply where decree has been granted under section 2 of this Act declaring the death of the missing person who is the heir in possession of an entailed estate.

(2) In the circumstances set out in subsection (1) above, the next heir may apply to the court for authority to disentail the estate and the court may make it a condition of granting such authority that the next heir gives security of such amount and in such manner as the court may direct to meet any contingent interest of the heir if he shall reappear and, within the period of five years beginning with the date of the said decree, application for the relative variation order shall be made.

(3) Where, in the circumstances set out in subsection (1) above—

(a) the estate has not been disentailed,

(b) the absent heir reappears,

(c) application for the relative variation order is made within the period of five years beginning with the date of the said decree, and

(d) the relative variation order is pronounced,

then, notwithstanding section 5 of this Act, the absent heir who reappears shall be entitled to resume possession of the estate but shall not be entitled to recover the fruits or income of the estate from any following heir in respect of the period of that heir's possession.

(4) In this section, 'the court' means the Court of Session.

17 Interpretation
In this Act, unless the context otherwise requires,

'action of declarator' has the meaning assigned to it by section 1 of this Act;

'any person having an interest' includes the Lord Advocate for the public interest;
'the court' means the Court of Session or the sheriff;
'insurer' includes a society registered under the Acts relating to friendly and industrial and provident societies and any person or body which provides for the payment of benefits on the death of another person;
'missing person' has the meaning assigned to it by section 1(1) of this Act;
'statutory tribunal' means a tribunal established by or under any enactment;
'trust' means—
(a)   any trust or executry for the administration of property which comes into operation as a result of a decree under section 2 of this Act, or
(b)   any trust under which property devolves upon or is transmitted to any person by reason of the death of the missing person;
and 'trustee' means the trustee, executor, judicial factor or other person administering any such property;
'variation order' has the meaning assigned to it by section 4(1) of this Act.

18, 19   [*Amendments and repeals*]

20   Short title, commencement and extent
(1)   This Act may be cited as the Presumption of Death (Scotland) Act 1977.
(2)   This Act, except this section, shall come into force on such date as the Lord Advocate may by order made by statutory instrument appoint.
(3)   This Act shall extend to Scotland only.

LAW REFORM (MISCELLANEOUS PROVISIONS) (SCOTLAND) ACT 1990
(1990, c 40)

Reorganisation of public trusts

9   Reorganisation of public trusts by the court
(1)   Where, in the case of any public trust, the court is satisfied—
(a)   that the purposes of the trust, whether in whole or in part—
(i)   have been fulfilled as far as it is possible to do so; or
(ii)   can no longer be given effect to, whether in accordance with the directions or spirit of the trust deed or other document constituting the trust or otherwise;
(b)   that the purposes of the trust provide a use for only part of the property available under the trust;
(c)   that the purposes of the trust were expressed by reference to—
(i)   an area which has, since the trust was constituted, ceased to have effect for the purpose described expressly or by implication in the trust deed or other document constituting the trust; or
(ii)   a class of persons or area which has ceased to be suitable or appropriate, having regard to the spirit of the trust deed or other document constituting the trust, or as regards which it has ceased to be practicable to administer the property available under the trust; or
(d)   that the purposes of the trust, whether in whole or in part, have, since the trust was constituted—
(i)   been adequately provided for by other means; or
(ii)   ceased to be such as would enable the trust to [be entered in the Scottish Charity Register]; or
(iii)   ceased in any other way to provide a suitable and effective method of using the property available under the trust, having regard to the spirit of the trust deed or other document constituting the trust,
the court, on the application of the trustees, may, subject to subsection (2) below, approve a scheme for the variation or reorganisation of the trust purposes.
(2)   The court shall not approve a scheme as mentioned in subsection (1)

above unless it is satisfied that the trust purposes proposed in the scheme will enable the resources of the trust to be applied to better effect consistently with the spirit of the trust deed or other document constituting the trust, having regard to changes in social and economic conditions since the time when the trust was constituted.

(3)　Where any of paragraphs (a) to (d) of subsection (1) above applies to a public trust, an application may be made under this section for the approval of a scheme—

　　(a)　for the transfer of the assets of the trust to another public trust, whether involving a change to the trust purposes of such other trust or not; or

　　(b)　for the amalgamation of the trust with one or more public trusts, and the court, if it is satisfied that the conditions specified in subsection (2) above are met, may approve such a scheme.

(4)　Subject to subsection (5) below, an application for approval of a scheme under this section shall be made to the Court of Session.

(5)　From such day as the Lord Advocate may, by order, appoint, an application for approval of a scheme under this section may be made by a public trust having an annual income not exceeding such amount as the Secretary of State may, by order, prescribe—

　　(a)　to the sheriff for the place with which the trust has its closest and most real connection;

　　(b)　where there is no such place as is mentioned in paragraph (a) above, to the sheriff for the place where any of the trustees resides;

　　(c)　where neither paragraph (a) nor (b) above applies, to the sheriff of Lothian and Borders at Edinburgh.

(6)　Every application under this section shall be intimated to the Lord Advocate who shall be entitled to enter appearance as a party in any proceedings on such application, and he may lead such proof and enter such pleas as he thinks fit; and no expenses shall be claimable by or against the Lord Advocate in any proceedings in which he has entered appearance under this subsection.

(7)　This section shall be without prejudice to the power of the Court of Session to approve a cy pres scheme in relation to any public trust.

10　Small trusts

(1)　Where a majority of the trustees of any public trust having an annual income not exceeding £5,000 are of the opinion—

　　(a)　that the purposes of the trust, whether in whole or in part—

　　　　(i)　have been fulfilled as far as it is possible to do so; or

　　　　(ii)　can no longer be given effect to, whether in accordance with the directions or spirit of the trust deed or other document constituting the trust or otherwise;

　　(b)　that the purposes of the trust provide a use for only part of the property available under the trust;

　　(c)　that the purposes of the trust were expressed by reference to—

　　　　(i)　an area which has, since the trust was constituted, ceased to have effect for the purpose described expressly or by implication in the trust deed or other document constituting the trust; or

　　　　(ii)　a class of persons or area which has ceased to be suitable or appropriate, having regard to the spirit of the trust deed or other document constituting the trust, or as regards which it has ceased to be practicable to administer the property available under the trust; or

　　(d)　that the purposes of the trust, whether in whole or in part, have, since the trust was constituted—

　　　　(i)　been adequately provided for by other means; or

　　　　(ii)　ceased to be such as would enable the trust to [be entered in the Scottish Charity Register]; or

(iii) ceased in any other way to provide a suitable and effective method of using the property available under the trust, having regard to the spirit of the trust deed or other document constituting the trust,

subsection (2) below shall apply in respect of the trust.

(2) Where this subsection applies in respect of a trust, the trustees may determine that, to enable the resources of the trust to be applied to better effect consistently with the spirit of the trust deed or other document constituting the trust—

(a) a modification of the trust's purposes should be made;

(b) the whole assets of the trust should be transferred to another public trust; or

(c) that the trust should be amalgamated with one or more public trusts.

(3) Where the trustees of a trust determine as mentioned in subsection (2)(a) above, they may, subject to subsections (4) to (6) below, pass a resolution that the trust deed be modified by replacing the trust purposes by other purposes specified in the resolution.

(4) The trustees shall ensure that, so far as is practicable in the circumstances, the purposes so specified are not so far dissimilar in character to those of the purposes set out in the original trust deed or other document constituting the trust that such modification of the trust deed would constitute an unreasonable departure from the spirit of such trust deed or other document.

(5) Before passing a resolution under subsection (3) above the trustees shall have regard—

(a) where the trust purposes relate to a particular locality, to the circumstances of the locality; and

(b) to the extent to which it may be desirable to achieve economy by amalgamating two or more trusts.

[. . .]

(7) Subject to subsection (14) below, a modification of trust purposes under this section shall not have effect before the expiry of a period of two months commencing with the date on which any advertisement in pursuance of regulations made under subsection (13) below is first published.

(8) Where the trustees determine as mentioned in subsection (2)(b) above they may pass a resolution that the trust be wound up and that the assets of the trust be transferred to another trust or trusts the purposes of which are not so dissimilar in character to those of the trust to be wound up as to constitute an unreasonable departure from the spirit of the trust deed or other document constituting the trust to be wound up.

(9) Before passing a resolution under subsection (8) above, the trustees shall—

(a) where the trust purposes relate to a particular locality, have regard to the circumstances of the locality; and

[. . .]

(c) ascertain that the trustees of the trust to which it is proposed to transfer the assets will consent to the transfer of the assets.

(10) Where the trustees determine as mentioned in subsection (2)(c) above, they may pass a resolution that the trust be amalgamated with one or more other trusts so that the purposes of the trust constituted by such amalgamation will not be so dissimilar in character to those of the trust to which the resolution relates as to constitute an unreasonable departure from the spirit of the trust deed or other document constituting the last mentioned trust.

(11) Before passing a resolution under subsection (10) above, the trustees shall—

(a) where the trust purposes relate to a particular locality, have regard to the circumstances of the locality; and

[. . .]

(c) ascertain that the trustees of any other trust with which it is proposed that the trust will be amalgamated will agree to such amalgamation.

(12) Subject to subsection (14) below, a transfer of trust assets or an amalgamation of two or more trusts under this section shall not be effected before the expiry of a period of two months commencing with the date on which any advertisement in pursuance of regulations made under subsection (13) below is first published.

(13) The Secretary of State may, by regulations, prescribe the procedure to be followed by trustees following upon a resolution passed under subsection (3), (8) or (10) above, and such regulations may, without prejudice to the generality, include provision as to advertisement of the proposed modification or winding up, the making of objections by persons with an interest in the purposes of the trust, notification to the Lord Advocate of the terms of the resolution and the time within which anything requires to be done.

(14) If it appears to the Lord Advocate, whether in consideration of any objections made in pursuance of regulations made under subsection (13) above or otherwise—

(a) that the trust deed should not be modified as mentioned in subsection (3) above;

(b) that the trust should not be wound up as mentioned in subsection (8) above; or

(c) that the trust should not be amalgamated as mentioned in subsection (10) above,

he may direct the trust not to proceed with the modification or, as the case may be winding up and transfer of funds or amalgamation.

(15) The Secretary of State may, by order, amend subsection (1) above by substituting a different figure for the figure, for the time being, mentioned in that subsection.

(16) This section shall apply to any trust to which section 223 of the Local Government (Scotland) Act 1973 (property held on trust by local authorities) applies.

11 Expenditure of capital

(1) This section applies to any public trust which has an annual income not exceeding £1,000 where the trust deed or other document constituting the trust prohibits the expenditure of any of the trust capital.

(2) In the case of any trust to which this section applies where the trustees—

(a) have resolved unanimously that, having regard to the purposes of the trust, the income of the trust is too small to enable the purposes of the trust to be achieved; and

(b) are satisfied that either there is no reasonable prospect of effecting a transfer of the trust's assets under section 10 of this Act or that the expenditure of capital is more likely to achieve the purposes of the trust,

they may, subject to subsection (3) below, proceed with the expenditure of capital.

(3) Not less than two months before proceeding to expend capital, the trustees shall advertise their intention to do so in accordance with regulations made by the Secretary of State and shall notify the Lord Advocate of such intention.

(4) If it appears to the Lord Advocate that there are insufficient grounds for the expenditure of capital he may apply to the court for an order prohibiting such expenditure, and if the court is satisfied that there are such insufficient grounds it may grant the order.

(5) The Secretary of State may, by order, amend subsection (1) above by substituting a different figure for the figure, for the time being, mentioned in that subsection.

CIVIL PARTNERSHIP ACT 2004
(2004, c 33)

131   Succession: legal rights arising by virtue of civil partnership

(1)   Where a person dies survived by a civil partner then, unless the circumstance is as mentioned in subsection (2), the civil partner has right to half of the moveable net estate belonging to the deceased at the time of death.

(2)   That circumstance is that the person is also survived by issue, in which case the civil partner has right to a third of that moveable net estate and those issue have right to another third of it.

(3)   In this section—

'issue' means issue however remote, and

'net estate' has the meaning given by section 36(1) (interpretation) of the Succession (Scotland) Act 1964 (c 41).

(4)   Every testamentary disposition executed after the commencement of this section by which provision is made in favour of the civil partner of the testator and which does not contain a declaration to the effect that the provision so made is in full and final satisfaction of the right to any share in the testator's estate to which the civil partner is entitled by virtue of subsection (1) or (2), has effect (unless the disposition contains an express provision to the contrary) as if it contained such a declaration.

(5)   In section 36(1) of the Succession (Scotland) Act 1964 (c 41), in the definition of 'legal rights', for 'and legitim' substitute 'legitim and rights under section 131 of the Civil Partnership Act 2004'.

INDEX

Access rights
acquisition of land, 219–20
byelaws, 218–19, 225
core paths plan—
  drawing up, 220
  maintenance, 221
  procedure for, 220–21
  review and amendment, 221–22
exclusions, 213, 215
exemption of particular land, 216–17
exercise of, 211–12
generally, 211
guidance, 224
judicial determination, 224–25
local access forums, 223–24
local authority duty to uphold, 218
local authority functions, 218–24
modifications, 212, 215
obstructions and impediments, 218–24
path agreement, 222
path order, 222
ploughing, 222–23
powers of entry, 224
protection of natural and cultural
  heritage, 225
qualifications, 213–15
rangers, 223
reciprocal obligations of owners, 212
relationship with other rights, 212–13
rights of way, 225
safety measures, 219
Scottish Outdoor Access Code, 215–16

Baronies
abolition of feudal tenure, 177

Charge certificate, 86, 319, 339–41
Civil partnership
property rights, 119–20
succession rights, 398
Common interest
abolition, 294
Community burden
adjacent unit, 240
affected unit, 240
binding decisions, 240
community consultation notice, 250, 286
common maintenance, 238–40
creation, 237
effect, 238
manager—
  appointment, 238, 250
  dismissal, 250
  remuneration, 240
meaning, 237
qualifications, 240
variation, discharge etc—
  adjacent owners, by, 242

Community burden—contd
variation, discharge etc—contd
  intimation of, 242–43
  Lands Tribunal, by, 261
  majority, by, 240–42
  preservation, 243
  registration, 281–84
Company charges
company's register of charges, 124–25
copies of instruments creating, 124
floating charges, 125–27
inspection, rights of, 125
register—
  entries of satisfaction and relief, 123–24
  rectification, 124
  registrar of companies, 122–23
registration—
  certificate of, 123
  company's duty, 122
  debentures, associated with, 121–22
  ex facie disposition etc, 122
  negotiable instrument to secure book
    debts, 121
  property outside UK, 121
  requirement for, 120–21
Compulsory acquisition
extinction of real burdens, 267–68
Conservation burden
abolition of feudal tenure and, 166–67
assignation, 244
completion of title, 244
conservation body, nomination, 199–201
creation, 243–44
enforcement, 167, 244
extinction, 244
nominating body, 166–67
preserving rights, notice of, 166, 198–99
Scottish Ministers, nomination, 199–201
Conservation bodies, 356–57
Contract
damages for breach, 153
extrinsic evidence of terms, 153
rectification of documents, 127–28
supersession, 153
Conveyance
additional sheets, 15–16
assignations, imports, 10–11
date of entry, 19
decree of division, 19
description of lands, 17, 21, 29, 38–39
direction clause, 11, 17
disposition by person uninfeft, 27, 35
duplicate plans, 34
errors in, 16
ex facie absolute, discharge of security,
  51, 66–67
extract decree of reduction, 33
formal clauses, 17

INDEX OF STATUTES